NEW Achieve for *Microeconomics*

Engage Every Student

Achieve is a comprehensive set of interconnected teaching and assessment tools. It incorporates the most effective elements from Macmillan's market-leading solutions in a single, easy-to-use platform. Our resources were co-designed with instructors and students, using a foundation of learning research and rigorous testing.

Everything You Need in a Single Learning Path

Achieve is an online learning system that supports students and instructors at every step, from the first point of contact with new content to demonstrating mastery of concepts and skills. Powerful resources including an integrated e-book, robust homework, and a wealth of interactives create an extraordinary learning resource for students.

Learning Objectives Provide Powerful Insights

Every asset you can assign in Achieve is tagged to a learning objective. Insights and reporting help instructors and students understand how they are performing against objectives, enabling more efficient and effective interventions.

PRE-CLASS

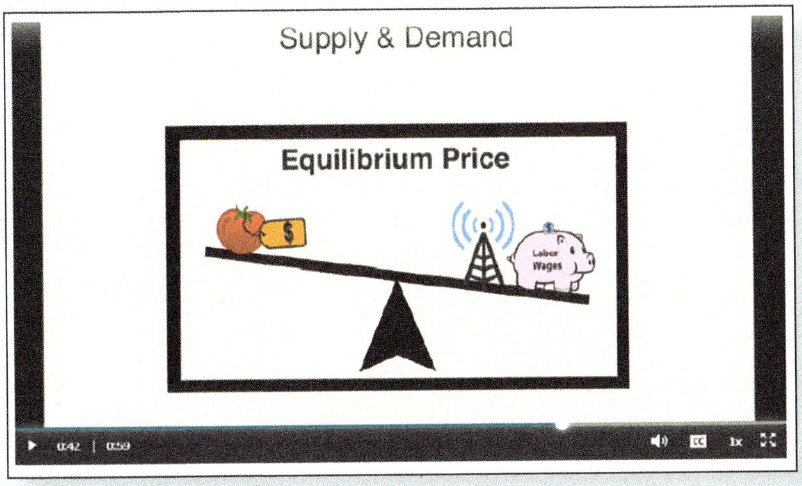

▲ **Pre-Class Tutorials with Bridge Questions** Developed by two pioneers in active-learning methods—Eric Chiang, Florida Atlantic University, and José Vazquez, University of Illinois at Urbana-Champaign—pre-class tutorials foster basic understanding of core economic concepts before students ever set foot in class. Students watch pre-lecture videos and complete bridge questions that prepare them to engage in class. Instructors receive data about student comprehension that can inform the lecture preparation.

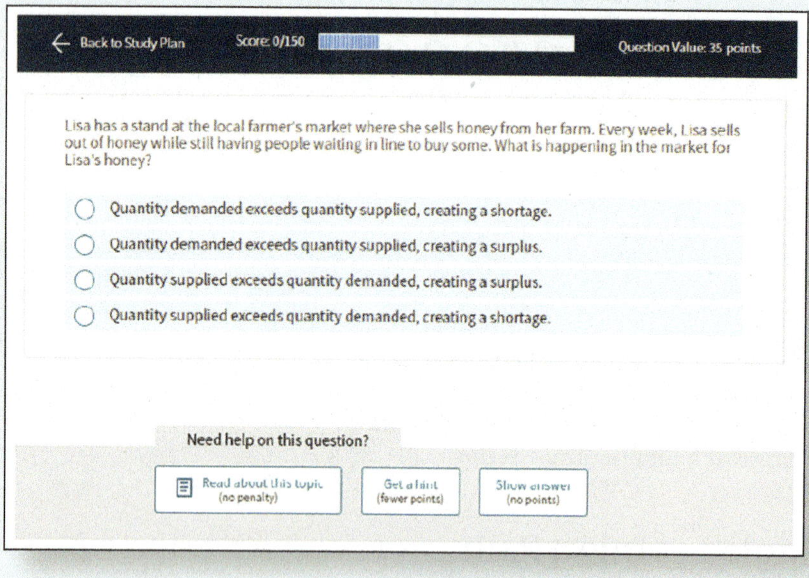

LearningCurve Adaptive Quizzing With a game-like interface, this popular and effective quizzing engine offers students a low-stakes way to brush up on concepts and help identify knowledge gaps. Questions are linked to relevant e-book sections, providing both the incentive to read and a framework for an efficient reading experience.

IN-CLASS

Instructor Activity Guides The guides provide instructors with a structured plan to facilitate an activity that encourages student engagement in both face-to-face and remote learning courses. Each guide is based on a single topic and allows students to participate through questions, group work, presentations, and/or simulations. The guide displays the activity type, estimated prep and class time, implementation instructions, suggestions for remote implementation where applicable, and Learning Objectives and Bloom's level for ease of use. Our Instructor Activity Guides encourage engagement from a Pre-Class Reflection question to prime student interest and offer follow-up iClicker questions to measure comprehension.

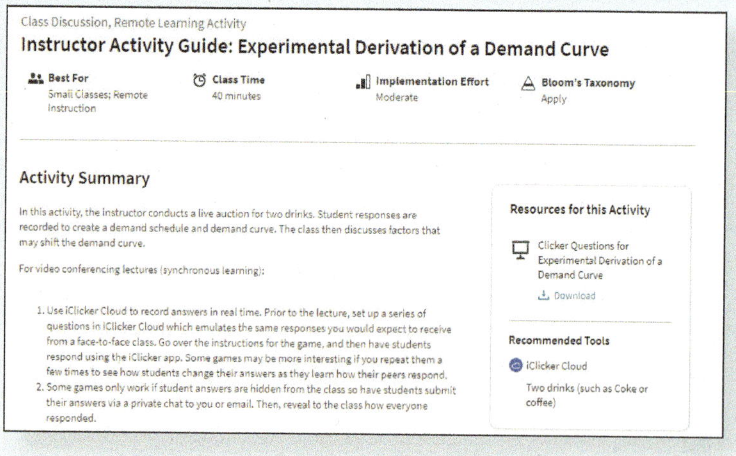

POST-CLASS

Interactive E-Book The Achieve e-book allows students to highlight and take notes; instructors can choose to assign sections of the e-book as part of their course assignments. The e-book includes step-by-step graphs for complex figures.

Step-by-Step Graphs Available in the e-book, step-by-step graphs mirror how an instructor constructs graphs in the classroom. By breaking down the process into its components, these graphs create more manageable "chunks" for students to understand each step of the process.

Discovering Data These exercises require students to use the Federal Reserve Economic Database (FRED) related to the concepts discussed in the chapter. Students will get practical experience manipulating data by being asked, for example, to track the impact of a sales tax on tobacco sales. In working these problems, students will gain a greater understanding of core concepts while also working with an impressive data resource.

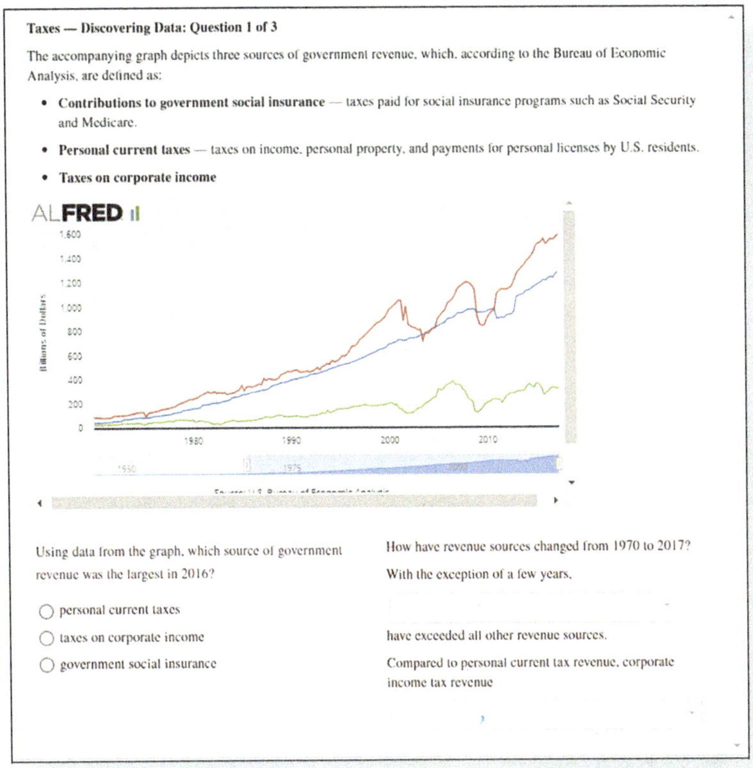

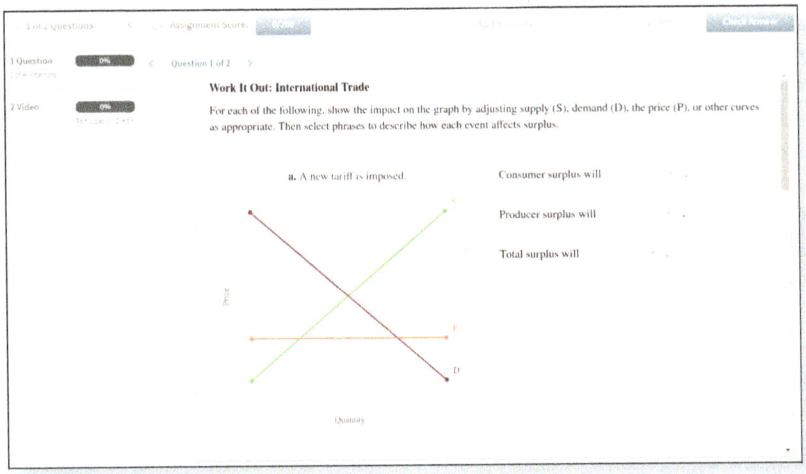

Work It Out These skill-building activities pair sample end-of-section problems with targeted feedback and video explanations to help students solve problems step by step. This approach allows students to work independently, tests their comprehension of concepts, and prepares them for class and exams.

End-of-Section Questions Developed by economists active in the classroom, these multistep problems are paired with rich feedback for incorrect and correct responses that guide students through the process of problem solving. These questions also feature our user-friendly graphing tool, designed so students focus entirely on economics and not on how to use the application.

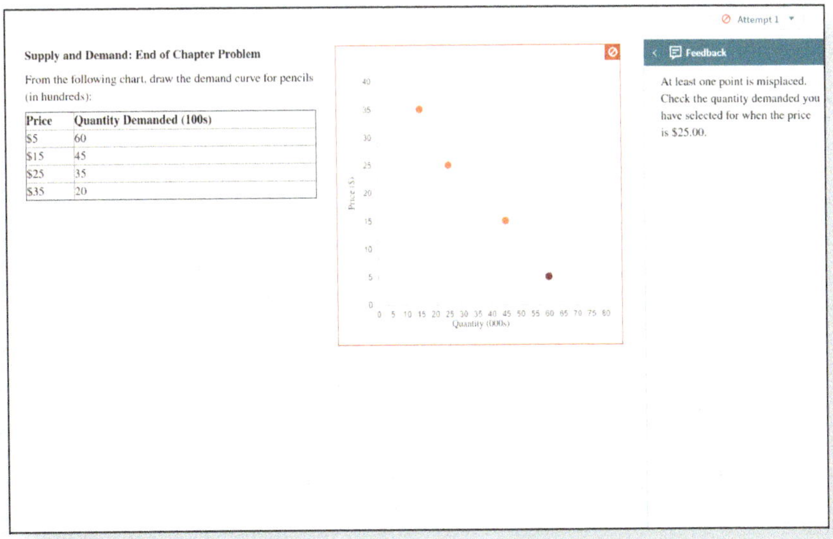

Homework Curated homework problems feature algorithmically generated variables and our user-friendly graphing tool. These problems are multistep with a variety of answer inputs—each with detailed and targeted feedback specific to that answer.

EconoFact Analysis Macmillan Learning has partnered with EconoFact to bring incisive and accessible analysis of current economic and policy trends into the economics classroom. The EconoFact Network provides even-handed and timely analysis of economic issues drawing on relevant data, historical experience, and well-regarded economic frameworks presented in the form of a short memo. In Achieve, instructors can access in-class activity guides to help integrate the memos into their own lectures. Instructors can also access and assign assessment on each memo that starts with basic reading comprehension and builds up to applying the analytical tools students have learned in their course to the economic or policy issue covered in the memo.

Practice Quizzes Designed to be used as a study tool, these quizzes feature questions from the Test Bank and allow for multiple attempts as students familiarize themselves with content.

Powerful Support for Instructors

Test Bank This comprehensive Test Bank contains multiple-choice and short-answer questions to help instructors assess students' comprehension, interpretation, and ability to synthesize.

Lecture Slides These brief, interactive, and visually interesting slides are designed to hold students' attention in class with graphics and animations demonstrating key concepts and real-world examples.

Clicker Slides These slides contain questions to incorporate active learning in the classroom. Students can participate by using the iClicker app on their smartphone or laptop.

iClicker Integration With Achieve's seamless integration with iClicker, you can help any student participate—in the classroom or virtually. iClicker's attendance feature gets students in class, then instructors can choose from flexible polling and quizzing options to engage, check understanding, and get feedback from students in real time. iClicker also allows students to participate using laptops, mobile devices, or iClicker remotes—whichever each student prefers. Additionally, we offer Instructor Activity Guides and book-specific iClicker question slides within Achieve to make the most out of your class time. It's no surprise that over a decade after being founded by educators, iClicker still leads the market. And thousands of instructors continue to give every student a voice with our simple, award-winning student engagement solutions.

Instructor's Resource Manual The Instructor's Resource Manual offers instructors teaching materials and tips to enhance the classroom experience, along with chapter objectives, outlines, and a breakdown of the large library of MRU videos.

Gradebook Assignment scores are collected into a comprehensive gradebook providing instructors reporting on individuals and overall course performance.

LMS Integration LMS Integration is included so that all students' scores in Achieve can easily integrate into a school's learning management system and that an instructor's gradebook and roster are always in sync.

Customer Support Our Achieve Client Success Specialist Team—dedicated platform experts—provides collaboration, software expertise, and consulting to tailor each course to fit your instructional goals and student needs. Start with a demo at a time that works for you to learn more about how to set up your customized course. Talk to your sales representative or visit https://www.macmillanlearning.com/college/us/contact-us/training-and-demos for more information.

Pricing and bundling options are available at the Macmillan student store: store.macmillanlearning.com/

WHAT'S NEW IN THIS EDITION?

There are 15 new Business Cases and Economics in Action applications in this edition—ensuring that the fifth edition is truly current and relevant. Other stories have been updated and refreshed.

Larry Busacca/PW18/ Getty Images

5 New Business Cases

Ticket Prices and Music's Reigning Couple
Beyond Impossible: McDonald's and Burger King's Beef-Free Battle
The Rise of the Machine at Amazon
Retail Wars: Big Box Stores in the Age of Amazon
Walmart Revolutionizes Its Labor Practices

VH Collection/Age Fotostock

10 New Economics in Action Applications

The China Shock
The Steel Tariffs of 2018–2019
Trade War, What Is It Good For?
How the Sharing Economy Reduces Fixed Cost
Global Pork Shortage Hits Chinese Diners Hard
Are Antitrust Policy Makers Behind the Digital Times?
The Ups and Downs of a Cartel: OPEC Hits the Skids on U.S. Shale Oil
Over 3,500 Economists Agree: Tax Greenhouse Gas Emissions
Marginal Productivity and the Minimum Wage Puzzle
The Real Housewives of the United States

MICROECONOMICS IN MODULES

Fifth Edition

for University of Wisconsin La Crosse

Paul Krugman • Robin Wells

Graduate Center of the City University of New York

worth publishers
Macmillan Learning
New York

Executive Vice President, General Manager: Charles Linsmeier
Program Director, Social Sciences: Shani Fisher
Senior Executive Program Manager: Simon Glick
Senior Development Editor: Lukia Kliossis
Consultant: Ryan Herzog
Director of Media Editorial and Assessment: Noel Hohnstine
Senior Assessment Editor: Joshua Hill
Senior Media Editor: Stephany Harrington
Assistant Editor: Amanda Gaglione
Marketing Manager: Clay Bolton
Marketing Assistant: Steven Huang
Director, Content Management Enhancement: Tracey Kuehn
Associate Director, Content Standards: Betsy Granger
Senior Managing Editor: Lisa Kinne
Senior Content Project Manager: Edgar Doolan
Director of Design, Content Management: Diana Blume
Design Services Manager: Natasha Wolfe
Cover Design: John Callahan
Executive Photo Editor: Cecilia Varas
Senior Workflow Project Managers: Susan Wein and Paul Rohloff
Production Supervisor: Lawrence Guerra
Media Project Manager: Andrew Vaccaro
Composition: Lumina Datamatics, Inc.
Printing and Binding: King Printing Co., Inc.

ISBN: 978-1-319-50560-8 (University of Wisconsin La Crosse Edition)

Library of Congress Control Number: 2021909900

2 3 4 5 6 27 26 25 24 23

Macmillan Learning Curriculum Solutions
14903 Pilot Drive
Plymouth, MI 48170
(macmillanlearning.com)

Front Cover

First Row (left to right): Shopping outdoors: Peathegee Inc/AGE Fotostock; Diamonds: The Adventurer/Shutterstock; Train: tovovan/Shutterstock; Baby at doctor's office: FatCamera/Getty Images; Electric Car charging: Oscar Bjarnason/Getty Images; 1040 Tax Form: Constantine Johnny/Getty Images; Graduates: Prasit Rodphan/Shutterstock

Second Row: Currency: Lucia Pitter/Shutterstock; Night Traffic: Artens/Shutterstock; Looking through microscope: Tetra Images/AGE Fotostock; Construction Workers: mikeledray/Shutterstock; Cupcakes: Tobias Titz/AGE Fotostock

Third Row: Fruit stand: Richard A McMillin/Shutterstock; Combines: Teri Virbickis/Getty Images; Cows: Stockbyte/Photodisc; Engineers: Maskot/Getty Images

Fourth Row: Stacked Wood: Fedor Selivanov/Shutterstock; Wall Street Sign: Thinkstock; Shenzhen at night: zhangyang13576997233/Shutterstock; Cargo Ship: EvrenKalinbacak/Shutterstock; Fish: John_Walker/Shutterstock; Soy Bean farm: Fotokostic/Shutterstock

Fifth Row: Scientist in lab: Kasipat Phonlamai/EyeEm/Getty Images; Printing US Money: matthiashaas/Thinkstock; Depression Era Worker: akg-images/The Image Works; Couple shopping for phones: Juice Images/AGE Fotostock

Back Cover

First Row (left to right): Busy Market: Peter Adams/Getty Images; Solar panels: iurii/Shutterstock; Paramedic: Granger Wootz/Getty Images; Stacked Copper Wires: Arsel Ozgurdal/Shutterstock; Friends eating burgers: PeopleImages/Getty Images; Smoke Stacks: iStockphoto/Thinkstock; Fracking: CSP_LonnyGarris/AGE Fotostock

Second Row: Sushi: Ipatov/Shutterstock; Walking Dog: Gregory Whitaker/EyeEm/Getty Images; Robot: istockphoto/Thinkstock; Recording concert: Wittybear/Shutterstock; Flags: yui/Shutterstock; Powerlines: Steve Allen/Stockbyte/Getty Images; Currency Exchange: Bankoo/Shutterstock; Warehouse employee: JulieanneBirch/Getty Images

Third Row: Plane Factory: Vince Streano/Getty Images

ABOUT THE AUTHORS

Ligaya Franklin

Paul Krugman, recipient of the 2008 Nobel Memorial Prize in Economic Sciences, is a faculty member of the Graduate Center of the City University of New York, associated with the Luxembourg Income Study, which tracks and analyzes income inequality around the world. Prior to that, he taught at Princeton University for 14 years. He received his BA from Yale and his PhD from MIT. Before Princeton, he taught at Yale, Stanford, and MIT. He also spent a year on the staff of the Council of Economic Advisers in 1982–1983. His research has included pathbreaking work on international trade, economic geography, and currency crises. In 1991, Krugman received the American Economic Association's John Bates Clark medal. In addition to his teaching and academic research, Krugman writes extensively for nontechnical audiences. He is a regular op-ed columnist for the *New York Times*. His best-selling trade books include *End This Depression Now!*, *The Return of Depression Economics and the Crisis of 2008*, a history of recent economic troubles and their implications for economic policy, and *The Conscience of a Liberal*, a study of the political economy of economic inequality and its relationship with political polarization from the Gilded Age to the present. His earlier books, *Peddling Prosperity* and *The Age of Diminished Expectations*, have become modern classics.

Robin Wells was a Lecturer and Researcher in Economics at Princeton University. She received her BA from the University of Chicago and her PhD from the University of California at Berkeley; she then did postdoctoral work at MIT. She has taught at the University of Michigan, the University of Southampton (United Kingdom), Stanford, and MIT.

An Innovative Modular Format

For some time, we have been hearing from instructors who want to use the Krugman/Wells text in their principles course but would prefer a version that focuses on the essentials, with less in the way of comprehensive theory and analytics. What you are holding in your hands is our response to these requests. ***Microeconomics in Modules* is a streamlined text that incorporates an accessible format that is geared toward how students learn today.**

Short, Accessible Modules

- Rather than tackling 20 chapters of about 25 to 40 pages each, students work through 6- to 10-page modules (grouped by Section) designed to be read in a single sitting
- Users and reviewers consistently describe the modules as "short, digestible chunks" of text that students actually read
- Each module is an easy-to-manage, student-friendly reading assignment, but each one is informative and provides thorough coverage

The Science Behind the Modular Format

Research confirms what we have all seen: students are reading less and for shorter periods of time, and they struggle with comprehension. So, when we began thinking about developing a more student-friendly principles text, we considered alternative formats and settled on modules, a format popular in other disciplines. They offer an appealing answer to the dilemma cited by the research, and the structure is supported by science and lauded by users:

- Cognitive psychologists have demonstrated that comprehension is best attained when material is "chunked" into smaller reading assignments, reinforced with frequent questioning (the "testing effect"), and incentivized by the sense of accomplishment earned from completing discrete reading tasks. These findings inform the modular format of this text and shape its pedagogy.
- Instructor response to the modular format has been overwhelming! Many report an almost identical story: students were actually completing their reading assignments, something that was rare with traditional textbooks. Overall, they found that students were coming to lectures better prepared. And, none of the instructors could imagine returning to a textbook with a more traditional format.

Consistent, Student-Friendly Pedagogy

Check Your Understanding 6-2

1. In the following three situations, the market is initially in equilibrium. Explain the changes in either supply or demand that will result from each event. After each event described below, does a surplus or shortage exist at the original equilibrium price? What will happen to the equilibrium price as a result?
   a. 2015 was a very good year for California wine-grape growers, who produced a bumper crop.
   b. After a hurricane, Florida hoteliers often find that many people cancel their upcoming vacations, leaving them with empty hotel rooms.
   c. After a heavy snowfall, many people want to buy second-hand snowblowers at the local tool shop.

- At the end of each numbered module section, **Check Your Understanding questions** allow students to test their comprehension of module content. The answers to the questions appear at the end of the book, so students can actually see how well they've mastered concepts.

PITFALLS

WHICH CURVE IS IT, ANYWAY?

A common mistake, both in economics classes and in real life, is to imagine that something is free if you don't have to buy it.

- But even if a taxi driver doesn't actually buy his medallion.
- The fact that he could have sold it means.
- That using it carries an opportunity cost.

- **Pitfalls** boxes teach students to identify and avoid common misconceptions about economic concepts.

>> Quick Review

- Profit maximization can be analyzed in terms of the choice of output instead of the choice of input.
- The **marginal production revenue,** or simply the of a producer is the increase in revenue from producing one more unit.
- The **marginal production cost,** or simply **marginal cost,** is the increase in cost from producing one more unit. It is equal to the marginal **input** cost divided by the input's marginal physical product.

- A **Quick Review,** also at the end of each numbered module section, recaps key concepts covered to that point in the module.
- There is additional review at the end of each Section: a **review** of concepts by module, a **key terms list.** In Achieve, end of section **problems** that test related concepts across all modules in a Section can be assigned as homework. These problems encourage students to make connections among ideas as well as to apply and practice what they've learned.

REVIEW

MODULE 5

1. The **supply and demand model** illustrates how a **competitive market,** one with many buyers and sellers, none of whom can influence the market price, works.
2. The **demand schedule** shows the **quantity demanded** at each price and is represented graphically by a **demand curve.** The **law of demand** says that demand curves slope downward; that is, a higher price for a good or service leads people to demand a smaller quantity, other things equal.
3. A **movement along the demand curve** occurs when a price change leads to a change in the quantity demanded. When economists talk of increasing or decreasing demand, they mean **shifts of the demand curve**—a change in the quantity demanded at any given price. An increase in demand causes a rightward shift of the demand curve. A decrease in demand causes a leftward shift.
4. There are five main factors that shift the demand curve:
   - A change in the prices of related goods or services, such as **substitutes** or **complements**
   - A change in income: when income rises, the demand for **normal goods** increases and the demand for **inferior goods** decreases
   - A change in tastes
   - A change in expectations
   - A change in the number of consumers
5. The market demand curve for a good or service is the horizontal sum of the **individual demand curves** of all consumers in the market.

MODULE 6

1. The **supply schedule** shows the **quantity supplied** at each price and is represented graphically by a **supply curve**. Supply curves usually slope upward.
2. A **movement along the supply curve** occurs when a price change leads to a change in the quantity supplied. When economists talk of increasing or decreasing supply, they mean **shifts of the supply curve**—a change in the quantity supplied at any given price. An increase in supply causes a rightward shift of the supply curve. A decrease in supply causes a leftward shift.
3. There are five main factors that shift the supply curve:
   - A change in **input** prices
   - A change in the prices of related goods and services
   - A change in technology
   - A change in expectations
   - A change in the number of producers
4. The market supply curve for a good or service is the horizontal sum of the **individual supply curves** of all producers in the market.
5. An economic situation is in equilibrium when no individual would be better off doing something different. At this point, the price in a market moves to its **equilibrium price,** or **market-clearing price,** the price at which the quantity demanded is equal to the quantity supplied. This quantity is the **equilibrium quantity.** When the price is above its market-clearing level, there is a **surplus** that pushes the price down. When the price is below its market-clearing level, there is a **shortage** that pushes the price up.

MODULE 7

1. An increase in demand increases both the equilibrium price and the equilibrium quantity; a decrease in demand has the opposite effect. An increase in supply reduces the equilibrium price and increases the equilibrium quantity; a decrease in supply has the opposite effect.
2. Shifts of the demand curve and the supply curve can happen simultaneously. When they shift in opposite directions, the change in equilibrium price is predictable but the change in equilibrium quantity is not. When they shift in the same direction, the change in equilibrium quantity is predictable but the change in equilibrium price is not. In general, the curve that shifts the greater distance has a greater effect on the changes in equilibrium price and quantity.

Engaging Students in the Study of *Microeconomics*

We are committed to the belief that students learn best from a complete textbook program, one built around narratives steeped in real-life and current events, with a strong emphasis on global matters, and with proven technology that supports student success.

Narrative Approach

This is a textbook built around narratives and stories, many pulled from real life. In every Section, stories teach core concepts and motivate learning. We believe that the best way to introduce concepts and reinforce them is to use memorable, real-world stories; students simply relate more easily to them.

Global Focus

This book is unrivaled in the attention it pays to global matters. We have thoroughly integrated an international perspective into the text, by means of the numerous applications, business cases, and stories.

Technology That Builds Success

Microeconomics in Modules is not just a textbook. With Achieve, it has evolved into a complete program whose interactive features are designed to extend the goals of the text. This program focus encourages even stronger student engagement, mastery of the material, and success in the course.

What's New in the Fifth Edition?

Technology That Offers the Best Value and Price.

Because students' needs are changing, our most powerful learning option is now our most affordable. Achieve is a new digital solution that brings all of the best aspects of Krugman/Wells and Macmillan's digital resources together in one place. Built on best practices in learning science, Achieve provides students with robust tools to succeed in economics while giving instructors insights into their students' understanding and performance.

Current Events Framed by the World's Best Communicators of Economics.

No other text stays as fresh as this one. This edition includes essential coverage of the global effects of COVID-19. For this edition, we've also added cutting-edge online features, including EconoFact Analysis with memos and Bloomberg Analysis with videos. These activities pair journalistic takes on pressing issues with questions based on Bloom's taxonomy. This complements the text's unparalleled coverage of current topics: sustainability, the economic impact of technology, pressing policy debates, and much more.

A Richer Commitment to Broadening Students' Understanding of the Global Economy.

With unparalleled insight and clarity, the authors use their hallmark narrative approach to take students outside of the classroom and into our global world, starting in Section 1 with a new principle on how increases in the economy's potential lead to economic growth over time. To reflect our rapidly world, there is an expanded section on market power and the digital economy and incisive new look at externalities.

Engaging Students with a Narrative Approach

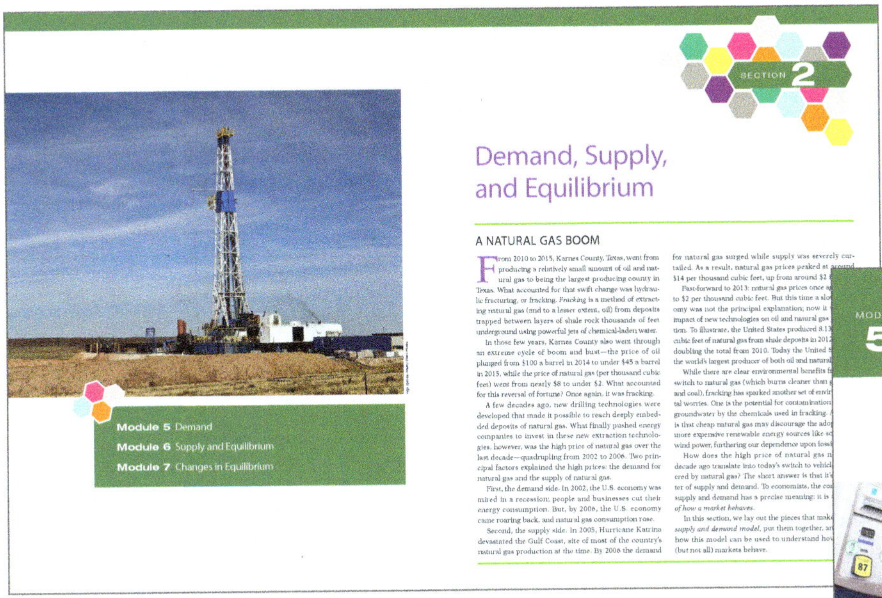

To engage students, every Section begins with a compelling story. There are two to four modules within each Section of the text. At the beginning of each module, **What You Will Learn** questions help students focus on key concepts in the module.

So students can immediately see economic concepts applied in the real world, **Economics in Action** applications appear at the end of each module.

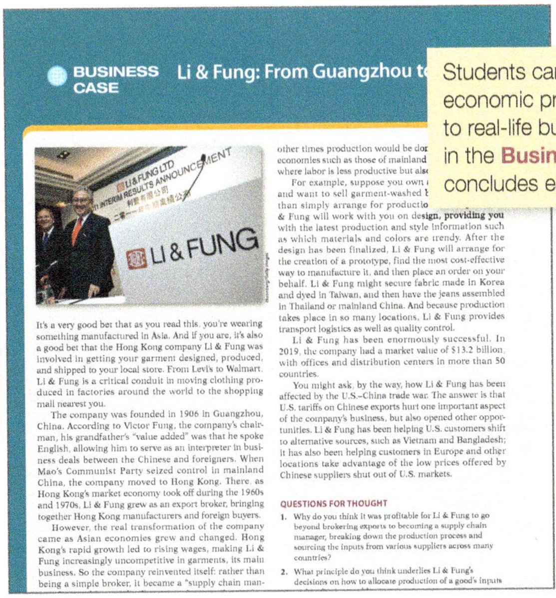

Students can see key economic principles applied to real-life business situations in the **Business Case** that concludes each section.

Acknowledgments

Our deep appreciation and heartfelt thanks go out to **Ryan Herzog,** Gonzaga University, for his hard work and extensive contributions during every stage of this revision. Ryan's creativity and insights helped make this fifth edition possible.

We must also thank the many people at Worth Publishers for their work on this edition: Chuck Linsmeier, Shani Fisher, Simon Glick, Lukia Kliossis, Stephany Harrington, Joshua Hill, and Amanda Gaglione in editorial. We thank Clay Bolton and Travis Long for their enthusiastic and tireless advocacy of this book. Many thanks to the incredible production, design, photo, and media teams: Tracey Kuehn, Betsy Granger, Lisa Kinne, Susan Wein, Paul Rohloff, Edgar Doolan, Natasha Wolfe, John Callahan, Cecilia Varas, Chris Efstratiou, and Andrew Vaccaro.

We are indebted to the following reviewers, class testers, focus group participants, and other consultants for their suggestions and advice on this edition and previous editions.

Charlene Abbott, *McNeese State University*
Carlos Aguilar, *El Paso Community College*
Terence Alexander, *Iowa State University*
Morris Altman, *University of Saskatchewan*
Farhad Ameen, *State University of New York, Westchester Community College*
Lindsay N. Amiel, *Madison College*
Miki Brunyer Anderson, *Pikes Peak Community College*
Giuliana Campanelli Andreopoulos, *William Paterson University*
Becca Arnold, *San Diego Mesa College*
Margaret apRoberts-Warren, *University of California–Santa Cruz*
Robert Baden, *University of California–Santa Cruz*
Christopher P. Ball, *Quinnipiac University*
Sue Bartlett, *University of South Florida*
Scott Beaulier, *Mercer University*
David Bernotas, *University of Georgia*
Marc Bilodeau, *Indiana University–Purdue University, Indianapolis*
Kelly Blanchard, *Purdue University*
Emily Blank, *Howard University*
Anne Bresnock, *California State Polytechnic University*
Douglas M. Brown, *Georgetown University*
Joseph Calhoun, *Florida State University*
Douglas Campbell, *University of Memphis*
Kevin Carlson, *University of Massachusetts, Boston*
Bryce Casavant, *University of Connecticut*
Andrew J. Cassey, *Washington State University*
Shirley Cassing, *University of Pittsburgh*
Sewin Chan, *New York University*
Mitchell M. Charkiewicz, *Central Connecticut State University*
Joni S. Charles, *Texas State University, San Marcos*
Adhip Chaudhuri, *Georgetown University*
Eric P. Chiang, *Florida Atlantic University*
Hayley H. Chouinard, *Washington State University*
Kenny Christianson, *Binghamton University*
Jan E. Christopher, *Delaware State University*
Lisa Citron, *Cascadia Community College*
Steven L. Cobb, *University of North Texas*
Barbara Z. Connolly, *Westchester Community College*
Stephen Conroy, *University of San Diego*
Thomas E. Cooper, *Georgetown University*
Cesar Corredor, *Texas A&M University and University of Texas, Tyler*
Jim F. Couch, *University of Northern Alabama*
Dixie Dalton, *College of the Low Country*
Daniel Daly, *Regis University*
H. Evren Damar, *Pacific Lutheran University*
Satarupa Das, *Montgomery College, Takoma Park*
Antony Davies, *Duquesne University*
Greg Delemeester, *Marietta College*
Ron Deiter, *Iowa State University*
Patrick Dolenc, *Keene State College*
Christine Doyle-Burke, *Framingham State College*
Ding Du, *South Dakota State University*
Jerry Dunn, *Southwestern Oklahoma State University*
Robert R. Dunn, *Washington and Jefferson College*
Ann Eike, *University of Kentucky*
Tisha L. N. Emerson, *Baylor University*
Hadi Salehi Esfahani, *University of Illinois*
William Feipel, *Illinois Central College*
Rudy Fichtenbaum, *Wright State University*
David W. Findlay, *Colby College*
Mary Flannery, *University of California, Santa Cruz*
Robert Francis, *Shoreline Community College*
Shelby Frost, *Georgia State University*
Frank Gallant, *George Fox University*
Robert Gazzale, *Williams College*
Seth Gitter, *Towson University*
Robert Godby, *University of Wyoming*
Julie Gonzalez, *University of California, Santa Cruz*
Michael Goode, *Central Piedmont Community College*
Douglas E. Goodman, *University of Puget Sound*
Marvin Gordon, *University of Illinois at Chicago*
Kathryn Graddy, *Brandeis University*
Mike Green, *College of Southern Maryland*
Yoseph Gutema, *Howard Community College*
Alan Day Haight, *State University of New York, Cortland*
Mehdi Haririan, *Bloomsburg University*
Clyde A. Haulman, *College of William and Mary*
Richard R. Hawkins, *University of West Florida*
Michael Heslop, *Northern Virginia Community College, Annandale*
Mickey A. Hepner, *University of Central Oklahoma*
Michael Hilmer, *San Diego State University*
Tia Hilmer, *San Diego State University*
Jane Himarios, *University of Texas, Arlington*
Jim Holcomb, *University of Texas, El Paso*
Don Holley, *Boise State University*
Alexander Holmes, *University of Oklahoma*

Julie Holzner, *Los Angeles City College*
Robert N. Horn, *James Madison University*
Steven Husted, *University of Pittsburgh*
John O. Ifediora, *University of Wisconsin, Platteville*
Samia Islam, *Washington State University*
Hiro Ito, *Portland State University*
Mike Javanmard, *Rio Hondo Community College*
Robert T. Jerome, *James Madison University*
Shirley Johnson-Lans, *Vassar College*
David Kalist, *Shippensburg University*
Lillian Kamal, *Northwestern University*
Roger T. Kaufman, *Smith College*
Herb Kessel, *St. Michael's College*
Rehim Kiliç, *Georgia Institute of Technology*
Grace Kim, *University of Michigan, Dearborn*
Michael Kimmitt, *University of Hawaii, Manoa*
Robert Kling, *Colorado State University*
Janet Koscianski, *Shippensburg University*
Sherrie Kossoudji, *University of Michigan*
Andrew Kozak, *St. Mary's College of Maryland*
Charles Kroncke, *College of Mount Saint Joseph*
Reuben Kyle, *Middle Tennessee State University (retired)*
Katherine Lande-Schmeiser, *University of Minnesota, Twin Cities*
Sang Lee, *Southeastern Louisiana University*
David Lehr, *Longwood College*
Mary Jane Lenon, *Providence College*
Mary H. Lesser, *Iona College*
Solina Lindahl, *California Polytechnic State University, San Luis Obispo*
Haiyong Liu, *East Carolina University*
Jane S. Lopus, *California State University, East Bay*
María José Luengo-Prado, *Northeastern University*
Rotua Lumbantobing, *North Carolina State University*
Ed Lyell, *Adams State College*
Mireille Makambira, *Montgomery College, Rockville*
John Marangos, *Colorado State University*
Ralph D. May, *Southwestern Oklahoma State University*
Wayne McCaffery, *University of Wisconsin, Madison*
Dennis McCornac, *Anne Arundel Community College*
Bill McLean, *Oklahoma State University*
Christopher McMahan, *University of Colorado–Boulder*
Larry McRae, *Appalachian State University*
Mary Ruth J. McRae, *Appalachian State University*
Ellen E. Meade, *American University*
Meghan Millea, *Mississippi State University*
Norman C. Miller, *Miami University (of Ohio)*
Khan A. Mohabbat, *Northern Illinois University*
Myra L. Moore, *University of Georgia*
Jay Morris, *Champlain College in Burlington*
Akira Motomura, *Stonehill College*
Kevin J. Murphy, *Oakland University*
Robert Murphy, *Boston College*
Ranganath Murthy, *Bucknell University*
Anthony Myatt, *University of New Brunswick, Canada*
Randy A. Nelson, *Colby College*
Charles Newton, *Houston Community College*
Daniel X. Nguyen, *Purdue University*
Dmitri Nizovtsev, *Washburn University*
Joan Nix, *Queens College*
Thomas A. Odegaard, *Baylor University*
Constantin Oglobin, *Georgia Southern University*
Charles C. Okeke, *College of Southern Nevada*
Terry Olson, *Truman State University*
Una Okonkwo Osili, *Indiana University–Purdue University, Indianapolis*
Chris Osuanah, *J. Sargeant Reynolds Community College, Downtown*
Maxwell Oteng, *University of California, Davis*
P. Marcelo Oviedo, *Iowa State University*
Jeff Owen, *Gustavus Adolphus College*
Dimitrios Pachis, *Eastern Connecticut State University*
James Palmieri, *Simpson College*
Walter G. Park, *American University*
Elliott Parker, *University of Nevada, Reno*
Michael Perelman, *California State University, Chico*
Nathan Perry, *Utah State University*
Dean Peterson, *Seattle University*
Ken Peterson, *Furman University*
Paul Pieper, *University of Illinois at Chicago*
Dennis L. Placone, *Clemson University*
Mike Pogodzinski, *San José State University*
Michael Polcen, *Northern Virginia Community College*
Raymond A. Polchow, *Zane State College*
Linnea Polgreen, *University of Iowa*
Michael A. Quinn, *Bentley University*
Eileen Rabach, *Santa Monica College*
Matthew Rafferty, *Quinnipiac University*
Jaishankar Raman, *Valparaiso University*
Margaret Ray, *Mary Washington College*
Helen Roberts, *University of Illinois, Chicago*
Jeffrey Rubin, *Rutgers University, New Brunswick*
Rose M. Rubin, *University of Memphis*
Lynda Rush, *California State Polytechnic University, Pomona*
Matthew S. Rutledge, *Boston College*
Michael Ryan, *Western Michigan University*
Sara Saderion, *Houston Community College*
Djavad Salehi-Isfahani, *Virginia Tech*
Matt Saltanovitz, *Indiana University Northwest*
Elizabeth Sawyer-Kelly, *University of Wisconsin, Madison*
Robert Schlack, *Carthage College*
Jesse A. Schwartz, *Kennesaw State University*
Chad Settle, *University of Tulsa*
Steve Shapiro, *University of North Florida*
Robert L. Shoffner III, *Central Piedmont Community College*
Galina Shogan, *Harper College*
Joseph Sicilian, *University of Kansas*
Fahlino Sjuib, *Framingham State University*
Judy Smrha, *Baker University*
Bryan Snyder, *Bentley University*
John Solow, *University of Iowa*
John Somers, *Portland Community College*
Stephen Stageberg, *University of Mary Washington*
Monty Stanford, *DeVry University*
Rebecca Stein, *University of Pennsylvania*
William K. Tabb, *Queens College, City University of New York (retired)*
Sarinda Taengnoi, *University of Wisconsin, Oshkosh*
Henry Terrell, *University of Maryland*
Rebecca Achée Thornton, *University of Houston*
Michael Toma, *Armstrong Atlantic State University*
Brian Trinque, *University of Texas, Austin*
Boone A. Turchi, *University of North Carolina, Chapel Hill*
Nora Underwood, *University of Central Florida*
J. S. Uppal, *State University of New York, Albany*
John Vahaly, *University of Louisville*
Jose J. Vazquez-Cognet, *University of Illinois at Urbana-Champaign*
Daniel Vazzana, *Georgetown College*
Roger H. von Haefen, *North Carolina State University*
Cheryl Wachenheim, *North Dakota State University*
Andreas Waldkirch, *Colby College*
Christopher Waller, *University of Notre Dame*
Gregory Wassall, *Northeastern University*
Robert Whaples, *Wake Forest University*
Thomas White, *Assumption College*
Jennifer P. Wissink, *Cornell University*
Mark Witte, *Northwestern University*
Kristen M. Wolfe, *St. Johns River Community College*
Larry Wolfenbarger, *Macon State College*
Louise B. Wolitz, *University of Texas, Austin*
Gavin Wright, *Stanford University*
Melissa A. Wright, *Washington State University*
Bill Yang, *Georgia Southern University*
Kiana Yektansani, *Washington State University*
Kristen L. Zaborski, *State College of Florida*
Jason Zimmerman, *South Dakota State University*

Organization of This Book

This text contains 12 sections with two to four modules in each.

An introduction to basic economic principles that will help students develop an understanding of economic models and the nature of markets. Expanded for this edition to include 12 principles of economics.

Moved up to follow Section 1, this appendix covers a review of math and graphing skills for students who would find this background helpful for this course.

Individual modules are devoted to each component of the supply and demand model so students can master the model incrementally.

Introduces students to market efficiency and the way markets fail. Then students immediately see how the government applies these concepts through price controls.

Moved to follow market efficiency, the section introduces the various elasticity measures—trice, cross-price, and income elasticity of demand. It concludes with a module on the benefits and costs of taxation.

This expanded section on trade offers integrated early coverage for those instructors who wish to expand on the earlier treatment of comparative advantage in Module 3.

This section introduces rational choice and behavioral economics. The section concludes with coverage of utility maximization, including income and substitution effects.

Contents

Bloomberg/Getty Images

ROGER KISBY/The New York Times /Redux

Terrance Klassen/AGE Fotostock

Richard Levine/Corbis via Getty Images

mevans/istockphoto

UKraft/Alamy Stock Photo

Ariel Skelley/DigitalVision/Getty Images; Wichita Eagle/Getty Images

Monika Graff/The Image Works

Xinhua/Alamy Stock Photo

SECTION 1

Basic Economic Concepts

A DAY IN THE MEGACITY

London, New York, and Tokyo have something in common: they are megacities—huge metropolitan complexes that contain tens of millions of people and are spread over immense tracts of land. While most people are familiar with these megacities, not everyone knows about the biggest of them all: China's vast urban complex known as Pearl River Delta (PRD). The PRD is home to more than 65 million people.

What are all those people doing? A significant percentage of them are engaged in producing goods for world markets, especially, but by no means only, electronic components: just about every smartphone, tablet, and computer contains components produced in the PRD. But the megacity's residents are consumers as well as producers.

While the wage of an average worker in the PRD is relatively low by U.S. standards, overall wages and income are high enough to support a vast retail sector, ranging from mom-and-pop local stores to shops selling expensive luxury goods. But not so long ago, neither the PRD nor the economic dynamism it embodies was visible. As recently as 1980, 800 million people in China subsisted on less than \$1.50 a day. The average Chinese citizen more or less had enough to eat and a roof over their head, but not much more than that. In fact, the standard of living wasn't much higher than it had been centuries earlier. And from 1959 to 1961, the Chinese government got the economy so wrong that millions of Chinese died from human-made famine.

In the years since 1980, however, Chinese incomes have soared more than twentyfold in real terms as the poverty rate (the percentage of the population subsisting on less than \$1.90 a day) has fallen from 88% in 1981 to 0.5% in 2016. The rise of the PRD is one chapter of an incredible success story in which hundreds of millions of Chinese have been lifted out of abject poverty over the past few decades. Never in human history have so many seen so much progress.

Although this is a remarkable story, it is not entirely unprecedented. From 1840 to 1910, British workers also experienced a marked rise in their standard of living. And this success was repeated soon afterward in the United States, setting the stage for the high levels of prosperity we now enjoy.

These unprecedented sets of events have touched our lives today in a dizzying number of ways. You are using smartphones, tablets, and laptops that are manufactured in the PRD as you pursue a first-rate education in the United States, one of the richest countries in the world.

In this section, we'll introduce you to key terms in economics and look in detail at eleven basic principles of economics. This will lead to looking at two important economic models and a revealing diagram about the flows of money, goods, and services in an economy to understand how economists think and illustrate why models are so useful.

MODULE 1

First Principles

WHAT YOU WILL LEARN

- How does the **invisible hand** govern modern economies?
- How can the individual pursuit of self-interest lead to **market failures?**
- What four principles guide the choices made by individuals?
- What four principles govern how individual choices interact?
- What three principles illustrate economy-wide interactions?

holgs/Getty Images

A booming marketplace in today's China.

1.1 The Invisible Hand

The massive industrial and consumer complex that is today's Pearl River Delta is a quite new creation. How did this small, poor fishing village turn into the electronics workshop of the world within the past 40 years, making it a dynamic creator of wealth?

To achieve the level of prosperity we have in America, a level the average resident of the PRD can only now begin to aspire to, you need a well-functioning system for coordinating productive activities—the activities that create the goods and services people want and then get them to the people who want them. That kind of system is what we mean when we talk about the **economy.** And **economics** is the social science that studies the production, distribution, and consumption of goods and services.

An economy succeeds to the extent that it, literally, delivers the goods. And as we've discussed, over the past 40 years the Chinese economy has achieved a spectacular increase in the amount of goods it delivers both to its own citizens and to the rest of the world.

So, China's economy must be doing something right, and we might want to compliment the people in charge. But guess what? There isn't anyone in charge—not anymore.

In the 1970s, before the incredible rise of PRD, China was a *command economy,* in which decisions about what factories would produce and what goods would be delivered to households were made by government officials. But experience has shown that command economies don't work very well. Producers in command economies like China before 1980 or the Soviet Union before 1991 routinely found themselves unable to produce because they did not have crucial raw materials, or if they succeeded in producing, they found that nobody wanted their products. Consumers were often unable to find necessities like toilet paper or milk. From 1959 to 1961, in what is now known as "The Great Leap Backward," the Chinese government got its command economy terribly wrong, inflicting enormous hardship and causing millions of unnecessary deaths.

An **economy** is a system for coordinating society's productive activities.

Economics is the social science that studies the production, distribution, and consumption of goods and services.

In 1978, the Chinese government finally admitted that its economic model wasn't working, and it began a remarkable transformation into a **market economy,** one in which production and consumption are the result of decentralized decisions by many firms and individuals. The United States has a market economy. And in today's China there is no central authority telling people what to produce or where to ship it. Each individual producer makes what they think will be most profitable; each consumer buys what they choose.

If you had never seen a market economy in action, you might imagine that it would be chaotic. After all, nobody is in charge. But market economies are able to coordinate even highly complex activities and reliably provide consumers with the goods and services they want. Indeed, people quite casually trust their lives to the market system: residents of any major city would starve in days if the unplanned yet somehow orderly actions of thousands of businesses did not deliver a steady supply of food. Surprisingly, the unplanned "chaos" of a market economy turns out to be far more orderly than the planning of a command economy. And that's why almost every country in the world—North Korea and Cuba are the only exceptions—has become a market economy.

In 1776, in a famous passage in his book *The Wealth of Nations,* the pioneering Scottish economist Adam Smith wrote about how individuals, in pursuing their own interests, often end up serving the interests of society as a whole. Of a businessman whose pursuit of profit makes the nation wealthier, Smith wrote: "[H]e intends only his own gain, and he is in this, as in many other cases, led by an invisible hand to promote an end which was no part of his intention." Ever since, economists have used the term **invisible hand** to refer to the way a market economy manages to harness the power of self-interest for the good of society.

The study of how individuals make decisions and how these decisions interact is called **microeconomics.** One of the key themes in microeconomics is the validity of Adam Smith's insight: individuals pursuing their own interests often do promote the interests of society as a whole.

But the invisible hand isn't always our friend. It's also important to understand when and why the individual pursuit of self-interest can lead to counterproductive behavior.

A **market economy** is an economy in which decisions about production and consumption are made by individual producers and consumers.

The **invisible hand** refers to the way in which the individual pursuit of self-interest can lead to good results for society as a whole.

Microeconomics is the branch of economics that studies how people make decisions and how these decisions interact.

Market failure is when the individual pursuit of self-interest actually makes society worse off.

My Benefit, Your Cost

In most ways, life in the PRD is immensely better today than it was in 1980. Two things have, however, gotten much worse: traffic congestion and air quality. At rush hour, the average speed on the PRD's roads is only around 12 miles an hour and the air is seriously unhealthy much of the year.

Why do these problems represent failures of the invisible hand? Consider the case of traffic congestion. When traffic is congested, each driver is imposing a cost on all the other drivers on the road—he is literally getting in their way (and they are getting in his way). This cost can be substantial: one estimate found that someone driving a car into lower Manhattan on a weekday causes more than three hours of delays to other drivers, and around $160 in monetary losses. Yet when deciding whether to drive, commuters have no incentive to take the costs they impose on others into account.

Traffic congestion is a familiar example of a much broader problem: **market failure,** which happens when the individual pursuit of one's own interest, instead of promoting the interests of society as a whole, actually makes society worse off. Another important example of market failure is air pollution, which is all too visible, literally, in the PRD. Water pollution and the overexploitation of natural resources such as fish and forests reflect the same problem.

The environmental costs of self-interested behavior can sometimes be huge. And as the world becomes more crowded and the environmental footprint of human activity continues to grow, issues like climate change and ocean acidification will become increasingly important.

The good news, as you will learn if you study microeconomics, is that economic analysis can be used to diagnose cases of market failure. And often, economic analysis can also be used to devise solutions for the problem.

Good Times, Bad Times

China has become an enormous economic powerhouse in the last 40 years. (And, depending upon the data source used, China and the United States vie for top place among the world's economies.) One somewhat ironic consequence of China's rise is that people around the world get nervous at any signs of trouble in Chinese industry, because it's such a big source of demand for raw materials. And in early 2020, there was a lot to be nervous about. Many economic indicators pointed to a sharp slowdown in the Chinese economy, which was caused by the coronavirus pandemic. Ultimately, both the virus and the economic slowdown spread throughout the rest of the world.

Such troubled periods are a regular feature of modern economies. The fact is that the economy does not always run smoothly: it experiences fluctuations, a series of ups and downs. By middle age, a typical American will have experienced three or four downs, known as **recessions.** The U.S. economy experienced serious recessions beginning in 1973, 1981, 1990, 2001, 2007, and 2020. During a severe recession, millions of workers may be laid off.

Like market failure, recessions are a fact of life; but also like market failure, they are a problem for which economic analysis offers some solutions. Recessions are one of the main concerns of the branch of economics known as **macroeconomics,** which is concerned with the overall ups and downs of the economy. If you study macroeconomics, you will learn how economists explain recessions and how government policies can be used to minimize the damage from economic fluctuations.

Despite the occasional recession, however, over the long run the stories of all major economies contain many more ups than downs. And that long-run ascent is the subject of our final question.

Onward and Upward

The overall standard of living of the average resident of the PRD, while immensely higher now than it was in 1980, is still pretty low by American standards. But then, America wasn't always as rich as it is today. Indeed, at the beginning of the twentieth century, most Americans lived under conditions that we would now think of as extreme poverty. Only 10% of homes had flush toilets, only 8% had central heating, only 2% had electricity, and almost nobody had a car, let alone a washing machine or air conditioning. But, over the course of the following century, America achieved a remarkable rise in living standards that ultimately led to the great wealth that we see around us today.

Such comparisons are a stark reminder of how much lives around the world have been changed by **economic growth,** the increasing ability of the economy to produce goods and services. Why does the economy grow over time? And why does economic growth occur faster in some places and times than in others? These are key questions for economics, because economic growth is a good thing, as the residents of the PRD can attest, and most of us want more of it.

However, it is important for economic growth to take place without irreparable damage to the environment. What we need is *sustainable long-run economic growth,* which is economic growth over time that balances protection of the environment with improved living standards for current and future generations.

A **recession** is a downturn in the economy.

Macroeconomics is the branch of economics that is concerned with overall ups and downs in the economy.

Economic growth is the growing ability of the economy to produce goods and services.

Today, the goal of balancing the production of goods and services with the health of the environment is an increasingly pressing concern. Economic analysis has a key role to play here because environmental degradation is typically a result of market failure.

Check Your Understanding 1-1

1. For each of the following scenarios, determine if this scenario best represents a market economy or a command economy decision.
   a. King George mandates that everyone in his kingdom must own two pairs of shoes and three pairs of pants.
   b. George recently got hired in a new position. He goes to the mall to pick up some casual business attire to wear to work: two pairs of shoes and three pairs of pants.
   c. For 30 years Hillary purchased groceries for her family. In all that time the grocery stores always had her favorite products.
2. Ruth prefers driving her car to work and values the ability to drive to work at $50. However, when Ruth drives to work, she contributes to traffic congestion that is significant. Suppose you are told that Ruth's decision to drive to work rather than taking the bus with others is an example of market failure. What do you infer must be true about the costs to society of Ruth's driving to work?
3. Economies go through business cycles, and it is these ups and downs that are studied in macroeconomics. For each of the following scenarios, determine whether this is a description of an economic recession, economic boom, or economic growth.
   a. In 2007, many workers lost their jobs or found their working hours reduced.
   b. In the 1990s, there was strong economic activity that led to unemployment levels being unusually low.
   c. Over the past 100 years, the average standard of living in the United States has improved dramatically.

Solutions appear at back of book.

>> Quick Review

- **Economics** is the study of the production, distribution, and consumption of goods and services and how the **economy** coordinates these activities. In a **market economy,** the **invisible hand** works through individuals pursuing their own self-interest.
- **Microeconomics** is the study of how individuals make decisions and how these decisions interact, which sometimes leads to **market failure. Macroeconomics** is concerned with economics fluctuations, such as **recessions,** that can temporarily slow **economic growth.**

1.2 Principles That Underlie Individual Choice: The Core of Economics

All economic analysis is based on a set of common principles that apply to many different issues.

Four of these principles involve *individual choice*—economics is, first of all, about the choices that individuals make. Do you save your money and take the bus or do you buy a car? Do you keep your old phone or upgrade to a new one? These decisions involve *making a choice* from among a limited number of alternatives—limited because no one can have everything that they want. Every question in economics at its most basic level involves individuals making choices.

Every person must make decisions in an environment that is shaped by the decisions of others. Indeed, in a modern economy even the simplest decisions you make—say, what to have for breakfast—are shaped by the decisions of thousands of other people. Because each of us in a market economy depends on so many others—and they, in turn, depend on us—our choices interact. At a basic level, economics is about individual choice, but to understand how market economies behave we must also understand *economic interaction.* To that end, in this module you will study the four principles that govern how individual choices interact in the economy.

Many important economic interactions can be understood by looking at the markets for individual goods. However, when we consider the economy as a whole, we see that it is composed of an enormous number of markets for those goods. As

TABLE 1-1 The Principles of Individual Choice

1. People must make choices because resources are scarce.
2. The opportunity cost of an item—what you must give up to get it—is its true cost.
3. "How much" decisions require making trade-offs at the margin: comparing the costs and benefits of doing a little bit more of an activity versus doing a little bit less.
4. People usually respond to incentives, exploiting opportunities to make themselves better off.

a result, the larger economy experiences ups and downs related to the individual markets. To understand economy-wide interactions, in this module we will study the three principles that underlie their behavior.

Every economic issue involves, at its most basic level, **individual choice**—decisions by an individual about what to do and what not to do. In fact, you might say that it isn't economics if it isn't about choice.

Take Walmart or Amazon. There are thousands of different products available, and it is extremely unlikely that you—or anyone else—could afford to buy everything you might want to have. And anyway, there's only so much space in your dorm room or apartment. So will you buy another bookcase or a mini-refrigerator? Given limitations on your budget and your living space, you must choose which products to buy and which to leave in your cart.

The fact that those products are on the shelf in the first place involves choice—the store manager chose to put them there, and the manufacturers of the products chose to produce them. Four economic principles underlie the economics of individual choice, as shown in Table 1-1. We'll now examine each of these four principles.

Ben Heys/Shutterstock

Resources are scarce.

Principle #1: Choices Are Necessary Because Resources Are Scarce

You can't always get what you want. Everyone would like to have a beautiful house in a great location, a new car or two, and a nice vacation in a fancy hotel. But even in a rich country like the United States, not many families can afford all that. So they must make choices.

Limited income isn't the only thing that keeps people from having everything they want. Time is also in limited supply: there are only 24 hours in a day. Choosing to spend time on one activity means choosing not to spend time on a different activity—studying for an exam means forgoing watching a movie. Indeed, many people faced with the limited number of hours in the day are willing to trade money for time. For example, convenience stores normally charge higher prices than a regular supermarket. But they fulfill a valuable role by catering to time-pressed customers who would rather pay more than travel farther to the supermarket.

Why do individuals have to make choices? The ultimate reason is that *resources are scarce.*

A **resource** is anything that can be used to produce something else. Lists of the economy's resources usually begin with **land, labor** (the time of workers), **physical capital** (machinery, buildings, and other man-made productive assets), and **human capital** (the educational achievements and skills of workers).

A resource is **scarce** when there's not enough of the resource available to satisfy all the ways a society wants to use it. For example, there is a limited supply of natural resources that come from the physical environment, such as minerals, lumber, and petroleum. There is also a limited quantity of human resources, such as labor, skill, and intelligence. And in a growing world economy with a rapidly increasing human population, even clean air and water have become scarce resources.

Just as individuals must make choices, the scarcity of resources means that society as a whole must make choices. One way a market economy makes choices is by allowing the choices to emerge as the result of many individual choices. For example, Americans as a group have only so many hours in a week: how many of those hours will they spend going to supermarkets to get lower prices, rather than saving time by shopping at convenience stores? The answer is the sum of

Individual choice is the decision by an individual of what to do, which necessarily involves a decision of what not to do.

A **resource** is anything that can be used to produce something else.

Land is a resource supplied by nature.

Labor is the economy's pool of workers.

Physical capital includes machinery, buildings, and other man-made productive assets.

Human capital is the educational achievements and skills of workers.

Resources are **scarce**—not enough of the resources are available to satisfy all the various ways a society wants to use them.

individual decisions: each of the millions of individuals in the economy makes a choice about where to shop, and the overall choice is simply the sum of those individual decisions.

The real cost of an item is its **opportunity cost:** what you must give up to get it.

Principle #2: The True Cost of Something Is Its Opportunity Cost

It is the last term before you graduate, and your class schedule allows you to take only one elective. There are two, however, that you would really like to take: Data Visualization Basics and Introduction to Chinese.

Suppose you decide to take the Introduction to Chinese course. What's the cost of that decision? It is the fact that you can't take the web design class, your next-best alternative choice. Economists call that kind of cost—what you must give up to get an item you want—the **opportunity cost** of that item.

So the opportunity cost of taking the Introduction to Chinese class is the benefit you would have derived from the Data Visualization Basics class. The concept of opportunity cost is crucial to understanding individual choice because, in the end, all costs are opportunity costs. That's because every choice you make means forgoing some other alternative.

Sometimes critics claim that economists are concerned only with costs and benefits that can be measured in dollars and cents. But that is not true. Much economic analysis involves cases like our elective course example, where it costs no extra tuition to take one elective course—that is, there is no direct monetary cost. Nonetheless, the elective you choose has an opportunity cost—the other desirable elective course that you must forgo because your limited time permits taking only one. More specifically, the opportunity cost of a choice is what you forgo by not choosing your next-best alternative.

You might think that opportunity cost is an add-on—that is, something *additional* to the monetary cost of an item. Suppose that an elective class costs additional tuition of $750; now there is a monetary cost to taking Introduction to Chinese. Is the opportunity cost of taking that course something separate from that monetary cost?

Yes, it is. Consider that you will have to spend that $750 no matter which class you take. So what you give up to take the Intro to Chinese class is still the Data Visualization class, period. But suppose there isn't any fee for the Data Visualization class. In that case, what you give up to take the Intro to Chinese class is the benefit from the Data Visualization class *plus* the benefit you could have gained from spending the $750 on other things.

Either way, the real cost of taking your preferred class is what you must give up to get it. As you expand the set of decisions that underlie each choice—whether to take an elective or not, whether to finish this term or not, whether to drop out or not—you'll realize that all costs are ultimately opportunity costs.

Sometimes the money you have to pay for something is a good indication of its opportunity cost. But many times it is not.

One very important example of how poorly monetary cost can indicate opportunity cost is the cost of attending college. Tuition and housing are major monetary expenses for most students; but even if these things were free, attending college would still be an expensive proposition because most college students, if they were not in college, would have a job. That is, by going to college, students *forgo* the income they could have earned if they had worked instead. This means that the opportunity cost of attending college is what you pay for tuition plus the forgone income you would have earned in a job.

It's easy to see that the opportunity cost of going to college is especially high for people who could be earning a lot during what would otherwise have been

Justin Sullivan/Getty Images

Mark Zuckerberg understood the concept of opportunity cost.

their college years. That is why star athletes like LeBron James and entrepreneurs like Mark Zuckerberg often skip or drop out of college.

Principle #3: "How Much" Is a Decision at the Margin

Some important decisions involve an "either–or" choice—for example, you decide either to go to college or to begin working; you decide either to take economics or to take something else. But other important decisions involve "how much" choices—for example, if you are taking both economics and chemistry this semester, you must decide how much time to spend studying for each. When it comes to understanding "how much" decisions, economics has an important insight to offer: "how much" is a decision made at the margin. Suppose you are taking both economics and chemistry. And suppose you are a pre-med student. Now your grade in chemistry matters more to you than your grade in economics. Does that therefore imply that you should spend *all* your study time on chemistry and wing it on the economics exam? Probably not; even if you think your chemistry grade is more important, you should put some effort into studying economics.

Spending more time studying chemistry involves a benefit (a higher expected grade in that course) and a cost (you could have spent that time doing something else, such as studying to get a higher grade in economics). That is, your decision involves a **trade-off**—a comparison of costs and benefits.

How do you decide this kind of "how much" question? The typical answer is that you make the decision a bit at a time, by asking how you should spend the next hour. Say both exams are on the same day, and the night before you spend time reviewing your notes for both courses. At 6:00 P.M., you decide that it's a good idea to spend at least an hour on each course. At 8:00 P.M., you decide you'd better spend another hour on each course. At 10:00 P.M., you are getting tired and figure you have one more hour to study before bed—chemistry or economics? If you are pre-med, it's likely to be chemistry; if you are a business major, it's likely to be economics.

Note how you've made the decision to allocate your time: at each point the question is whether to spend *one more hour* on either course. And in deciding whether to spend another hour studying for chemistry, you weigh the costs (an hour forgone of studying for economics or an hour forgone of sleeping) versus the benefits (a likely increase in your chemistry grade). As long as the benefit of studying chemistry for one more hour outweighs the cost, you should choose to study for that additional hour.

Decisions of this type—whether to do a bit more or a bit less of an activity, like what to do with your next hour, your next dollar, and so on—are **marginal decisions.** This brings us to our third principle of individual choice: *"How much" decisions require making trade-offs at the margin: comparing the costs and benefits of doing a little bit more of an activity versus doing a little bit less.*

The study of such decisions is known as **marginal analysis.** Many of the questions that we face in real life involve marginal analysis: How many minutes should I exercise? How many workers should I hire? Marginal analysis plays a central role in economics because it is the key to deciding "how much" of an activity to do.

You make a **trade-off** when you compare the costs with the benefits of doing something.

Decisions about whether to do a bit more or a bit less of an activity are **marginal decisions.**

The study of marginal decisions is known as **marginal analysis.**

Principle #4: People Usually Respond to Incentives, Exploiting Opportunities to Make Themselves Better Off

While listening to the news one day, the authors heard a great tip about how to park cheaply in Manhattan. Garages in the Wall Street area charge as much as $30 per day. But according to this news report, some people had found a better way: instead of parking in a garage, they had their oil changed at the Manhattan Jiffy Lube for $19.95—and Jiffy Lube keeps your car all day!

It's a great story, but unfortunately it turned out not to be true—in fact, there is no Jiffy Lube in Manhattan. But if there were, you can be sure there would be a lot of oil changes there. Why? Because when people are offered opportunities to make themselves better off, they normally take them—and if they could find a way to park their car all day for $19.95 rather than $30, they would.

In this example, economists say that people are responding to an **incentive**—an opportunity to make themselves better off. This leads us to our fourth principle of individual choice: *People respond to incentives, exploiting opportunities to make themselves better off.*

An **incentive** is anything that offers rewards to people to change their behavior.

When you try to predict how individuals will behave in an economic situation, it is a very good bet that they will respond to incentives—that is, exploit opportunities to make themselves better off. Furthermore, individuals will *continue* to exploit these opportunities until they have been fully exhausted. If there really were a Manhattan Jiffy Lube and an oil change really were a cheap way to park your car, we can safely predict that before long the waiting list for oil changes would be weeks, if not months.

In fact, the principle that people will exploit opportunities to make themselves better off is the basis of *all* predictions by economists about individual behavior.

If the earnings of those who get MBAs soar while the earnings of those who get law degrees decline, expect more students to go to business school and fewer to go to law school. If the price of gasoline rises and stays high for an extended period of time, expect people to buy smaller cars with higher gas mileage—making themselves better off by driving more fuel-efficient cars.

One last point: economists tend to be skeptical of any attempt to change behavior that *doesn't* change incentives. For example, a plan that calls on manufacturers to reduce pollution voluntarily probably won't be effective. In contrast, a plan that gives them a financial reward to reduce pollution is a lot more likely to succeed because it has changed manufacturers' incentives.

So are we ready to do economics? Not yet—because most of the interesting things that happen in the economy are the result not merely of individual choices but of the way in which individual choices interact.

Check Your Understanding 1-2

1. Explain how each of the following illustrates one of the four principles of individual choice.
   a. You are on your third trip to a restaurant's all-you-can-eat dessert buffet and are feeling very full. Although it would cost you no additional money, you forgo a slice of coconut cream pie but have a slice of chocolate cake.
   b. Even if there were more resources in the world, there would still be scarcity.
   c. Different teaching assistants teach several Economics 101 tutorials. Those taught by the teaching assistants with the best reputations fill up quickly, with spaces left unfilled in the ones taught by assistants with poor reputations.
   d. To decide how many hours per week to exercise, you compare the health benefits of one more hour of exercise to the effect on your grades of one fewer hour spent studying.
2. You make $50,000 per year. Which of the following are elements of the opportunity cost of accepting the new job at Brainiacs, Inc.?
   a. The increased time spent commuting to your new job
   b. The $45,000 salary from your old job
   c. The more spacious office at your new job

Solutions appear at back of book.

>> Quick Review

- All economic activities involve **individual choice.**
- People must make choices because **resources** are **scarce.** The four categories of resources are **land, labor, physical capital,** and **human capital.**
- The real cost of something is its **opportunity cost**—what you must give up to get it. All costs are opportunity costs. Monetary costs are sometimes a good indicator of opportunity costs, but not always.
- Many choices involve not whether to do something but how much of it to do. "How much" choices call for making a **trade-off** at the margin. The study of **marginal decisions** is called **marginal analysis.**
- Because people usually exploit opportunities to make themselves better off, **incentives** can change people's behavior.

1.3 Interaction: How Economies Work

An economy is a system for coordinating the productive activities of many people. In a market economy like the one we live in, coordination takes place without any coordinator: each individual makes their own choices.

Yet those choices are by no means independent of one another: each individual's opportunities, and hence choices, depend to a large extent on the choices made by other people. So to understand how a market economy behaves, we have to examine this **interaction** in which my choices affect your choices, and vice versa.

When we study economic interaction, we quickly learn that the end result of individual choices may be quite different from what any one individual intends. For example, over the past century farmers in the United States have eagerly adopted new farming techniques and crop strains that have reduced their costs and increased their yields. Clearly, it's in the interest of each farmer to keep up with the latest farming techniques.

The end result of each farmer trying to increase their own income, however, has actually been to drive many farmers out of business. Because American farmers have been so successful at producing larger yields, agricultural prices have steadily fallen. These falling prices have reduced the incomes of many farmers, resulting in fewer people finding farming worth doing. That is, an individual farmer who plants a better variety of corn is better off, but when many farmers plant a better variety of corn, the result may be to make farmers as a group worse off.

The farmer who plants a new, more productive corn variety doesn't just grow more corn. Such a farmer also affects the market for corn through the increased yields attained, with consequences that will be felt by other farmers, consumers, and beyond.

Just as there are four economic principles that underlie individual choice, there are four principles underlying the economics of interaction. These principles are summarized in Table 1-2.

TABLE 1-2 The Principles of the Interaction of Individual Choices

5. There are gains from trade.
6. Markets move toward equilibrium.
7. Resources should be used efficiently to achieve society's goals.
8. Markets usually lead to efficiency, but when they don't government intervention can improve society's welfare.

Interaction of choices—my choices affect your choices, and vice versa—is a feature of most economic situations. The results of this interaction are often quite different from what the individuals intend.

In a market economy, individuals engage in **trade:** they provide goods and services to others and receive goods and services in return.

There are **gains from trade:** people can get more of what they want through trade than they could if they tried to be self-sufficient.

This increase in output is due to **specialization:** each person specializes in the task that he or she is good at performing.

Principle #5: There Are Gains from Trade

Why do the choices I make interact with the choices you make? A family could try to take care of all its own needs—growing its own food, sewing its own clothing, providing itself with entertainment, writing its own economics textbooks. But trying to live that way would be very hard.

The key to a much better standard of living for everyone is **trade,** in which people divide tasks among themselves and each person provides a good or service that other people want in return for different goods and services that they want.

The reason we have an economy, and not many self-sufficient individuals, is that there are **gains from trade:** by dividing tasks and trading, two people (or 7 billion people) can each get more of what they want than they could get by being self-sufficient.

Gains from trade arise from this division of tasks, which economists call **specialization**—a situation in which different people each engage in a different task, specializing in those tasks that they are good at performing. The advantages of specialization, and the resulting gains from trade, were the starting point for Adam Smith's 1776 book *The Wealth of Nations,* which many regard as the beginning of economics as a discipline. Smith famously noted, *the economy, as a whole, can produce more when each person specializes in a task and trades with others.*

The benefits of specialization are the reason a person typically chooses only one career. It takes many years of study and experience to become a doctor or a commercial airline pilot. Many doctors might well have had the potential to become excellent pilots, and vice versa; but it is very unlikely that anyone who decided to pursue both careers would be as good a pilot or as good a doctor as someone who decided at the beginning to specialize in that field. So it is to everyone's advantage that individuals specialize in their career choices.

"I hunt and she gathers—otherwise, we couldn't make ends meet."

Markets are what allow a doctor and a pilot to specialize in their own fields. Because markets for commercial flights and for doctors' services exist, a doctor is assured that they can find a flight and a pilot is assured that they can find a doctor. As long as individuals know that they can find the goods and services they want in the market, they are willing to forgo self-sufficiency and to specialize.

Principle #6: Markets Move Toward Equilibrium

It's a busy afternoon at the supermarket; there are long lines at the checkout counters. Then one of the previously closed cash registers opens. What happens? The first thing, of course, is a rush to that register. After a couple of minutes, however, things will have settled down; shoppers will have rearranged themselves so that the line at the newly opened register is about the same length as the lines at all the other registers.

Witness equilibrium in action at the checkout line.

How do we know that? We know people will exploit opportunities to make themselves better off. This means that people will rush to the newly opened register to save time standing in line. And things will settle down when shoppers can no longer improve their position by switching lines—that is, when the opportunities to make themselves better off have all been exploited.

This story about supermarket checkout lines illustrates an important economic principle. A situation in which individuals cannot make themselves better off by doing something different—switching checkout lines—is what economists call an **equilibrium.**

Recall the story about the mythical Jiffy Lube, where it was supposedly cheaper to leave your car for an oil change than to pay for parking. If the opportunity had really existed and people were still paying $30 to park in garages, the situation would *not* have been an equilibrium. And that should have been a giveaway that the story couldn't be true. In reality, people would have seized an opportunity to park cheaply, just as they seize opportunities to save time at the checkout line. And in so doing they would have eliminated the opportunity! Either it would have become very hard to get an appointment for an oil change or the price of that oil job would have increased to the point that it was no longer an attractive option (unless you really needed an oil change). This brings us to our sixth principle: *Because people respond to incentives, markets move toward equilibrium.*

As we will see, markets usually reach equilibrium via changes in prices, which rise or fall until no opportunities for individuals to make themselves better off remain.

The concept of equilibrium is extremely helpful in understanding economic interactions because it provides a way of cutting through the sometimes complex details of those interactions. To understand what happens when a new line is opened at a supermarket, you don't need to worry about exactly how shoppers rearrange themselves, who moves ahead of whom, which register just opened, and

An economic situation is at **equilibrium** when no individual would be better off doing something different.

so on. What you need to know is that anytime there is a change, the situation will move to an equilibrium.

The fact that markets move toward equilibrium is why we can depend on them to work in a predictable way. In fact, we can trust markets to supply us with the essentials of life. For example, people who live in big cities can be sure that the supermarket shelves will always be fully stocked. Why? Because if some merchants who distribute food *didn't* make deliveries, a big profit opportunity would be created for any merchant who did—and there would be a rush to supply food, just like the rush to a newly opened cash register.

So the market ensures that food will always be available for city dwellers. And, returning to our fifth principle, this allows city dwellers to be city dwellers—to specialize in doing city jobs rather than living on farms and growing their own food.

A market economy, as we have seen, allows people to achieve gains from trade. But how do we know how well such an economy is doing? The next principle gives us a standard to use in evaluating an economy's performance.

Principle #7: Resources Should Be Used Efficiently to Achieve Society's Goals

You are taking a course in which the classroom is too small for the number of students—many people are forced to stand or sit on the floor—despite the fact that large, empty classrooms are available nearby. You would say, correctly, that this is no way to run a college. Economists would call this an *inefficient* use of resources. But if an inefficient use of resources is undesirable, just what does it mean to use resources *efficiently?*

You might imagine that the efficient use of resources has something to do with money, maybe that it is measured in dollars-and-cents terms. But in economics, as in life, money is only a means to other ends. The measure that economists really care about is not money but people's happiness or welfare. Economists say that *an economy's resources are used efficiently when they are used in a way that has fully exploited all opportunities to make everyone better off.* To put it another way, an economy is **efficient** if it takes all opportunities to make some people better off without making other people worse off.

In our classroom example, there clearly was a way to make everyone better off—moving the class to a larger room would make people in the class better off without hurting anyone else in the college. Assigning the course to the smaller classroom was an inefficient use of the college's resources, whereas assigning the course to the larger classroom would have been an efficient use of the college's resources.

When an economy is efficient, it is producing the maximum gains from trade possible given the resources available. Why? Because there is no way to rearrange how resources are used so that everyone can be made better off. When an economy is efficient, one person can be made better off by rearranging how resources are used *only* by making someone else worse off.

Back to our classroom example: if all larger classrooms were already occupied, the college would have been run in an efficient way. Your class could be made better off by moving to a larger classroom only by making people in the larger classroom worse off by making them move to a smaller classroom. This leads to our seventh principle: *Resources should be used as efficiently as possible to achieve society's goals.*

An economy is **efficient** if it takes all opportunities to make some people better off without making other people worse off.

Should policy makers always strive to achieve economic efficiency? Well, not quite, because efficiency is only a means to achieving society's goals. Sometimes efficiency may conflict with a goal that society has deemed worthwhile to achieve. For example, in most societies, people also care about issues of fairness, or **equity.** And there is typically a trade-off between equity and efficiency: policies that promote equity often come at a cost of decreased efficiency in the economy, and vice versa.

To see this, consider the case of disabled-designated parking spaces in public parking lots. Many people have difficulty walking due to age or disability, so it seems only fair to assign closer parking spaces specifically for their use. You may have noticed, however, that a certain amount of inefficiency is involved. To make sure that there is always a parking space available should a person with a disability want one, there are typically more such spaces available than there are people with disabilities who want one. As a result, desirable parking spaces are unused. (And the temptation for people without disabilities to use them is so great that they must be dissuaded by fear of getting a ticket.)

So, short of hiring parking valets to allocate spaces, there is a conflict between *equity,* making life "fairer" for people with disabilities, and *efficiency,* making sure that all opportunities to make people better off have been fully exploited by never letting close-in parking spaces go unused.

Exactly how far policy makers should go in promoting equity over efficiency is a difficult question that goes to the heart of the political process. As such, it is not a question that economists can answer. What is important for economists, however, is always to seek to use the economy's resources as efficiently as possible in the pursuit of society's goals, whatever those goals may be.

Construction Photography/Corbis

Sometimes equity trumps efficiency.

Principle #8: Markets Usually Lead to Efficiency, But When They Don't, Government Intervention Can Improve Society's Welfare

No branch of the U.S. government is entrusted with ensuring the general economic efficiency of our market economy—we don't have agents tasked with checking that brain surgeons aren't plowing fields or that Minnesota farmers aren't trying to grow oranges. The government doesn't need to enforce the efficient use of resources, because in most cases the *invisible hand* does the job. Economists have used the term *invisible hand* to refer to the way a market economy manages to harness the power of self-interest for the good of society.

The incentives built into a market economy ensure that resources are usually put to good use and that opportunities to make people better off are not wasted. If a college were known for its habit of crowding students into small classrooms while large classrooms went unused, it would soon find its enrollment dropping, putting the jobs of its administrators at risk. The "market" for college students would respond in a way that induced administrators to run the college efficiently.

A detailed explanation of why markets are usually very good at making sure that resources are used well will have to wait until we have studied how markets actually work. But the most basic reason is that in a market economy, in which individuals are free to choose what to consume and what to produce, people normally take opportunities for mutual gain—that is, gains from trade.

If there is a way in which some people can be made better off, people will usually be able to take advantage of that opportunity. And that is exactly what defines efficiency: all the opportunities to make some people better off without making other people worse off have been exploited. We have now arrived at the first half of our eighth principle: *Because people usually exploit gains from trade, markets usually lead to efficiency.*

However, there are exceptions to this principle that markets are generally efficient. In cases of *market failure,* the individual pursuit of self-interest found in markets makes society worse off—that is, the market outcome is inefficient.

Consider traffic congestion. Too many cars on the road cause traffic congestion, resulting in costly delays for everyone on the road as well as air pollution. Yet, no individual driver, when deciding whether to drive alone in their own car, has an incentive to take into account the increased congestion and pollution they

Equity means that everyone gets their fair share. Since people can disagree about what's "fair," equity isn't as well defined a concept as efficiency.

inflict on others. This is a type of market failure, in which the individual pursuit of self-interest makes everyone worse off.

There are several possible remedies to market failure; examples include charging road tolls, subsidizing the cost of public transportation, and taxing gasoline sales to individual drivers. These remedies would change the incentives of would-be drivers, motivating them to drive alone less often. But they also share another feature: each relies on government intervention in the market, which leads us to the second half of this principle: *When markets don't achieve efficiency, government intervention can improve society's welfare.*

Yet, short of instances of market failure, the general rule is that markets are a remarkably good way of organizing an economy.

>> Quick Review

- Most economic situations involve the **interaction** of choices, sometimes with unintended results. In a market economy, interaction occurs via **trade** between individuals.
- Individuals trade because there are **gains from trade,** which arise from **specialization.** Markets usually move toward **equilibrium** because people exploit gains from trade.
- To achieve society's goals, the use of resources should be **efficient.** But **equity,** as well as efficiency, may be desirable in an economy. There is often a trade-off between equity and efficiency.
- Except for certain well-defined exceptions, markets are normally efficient. When markets fail to achieve efficiency, government intervention can improve society's welfare.

Check Your Understanding 1-3

1. Explain how each of the following illustrates one of the five principles of interaction.
   a. Using Amazon any student who wants to sell a used textbook for at least $30 is able to sell it to someone who is willing to pay $30.
   b. At a college tutoring co-op, students can arrange to provide tutoring in subjects they are good in (like economics) in return for receiving tutoring in subjects they struggle with (like philosophy).
   c. The local municipality imposes a law that requires bars and nightclubs near residential areas to keep their noise levels below a certain threshold.
   d. To provide better care for low-income patients, the local municipality has decided to close some underutilized neighborhood clinics and shift funds to the main hospital.
   e. On Amazon's website, books of a given title with approximately the same level of wear and tear sell for about the same price.
2. Which of the following describes an equilibrium situation? Which does not? Explain your answer.
   a. The restaurants across the street from the university dining hall serve better-tasting and cheaper meals than those served at the university dining hall. The vast majority of students continue to eat at the dining hall.
   b. You currently take the subway to work. Although taking the bus is cheaper, the ride takes longer. So you are willing to pay the higher subway fare to save time.

Solutions appear at back of book.

1.4 Economy-Wide Interactions

The economy as a whole has its ups and downs: good economic times when the economy grows (called *recoveries*) alternate with bad economic times when the economy shrinks (called *recessions*). These cyles usually last less than a decade. However, over the longer run, a period of at least 10 years, the economy typically grows larger and larger. So if you were to draw a line plotting the size of the economy over time, it would look a lot like a car riding up the side of a mountain: you will drive over hills and valleys over the short run during your journey, as you slowly, but inevitably, ascend to your destination over the long run.

To understand recessions and recoveries and long-run economic growth, we need to understand economy-wide interactions, and understanding the big picture of the economy requires three more economic principles, which are summarized in Table 1-3.

TABLE 1-3 The Principles of Economy-Wide Interactions
9. One person's spending is another person's income.
10. Overall spending sometimes gets out of line with the economy's productive capacity; when it does, government policy can change spending.
11. Increases in the economy's potential lead to economic growth over time.

Principle #9: One Person's Spending Is Another Person's Income

Between 2005 and 2011, home construction in America plunged more than 60% because builders found it increasingly hard to make sales. At first the damage was mainly limited to the construction industry. But over time the slump spread into just about every part of the economy, with consumer spending falling across the board.

But why should a fall in home construction mean empty stores in shopping malls? After all, malls are places where families, not builders, do their shopping. The answer is that lower spending on construction led to lower incomes throughout the economy; people who had been employed either directly in construction, producing goods and services builders need (like roofing shingles), or in producing goods and services new homeowners need (like new furniture), either lost their jobs or were forced to take pay cuts. And as incomes fell, so did spending by consumers. This example illustrates our ninth principle: *One person's spending is another person's income.*

In a market economy, people make a living selling things—including their labor—to other people. If some group in the economy decides, for whatever reason, to spend more, the income of other groups will rise. If some group decides to spend less, the income of other groups will fall.

Because one person's spending is another person's income, a chain reaction of changes in spending behavior tends to have repercussions that spread through the economy. For example, a fall in consumer spending at shopping malls leads to reduced family incomes; families respond by reducing consumer spending; this leads to another round of income cuts; and so on. These repercussions play an important role in our understanding of recessions and recoveries.

Principle #10: Overall Spending Sometimes Gets Out of Line with the Economy's Productive Capacity; When It Does, Government Policy Can Change

The coronavirus pandemic harkened back to a period in the 1930s, known as the Great Depression. Then, as now, a collapse in spending in the economy by consumers and businesses led to a plunge in overall spending. In both periods, the plunge in spending led to very high unemployment. Macroeconomics emerged as a separate branch of economics in the 1930s in order to understand the Great Depression.

What economists learned from the troubles of the 1930s is that overall spending—the amount of goods and services that consumers and businesses want to buy—sometimes doesn't match the amount of goods and services the economy is capable of producing. In the 1930s, as in 2020, spending fell far short of what was needed to keep American workers employed, and the result was a severe economic slump. In fact, shortfalls in spending are responsible for most, though not all, recessions.

It's also possible for overall spending to be too high. In that case, the economy experiences *inflation,* a rise in prices throughout the economy. This rise in prices occurs because when the amount that people want to buy outstrips the supply, producers can raise their prices and still find willing customers.

When the economy experiences either shortfalls in spending or excesses in spending, government policies can be used to address the imbalances, which leads to our tenth principle: *Overall spending sometimes gets out of line with the economy's productive capacity. When it does, government policy can change.*

Overall spending sometimes gets out of line with the economy's productive capacity. The U.S. government spends a lot, on everything from military equipment to health care and teachers. Moreover, it can choose to spend more or less, depending upon the state of the economy. Likewise, the government can also vary how much it collects from the public in taxes, which in turn affects how much income consumers and businesses have left to spend. And the government's control of the quantity of money in circulation gives it another powerful tool with which to affect total spending. Government spending, taxes, and control of money are the tools of *macroeconomic policy.*

Modern governments deploy these macroeconomic policy tools in an effort to manage overall spending in the economy, trying to steer it between the perils of recession and inflation. These efforts aren't always successful—recessions still happen, and so do periods of inflation. But it's widely believed that aggressive efforts to sustain spending in 2008 and 2009 helped prevent the financial crisis of 2008 from turning into a full-blown depression. And in 2020, Congress passed a $2.2 trillion relief package for American workers and businesses to cushion the blow from the coronavirus pandemic.

Principle #11: Increases in the Economy's Potential Lead to Economic Growth over Time

The U.S. economy today is different from the economy of 20 years ago, and drastically different from the U.S. economy of a century ago. The same could be said of many economies around the world. These changes are due to economic growth and the increase in living standards over time, which has made the United States and other countries far richer. Like a car climbing up the mountain range, despite the valleys and hills along the way, the overall path of economies has been upward in the long run, as Figure 1-1 illustrates.

What accounts for this growth over time? It is due to the emergence of new technologies and increases in the resources available for production—land, labor, physical capital, and human capital, which we introduced earlier. Possessing new technology and the increased availability of the resources of production make it possible for a country to increase its economic *potential,* the total amount of goods and services it can produce, which leads to higher living standards. For example, in 1820, 80% of American workers were engaged in farming; now, that figure is 2%. Yet there is a far greater quantity and variety of food available now than 200 years ago. The increased mechanization and technological sophistication of agriculture—humongous tractors and satellite imaging—are changes to the resources available for production. As a result, the economy's potential has risen: American farmers can now produce vastly more food than before and American consumers can now consume vastly more food as well. We have now arrived at our eleventh and final principle: *Increases in the economy's potential lead to economic growth over time.*

Economic growth has benefited a vast number of people worldwide who enjoy an increased *standard of living,* which is a measure of the array of goods and

FIGURE 1-1 Growth in the U.S. Economy over Time

The overall path of the U.S. economy for the last 200 years, from 1800 to 2000, has been upward, with the inevitable short-term ups and downs along the way.

Data from: Maddison Project Database, version 2018. Jutta Bolt, Robert Inklaar, Hermong de Jong, and Jan Luiten van Zandem (2018).

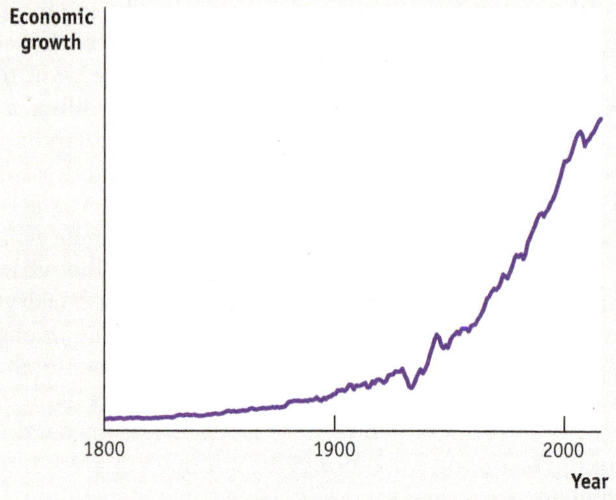

services produced and available for purchase in an economy. It includes everything from automobiles to zambonis.

At the same time, the benefits of economic growth are usually distributed unequally among a country's citizens in the short term. Some people will not benefit from growth, so that at any given time an increase in a country's economic potential creates *winners and losers*. For example, over the past 20 years, technological advancements have revolutionized the way energy is produced in the United States. New drilling techniques have made natural gas abundant, and alternative energy sources such as solar and wind power have become more efficient. These new sources of energy, which pollute less than older sources such as coal, benefit both the economy and the environment—the winners in our example. But reduced demand for coal has hurt communities where mining has been a primary source of employment, leading to job losses, reduced tax revenue for local governments, and depressed local economies in once thriving coal-mining towns in coal-producing states such as Wyoming, West Virginia, and Kentucky—these are the losers in our example.

Yet, in a dynamic market economy, losers won't always stay losers. The cyclical nature of the overall economy ensures this: good economic times will alternate with bad ones as the economy proceeds in its slow, inexorable upward climb. Because people usually respond to incentives (Principle #4), the unemployed may eventually migrate to other sectors of the economy where they can find work. If not, government has the option of reaching into its macroeconomic policy toolkit to improve society's welfare and provide relief, with assistance programs that could cushion dislocated workers during times of economic instability and change (Principle #9).

In the end, just as increases in an economy's potential lead to economic growth over time, economic growth inevitably leads to fundamental economic and social change. With these changes come questions (and debates) that are as relevant today as they were back in the eighteenth century.

Check Your Understanding 1-4

1. Explain how each of the following illustrates one of the three principles of economy-wide interactions.
   a. The price of solar panels has fallen by nearly 99% over the past 40 years. Prices are projected to continue falling over the next 30 years.
   b. The financial crisis of 2008 caused unemployment to soar. In response, the White House urged Congress to pass a package of temporary spending increases and tax cuts early in 2009.
   c. With oil prices plummeting, Canadian and U.S. oil companies have been forced to shut down their productive wells. In cities throughout North Dakota, Wyoming, Texas, and Alaska, restaurants and other consumer businesses are failing.

Solutions appear at back of book.

>> Quick Review

- In a market economy, one person's spending is another person's income. As a result, changes in spending behavior have repercussions that spread through the economy.
- Overall spending sometimes gets out of line with the economy's capacity to produce goods and services. When spending is too low, the result is a recession. When spending is too high, it causes inflation.
- When spending is out of line, governments can use macroeconomic policy tools to affect the overall level of spending in an effort to steer the economy between recession and inflation.
- Despite the economy's ups and downs, increases in the economy's potential lead to economic growth in the long term, while creating winners and losers in the short term.

MODULE

2

Models and the Production Possibility Frontier

WHAT YOU WILL LEARN

- Why are **models** an important tool in the study of economics?
- What does the **production possibility frontier** tell us about efficiency, growth, and opportunity cost?
- How are increases in the availability of resources and improvements in **technology** two sources of economic growth?

Ross D. Franklin/AP Images

The Wright brothers' model made modern airplanes, including the Dreamliner, possible.

2.1 Models Take Flight in Economics

In this module, we will look at why models are useful to economists. A good economic model can be a tremendous aid to understanding. Later in this module, we look at the production possibility frontier, a model that helps economists think about the trade-offs every economy faces. The production possibility frontier helps us understand three important aspects of the real economy: efficiency, opportunity cost, and economic growth.

A **model** is any simplified representation of reality that is used to better understand real-life situations. Models play a crucial role in economics and in almost all scientific research. Consider how Boeing went about building its newest jet, the 787 Dreamliner—a super-efficient, revolutionary plane designed to cut operating costs and the first to use superlight composite materials. Instead of building a full-scale version of the Dreamliner and hoping it would fly, Boeing engineers experimented with a miniature model of the plane inside of a wind tunnel. This simplified representation of the real thing allowed them to answer critical questions such as how much lift a given wing shape will generate at a certain air speed. Whatever form it takes, a good model can be a tremendous aid to understanding. But how do we create a simplified representation of an economic situation?

A **model** is a simplified representation of a real situation that is used to better understand real-life situations.

One possibility—an economist's equivalent of a wind tunnel—is to find or create a real but simplified economy. Take, for example, an economist who wants to know how an increase in the government-mandated minimum wage would affect the U.S. economy. It would be impossible to do an experiment that involved raising the minimum wage across the country and seeing what happens. Instead, the economist will observe the effects of a smaller economy that is raising its minimum wage (like the city of Seattle did in 2015) and then extrapolate those results to the larger U.S. economy.

Another possibility is to simulate the workings of the economy on a computer. For example, when changes in tax law are proposed, government officials use *tax models*—large mathematical computer programs—to assess how the proposed changes would affect different types of people.

Models are important because their simplicity allows economists to focus on the effects of only one change at a time. That is, they allow us to hold everything else constant and study how one change affects the overall economic outcome. So, an important assumption when building economic models is the **other things equal assumption,** which means that all other relevant factors remain unchanged.

But you can't always find or create a small-scale version of the whole economy, and a computer program is only as good as the data it uses. For many purposes, the most effective form of economic modeling is the construction of "thought experiments": simplified, hypothetical versions of real-life situations.

In discussing these models, we make considerable use of graphs to represent mathematical relationships. Graphs play an important role throughout this book. If you are already familiar with how graphs are used, you can skip the appendix to this section, which provides a brief introduction to the use of graphs in economics. If not, this would be a good time to turn to it.

2.2 Trade-Offs: The Production Possibility Frontier

One of the important principles of economics we introduced in Module 1 is that resources are scarce. As a result, any economy—whether it's an isolated group of a few dozen hunter-gatherers or the 7 billion people making up the twenty-first-century global economy—faces trade-offs. No matter how lightweight the Boeing Dreamliner is, no matter how efficient Boeing's assembly line, producing Dreamliners means using resources that therefore can't be used to produce something else.

To think about the trade-offs that face any economy, economists often use the model known as the **production possibility frontier.** The idea behind this model is to improve our understanding of trade-offs by considering a simplified economy that produces only two goods. This simplification enables us to show the trade-off graphically.

Suppose, for a moment, that the United States was a one-company economy, with Boeing its sole employer and aircraft its only product. But there would still be a choice of what kinds of aircraft to produce—say, Dreamliners versus small commuter jets.

Figure 2-1 shows a hypothetical production possibility frontier (PPF) representing the trade-off this one-company economy would face. The frontier—the line in the diagram—shows the maximum quantity of small jets that Boeing can produce per year *given* the quantity of Dreamliners it produces per year, and vice versa. That is, it answers questions of the form, "What is the maximum quantity of small jets that Boeing can produce in a year if it also produces 9 (or 15, or 30) Dreamliners that year?"

There is a crucial distinction between points *inside* or *on* the production possibility frontier (the shaded area) and *outside* the frontier. If a production point lies inside or on the frontier—like point *C*, at which Boeing produces 20 small jets and 9 Dreamliners in a year—it is feasible. After all, the frontier tells us that if Boeing produces 20 small jets, it could also produce a maximum of 15 Dreamliners that year, so it could certainly make 9 Dreamliners.

The **other things equal assumption** means that all other relevant factors remain unchanged.

The **production possibility frontier** illustrates the trade-offs facing an economy that produces only two goods. It shows the maximum quantity of one good that can be produced for any given quantity produced of the other.

FIGURE 2-1 The Production Possibility Frontier

The production possibility frontier (PPF) illustrates the trade-offs Boeing faces in producing Dreamliners and small jets. It shows the maximum quantity of one good that can be produced given the quantity of the other good produced. Here, the maximum quantity of Dreamliners manufactured per year depends on the quantity of small jets manufactured that year, and vice versa. Boeing's feasible production is shown by the area *inside* or *on* the curve. Production at point *C* is feasible but not efficient. Points *A* and *B* are feasible and efficient in production, but point *D* is not feasible.

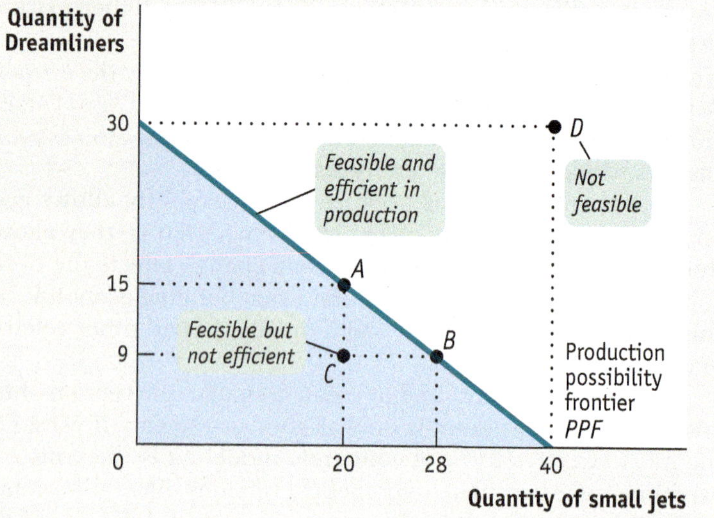

However, a production point that lies outside the frontier—such as the hypothetical production point *D*, where Boeing produces 40 small jets and 30 Dreamliners—isn't feasible. Boeing can produce 40 small jets and no Dreamliners, *or* it can produce 30 Dreamliners and no small jets, but it can't do both.

In Figure 2-1 the production possibility frontier intersects the horizontal axis at 40 small jets. This means that if Boeing dedicated all its production capacity to making small jets, it could produce 40 small jets per year but could produce no Dreamliners. The production possibility frontier intersects the vertical axis at 30 Dreamliners. This means that if Boeing dedicated all its production capacity to making Dreamliners, it could produce 30 Dreamliners per year but no small jets.

The figure also shows less extreme trade-offs. For example, if Boeing's managers decide to make 20 small jets this year, they can produce at most 15 Dreamliners; this production choice is illustrated by point *A*. And if Boeing's managers decide to produce 28 small jets, they can make at most 9 Dreamliners, as shown by point *B*.

Thinking in terms of a production possibility frontier simplifies the complexities of reality. The real-world U.S. economy produces millions of different goods. Even Boeing can produce more than two different types of planes. Yet it's important to realize that even in its simplicity, this stripped-down model gives us important insights about the real world.

By simplifying reality, the production possibility frontier helps us understand some aspects of the real economy better than we could without the model: efficiency, opportunity cost, and economic growth.

Efficiency

First of all, the production possibility frontier is a good way to illustrate the general economic concept of *efficiency*. Recall from Module 1 that an economy is efficient if there are no missed opportunities—there is no way to make some people better off without making other people worse off.

One key element of efficiency is that there are no missed opportunities in production—there is no way to produce more of one good without producing less of other goods. Returning to our Boeing example, as long as Boeing operates on its production possibility frontier, its production is efficient. At point *A*, 15 Dreamliners are the maximum quantity feasible given that Boeing has also committed to producing 20 small jets; at point *B*, 9 Dreamliners are the maximum number that can be made given the choice to produce 28 small jets; and so on.

But suppose for some reason that Boeing was operating at point *C*, making 20 small jets and 9 Dreamliners. In this case, it would not be operating efficiently and would therefore be *inefficient:* it could be producing more of both planes.

Although we have used an example of the production choices of a one-firm, two-good economy to illustrate efficiency and inefficiency, these concepts also carry over to the real economy, which contains many firms and produces many goods. If the economy as a whole could not produce more of any one good without producing less of something else—that is, if it is on its production possibility frontier—then we say that the economy is *efficient in production.*

If, however, the economy could produce more of some things without producing less of others—which typically means that it could produce more of everything—then it is *inefficient in production.* For example, an economy in which large numbers of workers are involuntarily unemployed is clearly inefficient in production. And that's a bad thing, as these workers could be employed in the production of more useful goods and services.

Although the production possibility frontier helps clarify what it means for an economy to be efficient in production, it's important to understand that efficiency in production is only *part* of what's required for the economy as a whole to be efficient. Efficiency also requires that the economy allocate its resources so that consumers are as well off as possible. If an economy does this, we say that it is *efficient in allocation.*

To see why efficiency in allocation is as important as efficiency in production, notice that points *A* and *B* in Figure 2-1 both represent situations in which the economy is efficient in production, because in each case it can't produce more of one good without producing less of the other. But these two situations may not be equally desirable from society's point of view. Suppose that society prefers to have more small jets and fewer Dreamliners than at point *A;* say, it prefers to have 28 small jets and 9 Dreamliners, corresponding to point *B*. In this case, point *A* is inefficient in allocation from the point of view of the economy as a whole because it would rather have Boeing produce at point *B* instead of point *A*.

This example shows that efficiency for the economy as a whole requires *both* efficiency in production and efficiency in allocation: to be efficient, an economy must produce as much of each good as it can given the production of other goods, and produce the mix of goods that people want to consume.

Opportunity Cost

The production possibility frontier is also useful as a reminder of the fundamental point that the true cost of any good isn't the money it costs to buy, but what must be given up to get that good—the *opportunity cost.* If, for example, Boeing decides to change its production from point *A* to point *B*, it will produce 8 more small jets but 6 fewer Dreamliners. So the opportunity cost of 8 small jets is 6 Dreamliners—the 6 Dreamliners that must be forgone to produce 8 more small jets. This means that each small jet has an opportunity cost of $6/8 = 3/4$ of a Dreamliner.

lindenblade/iStockphoto

If Boeing decides to produce more small jets, the opportunity cost is the Dreamliners it must forego producing.

Is the opportunity cost of an extra small jet in terms of Dreamliners always the same, no matter how many small jets and Dreamliners are currently produced? In the example illustrated by Figure 2-1, the answer is yes. If Boeing increases its production of small jets from 28 to 40, the number of Dreamliners it produces falls from 9 to zero.

So Boeing's opportunity cost per additional small jet is $9/12 = 3/4$ of a Dreamliner, the same as it was when Boeing went from 20 small jets produced to 28.

However, the fact that in this example the opportunity cost of a small jet in terms of a Dreamliner is always the same is a result of an assumption we've made, an assumption that's reflected in how Figure 2-1 is drawn. Specifically, whenever we assume that the opportunity cost of an additional unit of a good doesn't change regardless of the output mix, the production possibility frontier is a straight line.

Moreover, as you might have already guessed, the slope of a straight-line production possibility frontier is equal to the opportunity cost—specifically, the opportunity cost for the good measured on the horizontal axis in terms of the good measured on the vertical axis. In Figure 2-1, the production possibility frontier has a *constant slope* of $-3/4$, implying that Boeing faces a *constant opportunity cost* for 1 small jet equal to $3/4$ of a Dreamliner. (A review of how to calculate the slope of a straight line is found in this section's appendix.) This is the simplest case, but the production possibility frontier model can also be used to examine situations in which opportunity costs change as the mix of output changes.

Figure 2-2 illustrates a different assumption, a case in which Boeing faces *increasing opportunity cost*. Here, the more small jets it produces, the more costly it is to produce yet another small jet in terms of forgone production of a Dreamliner. And the same holds true in reverse: the more Dreamliners Boeing produces, the more costly it is to produce yet another Dreamliner in terms of forgone production of small jets. For example, to go from producing zero small jets to producing 20, Boeing has to forgo producing 5 Dreamliners. That is, the opportunity cost of those 20 small jets is 5 Dreamliners. But to increase its production of small jets to 40—that is, to produce an additional 20 small jets—it must forgo producing 25 more Dreamliners, a much higher opportunity cost. As you can see in Figure 2-2, when opportunity costs are increasing rather than constant, the production possibility frontier is a bowed-out curve rather than a straight line.

Although it's often useful to work with the simple assumption that the production possibility frontier is a straight line, economists believe that in reality opportunity costs are typically increasing. When only a small amount of a good is produced, the opportunity cost of producing that good is relatively low because the economy needs to use only those resources that are especially well suited for its production.

FIGURE 2-2 Increasing Opportunity Cost

The bowed-out shape of the production possibility frontier (PPF) reflects increasing opportunity cost. In this example, to produce the first 20 small jets, Boeing must forgo producing 5 Dreamliners. But to produce an additional 20 small jets, Boeing must forgo manufacturing 25 more Dreamliners.

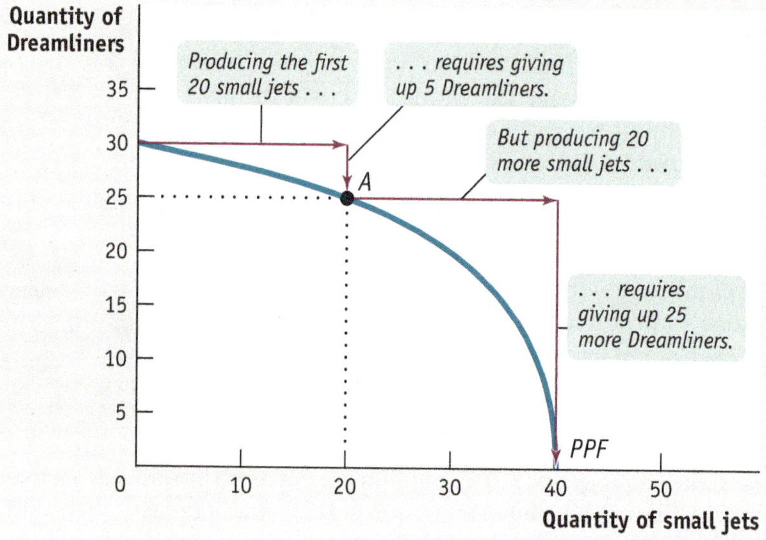

For example, if an economy grows only a small amount of corn, that corn can be grown in places where the soil and climate are perfect for corn-growing but less suitable for growing anything else, like wheat. So growing that corn involves giving up only a small amount of potential wheat output. Once the economy grows a lot of corn, however, land that is well suited for wheat but isn't so great for corn must be used to produce corn anyway. As a result, the additional corn production involves sacrificing considerably more wheat production. In other words, as more of a good is produced, its opportunity cost typically rises because well-suited inputs are used up and less adaptable inputs must be used instead.

Factors of production are resources used to produce goods and services.

Economic Growth

Finally, the production possibility frontier helps us understand what it means to talk about economic growth, which we've defined as the growing ability of the economy to produce goods and services. Economic growth is one of the fundamental features of the real economy. But are we really justified in saying that the economy has grown over time? After all, although the U.S. economy produces more of many things than it did a century ago, it produces less of other things—for example, horse-drawn carriages. Production of many goods, in other words, is actually down. So how can we say for sure that the economy as a whole has grown?

The answer is illustrated in Figure 2-3, where we have drawn two hypothetical production possibility frontiers for the economy. In them we have assumed once again that everyone in the economy works for Boeing and, consequently, the economy produces only two goods, Dreamliners and small jets. Notice how the two curves are nested, with the one labeled "Original *PPF*" lying completely inside the one labeled "New *PPF*." Now we can see graphically what we mean by economic growth of the economy: economic growth means an *expansion of the economy's production possibilities;* that is, the economy *can* produce more of everything.

For example, if the economy initially produces at point *A* (25 Dreamliners and 20 small jets), economic growth means that the economy could move to point *E* (30 Dreamliners and 25 small jets). *E* lies outside the original frontier; so in the production possibility frontier model, growth is shown as an outward shift of the frontier.

What can lead the production possibility frontier to shift outward? There are basically two sources of economic growth. One is an increase in the economy's **factors of production,** the resources used to produce goods and services.

FIGURE 2-3 Economic Growth

Economic growth results in an *outward shift* of the production possibility frontier (PPF) because production possibilities are expanded. The economy can now produce more of everything. For example, if production is initially at point *A* (25 Dreamliners and 20 small jets), economic growth means that the economy could move to point *E* (30 Dreamliners and 25 small jets).

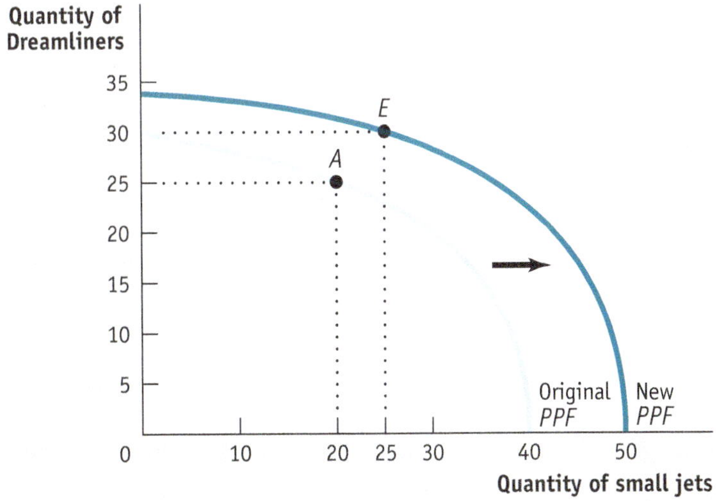

czbalazs/Getty Images; Jupiterimages/Getty Images; istockphoto/Thinkstock; Goodluz/Thinkstock/Getty Images

The four factors of production: land, labor, physical capital, and human capital.

Economists usually use the term *factor of production* to refer to a resource that is not used up in production. For example, in traditional airplane manufacture workers used riveting machines to connect metal sheets when constructing a plane's fuselage; the workers and the riveters are factors of production, but the rivets and the sheet metal are not. Once a fuselage is made, a worker and riveter can be used to make another fuselage, but the sheet metal and rivets used to make one fuselage cannot be used to make another.

Broadly speaking, the main factors of production are the resources land, labor, physical capital, and human capital. Land is a resource supplied by nature; labor is the economy's pool of workers; physical capital refers to created resources such as machines and buildings; and human capital refers to the educational achievements and skills of the labor force, which enhance its productivity. To see how adding to an economy's factors of production leads to economic growth, suppose that Boeing builds another construction hangar that allows it to increase the number of planes—small jets or Dreamliners or both—it can produce in a year. The new construction hangar is a factor of production, a resource Boeing can use to increase its yearly output. We can't say how many more planes of each type Boeing will produce; that's a management decision that will depend on, among other things, customer demand. But we can say that Boeing's production possibility frontier has shifted outward because it can now produce more small jets without reducing the number of Dreamliners it makes, or it can make more Dreamliners without reducing the number of small jets produced.

The other source of economic growth is progress in **technology,** the technical means for the production of goods and services. Composite materials had been used in some parts of aircraft before the Boeing Dreamliner was developed. But Boeing engineers realized that there were large additional advantages to building a whole plane out of composites, such as fiberglass, carbon fiber, and fiber-reinforced matrix systems. The plane would be lighter, stronger, and have better aerodynamics than a plane built in the traditional way. It would therefore have longer range, be able to carry more people, and use less fuel, in addition to being able to maintain higher cabin pressure. So in a real sense Boeing's innovation—a whole plane built out of composites—was a way to do more with any given amount of resources, pushing out the production possibility frontier.

Because improved jet technology has pushed out the production possibility frontier, it has made it possible for the economy to produce more of everything, not just jets and air travel. Over the past 30 years, the biggest technological advances have taken place in information technology, not in construction or food services. Yet some Americans have chosen to buy bigger houses and eat out more than they used to because the economy's growth has made it possible to do so.

Technology is the technical means for producing goods and services.

The production possibility frontier is a very simplified model of an economy. Yet it teaches us important lessons about real-life economies. It gives us our first clear sense of what constitutes economic efficiency, it illustrates the concept of opportunity cost, and it makes clear what economic growth is all about.

ECONOMICS >> *in Action*

Lights, Camera—But Where's the Action Figure?

In business terms, *Star Wars* isn't just a movie franchise. A lot of the money the series makes comes from sales of affiliated merchandise, everything from lunch boxes and T-shirts to action figures.

But to make the most of the marketing opportunity created by each new installment, *Star Wars* merchandise needs to be in the stores almost as soon as the new movie hits theaters. This means it has to have been manufactured in advance. This in turn means that the companies who produce and sell that merchandise have to predict sales. Produce too few of a highly desired item, and they will frustrate would-be buyers and miss a lot of potential sales. Produce too many, and they will take a loss on all the unsold stuff.

In the attempt to get an accurate prediction, toymakers like Hasbro create a model of sales based on the number and kinds of toys that sold when earlier blockbusters came out. In the past, these models have usually provided pretty good predictions of the number of people who will go to see a new movie (if it's *Star Wars,* basically everyone), and how many of those people will want to buy T-shirts, action figures, and so on.

But in 2015, when *The Force Awakens* came out, toymakers got it very, very wrong. If you've seen the movie, you know that the central heroic figure is a young woman named Rey. Yet when the movie was released, there was very little Rey merchandise available—and no Rey action figures at all. (Also neglected: the villainess Captain Phasma.) And fans were furious.

What happened? Movie industry executives were convinced and insisted to toymakers that only boys want action figures, and that they wouldn't be interested in figures of female characters—even if one of those characters was the movie's hero, and the other its most entertaining villain. Needless to say, their model of consumers' behavior was wrong.

The Force Awakens made a lot of money, but it would have made considerably more—millions, maybe tens of millions more—if Hollywood executives hadn't underestimated the extent to which the Force was with Rey.

Check Your Understanding 2-1

1. True or false? Explain your answer.
   - a. An increase in the amount of resources available to Boeing for use in producing Dreamliners and small jets does not change its production possibility frontier.
   - b. A technological change that allows Boeing to build more small jets for any amount of Dreamliners built results in a change in its production possibility frontier.
   - c. The production possibility frontier is useful because it illustrates how much of one good an economy must give up to get more of another good, regardless of whether resources are being used efficiently.

Solutions appear at back of book.

>> Quick Review

- Most economic **models** are "thought experiments" or simplified representations of reality that rely on the **other things equal assumption.**
- The **production possibility frontier** model illustrates the concepts of efficiency, opportunity cost, and economic growth.

MODULE 3

Comparative Advantage and Trade

WHAT YOU WILL LEARN

- How does trade lead to gains for an individual or an economy?
- What is the difference between **absolute advantage** and **comparative advantage?**
- How does comparative advantage lead to gains from trade in the global marketplace?
- How is opportunity cost related to comparative advantage and specialization?

Kees Metselaar/Alamy

Why do the choices I make interact with the choices you make? This next model we will discuss, comparative advantage, clarifies the principle of gains from trade—trade both between individuals and between countries.

3.1 Comparative Advantage and Gains from Trade

Another one of the eleven principles of economics described in Module 1 is the principle of *gains from trade*—the mutual gains that individuals can achieve by specializing in doing different things and trading with one another. Our second illustration of an economic model is a particularly useful model of gains from trade—trade based on *comparative advantage*.

How can we model the gains from trade? Let's stay with our aircraft example and once again imagine that the United States is a one-company economy where everyone works for Boeing, producing airplanes. Let's now assume, however, that the United States has the ability to trade with Brazil—another one-company economy where everyone works for the Brazilian aircraft company Embraer, which is, in the real world, a successful producer of small commuter jets. (If you fly from one major U.S. city to another, your plane is likely to be a Boeing, but if you fly into a small city, the odds are good that your plane will be an Embraer.)

In our example, the only two goods produced are large jets and small jets. Both countries could produce both kinds of jets. But as we'll see in a moment, they can gain by producing different things and trading with each other. For the purposes of this example, let's return to the simpler case of straight-line production possibility frontiers. The U.S. production possibilities are represented by the production

FIGURE 3-1 Production Possibilities for Two Countries

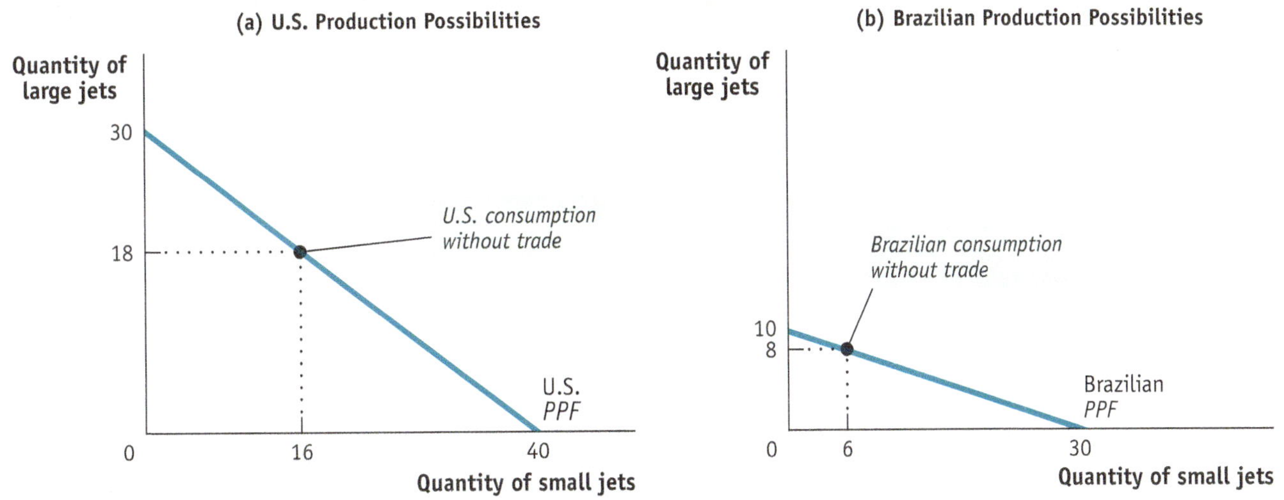

Here, both the United States and Brazil have a constant opportunity cost of small jets, illustrated by a straight-line production possibility frontier (PPF). For the United States, each small jet has an opportunity cost of ¾ of a large jet. Brazil has an opportunity cost of a small jet equal to ⅓ of a large jet.

possibility frontier in panel (a) of Figure 3-1, which is similar to the production possibility frontier presented in Module 2. According to this diagram, the United States can produce 40 small jets if it makes no large jets and can manufacture 30 large jets if it produces no small jets. Recall that this means that the slope of the U.S. production possibility frontier is: its opportunity cost of 1 small jet is ¾ of a large jet.

Panel (b) of Figure 3-1 shows Brazil's production possibilities. Like the United States, Brazil's production possibility frontier is a straight line, implying a constant opportunity cost of a small jet in terms of large jets. Brazil's production possibility frontier has a constant slope of −⅓. Brazil can't produce as much of anything as the United States can: at most it can produce 30 small jets or 10 large jets. But it is relatively better at manufacturing small jets than the United States; whereas the United States sacrifices ¾ of a large jet per small jet produced, for Brazil the opportunity cost of a small jet is only ⅓ of a large jet. Table 3-1 summarizes the two countries' opportunity costs of small jets and large jets.

Now, the United States and Brazil could each choose to make their own large and small jets, not trading any airplanes and consuming within its own country only what each produced. Let's suppose that the two countries start out this way and make the consumption choices shown in Figure 3-1: in the absence of trade, the United States produces and consumes 16 small jets and 18 large jets per year, while Brazil produces and consumes 6 small jets and 8 large jets per year.

But is this the best the two countries can do? No, it isn't. Given that the two producers—and therefore the two countries—have different opportunity costs, theUnited States and Brazil can strike a deal that makes both of them better off.

Table 3-2 shows how such a deal works: the United States specializes in the production of large jets, manufacturing 30 per year, and sells 10 to Brazil. Meanwhile, Brazil specializes in the production of small jets, producing 30 per year, and sells 20 to the United States. The result is shown in Figure 3-2. The United States now consumes more of both small jets and large jets than before: instead of 16 small jets and 18 large jets, it now consumes 20 small jets and 20 large jets. Brazil also consumes more, going from 6 small jets and 8 large jets to 10 small jets and 10 large jets.

TABLE 3-1 U.S. and Brazilian Opportunity Costs of Small Jets and Large Jets

	U.S. Opportunity Cost	Brazilian Opportunity Cost
1 small jet	¾ large jet > large jet	
1 large jet	4/3 small jets	

TABLE 3-2 How the United States and Brazil Gain from Trade

		Without Trade		With Trade		Gains from Trade
		Production	Consumption	Production	Consumption	
United States	Large jets	18	18	30	20	+2
	Small jets	16	16	0	20	+4
Brazil	Large jets	8	8	0	10	+2
	Small jets	6	6	30	10	+4

As Table 3-2 also shows, both the United States and Brazil reap gains from trade, consuming more of both types of plane than they would have without trade.

Both countries are better off when they each specialize in what they are good at and then trade. It's a good idea for the United States to specialize in the production of large jets because its opportunity cost of a large jet is smaller than Brazil's: $4/3 < 3$. Correspondingly, Brazil should specialize in the production of small jets because its opportunity cost of a small jet is smaller than the United States: $1/3 < 3/4$.

What we would say in this case is that the United States has a comparative advantage in the production of large jets and Brazil has a comparative advantage in the production of small jets. A country has a **comparative advantage** in producing something if the opportunity cost of that production is lower for that country than for other countries. The same concept applies to firms and people: a firm or an individual has a comparative advantage in producing something if its, his, or her opportunity cost of production is lower than for others.

A country has a **comparative advantage** in producing a good or service if its opportunity cost of producing the good or service is lower than other countries'. Likewise, an individual has a comparative advantage in producing a good or service if his or her opportunity cost of producing the good or service is lower than that for other people.

One point of clarification before we proceed further. You may have wondered why the United States traded 10 large jets to Brazil in return for 20 small jets. Why not some other deal, like trading 10 large jets for 12 small jets? The answer to that question has two parts. First, there may indeed be other trades that the United States and Brazil might agree to. Second, there are some deals that we can safely rule out—one like 10 large jets for 10 small jets.

To understand why, reexamine Table 3-1 and consider the United States first. Without trading with Brazil, the U.S. opportunity cost of a small jet is $3/4$ of a large

FIGURE 3-2 Comparative Advantage and Gains from Trade

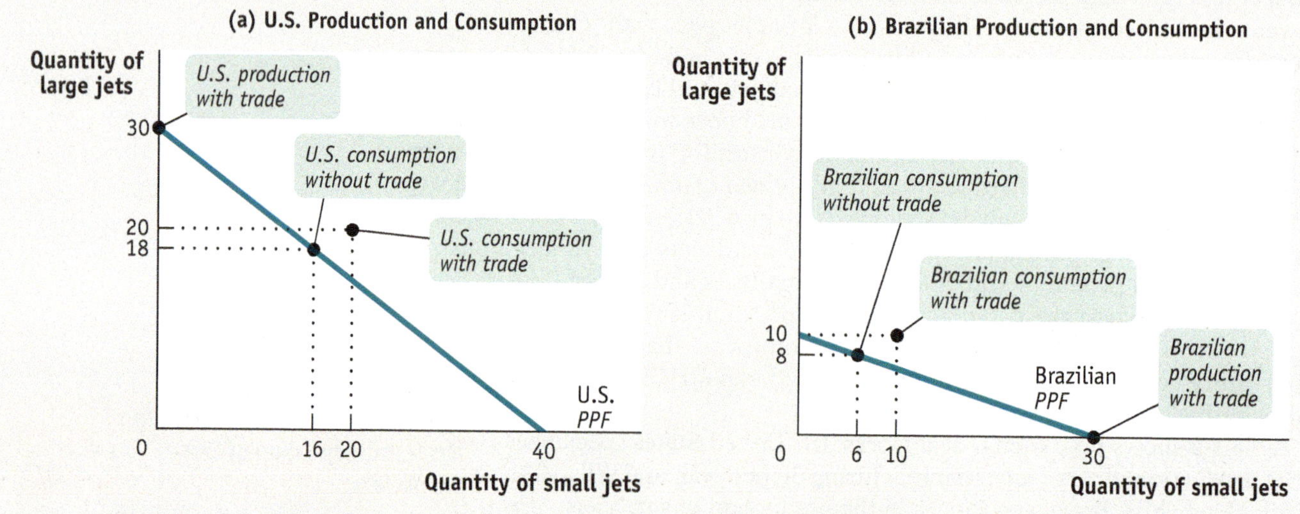

By specializing and trading, the United States and Brazil can produce and consume more of both large jets and small jets. The United States specializes in manufacturing large jets, its comparative advantage, and Brazil—which has an *absolute* disadvantage in both goods but a *comparative* advantage in small jets—specializes in manufacturing small jets. With trade, both countries can consume more of both goods than either could without trade.

jet. So it's clear that the United States will not accept any trade that requires it to give up more than ¾ of a large jet for a small jet. Trading 10 large jets in return for 12 small jets would require the United States to pay an opportunity cost of $10/12 = 5/6$ of a large jet for a small jet. Because ⅚ is greater than ¾, this is a deal that the United States would reject. Similarly, Brazil won't accept a trade that gives it less than ⅓ of a large jet for a small jet.

The point to remember is that the United States and Brazil will be willing to trade only if the "price" of the good each country obtains in the trade is less than its own opportunity cost of producing the good domestically. Moreover, this is a general statement that is true whenever two parties—countries, firms, or individuals—trade voluntarily.

While our story clearly simplifies reality, it teaches us some very important lessons that apply to the real economy, too. First, the model provides a clear illustration of the gains from trade: through specialization and trade, both countries produce more and consume more than if they were self-sufficient. Second, the model demonstrates a very important point that is often overlooked in real-world arguments: each country has a comparative advantage in producing something. This applies to firms and people as well: *everyone has a comparative advantage in something, and everyone has a comparative disadvantage in something.*

Crucially, in our example it doesn't matter if, as is probably the case in real life, U.S. workers are just as good as or even better than Brazilian workers at producing small jets. Suppose that the United States is actually better than Brazil at all kinds of aircraft production. In that case, we would say that the United States has an **absolute advantage** in both large-jet and small-jet production: in an hour, an American worker can produce more of either a large jet or a small jet than a Brazilian worker. You might be tempted to think that in that case the United States has nothing to gain from trading with the less productive Brazil.

But we've just seen that the United States can indeed benefit from trading with Brazil because *comparative, not absolute, advantage is the basis for mutual gain.* It doesn't matter whether it takes Brazil more resources than the United States to make a small jet; what matters for trade is that for Brazil the opportunity cost of a small jet is lower than the U.S. opportunity cost. So Brazil, despite its absolute disadvantage, even in small jets, has a comparative advantage in the manufacture of small jets. Meanwhile the United States, which can use its resources most productively by manufacturing large jets, has a comparative *dis*advantage in manufacturing small jets.

A country has an **absolute advantage** in producing a good or service if the country can produce more output per worker than other countries. Likewise, an individual has an absolute advantage in producing a good or service if he or she is better at producing it than other people are. Having an absolute advantage is not the same thing as having a comparative advantage.

Comparative Advantage and International Trade, in Reality

Look at the label on a manufactured good sold in the United States, and there's a good chance you will find that it was produced in some other country—in China, or Japan, or even in Canada. On the other side, many U.S. industries sell a large fraction of their output overseas. This is particularly true of agriculture, high technology, and entertainment.

Should all this international exchange of goods and services be celebrated, or is it cause for concern? Politicians and the public often question the desirability of international trade, arguing that the nation should produce goods for itself rather

PITFALLS

COMPARATIVE OR ABSOLUTE ADVANTAGE?

Students, pundits, and politicians confuse *comparative advantage* with *absolute advantage* all the time. For example, back in the 1980s, when the U.S. economy seemed to be lagging behind that of Japan, one often heard commentators warn that if we didn't improve our productivity, we would soon have no comparative advantage in anything.

What those commentators meant was that we would have no *absolute advantage* in anything—that there might come a time when the Japanese were better at everything than we were. (It didn't turn out that way, but that's another story.) And they had the idea that in that case we would no longer be able to benefit from trade with Japan.

But just as Brazil, in our example, was able to benefit from trade with the United States (and vice versa) despite the fact that the United States was better at manufacturing both large and small jets, in real life, nations can still gain from trade even if they are less productive in all industries than the countries they trade with.

than buying them from foreigners. Industries around the world demand protection from foreign competition: Japanese farmers want to keep out American rice, American steelworkers want to keep out European steel. And these demands are often supported by public opinion.

Economists, however, have a very positive view of international trade. Why? Because they view it in terms of comparative advantage. As we learned from our example of U.S. large jets and Brazilian small jets, international trade benefits both countries. Each country can consume more than if it doesn't trade and remains self-sufficient. Moreover, these mutual gains don't depend on each country being better than other countries at producing one kind of good. Even if one country has, say, higher output per worker in both industries—that is, even if one country has an absolute advantage in both industries—there are still gains from trade.

ECONOMICS >> *in Action*

Rich Nation, Poor Nation

Jeff Holt/Bloomberg via Getty Images

Although less productive than American workers, Bangladeshi workers have a comparative advantage in clothing production.

Try taking off your clothes—at a suitable time and in a suitable place, of course—and taking a look at the labels inside that say where the garments were made. It's a very good bet that much, if not most, of your clothes were manufactured overseas, in a country that is much poorer than the United States—say, in El Salvador, Sri Lanka, or Bangladesh.

Why are these countries so much poorer than we are? The immediate reason is that their economies are much less *productive*—firms in these countries are just not able to produce as much from a given quantity of resources as comparable firms in the United States or other wealthy countries. Why countries differ so much in productivity is a deep question—indeed, one of the main questions that preoccupy economists. But in any case, the difference in productivity is a fact.

But if the economies of these countries are so much less productive than ours, how is it that they make so much of our clothing? Why don't we do it for ourselves?

The answer is "comparative advantage." Just about every industry in Bangladesh is much less productive than the corresponding industry in the United States. But the productivity difference between rich and poor countries varies across goods; it is very large in the production of sophisticated goods like aircraft but not that large in the production of simpler goods like clothing. So Bangladesh's position with regard to clothing production is like Embraer's position with respect to producing small jets: it's not as good at it as Boeing, but it's the thing Embraer does comparatively well.

Bangladesh has a comparative advantage in clothing production, although it is at an absolute disadvantage compared with the United States in almost everything. This means that both the United States and Bangladesh are able to consume more because they specialize in producing different things, with Bangladesh supplying our clothes and the United States supplying Bangladesh with more sophisticated goods.

>> *Quick Review*

- Every person and every country has a **comparative advantage** in something, giving rise to gains from trade.
- Comparative advantage is often confused with **absolute advantage.**

Check Your Understanding 3-1

1. In Italy, an automobile can be produced by 8 workers in one day and a washing machine by 3 workers in one day. In the United States, an automobile can be produced by 6 workers in one day and a washing machine by 2 workers in one day.
   - **a.** Which country has an absolute advantage in the production of automobiles? In washing machines?
   - **b.** Which country has a comparative advantage in the production of washing machines? In automobiles?
   - **c.** What pattern of specialization results in the greatest gains from trade between the two countries?
2. Using the numbers from Table 3-1, explain why the United States and Brazil are willing to engage in a trade of 10 large jets for 15 small jets.

Solutions appear at back of book.

The Circular-Flow Diagram

MODULE 4

WHAT YOU WILL LEARN

- How do you interpret the **circular-flow diagram** of the economy?
- How do individual decisions affect the larger economy?
- How do you interpret **positive** and **normative** statements?

The model economies that we saw in Module 3—each containing only one firm—are huge simplifications. We've also greatly simplified trade between the United States and Brazil, assuming that they engage only in the simplest of economic transactions, **barter,** in which one party directly trades a good or service for another good or service without using money. In a modern economy, simple barter is rare: usually people trade goods or services for money—pieces of colored paper with no inherent value—and then trade those pieces of colored paper for the goods or services they want. That is, they sell goods or services and buy a lot of different goods or services. We'll next look at a diagram that is a schematic representation that helps us understand how flows of money, goods, and services are channeled through the economy.

ginosphotos/Thinkstock/Getty Images

4.1 The Circular-Flow Diagram

The U.S. economy is a vastly complex entity, with more than a hundred million workers employed by millions of companies, producing millions of different goods and services. Yet you can learn some very important things about the economy by considering the simple graphic shown in Figure 4-1, the **circular-flow diagram.** This diagram represents the transactions that take place in an economy by two kinds of flows around a circle: flows of physical things such as goods, services, labor, or raw materials in one direction, and flows of money that pay for these physical things in the opposite direction. In this case the physical flows are shown in blue, the money flows in green.

The simplest circular-flow diagram illustrates an economy that contains only two kinds of inhabitants: **households** and **firms.** A household consists of either an individual or a group of people (usually, but not necessarily, a family) that

Trade takes the form of **barter** when people directly exchange goods or services that they have for goods or services that they want.

The **circular-flow diagram** uses flows around a circle to represent the transactions in an economy.

A **household** is a person or a group of people that share their income.

A **firm** is an organization that produces goods and services for sale.

FIGURE 4-1 The Circular-Flow Diagram

This diagram represents the flows of money and of goods and services in the economy. In the markets for goods and services, households purchase goods and services from firms, generating a flow of money to the firms and a flow of goods and services to the households. The money flows back to households as firms purchase factors of production from the households in factor markets.

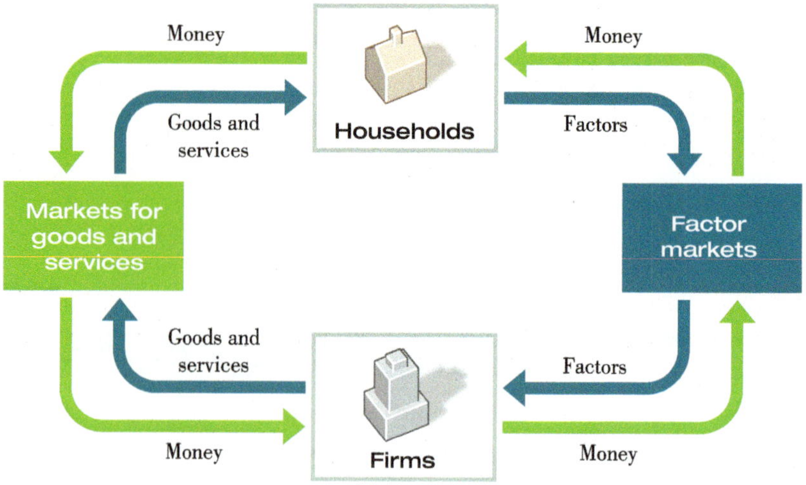

Firms sell goods and services that they produce to households in **markets for goods and services.**

Firms buy the resources they need to produce goods and services in **factor markets.**

An economy's **income distribution** is the way in which total income is divided among the owners of the various factors of production.

share their income. A firm is an organization that produces goods and services for sale—and that employs members of households.

As you can see in Figure 4-1, there are two kinds of markets in this simple economy. On the left side, there are **markets for goods and services** in which households buy the goods and services they want from firms. This produces a flow of goods and services to households and a return flow of money to firms.

On the right side, there are **factor markets,** in which firms buy the resources they need to produce goods and services. Recall from earlier that the main factors of production are land, labor, physical capital, and human capital.

The factor market most of us know best is the *labor market,* in which workers sell their services. In addition, we can think of households as owning and selling the other factors of production to firms. For example, when a firm buys physical capital in the form of machines, the payment ultimately goes to the households that own the machine-making firm. In this case, the transactions occur in the *capital market,* the market in which capital is bought and sold. As we'll examine in detail later, factor markets ultimately determine an economy's **income distribution,** how the total income created in an economy is allocated between less skilled workers, highly skilled workers, and the owners of capital and land.

The circular-flow diagram ignores a number of real-world complications in the interests of simplicity. A few examples:

- In the real world, the distinction between firms and households isn't always that clear-cut. Consider a small, family-run business—a farm, a shop, a small hotel. Is this a firm or a household? A more complete picture would include a separate box for family businesses.
- Many of the sales firms make are not to households but to other firms; for example, steel companies sell mainly to other companies such as auto manufacturers, not to households. A more complete picture would include these flows of goods, services, and money within the business sector.
- The figure doesn't show the government, which in the real world takes a lot of money out of the circular flow in the form of taxes but also injects a lot of money back into the flow in the form of spending.

Figure 4-1, in other words, is by no means a complete picture either of all the types of inhabitants of the real economy or of all the flows of money and physical items that take place among these inhabitants.

Despite its simplicity, the circular-flow diagram is a very useful aid to thinking about how the economy works and how the participants are interconnected. Next we'll take a closer look at the relationship between individual decision making and broader economic outcomes.

Check Your Understanding 4-1

1. Use the circular-flow diagram to explain how an increase in the amount of money spent by households results in an increase in the number of jobs in the economy. Describe in words what the circular-flow diagram predicts.

Solutions appear at back of book.

>> Quick Review

- In the simplest economies people **barter** rather than transact with money. The **circular-flow diagram** illustrates transactions within the economy as flows of goods and services, **factors of production,** and money between **households** and **firms.**
- These transactions occur in **markets for goods and services** and **factor markets.** Ultimately, factor markets determine the economy's **income distribution.**

4.2 Positive versus Normative Economics

Economic analysis, as we will see throughout the book, draws on a set of basic economic principles. As discussed in this section, economists create models that apply these principles to a particular situation. But what do economists actually do with their models?

Imagine that you are an economic adviser to the governor of your state. What kinds of questions might the governor ask you to answer?

Well, here are three possible questions:

1. How much revenue will the tolls on the state turnpike yield next year?
2. How much would that revenue increase if the toll were raised from $1 to $1.50?
3. Should the toll be raised, bearing in mind that a toll increase will reduce traffic and air pollution near the road but will impose some financial hardship on frequent commuters?

There is a big difference between the first two questions and the third one. The first two are questions about facts. Your forecast of next year's toll collection will be proved right or wrong when the numbers actually come in. Your estimate of the impact of a change in the toll is a little harder to check—revenue depends on other factors besides the toll, and it may be hard to disentangle the causes of any change in revenue. Still, in principle there is only one right answer.

But the question of whether tolls should be raised may not have a "right" answer—two people who agree on the effects of a higher toll could still disagree about whether raising the toll is a good idea. For example, someone who lives near the turnpike but doesn't commute on it will care a lot about noise and air pollution but not so much about commuting costs. A regular commuter who doesn't live near the turnpike will have the opposite priorities.

This example highlights a key distinction between two roles of economic analysis. Analysis that tries to answer questions about the way the world works, which have definite right and wrong answers, is known as **positive economics.** In contrast, analysis that involves saying how the world *should* work is known as **normative economics.** To put it another way, positive economics is about description; normative economics is about prescription.

Positive economics is the branch of economic analysis that describes the way the economy actually works.

Normative economics makes prescriptions about the way the economy should work.

Positive economics occupies most of the time and effort of the economics profession. And models play a crucial role in almost all positive economics. As we mentioned earlier, the U.S. government uses a computer model to assess proposed

A **forecast** is a simple prediction of the future.

changes in national tax policy, and many state governments have similar models to assess the effects of their own tax policy.

It's worth noting that there is a subtle but important difference between the first and second questions we imagined the governor asking. Question 1 asked for a simple prediction about next year's revenue—a **forecast.** Question 2 was a "what if" question, asking how revenue would change if the tax law were changed. Economists are often called upon to answer both types of questions, but models are especially useful for answering "what if" questions.

Suppose your economic model tells you that the governor's proposed increase in highway tolls will raise property values in communities near the road but will hurt people who must take the turnpike to get to work. Does that make this proposed toll increase a good idea or a bad one? It depends on whom you ask. As we've just seen, someone who is very concerned with the communities near the road will support the increase, but someone who is very concerned with the welfare of drivers will feel differently. That's a value judgment—it's not a question of economic analysis.

Still, economists often do engage in normative economics and give policy advice. How can they do this when there may be no "right" answer?

One answer is that economists are also citizens, and we all have our opinions. But economic analysis can often be used to show that some policies are clearly better than others, regardless of anyone's opinions.

Suppose that policies A and B achieve the same goal, but policy A makes everyone better off than policy B—or at least makes some people better off without making other people worse off. Then A is clearly more efficient than B. That's not a value judgment: we're talking about how best to achieve a goal, not about the goal itself.

For example, two different policies have been used to help low-income families obtain housing: rent control, which limits the rents landlords are allowed to charge, and rent subsidies, which provide families with additional money to pay rent. Almost all economists agree that subsidies are the more efficient policy. And so the great majority of economists, whatever their personal politics, favor subsidies over rent control.

>> Quick Review

- **Positive economics**—the focus of most economics research—is the analysis of the way the world works, in which there are definite right and wrong answers. It often involves making **forecasts.** But **normative economics,** which makes prescriptions about how things ought to be, inevitably involves value judgments.

Check Your Understanding 4-2

1. Which of the following statements is a positive statement? Which is a normative statement?
   - **a.** Society should take measures to prevent people from engaging in dangerous personal behavior.
   - **b.** People who engage in dangerous personal behavior impose higher costs on society through higher medical costs.

Solutions appear at back of book.

BUSINESS CASE

Efficiency, Opportunity Cost, and the Logic of Lean Production

Dan Lamont/Alamy

In January 2020, the Boeing 777x, an update to the widely popular 777, took its maiden flight. The 777x was the product of what Boeing calls its *advanced manufacturing* process. With it, Boeing extended its extremely successful process known as *lean production* to newer production methods, such as robotics.

Lean manufacturing, pioneered by Toyota Motors of Japan, is based on the practice of having parts arrive on the factory floor just as they are needed for production. This reduces the amount of parts Boeing holds in inventory as well as the amount of space on the factory floor needed for production. To help move from lean production to advanced manufacturing Boeing has turned to Toyota, hiring some of that company's top engineers.

Boeing first adopted lean manufacturing in 1999 in the manufacture of the 737, the most popular commercial airplane. By 2005, after constant refinement, it achieved a 50% reduction in the time it takes to produce a plane and a nearly 60% reduction in parts inventory. An important feature is a continuously moving assembly line, moving products from one assembly team to the next at a steady pace and eliminating the need for workers to wander across the factory floor from task to task or in search of tools and parts.

Toyota's lean production techniques have been the most widely adopted, revolutionizing manufacturing worldwide. In simple terms, lean production is focused on organization and communication. Workers and parts are organized so as to ensure a smooth and consistent workflow that minimizes wasted effort and materials. Lean production is also designed to be highly responsive to changes in the desired mix of output—for example, quickly producing more SUVs and fewer sedans according to changes in customer demand.

Toyota's methods were so successful that they transformed the global auto industry and severely threatened once-dominant American automakers. Until the 1980s, the "Big Three"—Chrysler, Ford, and General Motors—dominated the American auto industry, with virtually no foreign-made cars sold in the United States. In the 1980s, however, Toyotas became increasingly popular due to their high quality and relatively low price—so popular that the Big Three eventually prevailed upon the U.S. government to protect them by restricting the sale of Japanese autos in the United States. Over time, Toyota responded by building assembly plants in the United States, bringing along its lean production techniques, which then spread throughout American manufacturing.

QUESTIONS FOR THOUGHT

1. What is the opportunity cost associated with having a worker wander across the factory floor from task to task or in search of tools and parts?
2. Explain how lean manufacturing improves the economy's efficiency in allocation.
3. Before lean manufacturing innovations, Japan mostly sold consumer electronics to the United States. How did lean manufacturing innovations alter Japan's comparative advantage vis-à-vis the United States?
4. How do you think the shift in the location of Toyota's production from Japan to the United States has altered the pattern of comparative advantage in automaking between the two countries?

REVIEW

MODULE 1

1. **Economics** is the study of scarcity and choices. Everyone has to make choices about what to do and what *not* to do. The **economy** is a system that coordinates choices about production and consumption. In a **market economy,** these choices are made by many firms and individuals. Economists have used the term **invisible hand** to refer to the way a market economy manages to harness the power of self-interest for the good of society.

2. **Microeconomics** is the branch of economics that studies how people make decisions and how these decisions interact. **Market failure** occurs when the individual pursuit of self-interest leads to bad results for society as a whole.

3. **Macroeconomics** is the branch of economics that is concerned with economy-wide interactions, the ups and downs of the economy. Despite occasional **recessions,** the U.S. economy has achieved long-run **economic growth.**

4. All economic analysis is based on a set of basic principles that apply to three levels of economic activity. First, we study how individuals make choices; second, we study how these choices interact; and third, we study how the economy functions overall.

5. **Individual choice** is the basis of economics—if it doesn't involve choice, it isn't economics. The reason choices must be made is that **resources**—anything that can be used to produce something else—are **scarce.** The four categories of resources are **land, labor, physical capital,** and **human capital.** Individuals are limited in their choices by money and time; economies are limited by their supplies of human and natural resources. Because you must choose among limited alternatives, the truest cost of anything is what you must give up to get it—all costs are **opportunity costs.** Many economic decisions involve questions not of "whether" but of "how much"—how much to spend on some good, how much to produce, and so on. Such decisions must be made by performing a **trade-off** at the margin—by comparing the costs and benefits of doing a bit more or a bit less. Decisions of this type are called **marginal decisions,** and the study of them, **marginal analysis,** plays a central role in economics. The study of how people *should* make decisions is also a good way to understand actual behavior. Individuals usually respond to **incentives**—exploiting opportunities to make themselves better off.

6. The next level of economic analysis is the study of **interaction**—how my choices depend on your choices, and vice versa. When individuals interact, the end result may be different from what anyone intends. Individuals interact because there are **gains from trade:** by engaging in the **trade** of goods and services with one another, the members of an economy can all be made better off. **Specialization**—each person specializes in the task he or she is good at—is the source of gains from trade. Because individuals usually respond to incentives, markets normally move toward **equilibrium**—a situation in which no individual can make himself or herself better off by taking a different action. An economy is **efficient** if all opportunities to make some people better off without making other people worse off are taken. Resources should be used as efficiently as possible to achieve society's goals. But efficiency is not the sole way to evaluate an economy: **equity,** or fairness, is also desirable, and there is often a trade-off between equity and efficiency. Markets usually lead to efficiency, with some well-defined exceptions. When markets fail and do not achieve efficiency, government intervention can improve society.

7. Because people in a market economy earn income by selling things, one person's spending is another person's income. Overall spending in an economy can get out line with the economy's production capacity. Spending below the economy's productive capacity leads to a recession; spending in excess leads to inflation. When spending gets out of line, governments can use macroeconomic policy tools to steer the economy between recession and inflation. Increases in the economy's potential lead to economic growth over time. Although economic growth leads to higher living standards for everyone over time, in the short run, increases in the economy's potential lead to both winners and losers.

MODULE 2

1. Almost all economics is based on **models,** "thought experiments" or simplified versions of reality, many of which use mathematical tools such as graphs. An important assumption in economic models is the **other things equal assumption,** which allows analysis of the effect of a change in one factor by holding all other relevant factors unchanged.

2. One important economic model is the **production possibility frontier,** which illustrates the **trade-offs** facing an economy that produces only two goods. The PPF illustrates three elements: *opportunity cost* (showing how much less of one good can be produced if more of the other good is produced), *efficiency* (an economy is **efficient** in production if it produces on the production possibility frontier and efficient

in allocation if it produces the mix of goods and services that people want to consume), and *economic growth* (an outward shift of the production possibility frontier). There are two basic sources of growth: an increase in **factors of production**—resources such as land, labor, capital, and human capital, inputs that are not used up in production—and improved **technology.**

MODULE 3

1. Another important model is **comparative advantage,** which explains the source of gains from trade between individuals and countries. Everyone has a comparative advantage in something—some good or service in which that person has a lower opportunity cost than everyone else. But it is often confused with **absolute advantage,** an ability to produce a particular good or service better than anyone else. This confusion leads some to erroneously conclude that there are no gains from trade between people or countries.

MODULE 4

1. In the simplest economies people **barter**—trade goods and services, one for one another—rather than trade them for money, as in a modern economy. The **circular-flow diagram** represents transactions within the economy as flows of goods, services, and money between **households** and **firms.** These transactions occur in **markets for goods and services** and **factor markets,** markets for factors of production—land, labor, physical capital, and human capital. It is useful in understanding how spending, production, employment, income, and growth are related in the economy. Ultimately, factor markets determine the economy's **income distribution,** how an economy's total income is allocated to the owners of the factors of production.
2. Economists use economic models for both **positive economics,** which describes how the economy works, and **normative economics,** which prescribes how the economy *should* work. Positive economics often involves making **forecasts.** Economists can determine the correct answer for positive questions but typically not for normative questions, which involve value judgments. The exceptions are when policies designed to achieve a certain objective can be clearly ranked in terms of efficiency.

KEY TERMS

1

APPENDIX

Graphs in Economics

Getting the Picture

When you're reading about economics in the *Wall Street Journal* or in your economics textbook, you will see many graphs. Visual images can make it much easier to understand verbal descriptions, numerical information, or ideas. In economics, graphs are the type of visual image used to facilitate understanding. So, you need to be familiar with how to interpret and construct these visual aids. This appendix explains how to do that.

Graphs, Variables, and Economic Models

One reason to attend college is that a bachelor's degree provides access to higher-paying jobs. Additional degrees, such as MBAs or law degrees, increase earnings even more. If you were to read an article about the relationship between educational attainment and income, you would probably see a graph showing the income levels for workers with different amounts of education. The graph would depict the idea that, in general, more education increases income.

Like most graphs in economics, this graph would depict the relationship between two economic variables. A **variable** is a quantity that can take on more than one value, such as the number of years of education a person has, the price of a can of soda, or a household's income.

As you learned in this section, economic analysis relies heavily on *models*, simplified descriptions of real situations. Most economic models describe the relationship between two variables, simplified by holding constant other variables that may affect the relationship.

For example, an economic model might describe the relationship between the price of a can of soda and the number of cans of soda that consumers will buy, assuming that everything else affecting consumers' purchases of soda stays constant. This type of model can be described mathematically or verbally, but illustrating the relationship in a graph makes it easier to understand, as you'll see next.

How Graphs Work

Most graphs in economics are based on a grid built around two perpendicular lines that show the values of two variables, helping you visualize the relationship between them. Let's see how this works.

Two-Variable Graphs

A quantity that can take on more than one value is called a **variable.**

Figure 1A-1 shows a typical two-variable graph. It illustrates the data in the accompanying table on outside temperature and the number of sodas a typical vendor can expect to sell at a baseball stadium during one game. The first column

FIGURE 1A-1 Plotting Points on a Two-Variable Graph

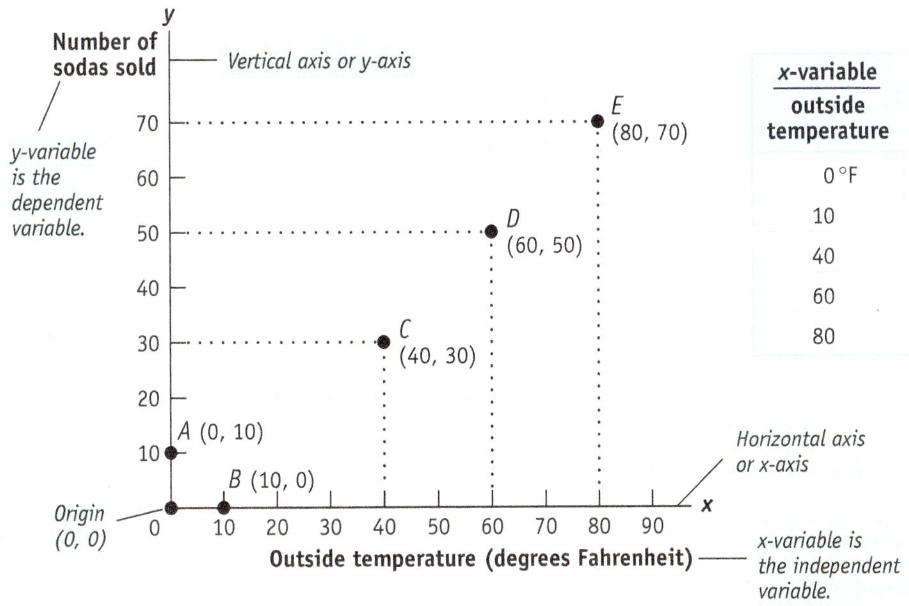

x-variable outside temperature	*y*-variable number of sodas sold	Point
0 °F	10	*A*
10	0	*B*
40	30	*C*
60	50	*D*
80	70	*E*

The data from the table are plotted where outside temperature (the independent variable) is measured along the horizontal axis and number of sodas sold (the dependent variable) is measured along the vertical axis. Each of the five combinations of temperature and sodas sold is represented by a point: *A*, *B*, *C*, *D*, and *E*. Each point in the graph is identified by a pair of values. For example, point *C* corresponds to the pair (40, 30)—an outside temperature of 40°F (the value of the *x*-variable) and 30 sodas sold (the value of the *y*-variable).

shows the values of outside temperature (the first variable) and the second column shows the values of the number of sodas sold (the second variable). Five combinations or pairs of the two variables are shown, each denoted by *A* through *E* in the third column.

Now let's turn to graphing the data in this table. In any two-variable graph, one variable is called the *x*-variable and the other is called the *y*-variable. Here we have made outside temperature the *x*-variable and number of sodas sold the *y*-variable. The solid horizontal line in the graph is called the **horizontal axis** or ***x*-axis,** and values of the *x*-variable—outside temperature—are measured along it. Similarly, the solid vertical line in the graph is called the **vertical axis** or ***y*-axis,** and values of the *y*-variable—number of sodas sold—are measured along it.

At the **origin,** the point where the two axes meet, each variable is equal to zero. As you move rightward from the origin along the *x*-axis, values of the *x*-variable are positive and increasing. As you move up from the origin along the *y*-axis, values of the *y*-variable are positive and increasing.

You can plot each of the five points *A* through *E* on this graph by using a pair of numbers—the values that the *x*-variable and the *y*-variable take on for a given point. In Figure 1A-1, at point *C*, the *x*-variable takes on the value 40 and the *y*-variable takes on the value 30. You plot point *C* by drawing a line straight up from 40 on the *x*-axis and a horizontal line across from 30 on the *y*-axis. We write point *C* as (40, 30). We write the origin as (0, 0).

Looking at point *A* and point *B* in Figure 1A-1, you can see that when one of the variables for a point has a value of zero, it will lie on one of the axes. If the value of the *x*-variable is zero, the point will lie on the vertical axis, like point *A*. If the value of the *y*-variable is zero, the point will lie on the horizontal axis, like point *B*.

The line along which values of the *x*-variable are measured is called the **horizontal axis** or ***x*-axis.** The line along which values of the *y*-variable are measured is called the **vertical axis** or ***y*-axis.** The point where the axes of a two-variable graph meet is the **origin.**

Most graphs that depict relationships between two economic variables represent a **causal relationship,** a relationship in which the value taken by one variable directly influences or determines the value taken by the other variable. In a causal relationship, the determining variable is called the **independent variable;** the variable it determines is called the **dependent variable.** In our example of soda sales, the outside temperature is the independent variable. It directly influences the number of sodas that are sold, the dependent variable in this case.

A **causal relationship** exists between two variables when the value taken by one variable directly influences or determines the value taken by the other variable. In a causal relationship, the determining variable is called the **independent variable;** the variable it determines is called the **dependent variable.**

By convention, we put the independent variable on the horizontal axis and the dependent variable on the vertical axis. Figure 1A-1 is constructed consistent with this convention; the independent variable (outside temperature) is on the horizontal axis and the dependent variable (number of sodas sold) is on the vertical axis.

An important exception to this convention is in graphs that show the economic relationship between the price of a product and the quantity of the product: although price is generally the independent variable that determines quantity, it is always measured on the vertical axis.

A **curve** is a line on a graph that depicts a relationship between two variables. It may be either a straight line or a curved line. If the curve is a straight line, the variables have a **linear relationship.** If the curve is not a straight line, the variables have a **nonlinear relationship.**

Curves on a Graph

Panel (a) of Figure 1A-2 contains some of the same information as Figure 1A-1, with a line drawn through the points *B, C, D,* and *E.* Such a line on a graph is called a **curve,** regardless of whether it is a straight line or a curved line. If the curve that shows the relationship between two variables is a straight line, or linear, the variables have a **linear relationship.** When the curve is not a straight line, or nonlinear, the variables have a **nonlinear relationship.**

FIGURE 1A-2 Drawing Curves

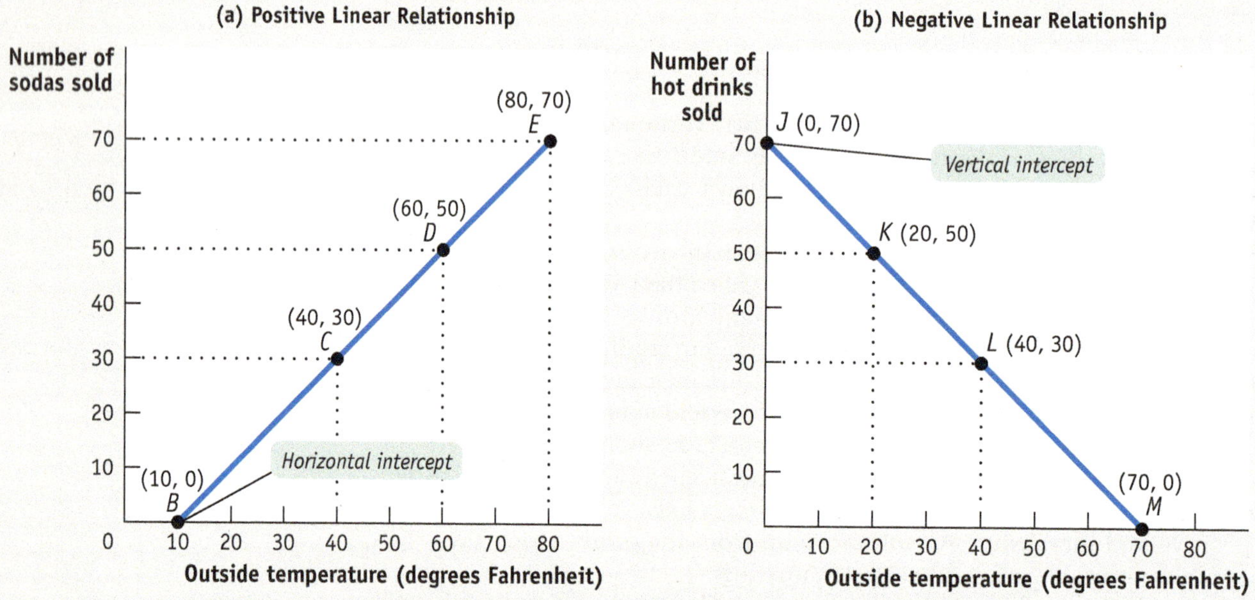

The curve in panel (a) illustrates the relationship between the two variables, outside temperature and number of sodas sold. The two variables have a positive linear relationship: positive because the curve has an upward tilt, and linear because it is a straight line. This relationship implies that an increase in the *x*-variable (outside temperature) leads to an increase in the *y*-variable (number of sodas sold). The curve in panel (b) is also a straight line, but it tilts downward. The two variables here, outside temperature and number of hot drinks sold, have a negative linear relationship: an increase in the *x*-variable (outside temperature) leads to a decrease in the *y*-variable (number of hot drinks sold). The curve in panel (a) has a horizontal intercept at point *B*, where it hits the horizontal axis. The curve in panel (b) has a vertical intercept at point *J*, where it hits the vertical axis, and a horizontal intercept at point *M*, where it hits the horizontal axis.

A point on a curve indicates the value of the *y*-variable for a specific value of the *x*-variable. For example, point *D* indicates that at a temperature of 60°F, a vendor can expect to sell 50 sodas. The shape and orientation of a curve reveal the general nature of the relationship between the two variables. The upward tilt of the curve in panel (a) of Figure 1A-2 means that vendors can expect to sell more sodas at higher outside temperatures.

When variables are related this way—that is, when an increase in one variable is associated with an increase in the other variable—the variables are said to have a **positive relationship.** It is illustrated by a curve that slopes upward from left to right. Because this curve is also linear, the relationship between outside temperature and number of sodas sold illustrated by the curve in panel (a) of Figure 1A-2 is a positive linear relationship.

When an increase in one variable is associated with a decrease in the other variable, the two variables are said to have a **negative relationship.** It is illustrated by a curve that slopes downward from left to right, like the curve in panel (b) of Figure 1A-2. Because this curve is also linear, the relationship it depicts is a negative linear relationship. Two variables that might have such a relationship are the outside temperature and the number of hot drinks a vendor can expect to sell at a baseball stadium.

Return for a moment to the curve in panel (a) of Figure 1A-2. Notice that it hits the horizontal axis at point *B*. This point, known as the **horizontal intercept,** shows the value of the *x*-variable when the value of the *y*-variable is zero. In panel (b) of Figure 1A-2, the curve hits the vertical axis at point *J*. This point, called the **vertical intercept,** indicates the value of the *y*-variable when the value of the *x*-variable is zero.

Two variables have a **positive relationship** when an increase in the value of one variable is associated with an increase in the value of the other variable. It is illustrated by a curve that slopes upward from left to right.

Two variables have a **negative relationship** when an increase in the value of one variable is associated with a decrease in the value of the other variable. It is illustrated by a curve that slopes downward from left to right.

The **horizontal intercept** of a curve is the point at which it hits the horizontal axis; it indicates the value of the *x*-variable when the value of the *y*-variable is zero.

The **vertical intercept** of a curve is the point at which it hits the vertical axis; it shows the value of the *y*-variable when the value of the *x*-variable is zero.

The **slope** of a line or curve is a measure of how steep it is. The slope of a line is measured by "rise over run"—the change in the *y*-variable between two points on the line divided by the change in the *x*-variable between those same two points.

A Key Concept: The Slope of a Curve

The **slope** of a curve is a measure of how steep it is and indicates how sensitive the *y*-variable is to a change in the *x*-variable. In our example of outside temperature and the number of cans of soda a vendor can expect to sell, the slope of the curve would indicate how many more cans of soda the vendor could expect to sell with each 1-degree increase in temperature. Interpreted this way, the slope gives meaningful information. Even without numbers for *x* and *y*, it is possible to arrive at important conclusions about the relationship between the two variables by examining the slope of a curve at various points.

The Slope of a Linear Curve

Along a linear curve, the slope, or steepness, is measured by dividing the *rise* between two points on the curve by the *run* between those same two points. The rise is the amount that *y* changes, and the run is the amount that *x* changes. Here is the formula:

$$\frac{\text{Change in } y}{\text{Change in } x} = \frac{\Delta y}{\Delta x} = \text{Slope}$$

In the formula, the symbol Δ (the Greek uppercase delta) stands for *change in*. When a variable increases, the change in that variable is positive; when a variable decreases, the change in that variable is negative.

The slope of a curve is positive when the rise (the change in the *y*-variable) has the same sign as the run (the change in the *x*-variable). That's because when two numbers have the same sign, the ratio of those two numbers is positive. The curve in panel (a) of Figure 1A-2 has a positive slope: along the curve, both the *y*-variable and the *x*-variable increase.

FIGURE 1A-3 Calculating the Slope

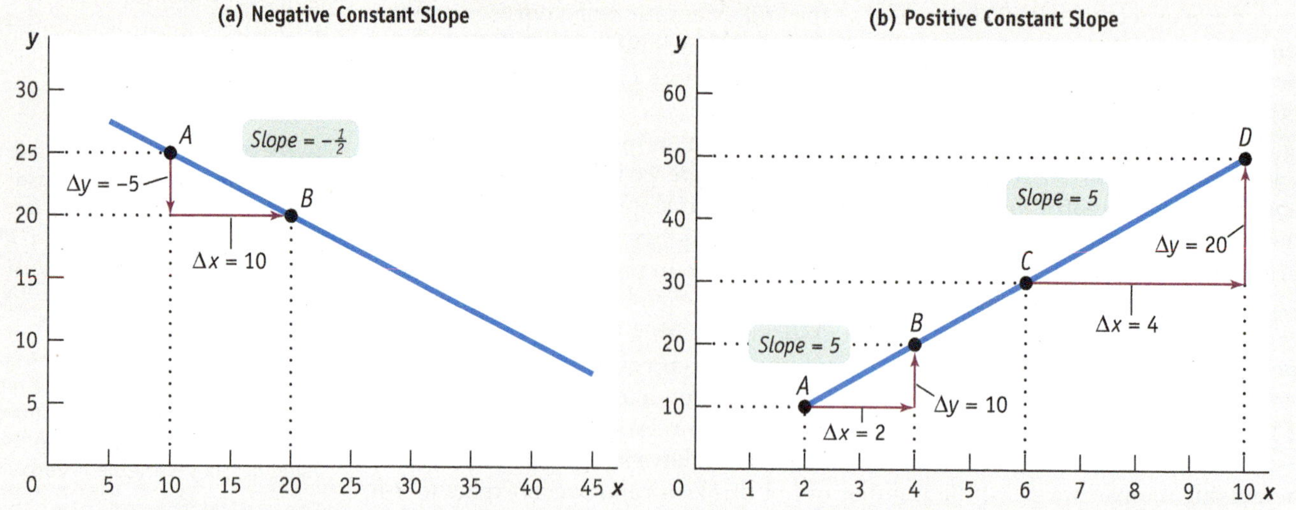

Panels (a) and (b) show two linear curves. Between points *A* and *B* on the curve in panel (a), the change in *y* (the rise) is −5 and the change in *x* (the run) is 10. So the slope from *A* to *B* is $\frac{\Delta y}{\Delta x} = \frac{-5}{10} = -\frac{1}{2} = -0.5$, where the negative sign indicates that the curve is downward sloping. In panel (b), the curve has a slope from *A* to *B* of $\frac{\Delta y}{\Delta x} = \frac{10}{2} = 5$. The slope from *C* to *D* is $\frac{\Delta y}{\Delta x} = \frac{20}{4} = 5$. The slope is positive, indicating that the curve is upward sloping. Furthermore, the slope between *A* and *B* is the same as the slope between *C* and *D*, making this a linear curve. The slope of a linear curve is constant: it is the same regardless of where it is measured along the curve.

The slope of a curve is negative when the rise and the run have different signs. That's because when two numbers have different signs, the ratio of those two numbers is negative. The curve in panel (b) of Figure 1A-2 has a negative slope: along the curve, an increase in the *x*-variable is associated with a decrease in the *y*-variable.

Figure 1A-3 illustrates how to calculate the slope of a linear curve. Let's focus first on panel (a). From point *A* to point *B*, the value of the *y*-variable changes from 25 to 20 and the value of the *x*-variable changes from 10 to 20. So the slope of the line between these two points is:

$$\frac{\text{Change in } y}{\text{Change in } x} = \frac{\Delta y}{\Delta x} = \frac{-5}{10} = -\frac{1}{2} = -0.5$$

Because a straight line is equally steep at all points, the slope of a straight line is the same at all points. In other words, a straight line has a constant slope. You can check this by calculating the slope of the linear curve between points *A* and *B* and between points *C* and *D* in panel (b) of Figure 1A-3.

Between *A* and *B*: $\frac{\Delta y}{\Delta x} = \frac{10}{2} = 5$

Between *C* and *D*: $\frac{\Delta y}{\Delta x} = \frac{20}{4} = 5$

Horizontal and Vertical Curves and Their Slopes

When a curve is horizontal, the value of the *y*-variable along that curve never changes—it is constant. Everywhere along the curve, the change in *y* is zero. Zero divided by any number is zero. So, regardless of the value of the change in *x*, the slope of a horizontal curve is always zero.

If a curve is vertical, the value of the x-variable along the curve never changes—it is constant. Everywhere along the curve, the change in x is zero. This means that the slope of a vertical curve is a ratio with zero in the denominator. A ratio with zero in the denominator is equal to infinity—that is, an infinitely large number. So the slope of a vertical curve is equal to infinity.

A vertical curve or a horizontal curve has a special implication: it means that the x-variable and the y-variable are unrelated. Two variables are unrelated when a change in one variable (the independent variable) has no effect on the other variable (the dependent variable). Or to put it in a slightly different way, two variables are unrelated when the dependent variable is constant regardless of the value of the independent variable. If, as is usual, the y-variable is the dependent variable, the curve is horizontal. If the dependent variable is the x-variable, the curve is vertical.

A **nonlinear curve** is one in which the slope is not the same between every pair of points.

The **absolute value** of a negative number is the value of the negative number without the minus sign.

The Slope of a Nonlinear Curve

A **nonlinear curve** is one in which the slope changes as you move along it. Panels (a), (b), (c), and (d) of Figure 1A-4 show various nonlinear curves. Panels (a) and (b) show nonlinear curves whose slopes change as you move along them, but the slopes always remain positive. Although both curves tilt upward, the curve in panel (a) gets steeper as you move from left to right in contrast to the curve in panel (b), which gets flatter.

A curve that is upward sloping and gets steeper, as in panel (a), is said to have *positive increasing* slope. A curve that is upward sloping but gets flatter, as in panel (b), is said to have *positive decreasing* slope.

When we calculate the slope along these nonlinear curves, we obtain different values for the slope at different points. How the slope changes along the curve determines the curve's shape. For example, in panel (a) of Figure 1A-4, the slope of the curve is a positive number that steadily increases as you move from left to right, whereas in panel (b), the slope is a positive number that steadily decreases.

The slopes of the curves in panels (c) and (d) are negative numbers. Economists often prefer to express a negative number as its **absolute value,** which is the value of the negative number without the minus sign. In general, we denote the absolute value of a number by two parallel bars around the number; for example, the absolute value of −4 is written as $|-4| = 4$.

In panel (c), the absolute value of the slope steadily increases as you move from left to right. The curve therefore has *negative increasing* slope. In panel (d), the absolute value of the slope of the curve steadily decreases along the curve. This curve therefore has *negative decreasing* slope.

Calculating the Slope Along a Nonlinear Curve

We've just seen that along a nonlinear curve, the value of the slope depends on where you are on that curve. So how do you calculate the slope of a nonlinear curve? We will focus on two methods: the *arc method* and the *point method.*

The Arc Method of Calculating the Slope An arc of a curve is some piece or segment of that curve. For example, panel (a) of Figure 1A-4 shows an arc consisting of the segment of the curve between points *A* and *B*. To calculate the slope along a nonlinear curve using the arc method, you draw a straight line between the two endpoints of the arc. The slope of that straight line is a measure of the average slope of the curve between those two endpoints.

FIGURE 1A-4 Nonlinear Curves

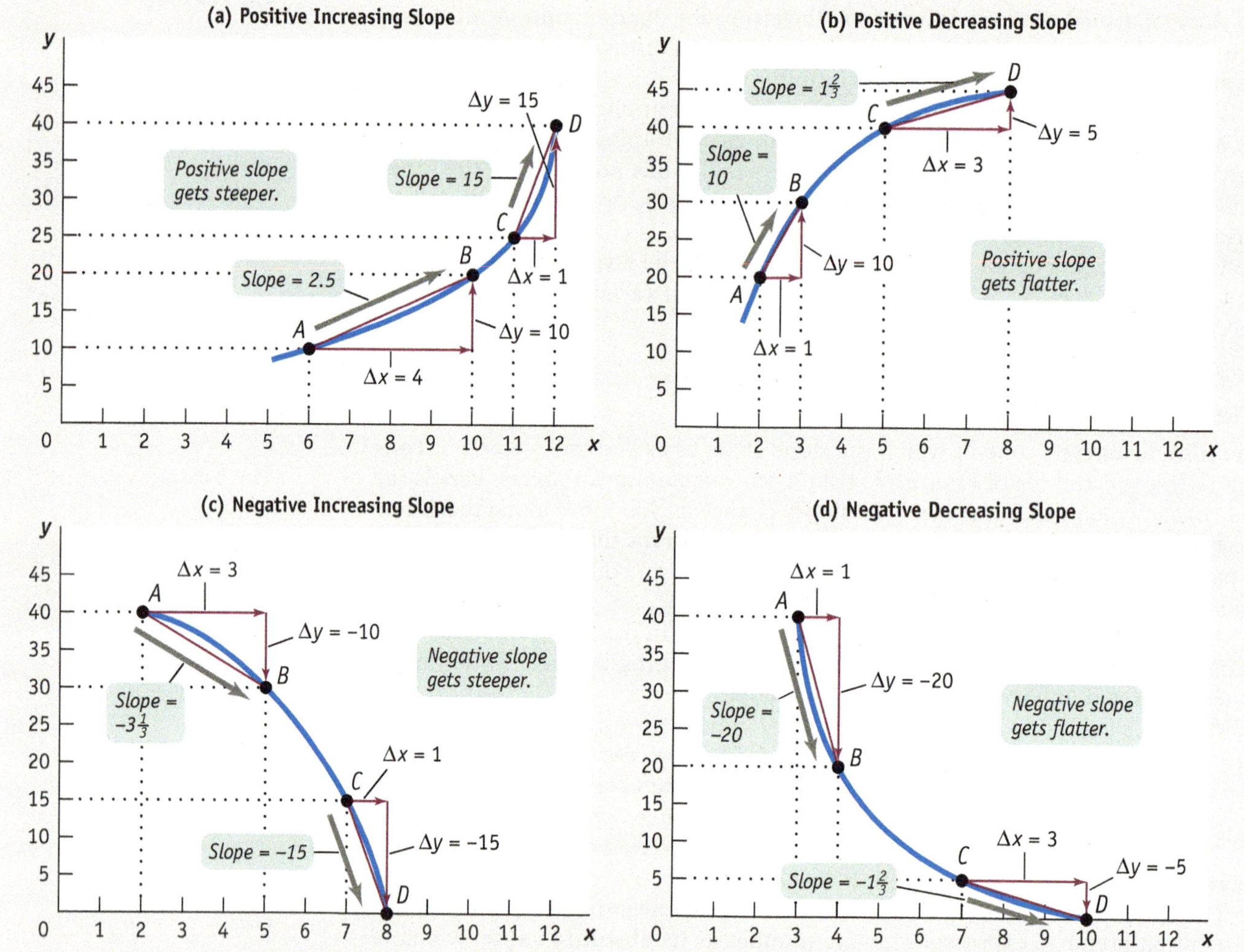

In panel (a), the slope of the curve from A to B is $\frac{y}{x} = \frac{10}{4} = 2.5$, and from C to D it is $\frac{\Delta y}{\Delta x} = \frac{15}{1} = 15$. The slope is positive and increasing; the curve gets steeper as you move to the right. In panel (b), the slope of the curve from A to B is $\frac{\Delta y}{\Delta x} = \frac{10}{1} = 10$, and from C to D it is $\frac{\Delta y}{\Delta x} = \frac{5}{3} = 1\frac{2}{3}$. The slope is positive and decreasing; the curve gets flatter as you move to the right. In panel (c), the slope from A to B is $\frac{\Delta y}{\Delta x} = \frac{-10}{3} = -3\frac{1}{3}$, and from C to D it is $\frac{\Delta y}{\Delta x} = \frac{-15}{1} = -15$. The slope is negative and increasing; the curve gets steeper as you move to the right. And in panel (d), the slope from A to B is $\frac{\Delta y}{\Delta x} = \frac{-20}{1} = -20$, and from C to D it is $\frac{\Delta y}{\Delta x} = \frac{-5}{3} = -1\frac{2}{3}$. The slope is negative and decreasing; the curve gets flatter as you move to the right. The slope in each case has been calculated by using the arc method—that is, by drawing a straight line connecting two points along a curve. The average slope between those two points is equal to the slope of the straight line between those two points.

You can see from panel (a) of Figure 1A-4 that the straight line drawn between points A and B increases along the x-axis from 6 to 10 (so that $\Delta x = 4$) as it increases along the y-axis from 10 to 20 (so that $\Delta y = 10$). Therefore the slope of the straight line connecting points A and B is:

$$\frac{\Delta y}{\Delta x} = \frac{10}{4} = 2.5$$

This means that the average slope of the curve between points A and B is 2.5.

Now consider the arc on the same curve between points C and D. A straight line drawn through these two points increases along the x-axis from 11 to 12 ($\Delta x = 1$) as it increases along the y-axis from 25 to 40 ($\Delta y = 15$). So the average slope between points C and D is:

$$\frac{\Delta y}{\Delta x} = \frac{15}{1} = 15$$

Therefore the average slope between points C and D is larger than the average slope between points A and B. These calculations verify what we have already observed—that this upward-tilted curve gets steeper as you move from left to right and therefore has positive increasing slope.

The Point Method of Calculating the Slope The point method calculates the slope of a nonlinear curve at a specific point on that curve. Figure 1A-5 illustrates how to calculate the slope at point B on the curve. First, we draw a straight line that just touches the curve at point B. Such a line is called a **tangent line:** the fact that it just touches the curve at point B and does not touch the curve at any other point on the curve means that the straight line is *tangent* to the curve at point B. The slope of this tangent line is equal to the slope of the nonlinear curve at point B.

You can see from Figure 1A-5 how the slope of the tangent line is calculated. From point A to point C, the change in y is 15 and the change in x is 5, generating a slope of:

$$\frac{\Delta y}{\Delta x} = \frac{15}{5} = 3$$

FIGURE 1A-5 Calculating the Slope Using the Point Method

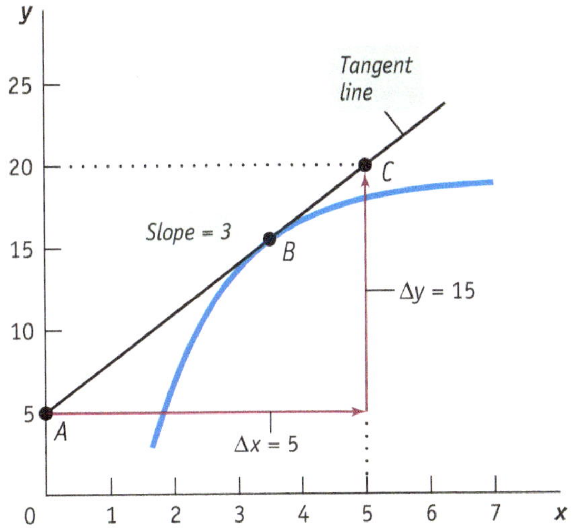

Here a tangent line has been drawn, a line that just touches the curve at point B. The slope of this line is equal to the slope of the curve at point B. The slope of the tangent line, measuring from A to C, is $\frac{\Delta y}{\Delta x} = \frac{15}{5} = 3$.

By the point method, the slope of the curve at point B is equal to 3.

A natural question to ask at this point is which method should I use—the arc method or the point method—in calculating the slope of a nonlinear curve? The answer depends on the curve itself and the data used to construct it.

Use the arc method when you don't have enough information to be able to draw a smooth curve. For example, suppose that in panel (a) of Figure 1A-4 you have only the data represented by points A, C, and D and don't have the data represented by point B or any of the rest of the curve. Clearly, then, you can't use the point method to calculate the slope at point B; you would have to use the arc method to approximate the slope of the curve in this area by drawing a straight line between points A and C.

But if you have sufficient data to draw the smooth curve shown in panel (a) of Figure 1A-4, then you could use the point method to calculate the slope at point B—and at every other point along the curve as well.

Maximum and Minimum Points

The slope of a nonlinear curve can change from positive to negative, or vice versa. When the slope of a curve changes from positive to negative, it creates what is called a *maximum* point of the curve. When the slope of a curve changes from negative to positive, it creates a *minimum* point.

Panel (a) of Figure 1A-6 illustrates a curve in which the slope changes from positive to negative as you move from left to right. When x is between 0 and 50, the slope of the curve is positive. At x equal to 50, the curve attains its highest point—the largest value of y along the curve. This point is called the **maximum** of the curve. When x exceeds 50, the slope becomes negative as the curve turns downward. Many

A **tangent line** is a straight line that just touches, or is tangent to, a nonlinear curve at a particular point. The slope of the tangent line is equal to the slope of the nonlinear curve at that point.

A nonlinear curve may have a **maximum** point, the highest point along the curve. At the maximum, the slope of the curve changes from positive to negative.

FIGURE 1A-6 Maximum and Minimum Points

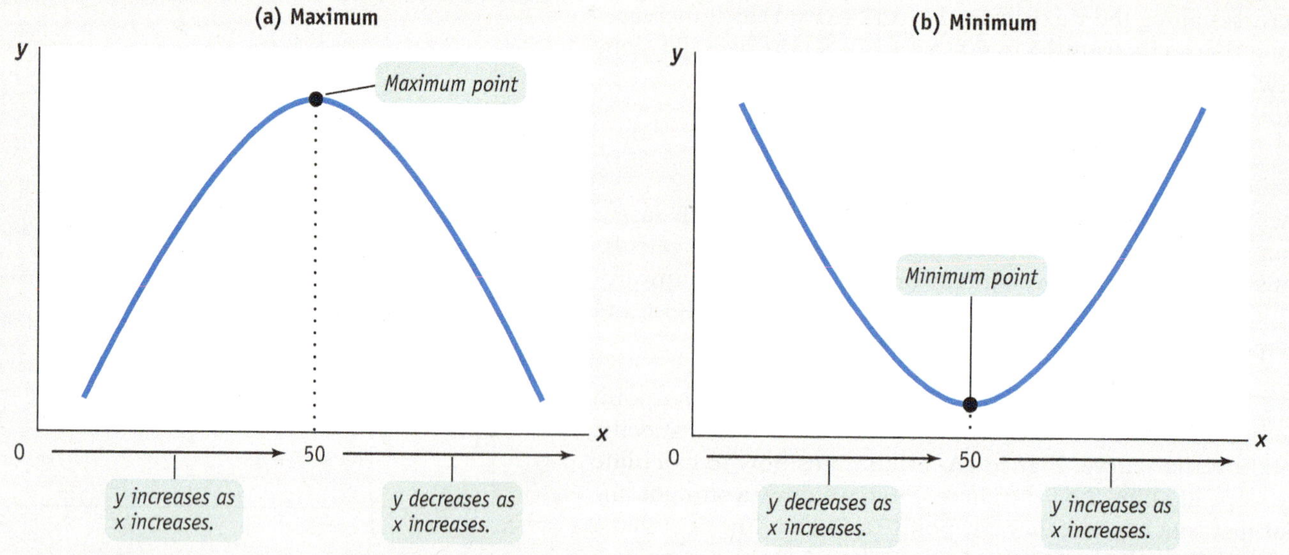

Panel (a) shows a curve with a maximum point, the point at which the slope changes from positive to negative. Panel (b) shows a curve with a minimum point, the point at which the slope changes from negative to positive.

important curves in economics, such as the curve that represents how the profit of a firm changes as it produces more output, are hill-shaped like this.

In contrast, the curve shown in panel (b) of Figure 1A-6 is U-shaped: it has a slope that changes from negative to positive. At x equal to 50, the curve reaches its lowest point—the smallest value of y along the curve. This point is called the **minimum** of the curve. Various important curves in economics are U-shaped like this.

Calculating the Area Below or Above a Curve

It is useful to know how to measure the size of the area below or above a curve. For the sake of simplicity, we'll only calculate the area below or above a linear curve.

How large is the shaded area below the linear curve in panel (a) of Figure 1A-7? First note that this area has the shape of a right triangle. A right triangle is a triangle that has two sides that make a right angle with each other. We will refer to one of these sides as the *height* of the triangle and the other side as the *base* of the triangle. For our purposes, it doesn't matter which of these two sides we refer to as the base and which as the height.

Calculating the area of a right triangle is straightforward: multiply the height of the triangle by the base of the triangle, and divide the result by 2. The height of the triangle in panel (a) of Figure 1A-7 is $10 - 4 = 6$. The base of the triangle is $3 - 0 = 3$. So the area of that triangle is

$$\frac{6 \times 3}{2} = 9$$

How about the shaded area above the linear curve in panel (b) of Figure 1A-7? We can use the same formula to calculate the area of this right triangle. The height of the triangle is $8 - 2 = 6$ and the base of the triangle is $4 - 0 = 4$. So the area of that triangle is

$$\frac{6 \times 4}{2} = 12$$

A nonlinear curve may have a **minimum** point, the lowest point along the curve. At the minimum, the slope of the curve changes from negative to positive.

A **time-series graph** has dates on the horizontal axis and values of a variable that occurred on those dates on the vertical axis.

FIGURE 1A-7 Calculating the Area Below and Above a Linear Curve

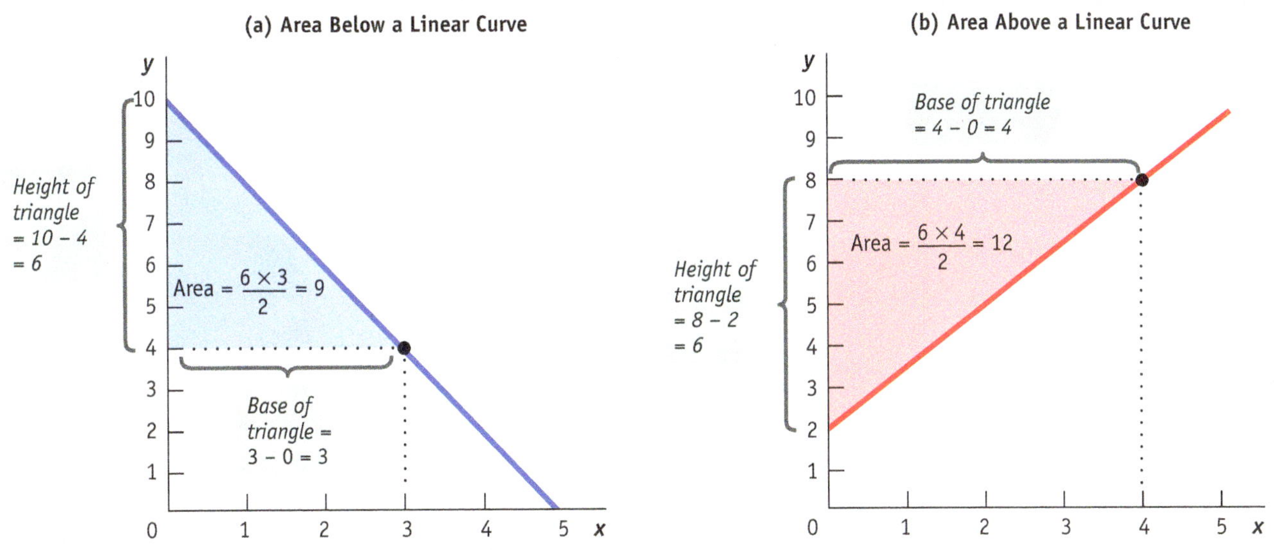

The area above or below a linear curve forms a right triangle. The area of a right triangle is calculated by multiplying the height of the triangle by the base of the triangle, and dividing the result by 2. In panel (a), the area of the shaded triangle is $6 \times \frac{3}{2} = 9$. In panel (b), the area of the shaded triangle is $6 \times \frac{4}{2} = 12$.

Graphs That Depict Numerical Information

Graphs are also a convenient way to summarize and display data without assuming some underlying causal relationship. Graphs that simply display numerical information are called *numerical graphs*. Here we will consider four types of numerical graphs: *time-series graphs, scatter diagrams, pie charts,* and *bar graphs*. These are widely used to display real, empirical data about different economic variables because they often help economists and policy makers identify patterns or trends in the economy. But it's important to be aware of both the usefulness and the limitations of numerical graphs to avoid misinterpreting them or drawing unwarranted conclusions from them.

Types of Numerical Graphs

You have probably seen graphs that show what has happened over time to economic variables such as the unemployment rate or stock prices. A **time-series graph** has successive dates on the horizontal axis and the values of a variable that occurred on those dates on the vertical axis.

For example, Figure 1A-8 shows real gross domestic product (GDP) per capita—a rough measure of a country's standard of living—in the United States from 1950 to 2019. A line connecting the points that correspond to real GDP per capita for each calendar quarter during those years gives a clear idea of the overall trend in the standard of living over these years.

FIGURE 1A-8 Time-Series Graph

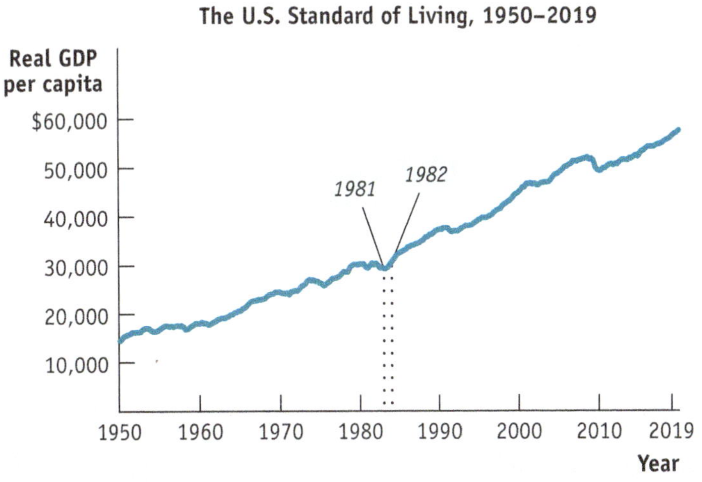

Time-series graphs show successive dates on the *x*-axis and values for a variable on the *y*-axis. This time-series graph shows real gross domestic product per capita, a measure of a country's standard of living, in the United States from 1950 to early 2019.

Data from: The Federal Reserve Bank of St. Louis.

FIGURE 1A-9 Scatter Diagram

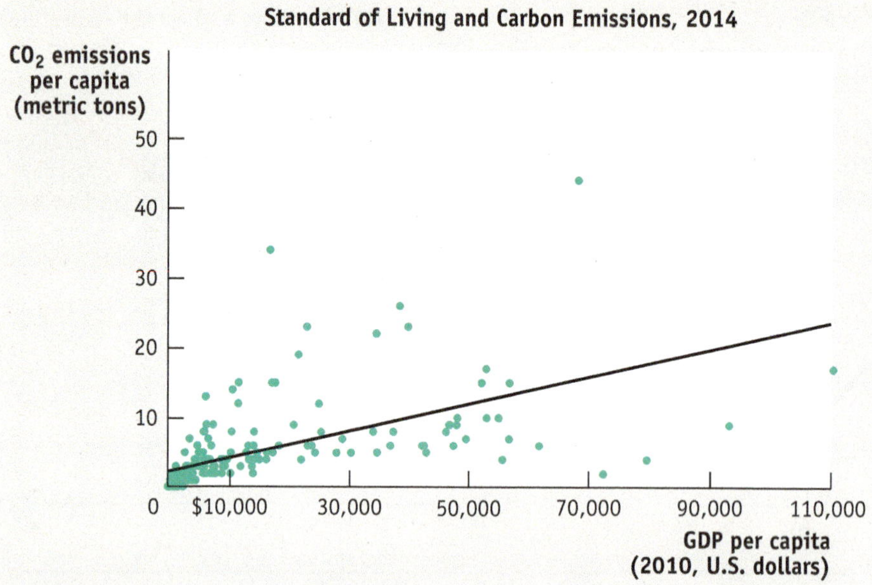

In a scatter diagram, each point represents the corresponding values of the *x*- and *y*-variables for a given observation. Here, each point indicates the GDP per capita and the amount of carbon emissions per capita for a given country for a sample of 180 countries. The upward-sloping fitted line here is the best approximation of the general relationship between the two variables.

Data from: World Development Indicators.

FIGURE 1A-10 Pie Chart

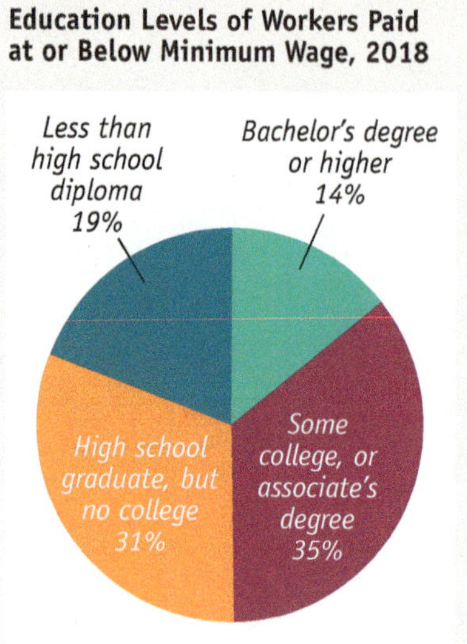

A pie chart shows the percentages of a total amount that can be attributed to various components. This pie chart shows the percentages of workers with given education levels who were paid at or below the federal minimum wage in 2018. (Numbers may not add to 100 due to rounding.)

Data from: Bureau of Labor Statistics.

Figure 1A-9 is an example of a different kind of numerical graph. It represents information from a sample of 180 countries on the standard of living, again measured by GDP per capita, and the amount of carbon emissions per capita, a measure of environmental pollution. Each point here indicates an average resident's standard of living and their annual carbon emissions for a given country.

The points lying in the upper right of the graph, which show combinations of a high standard of living and high carbon emissions, represent economically advanced countries such as the United States. (The country with the highest carbon emissions, at the top of the graph, is Qatar.) Points lying in the bottom left of the graph, which show combinations of a low standard of living and low carbon emissions, represent economically less advanced countries such as Afghanistan and Sierra Leone.

The pattern of points indicates that there is a positive relationship between living standard and carbon emissions per capita: on the whole, people create more pollution in countries with a higher standard of living.

A **scatter diagram** shows points that correspond to actual observations of the *x*- and *y*-variables. A curve is usually fitted to the scatter of points.

A **pie chart** shows how some total is divided among its components, usually expressed in percentages.

A **bar graph** uses bars of varying heights or lengths to show the comparative sizes of different observations of a variable.

This type of graph is called a **scatter diagram,** and each point corresponds to an actual observation of the *x*-variable and the *y*-variable. In scatter diagrams, a curve is typically fitted to the scatter of points; that is, a curve is drawn that approximates as closely as possible the general relationship between the variables. As you can see, the fitted line in Figure 1A-9 is upward sloping, indicating the underlying positive relationship between the two variables. Scatter diagrams are often used to show how a general relationship can be inferred from a set of data.

A **pie chart** shows the share of a total amount that is accounted for by various components, usually expressed in percentages. For example, Figure 1A-10 is

FIGURE 1A-11 Bar Graph

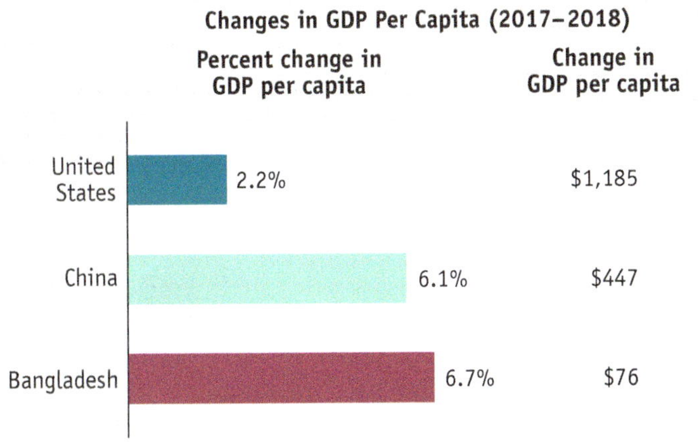

A bar graph measures a variable by using bars of various heights or lengths. This bar graph shows the percent change in GDP per capita (measured in 2010 dollars) for the United States, China, and Bangladesh.

Data from: World Bank, World Development Indicators.

a pie chart that depicts the education levels of workers who in 2018 were paid the federal minimum wage or less. As you can see, the majority of workers paid at or below the minimum wage had no college degree. Only 14% of workers who were paid at or below the minimum wage had a bachelor's degree or higher.

Bar graphs use bars of various heights or lengths to indicate values of a variable. In the bar graph in Figure 1A-11, the bars show the percent change in GDP per capita from 2017 to 2018 for the United States, China, and Bangladesh. Exact values of the variable that is being measured may be written at the end of the bar, as in this figure. For instance, GDP per capita for China increased by 6.1% between 2017 and 2018. But even without the precise values, comparing the heights or lengths of the bars can give useful insight into the relative magnitudes of the different values of the variable.

inga spence/Alamy Stock Photo

Module 5 Demand

Module 6 Supply and Equilibrium

Module 7 Changes in Equilibrium

SECTION 2

Demand, Supply, and Equilibrium

A NATURAL GAS BOOM

From 2010 to 2015, Karnes County, Texas, went from producing a relatively small amount of oil and natural gas to being the largest producing county in Texas. What accounted for that swift change was hydraulic fracturing, or fracking. *Fracking* is a method of extracting natural gas (and to a lesser extent, oil) from deposits trapped between layers of shale rock thousands of feet underground using powerful jets of chemical-laden water.

In those few years, Karnes County also went through an extreme cycle of boom and bust—the price of oil plunged from $100 a barrel in 2014 to under $45 a barrel in 2015, while the price of natural gas (per thousand cubic feet) went from nearly $8 to under $2. What accounted for this reversal of fortune? Once again, it was fracking.

A few decades ago, new drilling technologies were developed that made it possible to reach deeply embedded deposits of natural gas. What finally pushed energy companies to invest in these new extraction technologies, however, was the high price of natural gas over the last decade—quadrupling from 2002 to 2006. Two principal factors explained the high prices: the demand for natural gas and the supply of natural gas.

First, the demand side. In 2002, the U.S. economy was mired in a recession; people and businesses cut their energy consumption. But, by 2006, the U.S. economy came roaring back, and natural gas consumption rose.

Second, the supply side. In 2005, Hurricane Katrina devastated the Gulf Coast, site of most of the country's natural gas production at the time. By 2006 the demand for natural gas surged while supply was severely curtailed. As a result, natural gas prices peaked at around $14 per thousand cubic feet, up from around $2 in 2002.

Fast-forward to 2013: natural gas prices once again fell to $2 per thousand cubic feet. But this time a slow economy was not the principal explanation; now it was the impact of new technologies on oil and natural gas production. To illustrate, the United States produced 8.13 trillion cubic feet of natural gas from shale deposits in 2012, nearly doubling the total from 2010. Today the United States is the world's largest producer of both oil and natural gas.

While there are clear environmental benefits from the switch to natural gas (which burns cleaner than gasoline and coal), fracking has sparked another set of environmental worries. One is the potential for contamination of local groundwater by the chemicals used in fracking. Another is that cheap natural gas may discourage the adoption of more expensive renewable energy sources like solar and wind power, furthering our dependence upon fossil fuel.

How does the high price of natural gas nearly a decade ago translate into today's switch to vehicles powered by natural gas? The short answer is that it's a matter of supply and demand. To economists, the concept of supply and demand has a precise meaning: it is a *model of how a market behaves.*

In this section, we lay out the pieces that make up the *supply and demand model,* put them together, and show how this model can be used to understand how many (but not all) markets behave.

MODULE 5

Demand

WHAT YOU WILL LEARN

- What is a **competitive market?**
- What is a **demand curve?**
- What are the differences between the movements along the demand curve and changes in demand?
- What are the factors that shift the demand curve?

Hirkophoto/Getty Images

5.1 Supply and Demand: A Model of a Competitive Market

Natural gas sellers and natural gas buyers constitute a market—a group of producers and consumers who exchange a good or service for payment. In this section, we'll focus on a particular type of market known as a *competitive market*. A **competitive market** is a market in which there are many buyers and sellers of the same good or service. More precisely, the key feature of a competitive market is that no individual's actions have a noticeable effect on the price at which the good or service is sold. It's important to understand, however, that this is *not* an accurate description of every market.

For example, it's not an accurate description of the market for cola beverages. That's because in this market, Coca-Cola and Pepsi account for such a large proportion of total sales that they are able to influence the price at which cola beverages are bought and sold. But it is an accurate description of the market for natural gas. The global marketplace for natural gas is so huge that even the biggest U.S. driller for natural gas—Exxon Mobil—accounts for such a small share of total global transactions that it is unable to influence the price at which natural gas is bought and sold.

It's a little hard to explain why competitive markets are different from other markets until we've seen how a competitive market works. For now, let's just say that it's easier to model competitive markets than other markets. Just as when taking an exam, it's always a good strategy to begin by answering the easier questions, we are, in this book, going to talk about the easier model: competitive markets.

A **competitive market** is a market in which there are many buyers and sellers of the same good or service, none of whom can influence the price at which the good or service is sold.

The **supply and demand model** is a model of how a competitive market behaves.

When a market is competitive, its behavior is well described by the **supply and demand model.** And, because many markets are competitive, the supply and demand model is a very useful one indeed.

There are five key elements in this model:

- The *demand curve*
- The *supply curve*
- The set of factors that cause the demand curve to shift and the set of factors that cause the supply curve to shift
- The *market equilibrium*, which includes the *equilibrium price* and *equilibrium quantity*
- The way the market equilibrium changes when the supply curve or demand curve shifts

To understand the supply and demand model, we will examine each of these elements.

5.2 The Demand Curve

How much natural gas will American consumers want to buy in a given year? You might at first think that we can answer this question by simply adding up the amounts each American household and business consumes in that year. That's not enough to answer the question, however, because how much natural gas Americans want to buy depends on the price of natural gas.

When the price of natural gas falls, as it did from 2006 to 2015, consumers will generally respond to the lower price by using more natural gas—for example, by turning up their thermostats to keep their houses warmer in the winter or switching to vehicles powered by natural gas. In general, the amount of natural gas, or of any good or service that people want to buy, depends on the price. The higher the price, the less of the good or service people want to purchase; alternatively, the lower the price, the more they want to purchase.

So the answer to the question "How many units of natural gas do consumers want to buy?" depends on the price of a unit of natural gas. If you don't yet know what the price will be, you can start by making a table of how many units of natural gas people would want to buy at a number of different prices. Such a table is known as a *demand schedule*. This, in turn, can be used to draw a *demand curve*, which is one of the key elements of the supply and demand model.

The Demand Schedule and the Demand Curve

A **demand schedule** is a table showing how much of a good or service consumers will want to buy at different prices. At the right of Figure 5-1, we show a hypothetical demand schedule for natural gas. It's expressed in BTUs (British thermal units), a commonly used measure of quantity of natural gas. It's a hypothetical demand schedule—it doesn't use actual data on American demand for natural gas.

According to the table, if a BTU of natural gas costs $3, consumers will want to purchase 10 trillion BTUs of natural gas over the course of a year. If the price is $3.25 per BTU, they will want to buy only 8.9 trillion BTUs; if the price is only $2.75 per BTU, they will want to buy 11.5 trillion BTUs. The higher the price, the fewer BTUs of natural gas consumers will want to purchase. So, as the price rises, the **quantity demanded** of natural gas—the actual amount consumers are willing to buy at some specific price—falls.

The graph in Figure 5-1 is a visual representation of the information in the table. (You might want to review, in the appendix to Section 1, the discussion of the kinds of graphs used in economics.) The vertical axis shows the price of

A **demand schedule** shows how much of a good or service consumers will want to buy at different prices.

The **quantity demanded** is the actual amount of a good or service consumers are willing to buy at some specific price.

FIGURE 5-1 The Demand Schedule and the Demand Curve

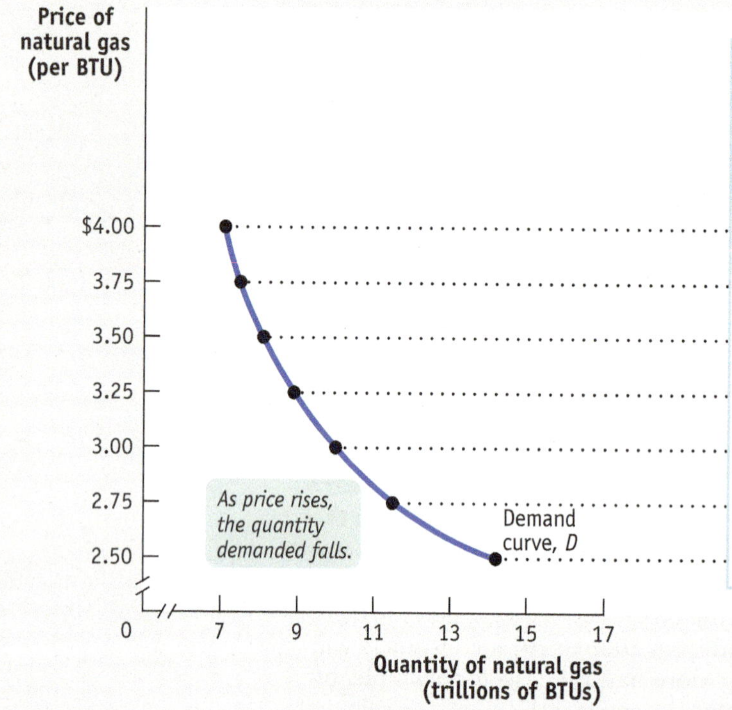

Demand Schedule for Natural Gas

Price of natural gas (per BTU)	Quantity of natural gas demanded (trillions of BTUs)
$4.00	7.1
3.75	7.5
3.50	8.1
3.25	8.9
3.00	10.0
2.75	11.5
2.50	14.2

The demand schedule for natural gas yields the corresponding demand curve, which shows how much of a good or service consumers want to buy at any given price. The demand curve and the demand schedule reflect the law of demand: as price rises, the quantity demanded falls. Similarly, a fall in price raises the quantity demanded. As a result, the demand curve is downward sloping.

a BTU of natural gas and the horizontal axis shows the quantity of natural gas in trillions of BTUs. Each point on the graph corresponds to one of the entries in the table. The curve that connects these points is a **demand curve.** A demand curve is a graphical representation of the demand schedule, another way of showing the relationship between the quantity demanded and price.

Note that the demand curve shown in Figure 5-1 slopes downward. This reflects the inverse relationship between price and the quantity demanded: a higher price reduces the quantity demanded, and a lower price increases the quantity demanded. We can see this from the demand curve in Figure 5-1. As price falls, we move down the demand curve and quantity demanded increases. And as price increases, we move up the demand curve and quantity demanded falls.

In the real world, demand curves almost always *do* slope downward. (The exceptions are so rare that for practical purposes we can ignore them.) Generally, the proposition that a higher price for a good, *other things equal,* leads people to demand a smaller quantity of that good is so reliable that economists are willing to call it a "law"—the **law of demand.**

A **demand curve** is a graphical representation of the demand schedule. It shows the relationship between quantity demanded and price.

The **law of demand** says that a higher price for a good or service, other things equal, leads people to demand a smaller quantity of that good or service.

Shifts of the Demand Curve

Although natural gas prices in 2006 were higher than they had been in 2002, U.S. consumption of natural gas was higher in 2006. How can we reconcile this fact with the law of demand, which says that a higher price reduces the quantity demanded, other things equal?

The answer lies in the crucial phrase *other things equal*. In this case, other things were not equal: the U.S. economy had changed between 2002 and 2006 in ways that increased the amount of natural gas demanded at any given price. For one thing, the U.S. economy was much stronger in 2006 than it was in 2002. Figure 5-2 illustrates this phenomenon using the demand schedule and demand curve for natural gas. (As before, the numbers in Figure 5-2 are hypothetical.)

The table in Figure 5-2 shows two demand schedules. The first is the demand schedule for 2002, the same as shown in Figure 5-1. The second is the demand schedule for 2006. It differs from the 2002 schedule because of the stronger U.S. economy, leading to an increase in the quantity of natural gas demanded at any given price. So at each price the 2006 schedule shows a larger quantity demanded than the 2002 schedule. For example, the quantity of natural gas that consumers wanted to buy at a price of $3 per BTU increased from 10 trillion to 12 trillion BTUs per year; the quantity demanded at $3.25 per BTU went from 8.9 trillion to 10.7 trillion, and so on.

What is clear from this example is that the changes that occurred between 2002 and 2006 generated a *new* demand schedule, one in which the quantity demanded was greater at any given price than in the original demand schedule. The two curves in Figure 5-2 show the same information graphically. As you can see, the demand schedule for 2006 corresponds to a new demand curve, D_2, that is to the right of the demand schedule for 2002, D_1. This **shift of the demand curve** shows the change in the quantity demanded at any given price, represented by the change in position of the original demand curve D_1 to its new location at D_2.

A **shift of the demand curve** is a change in the quantity demanded at any given price, represented by the shift of the original demand curve to a new position, denoted by a new demand curve.

FIGURE 5-2 An Increase in Demand

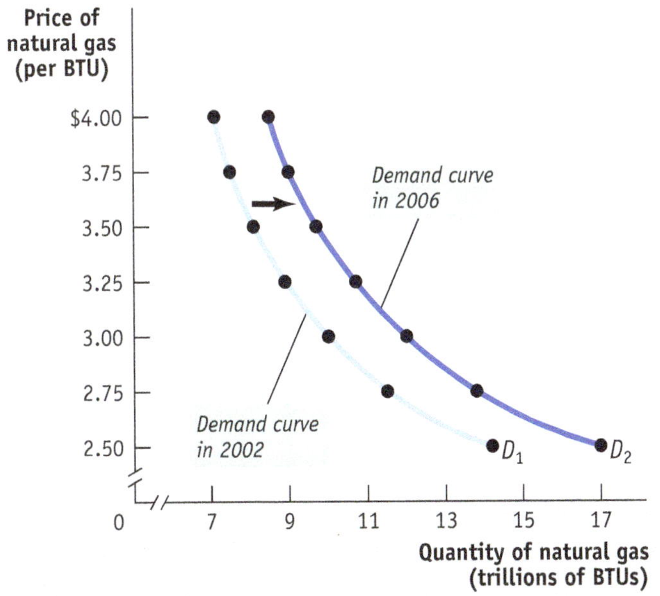

Demand Schedules for Natural Gas

Price of natural gas (per BTU)	Quantity of natural gas demanded (trillions of BTUs) in 2002	in 2006
$4.00	7.1	8.5
3.75	7.5	9.0
3.50	8.1	9.7
3.25	8.9	10.7
3.00	10.0	12.0
2.75	11.5	13.8
2.50	14.2	17.0

A strong economy is one factor that increases the demand for natural gas—a rise in the quantity demanded at any given price. This is represented by the two demand schedules—one showing the demand in 2002, when the economy was weak; the other showing the demand in 2006, when the economy was strong—and their corresponding demand curves. The increase in demand shifts the demand curve to the right.

GLOBAL COMPARISION PAY MORE, PUMP LESS

For a real-world illustration of the law of demand, consider how gasoline consumption varies according to the prices consumers pay at the pump. Because of high taxes, gasoline and diesel fuel are more than twice as expensive in most European countries and in many East Asian countries than in the United States. According to the law of demand, this should lead Europeans to buy less gasoline than Americans—and they do. As you can see from the figure, per person, Europeans consume less than half as much fuel as Americans, mainly because they drive smaller cars with better mileage.

Prices aren't the only factor affecting fuel consumption, but they're probably the main cause of the difference between European and American fuel consumption per person.

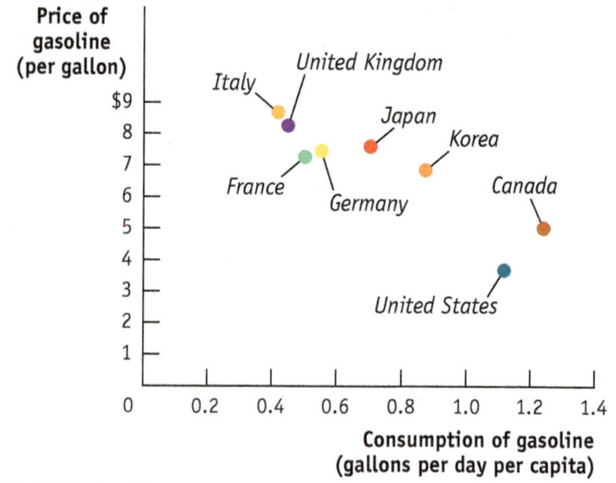

Data from: World Development Indicators and U.S. Energy Information Administration, 2013.

A **movement along the demand curve** is a change in the quantity demanded of a good arising from a change in the good's price.

It's crucial to make the distinction between such shifts of the demand curve and **movements along the demand curve,** changes in the quantity demanded of a good arising from a change in that good's price. Figure 5-3 illustrates the difference.

The movement from point *A* to point *B* is a movement along the demand curve: the quantity demanded rises due to a fall in price as you move down D_1. Here, a fall in the price of natural gas from $3.50 to $3 per BTU generates a rise in the quantity demanded from 8.1 trillion to 10 trillion BTUs per year. But the quantity demanded can also rise when the price is unchanged if there is an *increase in*

FIGURE 5-3 Movement Along the Demand Curve versus Shift of the Demand Curve

The rise in quantity demanded when going from point *A* to point *B* reflects a movement along the demand curve: it is the result of a fall in the price of the good. The rise in quantity demanded when going from point *A* to point *C* reflects a shift of the demand curve: it is the result of a rise in the quantity demanded at any given price.

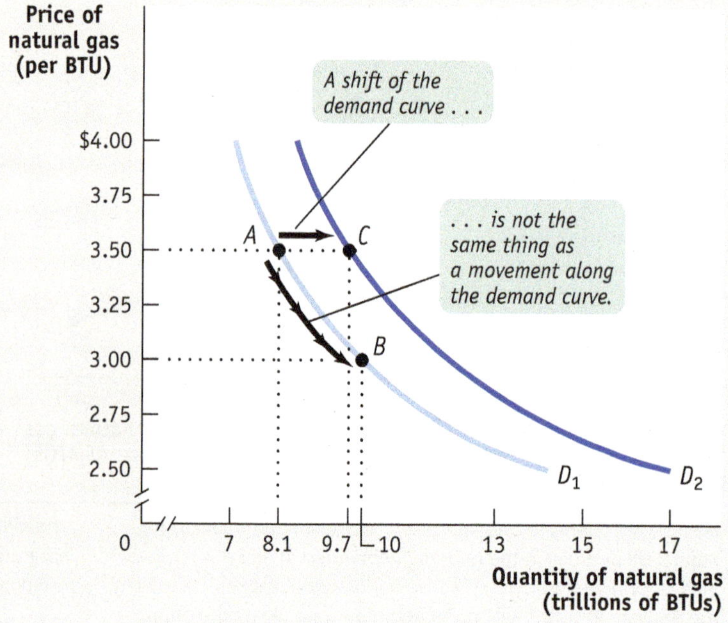

PITFALLS

DEMAND VERSUS QUANTITY DEMANDED

When economists say "an increase in demand," they mean a rightward shift of the demand curve, and when they say "a decrease in demand," they mean a leftward shift of the demand curve—that is, when they're being careful. In ordinary speech most people, including professional economists, use the word *demand* casually. For example, an economist might say "the demand for air travel has doubled over the past 15 years, partly because of falling airfares" when they really mean that the *quantity demanded* has doubled.

It's OK to be a bit sloppy in ordinary conversation. But when you're doing economic analysis, it's important to make the distinction between changes in the quantity demanded, which involve movements along a demand curve, and shifts of the demand curve (see Figure 5-3 for an illustration). Sometimes students end up writing something like this: "If demand increases, the price will go up, but that will lead to a fall in demand, which pushes the price down . . ." and then go around in circles.

If you make a clear distinction between changes in *demand*, which mean shifts of the demand curve, and changes in *quantity demanded*, which means movement along the demand curve, you can avoid a lot of confusion.

demand—a rightward shift of the demand curve. This is illustrated in Figure 5-3 by the shift of the demand curve from D_1 to D_2. Holding the price constant at \$3.50 per BTU, the quantity demanded rises from 8.1 trillion BTUs at point A on D_1 to 9.7 trillion BTUs at point C on D_2.

When economists say "the demand for X increased" or "the demand for Y decreased," they mean that the demand curve for X or Y shifted—not that the quantity demanded rose or fell because of a change in the price.

Understanding Shifts of the Demand Curve

Figure 5-4 illustrates the two basic ways in which demand curves can shift.

1. When economists talk about an increase in demand, they mean a *rightward* shift of the demand curve: at any given price, consumers demand a larger quantity of the good or service than before. This is shown by the rightward shift of the original demand curve D_1 to curve D_2.
2. When economists talk about a decrease in demand, they mean a *leftward* shift of the demand curve: at any given price, consumers demand a smaller quantity of the good or service than before. This is shown by the leftward shift of the original demand curve D_1 to curve D_3.

FIGURE 5-4 Shifts of the Demand Curve

Any event that increases demand shifts the demand curve to the right, reflecting a rise in the quantity demanded at any given price. Any event that decreases demand shifts the demand curve to the left, reflecting a fall in the quantity demanded at any given price.

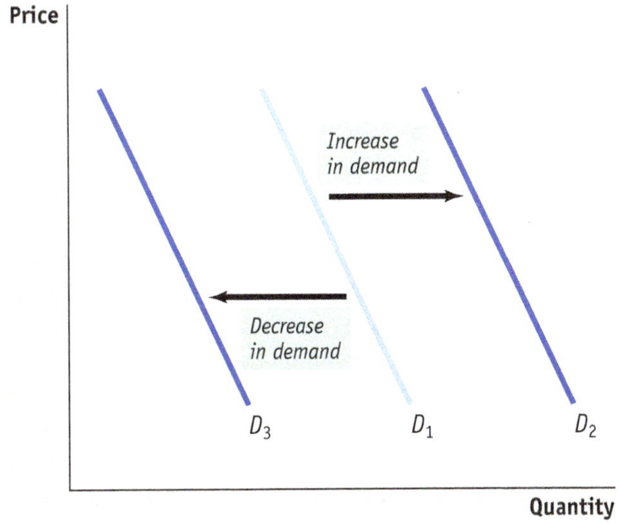

What caused the demand curve for natural gas to shift? As we mentioned earlier, the reason was the stronger U.S. economy in 2006 compared to 2002. If you think about it, you can come up with other factors that would be likely to shift the demand curve for natural gas. For example, suppose that the price of heating oil rises. This will induce some consumers, who heat their homes and businesses in winter with heating oil, to switch to natural gas instead, increasing the demand for natural gas.

Economists believe that there are five principal factors that shift the demand curve for a good or service:

- Changes in the prices of related goods or services
- Changes in income
- Changes in tastes
- Changes in expectations
- Changes in the number of consumers

Although this is not an exhaustive list, it contains the five most important factors that can shift demand curves. When we say that the quantity of a good or service demanded falls as its price rises, *other things equal,* we are in fact stating that the factors that shift demand are remaining unchanged. Let's now explore how those factors shift the demand curve.

Changes in the Prices of Related Goods or Services Heating oil is what economists call a *substitute* for natural gas. A pair of goods are **substitutes** if a rise in the price of one good (heating oil) makes consumers more likely to buy the other good (natural gas). Substitutes are usually goods that in some way serve a similar function: coffee and tea, muffins and doughnuts, train rides and air flights. A rise in the price of the alternative good induces some consumers to purchase the original good *instead* of the substitute, shifting demand for the original good to the right.

But sometimes a rise in the price of one good makes consumers *less* willing to buy another good. Such pairs of goods are known as **complements.** Complements are usually goods that in some sense are consumed together: smartphones and apps, coffee and Egg McMuffins, cars and gasoline. Because consumers like to consume a good and its complement together, a change in the price of one of the goods will affect the demand for its complement. In particular, when the price of one good rises, the demand for its complement decreases, shifting the demand curve for the complement to the left. So, for example, when the price of gasoline began to rise in 2009 from under $3 per gallon to close to $4 per gallon in 2011, the demand for gas-guzzling cars fell.

Changes in Income Why did the stronger economy in 2006 lead to an increase in the demand for natural gas compared to the demand during the weak economy of 2002? It was because the economy was stronger and Americans had more income, making them more likely to purchase more of *most* goods and services at any given price. For example, with a higher income you are likely to keep your house warmer in the winter than if your income is low.

And, the demand for natural gas, a major source of fuel for electricity-generating power plants, is tied to the demand for other goods and services. For example, businesses must consume power to provide goods and services to households. So when the economy is strong and household incomes are high, businesses will consume more electricity and, indirectly, more natural gas.

Why do we say that people are likely to purchase more of "most goods," not purchase more of "all goods"? Most goods are **normal goods**—the demand for them increases when consumer income rises. However, the demand for some products falls when income rises. Goods for which demand decreases when income rises are known as **inferior goods.** Usually an inferior good is considered less desirable than more expensive alternatives—such as a bus ride versus a taxi ride. When they can afford to, people stop buying an inferior good and switch their

Two goods are **substitutes** if a rise in the price of one of the goods leads to an increase in the demand for the other good.

Two goods are **complements** if a rise in the price of one good leads to a decrease in the demand for the other good.

When a rise in income increases the demand for a good—the normal case—it is a **normal good.**

When a rise in income decreases the demand for a good, it is an **inferior good.**

consumption to the preferred, more expensive alternative. Thus, when a good is inferior, a rise in income shifts the demand curve to the left. And, not surprisingly, a fall in income shifts the demand curve to the right.

One example of the distinction between normal and inferior goods that has drawn attention in the business press is the difference between so-called casual-dining restaurants such as Red Lobster or Olive Garden and fast-food chains such as Burger King or McDonald's. When their incomes rise, Americans tend to eat out more at casual-dining restaurants. However, some of that increased dining out comes at the expense of fast-food venues—to some extent, people visit McDonald's less often once they can afford to move upscale. So casual dining is a normal good, whereas fast-food consumption appears to be an inferior good.

Changes in Tastes Why do people want what they want? Fortunately, we don't need to answer that question—we just need to acknowledge that people generally have certain preferences, or tastes, that determine what they choose to consume and that these tastes can change. Economists usually lump together changes in demand due to trends, beliefs, cultural shifts, and so on, under the heading of changes in tastes or preferences.

For example, once upon a time men wore hats. Up until around World War II, a respectable man wasn't fully dressed unless he wore a dignified hat along with his suit. But after the war, returning troops adopted a more informal style, perhaps due to the rigors of the war. And President Eisenhower, who had been supreme commander of Allied Forces before becoming president, often went hatless. After World War II, the demand curve for hats had clearly shifted leftward, reflecting a decrease in the demand for hats.

Economists have relatively little to say about the forces that influence consumers' tastes (although marketers and advertisers have plenty to say about them!). However, a change in tastes does have a predictable impact on demand. When tastes change in favor of a good, more people want to buy it at any given price, so the demand curve shifts to the right. When tastes change against a good, fewer people want to buy it at any given price, so the demand curve shifts to the left.

Changes in Expectations When consumers have some choice about when to make a purchase, current demand for a good is often affected by expectations about its future price. For example, savvy shoppers often wait for seasonal sales—say, buying next year's holiday gifts during the post-holiday markdowns. In this case, expectations of a future drop in price lead to a decrease in demand today. Alternatively, expectations of a future rise in price are likely to cause an increase in demand today.

In addition, the fall in gas prices in recent years to around $2 per BTU has spurred more consumers to switch to natural gas from other fuel types than when natural gas fell to $2 per BTU in 2002. But why are consumers more willing to switch now? Because in 2002, consumers didn't expect the fall in the price of natural gas to last—and they were right.

In 2002, natural gas prices fell because of the weak economy. That situation changed in 2006 when the economy had come roaring back and the price of natural gas rose dramatically. In contrast, consumers have come to expect that the more recent fall in the price of natural gas will not be temporary because it is based on a permanent change: the ability to tap much larger deposits of natural gas.

Expected changes in future income can also lead to changes in demand: if you expect your income to rise in the future, you will typically borrow today and increase your demand for certain goods; if you expect your income to fall in the future, you are likely to save today and reduce your demand for some goods.

Changes in the Number of Consumers Another factor that can cause a change in demand is a change in the number of consumers of a good or service. For example, population growth in the United States eventually leads to a higher demand for natural gas since more homes and businesses need to be heated in the winter and cooled in the summer.

FIGURE 5-5 Individual Demand Curves and the Market Demand Curve

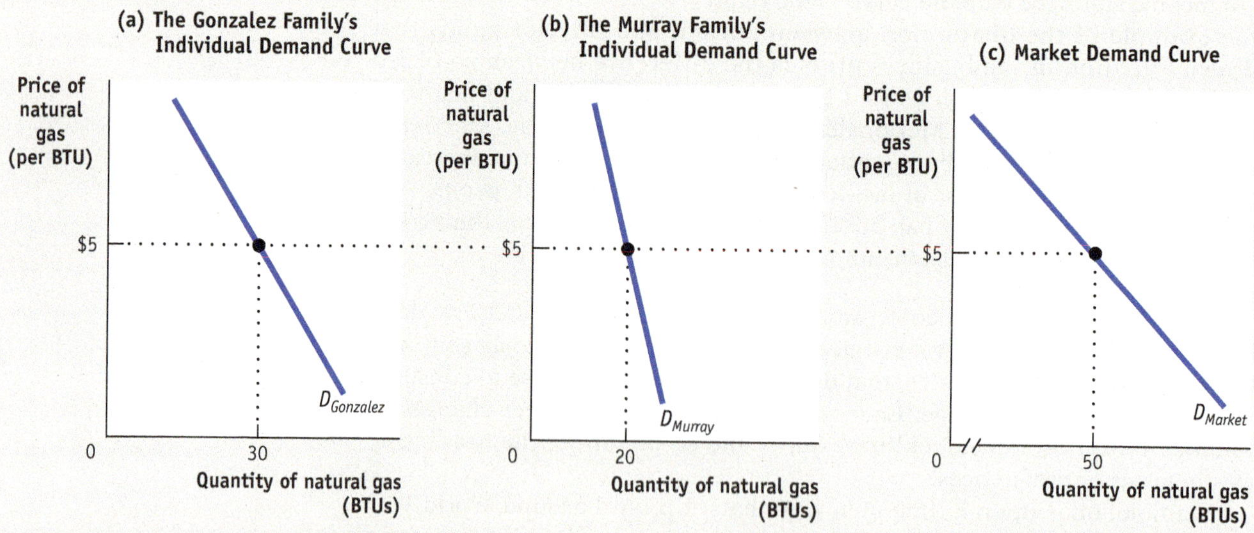

The Gonzalez family and the Murray family are the only two consumers of natural gas in the market. Panel (a) shows the Gonzalez family's individual demand curve: the number of BTUs they will buy per year at any given price. Panel (b) shows the Murray family's individual demand curve. Given that the Gonzalez family and the Murray family are the only two consumers, the *market demand curve,* which shows the quantity of BTUs demanded by all consumers at any given price, is shown in panel (c). The market demand curve is the *horizontal sum* of the individual demand curves of all consumers. In this case, at any given price, the quantity demanded by the market is the sum of the quantities demanded by the Gonzalez family and the Murray family.

Let's introduce a new concept: the **individual demand curve,** which shows the relationship between quantity demanded and price for an individual consumer. For example, suppose that the Gonzalez family is a consumer of natural gas for heating and cooling their home. Panel (a) of Figure 5-5 shows how many BTUs of natural gas they will buy per year at any given price. The Gonzalez family's individual demand curve is $D_{Gonzalez}$.

The *market demand curve,* panel (c), shows how the combined quantity demanded by all consumers depends on the market price of the good. (Most of the time when economists refer to the demand curve, they mean the market demand curve.) The market demand curve is the *horizontal sum* of the individual demand curves of all consumers in that market.

To see what we mean by the term *horizontal sum,* assume for a moment that there are only two consumers of natural gas, the Gonzalez family and the Murray family. The Murray family consumes natural gas to fuel their natural gas–powered car. The Murray family's individual demand curve, D_{Murray}, is shown in panel (b). Panel (c) shows the market demand curve. At any given price, the quantity demanded by the market is the sum of the quantities demanded by the Gonzalez family and the Murray family. For example, at a price of $5 per BTU, the Gonzalez family demands 30 BTUs of natural gas per year and the Murray family demands 20 BTUs per year. So the quantity demanded by the market is 50 BTUs per year, as seen on the market demand curve, D_{Market}.

Clearly, the quantity demanded by the market at any given price is larger with the Murray family present than it would be if the Gonzalez family were the only consumer. The quantity demanded at any given price would be even larger if we added a third consumer, then a fourth, and so on. So an increase in the number of consumers leads to an increase in demand.

For a review of the factors that shift demand, see Table 5-1.

An **individual demand curve** illustrates the relationship between quantity demanded and price for an individual consumer.

TABLE 5-1 Factors That Shift Demand

When this happens . . .		. . . demand increases	But when this happens . . .		. . . demand decreases
When the price of a substitute rises . . .	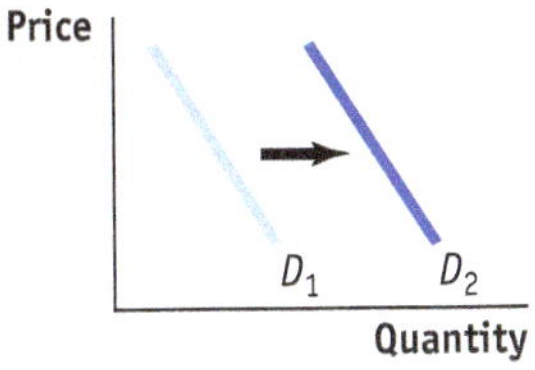	. . . demand for the original good increases.	When the price of a substitute falls . . .	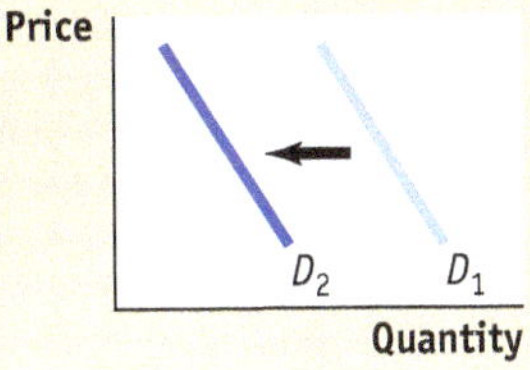	. . . demand for the original good decreases.
When the price of a complement falls . . .	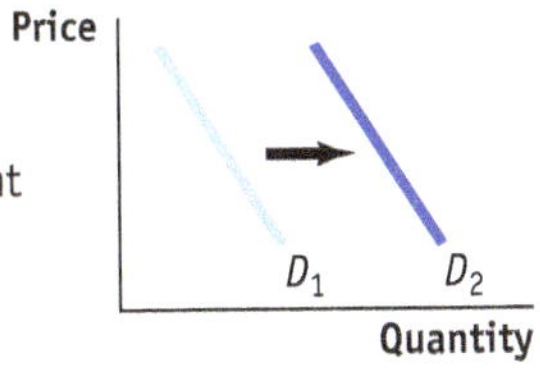	. . . demand for the original good increases.	When the price of a complement rises . . .	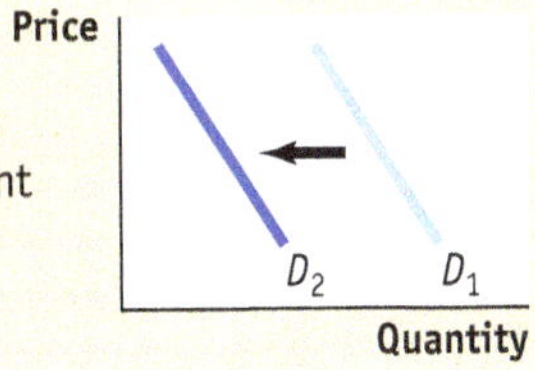	. . . demand for the original good decreases.
When income rises . . .	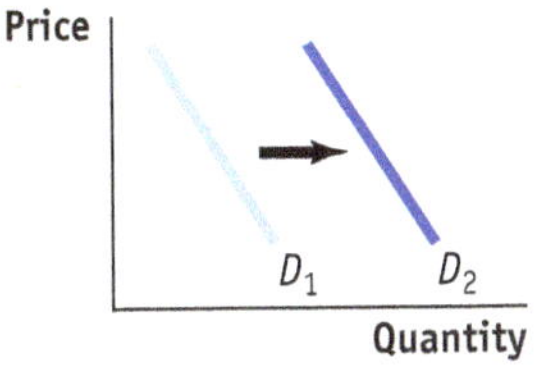	. . . demand for a normal good increases.	When income falls . . .	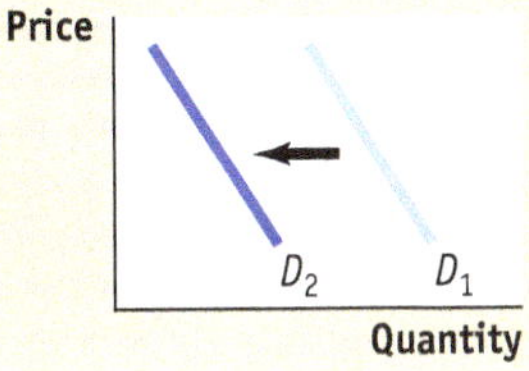	. . . demand for a normal good decreases.
When income falls . . .	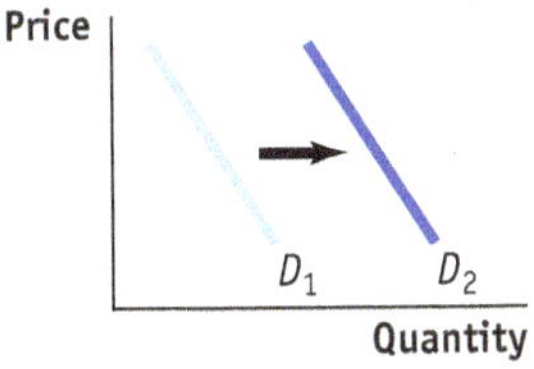	. . . demand for an inferior good increases.	When income rises . . .	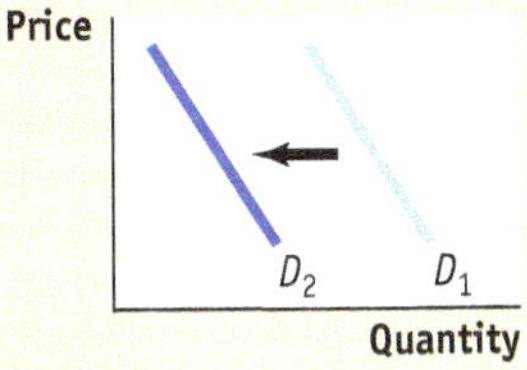	. . . demand for an inferior good decreases.
When tastes change in favor of a good . . .	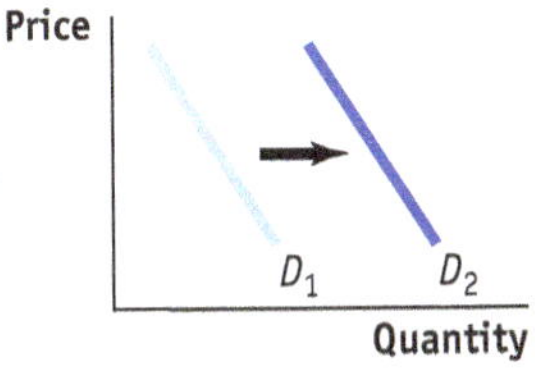	. . . demand for the good increases.	When tastes change against a good . . .	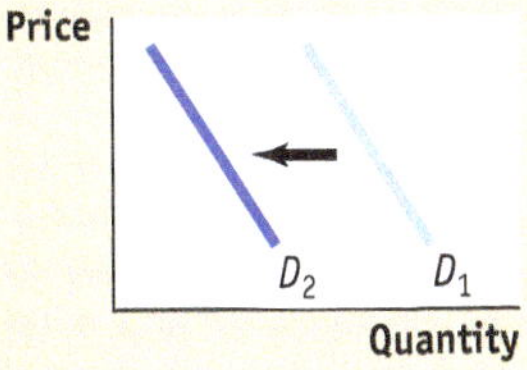	. . . demand for the good decreases.
When the price is expected to rise in the future . . .	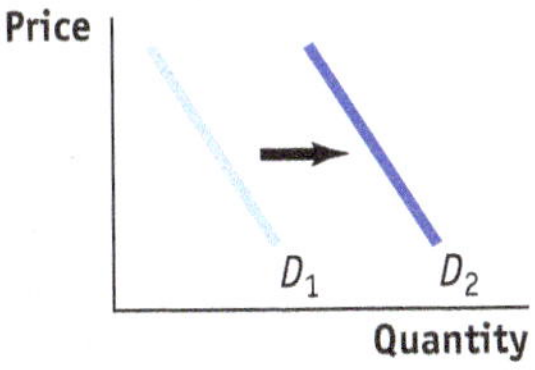	. . . demand for the good increases today.	When the price is expected to fall in the future . . .	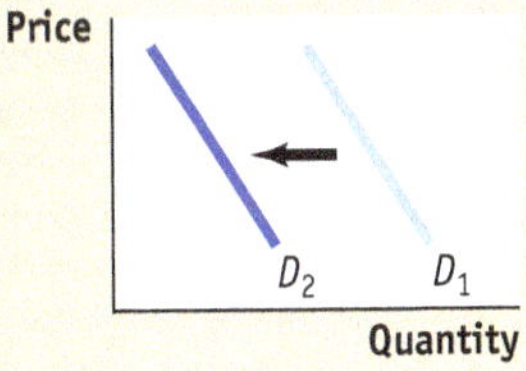	. . . demand for the good decreases today.
When the number of consumers rises . . .	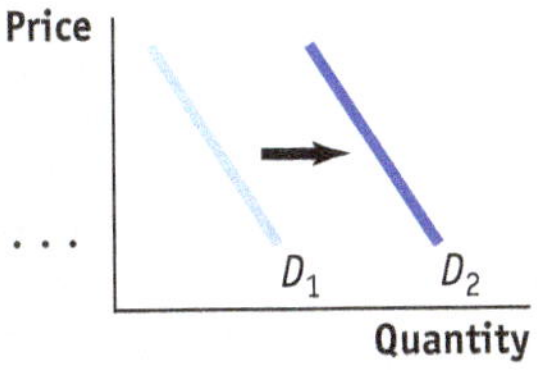	. . . market demand for the good increases.	When the number of consumers falls . . .	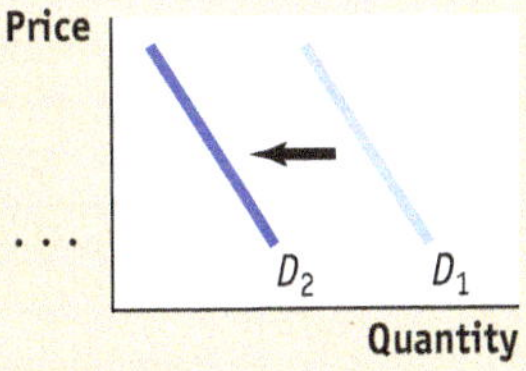	. . . market demand for the good decreases.

PA Images/Alamy Stock Photo

Cities can reduce traffic congestion by raising the price of driving.

ECONOMICS >> in Action

Beating the Traffic

All big cities have traffic problems, and many local authorities try to discourage driving in the crowded city center. If we think of an auto trip to the city center as a good that people consume, we can use the economics of demand to analyze anti-traffic policies.

One common strategy is to reduce the demand for auto trips by lowering the prices of substitutes. Many metropolitan areas subsidize bus and rail service, hoping to lure commuters out of their cars. An alternative is to raise the price of complements: several major U.S. cities impose high taxes on commercial parking garages and impose short time limits on parking meters, both to raise revenue and to discourage people from driving into the city.

A few major cities—including Singapore, London, Oslo, Stockholm, and Milan—have been willing to adopt a direct and politically controversial approach: reducing congestion by raising the price of driving. Under *congestion pricing,* a charge is imposed on cars entering the city center during business hours. Drivers buy passes that are debited electronically as the cars drive by monitoring stations. Compliance is monitored with cameras that photograph license plates.

In 2012, Moscow adopted a modest charge for parking in certain areas in the city in an attempt to reduce its traffic jams, considered the worst of all major cities. After the approximately $1.60 charge was applied, city officials estimated that Moscow traffic decreased by 4%.

The standard cost of driving into London is currently £11.50 (about $19). Drivers who don't pay and are caught pay a fine of £130 (about $215) for each transgression.

Studies have shown, not surprisingly, that after the implementation of congestion pricing, traffic does decrease. In the 1990s, London had some of the worst traffic in Europe. The introduction of its congestion charge in 2003 immediately reduced traffic in the city center by about 15%. And there has been increased use of substitutes, such as public transportation, bicycles, and ride-sharing. From 2001 to 2011, bike trips in London increased by 79%, and bus usage was up by 30%.

And, less congestion led not just to fewer accidents, but to a lower *rate* of accidents as fewer cars jostled for space. One study found that from 2000 to 2010 the number of accidents per mile driven in London fell by 40%. Stockholm experienced effects similar to those in London: traffic fell by 22% in 2013 compared to pre-congestion charge levels, transit times fell by one-third to one-half, and air quality measurably improved.

>> Quick Review

- The **supply and demand model is a model** of a **competitive market**—one in which there are many buyers and sellers of the same good or service.
- The **demand schedule** shows how the **quantity demanded** changes as the price changes. A **demand curve** illustrates this relationship.
- The **law of demand** asserts that a higher price reduces the quantity demanded. Thus, demand curves normally slope downward.
- An increase in demand leads to a rightward **shift of the demand curve:** the quantity demanded rises for any given price. A decrease in demand leads to a leftward shift: the quantity demanded falls for any given price. A change in price results in a change in the quantity demanded and a **movement along the demand curve.**
- The five main factors that can shift the demand curve are changes in (1) the price of a related good, such as a **substitute** or a **complement,** (2) income, (3) tastes, (4) expectations, and (5) the number of consumers.
- The market demand curve is the horizontal sum of the **individual demand curves** of all consumers in the market.

Check Your Understanding 5-1

1. Explain whether each of the following events represents (i) a *shift of* the demand curve or (ii) a *movement along* the demand curve.
   a. A store owner finds that customers are willing to pay more for umbrellas on rainy days.
   b. When Circus Cruise Lines offered reduced prices for summer cruises in the Caribbean, their number of bookings increased sharply.
   c. People buy more long-stem roses the week of Valentine's Day, even though the prices are higher than at other times during the year.
   d. When there is a sharp rise in the price of gasoline, many commuters join carpools to reduce their gasoline purchases.

Solutions appear at back of book.

Supply and Equilibrium

MODULE 6

WHAT YOU WILL LEARN

- What is the **supply curve?**
- What is the difference between movements along the supply curve and changes in supply?
- How do supply and demand curves lead to an **equilibrium price** and **equilibrium quantity** in the market?
- What are **shortages** and **surpluses** and why do price movements eliminate them?

6.1 The Supply Curve

Some deposits of natural gas are easier to tap than others. Before the widespread use of fracking, drillers would limit their natural gas wells to deposits that lay in easily reached pools beneath the earth. How much natural gas they would tap from existing wells, and how extensively they searched for new deposits and drilled new wells, depended on the price they expected to get for the natural gas. The higher the price, the more they would tap existing wells as well as drill and tap new wells.

So, just as the quantity of natural gas that consumers want to buy depends on the price they have to pay, the quantity that producers of natural gas, or of any good or service, are willing to produce and sell—the **quantity supplied**—depends on the price they are offered.

chain45154/Getty Images

The Supply Schedule and the Supply Curve

The table in Figure 6-1 shows how the quantity of natural gas made available varies with the price—that is, it shows a hypothetical **supply schedule** for natural gas.

A supply schedule works the same way as the demand schedule shown in Figure 5-1: in this case, the table shows the number of BTUs of natural gas that producers are willing to sell at different prices. At a price of $2.50 per BTU, producers are willing to sell only 8 trillion BTUs of natural gas per year. At $2.75 per BTU, they're willing to sell 9.1 trillion BTUs. At $3, they're willing to sell 10 trillion BTUs, and so on.

The **quantity supplied** is the actual amount of a good or service people are willing to sell at some specific price.

A **supply schedule** shows how much of a good or service would be supplied at different prices.

FIGURE 6-1 The Supply Schedule and the Supply Curve

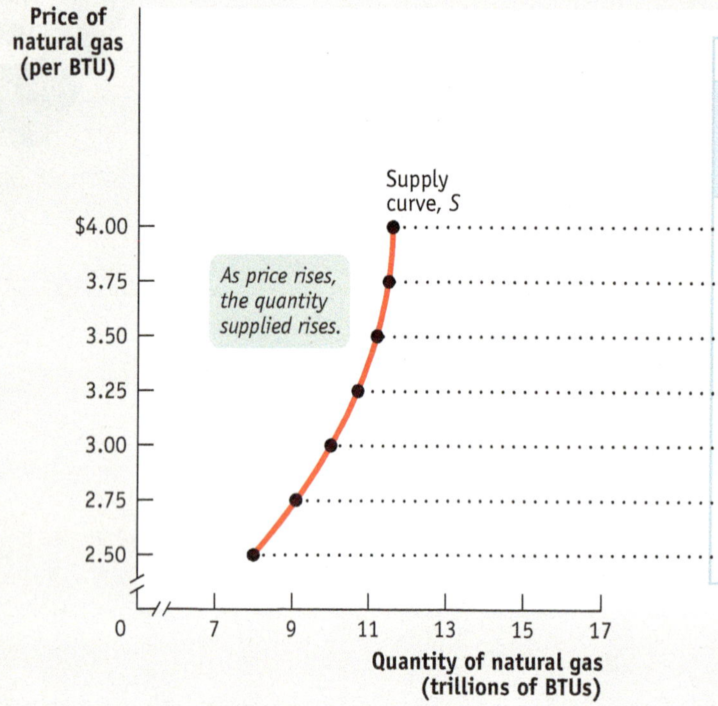

Supply Schedule for Natural Gas

Price of natural gas (per BTU)	Quantity of natural gas supplied (trillions of BTUs)
$4.00	11.6
3.75	11.5
3.50	11.2
3.25	10.7
3.00	10.0
2.75	9.1
2.50	8.0

The supply schedule for natural gas is plotted to yield the corresponding supply curve, which shows how much of a good producers are willing to sell at any given price. The supply curve and the supply schedule reflect the fact that supply curves are usually upward sloping: the quantity supplied rises when the price rises.

In the same way that a demand schedule can be represented graphically by a demand curve, a supply schedule can be represented by a **supply curve,** as shown in Figure 6-1. Each point on the curve represents an entry from the table.

Suppose that the price of natural gas rises from $3 to $3.25; we can see that the quantity of natural gas that producers are willing to sell rises from 10 trillion to 10.7 trillion BTUs. This is the normal situation for a supply curve, that a higher price leads to a higher quantity supplied. So just as demand curves normally slope downward, supply curves normally slope upward: the higher the price being offered, the more of any good or service producers will be willing to sell.

Shifts of the Supply Curve

Innovations in the technology of drilling natural gas deposits have led to a huge increase in U.S. production of natural gas—a 40% increase in daily production from 2005 through 2014. Figure 6-2 illustrates these events in terms of the supply schedule and the supply curve for natural gas. The table in Figure 6-2 shows two supply schedules. The schedule before improved natural gas–drilling technology was adopted is the same one as in Figure 6-1. The second schedule shows the supply of natural gas *after* the improved technology was adopted.

Just as a change in demand schedules leads to a shift of the demand curve, a change in supply schedules leads to a **shift of the supply curve**—a change in the quantity supplied at any given price. This is shown in Figure 6-2 by the shift of the supply curve before the adoption of new natural gas–drilling technology, S_1, to its new position after the adoption of new natural gas–drilling technology, S_2. Notice that S_2 lies to the right of S_1, a reflection of the fact that quantity supplied rises at any given price.

A **supply curve** shows the relationship between quantity supplied and price.

A **shift of the supply curve** is a change in the quantity supplied of a good or service at any given price. It is represented by the change of the original supply curve to a new position, denoted by a new supply curve.

FIGURE 6-2 An Increase in Supply

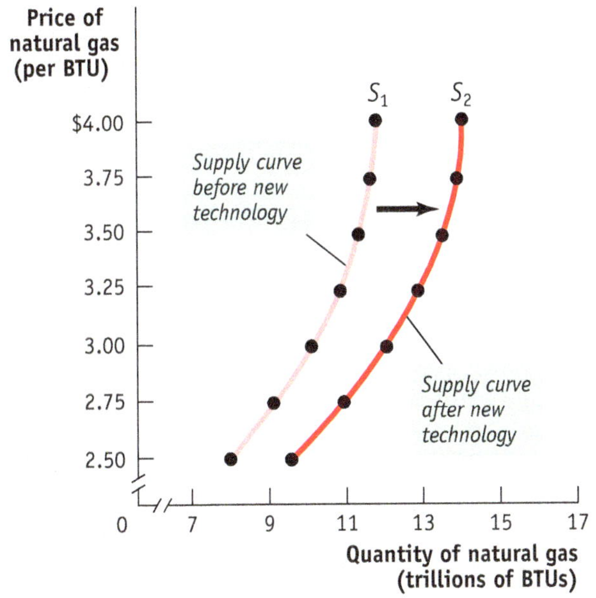

Supply Schedules for Natural Gas

Price of natural gas (per BTU)	Quantity of natural gas supplied (trillions of BTUs): Before new technology	After new technology
$4.00	11.6	13.9
3.75	11.5	13.8
3.50	11.2	13.4
3.25	10.7	12.8
3.00	10.0	12.0
2.75	9.1	10.9
2.50	8.0	9.6

The adoption of an improved natural gas–drilling technology generated an increase in supply—a rise in the quantity supplied at any given price. This event is represented by the two supply schedules—one showing supply before the new technology was adopted, the other showing supply after the new technology was adopted—and their corresponding supply curves. The increase in supply shifts the supply curve to the right.

As in the analysis of demand, it's crucial to draw a distinction between such shifts of the supply curve and **movements along the supply curve**—changes in the quantity supplied arising from a change in price. We can see this difference in Figure 6-3. The movement from point *A* to point *B* is a movement along the supply curve: the quantity supplied rises along S_1 due to a rise in price. Here, a rise in

A **movement along the supply curve** is a change in the quantity supplied of a good arising from a change in the good's price.

FIGURE 6-3 Movement Along the Supply Curve versus Shift of the Supply Curve

The increase in quantity supplied when going from point *A* to point *B* reflects a movement along the supply curve: it is the result of a rise in the price of a good. The increase in quantity supplied when going from point *A* to point *C* reflects a shift of the supply curve: it is the result of an increase in the quantity supplied at any given price.

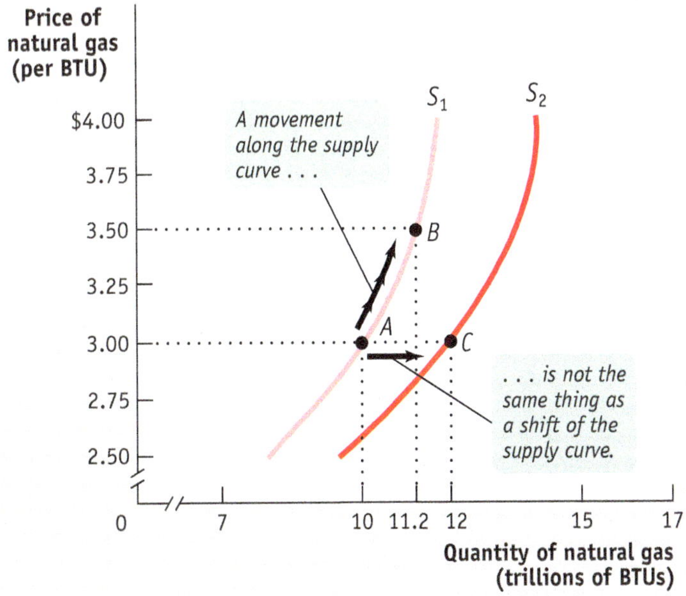

An **input** is a good or service that is used to produce another good or service.

price from \$3 to \$3.50 leads to a rise in the quantity supplied from 10 trillion to 11.2 trillion BTUs of natural gas. But the quantity supplied can also rise when the price is unchanged if there is an increase in supply—a rightward shift of the supply curve. This is shown by the rightward shift of the supply curve from S_1 to S_2. Holding the price constant at \$3, the quantity supplied rises from 10 trillion BTUs at point A on S_1 to 12 billion pounds at point C on S_2.

Understanding Shifts of the Supply Curve

Figure 6-4 illustrates the two basic ways in which supply curves can shift. When economists talk about an "increase in supply," they mean a *rightward* shift of the supply curve: at any given price, producers supply a larger quantity of the good than before. This is shown in Figure 6-4 by the rightward shift of the original supply curve S_1 to S_2. And when economists talk about a "decrease in supply," they mean a *leftward* shift of the supply curve: at any given price, producers supply a smaller quantity of the good than before. This is represented by the leftward shift of S_1 to S_3.

Economists believe that shifts of the supply curve for a good or service are mainly the result of five factors (though, as with demand, there are other possible causes):

- Changes in input prices
- Changes in the prices of related goods or services
- Changes in technology
- Changes in expectations
- Changes in the number of producers

Changes in Input Prices To produce output, you need inputs. For example, to make vanilla ice cream, you need vanilla beans, cream, sugar, and so on. An **input** is any good or service that is used to produce another good or service. Inputs, like outputs, have prices. And an increase in the price of an input makes the production of the final good more costly for those who produce and sell it. So producers are less willing to supply the final good at any given price, and the supply curve shifts to the left. That is, supply decreases. For example, fuel is a major cost for

FIGURE 6-4 Shifts of the Supply Curve

Any event that increases supply shifts the supply curve to the right, reflecting a rise in the quantity supplied at any given price. Any event that decreases supply shifts the supply curve to the left, reflecting a fall in the quantity supplied at any given price.

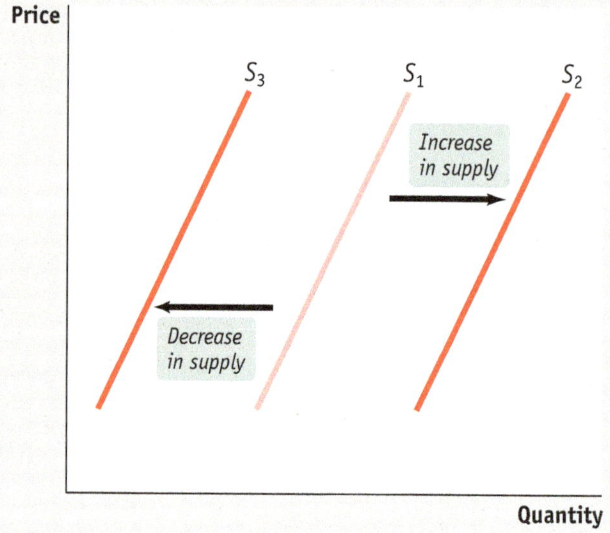

airlines. When oil prices surged in 2007–2008, airlines began cutting back on their flight schedules and some went out of business.

Similarly, a fall in the price of an input makes the production of the final good less costly for sellers. They are more willing to supply the good at any given price, and the supply curve shifts to the right. That is, supply increases.

Changes in the Prices of Related Goods or Services A single producer often produces a mix of goods rather than a single product. For example, an oil refinery produces gasoline from crude oil, but it also produces heating oil and other products from the same raw material. When a producer sells several products, the quantity of any one good it is willing to supply at any given price depends on the prices of its other co-produced goods.

This effect can run in either direction. An oil refiner will supply less gasoline at any given price when the price of heating oil rises, shifting the supply curve for gasoline to the left. But it will supply more gasoline at any given price when the price of heating oil falls, shifting the supply curve for gasoline to the right. This means that gasoline and other co-produced oil products are *substitutes in production* for refiners.

In contrast, due to the nature of the production process, other goods can be *complements in production*. Producers of natural gas often find that natural gas wells also produce oil as a by-product of extraction. The higher the price at which a driller can sell its oil, the more willing it will be to drill natural gas wells and the more natural gas it will supply at any given price. Higher oil prices then lead to more natural gas supplied at any given price because oil and natural gas can be tapped simultaneously. As a result, oil is a complement in the production of natural gas. The reverse is also true: natural gas is a complement in the production of oil.

Changes in Technology As the section's opening story illustrates, changes in technology affect the supply curve. Technology improvements enable producers to spend less on inputs (in this case, drilling equipment, labor, land purchases, and so on), yet still produce the same amount of output. When a better technology becomes available, reducing the cost of production, supply increases and the supply curve shifts to the right.

Improved technology enabled natural gas producers to more than double output in less than two years. Technology is also the main reason that natural gas has remained relatively cheap, even as demand has grown.

Changes in Expectations Just as changes in expectations can shift the demand curve, they can also shift the supply curve. When suppliers have some choice about when they put their good up for sale, changes in the expected future price of the good can lead a supplier to supply less or more of the good today.

Consider the fact that gasoline and other oil products are often stored for significant periods of time at oil refineries before being sold to consumers. In fact, storage is normally part of producers' business strategy. Knowing that the demand for gasoline peaks in the summer, oil refiners normally store some of their gasoline produced during the spring for summer sale. Similarly, knowing that the demand for heating oil peaks in the winter, they normally store some of their heating oil produced during the fall for winter sale.

In each case, there's a decision to be made between selling the product now versus storing it for later sale. The choice a producer makes depends on a comparison of the current price and the expected future price. This example illustrates how changes in expectations can alter supply: an increase in the anticipated future price of a good or service reduces supply today, a leftward shift of the supply curve. But a fall in the anticipated future price increases supply today, a rightward shift of the supply curve.

An **individual supply curve** illustrates the relationship between quantity supplied and price for an individual producer.

Changes in the Number of Producers Just as changes in the number of consumers affect the demand curve, changes in the number of producers affect the supply curve. Let's examine the **individual supply curve** by looking at panel (a) in Figure 6-5. The individual supply curve shows the relationship between quantity supplied and price for an individual producer. For example, suppose that Louisiana Drillers is a natural gas producer and that panel (a) of Figure 6-5 shows the quantity of BTUs it will supply per year at any given price. Then $S_{Louisiana}$ is its individual supply curve.

The *market supply curve* in panel (c) shows how the combined total quantity supplied by all individual producers in the market depends on the market price of that good. Just as the market demand curve is the horizontal sum of the individual demand curves of all consumers, the market supply curve is the horizontal sum of the individual supply curves of all producers. Assume for a moment that there are only two natural gas producers, Louisiana Drillers and Allegheny Natural Gas. Allegheny's individual supply curve is shown in panel (b). Panel (c) shows the market supply curve. At any given price, the quantity supplied to the market is the sum of the quantities supplied by Louisiana Drillers and Allegheny Natural Gas. For example, at a price of around \$2 per BTU, Louisiana Drillers supplies 200,000 BTUs and Allegheny Natural Gas supplies 100,000 BTUs per year, making the quantity supplied to the market 300,000 BTUs.

Clearly, the quantity supplied to the market at any given price is larger when Allegheny Natural Gas is also a producer than it would be if Louisiana Drillers were the only supplier. The quantity supplied at a given price would be even larger if we added a third producer, then a fourth, and so on. So an increase in the number of producers leads to an increase in supply and a rightward shift of the supply curve.

For a review of the factors that shift supply, see Table 6-1.

FIGURE 6-5 The Individual Supply Curve and the Market Supply Curve

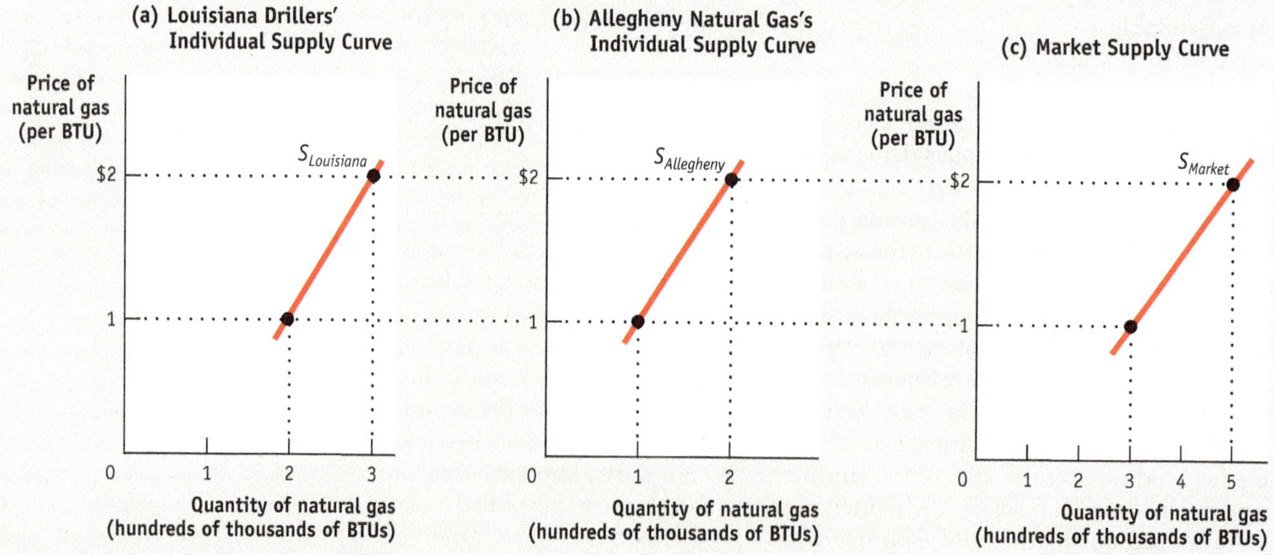

Panel (a) shows the individual supply curve for Louisiana Drillers $S_{Louisiana}$, the quantity it will sell at any given price. Panel (b) shows the individual supply curve for Allegheny Natural Gas, $S_{Allegheny}$. The market supply curve, which shows the quantity of natural gas supplied by all producers at any given price is shown in panel (c). The market supply curve is the horizontal sum of the individual supply curves of all producers.

TABLE 6-1 Factors That Shift Supply

When this happens . . .	. . . supply increases	But when this happens . . .	. . . supply decreases
When the price of an input falls . . .	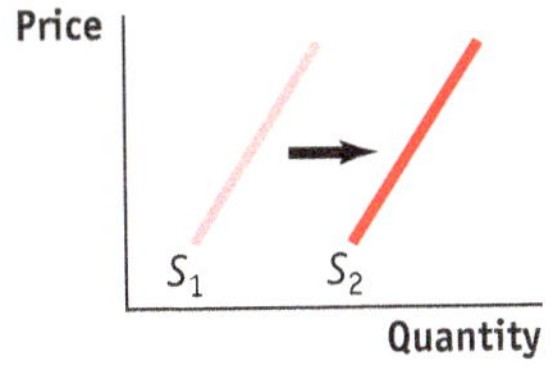 . . . supply of the good increases.	When the price of an input rises . . .	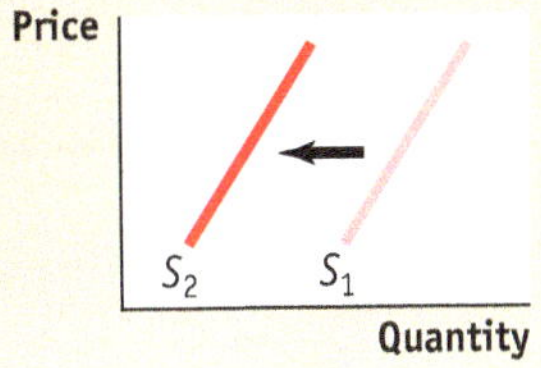 . . . supply of the good decreases.
When the price of a substitute in production falls . . .	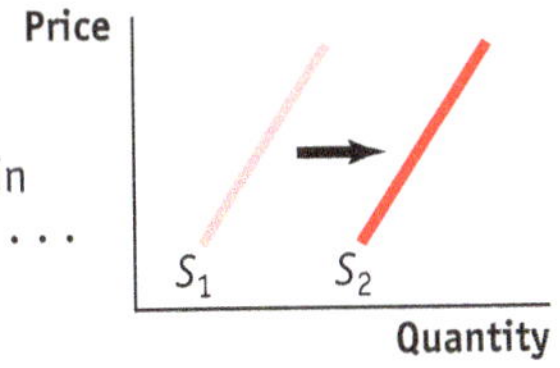 . . . supply of the original good increases.	When the price of a substitute in production rises . . .	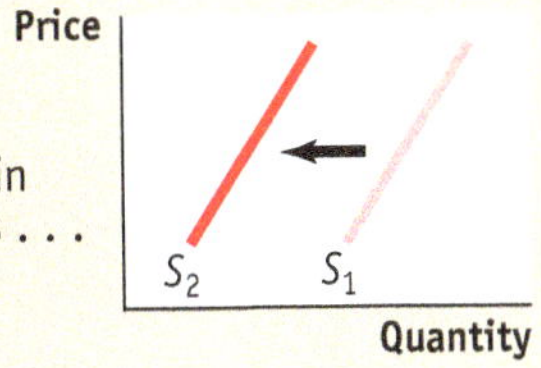 . . . supply of the original good decreases.
When the price of a complement in production rises . . .	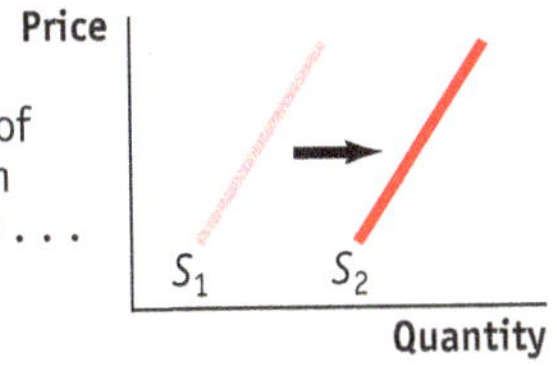 . . . supply of the original good increases.	When the price of a complement in production falls . . .	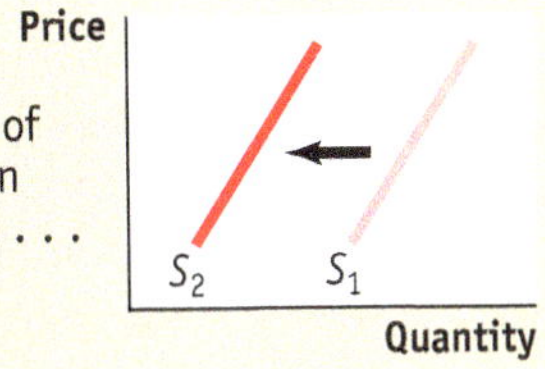 . . . supply of the original good decreases.
When the technology used to produce the good improves . . .	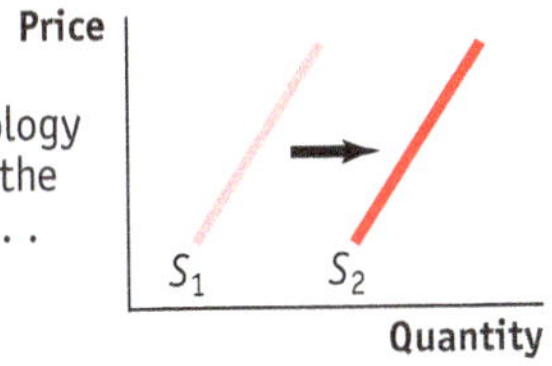 . . . supply of the good increases.	When the best technology used to produce the good is no longer available . . .	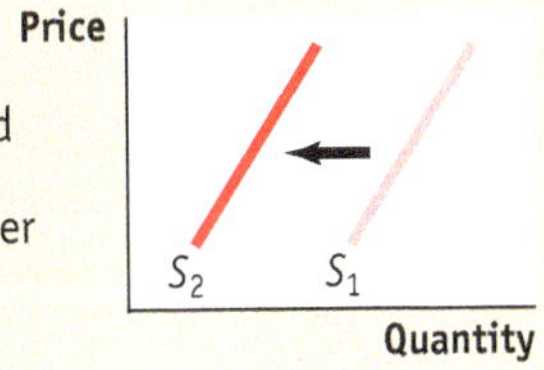 . . . supply of the good decreases.
When the price is expected to fall in the future . . .	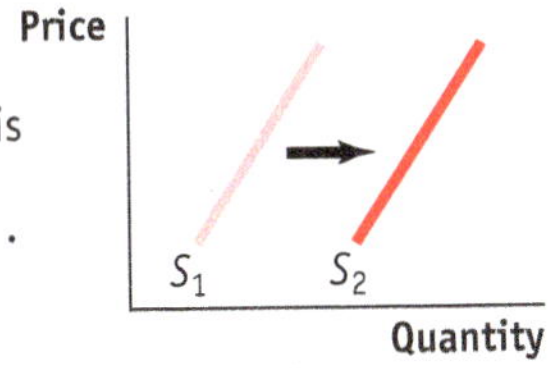 . . . supply of the good increases today.	When the price is expected to rise in the future . . .	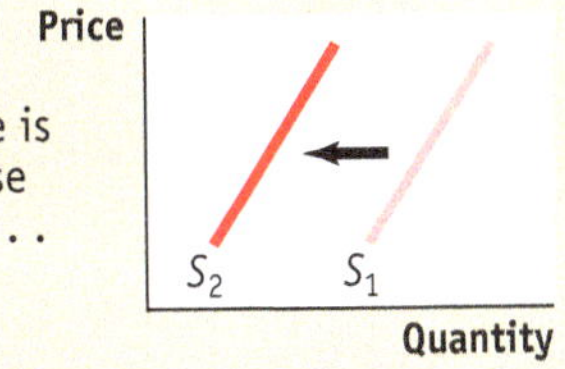 . . . supply of the good decreases today.
When the number of producers rises . . .	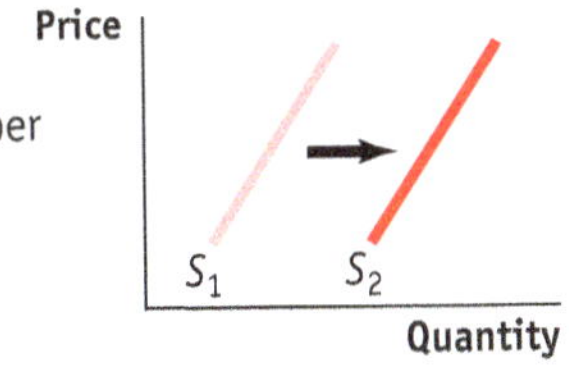 . . . market supply of the good increases.	When the number of producers falls . . .	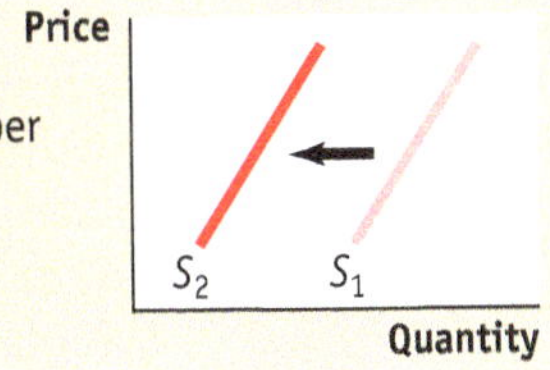 . . . market supply of the good decreases.

Check Your Understanding 6-1

1. Explain whether each of the following events represents (i) a *shift* of the supply curve or (ii) a *movement along* the supply curve.
   - **a.** As house prices rise, more homeowners put their houses up for sale.
   - **b.** Many strawberry farmers open temporary roadside stands during harvest season, even though prices are usually low at that time of year.
   - **c.** Immediately after the school year begins, fast-food chains must raise wages, which represent the price of labor, to attract workers.

d. Many construction workers temporarily move to areas that have suffered hurricane damage, lured by higher wages.

e. Since new technologies have made it possible to build larger cruise ships (which are cheaper to run per passenger), Caribbean cruise lines offer more cabins, at lower prices, than before.

Solutions appear at back of book.

6.2 Supply, Demand, and Equilibrium

We have now covered the first three key elements in the supply and demand model: the demand curve, the supply curve, and the set of factors that shift each curve. The next step is to put these elements together to show how they can be used to predict the actual price at which the good is bought and sold, as well as the actual quantity transacted.

What determines the price at which a good or service is bought or sold? What determines the quantity transacted of the good or service? In Module 1 we learned the general principle that *markets move toward equilibrium,* a situation in which no individual would be better off taking a different action. In the case of a competitive market, we can be more specific: a competitive market is in equilibrium when the price has moved to a level at which the quantity of a good demanded equals the quantity of that good supplied. At that price, no individual seller could make herself better off by offering to sell either more or less of the good and no individual buyer could make himself better off by offering to buy more or less of the good. In other words, at the market equilibrium, price has moved to a level that exactly matches the quantity demanded by consumers to the quantity supplied by sellers.

The price that matches the quantity supplied and the quantity demanded is the **equilibrium price;** the quantity bought and sold at that price is the **equilibrium quantity.** The equilibrium price is also known as the **market-clearing price:** it is the price that "clears the market" by ensuring that every buyer willing to pay that price finds a seller willing to sell at that price, and vice versa. So how do we find the equilibrium price and quantity?

A competitive market is in equilibrium when price has moved to a level at which the quantity of a good or service demanded equals the quantity of that good or service supplied. The price at which this takes place is the **equilibrium price,** also referred to as the **market-clearing price.** The quantity of the good or service bought and sold at that price is the **equilibrium quantity.**

Finding the Equilibrium Price and Quantity

The easiest way to determine the equilibrium price and quantity in a market is by putting the supply curve and the demand curve on the same diagram. Since the supply curve shows the quantity supplied at any given price and the demand curve shows the quantity demanded at any given price, the price at which the two curves cross is the equilibrium price: the price at which quantity supplied equals quantity demanded.

Figure 6-6 combines the demand curve from Figure 5-1 and the supply curve from Figure 6-1. They *intersect* at point *E,* which is the equilibrium of this market; \$3 is the equilibrium price and 10 trillion BTUs is the equilibrium quantity.

Let's confirm that point *E* fits our definition of equilibrium. At a price of \$3 per BTU, natural gas producers are willing to sell 10 trillion BTUs a year, and natural gas consumers want to buy 10 trillion BTUs a year. So, at the price of \$3 per BTU, the quantity of natural gas supplied equals the quantity demanded. Notice that at any other price the market would not clear: every willing buyer would not be able to find a willing seller, or vice versa. More specifically, if the price were more than \$3, the quantity supplied would exceed the quantity demanded; if the price were less than \$3, the quantity demanded would exceed the quantity supplied.

The model of supply and demand, then, predicts that given the demand and supply curves shown in Figure 6-5, 10 trillion BTUs would change hands at a price

FIGURE 6-6 Market Equilibrium

Market equilibrium occurs at point *E*, where the supply curve and the demand curve intersect. In equilibrium, the quantity demanded is equal to the quantity supplied. In this market, the equilibrium price is $3 per BTU and the equilibrium quantity is 10 trillion BTUs per year.

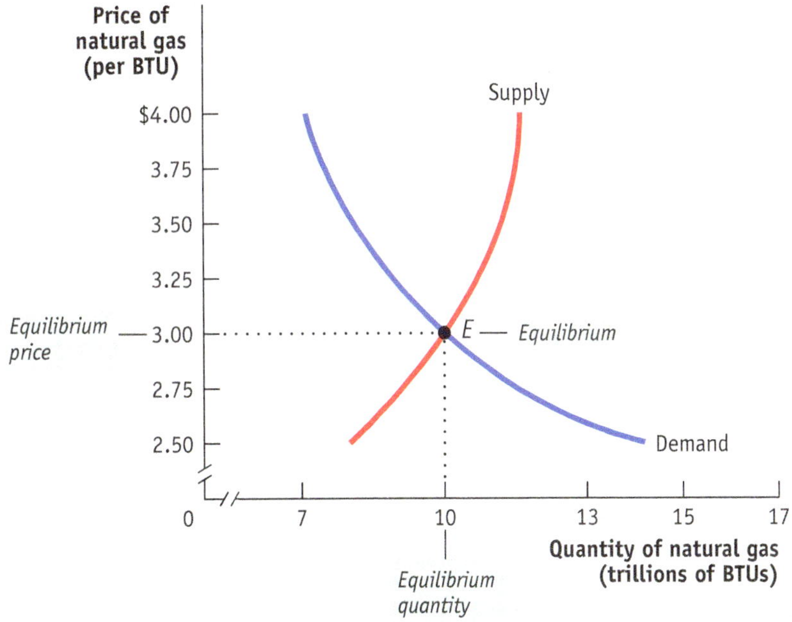

of $3 per BTU. But how can we be sure that the market will arrive at the equilibrium price? We begin by answering three simple questions:

1. Why do all sales and purchases in a market take place at the same price?
2. Why does the market price fall if it is above the equilibrium price?
3. Why does the market price rise if it is below the equilibrium price?

1. Why Do All Sales and Purchases in a Market Take Place at the Same Price?

There are some markets in which the same good can sell for many different prices, depending on who is selling or who is buying. For example, have you ever bought a souvenir in a tourist trap and then seen the same item on sale somewhere else for a lower price? Because tourists don't know which shops offer the best deals and don't have time for comparison shopping, sellers in tourist areas can charge different prices for the same good.

But, in any market in which both buyers and sellers have been around for some time, sales and purchases tend to converge at a generally uniform price, so we can safely talk about *the* market price. It's easy to see why. Suppose a seller offered a potential buyer a price noticeably above what the buyer knew other people to be paying. The buyer would clearly be better off shopping elsewhere—unless the seller were prepared to offer a better deal.

Witness equilibrium in action in the checkout line.

There is a **surplus** of a good or service when the quantity supplied exceeds the quantity demanded. Surpluses occur when the price is above its equilibrium level.

There is a **shortage** of a good or service when the quantity demanded exceeds the quantity supplied. Shortages occur when the price is below its equilibrium level.

Conversely, a seller would not be willing to sell for significantly less than the amount they knew most buyers were paying; the seller would be better off waiting to get a more reasonable customer. Thus, in any well-established, ongoing market, all sellers receive and all buyers pay approximately the same price. This is what we call the *market price.*

2. Why Does the Market Price Fall If It Is Above the Equilibrium Price?

Suppose the supply and demand curves are as shown in Figure 6-5 but the market price is above the equilibrium level of $3—say, $3.50. This situation is illustrated in Figure 6-7. Why can't the price stay there?

As the figure shows, at a price of $3.50 there would be more BTUs of natural gas available than consumers wanted to buy: 11.2 trillion BTUs versus 8.1 trillion BTUs. The difference of 3.1 trillion BTUs is the **surplus**—also known as the *excess supply*—of natural gas at $3.50.

This surplus means that some natural gas producers are frustrated: at the current price, they cannot find consumers who want to buy their natural gas. The surplus offers an incentive for those frustrated would-be sellers to offer a lower price to poach business from other producers and entice more consumers to buy. The result of this price cutting will be to push the prevailing price down until it reaches the equilibrium price. So the price of a good will fall whenever there is a surplus—that is, whenever the market price is above its equilibrium level.

3. Why Does the Market Price Rise If It Is Below the Equilibrium Price?

Now suppose the price is below its equilibrium level—say, at $2.75 per BTU, as shown in Figure 6-8. In this case, the quantity demanded, 11.5 trillion BTUs, exceeds the quantity supplied, 9.1 trillion BTUs, implying that there are would-be buyers who cannot find natural gas: there is a **shortage,** also known as an *excess demand,* of 2.4 trillion BTUs.

FIGURE 6-7 Price Above Its Equilibrium Level Creates a Surplus

The market price of $3.50 is above the equilibrium price of $3. This creates a surplus: at a price of $3.50, producers would like to sell 11.2 trillion BTUs but consumers want to buy only 8.1 trillion BTUs, so there is a surplus of 3.1 trillion BTUs. This surplus will push the price down until it reaches the equilibrium price of $3.

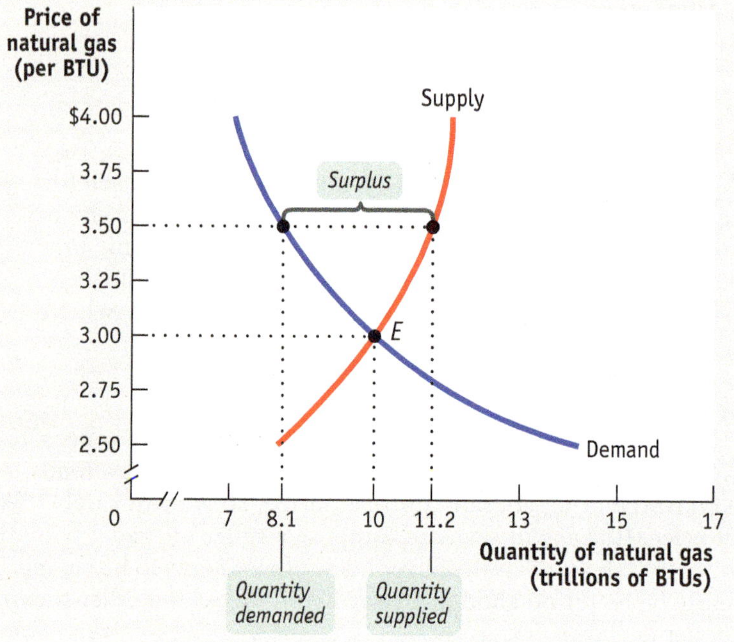

FIGURE 6-8 Price Below Its Equilibrium Level Creates a Shortage

The market price of $2.75 is below the equilibrium price of $3. This creates a shortage: consumers want to buy 11.5 trillion BTUs, but only 9.1 trillion BTUs are for sale, so there is a shortage of 2.4 trillion BTUs. This shortage will push the price up until it reaches the equilibrium price of $3.

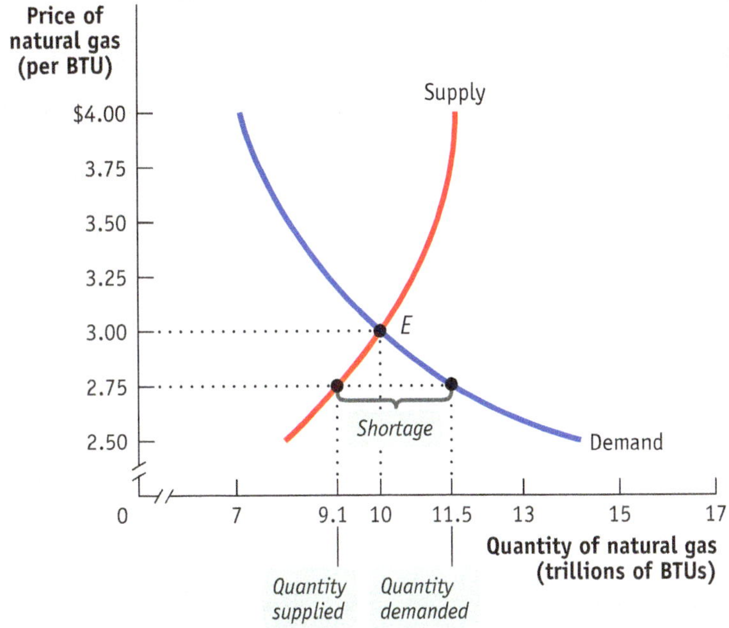

When there is a shortage, there are frustrated would-be buyers—people who want to purchase natural gas but cannot find willing sellers at the current price. In this situation, either buyers will offer more than the prevailing price or sellers will realize that they can charge higher prices. Either way, the result is to drive up the prevailing price.

This bidding up of prices happens whenever there are shortages—and there will be shortages whenever the price is below its equilibrium level. So the market price will always rise if it is below the equilibrium level.

Using Equilibrium to Describe Markets

We have now seen that a market tends to have a single price, the equilibrium price. If the market price is above the equilibrium level, the ensuing surplus leads buyers and sellers to take actions that lower the price. And if the market price is below the equilibrium level, the ensuing shortage leads buyers and sellers to take actions that raise the price. So the market price always *moves toward* the equilibrium price, the price at which there is neither surplus nor shortage.

ECONOMICS >> *in Action*

The Price of Admission

The market equilibrium, so the theory goes, is pretty egalitarian because the equilibrium price applies to everyone. That is, all buyers pay the same price—the equilibrium price—and all sellers receive that same price. But is this realistic?

The market for concert tickets is an example that seems to contradict the theory—there's one price at the box office, and there's another price (typically much higher) for the same event online where people who already have tickets resell them, such as StubHub.com or eBay. For example, compare the box office price for a Demi Lovato concert in Nashville, Tennessee in March 2018 to the

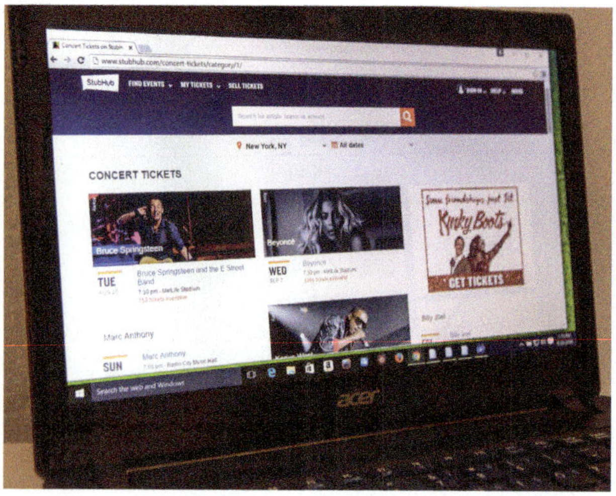

The Photo Works

The competitive market model determines the price you pay for concert tickets.

StubHub.com price for seats in the same location: $95.45 versus $169.98.

Puzzling as this may seem, there is no contradiction once we take opportunity costs and tastes into account. For major events, buying tickets from the box office means waiting in very long lines. Ticket buyers who use online resellers have decided that the opportunity cost of their time is too high to spend waiting in line. And tickets for major events being sold at face value by online box offices often sell out within minutes. In this case, some people who want to go to the concert badly but have missed out on the opportunity to buy cheaper tickets from the online box office are willing to pay the higher online reseller price.

Not only that, by comparing prices across sellers for seats close to one another, you can see that markets really do move to equilibrium. For example, for a seat in Section 107, Row 3, StubHub.com's price is $169.99 while ScoreBig's price for a nearby seat is $168. As the competitive market model predicts, units of the same good will end up selling for approximately the same price.

In fact, e-commerce is making markets move to equilibrium more quickly by doing the price comparisons for you. The website Seat Geek compares ticket prices across more than 100 ticket resellers, allowing customers to instantly choose the best deal. Tickets that are priced lower than those of competitors will be snapped up, while higher-priced tickets will languish unsold.

And tickets on StubHub.com can sell for less than their face value for events that have little appeal, while they can skyrocket for events in high demand. For example, in 2016 some fans paid over $20,000 to watch the Chicago Cubs win their first World Series Championship in 108 years. Even StubHub.com's chief executive says the site is "the embodiment of supply-and-demand economics."

So the theory of competitive markets isn't just speculation. If you want to experience it for yourself, try buying tickets to a concert (or the World Series).

Check Your Understanding 6-2

1. In the following three situations, the market is initially in equilibrium. Explain the changes in either supply or demand that will result from each event. After each event described below, does a surplus or shortage exist at the original equilibrium price? What will happen to the equilibrium price as a result?
   - **a.** 2015 was a very good year for California wine-grape growers, who produced a bumper crop.
   - **b.** After a hurricane, Florida hoteliers often find that many people cancel their upcoming vacations, leaving them with empty hotel rooms.
   - **c.** After a heavy snowfall, many people want to buy second-hand snowblowers at the local tool shop.

Solutions appear at back of book.

>> Quick Review

- The **supply schedule** shows how the **quantity supplied** depends on the price. The **supply curve** illustrates this relationship.
- Supply curves are normally upward sloping: at a higher price, producers are willing to supply more of a good or service.
- A change in price results in a **movement along the supply curve** and a change in the quantity supplied.
- Increases or decreases in supply lead to **shifts of the supply curve.** An increase in supply is a rightward shift: the quantity supplied rises for any given price. A decrease in supply is a leftward shift: the quantity supplied falls for any given price.
- The five main factors that can shift the supply curve are changes in (1) **input** prices, (2) prices of related goods or services, (3) technology, (4) expectations, and (5) number of producers.
- The market supply curve is the horizontal sum of the **individual supply** curves of all producers in the market.
- Price in a competitive market moves to the **equilibrium price,** or **market-clearing price,** where the quantity supplied is equal to the quantity demanded. This quantity is the **equilibrium quantity.**
- All sales and purchases in a competitive market take place at the same price. If the price is above its equilibrium level, there is a **surplus** that drives the price down to the equilibrium level. If the price is below its equilibrium level, there is a **shortage** that drives the price up to the equilibrium level.

Changes in Equilibrium

MODULE 7

WHAT YOU WILL LEARN

- How are equilibrium price and quantity affected when there is a change in either supply or demand?
- How are equilibrium price and quantity affected when there is a simultaneous change in both supply and demand?

7.1 Changes in Supply and Demand

The huge fall in the price of natural gas from $14 to $2 per BTU from 2006 to 2013 may have come as a surprise to consumers, but to suppliers it was no surprise at all. Suppliers knew that advances in drilling technology had opened up vast reserves of natural gas that had been too costly to tap in the past. And, predictably, an increase in supply reduced the equilibrium price.

The adoption of improved drilling technology is an example of an event that shifted the supply curve for a good without having an effect on the demand curve. There are many such events. There are also events that shift the demand curve without shifting the supply curve. For example, a medical report that chocolate is good for you increases the demand for chocolate but does not affect the supply. Events often shift either the supply curve or the demand curve, but not both; it is therefore useful to ask what is happening in each case.

We have seen that when a curve shifts, the equilibrium price and quantity change. We will now concentrate on exactly how the shift of a curve alters the equilibrium price and quantity.

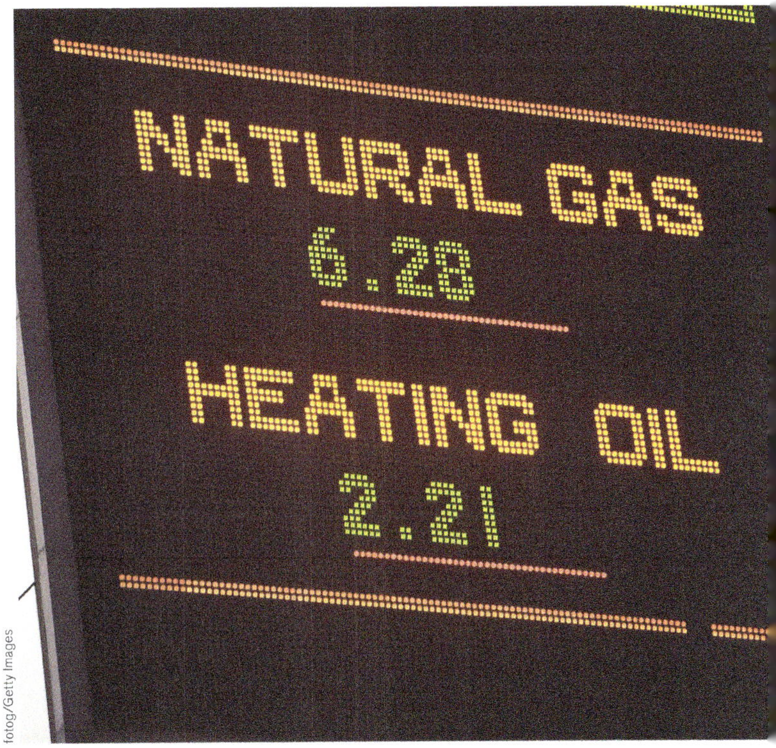

fotog/Getty Images

What Happens When the Demand Curve Shifts

Heating oil and natural gas are substitutes: if the price of heating oil rises, the demand for natural gas will increase, and if the price of heating oil falls, the demand for natural gas will decrease. But how does the price of heating oil affect the *market equilibrium* for natural gas?

Figure 7-1 shows the effect of a rise in the price of heating oil on the market for natural gas. The rise in the price of heating oil increases the demand for natural

FIGURE 7-1 Equilibrium and Shifts of the Demand Curve

The original equilibrium in the market for natural gas is at E_1, at the intersection of the supply curve and the original demand curve, D_1. A rise in the price of heating oil, a substitute, shifts the demand curve rightward to D_2. A shortage exists at the original price, P_1, causing both the price and quantity supplied to rise, a movement along the supply curve. A new equilibrium is reached at E_2, with a higher equilibrium price, P_2, and a higher equilibrium quantity, Q_2. When demand for a good or service increases, the equilibrium price and the equilibrium quantity of the good or service both rise.

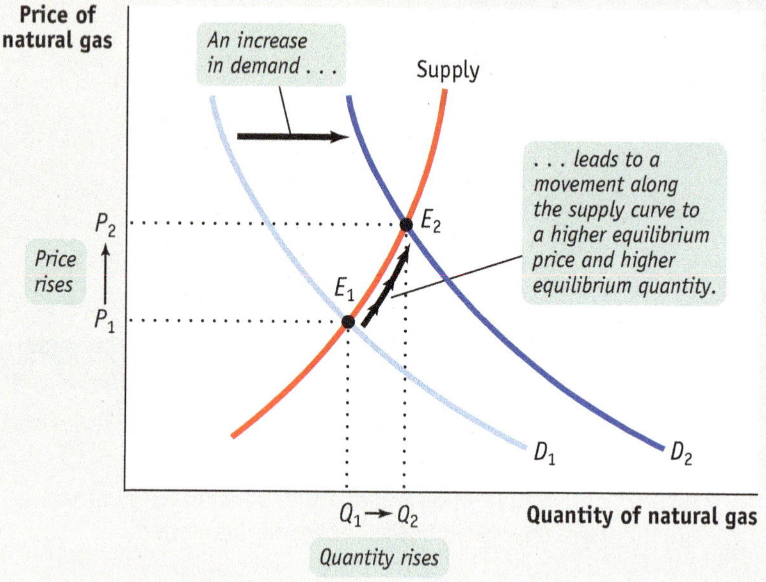

gas. Point E_1 shows the equilibrium corresponding to the original demand curve, with P_1 the equilibrium price and Q_1 the equilibrium quantity bought and sold.

An increase in demand is indicated by a *rightward* shift of the demand curve from D_1 to D_2. At the original market price P_1, this market is no longer in equilibrium: a shortage occurs because the quantity demanded exceeds the quantity supplied. The price of natural gas then rises and generates an increase in the quantity supplied, an upward *movement along the supply curve*. A new equilibrium is established at point E_2, with a higher equilibrium price, P_2, and higher equilibrium quantity, Q_2. This sequence of events reflects a general principle: *When demand for a good or service increases, the equilibrium price and the equilibrium quantity of the good or service both rise.*

What would happen in the reverse case, a fall in the price of heating oil? A fall in the price of heating oil reduces the demand for natural gas, shifting the demand curve to the *left*. At the original price, a surplus occurs as quantity supplied exceeds quantity demanded. The price falls and leads to a decrease in the quantity supplied, resulting in a lower equilibrium price and a lower equilibrium quantity. This illustrates another general principle: *When demand for a good or service decreases, the equilibrium price and the equilibrium quantity of the good or service both fall.*

To summarize how a market responds to a change in demand: *An increase in demand leads to a rise in both the equilibrium price and the equilibrium quantity. A decrease in demand leads to a fall in both the equilibrium price and the equilibrium quantity.*

What Happens When the Supply Curve Shifts

For most goods and services, it is a bit easier to predict changes in supply than changes in demand. Physical factors that affect supply, like weather or the availability of inputs, are easier to get a handle on than the fickle tastes that affect demand. Still, with supply as with demand, what we can best predict are the *effects* of shifts of the supply curve.

As we mentioned in the opening story, improved drilling technology significantly increased the supply of natural gas from 2006 onward. Figure 7-2 shows how this shift affected the market equilibrium. The original equilibrium is at E_1,

FIGURE 7-2 Equilibrium and Shifts of the Supply Curve

The original equilibrium in the market is at E_1. Improved technology causes an increase in the supply of natural gas and shifts the supply curve rightward from S_1 to S_2. A new equilibrium is established at E_2, with a lower equilibrium price, P_2, and a higher equilibrium quantity, Q_2.

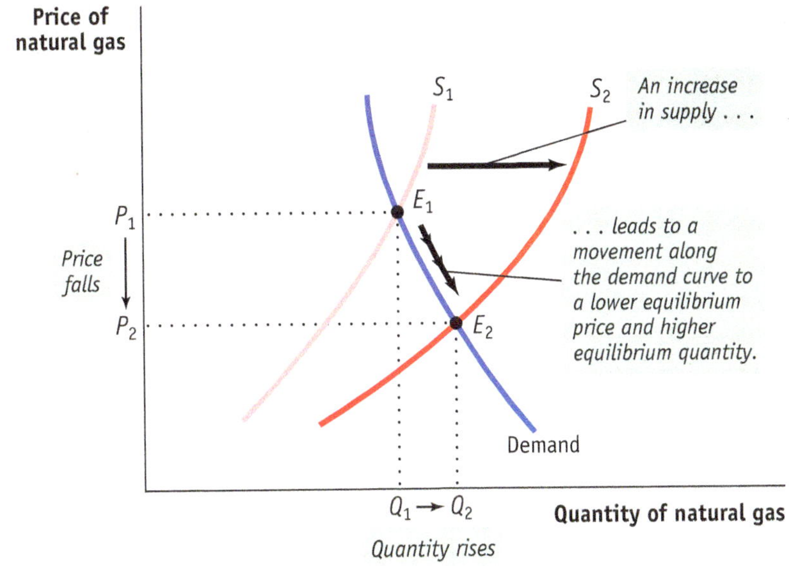

the point of intersection of the original supply curve, S_1, with an equilibrium price P_1 and equilibrium quantity Q_1. As a result of the improved technology, supply increases and S_1 shifts *rightward* to S_2. At the original price P_1, a surplus of natural gas now exists and the market is no longer in equilibrium. The surplus causes a fall in price and an increase in the quantity demanded, a downward movement along the demand curve. The new equilibrium is at E_2, with an equilibrium price P_2 and an equilibrium quantity Q_2. In the new equilibrium E_2, the price is lower and the equilibrium quantity is higher than before. This can be stated as a general principle: *When supply of a good or service increases, the equilibrium price of the good or service falls and the equilibrium quantity of the good or service rises.*

What happens to the market when supply falls? A fall in supply leads to a *leftward* shift of the supply curve. A shortage now exists at the original price; as a result, the equilibrium price rises and the quantity demanded falls. This describes what happened to the market for natural gas after Hurricane Katrina damaged natural gas production in the Gulf of Mexico in 2005. We can formulate a general principle: *When the supply of a good or service decreases, the equilibrium price of the good or service rises and the equilibrium quantity of the good or service falls.*

To summarize how a market responds to a change in supply: *An increase in supply leads to a fall in the equilibrium price and a rise in the equilibrium quantity. A decrease in supply leads to a rise in the equilibrium price and a fall in the equilibrium quantity.*

PITFALLS

WHICH CURVE IS IT, ANYWAY?

When the price of some good or service changes, we can, in general, say that this reflects a change in either supply or demand. But it is easy to get confused about which one. A helpful clue is the direction of change in the quantity. If the quantity sold changes in the *same* direction as the price—for example, if both the price and the quantity rise—this suggests that the demand curve has shifted. If the price and the quantity move in *opposite* directions, the likely cause is a shift of the supply curve.

Simultaneous Shifts of Supply and Demand Curves

Finally, it sometimes happens that events shift *both* the demand and supply curves at the same time. This is not unusual; in real life, supply curves and demand curves for many goods and services shift quite often because the economic environment is continually changing.

Figure 7-3 illustrates two examples of simultaneous shifts. In both panels there is an increase in supply—that is, a rightward shift of the supply curve from

FIGURE 7-3 Simultaneous Shifts of the Demand and Supply Curves

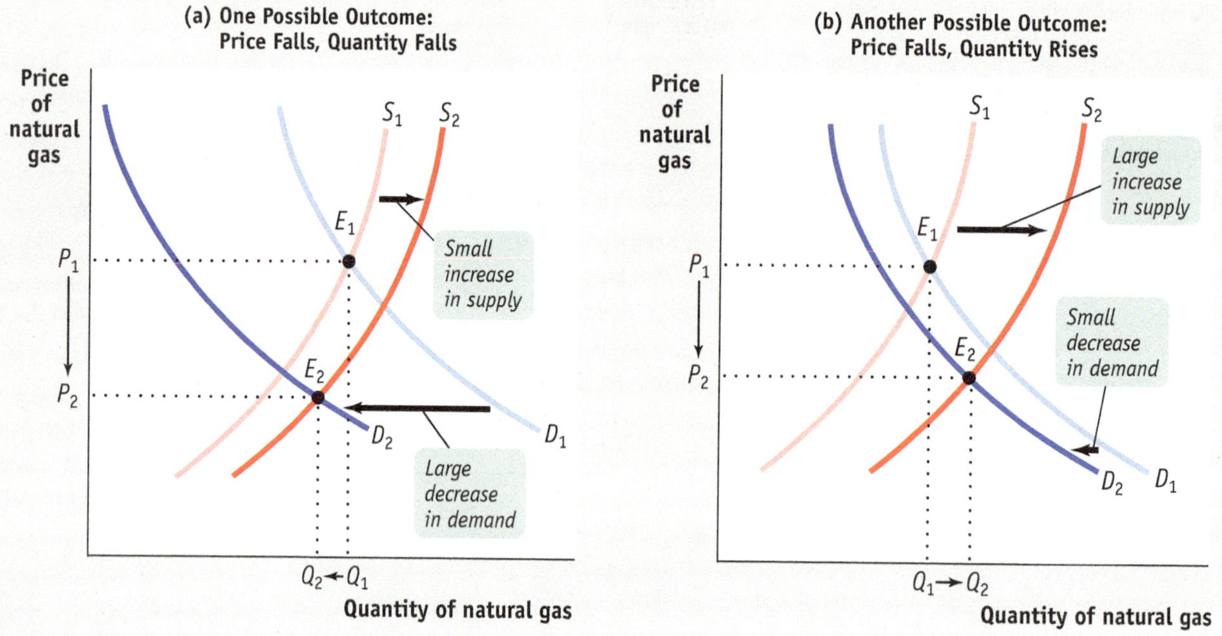

In panel (a) there is a simultaneous leftward shift of the demand curve and a rightward shift of the supply curve. Here the decrease in demand is relatively larger than the increase in supply, so the equilibrium quantity falls as the equilibrium price also falls. In panel (b) there is also a simultaneous leftward shift of the demand curve and rightward shift of the supply curve. Here the increase in supply is large relative to the decrease in demand, so the equilibrium quantity rises as the equilibrium price falls.

S_1 to S_2—representing, for example, adoption of an improved drilling technology. Notice that the rightward shift in panel (a) is smaller than the one in panel (b): we can suppose that panel (a) represents a small, incremental change in technology while panel (b) represents a big advance in technology.

Both panels show a decrease in demand—that is, a leftward shift from D_1 to D_2. Also notice that the leftward shift in panel (a) is relatively larger than the one in panel (b): we can suppose that panel (a) reflects the effect on demand of a deep recession in the overall economy, while panel (b) reflects the effect of a mild winter.

In both cases the equilibrium price falls from P_1 to P_2 as the equilibrium moves from E_1 to E_2. But what happens to the equilibrium quantity, the quantity of natural gas bought and sold? In panel (a) the decrease in demand is large relative to the increase in supply, and the equilibrium quantity falls as a result. In panel (b) the increase in supply is large relative to the decrease in demand, and the equilibrium quantity rises as a result. That is, when demand decreases and supply increases, the actual quantity bought and sold can go either way, depending on *how much* the demand and supply curves have shifted.

In general, when supply and demand shift in opposite directions, we can't predict what the ultimate effect will be on the quantity bought and sold. What we can say is that a curve that shifts a disproportionately greater distance than the other curve will have a disproportionately greater effect on the quantity bought and sold. That said, we can make the following prediction about the outcome when the supply and demand curves shift in opposite directions:

- When demand decreases and supply increases, the equilibrium price falls but the change in the equilibrium quantity is ambiguous.
- When demand increases and supply decreases, the equilibrium price rises but the change in the equilibrium quantity is ambiguous.

But suppose that the demand and supply curves shift in the same direction. This is what has happened in the United States as the economy made a gradual recovery from the recession of 2008; the result was an increase in both demand and supply. Can we safely make any predictions about the changes in price and quantity? In this situation, the change in quantity bought and sold can be predicted, but the change in price is ambiguous. The two possible outcomes when the supply and demand curves shift in the same direction are as follows:

- When both demand and supply increase, the equilibrium quantity rises but the change in equilibrium price is ambiguous.
- When both demand and supply decrease, the equilibrium quantity falls but the change in equilibrium price is ambiguous.

7.2 Competitive Markets—And Others

In Module 5, we defined a competitive market and explained that the supply and demand framework is a model of competitive markets. But why does it matter whether or not a market is competitive? Now that we've seen how the supply and demand model works, we can offer some explanation.

To understand why competitive markets are different from other markets, compare the problems facing two individuals: a wheat farmer who must decide whether to grow more wheat and the president of a giant aluminum company—say, Alcoa—who must decide whether to produce more aluminum.

For the wheat farmer, the question is simply whether the extra wheat can be sold at a price high enough to justify the extra production cost. The farmer need not worry about whether producing more wheat will affect the price of the wheat they were already planning to grow. That's because the wheat market is competitive. There are thousands of wheat farmers, and one farmer's decision will not impact the market price.

But for the Alcoa executive, the aluminum market is *not* competitive. There are only a few big producers, including Alcoa, and each of them is well aware that its actions *do* have a noticeable impact on the market price. This adds a whole new level of complexity to the decisions producers have to make. Alcoa can't decide whether or not to produce more aluminum just by asking whether the additional product will sell for more than it costs to make. The company also has to ask whether producing more aluminum will drive down the market price and reduce its *profit,* its net gain from producing and selling its output.

When a market is competitive, individuals can base decisions on less complicated analyses than those used in a noncompetitive market. This in turn means that it's easier for economists to build a model of a competitive market than of a noncompetitive market.

This doesn't mean that economic analysis has nothing to say about noncompetitive markets. On the contrary, economists can offer some very important insights into how other kinds of markets work. But those insights require other models that we will discuss later.

ECONOMICS >> *in Action*

Where's the Guacamole?

In 2015, a case of avocados could be purchased in California for $30 to $40. However, by August of 2017, the price had nearly tripled, to approximately $120 per case. And for consumers, average supermarket prices also shot up—doubling in many parts of the country. As one market trader commented at the time, "The avocado market is crazy right now."

Actually, it wasn't crazy—it was just responding to the forces of supply and demand. First, you can thank Americans' fast-growing appetite for all things

SherSor/Shutterstock

avocado: guacamole, avocado toast, avocado smoothies, and the like. The average American eats 7 pounds of guacamole per year, compared to 1.1 pounds per year in 1989, according to the Agriculture Marketing Resource Center. Adding to the increase in American demand is burgeoning demand in Europe and China.

Second, there's supply. Five years of high heat and drought in California, where about 10% of avocados consumed in the United States are grown, has sharply reduced the state's supply. In 2016, the California avocado harvest was only half of what it had been the year before. Mexico and Peru, which account for the lion's share of the remaining 90%, have had their own supply problems. Peru has experienced poor growing weather as well. And Mexico, which supplies 82% of U.S. consumption, has been hit by a "growers' strike."

Observing the rising prices of avocados in the United States owing to the California drought, Mexican avocado growers have become dissatisfied with the prices they received. So they are holding back their crop to get a higher price. In a typical week, about 40 million pounds of Mexican avocados are imported into the United States. But in the midst of the strike, that amount fell by nearly 68%, to only 13 million pounds per week. One producer buyer said, "[Mexican growers are] holding out for more money because the California season is running dry, and there's no other sources."

So an increase in demand coupled with a sharp fall in supply leads to sharply rising prices. It's economic logic, after all. Until demand falls, or supply rises, or both, the price of satisfying your avocado cravings is going to remain high.

>> *Quick Review*

- Changes in the equilibrium price and quantity in a market result from shifts of the supply curve, the demand curve, or both.
- An increase in demand increases both the equilibrium price and the equilibrium quantity. A decrease in demand decreases both the equilibrium price and the equilibrium quantity.
- An increase in supply drives the equilibrium price down but increases the equilibrium quantity. A decrease in supply raises the equilibrium price but reduces the equilibrium quantity.
- Often, fluctuations in markets involve shifts of both the supply and demand curves. When they shift in the same direction, the change in equilibrium quantity is predictable but the change in equilibrium price is not. When they shift in opposite directions, the change in equilibrium price is predictable but the change in equilibrium quantity is not. When there are simultaneous shifts of the demand and supply curves, the curve that shifts the greater distance has a greater effect on the change in equilibrium price and quantity.

Check Your Understanding 7-1

1. For each of the following, determine (i) the market in question; (ii) whether a shift in demand or supply occurred, the direction of the shift, and what induced the shift; and (iii) the effect of the shift on the equilibrium price and the equilibrium quantity.
   a. As U.S. gasoline prices fell during the 1990s, more people bought large cars.
   b. As technological innovation has lowered the cost of recycling used paper, fresh paper made from recycled stock is used more frequently.
   c. When a local cable company offers cheaper on-demand films, local movie theaters have more unfilled seats.
2. When a new, faster computer chip is introduced, demand for computers using the older, slower chips decreases. Simultaneously, computer makers increase their production of computers containing the old chips to clear out their stocks of old chips.
   a. Draw two diagrams of the market for computers containing the old chips: one in which the equilibrium quantity falls in response to these events and one in which the equilibrium quantity rises.
   b. What happens to the equilibrium price in each diagram?
3. Consider the market for bicycles which is initially in equilibrium. Analyze each of the following scenarios.
   a. Suppose that bicycles are a normal good. What happens to the equilibrium price and equilibrium quantity in this market if the producers find that the labor used to produce bicycles is now more expensive and, at the same time, that people's income has increased?
   b. Suppose a reputable medical group puts out a report stating that bicycling significantly improves health outcomes. At the same time several new firms enter the market to produce bicycles. What happens to the equilibrium price and equilibrium quantity in this market given this information and holding everything else constant?

Solutions appear at back of book.

BUSINESS CASE

Uber Gives Riders a Lesson in Supply and Demand

Imagine China/Newscom

Two young entrepreneurs, Garrett Camp and Travis Kalanick, created Uber in 2009 to alleviate a common frustration: how to find a taxi when there aren't any available. In a densely populated city like New York City, finding a taxi is relatively easy on most days—stand on a corner, stick out your arm, and before long a taxi will stop to pick you up. And you know exactly what taxi fare rates will be before you step into the car, because they are set by city regulators.

But at other times, it is not so easy to find a taxi, and you can wait a very long time for one—for example, on rainy days or during rush hour. As you wait, you will probably notice empty taxis passing you by—drivers who have quit working for the day and are headed home. Moreover, there are times when it is simply impossible to hail a taxi—such as during a snowstorm or on New Year's Eve.

Uber was created to address this problem. Using an app, Uber connects people who want a ride to drivers with cars. It also registers drivers, sets fares, and automatically collects payment from a registered rider's credit card. Uber then keeps 25% of the fare, with the rest going to the driver. As of 2019, Uber was operating in 65 countries and in more than 600 cities, and booked $11.3 billion in rides.

Studies have shown that Uber fares are either roughly equal to or less than regular taxi fares during normal driving hours. The qualification *during normal driving hours* is important because at other times Uber's rates fluctuate. When there are more people looking for a ride than cars available, Uber uses what it calls *surge pricing:* setting the rate higher until everyone who wants a car at the going price can get one. For example, during a snowstorm or on New Year's Eve, Uber rides cost around 9 to 10 times the standard price. Enraged, some Uber customers have accused it of price gouging.

But according to its founders, Uber's surge pricing is simply a method of keeping customers happy since the surge price is calculated to leave as few people as possible without a ride. As Kalanick explains, "We do not own cars nor do we employ drivers. Higher prices are required to get cars on the road and keep them on the road during the busiest times." However, with more drivers joining Uber's fleet, they are finding that it takes working longer hours to make sufficient income. So, in cities like San Diego, where passengers have limited access to taxi services, Uber drivers have banded together to take "synchronized breaks" during peak hours, such as Saturday nights. These breaks cause prices to surge, which then prompts the drivers to jump into their cars. Clearly, these Uber drivers know how supply and demand works.

QUESTIONS FOR THOUGHT

1. What accounts for the fact that before Uber's arrival on the scene, there were typically enough taxis available for everyone who wanted one on good weather days, but not enough available on bad weather days?
2. How does Uber's surge pricing solve the problem? Assess Kalanick's claim that the price is set to leave as few people as possible without a ride.
3. Use a supply and demand diagram to illustrate how Uber drivers can cause prices to surge by taking coordinated breaks. Why is this strategy unlikely to work in New York, a large city with an established fleet of taxis?

REVIEW

MODULE 5

1. The **supply and demand model** illustrates how a **competitive market,** one with many buyers and sellers, none of whom can influence the market price, works.
2. The **demand schedule** shows the **quantity demanded** at each price and is represented graphically by a **demand curve.** The **law of demand** says that demand curves slope downward; that is, a higher price for a good or service leads people to demand a smaller quantity, other things equal.
3. A **movement along the demand curve** occurs when a price change leads to a change in the quantity demanded. When economists talk of increasing or decreasing demand, they mean **shifts of the demand curve**—a change in the quantity demanded at any given price. An increase in demand causes a rightward shift of the demand curve. A decrease in demand causes a leftward shift.
4. There are five main factors that shift the demand curve:
   - A change in the prices of related goods or services, such as **substitutes** or **complements**
   - A change in income: when income rises, the demand for **normal goods** increases and the demand for **inferior goods** decreases
   - A change in tastes
   - A change in expectations
   - A change in the number of consumers
5. The market demand curve for a good or service is the horizontal sum of the **individual demand curves** of all consumers in the market.

MODULE 6

1. The **supply schedule** shows the **quantity supplied** at each price and is represented graphically by a **supply curve**. Supply curves usually slope upward.
2. A **movement along the supply curve** occurs when a price change leads to a change in the quantity supplied. When economists talk of increasing or decreasing supply, they mean **shifts of the supply curve**—a change in the quantity supplied at any given price. An increase in supply causes a rightward shift of the supply curve. A decrease in supply causes a leftward shift.
3. There are five main factors that shift the supply curve:
   - A change in **input** prices
   - A change in the prices of related goods and services
   - A change in technology
   - A change in expectations
   - A change in the number of producers
4. The market supply curve for a good or service is the horizontal sum of the **individual supply curves** of all producers in the market.
5. An economic situation is in equilibrium when no individual would be better off doing something different. At this point, the price in a market moves to its **equilibrium price,** or **market-clearing price,** the price at which the quantity demanded is equal to the quantity supplied. This quantity is the **equilibrium quantity.** When the price is above its market-clearing level, there is a **surplus** that pushes the price down. When the price is below its market-clearing level, there is a **shortage** that pushes the price up.

MODULE 7

1. An increase in demand increases both the equilibrium price and the equilibrium quantity; a decrease in demand has the opposite effect. An increase in supply reduces the equilibrium price and increases the equilibrium quantity; a decrease in supply has the opposite effect.
2. Shifts of the demand curve and the supply curve can happen simultaneously. When they shift in opposite directions, the change in equilibrium price is predictable but the change in equilibrium quantity is not. When they shift in the same direction, the change in equilibrium quantity is predictable but the change in equilibrium price is not. In general, the curve that shifts the greater distance has a greater effect on the changes in equilibrium price and quantity.

KEY TERMS

Competitive market p. 54
Supply and demand model p. 54
Demand schedule p. 55
Quantity demanded p. 55
Demand curve p. 56
Law of demand p. 56
Shift of the demand curve p. 57
Movement along the demand curve p. 58
Substitutes p. 60
Complements p. 60

Normal good p. 60
Inferior good p. 60
Individual demand curve p. 62
Quantity supplied p. 65
Supply schedule p. 65
Supply curve p. 66
Shift of the supply curve p. 66
Movement along the supply curve p. 67
Input p. 68
Individual supply curve p. 70
Equilibrium price p. 72
Equilibrium quantity p. 72
Market-clearing price p. 72
Surplus p. 74
Shortage p. 74

Norma Jean Gargasz/AGE Fotostock

Module 8 Consumer and Producer Surplus

Module 9 Efficiency and Markets

Module 10 Price Controls (Ceilings and Floors)

SECTION 3

Market Efficiency and Price Controls

MAKING GAINS BY THE BOOK

There is a lively market in second-hand college textbooks. At the end of each term, some students who took a course decide that the money they can make by selling their used books is worth more to them than keeping the books. And some students who are taking the course next term prefer to buy a somewhat battered but less expensive used textbook rather than buy a new one at full price.

Textbook publishers and authors are not happy about these transactions because they cut into sales of new books. But both the students who sell used books and those who buy them clearly benefit from the existence of second-hand textbook markets. That is why many college bookstores create them, buying used textbooks and selling them alongside the new books. And it is why there are several websites, such as Amazon.com, devoted to the buying and selling of second-hand textbooks. (And renting a textbook is just a form of buying a second-hand textbook: you are buying the *use* of a second-hand textbook for a given amount of time.)

Can we put a number on what used textbook buyers and sellers gain from these transactions? That is, Can we answer the question, "How much do the buyers and sellers of textbooks gain from the existence of the used-book market?"

Yes, we can. In this section we will see how to measure benefits, such as those to buyers of used textbooks, from being able to purchase a good—known as *consumer surplus*. And we will see that there is a corresponding measure, *producer surplus*, of the benefits sellers receive from being able to sell a good.

The concepts of consumer surplus and producer surplus are extremely useful for analyzing a wide variety of economic issues. They let us calculate how much benefit producers and consumers receive from the existence of a market. They also allow us to calculate how the welfare of consumers and producers is affected by changes in market prices. Such calculations play a crucial role in evaluating many economic policies.

What information do we need to calculate consumer and producer surplus? Surprisingly, all we need are the demand and supply curves for a good. That is, the supply and demand model isn't just a model of how a competitive market works—it's also a model of how much consumers and producers gain from participating in that market.

So, our first step will be to learn how consumer and producer surplus can be derived from the demand and supply curves. We will then see how these concepts can be applied to actual economic issues, specifically a government decision to regulate prices through price controls.

MODULE

8 Consumer and Producer Surplus

WHAT YOU WILL LEARN

- What is the meaning of **consumer surplus** and its relationship to the demand curve?
- What is the meaning of **producer surplus** and its relationship to the supply curve?

JenniferRae/Getty Images

8.1 Consumer Surplus and the Demand Curve

The market in used textbooks is a big business in terms of dollars and cents—several billion dollars each year. More importantly for us, it is a convenient starting point for developing the concepts of consumer and producer surplus. We'll use the concepts of consumer and producer surplus to understand exactly how buyers and sellers benefit from a competitive market and how big those benefits are. In addition, these concepts play important roles in analyzing what happens when competitive markets don't work well or there is interference in the market.

So let's begin by looking at the market for used textbooks, starting with the buyers. The key point, as we'll see in a minute, is that the demand curve is derived from their tastes or preferences—and that those same preferences also determine how much they gain from the opportunity to buy used books.

Willingness to Pay and the Demand Curve

A used book is not as good as a new book—it will be battered and coffee-stained, may include someone else's highlighting, and may not be completely up to date. How much this bothers you depends on your preferences. Some potential buyers would prefer to buy the used book even if it is only slightly cheaper than a new one; others would buy the used book only if it is considerably cheaper.

Let's define a potential buyer's **willingness to pay** as the maximum price at which they would buy a good, in this case a used textbook. An individual won't buy the good if it costs more than this amount but they are eager to do so if it costs less. If the price is just equal to an individual's willingness to pay, they are indifferent between buying and not buying. For the sake of simplicity, we'll assume that the individual buys the good in this case.

The table in Figure 8-1 shows five potential buyers of a used book that costs $100 new, listed in order of their willingness to pay. At one extreme is Aleisha, who will buy a second-hand book even if the price is as high as $59. Brad is less willing to have a used book and will buy one only if the price is $45 or less. Claudia is willing to pay only $35 and Darren, only $25. And Edwina, who really doesn't like the idea of a used book, will buy one only if it costs no more than $10.

How many of these five students will actually buy a used book? It depends on the price. If the price of a used book is $55, only Aleisha buys one; if the price is $40, Aleisha and Brad both buy used books, and so on. So the information in the table can be used to construct the *demand schedule* for used textbooks.

A consumer's **willingness to pay** for a good is the maximum price at which they would buy that good.

FIGURE 8-1 The Demand Curve for Used Textbooks

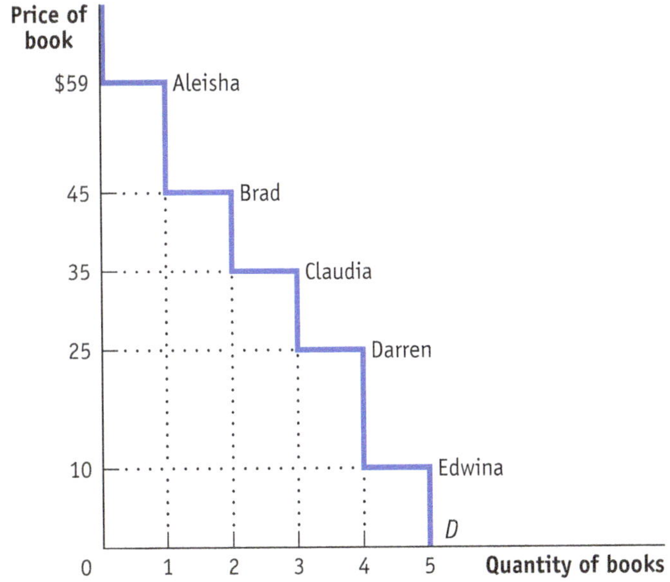

Potential buyers	Willingness to pay
Aleisha	$59
Brad	45
Claudia	35
Darren	25
Edwina	10

With only five potential consumers in this market, the demand curve is step-shaped. Each step represents one consumer, and its height indicates that consumer's willingness to pay—the maximum price at which they will buy a used textbook—as indicated in the table. Aleisha has the highest willingness to pay at $59, Brad has the next highest at $45, and so on down to Edwina with the lowest willingness to pay at $10. At a price of $59, the quantity demanded is one (Aleisha); at a price of $45, the quantity demanded is two (Aleisha and Brad); and so on until you reach a price of $10, at which all five students are willing to purchase a used textbook.

We can use this demand schedule to derive the market demand curve shown in Figure 8-1. Because we are considering only a small number of consumers, this curve doesn't look like the smooth demand curves from Section 2, where markets contained hundreds or thousands of consumers. Instead, this demand curve is step-shaped, with alternating horizontal and vertical segments. Each horizontal segment—each step—corresponds to one potential buyer's willingness to pay.

However, we'll see shortly that for the analysis of consumer surplus it doesn't matter whether the demand curve is step-shaped, as in this figure, or whether there are many consumers, making the curve smooth.

Willingness to Pay and Consumer Surplus

Suppose that the campus bookstore makes used textbooks available at a price of $30. In that case Aleisha, Brad, and Claudia will buy books. Do they gain from their purchases, and if so, how much?

The answer, shown in Table 8-1, is that each student who purchases a book does achieve a net gain but that the amount of the gain differs among students.

Aleisha would have been willing to pay $59, so her net gain is $59 – $30 = $29. Brad would have been willing to pay $45, so his net gain is $45 – $30 = $15. Claudia would have been willing to pay $35, so her net gain is $35 – $30 = $5. Darren and Edwina, however, won't be willing to buy a used book at a price of $30, so they neither gain nor lose.

The net gain that a buyer achieves from the purchase of a good is called that buyer's **individual consumer surplus.** What we learn from this example is that whenever a buyer pays a price less than their willingness to pay, the buyer achieves some individual consumer surplus.

Individual consumer surplus is the net gain to an individual buyer from the purchase of a good. It is equal to the difference between the buyer's willingness to pay and the price paid.

TABLE 8-1 Consumer Surplus If the Price of a Used Textbook = $30

Potential buyer	Willingness to pay	Price paid	Individual consumer surplus = Willingness to pay − Price paid
Aleisha	$59	$30	$29
Brad	45	30	15
Claudia	35	30	5
Darren	25	—	—
Edwina	10	—	—
All buyers			**Total consumer surplus = $49**

The sum of the individual consumer surpluses achieved by all the buyers of a good is known as the **total consumer surplus** achieved in the market. In Table 8-1, the total consumer surplus is the sum of the individual consumer surpluses achieved by Aleisha, Brad, and Claudia: $29 + $15 + $5 = $49.

Economists often use the term **consumer surplus** to refer to both individual and total consumer surplus. We will follow this practice; it will always be clear in context whether we are referring to the consumer surplus achieved by an individual or by all buyers.

Total consumer surplus can be represented graphically. Figure 8-2 reproduces the demand curve from Figure 8-1. Each step in that demand curve is one book wide and represents one consumer. For example, the height of Aleisha's step is $59, her willingness to pay. This step forms the top of a rectangle, with $30—the price she actually pays for a book—forming the bottom. The area of Aleisha's rectangle, ($59 − $30) × 1 = $29, is her consumer surplus from purchasing one book at $30. So the individual consumer surplus Aleisha gains is the *area of the dark blue rectangle* shown in Figure 8-2.

Total consumer surplus is the sum of the individual consumer surpluses of all the buyers of a good in a market.

The term **consumer surplus** is often used to refer both to individual and to total consumer surplus.

In addition to Aleisha, Brad and Claudia will also each buy a book when the price is $30. Like Aleisha, they benefit from their purchases, though not as much, because they each have a lower willingness to pay. Figure 8-2 also shows the

FIGURE 8-2 Consumer Surplus in the Used-Textbook Market

At a price of $30, Aleisha, Brad, and Claudia each buy a book but Darren and Edwina do not. Aleisha, Brad, and Claudia receive individual consumer surpluses equal to the difference between their willingness to pay and the price, illustrated by the areas of the shaded rectangles. Both Darren and Edwina have a willingness to pay less than $30, so they are unwilling to buy a book in this market; they receive zero consumer surplus. The total consumer surplus is given by the entire shaded area—the sum of the individual consumer surpluses of Aleisha, Brad, and Claudia—equal to $29 + $15 + $5 = $49.

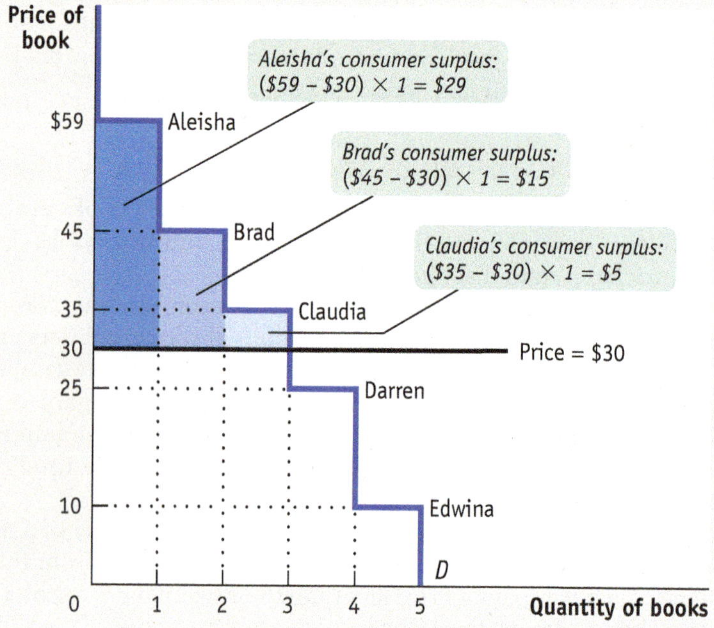

FIGURE 8-3 Consumer Surplus

The demand curve for iPhones is smooth because there are many potential buyers. At a price of $500, 1 million iPhones are demanded. The consumer surplus at this price is equal to the shaded area: the area below the demand curve but above the price. This is the total net gain to consumers generated from buying and consuming iPhones when the price is $500.

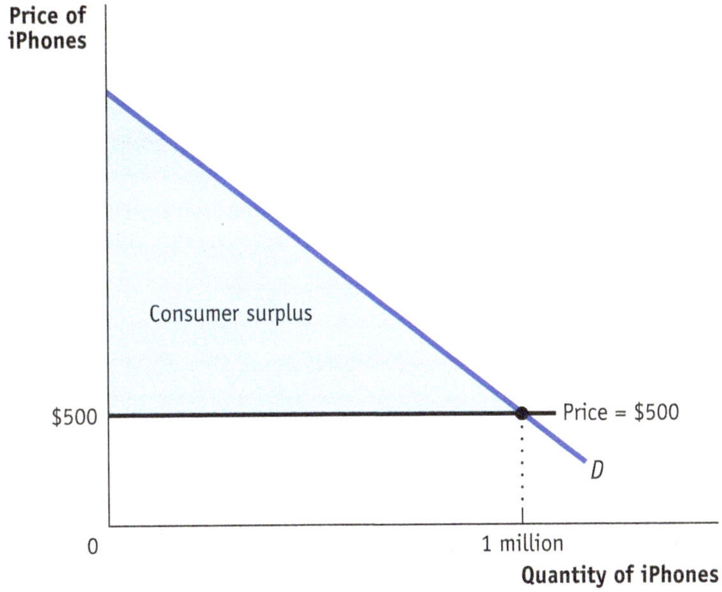

consumer surplus gained by Brad and Claudia; again, this can be measured by the areas of the appropriate rectangles. Darren and Edwina, because they do not buy books at a price of $30, receive no consumer surplus.

The total consumer surplus achieved in this market is just the sum of the individual consumer surpluses received by Aleisha, Brad, and Claudia. So total consumer surplus is equal to the combined area of the three rectangles—the entire shaded area in Figure 8-2. Another way to say this is that total consumer surplus is equal to the area below the demand curve but above the price.

Figure 8-2 illustrates the following general principle: *The total consumer surplus generated by purchases of a good at a given price is equal to the area below the demand curve but above that price.* The same principle applies regardless of the number of consumers.

When we consider large markets, this graphical representation of consumer surplus becomes extremely helpful. Consider, for example, the sales of iPhone to millions of potential buyers. Each potential buyer has a maximum price that they are willing to pay. With so many potential buyers, the demand curve will be smooth, like the one shown in Figure 8-3.

Suppose that at a price of $500, a total of 1 million iPhones are purchased. How much do consumers gain from being able to buy those 1 million iPhones? We could answer that question by calculating the individual consumer surplus of each buyer and then adding these numbers up to arrive at a total. But it is much easier just to look at Figure 8-3 and use the fact that total consumer surplus is equal to the shaded area. As in our original example, consumer surplus is equal to the area below the demand curve but above the price.

How Changing Prices Affect Consumer Surplus

It is often important to know how much consumer surplus *changes* when the price changes. For example, we may want to know how much consumers are hurt if a flood in cotton-growing areas of Pakistan drives up cotton prices or how much consumers gain if the introduction of fish farming makes salmon steaks less expensive. The same approach we have used to derive consumer surplus can be used to answer questions about how changes in prices affect consumers.

Let's return to the example of the market for used textbooks. Suppose that the bookstore decided to sell used textbooks for $20 instead of $30. How much would this fall in price increase consumer surplus?

The answer is illustrated in Figure 8-4. As shown in the figure, there are two parts to the increase in consumer surplus. The first part, shaded dark blue, is the gain of those who would have bought books even at the higher price of $30. Each of the students who would have bought books at $30—Aleisha, Brad, and Claudia—now pays $10 less, and therefore each gains $10 in consumer surplus from the fall in price to $20. So the dark blue area represents the $10 × 3 = $30 increase in consumer surplus to those three buyers.

The second part, shaded light blue, is the gain to those who would not have bought a book at $30 but are willing to pay more than $20. In this case that gain goes to Darren, who would not have bought a book at $30 but does buy one at $20. He gains $5—the difference between his willingness to pay of $25 and the new price of $20. So the light blue area represents a further $5 gain in consumer surplus.

The total increase in consumer surplus is the sum of the shaded areas, $35. Likewise, a rise in price from $20 to $30 would decrease consumer surplus by an amount equal to the sum of the shaded areas.

Figure 8-4 illustrates that when the price of a good falls, the area under the demand curve but above the price—which we have seen is equal to total consumer surplus—increases. Figure 8-5 shows the same result for the case of a smooth demand curve, the demand for iPhones. Here we assume that the price of iPhones falls from $2,000 to $500, leading to an increase in the quantity demanded from 200,000 to 1 million units.

As in the used-textbook example, we divide the gain in consumer surplus into two parts.

1. The dark blue rectangle in Figure 8-5 corresponds to the dark blue area in Figure 8-4: it is the gain to the 200,000 people who would have bought iPhones even at the higher price of $2,000. As a result of the price reduction, each receives additional surplus of $1,500.

FIGURE 8-4 Consumer Surplus and a Fall in the Price of Used Textbooks

There are two parts to the increase in consumer surplus generated by a fall in price from $30 to $20. The first is given by the dark blue rectangle: each person who would have bought at the original price of $30—Aleisha, Brad, and Claudia—receives an increase in consumer surplus equal to the total reduction in price, $10. So the area of the dark blue rectangle corresponds to an amount equal to 3 × $10 = $30. The second part is given by the light blue area: the increase in consumer surplus for those who would not have bought at the original price of $30 but who buy at the new price of $20—namely, Darren. Darren's willingness to pay is $25, so he now receives consumer surplus of $5. The total increase in consumer surplus is (3 × $10) + $5 = $35, represented by the sum of the shaded areas. Likewise, a rise in price from $20 to $30 would decrease consumer surplus by $35, the amount corresponding to the sum of the shaded areas.

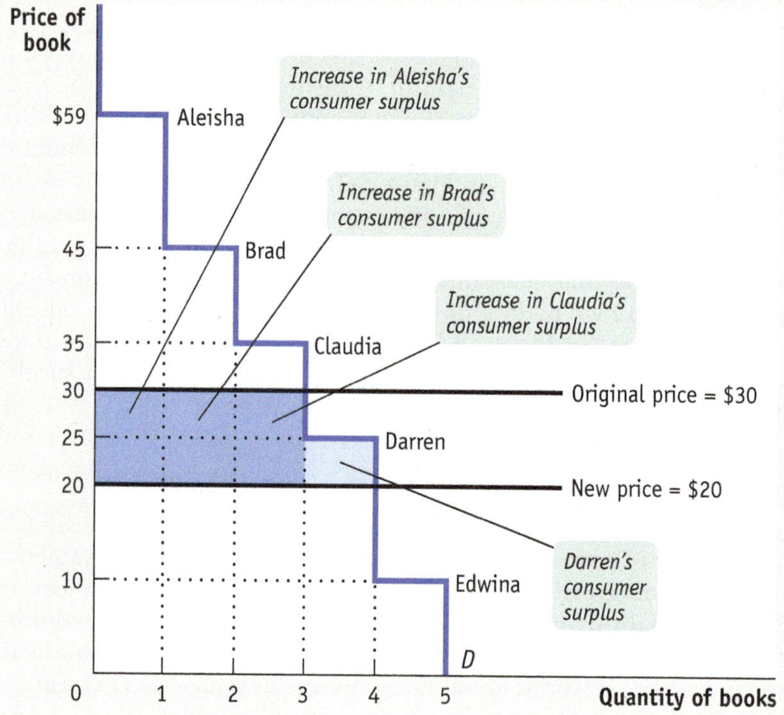

FIGURE 8-5 A Fall in the Price Increases Consumer Surplus

A fall in the price of an iPhone from $2,000 to $500 leads to an increase in the quantity demanded and an increase in consumer surplus. The change in total consumer surplus is given by the sum of the shaded areas: the total area below the demand curve and between the old and new prices. Here, the dark blue area represents the increase in consumer surplus for the 200,000 consumers who would have bought an iPhone at the original price of $2,000; they each receive an increase in consumer surplus of $1,500. The light blue area represents the increase in consumer surplus for those willing to buy at a price equal to or greater than $500 but less than $2,000. Similarly, a rise in the price of an iPhone from $500 to $2,000 generates a decrease in consumer surplus equal to the sum of the two shaded areas.

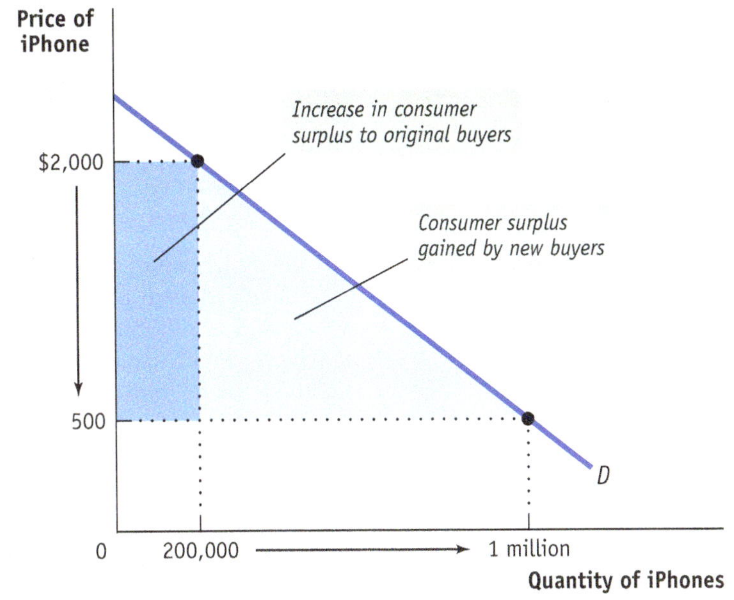

2. The light blue triangle in Figure 8-5 corresponds to the light blue area in Figure 8-4: it is the gain to people who would not have bought the good at the higher price but are willing to do so at a price of $500. For example, the light blue triangle includes the gain to someone who would have been willing to pay $1,000 for an iPhone and therefore gains $500 in consumer surplus when it is possible to buy an iPhone for only $500.

As before, the total gain in consumer surplus is the sum of the shaded areas: the increase in the area under the demand curve but above the price.

What would happen if the price of a good were to rise instead of fall? We would do the same analysis in reverse. Suppose that the price of iPhones rises from $500 to $2,000. This would lead to a fall in consumer surplus, equal to the sum of the shaded areas in Figure 8-5. This loss consists of two parts.

1. The dark blue rectangle represents the loss to consumers who would still buy an iPhone, even at a price of $2,000.
2. The light blue triangle represents the loss to consumers who decide not to buy an iPhone at the higher price.

>> *Quick Review*

- The demand curve for a good is determined by each potential consumer's **willingness to pay.**
- **Individual consumer surplus** is the net gain an individual consumer gets from buying a good.
- The **total consumer surplus** in a given market is equal to the area below the market demand curve but above the price.
- A fall in the price of a good increases **consumer surplus** through two channels: a gain to consumers who would have bought at the original price and a gain to consumers who are persuaded to buy by the lower price. A rise in the price of a good reduces consumer surplus in a similar fashion.

Check Your Understanding 8-1

1. Consider the market for cheese-stuffed jalapeno peppers. There are two consumers, Casey and Josey, and their willingness to pay for each pepper is given in the accompanying table. (Neither is willing to consume more than 4 peppers at any price.) Use the table (i) to construct the demand schedule for peppers for prices of $0.00, $0.10, and so on, up to $0.90, and (ii) to calculate the total consumer surplus when the price of a pepper is $0.40.

Quantity of peppers	Casey's willingness to pay	Josey's willingness to pay
1st pepper	$0.90	$0.80
2nd pepper	0.70	0.60
3rd pepper	0.50	0.40
4th pepper	0.30	0.30

Solutions appear at back of book.

8.2 Producer Surplus and the Supply Curve

Just as some buyers of a good would have been willing to pay more for their purchase than the price they actually pay, some sellers of a good would have been willing to sell it for less than the price they actually receive. So just as there are consumers who receive consumer surplus from buying in a market, there are producers who receive producer surplus from selling in a market.

Cost and Producer Surplus

Consider a group of students who are potential sellers of used textbooks. Because they have different preferences, the various potential sellers differ in the price at which they are willing to sell their books. The table in Figure 8-6 shows the prices at which several different students would be willing to sell. Andrew is willing to sell the book as long as he can get at least $5; Betty won't sell unless she can get at least $15; Carlos, unless he can get $25; Donna, unless she can get $35; Engelbert, unless he can get $45.

The lowest price at which a potential seller is willing to sell has a special name in economics: it is called the seller's **cost.** So Andrew's cost is $5, Betty's is $15, and so on.

Using the term *cost,* which people normally associate with the monetary cost of producing a good, may sound a little strange when applied to sellers of used textbooks. The students don't have to manufacture the books, so it doesn't cost the student who sells a used textbook anything to make that book available for sale, does it?

A seller's **cost** is the lowest price at which they are willing to sell a good.

Yes, it does. A student who sells a book won't have it later, as part of their personal collection. So there is an *opportunity* cost to selling a textbook, even if the owner has completed the course for which it was required. And remember that

FIGURE 8-6 The Supply Curve for Used Textbooks

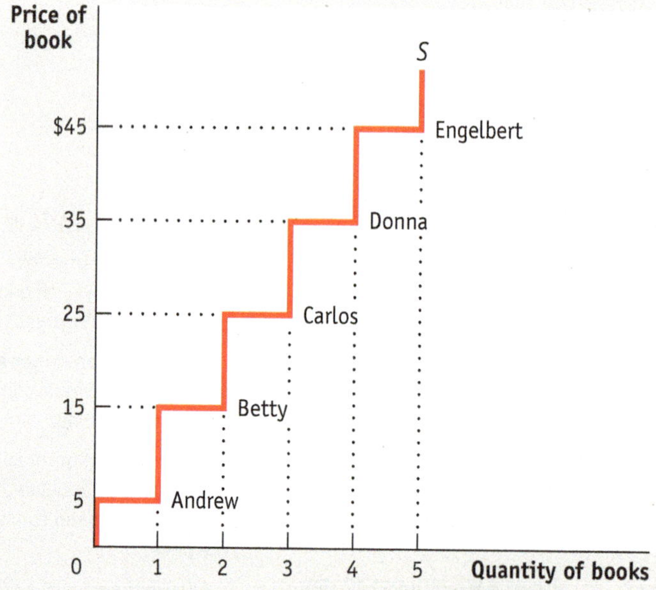

Potential sellers	Cost
Andrew	$5
Betty	15
Carlos	25
Donna	35
Engelbert	45

The supply curve illustrates seller's cost, the lowest price at which a potential seller is willing to sell the good, and the quantity supplied at that price. Each of the five students has one book to sell and each has a different cost, as indicated in the accompanying table. At a price of $5 the quantity supplied is one (Andrew), at $15 it is two (Andrew and Betty), and so on until you reach $45, the price at which all five students are willing to sell.

one of the basic principles of economics is that the true measure of the cost of doing something is always its opportunity cost. That is, the real cost of something is what you must give up to get it.

So it is good economics to talk of the minimum price at which someone will sell a good as the "cost" of selling that good, even if they don't spend any money to make the good available for sale. Of course, in most real-world markets the sellers are also those who produce the good and therefore *do* spend money to make it available for sale. In that case, the cost of making the good available for sale includes monetary costs, but it may also include other opportunity costs.

Getting back to the example, suppose that Andrew sells his book for $30. Clearly he has gained from the transaction: he would have been willing to sell for only $5, so he has gained $25. This net gain, the difference between the price he actually gets and his cost—the minimum price at which he would have been willing to sell—is known as his **individual producer surplus.**

Just as we derived the demand curve from the willingness to pay of different consumers, we can derive the supply curve from the cost of different producers. The step-shaped curve in Figure 8-6 shows the supply curve implied by the costs shown in the accompanying table. At a price less than $5, none of the students are willing to sell; at a price between $5 and $15, only Andrew is willing to sell, and so on.

As in the case of consumer surplus, we can add the individual producer surpluses of sellers to calculate the **total producer surplus,** the total net gain to all sellers in the market. Economists use the term **producer surplus** to refer to either individual or total producer surplus. Table 8-2 shows the net gain to each of the students who would sell a used book at a price of $30: $25 for Andrew, $15 for Betty, and $5 for Carlos. The total producer surplus is $25 + $15 + $5 = $45.

As with consumer surplus, the producer surplus gained by those who sell books can be represented graphically. Figure 8-7 reproduces the supply curve from Figure 8-6. Each step in that supply curve is one book wide and represents one seller. The height of Andrew's step is $5, his cost. This forms the bottom of a rectangle, with $30, the price he actually receives for his book, forming the top. The area of this rectangle, ($30 – $5) × 1 = $25, is his producer surplus. So the producer surplus Andrew gains from selling his book is the *area of the red rectangle* shown in the figure.

Let's assume that the campus bookstore is willing to buy all the used copies of this book that students are willing to sell at a price of $30. Then, in addition to Andrew, Betty and Carlos will also sell their books. They will also benefit from their sales, though not as much as Andrew, because they have higher costs. Andrew, as we have seen, gains $25. Betty gains a smaller amount: since her cost is $15, she gains only $15. Carlos gains even less, only $5.

Again, as with consumer surplus, we have a general rule for determining the total producer surplus from sales of a good: *The total producer surplus from*

Individual producer surplus is the net gain to an individual seller from selling a good. It is equal to the difference between the price received and the seller's cost.

Total producer surplus is the sum of the individual producer surpluses of all the sellers of a good in a market.

Economists use the term **producer surplus** to refer both to individual and to total producer surplus.

TABLE 8-2 Producer Surplus When the Price of a Used Textbook = $30

Potential seller	Cost	Price received	Individual producer surplus = Price received – Cost
Andrew	$5	$30	$25
Betty	15	30	15
Carlos	25	30	5
Donna	35	—	—
Engelbert	45	—	—
All sellers			**Total producer surplus = $45**

FIGURE 8-7 Producer Surplus in the Used-Textbook Market

At a price of $30, Andrew, Betty, and Carlos each sell a book but Donna and Engelbert do not. Andrew, Betty, and Carlos get individual producer surpluses equal to the difference between the price and their cost, illustrated here by the shaded rectangles. Donna and Engelbert each have a cost that is greater than the price of $30, so they are unwilling to sell a book and so receive zero producer surplus. The total producer surplus is given by the entire shaded area, the sum of the individual producer surpluses of Andrew, Betty, and Carlos, equal to $25 + $15 + $5 = $45.

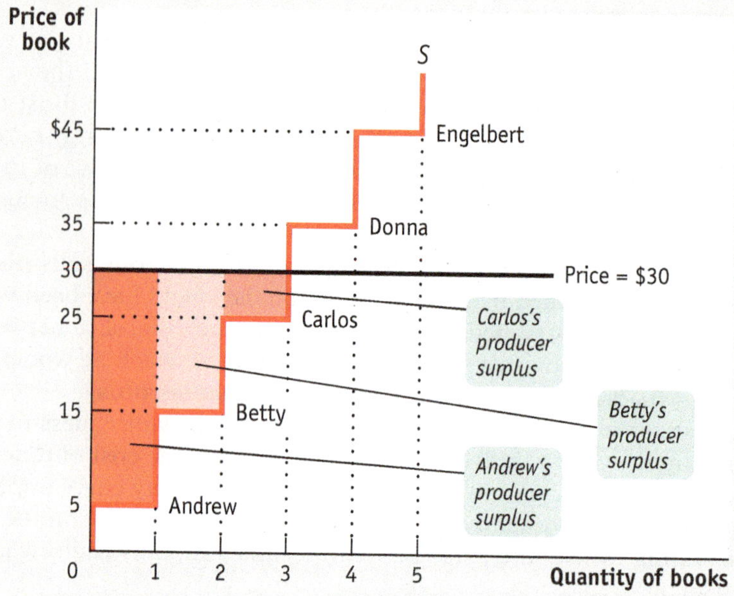

sales of a good at a given price is the area above the supply curve but below that price.

This rule applies both to examples like the one shown in Figure 8-7, where there are a small number of producers and a step-shaped supply curve, and to more realistic examples, where there are many producers and the supply curve is smooth.

Consider, for example, the supply of wheat. Figure 8-8 shows how producer surplus depends on the price per bushel. Suppose that, as shown in the figure, the price is $5 per bushel and farmers supply 1 million bushels. What is the benefit

FIGURE 8-8 Producer Surplus

Here is the supply curve for wheat. At a price of $5 per bushel, farmers supply 1 million bushels. The producer surplus at this price is equal to the shaded area: the area above the supply curve but below the price. This is the total gain to producers—farmers in this case—from supplying their product when the price is $5.

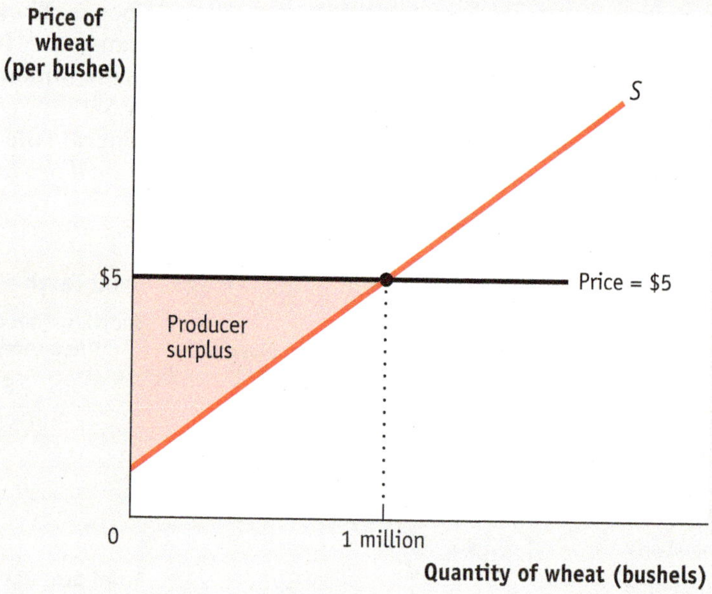

to the farmers from selling their wheat at a price of $5? Their producer surplus is equal to the shaded area in the figure—the area above the supply curve but below the price of $5 per bushel.

How Changing Prices Affect Producer Surplus

As with the case of consumer surplus, a change in price alters producer surplus. But the effects are opposite. While a fall in price increases consumer surplus, it reduces producer surplus. And a rise in price reduces consumer surplus but increases producer surplus.

To illustrate this, let's first consider a rise in the price of the good. Producers of the good will experience an increase in producer surplus, though not all producers gain the same amount. Some producers would have produced the good even at the original price; they will gain the entire price increase on every unit they produce. Other producers will enter the market because of the higher price; they will gain only the difference between the new price and their cost.

Figure 8-9 is the supply counterpart of Figure 8-5. It shows the effect on producer surplus of a rise in the price of wheat from $5 to $7 per bushel. The increase in producer surplus is the sum of the shaded areas, which consists of two parts. First, there is a red rectangle corresponding to the gains to those farmers who would have supplied wheat even at the original $5 price. Second, there is an additional pink triangle that corresponds to the gains to those farmers who would not have supplied wheat at the original price but are drawn into the market by the higher price.

If the price were to fall from $7 to $5 per bushel, the story would run in reverse. The sum of the shaded areas would now be the decline in producer surplus, the decrease in the area above the supply curve but below the price. The loss would consist of two parts, the loss to farmers who would still grow wheat at a price of $5 (the red rectangle) and the loss to farmers who cease to grow wheat because of the lower price (the pink triangle).

FIGURE 8-9 A Rise in the Price Increases Producer Surplus

A rise in the price of wheat from $5 to $7 leads to an increase in the quantity supplied and an increase in producer surplus. The change in total producer surplus is given by the sum of the shaded areas: the total area above the supply curve but between the old and new prices. The red area represents the gain to the farmers who would have supplied 1 million bushels at the original price of $5; they each receive an increase in producer surplus of $2 for each of these bushels. The triangular pink area represents the increase in producer surplus achieved by the farmers who supply the additional 500,000 bushels because of the higher price. Similarly, a fall in the price of wheat from $7 to $5 generates a reduction in producer surplus equal to the sum of the shaded areas.

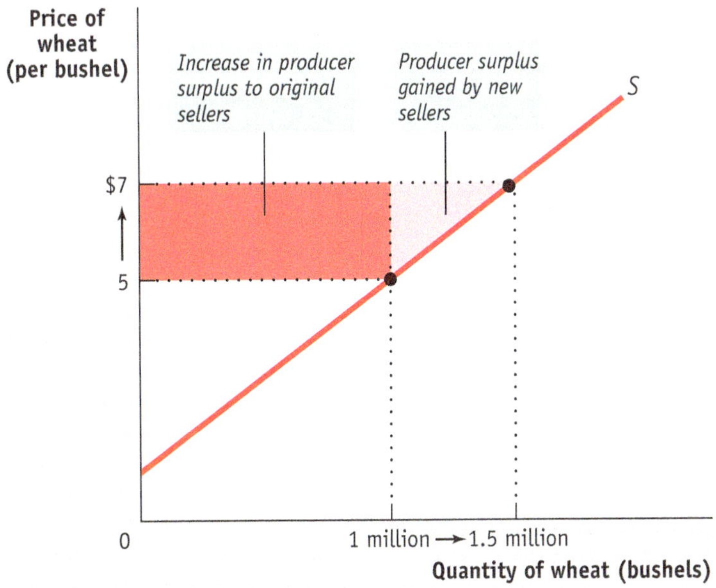

ECONOMICS >> *in Action*

A Matter of Life and Death

In 2016 an average of 22 Americans died every day because of a shortage of organs for transplant. In 2016, more than 115,000 people were wait-listed.

Since the number of people who need organs far exceeds organ availability, and the demand for organs continues to grow faster than the supply of them, what is the best way to allocate the available organs? A market isn't feasible. And for understandable reasons, the sale of human body parts is illegal in this country. So, the task for establishing a protocol for these situations has fallen to the nonprofit group United Network for Organ Sharing (UNOS).

deepstock/Shutterstock

Kidney transplants, the most common kind of transplant, were the focus of attention when UNOS reformulated its guidelines for allocating organs in 2013. Under the previous guidelines, a donated kidney would go to the person waiting the longest: an available kidney would, for example, go to a 75-year-old who had been waiting for two years rather than to a 25-year-old who had been waiting a year—despite the fact that the 25-year-old is likely to live longer and therefore benefit from the organ for a longer period of time.

So, UNOS formulated a new set of guidelines based on a concept called *net survival benefit*. Available kidneys are ranked according to how long they are likely to last; recipients are ranked according to how long they are likely to live once they receive a kidney. A kidney is then matched to the recipient expected to achieve the greatest survival time from that kidney. That is, a kidney expected to last many decades will be given to a young person, while a kidney with a shorter expected life span will be given to an older recipient.

So what does kidney transplantation have to do with consumer surplus? The UNOS concept of *net survival benefit* is a lot like individual consumer surplus—the individual consumer surplus generated from getting a new kidney. In essence, UNOS has devised a system that allocates a kidney according to who gets the greatest consumer surplus, thereby maximizing the total consumer surplus from the available pool of kidneys. In terms of results, the UNOS system operates a lot like a competitive market, but without the purchase and sale of kidneys.

>> *Quick Review*

- The supply curve for a good is determined by the **cost** of each seller.
- The difference between the price and cost is the seller's **individual producer surplus.**
- The **total producer surplus** is equal to the area above the market supply curve but below the price.
- When the price of a good rises, **producer surplus** increases through two channels: the gains of those who would have supplied the good at the original price and the gains of those who are induced to supply the good by the higher price. A fall in the price of a good similarly leads to a fall in producer surplus.

Check Your Understanding 8-2

1. Consider again the market for cheese-stuffed jalapeno peppers. There are two producers, Cara and Jamie, and their costs of producing each pepper are given in the accompanying table. (Neither is willing to produce more than 4 peppers at any price.)

Quantity of peppers	Cara's cost	Jamie's cost
1st pepper	$0.10	$0.30
2nd pepper	0.10	0.50
3rd pepper	0.40	0.70
4th pepper	0.60	0.90

a. Use the accompanying table to construct the supply schedule for peppers for prices of $0.00, $0.10, and so on, up to $0.90.

b. Calculate the total producer surplus when the price of a pepper is $0.70.

Solutions appear at back of book.

Efficiency and Markets

MODULE 9

WHAT YOU WILL LEARN

- What is **total surplus** and why is it used to illustrate the gains from trade in a market?
- What accounts for the importance of **property rights** and economic signals in a well-functioning market?
- Why can a market sometimes fail and be **inefficient?**

9.1 Consumer Surplus, Producer Surplus, and the Gains from Trade

vasiliki/Getty Images

One of the twelve core principles of economics is that markets are a remarkably effective way to organize economic activity: they generally make society as well off as possible given the available resources. The concepts of consumer surplus and producer surplus can help us deepen our understanding of why this is so.

The Gains from Trade

Let's return to the market in used textbooks but now consider a much bigger market—say, one at a large state university. There are many potential buyers and sellers, so the market is competitive. Let's line up incoming students who are potential buyers of a book in order of their willingness to pay, so that the entering student with the highest willingness to pay is potential buyer number 1, the student with the next-highest willingness to pay is number 2, and so on. Then we can use their willingness to pay to derive a demand curve like the one in Figure 9-1.

Similarly, we can line up outgoing students, who are potential sellers of the book, in order of their cost—starting with the student with the lowest cost, then the student with the next lowest cost, and so on—to derive a supply curve like the one shown in the same figure.

As we have drawn the curves, the market reaches equilibrium at a price of $30 per book, and 1,000 books are bought and sold at that price. The two shaded triangles show the consumer surplus (blue) and the producer surplus (red) generated by this market. The sum of consumer and producer surplus is known as the **total surplus** generated in a market.

The striking thing about this picture is that both consumers and producers gain. Both are made better off because there is a market in this

The **total surplus** generated in a market is the total net gain to consumers and producers from trading in the market. It is the sum of the producer and the consumer surplus.

FIGURE 9-1 Total Surplus

In the market for used textbooks, the equilibrium price is $30 and the equilibrium quantity is 1,000 books. Consumer surplus is given by the blue area, the area below the demand curve but above the price. Producer surplus is given by the red area, the area above the supply curve but below the price. The sum of the blue and the red areas is total surplus, the total benefit to society from the production and consumption of the good.

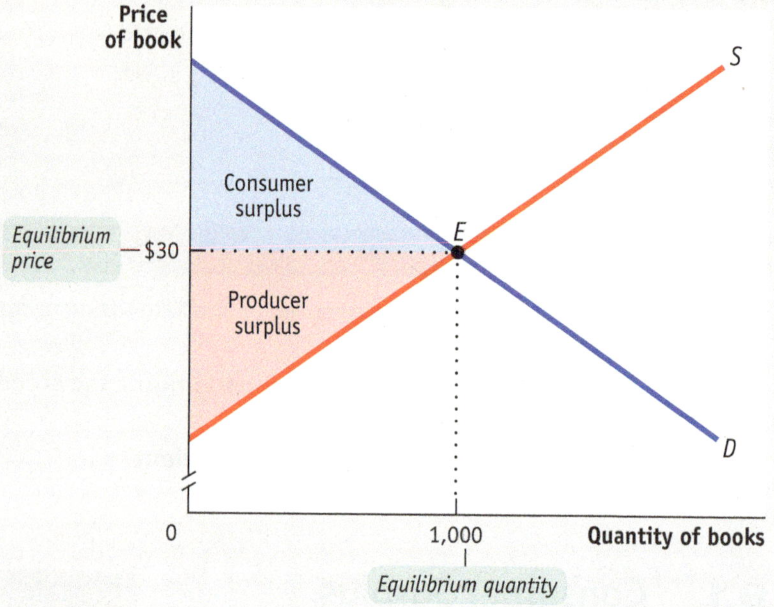

good this should come as no surprise—it illustrates another core principle of economics: *There are gains from trade.* Gains from trade are the reason everyone is better off participating in a market economy than being self-sufficient.

But are we as well off as we could be? This brings us to the question of the efficiency of markets.

The Efficiency of Markets

In Module 2, we learned about how the concept of efficiency applied to an entire economy. Here we will learn how the concept of efficiency applies to a single market within the economy. A market is *efficient* if, once the market has produced gains from trade, there is no way to change the market outcome in a way that makes some people better off without making other people worse off.

The analysis of consumer and producer surplus helps us understand why markets are usually efficient. To gain more intuition into why this is so, consider the fact that market equilibrium is just *one* way of deciding who consumes the good and who sells the good. There are other possible ways of making that decision.

Consider, again, the case of kidney transplants, in which a decision must be made about who receives one. It is not possible to use a market to decide because in this situation, human organs are involved. Instead, in the past, kidneys were allocated according to a recipient's wait time—a very inefficient method. It has since been replaced with a new system created by the United Network for Organ Sharing, or UNOS, based on *net survival benefit,* a concept an awful lot like consumer surplus that, although not a market system, succeeds in reproducing the efficiency of one.

To further our understanding of why markets usually work so well, imagine a committee charged with improving on the market equilibrium by deciding who gets and who gives up a used textbook. The committee's ultimate goal is to bypass the market outcome and devise another arrangement, one that would produce higher total surplus.

Let's consider the three ways in which the committee might try to increase the total surplus:

1. Reallocate consumption among consumers
2. Reallocate sales among sellers
3. Change the quantity traded

Reallocate Consumption Among Consumers The committee might try to increase total surplus by selling books to different consumers. Figure 9-2 shows why this will result in lower surplus compared to the market equilibrium outcome. Here we have smooth demand and supply curves because there are many buyers and sellers. Points *A* and *B* show the positions on the demand curve of two potential buyers of used books, Ana and Bob. As we can see from the figure, Ana is willing to pay $35 for a book, but Bob is willing to pay only $25. Since the market equilibrium price is $30, under the market outcome Ana buys a book and Bob does not.

Now suppose the committee reallocates consumption. This would mean taking the book away from Ana and giving it to Bob. Since the book is worth $35 to Ana but only $25 to Bob, this change *reduces total consumer surplus* by $35 – $25 = $10. Moreover, this result doesn't depend on which two students we pick. Every student who buys a book at the market equilibrium has a willingness to pay of $30 or more, and every student who doesn't buy a book has a willingness to pay of less than $30.

So reallocating the good among consumers always means taking a book away from a student who values it more and giving it to one who values it less. This necessarily reduces total consumer surplus.

FIGURE 9-2 Reallocating Consumption Lowers Consumer Surplus

Ana (point *A*) has a willingness to pay of $35. Bob (point *B*) has a willingness to pay of only $25. At the market equilibrium price of $30, Ana purchases a book but Bob does not. If we rearrange consumption by taking a book from Ana and giving it to Bob, consumer surplus declines by $10, and, as a result, total surplus declines by $10.

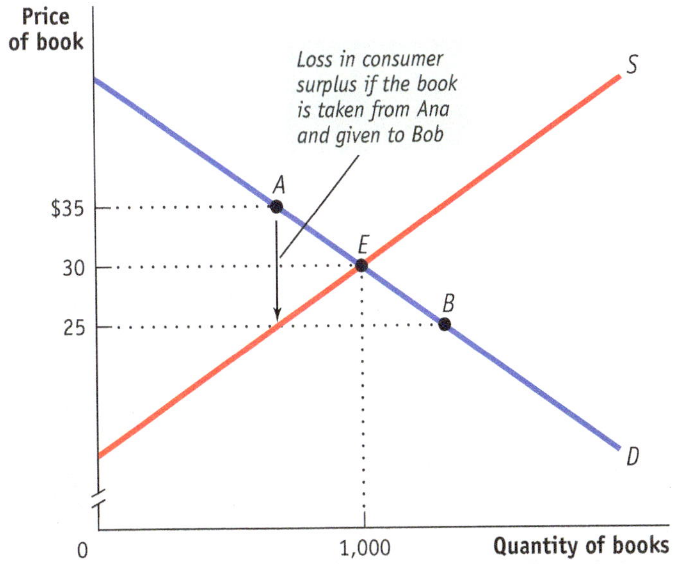

FIGURE 9-3 Reallocating Sales Lowers Producer Surplus

Yvonne (point *Y*) has a cost of $35, $10 more than Xavier (point *X*), who has a cost of $25. At the market equilibrium price of $30, Xavier sells a book but Yvonne does not. If we rearrange sales by preventing Xavier from selling his book and compelling Yvonne to sell hers, producer surplus declines by $10 and, as a result, total surplus declines by $10.

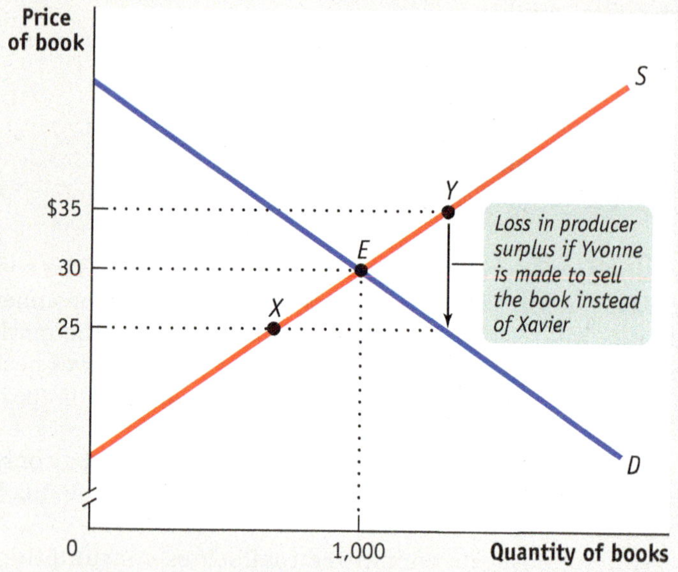

Reallocate Sales Among Sellers The committee might try to increase total surplus by altering who sells their books, taking sales away from sellers who would have sold their books at the market equilibrium and instead compelling those who would not have sold their books at the market equilibrium to sell them.

Figure 9-3 shows why this will result in lower surplus. Here points *X* and *Y* show the positions on the supply curve of Xavier, who has a cost of $25, and Yvonne, who has a cost of $35. At the equilibrium market price of $30, Xavier would sell his book but Yvonne would not sell hers. If the committee reallocated sales, forcing Xavier to keep his book and Yvonne to sell hers, total producer surplus would be reduced by $35 – $25 = $10.

Again, it doesn't matter which two students we choose. Any student who sells a book at the market equilibrium has a lower cost than any student who keeps a book. So reallocating sales among sellers necessarily increases total cost and reduces total producer surplus.

Change the Quantity Traded The committee might try to increase total surplus by compelling students to trade either more books or fewer books than the market equilibrium quantity.

Figure 9-4 shows why this will result in lower surplus. It shows all four students: potential buyers Ana and Bob, and potential sellers Xavier and Yvonne. To reduce sales, the committee will have to prevent a transaction that would have occurred in the market equilibrium—that is, prevent Xavier from selling to Ana. Since Ana is willing to pay $35 and Xavier's cost is $25, preventing this transaction reduces total surplus by $35 – $25 = $10.

Once again, this result doesn't depend on which two students we pick: any student who would have sold the book at the market equilibrium has a cost of $30 or less, and any student who would have purchased the book at the market equilibrium has a willingness to pay of $30 or more. Thus, preventing any sale that would have occurred in the market equilibrium necessarily reduces total surplus.

FIGURE 9-4 Changing the Quantity Lowers Total Surplus

If Xavier (point *X*) were prevented from selling his book to someone like Ana (point *A*), total surplus would fall by $10, the difference between Ana's willingness to pay ($35) and Xavier's ($25). This means that total surplus falls whenever fewer than 1,000 books—the equilibrium quantity—are transacted. Likewise, if Yvonne (point *Y*) were compelled to sell her book to someone like Bob (point *B*), total surplus would also fall by $10, the difference between Yvonne's cost ($35) and Bob's willingness to pay ($25). This means that total surplus falls whenever more than 1,000 books are transacted. These two examples show that at market equilibrium, all mutually beneficial transactions—and only mutually beneficial transactions—occur.

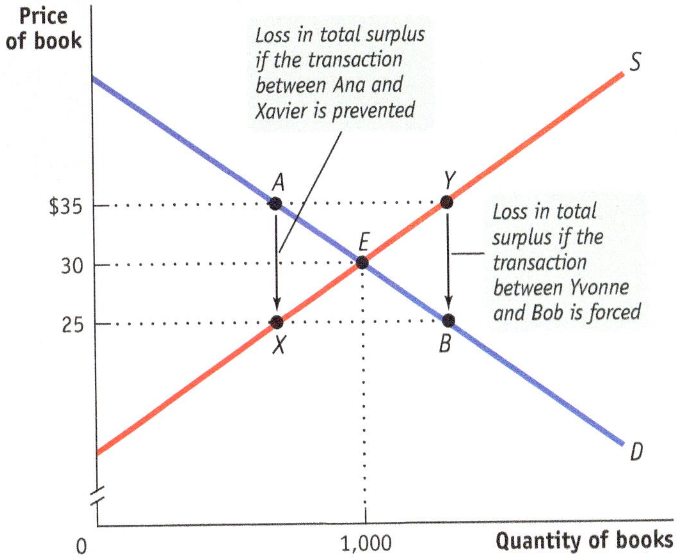

Finally, the committee might try to increase sales by forcing Yvonne, who would not have sold her book at the market equilibrium, to sell it to someone like Bob, who would not have bought a book at the market equilibrium. Because Yvonne's cost is $35, but Bob is only willing to pay $25, this transaction reduces total surplus by $10. And once again it doesn't matter which two students we pick—anyone who wouldn't have bought the book has a willingness to pay of less than $30, and anyone who wouldn't have sold has a cost of more than $30.

The key point to remember is that once this market is in equilibrium, there is no way to increase the gains from trade. Any other outcome reduces total surplus. We can summarize our results by stating that an efficient market performs four important functions:

1. It allocates consumption of the good to the potential buyers who most value it, as indicated by the fact that they have the highest willingness to pay.
2. It allocates sales to the potential sellers who most value the right to sell the good, as indicated by the fact that they have the lowest cost.
3. It ensures that every consumer who makes a purchase values the good more than every seller who makes a sale, so that all transactions are mutually beneficial.
4. It ensures that every potential buyer who doesn't make a purchase values the good less than every potential seller who doesn't make a sale, so that no mutually beneficial transactions are missed.

As a result of these four functions, *any way of allocating the good other than the market equilibrium outcome lowers total surplus.*

There are three caveats, however. First, although a market may be efficient, it isn't necessarily *fair.* In fact, fairness, or equity, is often in conflict with efficiency. We'll discuss this next.

The second caveat is that markets are only efficient under well-defined conditions as mentioned in Module 1. When these conditions are no longer met, markets can fail to deliver efficiency and no longer maximize total surplus.

Third, even when the market equilibrium maximizes total surplus, this does not mean that it results in the best outcome for every *individual* consumer and producer. Other things equal, each buyer would like to pay a lower price and each seller would like to receive a higher price. So if the government were to intervene in the market—say, by lowering the price below the equilibrium price to make consumers happy or by raising the price above the equilibrium price to make producers happy—the outcome would no longer be efficient. Although some people would be happier, total surplus would be lower.

Equity and Efficiency

It's easy to get carried away with the idea that markets are always right and that economic policies that interfere with efficiency are bad. That would be misguided, however, because there is another factor to consider: society cares about equity, or what's "fair."

There is often a trade-off between equity and efficiency: policies that promote equity often come at the cost of decreased efficiency, and policies that promote efficiency often result in decreased equity. So it's important to realize that a society's choice to sacrifice some efficiency for the sake of equity, however it defines equity, is a valid one.

Consider, for example, that to many patients who need kidney transplants, the new UNOS guidelines, covered earlier, were unwelcome news. Unsurprisingly, those who have been waiting years for a transplant have found the guidelines, which give precedence to younger patients, . . . well . . . unfair. And the guidelines raise other questions about fairness: Why limit potential transplant recipients to Americans? Why include younger patients with other chronic diseases? Why not give precedence to those who have made recognized contributions to society? And so on.

The point is that efficiency is about *how to achieve goals, not what those goals should be*. For example, UNOS decided that its goal is to maximize the life span of kidney recipients. Some might have argued for a different goal, and efficiency does not address which goal is the best. *What efficiency does address is the best way to achieve a goal once it has been determined*—in this case, using the UNOS concept of net survival benefit.

It's important to understand that fairness, unlike efficiency, can be very hard to define. Fairness is a concept about which well-intentioned people often disagree.

>> Quick Review

- **Total surplus** measures the gains from trade in a market.
- Markets are efficient except under some well-defined conditions. We can demonstrate the efficiency of a market by considering what happens to total surplus if we start from the equilibrium and reallocate consumption, reallocate sales, or change the quantity traded. Any outcome other than the market equilibrium reduces total surplus, which means that the market equilibrium is efficient.
- Because society cares about equity or fairness, government intervention in a market that reduces efficiency while increasing equity can be justified.

Check Your Understanding 9-1

1. Using the tables in Check Your Understanding 8-1 and 8-2, find the equilibrium price and quantity in the market for cheese-stuffed jalapeno peppers. What is total surplus in the equilibrium in this market, and who receives it?
2. Show how each of the following three actions reduces total surplus:
   - **a.** Having Josey consume one fewer pepper, and Casey one more pepper, than in the market equilibrium
   - **b.** Having Cara produce one fewer pepper, and Jamie one more pepper, than in the market equilibrium
   - **c.** Having Josey consume one fewer pepper, and Cara produce one fewer pepper, than in the market equilibrium
3. Suppose UNOS decides to further alter its guidelines for the allocation of donated kidneys, no longer relying solely on the concept of net survival benefit but also giving preference to patients with small children. If "total surplus" in this case is defined to be the total life span of kidney recipients, is this new guideline likely to reduce, increase, or leave total surplus unchanged? How might you justify this new guideline?

Solutions appear at back of book.

9.2 A Market Economy

As we learned earlier, in a market economy decisions about production and consumption are made via markets. In fact, the economy as a whole is made up of many *interrelated markets*. Up until now, to learn how markets work, we've been examining a single market—the market for used textbooks. But in reality, consumers and producers do not make decisions in isolated markets. For example, a student's decision in the market for used textbooks might be affected by how much interest must be paid on a student loan; thus, the decision in the used textbook market would be influenced by what is going on in the market for money.

We know that an efficient market equilibrium maximizes total surplus—the gains to buyers and sellers in that market. Is there a comparable result for an economy as a whole, an economy composed of a vast number of individual markets? The answer is yes, but with qualifications.

When each and every market in the economy maximizes total surplus, the economy as a whole is efficient. This is a very important result: just as it is impossible to make someone better off without making other people worse off in a single market when it is efficient, the same is true when each and every market in that economy is efficient. However, it is important to realize that this is a *theoretical* result: it is virtually impossible to find an economy in which every market is efficient.

For now, let's examine why markets and market economies typically work so well. Once we understand why, we can then briefly address why markets sometimes get it wrong.

Why Markets Typically Work So Well

Economists have written volumes about why markets are an effective way to organize an economy. In the end, well-functioning markets owe their effectiveness to two powerful features: *property rights* and the role of prices as *economic signals*.

Property Rights By **property rights** we mean a system in which valuable items in the economy have specific owners who can dispose of them as they choose. In a system of property rights, by purchasing a good you receive *ownership rights:* the right to use and dispose of the good as you see fit. Property rights are what make the mutually beneficial transactions in the used-textbook market, or any market, possible.

To see why property rights are crucial, imagine that students do not have full property rights in their textbooks and are prohibited from reselling them when the semester ends. This restriction on property rights would prevent many mutually beneficial transactions. Some students would be stuck with textbooks they will never reread when they would be much happier receiving some cash instead. Other students would be forced to pay full price for brand-new books when they would be happier getting slightly battered copies at a lower price.

Economic Signals Once a system of well-defined property rights is in place, the second necessary feature of well-functioning markets—prices as economic signals—can operate. An **economic signal** is any piece of information that helps people and businesses make better economic decisions. For example, business forecasters say that sales of cardboard boxes are a good early indicator of changes in industrial production: if businesses are buying lots of cardboard boxes, you can be sure that they will soon increase their production.

Property rights are the rights of owners of valuable items, whether resources or goods, to dispose of those items as they choose.

An **economic signal** is any piece of information that helps people make better economic decisions.

The Photo Works

Price is the most important economic signal in a market economy.

But prices are far and away the most important signals in a market economy, because they convey essential information about other people's costs and their willingness to pay. If the equilibrium price of used books is $30, this in effect tells everyone both that there are consumers willing to pay $30 and up and that there are potential sellers with a cost of $30 or less. The signal given by the market price ensures that total surplus is maximized by telling people whether to buy books, sell books, or do nothing at all.

Each potential seller with a cost of $30 or less learns from the market price that it's a good idea to sell their book; if they have a higher cost, it's a good idea to keep it. Likewise, each consumer willing to pay $30 or more learns from the market price that it's a good idea to buy a book; if they are unwilling to pay $30, then it's a good idea not to buy a book.

This example shows that the market price "signals" to consumers with a willingness to pay equal to or more than the market price that they should buy the good, just as it signals to producers with a cost equal to or less than the market price that they should sell the good. And since, in equilibrium, the quantity demanded equals the quantity supplied, all willing consumers will find willing sellers.

Prices can sometimes fail as economic signals. Sometimes a price is not an accurate indicator of how desirable a good is. When there is uncertainty about the quality of a good, price alone may not be an accurate indicator of the value of the good. For example, you can't infer from the price alone whether a used car is good or a "lemon." In fact, a well-known problem in economics is "the market for lemons," a market in which prices don't work well as economic signals.

A Few Words of Caution

Markets are an amazingly effective way to organize economic activity. But, as we've noted, markets can sometimes get it wrong—they can be *inefficient*. We first learned about this in Module 1 in our eighth principle: *When markets don't achieve efficiency, government intervention can improve society's welfare.*

When markets are **inefficient,** there are missed opportunities—ways in which production or consumption can be rearranged that would make some people better off without making other people worse off. In other words, there are gains from trade that go unrealized: total surplus could be increased. And when a market or markets are inefficient, the economy in which they are embedded is also inefficient.

Markets can be rendered inefficient for a number of reasons. Two of the most important are a lack of property rights and inaccuracy of prices as economic signals. When a market is inefficient, we have a **market failure.** We will examine various types of market failures in later sections. For now, let's review the four main ways in which markets sometimes fall short of efficiency.

A market or an economy is **inefficient** if there are missed opportunities: some people could be made better off without making other people worse off.

Market failure occurs when a market fails to be efficient.

1. *Market Power:* Markets can fail due to *market power,* which occurs when a firm has the ability to raise the market price. In this case the assumption that underlies supply and demand analysis—that no one can have a noticeable effect on the market price—is no longer valid. As we'll see in Section 9, the presence of market power leads to inefficiency as the firm manipulates the market price to increase profits and thereby prevents mutually beneficial trades from occurring.
2. *Externalities:* Markets can fail due to *externalities,* which arise when actions have side effects on the welfare of others. The most common example of an externality is pollution. Because the market price doesn't capture the negative effect pollution has on others, the market outcome is inefficient. In Section 11 we'll learn more about externalities and how societies try to cope with them.

3. *Public Goods and Common Resources:* Goods that fall into the category of being unsuited for efficient management by markets—public goods and common resources. Markets for these goods fail because of problems in limiting people's access to and consumption of the good; examples are fish in the sea and trees in the Amazonian rain forest. In these instances, markets generally fail due to incomplete property rights.
4. *Discrimination:* Discrimination, in which some people are denied opportunities based on personal characteristics that have no impact on their economic performance—characteristics such as race, gender, ethnicity, religion, national origin, class, people with disabilities, sexual orientation or gender identification—is a type of market failure. It represents a missed opportunity because those who are discriminated against are denied the opportunity to participate in the economy freely and equally, causing a loss to both them and to those who would have benefited from transacting with them. Society as whole suffers because valuable human capital is wasted. But why don't the forces of market competition eliminate discrimination? The answer is that social pressure and structures arising from historical circumstances tend to perpetuate discrimination over time. In some cases—such as those of Irish-Americans, Italian-Americans, and Jewish-Americans—changes in norms and market forces did indeed lead to a vast reduction in discrimination. For other groups, however, discrimination has been reduced somewhat but still endures.

But even with these limitations, it's remarkable how well markets work at maximizing gains from trade.

ECONOMICS >> *in Action*

A Great Leap—Backward

Of any country in the world, China is perhaps the one most associated with free-wheeling markets. From the endless street markets for food in Shanghai, to the bustling export-goods markets in Guanzhou that specialize in everything from eyeglasses to electronics, to the massive mall in Shenzen where you can find finely tailored custom suits and fake designer bags, the shopping possibilities in China are endless.

Yet, not so long ago, China was a country almost completely lacking in markets. That's because until the 1980s, China was largely a *planned economy,* an economy in which a central planner, rather than markets, makes consumption and production decisions. Russia, many Eastern European countries, and several Southeast Asian countries once had planned economies. In addition, India and Brazil once had significant parts of their economies under central planning.

VH Collection/Age Fotostock

Although some aspects of central planning remain, China's economy has moved closer to a free-market system.

Planned economies are notorious for their inefficiency, and probably the most compelling example of that is the so-called Great Leap Forward, an ambitious economic plan instituted in China during the late 1950s by its leader Mao Zedong. Its intention was to speed up the country's industrialization. Key to this plan was a shift from urban to rural manufacturing: farming villages were supposed to start producing heavy industrial goods such as steel. Unfortunately, the plan backfired.

Diverting farmers from their usual work led to a sharp fall in food production. Meanwhile, because raw materials for steel, such as coal and iron ore, were sent to ill-equipped and inexperienced rural producers rather than to urban factories, industrial output declined as well. The plan, in short, led to a fall in the production of everything in China.

Because China was a very low-income country to start with, the results were catastrophic. The famine that followed is estimated to have reduced China's population by as much as 30 million.

China's transition to a free-market system has put it on the path to greater economic growth, increased wealth, and the emergence of a middle class. But some aspects of central planning still remain, largely in the allocation of financial capital and in state-owned enterprises. As a result, significant inefficiencies persist. Many economists have observed that these inefficiencies must be addressed if China is to sustain its rapid growth and satisfy the aspirations of billions of Chinese.

>> Quick Review

- In a market economy, markets are interrelated. When each and every market in an economy is efficient, the economy as a whole is efficient. But in the real world, some markets in a market economy will almost certainly fail to be efficient.
- A system of **property rights** and the operation of prices as **economic signals** are two key factors that enable a market to be efficient. But under conditions in which property rights are incomplete or prices give inaccurate economic signals, markets can fail.
- Under certain conditions, **market failure** occurs and the market is **inefficient:** gains from trade are unrealized. There are four principal causes of market failure: market power; externalities; a good that, by its nature, makes it unsuitable for a market to allocate it efficiently; and discrimination.

Check Your Understanding 9-2

1. In some states that are rich in natural resources, such as oil, the law separates the right to above-ground use of the land from the right to drill below ground (called "mineral rights"). Someone who owns both the above-ground rights and the mineral rights can sell the two rights separately. Explain how this division of the property rights enhances efficiency compared to a situation in which the two rights must always be sold together.
2. Suppose that in the market for used textbooks the equilibrium price is $30, but it is mistakenly announced that the equilibrium price is $300. How does this affect the efficiency of the market? Be specific.
3. What is wrong with the following statement? "Markets are always the best way to organize economic activity. Any policies that interfere with markets reduce society's welfare."

Solutions appear at back of book.

Price Controls (Ceilings and Floors)

MODULE **10**

WHAT YOU WILL LEARN

- What is a market intervention and why are **price controls** the main forms it takes?
- Why do price controls create **deadweight losses?**

10.1 Why Governments Control Prices

Jay Lazarin/iStock/Getty Images Plus

In 2015, a real estate developer purchased a New York City apartment building and wanted to evict three elderly tenants who had lived in their apartment for decades. But inducing the tenants to leave was no easy matter because their apartment was one of 27,000 units covered by New York's rent control law. The law prevents landlords from raising rents or evicting tenants in rent-controlled apartments except when specifically given permission by a city agency. In fact, under the law it would have been virtually impossible to evict these tenants against their will. So, how was the situation resolved? After intense negotiations, the three tenants finally agreed to move after receiving a payment of $25 million from the developer. Yes, $25 million.

Why was the developer willing to pay so much? Because in New York City's highly lucrative housing market, with its shortage of places to live, the developer stood to make a lot more money by constructing a larger building with apartments that are not rent controlled and that will rent for very high prices. Some developers argue that the difficulty they have dislodging rent-controlled tenants in New York limits their ability to build more housing, leading to a shortage of all apartments, whether affordable or expensive.

Rent control is a type of market intervention, a policy imposed by government to prevail over the market forces of supply and demand—in this case, over the market forces of the supply and demand for New York City rental apartments. Although rent-control laws were introduced during World War II in many major American cities to protect the interests of tenants, their problems have led most cities to discard them. New York City and San Francisco are notable exceptions, although rent control covers only a small and diminishing proportion of apartments in both cities.

As you've learned, a market moves to equilibrium—price rises or falls to the level at which the quantity of a good that people are willing to supply is equal to

Price controls are legal restrictions on how high or low a market price may go. They can take two forms: a **price ceiling,** a maximum price sellers are allowed to charge for a good or service, or a **price floor,** a minimum price buyers are required to pay for a good or service.

the quantity that other people demand. But this equilibrium price does not necessarily please either buyers or sellers.

After all, buyers would always like to pay less if they could, and sometimes they can make a strong moral or political case that they should pay lower prices. For example, what if the equilibrium between supply and demand for apartments in a major city leads to rental rates that an average working person can't afford? In that case, a government might well be under pressure to impose limits on the rents landlords can charge.

Sellers, however, would always like to get more money for what they sell, and sometimes they can make a strong moral or political case that they should receive higher prices. For example, consider the labor market: the price for an hour of a worker's time is the wage rate. What if the equilibrium between supply and demand for less-skilled workers leads to wage rates that yield an income below the poverty level? In that case, a government might well be pressured to require employers to pay a rate no lower than some specified minimum wage.

In other words, there is often a strong political demand for governments to intervene in markets. And powerful interests can make a compelling case that a market intervention favoring them is "fair." When a government intervenes to regulate prices, we say that it imposes **price controls.** These controls typically take the form either of an upper limit, a **price ceiling,** or a lower limit, a **price floor.**

Unfortunately, it's not that easy to tell a market what to do. As we will now see, when a government tries to legislate prices—whether it legislates them down by imposing a price ceiling or up by imposing a price floor—there are certain predictable and unpleasant side effects.

We make an important assumption in this module: the markets in question are efficient before price controls are imposed. But markets can sometimes be inefficient—for example, a market dominated by a monopolist, a single seller that has the power to influence the market price. When markets are inefficient, price controls don't necessarily cause problems and can potentially move the market closer to efficiency.

In practice, however, price controls are often imposed on efficient markets—like the New York apartment market. And so the analysis in this module applies to many important real-world situations.

10.2 Price Ceilings

Aside from rent control, there are not many price ceilings in the United States today. But at times they have been widespread. Price ceilings are typically imposed during crises—wars, harvest failures, natural disasters—because these events often lead to sudden price increases that hurt many people but produce big gains for a lucky few.

The U.S. government imposed ceilings on many prices during World War II: the war sharply increased demand for raw materials, such as aluminum and steel, and price controls prevented those with access to these raw materials from earning profits. Price controls on oil were imposed in 1973, when an embargo by Arab oil-exporting countries seemed likely to generate huge profits for U.S. oil companies. Price controls were instituted again in 2012 by New York and New Jersey authorities in the aftermath of Hurricane Sandy, as gas shortages led to rampant price-gouging.

Rent control in New York is, as we mentioned in the opening story, a legacy of World War II: it was imposed because wartime production led to an economic boom that increased demand for apartments at a time when the labor and raw materials that might have been used to build them were being used to win the war instead. Although most price controls were removed soon after the war ended, New York's rent limits were retained and gradually extended to buildings not previously covered, leading to some very strange situations.

You can rent a one-bedroom apartment in Manhattan on fairly short notice—if you are able and willing to pay several thousand dollars a month and live in a less desirable area. Yet some people pay only a small fraction of this for comparable apartments, and others pay hardly more for bigger apartments in better locations.

Aside from producing great deals for some renters, however, what are the broader consequences of New York's rent-control system? To answer this question, we turn to the model we developed in Section 2: the supply and demand model.

Modeling a Price Ceiling

To see what can go wrong when a government imposes a price ceiling on an efficient market, consider Figure 10-1, which shows a simplified model of the market for apartments in New York. For the sake of simplicity, we imagine that all apartments are exactly the same and so they would rent for the same price in an unregulated market.

The table in Figure 10-1 shows the demand and supply schedules; the demand and supply curves are shown on the left. We show the quantity of apartments on the horizontal axis and the monthly rent per apartment on the vertical axis. You can see that in an unregulated market the equilibrium would be at point *E*: 2 million apartments would be rented for $1,000 each per month.

Now suppose that the government imposes a price ceiling, limiting rents to a price below the equilibrium price—say, no more than $800.

Figure 10-2 shows the effect of the price ceiling, represented by the line at $800. At the enforced rental rate of $800, landlords have less incentive to offer apartments, so they won't be willing to supply as many as they would at the equilibrium rate of $1,000. They will choose point *A* on the supply curve, offering only 1.8 million apartments for rent, 200,000 fewer than in the unregulated market.

At the same time, more people will want to rent apartments at a price of $800 than at the equilibrium price of $1,000; as shown at point *B* on the demand curve, at a monthly rent of $800 the quantity of apartments demanded rises to 2.2 million, 200,000 more than in the unregulated market and 400,000 more than

FIGURE 10-1 The Market for Apartments in the Absence of Price Controls

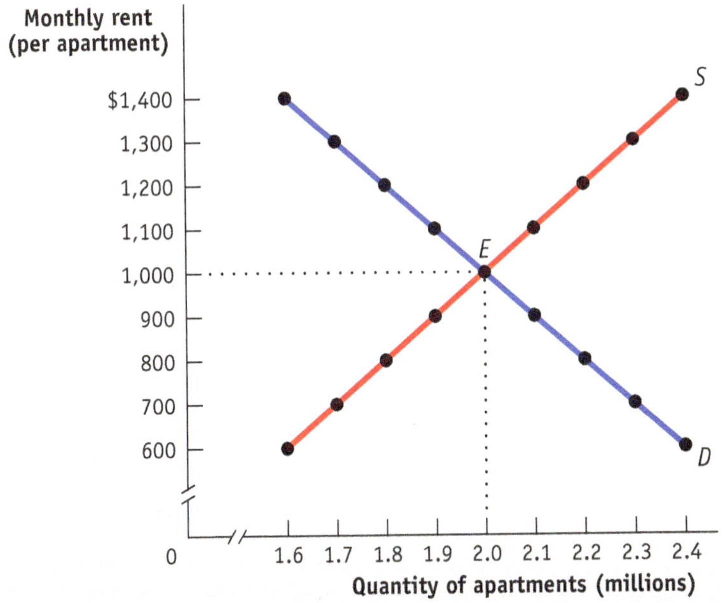

Monthly rent (per apartment)	Quantity of apartments (millions) Quantity demanded	Quantity supplied
$1,400	1.6	2.4
1,300	1.7	2.3
1,200	1.8	2.2
1,100	1.9	2.1
1,000	2.0	2.0
900	2.1	1.9
800	2.2	1.8
700	2.3	1.7
600	2.4	1.6

Without government intervention, the market for apartments reaches equilibrium at point *E* with a market rent of $1,000 per month and 2 million apartments rented.

FIGURE 10-2 The Effects of a Price Ceiling

The black horizontal line represents the government-imposed price ceiling on rents of $800 per month. This price ceiling reduces the quantity of apartments supplied to 1.8 million, point *A*, and increases the quantity demanded to 2.2 million, point *B*. This creates a persistent shortage of 400,000 units: 400,000 people who want apartments at the legal rent of $800 but cannot get them.

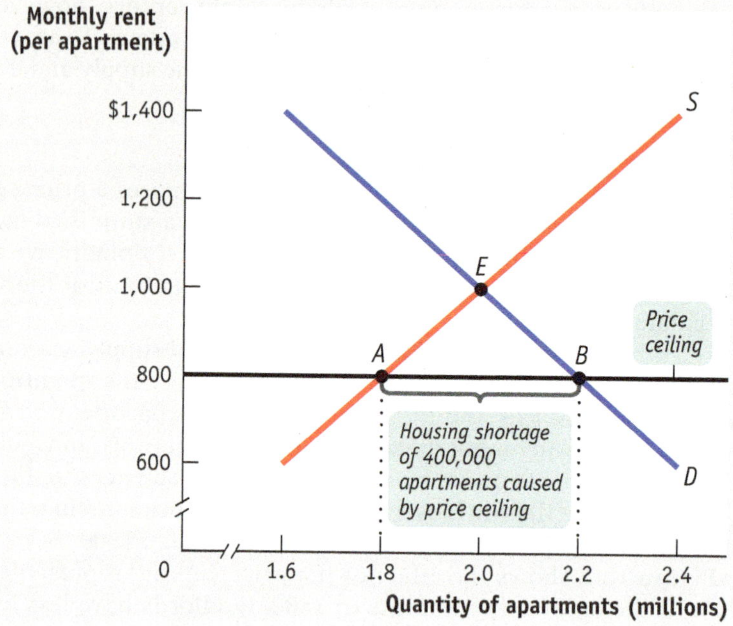

are actually available at the price of $800. So there is now a persistent shortage of rental housing: at that price, 400,000 more people want to rent than are able to find apartments.

Do price ceilings always cause shortages? No. If a price ceiling is set above the equilibrium price, it won't have any effect. Suppose that the equilibrium rental rate on apartments is $1,000 per month and the city government sets a ceiling of $1,200. Who cares? In this case, the price ceiling won't be *binding*—it won't actually constrain market behavior—and it will have no effect.

How a Price Ceiling Causes Inefficiency

The housing shortage shown in Figure 10-2 is not merely annoying: like any shortage induced by price controls, it can be seriously harmful because it leads to inefficiency. In other words, there are gains from trade that go unrealized.

Rent control, like all price ceilings, creates inefficiency in at least four distinct ways.

1. It reduces the quantity of apartments rented below the efficient level.
2. It typically leads to inefficient allocation of apartments among would-be renters.
3. It leads to wasted time and effort as people search for apartments.
4. It leads landlords to maintain apartments in inefficiently low quality or condition.

In addition to inefficiency, price ceilings give rise to illegal behavior as people try to circumvent them. We'll now look at each of these inefficiencies caused by price ceilings.

Inefficiently Low Quantity In Module 9 we learned that the market equilibrium of an efficient market leads to the "right" quantity of a good or service being bought and sold—that is, the quantity that maximizes the sum of producer and consumer surplus. Because rent controls reduce the number of apartments supplied, they reduce the number of apartments rented, too.

FIGURE 10-3 A Price Ceiling Causes Inefficiently Low Quantity

A price ceiling reduces the quantity supplied below the market equilibrium quantity, leading to a deadweight loss. The area of the shaded triangle corresponds to the amount of total surplus lost due to the inefficiently low quantity transacted.

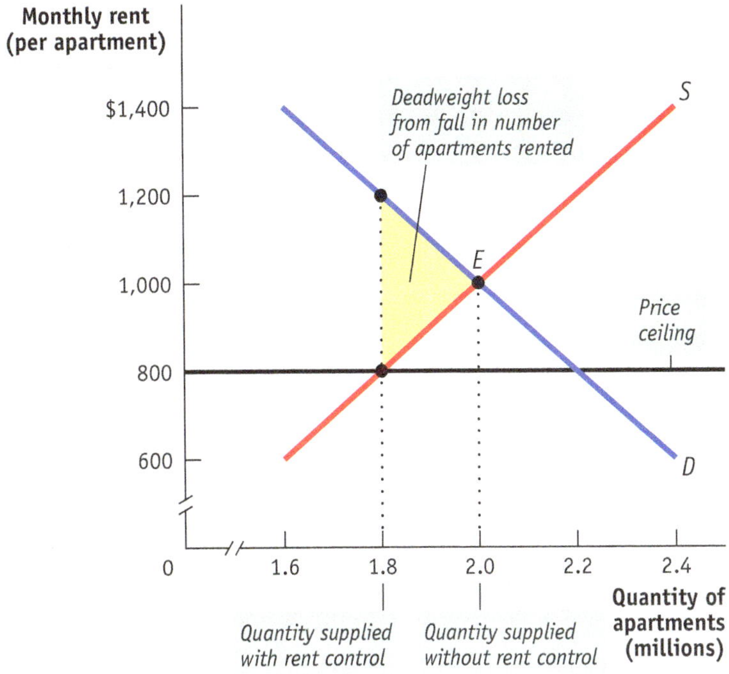

Figure 10-3 shows the implications for total surplus. Recall that total surplus is the sum of the area above the supply curve and below the demand curve. If the only effect of rent control was to reduce the number of apartments available, it would cause a loss of surplus equal to the area of the shaded triangle in the figure.

The area represented by that triangle has a special name in economics, **deadweight loss:** the lost surplus associated with the transactions that no longer occur due to the market intervention. In this example, the deadweight loss is the lost surplus associated with the apartment rentals that no longer occur due to the price ceiling, a loss that is experienced by both disappointed renters and frustrated landlords. Economists often call triangles like the one in Figure 10-3 a *deadweight-loss triangle.*

Deadweight loss is a key concept in economics, one that we will encounter whenever an action or a policy leads to a reduction in the quantity transacted below the efficient market equilibrium quantity. It is important to realize that deadweight loss is a *loss to society*—it is a reduction in total surplus, a loss in surplus that accrues to no one as a gain. It is not the same as a loss in surplus to one person that then accrues as a gain to someone else, what an economist would call a *transfer* of surplus from one person to another.

Deadweight loss is not the only type of inefficiency that arises from a price ceiling. The types of inefficiency created by rent control go beyond reducing the quantity of apartments available. These additional inefficiencies—inefficient allocation to consumers, wasted resources, and inefficiently low quality—lead to a loss of surplus over and above the deadweight loss.

Deadweight loss is the loss in total surplus that occurs whenever an action or a policy reduces the quantity transacted below the efficient market equilibrium quantity.

Inefficient Allocation to Consumers Rent control doesn't just lead to too few apartments being available. It can also lead to misallocation of the apartments that are available: people who badly need a place to live may not be able to find an apartment, but some apartments may be occupied by people with much less urgent needs.

In the case shown in Figure 10-2, 2.2 million people would like to rent an apartment at $800 per month, but only 1.8 million apartments are available. Of those 2.2 million who are seeking an apartment, some want one badly and are willing to pay a high price to get it. Others have a less urgent need and are only willing to pay a low price, perhaps because they have alternative housing or have sufficient income to offer a high price.

An efficient allocation of apartments would reflect these differences: people who really want an apartment will get one and people who aren't all that anxious to find an apartment won't. In an inefficient distribution of apartments, the opposite will happen: some people who are not especially anxious to find an apartment will get one and others who are very anxious to find an apartment won't.

Because people usually get apartments through luck or personal connections under rent control, it generally results in an **inefficient allocation to consumers** of the few apartments available.

To see the inefficiency involved, consider the plight of the Lees, a family with young children who have no alternative housing and would be willing to pay up to $1,500 for an apartment—but are unable to find one. Also consider George, a retiree who lives most of the year in Florida but still has a lease on the New York apartment he moved into 40 years ago. George pays $800 per month for this apartment, but if the rent were even slightly more—say, $850—he would give it up and stay with his children when he visits New York.

This allocation of apartments—George has one and the Lees do not—is a missed opportunity: there is a way to make the Lees and George both better off at no additional cost. The Lees would be happy to pay George, say, $1,200 a month to sublease his apartment, which he would happily accept since the apartment is worth no more than $849 a month to him. George would prefer the money he gets from the Lees to keeping his apartment; the Lees would prefer to have the apartment rather than the money. So both would be made better off by this transaction—and nobody else would be made worse off.

Generally, if people who really want apartments could sublease them from people who are less eager to live there, both those who gain apartments and those who trade their occupancy for money would be better off. However, subletting is illegal under rent control because it would occur at prices above the price ceiling.

The fact that subletting is illegal doesn't mean it never happens. In fact, chasing down illegal subletting is a major business for New York private investigators who are hired to prove that the legal tenants in rent-controlled apartments actually live somewhere else and have sublet their apartments at two or three times the controlled rent.

This subletting leads to the emergence of a black market, which we will discuss shortly. For now, just note that landlords and legal agencies actively discourage the practice. As a result, the problem of inefficient allocation of apartments remains.

Price ceilings often lead to inefficiency in the form of **inefficient allocation to consumers:** some people who want the good badly and are willing to pay a high price don't get it, and some who care relatively little about the good and are only willing to pay a low price do get it.

Price ceilings typically lead to inefficiency in the form of **wasted resources:** people expend money, effort, and time to cope with the shortages caused by the price ceiling.

Wasted Resources Another reason a price ceiling causes inefficiency is that it leads to **wasted resources:** people expend money, effort, and time to cope with the shortages caused by the price ceiling. Back in 1979, U.S. price controls on gasoline led to shortages that forced millions of Americans to wait in lines at gas stations for hours each week. The opportunity cost of the time spent in gas lines—the wages not earned, the leisure time not enjoyed—constituted wasted resources from the point of view of consumers and of the economy as a whole.

Because of rent control, the Lees will spend all their spare time for several months searching for an apartment, time they would rather have spent working or in family activities. That is, there is an opportunity cost to the Lees' prolonged search for an apartment—the leisure or income they had to forgo.

If the market for apartments worked freely, the Lees would quickly find an apartment at the equilibrium rent of $1,000, leaving them time to earn more or to enjoy themselves—an outcome that would make them better off without making anyone else worse off. Again, rent control creates missed opportunities.

Inefficiently Low Quality Yet another way a price ceiling creates inefficiency is by causing goods to be of inefficiently low quality. **Inefficiently low quality** means that sellers offer low-quality goods at a low price even though buyers would rather have higher quality and would be willing to pay a higher price for it.

Again, consider rent control. Landlords have no incentive to provide better conditions because they cannot raise rents to cover their repair costs but are able to find tenants easily. In many cases, tenants would be willing to pay much more for improved conditions than it would cost for the landlord to provide them—for example, upgrading an outdated electrical system that cannot safely run air conditioners or computers. But any additional payment for such improvements would be legally considered a rent increase, which is prohibited.

Indeed, rent-controlled apartments are notoriously badly maintained, rarely painted, subject to frequent electrical and plumbing problems, and sometimes even hazardous to inhabit. This whole situation is a missed opportunity—some tenants would be happy to pay for better conditions, and landlords would be happy to provide them for payment. But such an exchange would occur only if the market were allowed to operate freely.

Black Markets In addition to these four inefficiencies there is a final aspect of price ceilings: the incentive they provide for illegal activities, specifically the emergence of **black markets.** We have already described one kind of black market activity—illegal subletting by tenants. But it does not stop there. Clearly, there is a temptation for a landlord to say to a potential tenant, "Look, you can have the place if you slip me an extra few hundred in cash each month"—and for the tenant to agree if they are one of those people who would be willing to pay much more than the maximum legal rent.

What's wrong with black markets? In general, it's a bad thing if people break any law, because it encourages disrespect for the law in general. Worse yet, in this case illegal activity worsens the position of those who are honest. If the Lees are scrupulous about upholding the rent-control law but other people—who may need an apartment less than the Lees—are willing to bribe landlords, the Lees may never find an apartment.

So Why Are There Price Ceilings?

We have seen three common results of price ceilings:

- A persistent shortage of the good
- Inefficiency arising from this persistent shortage in the form of inefficiently low quantity (deadweight loss), inefficient allocation of the good to consumers, resources wasted in searching for the good, and the inefficiently low quality of the good offered for sale
- The emergence of illegal, black market activity

Given these unpleasant consequences of price ceilings, why do governments still sometimes impose them? Why does rent control, in particular, persist in New York?

One answer is that although price ceilings may have adverse effects, they do benefit some people. In practice, New York's rent-control rules—which are more complex than our simple model—hurt most residents but give a small minority of renters much cheaper housing than they would get in an unregulated market.

Price ceilings often lead to inefficiency in that the goods being offered are of **inefficiently low quality** sellers offer low-quality goods at a low price even though buyers would prefer a higher quality at a higher price.

A **black market** is a market in which goods or services are bought and sold illegally—either because it is illegal to sell them at all or because the prices charged are legally prohibited by a price ceiling.

And those who benefit from the controls are typically better organized and more vocal than those who are harmed by them.

Also, when price ceilings have been in effect for a long time, buyers may not have a realistic idea of what would happen without them. In our previous example, the rental rate in an unregulated market (Figure 10-1) would be only 25% higher than in the regulated market (Figure 10-2): $1,000 instead of $800. But how would renters know that? Indeed, they might have heard about black market transactions at much higher prices—the Lees or some other family paying George $1,200 or more—and would not realize that these black market prices are much higher than the price that would prevail in a fully unregulated market.

A last answer is that government officials often do not understand supply and demand analysis! It is a great mistake to suppose that economic policies in the real world are always sensible or well informed.

Check Your Understanding 10-1

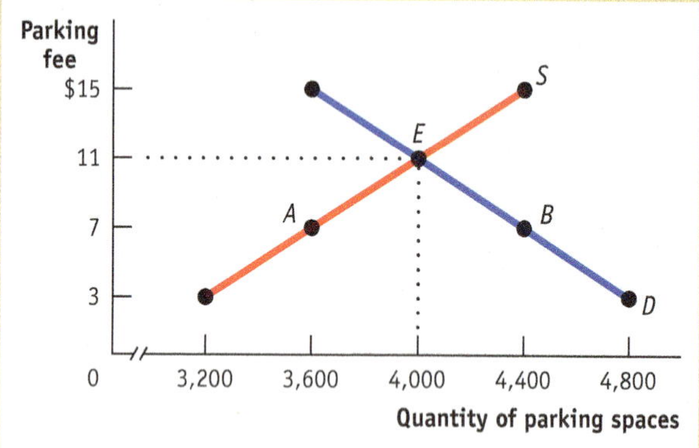

1. On game days, homeowners near Middletown University's stadium used to rent parking spaces in their driveways to fans at a going rate of $11. A new town ordinance now sets a maximum parking fee of $7. Use the accompanying supply and demand diagram to explain how each of the following corresponds to a price-ceiling concept.
   a. Some homeowners now think it's not worth the hassle to rent out spaces.
   b. Some fans who used to carpool to the game now drive alone.
   c. Some fans can't find parking and leave without seeing the game.

   Explain how each of the following adverse effects arises from the price ceiling.
   d. Some fans now arrive several hours early to find parking.
   e. Friends of homeowners near the stadium regularly attend games, even if they aren't big fans. But some serious fans have given up because of the parking situation.
   f. Some homeowners rent spaces for more than $7 but pretend that the buyers are nonpaying friends or family.
2. True or false? Explain your answer. A price ceiling below the equilibrium price of an otherwise efficient market does the following:
   a. Increases quantity supplied
   b. Makes some people who want to consume the good worse off
   c. Makes all producers worse off
3. Which of the following create deadweight loss? Which do not and are simply a transfer of surplus from one person to another? Explain your answers.
   a. You have been evicted from your rent-controlled apartment after the landlord discovered your pet boa constrictor. The apartment is quickly rented to someone else at the same price. You and the new renter do not necessarily have the same willingness to pay for the apartment.
   b. In a contest, you won a ticket to a jazz concert. But you can't go to the concert because of an exam, and the terms of the contest do not allow you to sell the ticket or give it to someone else. Would your answer to this question change if you could not sell the ticket but you could give it to someone else?
   c. Your school's dean of students, who is a proponent of a low-fat diet, decrees that ice cream can no longer be served on campus.
   d. Your ice-cream cone falls on the ground and your dog eats it. (Take the liberty of counting your dog as a member of society, and assume that, if he could, your dog would be willing to pay the same amount for the ice-cream cone as you would pay.)

Solutions appear at back of book.

>> Quick Review

- **Price controls** take the form of either legal maximum prices—**price ceilings**—or legal minimum prices—**price floors.**
- A price ceiling below the equilibrium price benefits successful buyers but causes predictable adverse effects such as persistent shortages, which lead to four types of inefficiencies: **deadweight loss, inefficient allocation to consumers, wasted resources,** and **inefficiently low quality.**
- A deadweight loss is a loss of total surplus that occurs whenever a policy or action reduces the quantity transacted below the efficient market equilibrium level.
- Price ceilings also lead to **black markets,** as buyers and sellers attempt to evade the price controls.

10.3 Price Floors

Sometimes governments intervene to push market prices up instead of down. *Price floors* have been widely legislated for agricultural products, such as wheat and milk, as a way to support the incomes of farmers. Historically, there were also price floors—legally mandated minimum prices—on such services as trucking and air travel, although these were phased out by the U.S. government in the 1970s.

If you have ever worked in a fast-food restaurant, you are likely to have encountered a price floor: governments in the United States and many other countries maintain a lower limit on the hourly wage rate of a worker's labor; that is, a floor on the price of labor called the **minimum wage.**

Just like price ceilings, price floors are intended to help some people but generate predictable and undesirable side effects. Figure 10-4 shows hypothetical supply and demand curves for butter. Left to itself, the market would move to equilibrium at point *E*, with 10 million pounds of butter bought and sold at a price of $1 per pound.

Now suppose that the government, to help dairy farmers, imposes a price floor on butter of $1.20 per pound. Its effects are shown in Figure 10-5, where the line at $1.20 represents the price floor. At a price of $1.20 per pound, producers would want to supply 12 million pounds (point *B* on the supply curve) but consumers would want to buy only 9 million pounds (point *A* on the demand curve). So the price floor leads to a persistent surplus of 3 million pounds of butter.

Does a price floor always lead to an unwanted surplus? No. Just as in the case of a price ceiling, the floor may not be binding—that is, it may be irrelevant. If the equilibrium price of butter is $1 per pound but the floor is set at only $0.80, the floor has no effect.

The **minimum wage** is a legal floor on the wage rate, which is the market price of labor.

FIGURE 10-4 The Market for Butter in the Absence of Government Controls

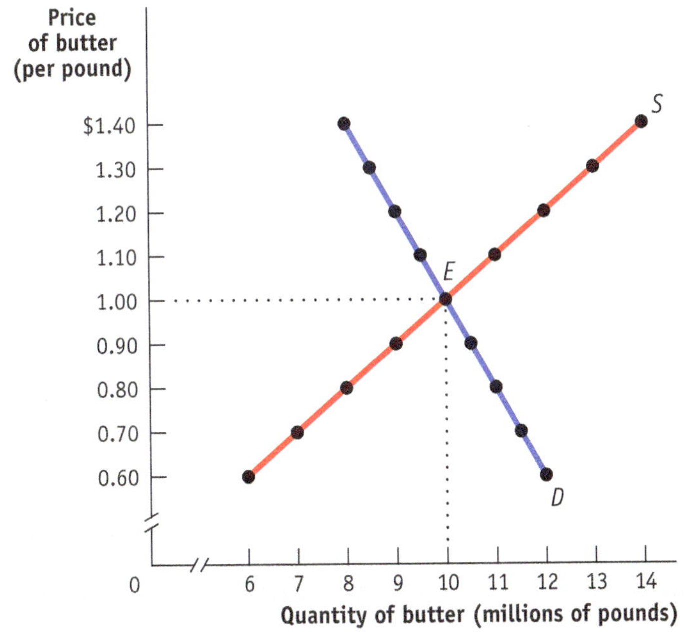

Price of butter (per pound)	Quantity of butter (millions of pounds)	
	Quantity demanded	Quantity supplied
$1.40	8.0	14.0
1.30	8.5	13.0
1.20	9.0	12.0
1.10	9.5	11.0
1.00	10.0	10.0
0.90	10.5	9.0
0.80	11.0	8.0
0.70	11.5	7.0
0.60	12.0	6.0

Without government intervention, the market for butter reaches equilibrium at a price of $1 per pound with 10 million pounds of butter bought and sold.

FIGURE 10-5 The Effects of a Price Floor

The black horizontal line represents the government-imposed price floor of $1.20 per pound of butter. The quantity of butter demanded falls to 9 million pounds, and the quantity supplied rises to 12 million pounds, generating a persistent surplus of 3 million pounds of butter.

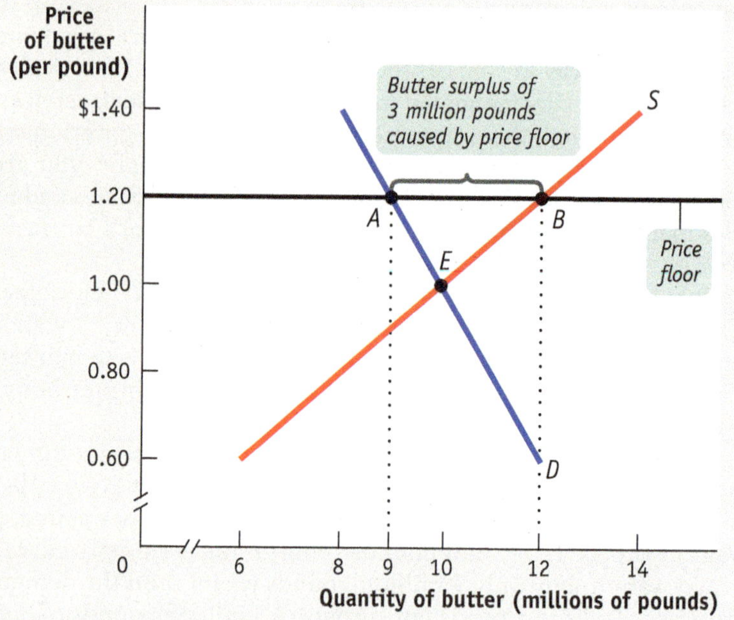

But suppose that a price floor is binding: what happens to the unwanted surplus? The answer depends on government policy. In the case of agricultural price floors, governments buy up unwanted surplus. As a result, the U.S. government, for example, has at times found itself warehousing thousands of tons of butter, cheese, and other farm products. (The European Commission, which administers price floors for a number of European countries, once found itself the owner of a so-called butter mountain, equal in weight to the entire population of Austria.) The government then has to find a way to dispose of these unwanted goods.

Some countries pay exporters to sell products at a loss overseas; this is the standard procedure for the European Union. The United States gives surplus food away to citizens in need as well as to schools, which use the products in school lunches. In some cases, governments have actually destroyed the surplus production.

When the government is not prepared to purchase the unwanted surplus, a price floor means that would-be sellers cannot find buyers. This is what happens when there is a price floor on the wage rate paid for an hour of labor, the minimum wage: when the minimum wage is above the equilibrium wage rate, some people who are willing to work—that is, sell labor—cannot find buyers—that is, employers—willing to give them jobs.

How a Price Floor Causes Inefficiency

The persistent surplus that results from a price floor creates missed opportunities—inefficiencies—that resemble those created by the shortage that results from a price ceiling. Like a price ceiling, a price floor creates inefficiency in at least four ways:

1. It creates deadweight loss by reducing the quantity transacted to below the efficient level.
2. It leads to an inefficient allocation of sales among sellers.
3. It leads to a waste of resources.
4. It leads to sellers providing an inefficiently high quality level.

In addition to inefficiency, like a price ceiling, a price floor leads to illegal behavior as people break the law to sell below the legal price.

Inefficiently Low Quantity Because a price floor raises the price of a good to consumers, it reduces the quantity of that good demanded; because sellers can't sell more units of a good than buyers are willing to buy, a price floor reduces the quantity of a good bought and sold below the market equilibrium quantity and leads to a deadweight loss. Notice that this is the *same* effect as a price ceiling. You might be tempted to think that a price floor and a price ceiling have opposite effects, but both have the effect of reducing the quantity of a good bought and sold (see the accompanying Pitfalls).

Since the equilibrium of an efficient market maximizes the sum of consumer and producer surplus, a price floor that reduces the quantity below the equilibrium quantity reduces total surplus. Figure 10-6 shows the implications for total surplus of a price floor on the price of butter. Total surplus is the sum of the area above the supply curve and below the demand curve.

By reducing the quantity of butter sold, a price floor causes a deadweight loss equal to the area of the shaded triangle in the figure. As in the case of a price ceiling, however, deadweight loss is only one of the forms of inefficiency that the price control creates.

Inefficient Allocation of Sales Among Sellers Like a price ceiling, a price floor can lead to *inefficient allocation*—in this case, an **inefficient allocation of sales among sellers:** sellers who are willing to sell at the lowest price are unable to make sales, while sales go to sellers who are only willing to sell at a higher price.

Price floors can lead to **inefficient allocation of sales among sellers:** sellers who are willing to sell at the lowest price are unable to make sales while sales go to sellers who are only willing to sell at a higher price.

One historical example of the inefficient allocation of selling opportunities caused by a price floor was the labor market situation in many European countries from the 1980s onward. A high minimum wage led to a two-tier labor system, composed of the fortunate who had good jobs in the formal labor market, and the rest who were locked out without any prospect of ever finding a good job.

FIGURE 10-6 A Price Floor Causes Inefficiently Low Quantity

A price floor reduces the quantity demanded below the market equilibrium quantity and leads to a deadweight loss.

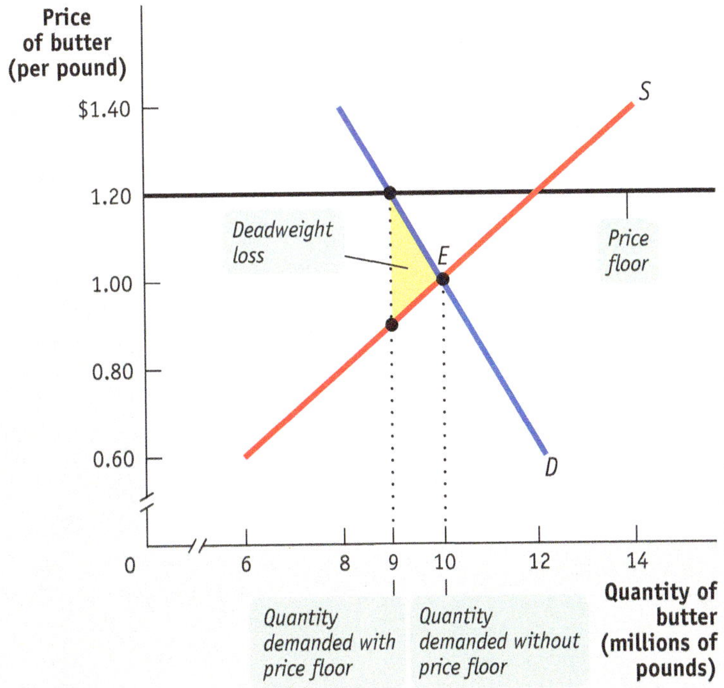

PITFALLS

CEILINGS, FLOORS, AND QUANTITIES

A price ceiling pushes the price of a good *down*. A price floor pushes the price of a good *up*. So it's easy to assume that the effects of a price floor are the opposite of the effects of a price ceiling. In particular, if a price ceiling reduces the quantity of a good bought and sold, doesn't a price floor increase the quantity?

No, it doesn't. In fact, both floors and ceilings reduce the quantity bought and sold. Why? When the quantity of a good supplied isn't equal to the quantity demanded, the actual quantity sold is determined by the "short side" of the market—whichever quantity is less. If sellers don't want to sell as much as buyers want to buy, it's the sellers who determine the actual quantity sold, because buyers can't force unwilling sellers to sell. If buyers don't want to buy as much as sellers want to sell, it's the buyers who determine the actual quantity sold, because sellers can't force unwilling buyers to buy.

Either unemployed or underemployed in dead-end jobs in the black market for labor, the unlucky ones were disproportionately young, from the ages of 18 to early 30s. Although eager for good jobs in the formal sector and willing to accept less than the minimum wage—that is, willing to sell their labor for a lower price—it was illegal for employers to pay them less than the minimum wage.

The inefficiency of unemployment and underemployment was compounded as a generation of young people was unable to get adequate job training, develop careers, and save for their future. These young people were also more likely to engage in crime. And many of these countries saw their best and brightest young people emigrate, leading to a permanent reduction in the future performance of their economies. The social losses grew to such an extent that in recent years European countries have undertaken labor market reforms that have significantly reduced the problem.

Wasted Resources Also like a price ceiling, a price floor generates inefficiency by *wasting resources*. The most graphic examples involve government purchases of the unwanted surpluses of agricultural products caused by price floors. The surplus production is sometimes destroyed, which is pure waste; in other cases, the stored produce goes, as officials euphemistically put it, "out of condition" and must be thrown away.

Price floors also lead to wasted time and effort. Consider the minimum wage. Would-be workers who spend many hours searching for jobs, or waiting in line in the hope of getting jobs, play the same role in the case of price floors as hapless families searching for apartments in the case of price ceilings.

Inefficiently High Quality Again like price ceilings, price floors lead to inefficiency in the quality of goods produced.

We saw that when there is a price ceiling, suppliers produce products that are of inefficiently low quality: buyers prefer higher-quality products and are willing to pay for them, but sellers refuse to improve the quality of their products because the price ceiling prevents their being compensated for doing so. This same logic applies to price floors, but in reverse: suppliers offer goods of **inefficiently high quality.**

How can this be? Isn't high quality a good thing? Yes, but only if it is worth the cost. Suppose that suppliers spend a lot to make goods of very high quality but that this quality isn't worth much to consumers, who would rather receive the money spent on that quality in the form of a lower price. This represents a missed opportunity: suppliers and buyers could make a mutually beneficial deal in which buyers got goods of lower quality for a much lower price.

A good example of the inefficiency of excessive quality comes from the days when transatlantic airfares were set artificially high by international treaty. Forbidden to compete for customers by offering lower ticket prices, airlines instead offered expensive services, like lavish in-flight meals that went largely uneaten—an especially wasteful practice, considering that what passengers really wanted was less food and lower airfares.

Price floors often lead to inefficiency in that goods of **inefficiently high quality** are offered: sellers offer high-quality goods at a high price, even though buyers would prefer a lower quality at a lower price.

Since the deregulation of U.S. airlines in the 1970s, American passengers have experienced a large decrease in ticket prices accompanied by a decrease in the quality of in-flight service—smaller seats, lower-quality food, and so on. Everyone complains about the service—but thanks to lower fares, the number of people flying on U.S. carriers has grown from 130 billion passenger miles when deregulation began to approximately 964 billion in 2017.

Illegal Activity In addition to the four inefficiencies we analyzed, price floors, like price ceilings, provide incentives for illegal activity. For example, in countries where the minimum wage is far above the equilibrium wage rate, workers desperate for jobs sometimes agree to work off the books for employers who conceal their employment from the government—or bribe the government inspectors. This practice, known in Europe as *black labor,* is especially common in Southern European countries such as Italy and Spain.

So Why Are There Price Floors?

To sum up, a price floor creates various negative side effects:

- A persistent surplus of the good
- Inefficiency arising from the persistent surplus in the form of inefficiently low quantity (deadweight loss), inefficient allocation of sales among sellers, wasted resources, and an inefficiently high level of quality offered by suppliers
- The temptation to engage in illegal activity, particularly bribery and corruption of government officials

So why do governments impose price floors when they have so many negative side effects? The reasons are similar to those for imposing price ceilings. Government officials often disregard warnings about the consequences of price floors either because they believe that the relevant market is poorly described by the supply and demand model or, more often, because they do not understand the model. Above all, just as price ceilings are often imposed because they benefit some influential buyers of a good, price floors are often imposed because they benefit some influential sellers.

ECONOMICS >> *in Action*

The Rise and Fall of the Unpaid Intern

The best-known example of a price floor is the minimum wage. Most economists believe, however, that the minimum wage has relatively little effect on the overall job market in the United States, mainly because the floor is set so low. In 1964, the U.S. minimum wage was 53% of the average wage of blue-collar production workers; by 2017, it had fallen to about 33%. However, there is one sector of the U.S. job market where it appears that the minimum wage can indeed be binding: the market for interns.

Starting in 2011, a spate of lawsuits brought by former unpaid interns claiming they were cheated out of wages brought the matter to public attention. A common thread in these complaints was that interns were assigned grunt work with no educational value, such as tracking lost cell phones. In other cases, unpaid interns complained that they were given the work of full-salaried employees. By 2015, many of those lawsuits proved successful: Condé Nast Publications settled for $5.8 million, Sirius XM Radio settled for $1.3 million, and Viacom Media settled for $7.2 million. In 2017, even the Olsen twins had to cough up $140,000 in payments to unpaid interns for their fashion company, Dualstar Entertainment.

"We have an opening for a part-time unpaid intern, which could lead to a full-time unpaid internship."

Aaron Bacall/www.Cartoonstock.com

As a result, unless their programs can clearly demonstrate an educational component such as course credit, companies have to pay their interns minimum wage or shut down their programs altogether.

Some observers worry that the end of the unpaid internship means that programs that once offered valuable training will be lost. But as one lawyer commented, "The law says that when you work, you have to get paid [at least the minimum wage]."

Check Your Understanding 10-2

1. The state legislature mandates a price floor for gasoline of P_F per gallon. Assess the following statements and illustrate your answer using the figure provided.

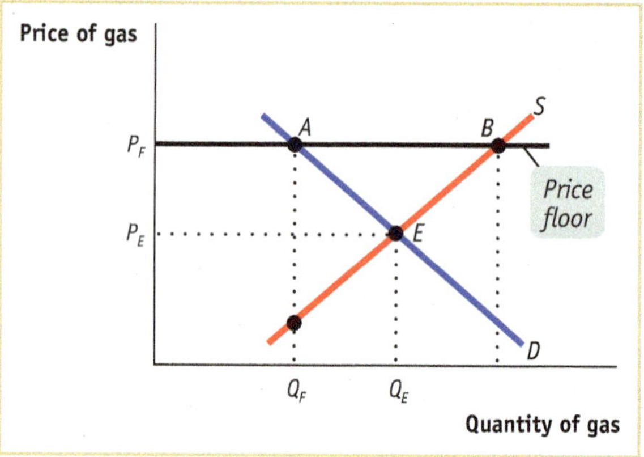

a. Proponents of the law claim it will increase the income of gas station owners. Opponents claim it will hurt gas station owners because they will lose customers.

b. Proponents claim consumers will be better off because gas stations will provide better service. Opponents claim consumers will be generally worse off because they prefer to buy gas at cheaper prices.

c. Proponents claim that they are helping gas station owners without hurting anyone else. Opponents claim that consumers are hurt and will end up doing things like buying gas in a nearby state or on the black market.

Solutions appear at back of book.

>> Quick Review

- The most familiar price floor is the **minimum wage.** Price floors are also commonly imposed on agricultural goods.
- A price floor above the equilibrium price benefits successful sellers but causes predictable adverse effects such as a persistent surplus, which leads to four kinds of inefficiencies: deadweight loss from inefficiently low quantity, **inefficient allocation of sales among sellers,** wasted resources, and **inefficiently high quality.**
- Price floors encourage illegal activity, such as workers who work off the books, often leading to official corruption.

BUSINESS CASE

Ticket Prices and Music's Reigning Couple, Beyoncé and Jay-Z

Larry Busacca/PW18/Getty Images

Beyoncé and Jay-Z are the reigning couple of music, estimated to be worth $1.4 billion. And a good chunk of that money was earned by touring. In 2018, their "On the Run II" tour grossed a staggering $253 million with nearly 2.2 million tickets sold. The couple also had a very profitable year in 2014 when their initial "On the Run" tour grossed over $100 million. One music industry expert noted that no one should be surprised by this. "With nearly 200 million records sold between them and 36 total Grammys, Beyoncé and Jay-Z are a creative force to be reckoned with. When their talents are combined, the sky is the limit—at least as far as ticket prices are concerned." And the market seems to agree. TicketIQ estimated that the average online reseller ticket price for the 2018 tour was $403.

Yet, despite the high demand for their tickets, Jay-Z and Beyoncé receive significantly less than this amount for an average ticket. Why? Omar Al-Joulani, the producer of the tour, explained that tickets were priced to be *inclusive*. At the MetLife Stadium event in New Jersey in 2018, prices for direct-sale tickets on Live Nation ranged from $25 to $380. Al-Joulani continued: "Our strategy was to price tickets so that wherever you were on that ticket chain you had an opportunity to attend the show."

So if you were able to obtain a ticket from a direct seller, you could have made a pretty penny by reselling your ticket at the market price. Perhaps this was Beyoncé and Jay-Z's way of sharing the wealth as well as their music.

QUESTIONS FOR THOUGHT

1. Use the concepts of consumer surplus and producer surplus to analyze the exchange between Beyoncé and Jay-Z and their fans in the absence of ticket resellers. (That is, assume that everyone buys a ticket directly and goes to the concert.) Draw a diagram to illustrate.
2. Referring to the diagram drawn in response to question 1, explain the effect of resellers on the allocation of consumer surplus and producer surplus among Beyoncé and Jay-Z and their fans.

REVIEW

MODULE 8

1. The **willingness to pay** of each individual consumer determines the demand curve. When price is less than or equal to the willingness to pay, the potential consumer purchases the good. The difference between willingness to pay and price is the net gain to the consumer, the **individual consumer surplus.**
2. **Total consumer surplus** in a market, the sum of all individual consumer surpluses in a market, is equal to the area below the market demand curve but above the price. A rise in the price of a good reduces consumer surplus; a fall in the price increases consumer surplus. The term **consumer surplus** is often used to refer to both individual and total consumer surplus.
3. The **cost** of each potential producer, the lowest price at which they are willing to supply a unit of a particular good, determines the supply curve. If the price of a good is above a producer's cost, a sale generates a net gain to the producer, known as the **individual producer surplus.**
4. **Total producer surplus** in a market, the sum of the individual producer surpluses in a market, is equal to the area above the market supply curve but below the price. A rise in the price of a good increases producer surplus; a fall in the price reduces producer surplus. The term **producer surplus** is often used to refer to both individual and total producer surplus.
5. **Total surplus,** the total gain to society from the production and consumption of a good, is the sum of consumer and producer surplus.

MODULE 9

1. Usually markets are efficient and achieve the maximum total surplus. Any possible reallocation of consumption or sales, or a change in the quantity bought and sold, reduces total surplus. However, society also cares about equity, or fairness. So government intervention in a market that reduces efficiency but increases equity can be a valid choice by society.
2. An economy composed of efficient markets is also efficient, although this is virtually impossible to achieve in reality. The keys to the efficiency of a market economy are **property rights** and the operation of prices as **economic signals.** Under certain conditions, **market failure** occurs, making a market **inefficient.** The three principal causes of market failure are market power, externalities, and a good that, by its nature, makes it unsuitable for a market to allocate efficiently.

MODULE 10

1. Even when a market is efficient, governments often intervene to pursue greater fairness or to please a powerful interest group. Interventions take the form of **price controls,** which generate predictable and undesirable side effects that consist of various forms of inefficiency and illegal activity.
2. A **price ceiling,** a maximum market price below the equilibrium price, benefits successful buyers but creates persistent shortages. Because the price is maintained below the equilibrium price, the quantity demanded is increased and the quantity supplied is decreased compared to the equilibrium quantity. This leads to predictable problems: inefficiencies in the form of **deadweight loss** from inefficiently low quantity, **inefficient allocation to consumers, wasted resources,** and **inefficiently low quality.** It also encourages illegal activity as people turn to **black markets** to get the good. Because of these problems, price ceilings have generally lost favor as an economic policy tool. But some governments continue to impose them either because they don't understand the effects or because the price ceilings benefit some influential group.
3. A **price floor,** a minimum market price above the equilibrium price, benefits successful sellers but creates persistent surplus. Because the price is maintained above the equilibrium price, the quantity demanded is decreased and the quantity supplied is increased compared to the equilibrium quantity. This leads to predictable problems: inefficiencies in the form of deadweight loss from inefficiently low quantity, **inefficient allocation of sales among sellers,** wasted resources, and **inefficiently high quality.** It also encourages illegal activity and black markets. The most well-known kind of price floor is the **minimum wage,** but price floors are also commonly applied to agricultural products.

KEY TERMS

Willingness to pay p. 88
Individual consumer surplus p. 89
Total consumer surplus p. 90
Consumer surplus p. 90
Cost p. 94
Individual producer surplus p. 95
Total producer surplus p. 95
Producer surplus p. 95
Total surplus p. 99
Property rights p. 105
Economic signal p. 105
Inefficient p. 106
Market failure p. 106
Price controls p. 110
Price ceiling p. 110
Price floor p. 110
Deadweight loss p. 113
Inefficient allocation to consumers p. 114
Wasted resources p. 114
Inefficiently low quality p. 115
Black market p. 115
Minimum wage p. 117
Inefficient allocation of sales among sellers p. 119
Inefficiently high quality p. 120

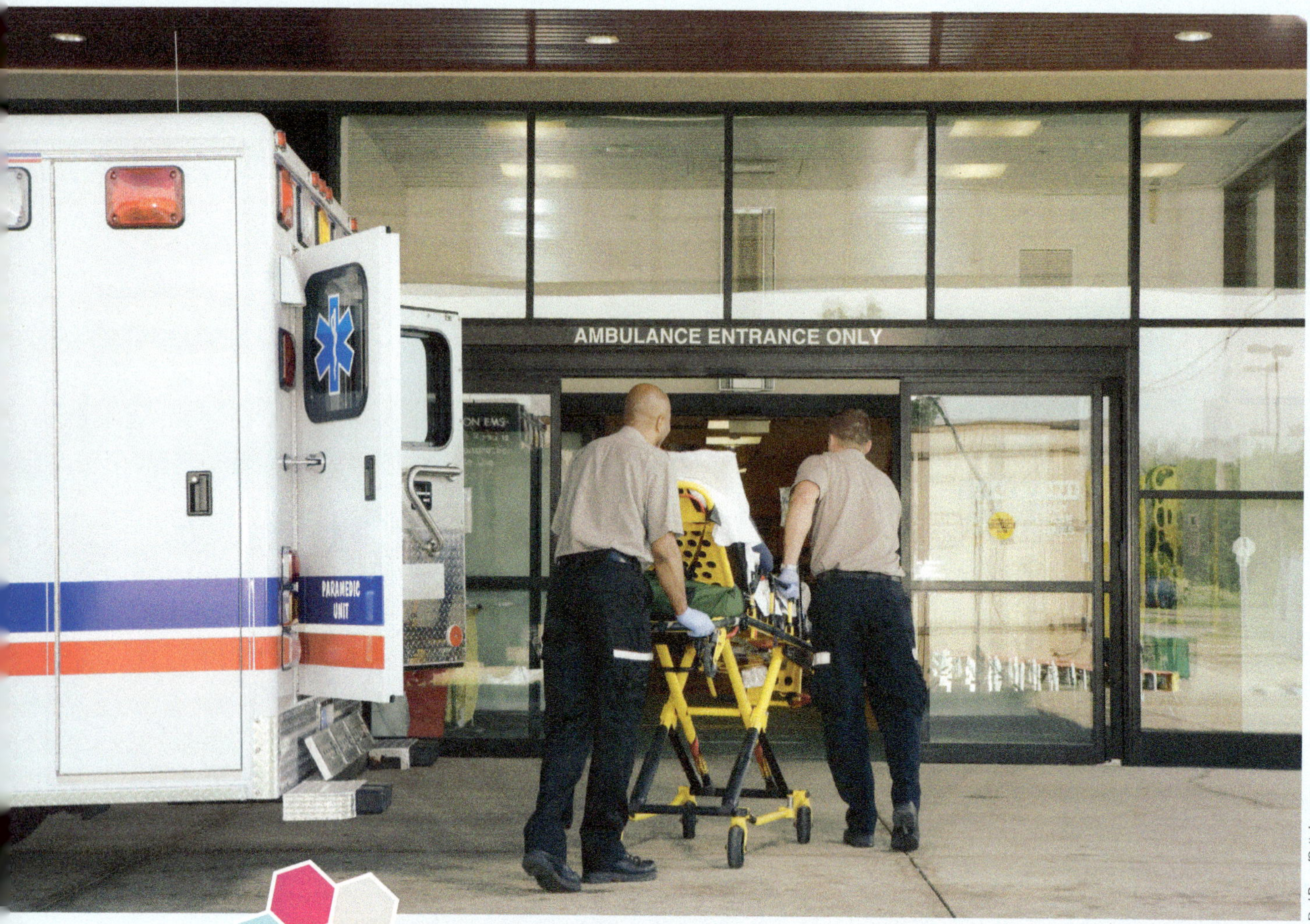

Paul Burns/Getty Images

Module 11 Defining and Measuring Elasticity

Module 12 Interpreting the Price Elasticity of Demand

Module 13 Other Elasticities

Module 14 The Benefits and Costs of Taxation

SECTION 4

Elasticity and Law of Demand

TAKEN FOR A RIDE

In a true emergency, you aren't likely to quibble about the price of an ambulance ride to the nearest emergency room. But what if it isn't an emergency? Kira Millas doesn't know who called an ambulance after she broke three teeth while swimming. Shaken, she accepted the ambulance ride to a hospital, 15 minutes away. A week later, she received the bill: $1,772.42. Stunned, she said: "We only drove nine miles and it was a non-life-threatening injury. I needed absolutely no emergency treatment."

Kira's experience is by no means exceptional. In a true medical emergency, a patient undoubtedly feels fortunate when an ambulance pulls up. But in nonemergency cases, many patients feel obliged to get into the ambulance once it arrives. And just like Kira, they are uninformed about the cost of the ride to the hospital.

Each year in the United States an estimated 40 million ambulance trips, at a cost of $14 billion, are provided. Sensing profit-making opportunities, in recent years companies have significantly expanded their operations, with one investor recently paying $3 billion for an ambulance provider. A similar dynamic has occurred in the air ambulance market, high profits have led to explosive growth, and with patients handed bills for tens of thousands of dollars for trips that would have been shorter and more safely taken by land.

How can ambulance operators charge thousands of dollars for a ride regardless of whether their services are actually needed? The answer to all these questions is *price unresponsiveness:* in the heat of the moment, many consumers—particularly those with true emergencies—are *unresponsive* to the price of an ambulance. And ambulance operators know this. A large increase in the price of an ambulance ride would leave the quantity demanded by a significant number of consumers relatively unchanged.

Let's consider a very different scenario. Suppose that the maker of a particular brand of breakfast cereal decided to charge 10 times the original price. It would be extremely difficult, if not impossible, to find consumers willing to pay the much higher price. In other words, consumers of breakfast cereal are much more responsive to price than are the consumers of ambulance rides.

But how do we define *responsiveness?* Economists measure responsiveness of consumers to price with a particular number, called the *price elasticity of demand.*

In this section we will show how the price elasticity of demand is calculated and why it is the best measure of how the quantity demanded responds to changes in price. We will then see that the price elasticity of demand is only one of a family of related concepts, including the *income elasticity of demand, cross-price elasticity of demand,* and *price elasticity of supply.*

MODULE 11

Defining and Measuring Elasticity

WHAT YOU WILL LEARN

- Why is **elasticity** used to measure the response to changes in prices or income?
- What are the different elasticity measures and what do they mean?

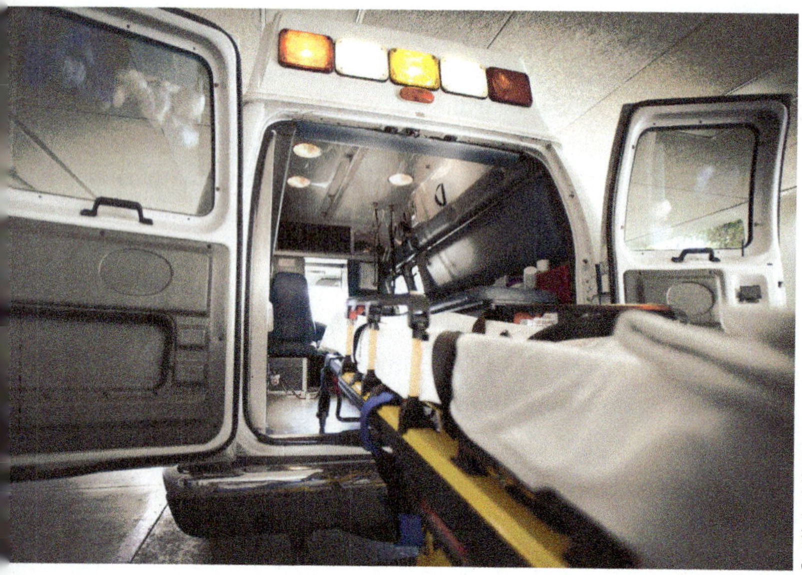

Scott Kochsiek/Getty Images

For investors to know whether they can earn significant profits in the ambulance business, they need to know the *price elasticity of demand* for ambulance rides. With this information, investors can accurately predict whether or not a significant rise in the price of an ambulance ride results in an increase in revenue.

11.1 Calculating the Price Elasticity of Demand

Figure 11-1 shows a hypothetical demand curve for an ambulance ride. At a price of $200 per ride, consumers would demand 10 million rides per year (point *A*); at a price of $210 per ride, consumers would demand 9.9 million rides per year (point *B*).

Figure 11-1, then, tells us the change in the quantity demanded for a particular change in the price. But how can we turn this into a measure of price responsiveness? The answer is to calculate the *price elasticity of demand.*

The **price elasticity of demand** is the ratio of the *percent change in quantity demanded* to the *percent change in price* as we move along the demand curve. As we'll see later in this module, the reason economists use percent changes is to obtain a measure that doesn't depend on the units in which a good is measured (say, a 1-mile ambulance trip versus a 10-mile ambulance trip). But before we get to that, let's look at how elasticity is calculated.

To calculate the price elasticity of demand, we first calculate the *percent change in the quantity demanded* and the corresponding *percent change in the price* as we move along the demand curve. These are defined as follows:

The **price elasticity of demand** is the ratio of the percent change in the quantity demanded to the percent change in the price as we move along the demand curve.

(11-1) $$\%\text{ change in quantity demanded} = \frac{\text{Change in quantity demanded}}{\text{Initial quantity demanded}} \times 100$$

and

FIGURE 11-1 The Demand for Ambulance Rides

At a price of $200 per ambulance ride, the quantity of ambulance rides demanded is 10 million per year (point *A*). When price rises to $210 per ambulance ride, the quantity demanded falls to 9.9 million ambulance rides per year (point *B*).

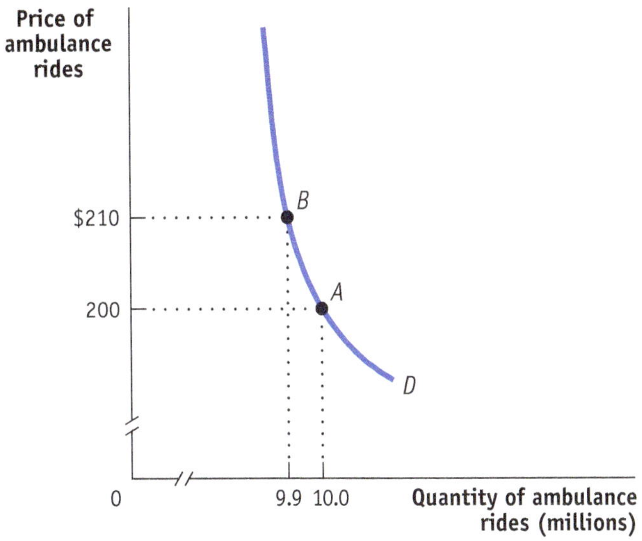

$$\textbf{(11-2)}\quad \%\text{ change in price} = \frac{\text{Change in price}}{\text{Initial price}} \times 100$$

In Figure 11-1, we see that when the price rises from $200 to $210, the quantity demanded falls from 10 million to 9.9 million rides, yielding a change in the quantity demanded of 0.1 million rides. So the percent change in the quantity demanded is

$$\%\text{ change in quantity demanded} = \frac{-0.1\text{ million rides}}{10\text{ million rides}} \times 100 = -1\%$$

The initial price is $200 and the change in the price is $10, so the percent change in price is

$$\%\text{ change in price} = \frac{\$10}{\$200} \times 100 = 5\%$$

To calculate the price elasticity of demand, we find the ratio of the percent change in the quantity demanded to the percent change in the price:

$$\textbf{(11-3)}\quad \text{Price elasticity of demand} = \frac{\%\text{ change in quantity demanded}}{\%\text{ change in price}}$$

In Figure 11-1, the price elasticity of demand is therefore

$$\text{Price elasticity of demand} = \frac{1\%}{5\%} = 0.2$$

Notice that the minus sign that appeared in the calculation of the percent change in the quantity demanded has been dropped when we calculate this last equation, the price elasticity of demand. Why have we done this?

The *law of demand* says that demand curves are downward sloping, so price and quantity demanded always move in opposite directions. In other words, a positive percent change in price (a rise in price) leads to a negative percent change in the quantity demanded; a negative percent change in price (a fall in price) leads to a positive percent change in the quantity demanded. This means that the price elasticity of demand is, in strictly mathematical terms, a negative number.

However, it is inconvenient to repeatedly write a minus sign. So, when economists talk about the price elasticity of demand, they usually drop the minus sign and report the *absolute value* of the price elasticity of demand. In this case, for example, economists would usually say "the price elasticity of demand is 0.2," taking it for granted that you understand they mean *minus* 0.2. We follow this convention here.

The larger the price elasticity of demand, the more responsive the quantity demanded is to the price. When the price elasticity of demand is large—when consumers change their quantity demanded by a large percentage compared to the percent change in the price—economists say that demand is highly elastic.

As we'll see shortly, a price elasticity of 0.2 indicates a small response of quantity demanded to price. That is, the quantity demanded will fall by a relatively small amount when price rises. This is what economists call *inelastic* demand. And inelastic demand is exactly what enables an ambulance operator to increase the total amount earned by raising the price of an ambulance ride.

An Alternative Way to Calculate Elasticities: The Midpoint Method

Price elasticity of demand compares the *percent change in quantity demanded* with the *percent change in price*. When we look at some other elasticities, which we will do shortly, we'll learn why it is important to focus on percent changes. But at this point we need to discuss a technical issue that arises when you calculate percent changes in variables.

The best way to understand the issue is with a real example. Suppose you were trying to estimate the price elasticity of demand for gasoline by comparing gasoline prices and consumption in different countries. Because of high taxes, gasoline usually costs about three times as much per gallon in Europe as it does in the United States. So what is the percent difference between American and European gas prices?

Well, it depends on which way you measure it. Because the price of gasoline in Europe is approximately three times higher than in the United States, it is 200% higher. Because the price of gasoline in the United States is one-third as high as in Europe, it is 66.7% lower.

This is a nuisance: we'd like to have a percent measure of the difference in prices that doesn't depend on which way you measure it. To avoid computing different elasticities for rising and falling prices we use the *midpoint method*.

The **midpoint method** replaces the usual definition of the percent change in a variable, X, with a slightly different definition:

$$\textbf{(11-4)}\quad \%\text{ change in } X = \frac{\text{Change in } X}{\text{Average value of } X} \times 100$$

where the average value of X is defined as

$$\text{Average value of } X = \frac{\text{Starting value of } X + \text{Final value of } X}{2}$$

When calculating the price elasticity of demand using the midpoint method, both the percent change in the price and the percent change in the quantity demanded are found using this method. To see how this method works, suppose you have the following data for some good:

The **midpoint method** is a technique for calculating the percent change. In this approach, we calculate changes in a variable compared with the average, or midpoint, of the starting and final values.

Situation	Price	Quantity demanded
A	$0.90	1,100
B	$1.10	900

To calculate the percent change in quantity going from situation A to situation B, we compare the change in the quantity demanded—a fall of 200 units—with the *average* of the quantity demanded in the two situations. So we calculate

$$\%\text{ change in quantity demanded} = \frac{-200}{(1{,}100 + 900)/2} \times 100 = \frac{-200}{1{,}000} \times 100 = -20\%$$

In the same way, we calculate

$$\%\text{ change in price} = \frac{\$0.20}{(\$0.90 + \$1.10)/2} \times 100 = \frac{\$0.20}{\$1.00} \times 100 = 20\%$$

So in this case we would calculate the price elasticity of demand to be

$$\text{Price elasticity of demand} = \frac{\%\text{ change in quantity demanded}}{\%\text{ change in price}} = \frac{20\%}{20\%} = 1$$

again dropping the minus sign.

The important point is that we would get the same result, a price elasticity of demand of 1, whether we go up the demand curve from situation A to situation B or down the demand curve from situation B to situation A.

To arrive at a more general formula for price elasticity of demand, suppose that we have data for two points on a demand curve. At point 1 the quantity demanded and price are (Q_1, P_1); at point 2 they are (Q_2, P_2). Then the formula for calculating the price elasticity of demand is:

$$\textbf{(11-5)}\quad \text{Price elasticity of demand} = \frac{\dfrac{Q_2 - Q_1}{(Q_1 + Q_2)/2}}{\dfrac{P_2 - P_1}{(P_1 + P_2)/2}}$$

As before, when finding a price elasticity of demand calculated by the midpoint method, we drop the minus sign and use the absolute value.

ECONOMICS >> *in Action*

Estimating Elasticities

You might think it's easy to estimate price elasticities of demand from real-world data: just compare percent changes in prices with percent changes in quantities demanded. Unfortunately, it's rarely that simple since changes in price aren't the only thing affecting changes in the quantity demanded: other factors—such as changes in income, changes in tastes, and changes in the prices of other goods—shift the demand curve, thereby changing the quantity demanded at any given price.

To estimate price elasticities of demand, economists must use careful statistical analysis to separate the influence of the change in price, holding other things equal.

Economists have estimated price elasticities of demand for a number of goods and services. Table 11-1 summarizes some of these and shows a wide range of price elasticities. There are some goods, like gasoline, for which demand hardly responds at all to changes in the price. There are other goods, such as airline travel for leisure, or Coke and Pepsi, for which the quantity demanded is very sensitive to the price.

TABLE 11-1 Some Estimated Price Elasticities of Demand

Good	Price elasticity of demand
Inelastic demand	
Gasoline (short-run)	0.09
Gasoline (long-run)	0.24
College (in-state tuition)	0.60–0.75
Airline travel (business)	0.80
Soda	0.80
Elastic demand	
Housing	1.2
College (out-of-state tuition)	1.2
Airline travel (leisure)	1.5
Coke/Pepsi	3.3

Notice that Table 11-1 is divided into two parts: inelastic and elastic demand. We'll explain the significance of that division in the next section.

>> Quick Review

- The **price elasticity of demand** is equal to the percent change in the quantity demanded divided by the percent change in the price as you move along the demand curve, and dropping any minus sign.
- In practice, percent changes are best measured using the **midpoint method,** in which the percent changes are calculated using the average of starting and final values.

Check Your Understanding 11-1

1. The price of strawberries falls from $1.50 to $1.00 per carton and the quantity demanded goes from 100,000 to 200,000 cartons. Use the midpoint method to find the price elasticity of demand.
2. At the present level of consumption, 4,000 movie tickets, and at the current price, $5 per ticket, the price elasticity of demand for movie tickets is 1. Using the midpoint method, calculate the percentage by which the owners of movie theaters must reduce price to sell 5,000 tickets.
3. The price elasticity of demand for ice-cream sandwiches is 1.2 at the current price of $0.50 per sandwich and the current consumption level of 100,000 sandwiches. Calculate the change in the quantity demanded when price rises by $0.05. Use Equations 11-1 and 11-2 to calculate percent changes and Equation 11-3 to relate price elasticity of demand to the percent changes.

Solutions appear at back of book.

Interpreting the Price Elasticity of Demand

MODULE 12

WHAT YOU WILL LEARN

- What factors influence the size of these various elasticities?
- Why is it vitally important to determine the size of the relevant elasticity before setting prices or government fees?

In a true emergency, a patient is unlikely to question the price of the ambulance ride to the hospital. But even in a nonemergency, like Kira's broken teeth, patients are often unlikely to respond to an increase in the price of an ambulance by reducing their demand, because they are not aware of the cost. As a result, investors in private ambulance companies see profit-making opportunities in delivering ambulance services, because the price elasticity of demand is small. But what does that mean? How low does a price elasticity have to be for us to classify it as low? How high does it have to be for us to consider it high? And what determines whether the price elasticity of demand is high or low anyway?

To answer these questions, we need to look more deeply at the price elasticity of demand.

robeo/Getty Images

12.1 How Elastic Is Elastic?

As a first step toward classifying price elasticities of demand, let's look at the extreme cases.

First, consider the demand for a good when people pay no attention to the price—say, snake anti-venom. Suppose that consumers will buy 1,000 doses of anti-venom per year regardless of the price. In this case, the demand curve for anti-venom would look like the curve shown in panel (a) of Figure 12-1: it would be a vertical line at 1,000 doses of anti-venom. Since the percent change in the quantity demanded is zero for *any* change in the price, the price elasticity of demand in this case is zero. The case of a zero price elasticity of demand is known as **perfectly inelastic** demand.

Demand is **perfectly inelastic** when the quantity demanded does not respond at all to changes in the price. When demand is perfectly inelastic, the demand curve is a vertical line.

The opposite extreme occurs when even a tiny rise in the price will cause the quantity demanded to drop to zero or even a tiny fall in the price will cause the quantity demanded to get extremely large.

Panel (b) of Figure 12-1 shows the case of pink tennis balls; we suppose that tennis players really don't care what color their balls are and that other

FIGURE 12-1 Two Extreme Cases of Price Elasticity of Demand

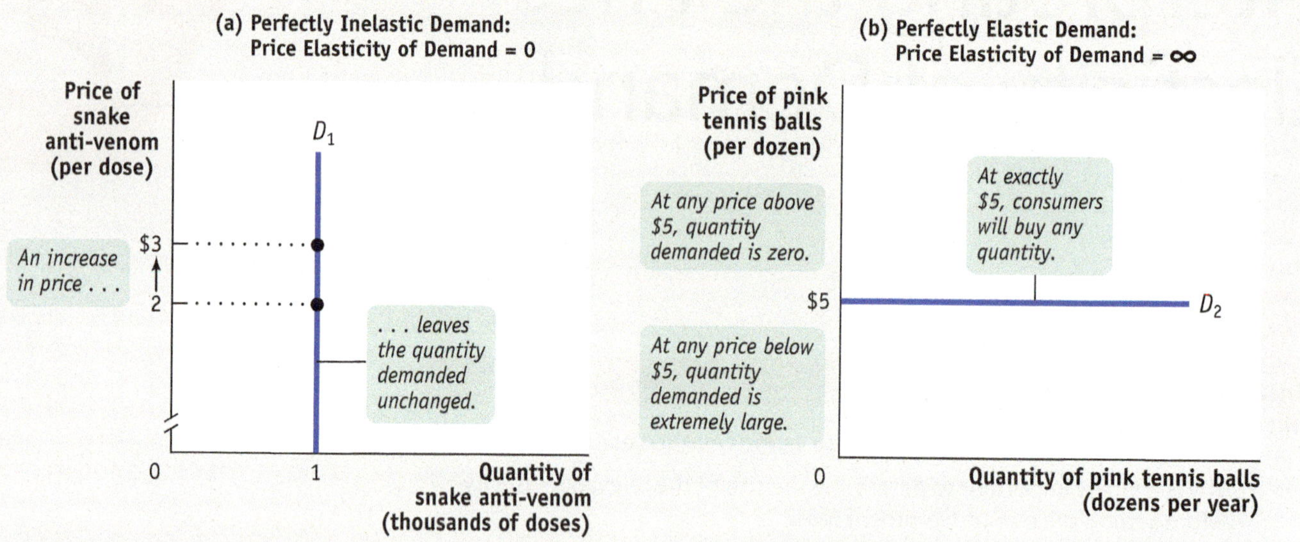

Panel (a) shows a perfectly inelastic demand curve, which is a vertical line. The quantity of snake anti-venom demanded is always 1,000 doses, regardless of price. As a result, the price elasticity of demand is zero—the quantity demanded is unaffected by the price. Panel (b) shows a perfectly elastic demand curve, which is a horizontal line. At a price of $5, consumers will buy any quantity of pink tennis balls, but they will buy none at a price above $5. If the price falls below $5, they will buy an extremely large number of pink tennis balls and none of any other color.

colors, such as neon green and vivid yellow, are available at $5 per dozen balls. In this case, consumers will buy no pink balls if they cost more than $5 per dozen but will buy only pink balls if they cost less than $5. The demand curve will therefore be a horizontal line at a price of $5 per dozen balls. As you move back and forth along this line, there is a change in the quantity demanded but no change in the price. Roughly speaking, when you divide a number by zero, you get infinity, denoted by the symbol ∞. So a horizontal demand curve implies an infinite price elasticity of demand. When the price elasticity of demand is infinite, economists say that demand is **perfectly elastic.**

The price elasticity of demand for the vast majority of goods is somewhere between these two extreme cases. Economists use one main criterion for classifying these intermediate cases: they ask whether the price elasticity of demand is greater than or less than 1. When the price elasticity of demand is greater than 1, economists say that demand is **elastic.** When the price elasticity of demand is less than 1, they say that demand is **inelastic.** The borderline case is **unit-elastic** demand, where the price elasticity of demand is—surprise!—exactly 1.

To see why a price elasticity of demand equal to 1 is a useful dividing line, let's consider a hypothetical example: a toll bridge operated by the state highway department. Other things equal, the number of drivers who use the bridge depends on the toll, the price the highway department charges vehicles to cross the bridge: the higher the toll, the fewer the drivers who use the bridge.

Demand is **perfectly elastic** when any price increase will cause the quantity demanded to drop to zero. When demand is perfectly elastic, the demand curve is a horizontal line.

Demand is **elastic** if the price elasticity of demand is greater than 1, **inelastic** if the price elasticity of demand is less than 1, and **unit-elastic** if the price elasticity of demand is exactly 1.

Figure 12-2 shows three hypothetical demand curves—one in which demand is unit-elastic, one in which it is inelastic, and one in which it is elastic. In each case, point *A* shows the quantity demanded if the toll is $0.90 and point *B* shows the quantity demanded if the toll is $1.10. An increase in the toll from $0.90 to $1.10 is an increase of 20% if we use the midpoint method to calculate percent changes.

Panel (a) shows what happens when the toll is raised from $0.90 to $1.10 and the demand curve is unit-elastic. Here the 20% price rise leads to a fall in the quantity of cars using the bridge each day from 1,100 cars to 900, which is a 20% decline (again using the midpoint method). So the price elasticity of demand is 20%/20% = 1.

FIGURE 12-2 Unit-Elastic Demand, Inelastic Demand, and Elastic Demand

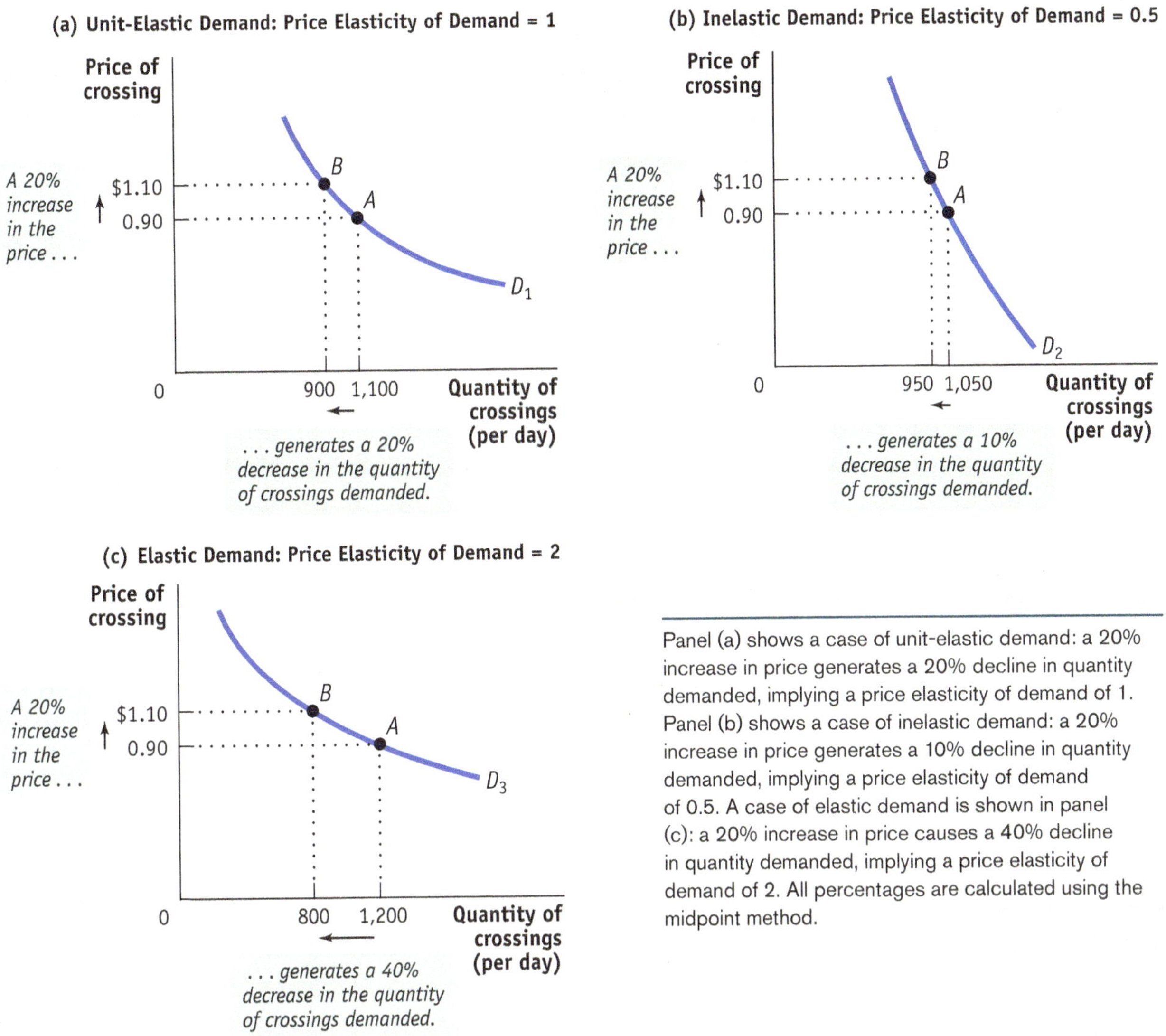

Panel (a) shows a case of unit-elastic demand: a 20% increase in price generates a 20% decline in quantity demanded, implying a price elasticity of demand of 1. Panel (b) shows a case of inelastic demand: a 20% increase in price generates a 10% decline in quantity demanded, implying a price elasticity of demand of 0.5. A case of elastic demand is shown in panel (c): a 20% increase in price causes a 40% decline in quantity demanded, implying a price elasticity of demand of 2. All percentages are calculated using the midpoint method.

Panel (b) shows a case of inelastic demand when the toll is raised from $0.90 to $1.10. The same 20% price rise reduces the quantity demanded from 1,050 to 950. That's only a 10% decline, so in this case the price elasticity of demand is 10%/20% = 0.5.

Panel (c) shows a case of elastic demand when the toll is raised from $0.90 to $1.10. The 20% price increase causes the quantity demanded to fall from 1,200 to 800—a 40% decline, so the price elasticity of demand is 40%/20% = 2.

Why does it matter whether demand is unit-elastic, inelastic, or elastic? Because this classification predicts how changes in the price of a good will affect the *total revenue* earned by producers from the sale of that good. In many real-life situations, it is crucial to know how price changes affect total revenue. **Total revenue** is defined as the total value of sales of a good or service, equal to the price multiplied by the quantity sold.

(12-1) Total revenue = Price × Quantity sold

The **total revenue** is the total value of sales of a good or service. It is equal to the price multiplied by the quantity sold.

Total revenue has a useful graphical representation that can help us understand why knowing the price elasticity of demand is crucial when we ask whether a price rise will increase or reduce total revenue. Panel (a) of Figure 12-3 shows the same demand curve as panel (a) of Figure 12-2. We see that 1,100 drivers will use the bridge if the toll is $0.90. So the total revenue at a price of $0.90 is $\$0.90 \times 1{,}100 = \$990$. This value is equal to the area of the green rectangle, which is drawn with the bottom left corner at the point (0, 0) and the top right corner at (1,100, 0.90). In general, the total revenue at any given price is equal to the area of a rectangle whose height is the price and whose width is the quantity demanded at that price.

To get an idea of why total revenue is important, consider the following scenario. Suppose that the toll on the bridge is currently $0.90 but that the highway department must raise extra money for road repairs. One way to do this is to raise the toll on the bridge. But this plan might backfire, since a higher toll will reduce the number of drivers who use the bridge. And if traffic on the bridge dropped a lot, a higher toll would actually reduce total revenue instead of increasing it. So, it's important for the highway department to know how drivers will respond to a toll increase.

We can see graphically how the toll increase affects total bridge revenue by examining panel (b) of Figure 12-3. At a toll of $0.90, total revenue is given by the sum of the areas *A* and *B*. After the toll is raised to $1.10, total revenue is given by the sum of areas *B* and *C*. So when the toll is raised, revenue represented by area *A* is lost but revenue represented by area *C* is gained.

These two areas have important interpretations. Area *C* represents the revenue gain that comes from the additional $0.20 paid by drivers who continue to use the bridge. That is, the 900 who continue to use the bridge contribute an additional $\$0.20 \times 900 = \$180$ per day to total revenue, represented by area *C*. But 200 drivers who would have used the bridge at a price of $0.90 no longer do so, generating a loss to total revenue of $\$0.90 \times 200 = \$180$ per day, represented by area *A*. (In this particular example, because demand is unit-elastic—the same as in panel (a) of Figure 12-2—the rise in the toll has no effect on total revenue; areas *A* and *C* are the same size.)

FIGURE 12-3 Total Revenue

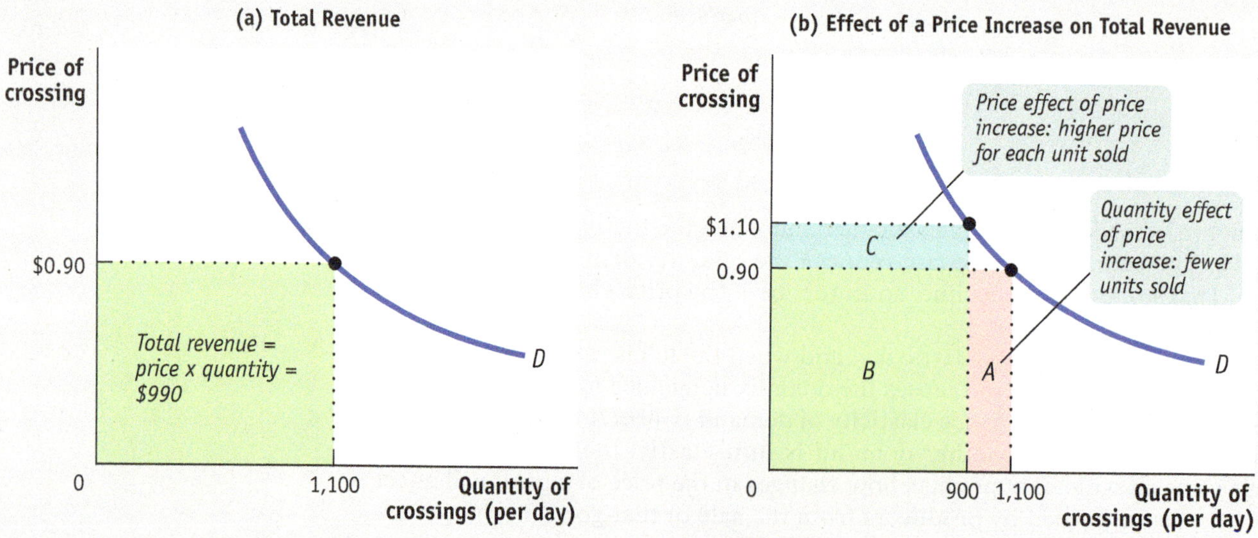

The green rectangle in panel (a) shows the total revenue generated from 1,100 drivers who each pay a toll of $0.90. Panel (b) shows how total revenue is affected when the price increases from $0.90 to $1.10. Due to the quantity effect, total revenue falls by area *A*. Due to the price effect, total revenue increases by the area *C*. In general, the overall effect can go either way, depending on the price elasticity of demand.

Except in the rare case of a good with perfectly elastic or perfectly inelastic demand, when a seller raises the price of a good, two countervailing effects are present:

- *A price effect:* After a price increase, each unit sold sells at a higher price, which tends to raise revenue.
- *A quantity effect:* After a price increase, fewer units are sold, which tends to lower revenue.

But then, you may ask, what is the ultimate net effect on total revenue: does it go up or down? The answer is that, in general, the effect on total revenue can go either way—a price rise may either increase total revenue or lower it. If the price effect, which tends to raise total revenue, is the stronger of the two effects, then total revenue goes up. If the quantity effect, which tends to reduce total revenue, is the stronger, then total revenue goes down. And if the strengths of the two effects are exactly equal—as in our toll bridge example, where a $180 gain offsets a $180 loss—total revenue is unchanged by the price increase.

The price elasticity of demand tells us what happens to total revenue when price changes: its size determines which effect—the price effect or the quantity effect—is stronger. Specifically:

- If demand for a good is *unit-elastic* (the price elasticity of demand is 1), an increase in price does not change total revenue. In this case, the quantity effect and the price effect exactly offset each other.
- If demand for a good is *inelastic* (the price elasticity of demand is less than 1), a higher price increases total revenue. In this case, the quantity effect is weaker than the price effect.
- If demand for a good is *elastic* (the price elasticity of demand is greater than 1), an increase in price reduces total revenue. In this case, the quantity effect is stronger than the price effect.

Scott Barrow/Getty Images

The highway department uses the price elasticity of demand to calculate the change in revenue from higher tolls.

Table 12-1 shows how the effect of a price increase on total revenue depends on the price elasticity of demand, using the same data as in Figure 12-2. An increase in the price from $0.90 to $1.10 leaves total revenue unchanged at $990 when demand is unit-elastic. When demand is inelastic, the quantity effect is dominated by the price effect; the same price increase leads to an increase in total revenue from $945 to $1,045. And when demand is elastic, the quantity effect dominates the price effect; the price increase leads to a decline in total revenue from $1,080 to $880.

The price elasticity of demand also predicts the effect of a *fall* in price on total revenue. When the price falls, the same two countervailing effects are present, but they work in the opposite directions, as compared to the case of a price rise. There is the price effect of a lower price per unit sold, which tends to lower revenue. This is countered by the quantity effect of more units sold, which tends to raise revenue. Which effect dominates depends on the price elasticity. Here is a quick summary:

- When demand is *unit-elastic,* the two effects exactly balance; so a fall in price has no effect on total revenue.
- When demand is *inelastic,* the quantity effect is dominated by the price effect; so a fall in price reduces total revenue.
- When demand is *elastic,* the quantity effect dominates the price effect; so a fall in price increases total revenue.

TABLE 12-1 Price Elasticity of Demand and Total Revenue

	Price of toll = $0.90	Price of toll = $1.10
Unit-elastic demand		
Quantity demanded	1,100	900
Total revenue	$990	$990
Inelastic demand		
Quantity demanded	1,050	950
Total revenue	$945	$1,045
Elastic demand		
Quantity demanded	1,200	800
Total revenue	$1,080	$880

12.2 Price Elasticity Along the Demand Curve

Suppose an economist says that "the price elasticity of demand for coffee is 0.25." What they mean is that *at the current price* the elasticity is 0.25. In the previous discussion of the toll bridge, what we were really describing was the elasticity *at the toll price* of $0.90. Why this qualification? Because for the vast majority of demand curves, the price elasticity of demand at one point along the curve is different from the price elasticity of demand at other points along the same curve.

To see this, consider the table in Figure 12-4, which shows a hypothetical demand schedule. It also shows in the last column the total revenue generated at each price and quantity combination in the demand schedule. The upper panel of the graph in Figure 12-4 shows the corresponding demand curve. The lower panel illustrates the same data on total revenue: the height of a bar at each quantity demanded—which corresponds to a particular price—measures the total revenue generated at that price.

In Figure 12-4, you can see that when the price is low, raising the price increases total revenue: starting at a price of $1, raising the price to $2 increases total revenue from $9 to $16. This means that when the price is low, demand is

FIGURE 12-4 The Price Elasticity of Demand Changes Along the Demand Curve

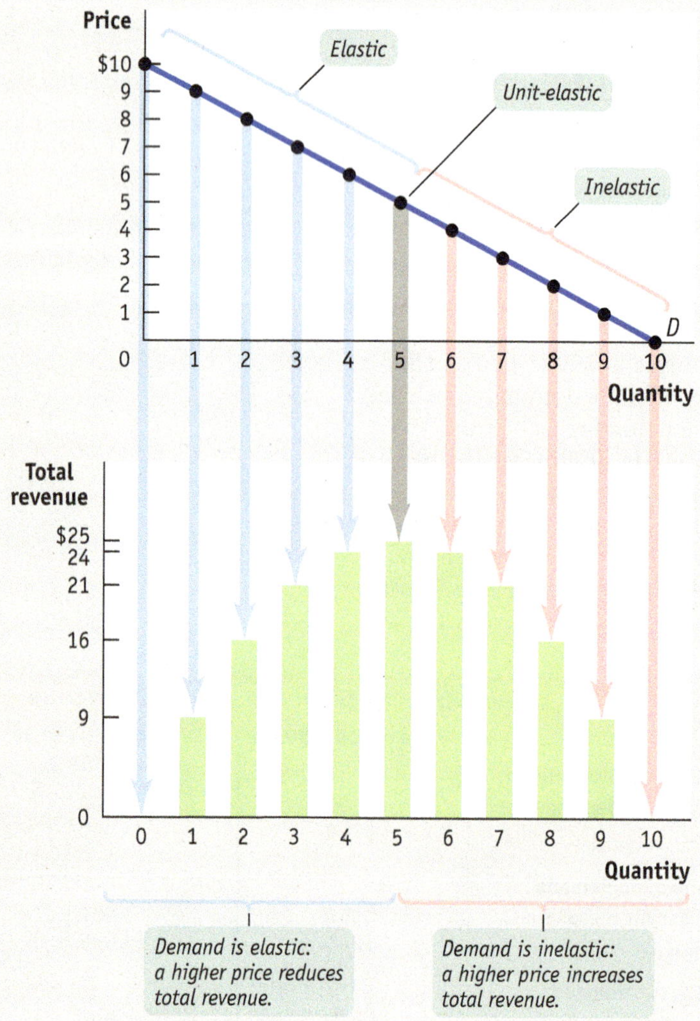

Demand Schedule and Total Revenue for a Linear Demand Curve

Price	Quantity demanded	Total revenue
$0	10	$0
1	9	9
2	8	16
3	7	21
4	6	24
5	5	25
6	4	24
7	3	21
8	2	16
9	1	9
10	0	0

The upper panel of the graph shows a demand curve corresponding to the demand schedule in the table. The lower panel shows how total revenue changes along that demand curve: at each price and quantity combination, the height of the bar represents the total revenue generated. You can see that at a low price, raising the price increases total revenue. So demand is inelastic at low prices. At a high price, however, a rise in price reduces total revenue. Demand is elastic at high prices.

inelastic. Moreover, you can see that demand is inelastic on the entire section of the demand curve from a price of $0 to a price of $5.

When the price is high, however, raising it further reduces total revenue: starting at a price of $8, raising the price to $9 reduces total revenue, from $16 to $9. This means that when the price is high, demand is elastic. Furthermore, you can see that demand is elastic over the section of the demand curve from a price of $5 to $10.

For the vast majority of goods, the price elasticity of demand changes along the demand curve. So whenever you measure a good's elasticity, you are really measuring it at a particular point or section of the good's demand curve.

12.3 What Factors Determine the Price Elasticity of Demand?

Investors in private ambulance companies believe that the price elasticity of demand for an ambulance ride is low for two important reasons. First, in many if not most cases, an ambulance ride is a medical necessity. Second, in an emergency there really is no substitute for the standard of care that an ambulance provides. And even among ambulances there are typically no substitutes because in any given geographical area there is usually only one ambulance provider. The exceptions are very densely populated areas, but even in those locations an ambulance dispatcher is unlikely to give you a choice of ambulance providers with an accompanying price list.

In general there are four main factors that determine elasticity: whether a good is a necessity or luxury, the availability of close substitutes, the share of income a consumer spends on the good, and how much time has elapsed since a change in price. We'll briefly examine each of these factors.

Whether the Good Is a Necessity or a Luxury

As our opening story illustrates, the price elasticity of demand tends to be low if a good is something you must have, like a life-saving ambulance ride to the hospital. The price elasticity of demand tends to be high if the good is a luxury—something you can easily live without. For example, most people would consider a 110-inch ultra-high-definition TV a luxury—nice to have, but something they can live without. Therefore, the price elasticity of demand for it will be much higher than for a life-saving ambulance ride to the hospital.

The Availability of Close Substitutes

As we just noted, the price elasticity of demand tends to be low if there are no close substitutes or if they are very difficult to obtain. In contrast, the price elasticity of demand tends to be high if there are other readily available goods that consumers regard as similar and would be willing to consume instead. For example, most consumers believe that there are fairly close substitutes to their favorite brand of breakfast cereal. As a result, if the maker of a particular brand of breakfast cereal raised the price significantly, that maker is likely to lose much—if not all—of its sales to other brands whose prices have not risen.

Share of Income Spent on the Good

Consider a good that some people consume frequently, such as gasoline—say, for a long commute to and from work every day. For these consumers,

spending on gasoline will typically absorb a significant share of their income. As a result, when the price of gasoline goes up, these consumers are likely to be very responsive to the price change and have a higher elasticity of demand. Why? Because when the good absorbs a significant share of these consumers' income, it is worth their time and effort to find a way to reduce their demand when the price goes up—such as switching to car-pooling instead of driving alone. In contrast, people who consume gasoline infrequently—for example, people who walk to work or take the bus—will have a low share of income spent on gasoline and therefore a lower elasticity of demand.

Time Elapsed Since Price Change

In general, the price elasticity of demand tends to increase as consumers have more time to adjust. This means that the long-run price elasticity of demand is often higher than the short-run elasticity.

A good illustration is the changes in Americans' behavior over the past two decades in response to higher gasoline prices. In 1998, a gallon of gasoline was only about $1. Over the years, however, gasoline prices steadily rose, so that by 2005 a gallon of gas cost over $4.00 in much of the United States. Over time, however, people changed their habits and choices in ways that enabled them to gradually reduce their gasoline consumption. But by 2016, gas prices had fallen to under $3 per gallon, and as expected, consumers responded by increasing gasoline consumption. These changes are reflected in the data on American gasoline consumption: the trend line of consumption fluctuated until about 2003, then took a nosedive. So by 2013, Americans were purchasing less than 350 million gallons of gas daily, less than the nearly 380 million gallons purchased daily in 2007, and far less than 450 million gallons a day, the amount Americans would have purchased if they had followed previous trends of ever-increasing gasoline consumption. This confirms that the long-run price elasticity of demand for gasoline is indeed much larger than the short-run elasticity.

Gas prices dropped dramatically from 2014 to 2017, with the average price down to around $2.25. Not surprisingly, gasoline consumption started to rise again. And by 2016, Americans consumed nearly 400 million gallons of gasoline per day, as consumers slowly switch back to their gas-guzzlers.

Students at two-year schools are more responsive to the price of tuition than students at four-year schools.

ECONOMICS >> *in Action*

Responding to Your Tuition Bill

If it seems like the cost of college keeps going up—it's because it has. It is estimated that over the past 10 years the average annual increase in tuition has exceeded the inflation rate by approximately 5% to 6% every year. An important question for educators and policy makers is whether the rise in tuition deters people from going to college. And if so, by how much?

Several studies have shown that tuition increases lead to consistently negative effects on enrollment numbers, with estimates of the price elasticity of demand ranging from 0.67 to 0.76 for four-year institutions. So a 3% rise in tuition at a four-year institution leads to a fall in enrollment of approximately 2% (3×0.67) to 2.3% (3×0.76). Two-year institutions were found to have a significantly higher response: a 3% increase in tuition leads to a 2.7% fall in enrollment, implying a price elasticity of demand of 0.9. For financial aid students, the price elasticity of demand rises to 1.18, implying that a 3% rise in tuition leads to a 3.54% fall in enrollment.

So the increase in tuition *is* a barrier to college, and it is more of a barrier for students at two-year institutions than four-year institutions. This makes sense in light of evidence suggesting that students at two-year schools are more likely to be paying their own way, so they are spending a higher share of income on tuition compared to students at four-year institutions (who are more likely to be counting on their parents' income).

Students at two-year schools are also more responsive to changes in the unemployment rate. Higher unemployment leads to higher enrollments, indicating that these students are making a trade-off by going to school instead of working and that they consider school a substitute for their time. Both of these factors—the high share of income spent on tuition and viewing school as a substitute for their time—will lead students at two-year colleges to be more responsive to changes in tuition than students at four-year colleges.

An increase in tuition is also more of a barrier for financial aid students than for students paying full tuition. Financial aid students may be more responsive to the full cost of tuition due to fear of losing their grant money or concerns about the cost of paying back their student loans.

Check Your Understanding 12-1

1. For each case, choose the condition that characterizes demand: elastic demand, inelastic demand, or unit-elastic demand.
   a. Total revenue decreases when price increases.
   b. The additional revenue generated by an increase in quantity sold is exactly offset by revenue lost from the fall in price received per unit.
   c. Total revenue falls when output increases.
   d. Producers in an industry find they can increase their total revenues by coordinating a reduction in industry output.
2. What is the elasticity of demand for the following goods? Explain. What is the shape of the demand curve?
   a. Demand for a blood transfusion by an accident victim
   b. Demand by students for green erasers

Solutions appear at back of book.

>> Quick Review

- Demand is **perfectly inelastic** if it is completely unresponsive to price. It is **perfectly elastic** if it is infinitely responsive to price.
- Demand is **elastic** if the price elasticity of demand is greater than 1. It is **inelastic** if the price elasticity of demand is less than 1. It is **unit-elastic** if the price elasticity of demand is exactly 1.
- When demand is elastic, the quantity effect of a price increase dominates the price effect and **total revenue** falls. When demand is inelastic, the quantity effect is dominated by the price effect and total revenue rises.
- Because the price elasticity of demand can change along the demand curve, economists refer to a particular point on the demand curve when speaking of "the" price elasticity of demand.
- Ready availability of close substitutes makes demand for a good more elastic, as does a longer length of time elapsed since the price change. Demand for a necessity is less elastic, and demand for a luxury good is more elastic. Demand tends to be inelastic for goods that absorb a small share of a consumer's income and elastic for goods that absorb a large share of income.

MODULE 13

Other Elasticities

WHAT YOU WILL LEARN

- How is the **cross-price elasticity of demand** related to the responsiveness of demand for one good to changes in the price of another good?
- What is the meaning and importance of the **income elasticity of demand?**
- What is the price elasticity of supply and why is it significant?
- What are the factors that influence the size of these various elasticities?

Msheldrake/Dreamstime.com

© Lauri Patterson/iStockphoto

The quantity of a good demanded depends not only on the price of that good but also on other variables. In particular, demand curves shift because of changes in the prices of related goods and changes in consumers' incomes. It is often important to have a measure of these other effects, and the best measures are—you guessed it—elasticities. Specifically, we can best measure how the demand for a good is affected by prices of other goods by using a measure called the *cross-price elasticity of demand,* and we can best measure how demand is affected by changes in income using the *income elasticity of demand.*

13.1 The Cross-Price Elasticity of Demand

In Section 2 you learned that the demand for a good is often affected by the prices of other, related goods—goods that are substitutes or complements. There you saw that a change in the price of a related good shifts the demand curve of the original good, reflecting a change in the quantity demanded at any given price. The strength of such a "cross" effect on demand can be measured by the **cross-price elasticity of demand,** defined as the ratio of the percent change in the quantity demanded of one good to the percent change in the price of the other. Like the price elasticity of demand, the cross-price elasticity is calculated using the midpoint method.

The **cross-price elasticity of demand** between two goods measures the effect of the change in one good's price on the quantity demanded of the other good. It is equal to the percent change in the quantity demanded of one good divided by the percent change in the other good's price.

(13-1) Cross-price elasticity of demand between goods A and B

$$= \frac{\%\text{ change in quantity of A demanded}}{\%\text{ change in price of B}}$$

When two goods are substitutes, like hot dogs and hamburgers, the cross-price elasticity of demand is positive: a rise in the price of hot dogs increases the demand for hamburgers—that is, it causes a rightward shift of the demand curve for hamburgers. If the goods are close substitutes, the cross-price elasticity will be positive and large; if they are not close substitutes, the cross-price elasticity will be positive and small. Thus, when the cross-price elasticity of demand is positive, its size is a measure of how closely substitutable the two goods are, with a higher number meaning the goods are closer substitutes.

When two goods are complements, like hot dogs and hot dog buns, the cross-price elasticity is negative: a rise in the price of hot dogs decreases the demand for hot dog buns—that is, it causes a leftward shift of the demand curve for hot dog buns. As with substitutes, the size of the cross-price elasticity of demand between two complements tells us how strongly complementary they are: if the cross-price elasticity is only slightly below zero, they are weak complements; if it is very negative, they are strong complements.

Note that in the case of the cross-price elasticity of demand, the sign (plus or minus) is very important: it tells us whether the two goods are complements or substitutes. So we cannot drop the minus sign as we did for the price elasticity of demand.

Our discussion of the cross-price elasticity of demand is a useful place to return to a point we made earlier: elasticity is a *unit-free* measure—that is, it doesn't depend on the units in which goods are measured.

To see how this could be a potential problem, suppose someone told you that "if the price of hot dog buns rises by $0.30, Americans will buy 10 million fewer hot dogs this year." If you've ever bought hot dog buns, you'll immediately wonder: is that a $0.30 increase in the price *per bun,* or is it a $0.30 increase in the price *per package?* Buns are usually sold in packages of eight. It makes a big difference what units we are talking about! However, if someone says that the cross-price elasticity of demand between buns and hot dogs is −0.3, it doesn't matter whether buns are sold individually or by the package. Thus, elasticity is defined as a ratio of percent changes, as a way of making sure that confusion over units doesn't arise.

Check Your Understanding 13-1

1. As the price of margarine rises by 20%, a manufacturer of baked goods increases its quantity of butter demanded by 5%. Calculate the cross-price elasticity of demand between butter and margarine. Are butter and margarine substitutes or complements for this manufacturer?

Solutions appear at back of book.

>> *Quick Review*

- Goods are substitutes when the **cross-price elasticity of demand** is positive. Goods are complements when the cross-price elasticity of demand is negative.

13.2 The Income Elasticity of Demand

The **income elasticity of demand** is a measure of how much the demand for a good is affected by changes in consumers' incomes. It allows us to determine whether a good is a normal or inferior good as well as to measure how intensely the demand for the good responds to changes in income.

$$\text{(13-2) Income elasticity of demand} = \frac{\%\ \text{change in quantity demanded}}{\%\ \text{change in income}}$$

Just as the cross-price elasticity of demand between two goods can be either positive or negative, depending on whether the goods are substitutes or complements, the income elasticity of demand for a good can also be either positive or negative. Recall from Section 2 that goods can be either *normal goods,* for which demand increases when income rises, or *inferior goods,* for which demand decreases when income rises. These definitions relate directly to the sign of the income elasticity of demand:

- When the income elasticity of demand is positive, the good is a normal good. In this case, the quantity demanded at any given price increases as income

The **income elasticity of demand** is the percent change in the quantity of a good demanded when a consumer's income changes divided by the percent change in the consumer's income.

increases. Correspondingly, the quantity demanded at any given price decreases as income falls.

- When the income elasticity of demand is negative, the good is an inferior good. In this case, the quantity demanded at any given price decreases as income increases. Likewise, the quantity demanded at any given price increases as income falls.

Economists often use estimates of the income elasticity of demand to predict which industries will grow most rapidly as the incomes of consumers grow over time. In doing this, they often find it useful to make a further distinction among normal goods, identifying which are *income-elastic* and which are *income-inelastic*.

The demand for a good is **income-elastic** if the income elasticity of demand for that good is greater than 1. When income rises, the demand for income-elastic goods rises *faster* than income. Luxury goods such as second homes and international travel tend to be income-elastic. The demand for a good is **income-inelastic** if the income elasticity of demand for that good is positive but less than 1. When income rises, the demand for income-inelastic goods rises, but more slowly than income. Necessities such as food and clothing tend to be income-inelastic.

>> Quick Review

- Inferior goods have a negative **income elasticity of demand.** Most goods are normal goods, which have a positive income elasticity of demand.
- Normal goods may be either **income-elastic,** with an income elasticity of demand greater than 1, or **income-inelastic,** with an income elasticity of demand that is positive but less than 1.

Check Your Understanding 13-2

1. After Chelsea's income increased from $12,000 to 18,000 a year, her purchases of album downloads increased from 10 to 40 downloads a year. Calculate Chelsea's income elasticity of demand for albums using the midpoint method.
2. Expensive restaurant meals are income-elastic goods for most people, including Sanjay. Suppose his income falls by 10% this year. What can you predict about the change in Sanjay's consumption of expensive restaurant meals?

Solutions appear at back of book.

13.3 The Price Elasticity of Supply

A fundamental characteristic of any market for ambulance services, no matter where it is located, is limited supply. For example, it would have been much harder to charge Kira Millas $1,772.42 for a 15-minute ride to the hospital if there had been many ambulance providers cruising nearby and offering a lower price. But there are good economic reasons why there are not: Who among those experiencing a true health emergency would trust their health and safety to a low-price ambulance? And who would want to be a supplier, paying the expense of providing quality ambulance services, without being able to charge high prices to recoup costs? Not surprisingly, then, in most locations there is only one ambulance provider available.

In sum, a critical element in the ability of ambulance providers to charge high prices is limited supply: a low responsiveness in the quantity of output supplied to the higher prices charged for an ambulance ride. To measure the response of ambulance providers to price changes, we need a measure parallel to the price elasticity of demand—the *price elasticity of supply,* as we'll see next.

The demand for a good is **income-elastic** if the income elasticity of demand for that good is greater than 1.

The demand for a good is **income-inelastic** if the income elasticity of demand for that good is positive but less than 1.

The **price elasticity of supply** is a measure of the responsiveness of the quantity of a good supplied to the price of that good. It is the ratio of the percent change in the quantity supplied to the percent change in the price as we move along the supply curve.

Measuring the Price Elasticity of Supply

The **price elasticity of supply** is defined the same way as the price elasticity of demand, although since it is always positive there is no minus sign to be eliminated:

$$\text{(13-3)}\quad \text{Price elasticity of supply} = \frac{\%\text{ change in quantity supplied}}{\%\text{ change in price}}$$

It is also calculated using the midpoint method. The only difference is that now we consider movements along the supply curve rather than movements along the demand curve.

Suppose that the price of tomatoes rises by 10%. If the quantity of tomatoes supplied also increases by 10% in response, the price elasticity of supply of tomatoes is 1 (10%/10%) and supply is unit-elastic. If the quantity supplied increases by 5%, the price elasticity of supply is 0.5 and supply is inelastic; if the quantity increases by 20%, the price elasticity of supply is 2 and supply is elastic.

As in the case of demand, the extreme values of the price elasticity of supply have a simple graphical representation. Panel (a) of Figure 13-1 shows the supply of cell phone frequencies, the portion of the radio spectrum that is suitable for sending and receiving cell phone signals. Governments own the right to sell the use of this part of the radio spectrum to cell phone operators inside their borders. But governments can't increase or decrease the number of cell phone frequencies that they have to offer—for technical reasons, the quantity of frequencies suitable for cell phone operation is a fixed quantity.

So the supply curve for cell phone frequencies is a vertical line, which we have assumed is set at the quantity of 100 frequencies. As you move up and down that curve, the change in the quantity supplied by the government is zero, whatever the change in price. So panel (a) illustrates a case in which the price elasticity of supply is zero. This is a case of **perfectly inelastic supply.**

Panel (b) shows the supply curve for pizza. We suppose that it costs $12 to produce a pizza, including all opportunity costs. At any price below $12, it would be unprofitable to produce pizza and all the pizza parlors in America would go out of business. Alternatively, there are many producers who could operate pizza parlors if they were profitable. The ingredients—flour, tomatoes, and cheese—are plentiful. And if necessary, more tomatoes could be grown, more milk could be produced to make mozzarella, and so on. So any price above $12 would elicit an extremely large quantity of pizzas supplied. The implied supply curve is therefore a horizontal line at $12.

Since even a tiny increase in the price would lead to a huge increase in the quantity supplied, the price elasticity of supply would be more or less infinite. This is a case of **perfectly elastic supply.**

There is **perfectly inelastic supply** when the price elasticity of supply is zero, so that changes in the price of the good have no effect on the quantity supplied. A perfectly inelastic supply curve is a vertical line.

There is **perfectly elastic supply** when even a tiny increase or reduction in the price will lead to very large changes in the quantity supplied, so that the price elasticity of supply is infinite. A perfectly elastic supply curve is a horizontal line.

FIGURE 13-1 Two Extreme Cases of Price Elasticity of Supply

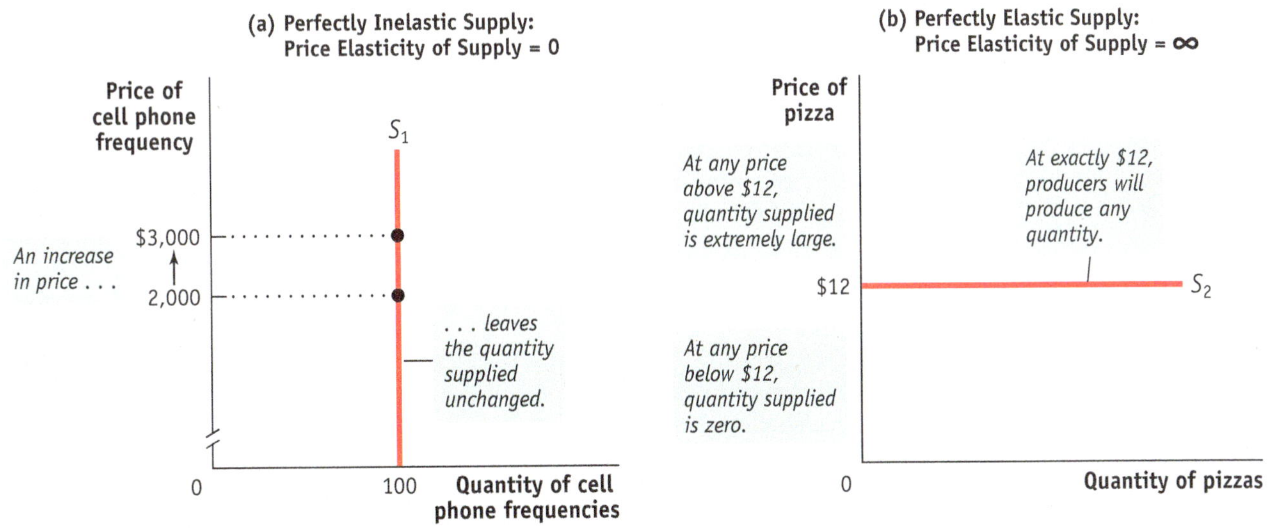

Panel (a) shows a perfectly inelastic supply curve, which is a vertical line. The price elasticity of supply is zero: the quantity supplied is always the same, regardless of price. Panel (b) shows a perfectly elastic supply curve, which is a horizontal line. At a price of $12, producers will supply any quantity, but they will supply none at a price below $12. If price rises above $12, they will supply an extremely large quantity.

As our cell phone frequencies and pizza examples suggest, real-world instances of both perfectly inelastic and perfectly elastic supply are easy to find—much easier than their counterparts in demand.

What Factors Determine the Price Elasticity of Supply?

Our examples tell us the main determinant of the price elasticity of supply: the availability of inputs. In addition, as with the price elasticity of demand, time may also play a role in the price elasticity of supply. Here we briefly summarize the two factors.

The Availability of Inputs The price elasticity of supply tends to be large when inputs are readily available and can be shifted into and out of production at a relatively low cost. It tends to be small when inputs are difficult to obtain—and can be shifted into and out of production only at a relatively high cost. In the case of ambulance services, the high cost of providing quality ambulance services is the crucial element in keeping the elasticity of supply very low.

Time The price elasticity of supply tends to grow larger as producers have more time to respond to a price change. This means that the long-run price elasticity of supply is often higher than the short-run elasticity.

The price elasticity of the supply of pizza is very high because the inputs needed to expand the industry are readily available. The price elasticity of cell phone frequencies is zero because an essential input—the radio spectrum—cannot be increased at all.

Many industries are like pizza production and have large price elasticities of supply: they can be readily expanded because they don't require any special or unique resources. In contrast, the price elasticity of supply is usually substantially less than perfectly elastic for goods that involve limited natural resources: minerals like gold or copper, agricultural products like coffee that flourish only on certain types of land, and renewable resources like ocean fish that can only be exploited up to a point without destroying the resource.

But given enough time, producers are often able to significantly change the amount they produce in response to a price change, even when production involves a limited natural resource or a very costly input. Agricultural markets provide a good example. When American farmers receive much higher prices for a given commodity, like wheat (because of a drought in a big wheat-producing country like Australia), in the next planting season they are likely to switch their acreage planted in other crops to wheat.

For this reason, economists often make a distinction between the short-run elasticity of supply, usually referring to a few weeks or months, and the long-run elasticity of supply, usually referring to several years. In most industries, the long-run elasticity of supply is larger than the short-run elasticity.

An Elasticity Menagerie

We've just run through quite a few different elasticities. Keeping them all straight can be a challenge, so in Table 13-1 we provide a summary of all the elasticities we have discussed and their implications.

TABLE 13-1 An Elasticity Menagerie

Price elasticity of demand $= \dfrac{\text{\% change in quantity demanded}}{\text{\% change in price}}$ **(dropping the minus sign)**	
0	**Perfectly inelastic:** price has no effect on quantity demanded (vertical demand curve).
Between 0 and 1	**Inelastic:** a rise in price increases total revenue.
Exactly 1	**Unit-elastic:** changes in price have no effect on total revenue.
Greater than 1, less than ∞	**Elastic:** a rise in price reduces total revenue.
∞	**Perfectly elastic:** any rise in price causes quantity demanded to fall to 0. Any fall in price leads to an infinite quantity demanded (horizontal demand curve).
Cross-price elasticity of demand $= \dfrac{\text{\% change in quantity demanded of } \textit{one good}}{\text{\% change in price of } \textit{another good}}$	
Negative	**Complements:** quantity demanded of one good falls when the price of another rises.
Positive	**Substitutes:** quantity demanded of one good rises when the price of another rises.
Income elasticity of demand $= \dfrac{\text{\% change in quantity demanded}}{\text{\% change in income}}$	
Negative	**Inferior good:** quantity demanded falls when income rises.
Positive, less than 1	**Normal good, income-inelastic:** quantity demanded rises when income rises, but not as rapidly as income.
Greater than 1	**Normal good, income-elastic:** quantity demanded rises when income rises, and more rapidly than income.
Price elasticity of supply $= \dfrac{\text{\% change in quantity supplied}}{\text{\% change in price}}$	
0	**Perfectly inelastic:** price has no effect on quantity supplied (vertical supply curve).
Greater than 0, less than ∞	Ordinary upward-sloping supply curve.
∞	**Perfectly elastic:** any fall in price causes quantity supplied to fall to 0. Any rise in price elicits an infinite quantity supplied (horizontal supply curve).

ECONOMICS >> *in Action*

China and the Global Commodities Glut of 2016

Over the past decade, the rapidly growing Chinese economy has been a voracious consumer of commodities—metals, foodstuffs, and fuel—as its economy rapidly expanded to become a global manufacturing powerhouse. As China's demand for commodities to support its transformation soared, the countries providing those commodities also saw their incomes soar.

However, in 2016, it all came to a screeching halt as the Chinese economy faltered. Global commodity producers saw the demand for their goods fall dramatically, just as many of them were investing in costly projects to increase supplies. For example, Chile, the world's major copper producer, had undertaken a massive expansion of its copper mines, digging up 1.7 billion tons of material as copper prices plummeted around the world. India was building railroad lines to connect its underused coal mines to the export market just as a worldwide glut of coal opened up. And Australia was planning to increase its natural gas production by 150% just as natural gas companies around the world went bankrupt due to shrinking fuel demand and plunging prices.

Because these countries had invested many billions of dollars into increasing their supply capacity over several years, they could not simply shut down production. It continued, making the existing glut of commodities even worse.

What the commodity producers appeared to have forgotten is the logic of the price elasticity of supply: combine persistently high prices with the easy availability of inputs to increase supply capacity (in this case, the chief input was financial capital), and the predictable result is a big increase in the supply of commodities (a rightward shift of the supply curve).

Also predictable is that once the growth in demand for the commodities slowed down, a steep fall in prices would result. As Michael Levi, a commodities expert at the Council of Foreign Relations said, "Producers ended up being their own worst enemies. No one ever worried they would produce too much, but that is exactly what has happened and gotten them into this mess."

>> *Quick Review*

- The **price elasticity of supply** is the percent change in the quantity supplied divided by the percent change in the price.
- Under **perfectly inelastic supply,** the quantity supplied is completely unresponsive to price and the supply curve is a vertical line. Under **perfectly elastic supply,** the supply curve is horizontal at some specific price. If the price falls below that level, the quantity supplied is zero. If the price rises above that level, the quantity supplied is extremely large.
- The price elasticity of supply depends on the availability of inputs, the ease of shifting inputs into and out of alternative uses, and the period of time that has elapsed since the price change.

Check Your Understanding 13-3

1. Using the midpoint method, calculate the price elasticity of supply for web-design services when the price per hour rises from $100 to $150 and the number of hours transacted increases from 300,000 to 500,000. Is supply elastic, inelastic, or unit-elastic?
2. Are each of the following statements true or false? Explain.
   a. If the demand for milk rose, then, in the long run, milk-drinkers would be better off if supply were elastic rather than inelastic.
   b. Long-run price elasticities of supply are generally larger than short-run price elasticities of supply. As a result, the short-run supply curves are generally flatter than the long-run supply curves.
   c. When supply is perfectly elastic, changes in demand have no effect on price.

Solutions appear at back of book.

MODULE 14

The Benefits and Costs of Taxation

WHAT YOU WILL LEARN

- How do taxes affect supply and demand?
- What factors determine who bears the burden of a tax?
- What are the costs and benefits of a tax, and why is the cost greater than the tax revenue generated?

Taxes are necessary: all governments need money to function. Without taxes, governments could not provide the services we want, from national defense to public parks. But taxes have a cost that normally exceeds the money actually paid to the government. That's because taxes distort incentives to engage in mutually beneficial transactions.

In this module, we will look at how taxes affect supply and demand and how they reduce total surplus, creating an inefficiency in the form of deadweight loss.

14.1 The Economics of Taxes: A Preliminary View

To understand the economics of taxes, it's helpful to look at a simple type of tax known as an **excise tax**—a tax charged on each unit of a good or service that is sold. Most tax revenue in the United States comes from other kinds of taxes, which we'll describe later in the module. But excise taxes are common. For example, there are excise taxes on gasoline, cigarettes, and foreign-made trucks, and many local governments impose excise taxes on services such as hotel room rentals. The lessons we'll learn from studying excise taxes apply to other, more complex taxes as well.

The Effect of an Excise Tax on Quantities and Prices

Suppose that the supply and demand for hotel rooms in the city of Potterville are as shown in Figure 14-1. We'll make the simplifying assumption that all hotel rooms are the same. In the absence of taxes, the equilibrium price of a room is \$80 per night and the equilibrium quantity of hotel rooms rented is 10,000 per night.

An **excise tax** is a tax on sales of a good or service.

FIGURE 14-1 The Supply and Demand for Hotel Rooms in Potterville

In the absence of taxes, the equilibrium price of hotel rooms is \$80 a night, and the equilibrium number of rooms rented is 10,000 per night, as shown by point *E*. The supply curve, *S*, shows the quantity supplied at any given price pre-tax. At a price of \$60 a night, hotel owners are willing to supply 5,000 rooms, shown by point *B*. But post-tax, hotel owners are willing to supply the same quantity only at a price of \$100: \$60 for themselves plus \$40 paid to the city as a tax. This is shown by point *A*.

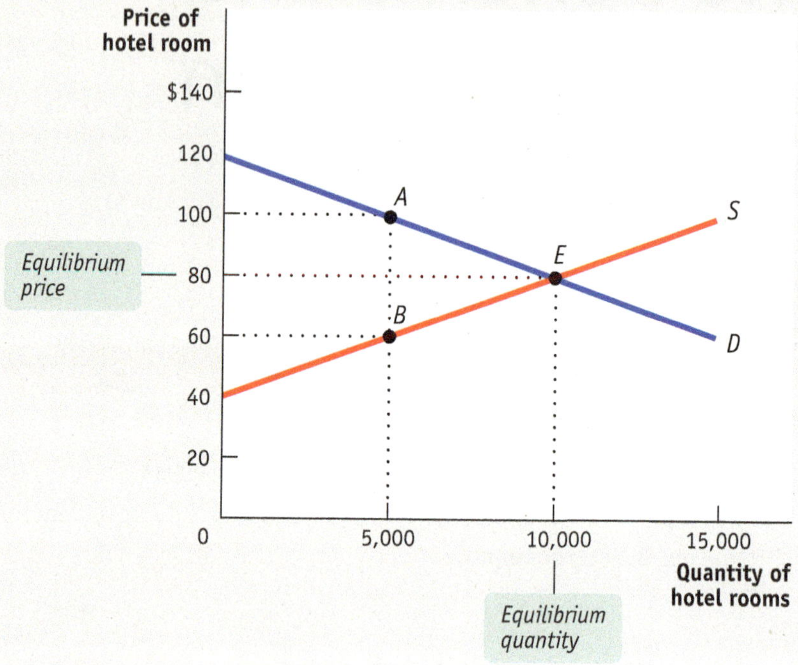

Now suppose that Potterville's government imposes an excise tax of \$40 per night on hotel rooms—that is, every time a room is rented for the night, the owner of the hotel must pay the city \$40. For example, if a customer pays \$80, \$40 is collected as a tax, leaving the hotel owner with only \$40. As a result, hotel owners are less willing to supply rooms at any given price.

What does this imply about the supply curve for hotel rooms in Potterville? To answer this question, we must compare the incentives of hotel owners *pre*-tax (before the tax is levied) to their incentives *post*-tax (after the tax is levied).

From Figure 14-1 we know that pre-tax, hotel owners are willing to supply 5,000 rooms per night at a price of \$60 per room. But after the \$40 tax per room is levied, they are willing to supply the same amount, 5,000 rooms, only if they receive \$100 per room—\$60 for themselves plus \$40 paid to the city as tax. This is shown by point *A*. In other words, for hotel owners to be willing to supply the same quantity post-tax as they would have pre-tax, they must receive an additional \$40 per room, the amount of the tax.

This implies that the post-tax supply curve shifts up, decreasing, by the amount of the tax compared to the pre-tax supply curve. At every quantity supplied, the supply price—the price that producers must receive to produce a given quantity—has increased by \$40.

The upward shift of the supply curve caused by the tax is shown in Figure 14-2, where S_1 is the pre-tax supply curve and S_2 is the post-tax supply curve. As you can see, as a result of the tax the market equilibrium moves from *E*, at the equilibrium price of \$80 per room and 10,000 rooms rented each night, to *A*, at a market price of \$100 per room and only 5,000 rooms rented each night. *A* is, of course, on both the demand curve *D* and the new supply curve S_2.

Although \$100 is the demand price of 5,000 rooms, hotel owners receive only \$60 of that price because they must pay \$40 of it in tax. From the point of view of hotel owners, it is as if they were on their original supply curve at point *B*.

Let's check this again. How do we know that 5,000 rooms will be supplied at a price of \$100? Because the price net of tax is \$60, and according to the original

FIGURE 14-2 An Excise Tax Imposed on Hotel Owners

A $40 per room tax imposed on hotel owners shifts the supply curve from S_1 to S_2, an upward shift of $40. The equilibrium price of hotel rooms rises from $80 to $100 per night, and the equilibrium quantity of rooms rented falls from 10,000 to 5,000. Although hotel owners pay the tax, they actually bear only half the burden: the price they receive net of tax falls only $20, from $80 to $60. Guests who rent rooms bear the other half of the burden, because the price they pay rises $20, from $80 to $100.

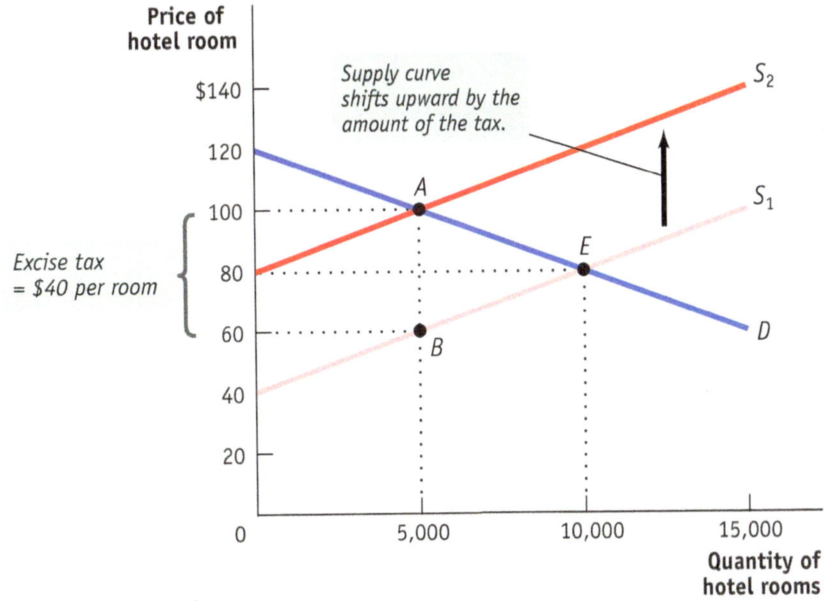

supply curve, 5,000 rooms will be supplied at a price of $60, as shown by point *B* in Figure 14-2.

An excise tax *drives a wedge* between the price paid by consumers and the price received by producers. As a result of this wedge, consumers pay more and producers receive less.

In our example, consumers—people who rent hotel rooms—end up paying $100 a night, $20 more than the pre-tax price of $80. At the same time, producers—the hotel owners—receive a price net of tax of $60 per room, $20 less than the pre-tax price. In addition, the tax creates missed opportunities: 5,000 potential consumers who would have rented hotel rooms—those willing to pay $80 but not $100 per night—are discouraged from doing so. Correspondingly, 5,000 rooms that would have been made available by hotel owners when they receive $80 are not offered when they receive only $60. This tax leads to inefficiency by distorting incentives and creating missed opportunities for mutually beneficial transactions.

It's important to recognize that as we've described it, Potterville's hotel tax is a tax on the hotel owners, not their guests—it's a tax on the producers, not the consumers. Yet the price received by producers, net of tax, falls by only $20, half the amount of the tax, and the price paid by consumers rises by $20. In effect, half the tax is being paid by consumers.

What would happen if the city levied a tax on consumers instead of producers? That is, suppose that instead of requiring hotel owners to pay $40 a night for each room they rent, the city required hotel *guests* to pay $40 for each night they stayed in a hotel. The answer is shown in Figure 14-3. If a hotel guest must pay a tax of $40 per night, then the price for a room paid by that guest must be reduced by $40 for the quantity of hotel rooms demanded post-tax to be the same as that demanded pre-tax. Thus the demand curve shifts *downward,* from D_1 to D_2, by the amount of the tax.

At every quantity demanded, the demand price—the price that consumers must be offered to demand a given quantity—has fallen by $40. This shifts the equilibrium from *E* to *B,* where the market price of hotel rooms is $60 and 5,000 hotel rooms are bought and sold. In effect, hotel guests pay $100 when the tax is

FIGURE 14-3 An Excise Tax Imposed on Hotel Guests

A $40 per room tax imposed on hotel guests shifts the demand curve from D_1 to D_2, a downward shift of $40. The equilibrium price of hotel rooms falls from $80 to $60 per night, and the quantity of rooms rented falls from 10,000 to 5,000. Although in this case the tax is officially paid by consumers, while in Figure 14-2 the tax was paid by producers, the outcome is the same: after taxes, hotel owners receive $60 per room but guests pay $100. This illustrates a general principle: *The incidence of an excise tax doesn't depend on whether consumers or producers officially pay the tax.*

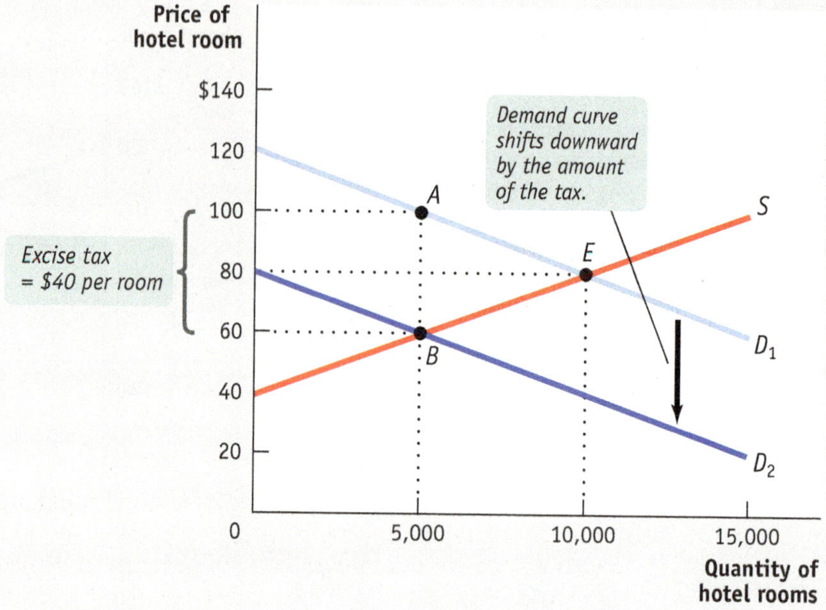

included. So, from the point of view of guests, it is as if they were on their original demand curve at point *A*.

If you compare Figures 14-2 and 14-3, you will immediately notice that they show equivalent outcomes. In both cases consumers pay $100, producers receive $60, and 5,000 hotel rooms are bought and sold. *In fact, it doesn't matter who officially pays the tax—the outcome is the same.*

This insight illustrates a general principle of the economics of taxation: the **incidence** of a tax—who really bears the burden of the tax—is typically not a question you can answer by asking who writes the check to the government. In this particular case, a $40 tax on hotel rooms is reflected in a $20 increase in the price paid by consumers and a $20 decrease in the price received by producers. Here, regardless of whether the tax is levied on consumers or producers, the incidence of the tax is evenly split between them.

Price Elasticities and Tax Incidence

We've just learned that the incidence of an excise tax doesn't depend on who officially pays it. In the example shown in Figures 14-1 through 14-3, a tax on hotel rooms falls equally on consumers and producers, no matter who the tax is levied on.

But it's important to note that this 50–50 split between consumers and producers is a result of our assumptions in this example. In the real world, the incidence of an excise tax usually falls unevenly between consumers and producers, as one group bears more of the burden than the other.

What determines how the burden of an excise tax is allocated between consumers and producers? The answer is that it depends on the shapes of the supply and the demand curves. *More specifically, the incidence of an excise tax depends on the price elasticity of supply and the price elasticity of demand.* We first look at a case in which consumers pay most of an excise tax, then at a case in which producers pay most of the tax.

The **incidence** of a tax is a measure of who really pays it.

When an Excise Tax Is Paid Mainly by Consumers Figure 14-4 shows an excise tax that falls mainly on consumers: an excise tax on gasoline, which we set at $1 per gallon. (There really is a federal excise tax on gasoline, although it is actually only about $0.18 per gallon in the United States. In addition, states impose excise taxes between $0.12 and $0.50 per gallon.) According to Figure 14-4, in the absence of the tax, gasoline would sell for $2 per gallon.

Two key assumptions are reflected in the shapes of the supply and demand curves in Figure 14-4.

1. The price elasticity of demand for gasoline is assumed to be very low, so the demand curve is relatively steep. Recall that a low price elasticity of demand means that the quantity demanded changes little in response to a change in price—a feature of a steep demand curve.
2. The price elasticity of supply of gasoline is assumed to be very high, so the supply curve is relatively flat. A high price elasticity of supply means that the quantity supplied changes a lot in response to a change in price—a feature of a relatively flat supply curve.

We have learned that an excise tax drives a wedge, equal to the size of the tax, between the price paid by consumers and the price received by producers. This wedge drives the price paid by consumers up and the price received by producers down. But as we can see from Figure 14-4, in this case those two effects are very unequal in size. The price received by producers falls only slightly, from $2.00 to $1.95, but the price paid by consumers rises by a lot, from $2.00 to $2.95. In this case consumers bear the greater share of the tax burden.

This example illustrates another general principle of taxation: *When the price elasticity of demand is low and the price elasticity of supply is high, the burden of an excise tax falls mainly on consumers.* Why? A low price elasticity of demand means that consumers have few substitutes, and therefore little alternative to buying higher-priced gasoline. In contrast, a high price elasticity of supply results from the fact that producers have many production substitutes for their gasoline (that is, other uses for the crude oil from which gasoline is refined).

This gives producers much greater flexibility in refusing to accept lower prices for their gasoline. And, not surprisingly, the party with the least flexibility—in this case, consumers—gets stuck paying most of the tax. This is a good description of how the burden of the most significant excise taxes actually collected in the

FIGURE 14-4 An Excise Tax Paid Mainly by Consumers

The relatively steep demand curve here reflects a low price elasticity of demand for gasoline. The relatively flat supply curve reflects a high price of elasticity of supply. The pre-tax price per gallon of gasoline is $2.00. When a tax of $1.00 per gallon is imposed, the price paid by consumers rises by $0.95 to $2.95. This reflects the fact that most of the burden of the tax falls on consumers. Only a small portion of the tax is borne by producers: the price they receive falls by only $0.05 to $1.95.

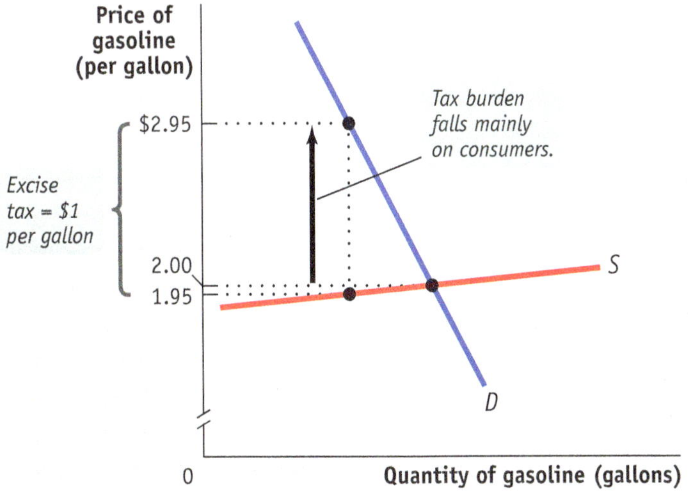

FIGURE 14-5 An Excise Tax Paid Mainly by Producers

The relatively flat demand curve here reflects a high price elasticity of demand for downtown parking, and the relatively steep supply curve results from a low price elasticity of supply. The pre-tax price of a daily parking space is $6.00 and a tax of $5.00 is imposed. The price received by producers falls a lot, to $1.50, reflecting the fact that they bear most of the tax burden. The price paid by consumers rises a small amount, $0.50 to $6.50, so they bear very little of the burden.

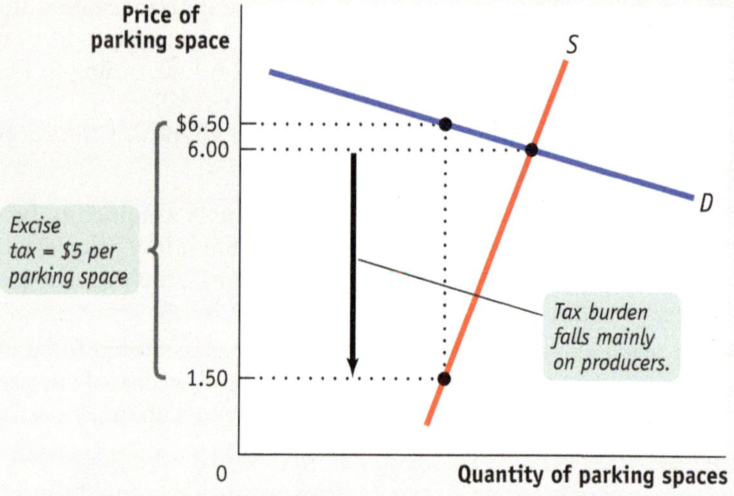

United States today, such as those on cigarettes and alcoholic beverages, is allocated between consumers and producers.

When an Excise Tax Is Paid Mainly by Producers Figure 14-5 shows an example of an excise tax paid mainly by producers, a $5.00 per day tax on downtown parking in a small city. In the absence of the tax, the market equilibrium price of parking is $6.00 per day.

We've assumed in this case that the price elasticity of supply is very low because the lots used for parking have very few alternative uses. This makes the supply curve for parking spaces relatively steep. The price elasticity of demand, however, is assumed to be high: substitutes are readily available as consumers can easily switch from the downtown spaces to other parking spaces a few minutes' walk from downtown, spaces that are not subject to the tax. This makes the demand curve relatively flat.

The tax drives a wedge between the price paid by consumers and the price received by producers. In this example, however, the tax causes the price paid by consumers to rise only slightly, from $6.00 to $6.50, but causes the price received by producers to fall a lot, from $6.00 to $1.50. In the end, consumers bear only $0.50 of the $5.00 tax burden, with producers bearing the remaining $4.50.

Again, this example illustrates a general principle: *When the price elasticity of demand is high and the price elasticity of supply is low, the burden of an excise tax falls mainly on producers.* A real-world example is a tax on purchases of existing houses. Before the collapse of the housing market that began in 2007, house prices in many American cities and towns rose significantly, as well-off outsiders moved into desirable locations and purchased homes from the less-well-off original occupants.

Some of these towns have imposed taxes on house sales intended to extract money from the new arrivals. But this ignores the fact that the price elasticity of demand for houses in a particular town is often high, because potential buyers can choose to move to other towns. Furthermore, the price elasticity of supply is often low because most sellers must sell their houses due to job transfers or to provide funds for their retirement. So taxes on home purchases are actually paid mainly by the less-well-off sellers—not, as town officials imagine, by wealthy buyers.

Putting It All Together We've just seen that when the price elasticity of supply is high and the price elasticity of demand is low, an excise tax falls mainly on consumers. And when the price elasticity of supply is low and the price elasticity of demand is high, an excise tax falls mainly on producers. This leads us to the general rule: *When the price elasticity of demand is higher than the price elasticity of supply, an excise tax falls mainly on producers. When the price elasticity of supply is higher than the price elasticity of demand, an excise tax falls mainly on consumers.*

So elasticity—not who officially pays the tax—determines the incidence of an excise tax.

Check Your Understanding 14-1

1. Consider the market for butter, shown in the accompanying figure. The government imposes an excise tax of $0.30 per pound of butter. What is the price paid by consumers post-tax? What is the price received by producers post-tax? What is the quantity of butter transacted? How is the incidence of the tax allocated between consumers and producers? Show this on the figure.

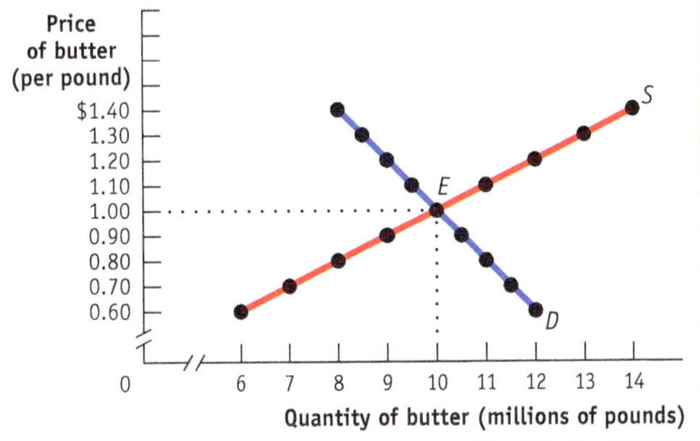

2. The demand for economics textbooks is very inelastic, but the supply is somewhat elastic. What does this imply about the incidence of an excise tax? Illustrate with a diagram.
3. True or false? When a substitute for a good is readily available to consumers, but it is difficult for producers to adjust the quantity of the good produced, then the burden of a tax on the good falls more heavily on producers. Explain your answer.
4. The supply of bottled spring water is very inelastic, but the demand for it is somewhat elastic. What does this imply about the incidence of a tax? Illustrate with a diagram.
5. True or false? Other things equal, consumers would prefer to face a less elastic supply curve for a good or service when an excise tax is imposed. Explain your answer.

Solutions appear at back of book.

>> Quick Review

- An **excise tax** drives a wedge between the price paid by consumers and that received by producers, leading to a fall in the quantity transacted. It creates inefficiency by distorting incentives and creating missed opportunities.
- The **incidence** of an excise tax doesn't depend on who the tax is officially levied on. Rather, it depends on the price elasticities of demand and of supply.
- The higher the price elasticity of supply and the lower the price elasticity of demand, the heavier the burden of an excise tax on consumers. The lower the price elasticity of supply and the higher the price elasticity of demand, the heavier the burden on producers.

14.2 The Benefits and Costs of Taxation

When a government is considering whether to impose a tax or how to design a tax system, it has to weigh the benefits of a tax against its costs. We don't usually think of a tax as something that provides benefits, but governments need money to provide things people want, such as national defense and health care for those unable to afford it. The benefit of a tax is the revenue it raises for the government to pay for these services. Unfortunately, this benefit comes at a cost—a cost that is normally greater than the amount consumers and producers pay. Let's look first at what determines how much money a tax raises, then at the costs a tax imposes.

The Revenue from an Excise Tax

How much revenue does the government collect from an excise tax? In our hotel tax example, the revenue is equal to the area of the shaded rectangle in Figure 14-6.

"What taxes would you like to see imposed on other people?"

To see why this area represents the revenue collected by a $40 tax on hotel rooms, notice that the height of the rectangle is $40, equal to the tax per room. It is also, as we've seen, the size of the wedge that the tax drives between the supply price (the price received by producers) and the demand price (the price paid by consumers). Meanwhile, the width of the rectangle is 5,000 rooms, equal to the equilibrium quantity of rooms given the $40 tax. With that information, we can make the following calculations.

The tax revenue collected is:

$$\text{Tax revenue} = \$40 \text{ per room} \times 5{,}000 \text{ rooms} = \$200{,}000$$

The area of the shaded rectangle is:

$$\text{Area} = \text{Height} \times \text{width} = \$40 \text{ per room} \times 5{,}000 \text{ rooms} = \$200{,}000$$

or

$$\text{Tax revenue} = \text{Area of shaded rectangle}$$

This is a general principle: *The revenue collected by an excise tax is equal to the area of the rectangle whose height is the tax wedge between the supply and demand curves and whose width is the quantity transacted under the tax.*

Tax Rates and Revenue

A **tax rate** is the amount of tax people are required to pay per unit of whatever is being taxed.

In Figure 14-6, $40 per room is the *tax rate* on hotel rooms. A **tax rate** is the amount of tax levied per unit of the taxed item. Sometimes tax rates are defined in terms of dollar amounts per unit of a good or service: for example, $2.46 per pack of cigarettes sold. In other cases, they are defined as a percentage of the price: for example, the payroll tax is 15.3% of a worker's earnings up to $127,200 in 2017.

There's obviously a relationship between tax rates and revenue. That relationship is not, however, one-for-one. In general, doubling the excise tax rate on a good or service won't double the amount of revenue collected, because the tax increase will reduce the quantity of the good or service transacted. And the relationship between the level of the tax and the amount of revenue collected may not even be positive: in some cases raising the tax rate actually *reduces* the amount of revenue the government collects.

FIGURE 14-6 The Revenue from an Excise Tax

The revenue from a $40 excise tax on hotel rooms is $200,000, equal to the tax rate, $40—the size of the wedge that the tax drives between the supply price and the demand price—multiplied by the number of rooms rented, 5,000. This is equal to the area of the shaded rectangle.

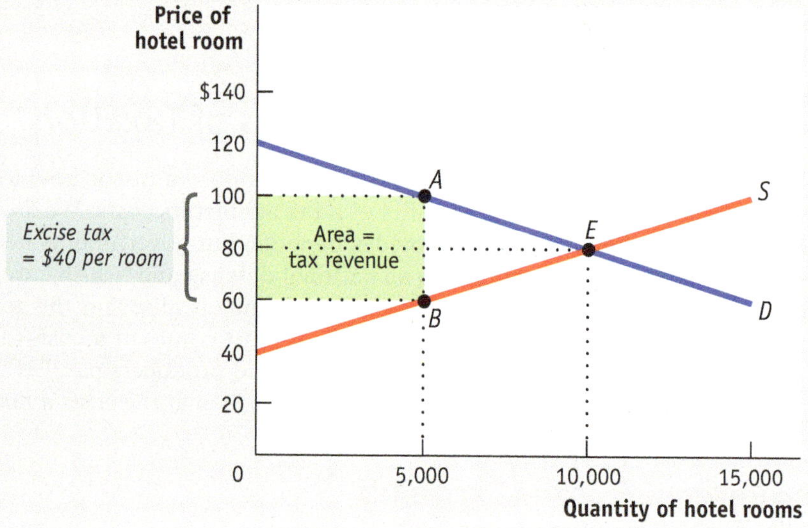

FIGURE 14-7 Tax Rates and Revenue

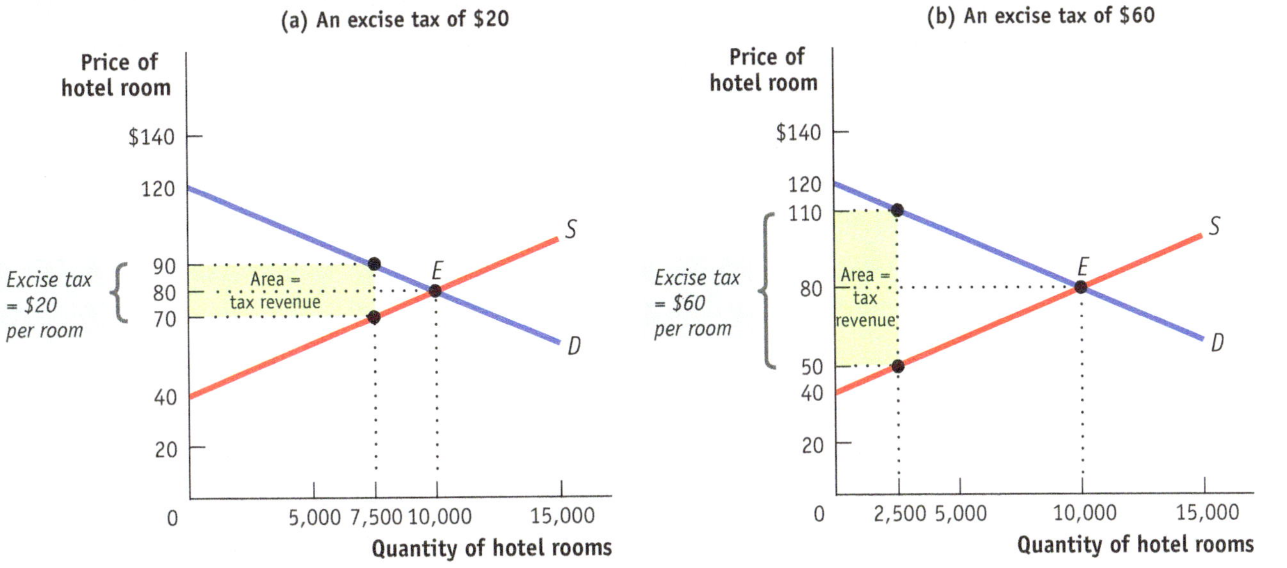

In general, doubling the excise tax rate on a good or service won't double the amount of revenue collected, because the tax increase will reduce the quantity of the good or service bought and sold. And the relationship between the level of the tax and the amount of revenue collected may not even be positive. Panel (a) shows the revenue raised by a tax of $20 per room, only half the tax rate in Figure 14-6. The tax revenue raised, equal to the area of the shaded rectangle, is $150,000. That is 75% of $200,000, the revenue raised by a $40 tax rate. Panel (b) shows that the revenue raised by a $60 tax is also $150,000. So raising the tax rate from $40 to $60 actually reduces tax revenue.

We can illustrate these points using our hotel room example. Figure 14-6 showed the revenue the government collects from a $40 tax on hotel rooms. Figure 14-7 shows the revenue the government would collect from two alternative tax rates—a lower tax of only $20 per room and a higher tax of $60 per room.

Panel (a) of Figure 14-7 shows the case of a $20 tax, equal to half the tax rate illustrated in Figure 14-6. At this lower tax rate, 7,500 rooms are rented, generating a tax revenue of:

$$\text{Tax revenue} = \$20 \text{ per room} \times 7{,}500 \text{ rooms} = \$150{,}000$$

Recall that the tax revenue collected from a $40 tax rate is $200,000. So the revenue collected from a $20 tax rate, $150,000, is only 75% of the amount collected when the tax rate is twice as high ($\$150{,}000/\$200{,}000 \times 100 = 75\%$). To put it another way, a 100% increase in the tax rate from $20 to $40 per room leads to only a one-third, or 33.3%, increase in revenue, from $150,000 to $200,000 $\left((\$200{,}000 - \$150{,}000)/\$150{,}000 \times 100 = 33.3\%\right)$.

Panel (b) depicts what happens if the tax rate is raised from $40 to $60 per room, leading to a fall in the number of rooms rented from 5,000 to 2,500. The revenue collected at a $60 per room tax rate is:

$$\text{Tax revenue} = \$60 \text{ per room} \times 2{,}500 \text{ rooms} = \$150{,}000$$

This is also *less* than the revenue collected by a $40 per room tax. So raising the tax rate from $40 to $60 actually reduces revenue. More precisely, in this case raising the tax rate by $50\%\left((\$60 - \$40)/\$40 \times 100 = 50\%\right)$ lowers the tax revenue by $25\%\left((\$150{,}000 - \$200{,}000)/\$200{,}000 \times 100 = -25\%\right)$. Why did this happen? Because the fall in tax revenue caused by the reduction in the number of rooms rented more than offset the increase in the tax revenue caused by the rise in the tax rate. In other words, setting a tax rate so high that it deters a significant number of transactions will likely lead to a fall in tax revenue.

One way to think about the revenue effect of increasing an excise tax is that the tax increase affects tax revenue in two ways. On one side, the tax increase means that the government raises more revenue for each unit of the good sold, which other things equal would lead to a rise in tax revenue. On the other side, the tax increase reduces the quantity of sales, which other things equal would lead to a fall in tax revenue. The end result depends both on the price elasticities of supply and demand and on the initial level of the tax.

If the price elasticities of both supply and demand are low, the tax increase won't reduce the quantity of the good sold very much, so tax revenue will definitely rise. If the price elasticities are high, the result is less certain; if they are high enough, the tax reduces the quantity sold so much that tax revenue falls. Also, if the initial tax rate is low, the government doesn't lose much revenue from the decline in the quantity of the good sold, so the tax increase will definitely increase tax revenue. If the initial tax rate is high, the result is again less certain. Tax revenue is likely to fall or rise very little from a tax increase only in cases in which the price elasticities are high and there is already a high tax rate.

The possibility that a higher tax rate can reduce tax revenue, and the corresponding possibility that cutting taxes can increase tax revenue, is a basic principle of taxation that policy makers take into account when setting tax rates. That is, when considering a tax created for the purpose of raising revenue (in contrast to taxes created to discourage undesirable behavior, known as *sin taxes*), a well-informed policy maker won't impose a tax rate so high that cutting the tax would increase revenue.

14.3 The Costs of Taxation

What is the cost of a tax? You might be inclined to answer that it is the money taxpayers pay to the government. In other words, you might believe that the cost of a tax is the tax revenue collected. But suppose the government uses the tax revenue to provide services that taxpayers want. Or suppose that the government simply hands the tax revenue back to taxpayers. Would we say in those cases that the tax didn't actually cost anything?

No—because a tax prevents mutually beneficial transactions from occurring. Consider Figure 14-6 once more. Here, with a \$40 tax on hotel rooms, guests pay \$100 per room but hotel owners receive only \$60 per room. Because of the wedge created by the tax, we know that some transactions don't occur that would have occurred without the tax.

For example, we know from the supply and demand curves that there are some potential guests who would be willing to pay up to \$90 per night and some hotel owners who would be willing to supply rooms if they received at least \$70 per night. If these two sets of people were allowed to trade with each other without the tax, they would engage in mutually beneficial transactions—hotel rooms would be rented.

But such deals would be illegal, because the \$40 tax would not be paid. In our example, 5,000 potential hotel room rentals that would have occurred in the absence of the tax, to the mutual benefit of guests and hotel owners, do not take place because of the tax. Specifically, 5,000 (the number of lost rentals) is equal to 10,000 (the equilibrium quantity at an untaxed rate of \$80) minus 5,000 (the rooms that are rented with the tax).

So an excise tax imposes costs—over and above the tax revenue collected—in the form of inefficiency, which occurs because the tax discourages mutually beneficial transactions. As we learned in Section 3, the cost to society of this kind of inefficiency—the value of the forgone mutually beneficial transactions—is called the deadweight loss. While all real-world taxes impose some deadweight loss, a badly designed tax imposes a larger deadweight loss than a well-designed one.

To measure the deadweight loss from a tax, we turn to the concepts of producer and consumer surplus. Figure 14-8 shows the effects of an excise tax on consumer and producer surplus. In the absence of the tax, the equilibrium is at *E*

FIGURE 14-8 A Tax Reduces Consumer and Producer Surplus

Before the tax, the equilibrium price and quantity are P_E and Q_E, respectively. After an excise tax of T per unit is imposed, the price to consumers rises to P_C and consumer surplus falls by the sum of the dark blue rectangle, labeled A, and the light blue triangle, labeled B. The tax also causes the price to producers to fall to P_P; producer surplus falls by the sum of the red rectangle, labeled C, and the pink triangle, labeled F. The government receives revenue from the tax equal to $Q_T \times T$, which is given by the sum of the areas A and C. Areas B and F represent the losses to consumer and producer surplus that are not collected by the government as revenue. They are the deadweight loss to society of the tax.

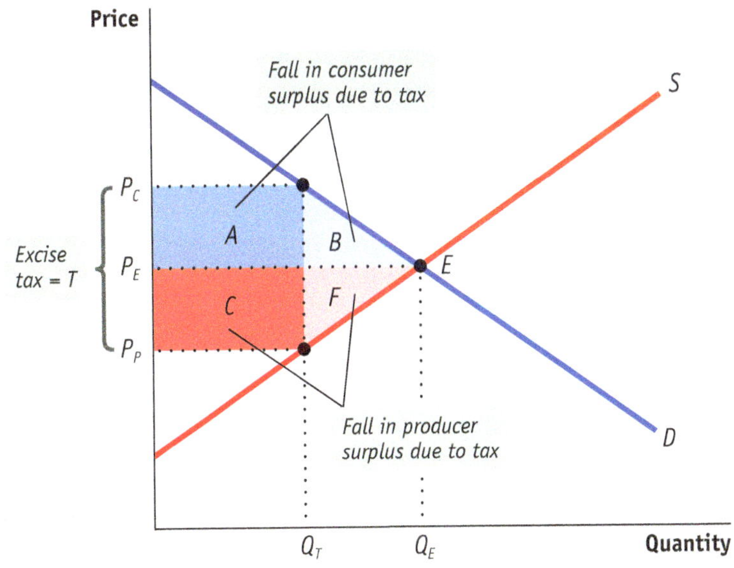

and the equilibrium price and quantity are P_E and Q_E, respectively. An excise tax drives a wedge equal to the amount of the tax between the price received by producers and the price paid by consumers, reducing the quantity sold. In this case, where the tax is T dollars per unit, the quantity sold falls to Q_T. The price paid by consumers rises to P_C, the demand price of the reduced quantity, Q_T, and the price received by producers falls to P_P, the supply price of that quantity. The difference between these prices, $P_C - P_P$, is equal to the excise tax, T.

Using the concepts of producer and consumer surplus, we can show exactly how much surplus producers and consumers lose as a result of the tax. From Figure 10-4 we learned that a fall in the price of a good generates a gain in consumer surplus that is equal to the sum of the areas of a rectangle and a triangle. Similarly, a price increase causes a loss to consumers that is represented by the sum of the areas of a rectangle and a triangle. So it's not surprising that in the case of an excise tax, the rise in the price paid by consumers causes a loss equal to the sum of the areas of a rectangle and a triangle: the dark blue rectangle labeled A and the area of the light blue triangle labeled B in Figure 14-8.

Meanwhile, the fall in the price received by producers leads to a fall in producer surplus. This, too, is equal to the sum of the areas of a rectangle and a triangle. The loss in producer surplus is the sum of the areas of the red rectangle labeled C and the pink triangle labeled F in Figure 14-8.

Of course, although consumers and producers are hurt by the tax, the government gains revenue. The revenue the government collects is equal to the tax per unit sold, T, multiplied by the quantity sold, Q_T. This revenue is equal to the area of a rectangle Q_T wide and T high. And we already have that rectangle in the figure: it is the sum of rectangles A and C. So the government gains part of what consumers and producers lose from an excise tax.

But a portion of the loss to producers and consumers from the tax is not offset by a gain to the government—specifically, the two triangles B and F. The deadweight loss caused by the tax is equal to the combined area of these two triangles. It represents the total surplus lost to society because of the tax—that is, the amount of surplus that would have been generated by transactions that now do not take place because of the tax.

Figure 14-9 is a version of Figure 14-8 that leaves out rectangles A (the surplus shifted from consumers to the government) and C (the surplus shifted from producers to the government) and shows only the deadweight loss, here drawn as a

FIGURE 14-9 The Deadweight Loss of a Tax

A tax leads to a deadweight loss because it creates inefficiency: some mutually beneficial transactions never take place because of the tax—namely, the transactions $Q_E - Q_T$. The yellow area here represents the value of the deadweight loss: it is the total surplus that would have been gained from the $Q_E - Q_T$ transactions. If the tax had not discouraged transactions—had the number of transactions remained at Q_E because of either perfectly inelastic supply or perfectly inelastic demand—no deadweight loss would have been incurred.

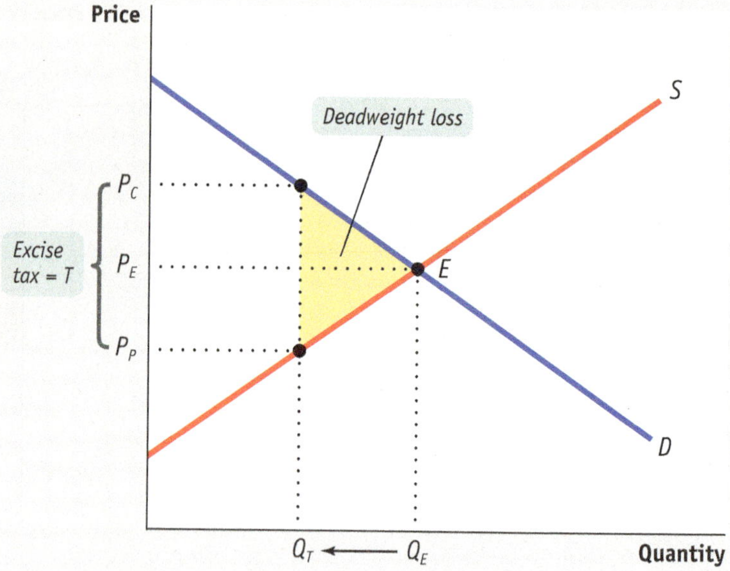

triangle shaded yellow. The base of that triangle is equal to the tax wedge, *T;* the height of the triangle is equal to the reduction in the quantity transacted due to the tax, $Q_E - Q_T$. Clearly, the larger the tax wedge and the larger the reduction in the quantity transacted, the greater the inefficiency from the tax.

But also note an important, contrasting point: if the excise tax somehow *didn't* reduce the quantity bought and sold in this market—if Q_T remained equal to Q_E after the tax was levied—the yellow triangle would disappear and the deadweight loss from the tax would be zero. This observation is simply the flip side of the principle found earlier in the section: a tax causes inefficiency because it discourages mutually beneficial transactions between buyers and sellers. So if a tax does not discourage transactions, which would be true if either supply or demand were perfectly inelastic, it causes no deadweight loss. In this case, the tax simply shifts surplus straight from consumers and producers to the government.

The **administrative costs** of a tax are the resources used for its collection, for the method of payment, and for any attempts to evade the tax.

Using a triangle to measure deadweight loss is a technique used in many economic applications. For example, triangles are used to measure the deadweight loss produced by types of taxes other than excise taxes. They are also used to measure the deadweight loss produced by monopoly, another kind of market distortion. And deadweight-loss triangles are often used to evaluate the benefits and costs of public policies besides taxation—such as whether to impose stricter safety standards on a product.

David Paul Morris/Bloomberg via Getty Images

Society ultimately pays the administrative costs of taxes.

In considering the total amount of inefficiency caused by a tax, we must also take into account something not shown in Figure 14-9: the resources actually used by the government to collect the tax, and by taxpayers to pay it, over and above the amount of the tax. These lost resources are called the **administrative costs** of the tax. The most familiar administrative cost of the U.S. tax system is the time individuals spend filling out their income tax forms or the money they pay for tax return preparation services like those provided by H&R Block and companies like it. (The latter is considered an inefficiency from the point of view of society because resources spent on return preparation could be used for other, non-tax-related purposes.)

Included in the administrative costs that taxpayers incur are resources used to evade the tax, both legally and illegally. The costs of operating the Internal Revenue Service, the arm of the federal government tasked with collecting the federal income tax, are actually quite small in comparison to the administrative costs paid by taxpayers.

So we get the result:

Total Inefficiency of Tax = Deadweight Loss + Administrative Costs

The general rule for economic policy is that, other things equal, a tax system should be designed to minimize the total inefficiency it imposes on society. In practice, other considerations also apply, but this principle nonetheless gives valuable guidance. Administrative costs are usually well known, more or less determined by the current technology of collecting taxes (for example, filing paper returns versus filing electronically).

But how can we predict the size of the deadweight loss associated with a given tax? Not surprisingly, as in our analysis of the incidence of a tax, the price elasticities of supply and demand play crucial roles in making such a prediction.

14.4 Elasticities and the Deadweight Loss of a Tax

We know that the deadweight loss from an excise tax arises because it prevents some mutually beneficial transactions from occurring. In particular, the producer and consumer surplus that is forgone because of these missing transactions is equal to the size of the deadweight loss itself. *This means that the larger the number of transactions that are prevented by the tax, the larger the deadweight loss.*

This fact gives us an important clue in understanding the relationship between elasticity and the size of the deadweight loss from a tax. Recall that when demand or supply is elastic, the quantity demanded or the quantity supplied is relatively responsive to changes in the price. So a tax imposed on a good for which either demand or supply, or both, is elastic will cause a relatively large decrease in the quantity transacted and a relatively large deadweight loss. In addition, the greater the elasticity of either demand or supply, the greater the deadweight loss from a tax. Correspondingly, a tax imposed when demand or supply, or both, is inelastic will cause a relatively small decrease in the quantity transacted and a relatively small deadweight loss.

The four panels of Figure 14-10 illustrate the positive relationship between a good's price elasticity of either demand or supply and the deadweight loss from taxing that good. Each panel represents the same amount of tax imposed but on a different good; the size of the deadweight loss is given by the area of the shaded triangle. In panel (a), the deadweight-loss triangle is large because demand for this good is relatively elastic—a large number of transactions fail to occur because of the tax. In panel (b), the same supply curve is drawn as in panel (a), but demand for this good is relatively inelastic; as a result, the triangle is small because only a small number of transactions are forgone. Likewise, panels (c) and (d) contain the same demand curve but different supply curves. In panel (c), an elastic supply curve gives rise to a large deadweight-loss triangle, but in panel (d) an inelastic supply curve gives rise to a small deadweight-loss triangle.

The implication of this result is clear: if you want to minimize the efficiency costs of taxation, you should choose to tax only those goods for which demand or supply, or both, is relatively inelastic. For such goods, a tax has little effect on behavior because behavior is relatively unresponsive to changes in the price. In the extreme case in which demand is perfectly inelastic (a vertical demand curve),

FIGURE 14-10 Deadweight Loss and Elasticities

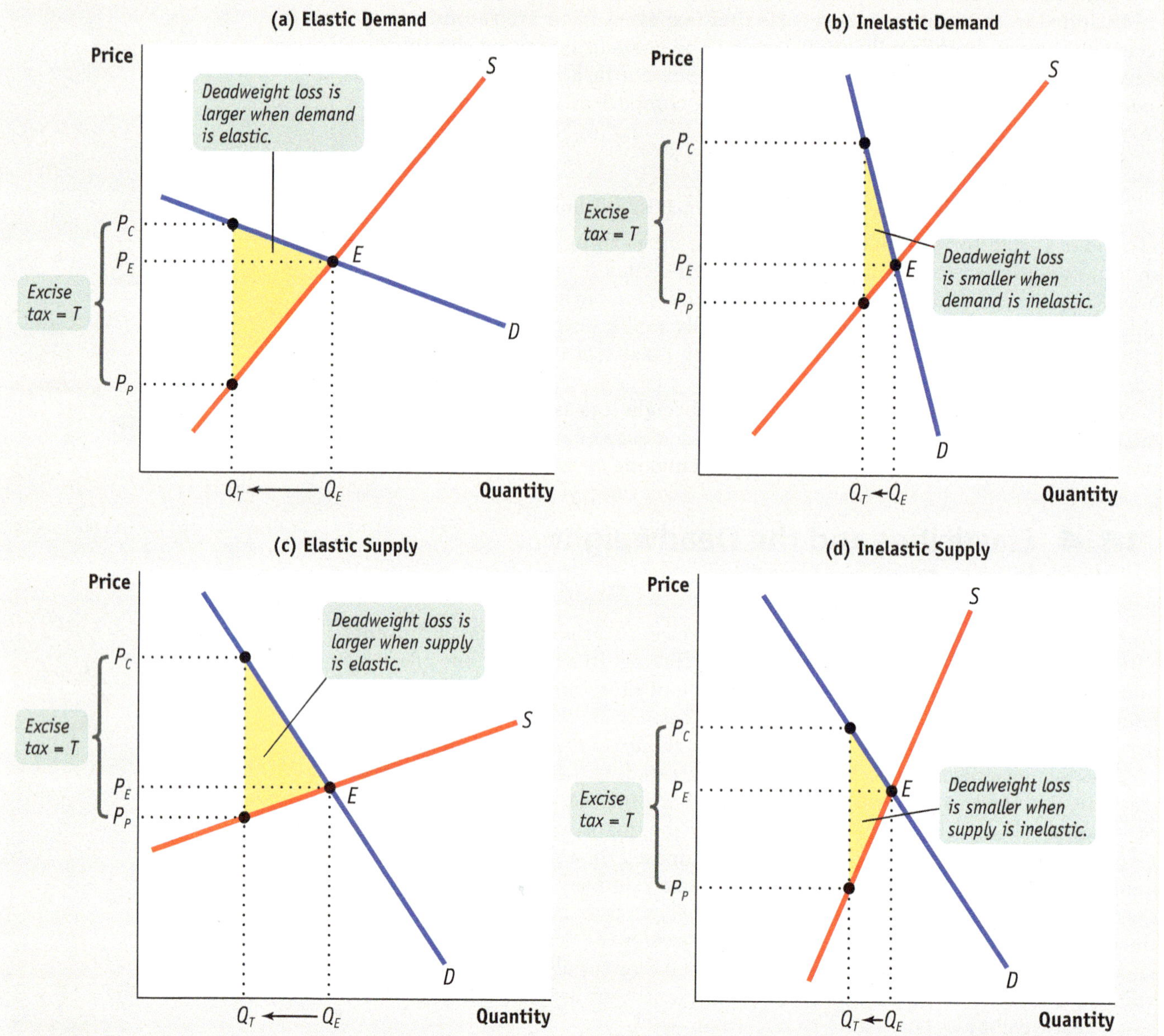

Demand is elastic in panel (a) and inelastic in panel (b), but the supply curves are the same. Supply is elastic in panel (c) and inelastic in panel (d), but the demand curves are the same. The deadweight losses are larger in panels (a) and (c) than in panels (b) and (d) because the greater the price elasticity of demand or supply, the greater the tax-induced fall in the quantity transacted. In contrast, the lower the price elasticity of demand or supply, the smaller the tax-induced fall in the quantity transacted and the smaller the deadweight loss.

the quantity demanded is unchanged by the imposition of the tax. As a result, the tax imposes no deadweight loss. Similarly, if supply is perfectly inelastic (a vertical supply curve), the quantity supplied is unchanged by the tax and there is also no deadweight loss.

So if the goal in choosing whom to tax is to minimize deadweight loss, then taxes should be imposed on goods and services that have the most inelastic response—that is, goods and services for which consumers or producers will change their behavior the least in response to the tax. (Unless they have a tendency to revolt, of course.) And this lesson carries a flip side: using a tax to purposely decrease the amount of a harmful activity, such as underage drinking, will have the most impact when that activity is elastically demanded or supplied.

ECONOMICS >> *in Action*

Taxing Tobacco

One of the most important excise taxes in the United States is the tax on cigarettes. The federal government imposes a tax of $1.01 a pack; state governments impose taxes that range from $0.17 cents per pack in Missouri to $4.35 per pack in New York; and many cities impose further taxes. In general, tax rates on cigarettes have increased over time, because more governments have seen them not just as a source of revenue but as a way to discourage smoking. But the rise in cigarette taxes has not been gradual. Usually, once a state government decides to raise cigarette taxes, it raises them a lot—which provides economists with useful data on what happens when there is a big tax increase.

Table 14-1 shows the results of big increases in cigarette taxes. In each case, sales fell, just as our analysis predicts. Although it's theoretically possible for tax revenue to fall after such a large tax increase, in reality tax revenue rose in each case. That's because cigarettes have a low price elasticity of demand.

TABLE 14-1 Results of Increases in Cigarette Taxes

State	Increase in tax (per pack)	New state tax (per pack)	Change in quantity transacted	Change in tax revenue
Illinois	$1.00	$1.98	−31.2%	39.0%
Minnesota	1.60	2.83	−24.0	56.0
New Mexico	0.75	1.66	−7.8	67.5
Florida	1.00	2.00	−27.8	193.2
Washington	1.00	3.03	−20.5	17.0

Data from: Orzechowski & Walker, Tax Burden on Tobacco. U.S. Alcohol and Tobacco Tax and Trade Bureau.

Check Your Understanding 14-2

1. The accompanying table shows four consumers' willingness to pay for one can of diet soda each, as well as four producers' costs of selling one can of diet soda each. Each consumer buys at most one can of soda; each producer sells at most one can of soda. The government asks your advice about the effects of an excise tax of $0.40 per can of diet soda. Assume that there are no administrative costs from the tax.

Consumer	Willingness to pay	Producer	Cost
Ana	$0.70	Zhang	$0.10
Bernice	0.60	Yves	0.20
Chizuko	0.50	Xavier	0.30
Dagmar	0.40	Walter	0.40

   a. Without the excise tax, what is the equilibrium price and the equilibrium quantity of soda transacted?
   b. The excise tax raises the price paid by consumers post-tax to $0.60 and lowers the price received by producers post-tax to $0.20. With the excise tax, what is the quantity of soda transacted?
   c. Without the excise tax, how much individual consumer surplus does each of the consumers gain? How much with the tax? How much total consumer surplus is lost as a result of the tax?
   d. Without the excise tax, how much individual producer surplus does each of the producers gain? How much with the tax? How much total producer surplus is lost as a result of the tax?

e. How much government revenue does the excise tax create?
f. What is the deadweight loss from the imposition of this excise tax?

2. In each of the following cases, focus on the price elasticity of demand and use a diagram to illustrate the likely size—small or large—of the deadweight loss resulting from a tax. Explain your reasoning.
a. Gasoline
b. Milk chocolate bars

Solutions appear at back of book.

>> *Quick Review*

- An excise tax generates tax revenue equal to the **tax rate** times the number of units of the good or service transacted but reduces consumer and producer surplus.
- The government tax revenue collected is less than the loss in total surplus because the tax creates inefficiency by discouraging some mutually beneficial transactions.
- The difference between the tax revenue from an excise tax and the reduction in total surplus is the deadweight loss from the tax. The total amount of inefficiency resulting from a tax is equal to the deadweight loss plus the **administrative costs** of the tax.
- The larger the number of transactions prevented by a tax, the larger the deadweight loss. As a result, taxes on goods with a greater price elasticity of supply or demand, or both, generate higher deadweight losses. There is no deadweight loss when the number of transactions is unchanged by the tax. (That is, when supply or demand is perfectly inelastic.)

BUSINESS CASE

The Airline Industry: Fly Less, Charge More

AP Photo/Ted S. Warren

In 2019, the top four intra-North American airlines accounted for 67% of all passenger air-miles traveled in the United States. In contrast, the top five intra-European airlines accounted for around 50% of all European air-miles traveled. Moreover, U.S. airlines are the most profitable in the world, earning more than twice as much profit per passenger as the global average. Since 2010, the U.S. airline industry has been profitable every year.

However, it wasn't always like this. The U.S. airline industry suffered heavy losses for many decades, accumulating an industry-wide loss of $52 billion between 1977 to 2009. Those years were also a time of greater fragmentation across the industry: then, the top four airlines accounted for only 49% of air-miles traveled, instead of the 67% share of today. As the accompanying table shows, from 2005 onward, consolidation among the 10 major American carriers led to the 4 major carriers left today: American, Delta, United, and Southwest.

Acquiring airline	Acquired airline	Date
American Airlines	TWA	2001
U.S. Airways	America West	2005
Delta	Northwest	2008
United	Continental	2010
Southwest	AirTran	2010

How did the airline industry achieve such a dramatic turnaround? Simple: fly less and charge more. The catalyst was a particularly nasty recession in 2008, which pushed the U.S. airline industry to the edge of disaster. When the economy cratered, people stopped flying, and the industry lost a staggering $11 billion that year. The largest carriers were forced to significantly slash their capacity—flying fewer planes—to match the lower demand for seats. Smaller carriers, saddled with years of losses, were no longer viable. They merged with their larger rivals and redundant flights were cut. As a result, starting in 2010 flights became a lot more crowded, with only about 1 in 7 seats empty.

Airlines also began charging more: beginning in 2010, the industry enjoyed several years of significant fare increases. One way the airlines accomplished this was by varying ticket prices according to the day and time of departure, as well as the day the ticket was purchased. For example, Wednesday became the cheapest day to fly, with Friday and Saturday the most expensive. The least expensive flight of the day is the first flight of the morning (the one that requires you to get up at 4 A.M.). And buying tickets on Tuesdays at 3 P.M. Eastern Standard Time results in the cheapest fares, while tickets purchased on the weekend cost the most.

And it doesn't stop there, as every beleaguered traveler knows. In 2010, airlines began imposing new fees and increased old ones—fees for food, blankets, baggage, the right to board first or choose your seat in advance. These fees are now a major source of airlines' revenue, all while providing a seemingly ever-shrinking amount of leg room.

However, recent events may be turning in consumers' favor. Since 2015 fare increases have been small as low-cost carriers like Spirit Air and Alaska Airlines have expanded as the economy gathered steam. One airline industry researcher, commenting on the long-term profitability of airlines, had this to say: "The wild card is always capacity discipline. All it takes is one carrier to begin to add capacity aggressively, and then we follow and we undo all the good work that's been done."

QUESTIONS FOR THOUGHT

1. How would you describe the price elasticity of demand for airline flights given the information in this case? Explain.
2. Using the concept of elasticity, explain why airlines would create such great variations in the price of a ticket depending on when it is purchased and the day and time the flight departs. Assume that some people are willing to spend time shopping for deals as well as fly at inconvenient times, but others are not.
3. Using the concept of elasticity, explain why airlines have imposed fees on things such as checked bags. Why might they try to hide or disguise fees?
4. Use an elasticity concept to explain under what conditions the airline industry will be able to maintain its high profitability in the future. Explain.

REVIEW

MODULE 11

1. Many economic questions depend on the size of consumer or producer responses to changes in prices or other variables. *Elasticity* is a general measure of responsiveness that can be used to answer such questions.

2. The **price elasticity of demand**—the percent change in the quantity demanded divided by the percent change in the price (dropping the minus sign)—is a measure of the responsiveness of the quantity demanded to changes in the price. In practical calculations, it is usually best to use the **midpoint method,** which calculates percent changes in prices and quantities based on the average of starting and final values.

MODULE 12

1. The responsiveness of the quantity demanded to price can range from **perfectly inelastic demand,** where the quantity demanded is unaffected by the price, to **perfectly elastic demand,** where there is a unique price at which consumers will buy as much or as little as they are offered. When demand is perfectly inelastic, the demand curve is a vertical line; when it is perfectly elastic, the demand curve is a horizontal line.

2. The price elasticity of demand is classified according to whether it is more or less than 1. If it is greater than 1, demand is **elastic;** if it is less than 1, demand is **inelastic;** if it is exactly 1, demand is **unit-elastic.** This classification determines how **total revenue,** the total value of sales, changes when the price changes. If demand is elastic, total revenue falls when the price increases and rises when the price decreases. If demand is inelastic, total revenue rises when the price increases and falls when the price decreases. If demand is unit-elastic, total revenue is unchanged by a change in price.

3. The price elasticity of demand depends on whether there are close substitutes for the good in question (it is higher), whether the good is a necessity (it is lower) or a luxury (it is higher), the share of income spent on the good (it is higher), and the length of time that has elapsed since the price change (it is higher).

MODULE 13

1. The **cross-price elasticity of demand** measures the effect of a change in one good's price on the quantity demanded of another good. The cross-price elasticity of demand can be positive, in which case the goods are substitutes, or negative, in which case they are complements.

2. The **income elasticity of demand** is the percent change in the quantity of a good demanded when a consumer's income changes divided by the percent change in income. The income elasticity of demand indicates how intensely the demand for a good responds to changes in income. It can be negative; in that case the good is an inferior good. Goods with positive income elasticities of demand are normal goods. If the income elasticity is greater than 1, a good is **income-elastic;** if it is positive and less than 1, the good is **income-inelastic.**

3. The **price elasticity of supply** is the percent change in the quantity of a good supplied divided by the percent change in the price. If the quantity supplied does not change at all, we have an instance of **perfectly inelastic supply;** the supply curve is a vertical line. If the quantity supplied is zero below some price but infinite above that price, we have an instance of **perfectly elastic supply;** the supply curve is a horizontal line.

4. The price elasticity of supply depends on time and the availability of resources to expand production. It is higher when inputs are available at relatively low cost and the longer the time that has elapsed since the price change.

MODULE 14

1. **Excise taxes**—taxes on the purchase or sale of a good—raise the price paid by consumers and reduce the price received by producers, driving a wedge between the two. The **incidence** of the tax—how the burden of the tax is divided between consumers and producers—does not depend on who officially pays the tax.

2. The incidence of an excise tax depends on the price elasticities of supply and demand. If the price elasticity of demand is higher than the price elasticity of supply, the tax falls mainly on producers; if the price elasticity of supply is higher than the price elasticity of demand, the tax falls mainly on consumers.

3. The tax revenue generated by a tax depends on the **tax rate** and on the number of taxed units transacted. Excise taxes cause inefficiency in the form of deadweight loss because they discourage some mutually beneficial transactions. Taxes also impose **administrative costs:** resources used to collect the

tax, to pay it (over and above the amount of the tax), and to evade it.

4. An excise tax generates revenue for the government but lowers total surplus. The loss in total surplus exceeds the tax revenue, resulting in a deadweight loss to society. This deadweight loss is represented by a triangle, the area of which equals the value of the transactions discouraged by the tax. The greater the elasticity of demand or supply, or both, the larger the deadweight loss from a tax. If either demand or supply is perfectly inelastic, there is no deadweight loss from a tax.

KEY TERMS

Price elasticity of demand p. 128
Midpoint method p. 130
Perfectly inelastic demand p. 133
Perfectly elastic demand p. 134
Elastic demand p. 134
Inelastic demand p. 134
Unit-elastic demand p. 134
Total revenue p. 135
Cross-price elasticity of demand p. 142
Income elasticity of demand p. 143
Income-elastic demand p. 144
Income-inelastic demand p. 144
Price elasticity of supply p. 144
Perfectly inelastic supply p. 145
Perfectly elastic supply p. 145
Excise tax p. 149
Incidence p. 152
Tax rate p. 156
Administrative costs p. 160

Bloomberg/Getty Images

Module 15 Gains from Trade

Module 16 Supply, Demand, and International Trade

SECTION 5

International Trade

THE EVERYWHERE PHONE

What do Americans do with their time? The answer is that they largely spend it staring at small screens. According to one survey, in 2018, the average American spent three hours and 43 minutes a day looking at a smartphone (especially an iPhone) or a tablet, more time than is spent watching TV.

Where do these small screens come from? Specifically, where does an iPhone come from?

Apple, which sells the iPhone, is an American company. But if you said that iPhones come from America, you're mostly wrong: Apple develops products, but contracts almost all of the manufacturing of those products to other, mainly overseas, companies. But it's not really right to answer "China," either, even though that's where iPhones are assembled. You see, assembly—the last phase of iPhone production, in which the pieces are put together in the familiar metal-and-glass case—only accounts for a small fraction of the phone's value.

In fact, a study of the iPhone X estimated that of the average wholesale price of about $800 per phone, less than $25 stayed in the Chinese economy. A substantially larger amount went to South Korean manufacturers, who supplied the display and memory chips. There were also substantial outlays for raw materials, which are sourced all over the world. And the biggest share of the price—more than half—consisted of Apple's profit margin, which was largely a reward for research, development, and design.

So where *do* iPhones come from? Lots of places. And the case of the iPhone isn't unusual: the car you drive, the clothing you wear, even the food you eat, are generally the end products of complex supply chains that span the globe.

Has this always been true? Yes and no. Large-scale international trade isn't new. By the early twentieth century, middle-class residents of London already ate bread made from Canadian wheat and beef from the Argentine Pampas, while wearing clothing woven from Australian wool and Egyptian cotton. In recent decades, however, new technologies for transportation and communication have interacted with pro-trade policies to produce an era of *hyperglobalization* in which international trade has soared, thanks to complex chains of production like the one that puts an iPhone in front of your nose.

These global supply chains make the world economy much more productive and, as a result, richer than it would be if each country tried to be self-sufficient. And it isn't just the world as a whole that benefits from international trade: it's almost certain that every country benefits, too. But international trade is nonetheless controversial, because it sometimes hurts particular groups within countries, while helping others. For these reasons, we must have a full picture of international trade to understand how national economies work.

This section examines the economics of international trade. We start from the model of comparative advantage, which, as we saw in Module 3, explains why there are gains from international trade. We will briefly recap that model here, then turn to a more detailed examination of the causes and consequences of globalization.

MODULE 15

Gains from Trade

WHAT YOU WILL LEARN

- What is comparative advantage and why does it lead to international trade?
- What are the sources of comparative advantage?

15.1 Comparative Advantage and International Trade

Raphye Alexius/Cultura Creative (RF)/Alamy

The United States buys smartphones—and many other goods and services—from other countries. At the same time, it sells many goods and services to other countries. Goods and services purchased from abroad are **imports;** goods and services sold abroad are **exports.**

As illustrated by the opening story, international trade plays an increasingly important role in the world economy. Panel (a) of Figure 15-1 shows the ratio of goods crossing national borders to *world GDP*—the total value of goods and services produced in the world as a whole—since 1870. As you can see, the long-term trend has been upward, although there have been some periods of declining trade—for example, the sharp but brief dip in trade during the global financial crisis of 2008 and its aftermath.

Panel (b) illustrates imports and exports as a percentage of GDP for a number of countries. What it shows is that foreign trade is significantly more important for many other countries than it is for the United States.

Foreign trade isn't the only way countries interact economically. In the modern world, investors from one country often invest funds in another nation; many companies are multinational, with subsidiaries operating in several countries; and a growing number of people work in a country different from the one in which they were born. The growth of all these forms of economic linkages among countries is often called **globalization.**

Globalization isn't a new phenomenon. As you can see from panel (a) of Figure 15-1, there was rapid growth in trade between 1870 and the beginning of World War I, as railroads and steamships effectively made shipping goods over long distances faster and cheaper, effectively shrinking the world. This growth of trade was accompanied by large-scale international investment and migration. However, globalization went into reverse for almost 40 years after World War I, as governments imposed limits on trade of the kind analyzed later in this section. And by several measures, globalization didn't return to 1913 levels until the 1980s.

Since then, however, there has been a further dramatic increase in international linkages, sometimes referred to as **hyperglobalization.** The manufacturing of

Goods and services purchased from other countries are **imports;** goods and services sold to other countries are **exports.**

Globalization is the phenomenon of growing economic linkages among countries.

Hyperglobalization is the phenomenon of extremely high levels of international trade.

FIGURE 15-1 The Growing Importance of International Trade

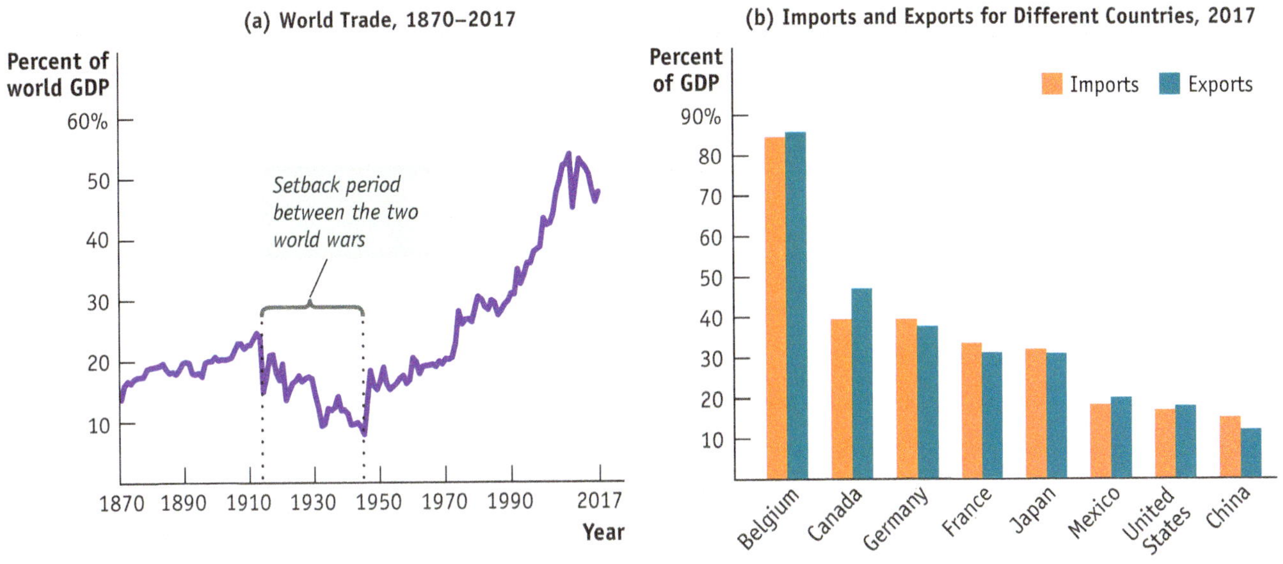

Panel (a) shows the long-term history of the ratio of world trade to world production. The trend has been generally upward, thanks to technological progress in transportation and communication, although there was a long setback during the period between the two world wars. Panel (b) demonstrates that international trade is significantly more important to many other countries than it is to the United States.

Data from: [panel (a)] Klasing, M. J., and P. Milionis, "Quantifying the Evolution of World Trade, 1870–1949," *Journal of International Economics* (2013); and Feenstra, Robert C., Robert Inklaar, and Marcel P. Timmer, "The Next Generation of the Penn World Table" *American Economic Review* 105, 10 (2015): 3150–3182, available for download at www.ggdc.net/pwt; [panel (b)] World Development Indicators.

iPhones and other high-tech goods, which often involves supply chains of production that span the globe, is an example of hyperglobalization. Each stage of a good's production takes place in a different country—all made possible by advances in communication and transportation technology. (For a real-life example, see this section's business case.)

One big question in international economics is whether the fast pace of hyperglobalization will continue in the decades ahead. Some even wonder whether there will be a reversal. As you can see from looking closely at Figure 15-1, the big rise in the ratio of exports to world GDP leveled off around 2005. Since then, many reports have appeared about companies deciding that the money they saved by buying goods from suppliers thousands of miles away is more than offset by the disadvantages of long shipping times and other inconveniences. (Even now, it takes around two weeks for a container ship from China to arrive in California, and a month to reach the East Coast.) As a result, there has been some move toward *reshoring,* bringing production closer to markets. In addition, there has been a resurgence of international disputes over trade in recent years, raising the specter of new restrictions to trade. We will discuss those conflicts later in this section.

Jay Mallin/Bloomberg via Getty Images

Thanks to cheap and fast ways of transporting goods, extremely high levels of international trade are a feature of today's economy.

As a result of these two issues—cost concerns and international trade disputes—it is possible that hyperglobalization may become less prevalent than it is today. Yet it would still remain an extraordinary part of the economy. To understand why international trade occurs and why economists believe it is beneficial to the economy, we will first review the concept of comparative advantage.

Production Possibilities and Comparative Advantage, Revisited

To produce phones, any country must use resources—land, labor, and capital—that could have been used to produce other things. The opportunity cost of that phone is the potential production of other goods a country must forgo to produce a phone.

In some cases, it's easy to see why the opportunity cost of producing a good is especially low in a given country. Consider, for example, shrimp—much of which now comes from seafood farms in Vietnam and Thailand. It's a lot easier to produce shrimp in Vietnam, where the climate is nearly ideal and there's plenty of coastal land suitable for shellfish farming, than it is in the United States.

Conversely, other goods are not produced as easily in Vietnam as in the United States. For example, Vietnam doesn't have the base of skilled workers and technological know-how that makes the United States so good at producing high-technology goods. So the opportunity cost of a ton of shrimp, in terms of other goods, such as aircraft, is much less in Vietnam than it is in the United States.

In other cases, matters are a little less obvious. It's as easy to assemble smartphones in the United States as it is in China, and Chinese electronics workers are, if anything, less productive than their U.S. counterparts. But Chinese workers are even less productive than the U.S. workers in other areas, such as automobile and aircraft production. This means that diverting a Chinese worker into assembling phones reduces output of other goods less than diverting a U.S. worker into assembling phones. So we say that China has a comparative advantage in producing smartphones. That is, the opportunity cost of smartphone assembly in China is less than it is in the United States.

Notice that we said the opportunity cost of phone *assembly*. As we've seen, most of the value of a "Chinese-made" phone actually comes from other countries. For the sake of exposition, however, let's ignore that complication and consider a hypothetical case in which China makes phones from scratch.

To begin, we say that China has a comparative advantage in producing smartphones. Let's repeat the definition of comparative advantage from Module 3: *A country has a comparative advantage in producing a good or service if the opportunity cost of producing the good or service is lower for that country than for other countries.*

Figure 15-2 provides a hypothetical numerical example of comparative advantage in international trade. We assume that only two goods are produced and consumed, phones and Caterpillar heavy trucks. (The United States doesn't export many ordinary trucks, but Caterpillar, which makes earth-moving equipment, is a major exporter.) And we assume that there are only two countries in the world, the United States and China. The figure shows hypothetical production possibility frontiers for the United States and China.

As in Module 2, we simplify the model by assuming that the production possibility frontiers are straight lines, as shown in Figure 2-1, rather than the more realistic bowed-out shape in Figure 2-2. The straight-line shape implies that the opportunity cost of a phone in terms of trucks in each country is constant—it does not depend on how many units of each good the country produces. The analysis of international trade under the assumption that opportunity costs are constant, which makes production possibility frontiers straight lines, is known as the **Ricardian model of international trade,** named after the English economist David Ricardo, who introduced this analysis in the early nineteenth century.

The **Ricardian model of international trade** analyzes international trade under the assumption that opportunity costs are constant.

In Figure 15-2 we show a situation in which the United States can produce 100,000 trucks if it produces no phones, or 100 million phones if it produces no trucks. Thus, the slope of the U.S. production possibility frontier, or *PPF,* is $-100{,}000/100 = -1{,}000$. That is, to produce an additional million phones, the United States must forgo the production of 1,000 trucks. Likewise, to produce one more truck, the United States must forgo 1,000 phones (equal to 1 million phones divided by 1,000 trucks).

FIGURE 15-2 Comparative Advantage and the Production Possibility Frontier

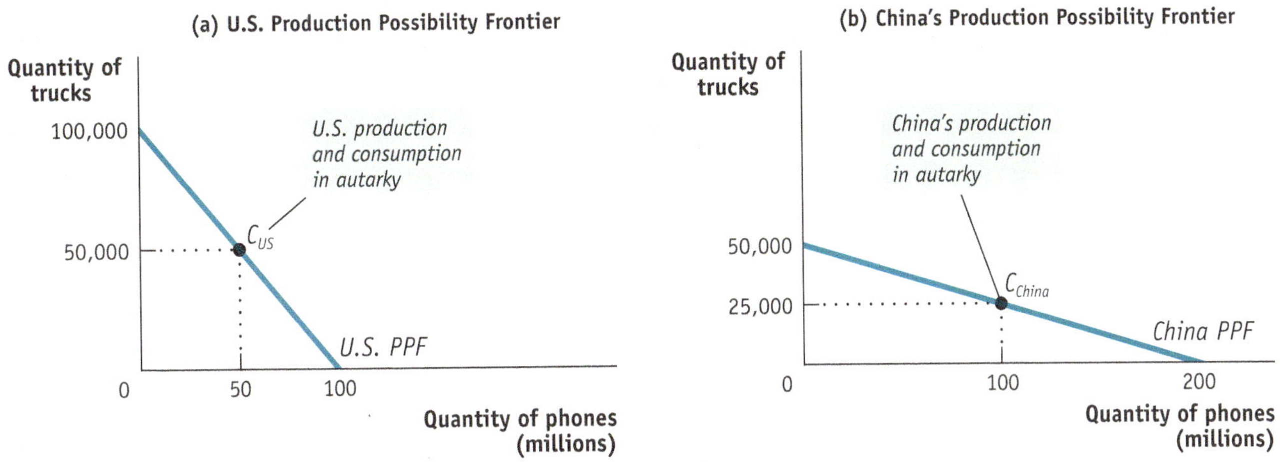

The U.S. opportunity cost of 1 million phones in terms of trucks is 1,000: for every 1 million phones, 1,000 trucks must be forgone. The Chinese opportunity cost of 1 million phones in terms of trucks is 250: for every additional 1 million phones, only 250 trucks must be forgone. As a result, the United States has a comparative advantage in truck production, and China has a comparative advantage in phone production. In autarky, each country is forced to consume only what it produces: 50,000 trucks and 50 million phones for the United States; 25,000 trucks and 100 million phones for China.

Similarly, China can produce 50,000 trucks if it produces no phones or 200 million phones if it produces no trucks. Thus, the slope of China's *PPF* is −50,000/200 = −250. That is, to produce an additional million phones, China must forgo the production of 250 trucks. Likewise, to produce one more truck, China must forgo 4,000 phones (1 million phones divided by 250 trucks).

Autarky is a situation in which a country does not trade with other countries.

Historically, countries have almost always traded with each other. Yet economists find it helpful as a first step to illustrate the choices a country would make if it were unable to engage in international trade. Economists use the term **autarky** to refer to a situation in which a country does not trade with other countries. In our example, we assume that in autarky the United States chooses to produce and consume 50 million phones and 50,000 trucks. We also assume that in autarky China produces 100 million phones and 25,000 trucks.

The trade-offs facing the two countries when they don't trade are summarized in Table 15-1. As you can see, the United States has a comparative advantage in the production of trucks because it has a lower opportunity cost in terms of phones than China has: producing a truck costs the United States only 1,000 phones, while it costs China 4,000 phones. Correspondingly, China has a comparative advantage in phone production: producing 1 million phones costs only 250 trucks, while it costs the United States 1,000 trucks.

As we learned in Module 3, each country can do better by engaging in trade than it could by not trading. A country can accomplish this by specializing in the production of the good in which it has a comparative advantage and exporting that good, while importing the good in which it has a comparative disadvantage.

Let's see how this works.

TABLE 15-1 U.S. and Chinese Opportunity Costs of Phones and Trucks

	U.S. Opportunity Cost		Chinese Opportunity Cost
1 million phones	1,000 trucks	>	250 trucks
1 truck	1,000 phones	<	4,000 phones

The Gains from International Trade

Figure 15-3 illustrates how both countries can gain from specialization and trade, by showing a hypothetical rearrangement of production and consumption that allows *each* country to consume more of *both* goods. Again, panel (a) represents the United States and panel (b) represents China. In each panel we indicate again the autarky production and consumption assumed in Figure 15-2.

Once trade becomes possible, however, everything changes. With trade, each country can move to producing only the good in which it has a comparative advantage—trucks for the United States and phones for China. Because the world production of both goods is now higher than in autarky, trade makes it possible for each country to consume more of both goods.

Table 15-2 sums up the changes as a result of trade and shows why both countries can gain. The left part of the table shows the autarky situation, before trade, in which each country must produce the goods it consumes. The right part of the table shows what happens as a result of trade. After trade, the United States specializes in the production of trucks, producing 100,000 trucks and no phones; China specializes in the production of phones, producing 200 million phones and no trucks.

The result is a rise in total world production of both goods. As you can see in the table, there are gains from trade to both countries:

- The United States can consume both more trucks (12,500 more) and phones (25 million more) than before, even though it no longer produces phones, because it can import phones from China.
- China can also consume more of both goods (12,500 more trucks and 25 million more phones), even though it no longer produces trucks, because it can import trucks from the United States.

The key to this mutual gain is the fact that trade liberates both countries from self-sufficiency—from the need to produce the same mixes of goods they consume. Because each country can concentrate on producing the good in which it has a comparative advantage, total world production rises, making a higher standard of living possible in both nations.

FIGURE 15-3 The Gains from International Trade

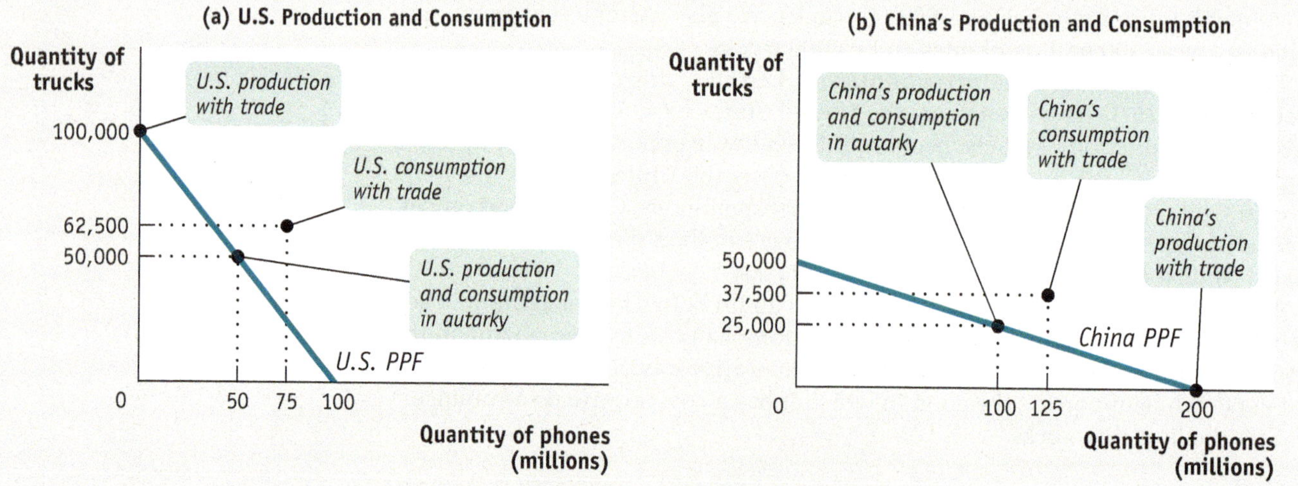

Trade increases world production of both phone and trucks, allowing both countries to consume more. Here, each country specializes its production as a result of trade: the United States concentrates on producing trucks, and China concentrates on producing phones. Total world production of both goods rises, which means that it is possible for both countries to consume more of both goods.

TABLE 15-2 How the United States and China Gain from Trade

		In Autarky		With Trade		
		Production	Consumption	Production	Consumption	Gains from Trade
United States	Million phones	50	50	0	75	+25
	Trucks	50,000	50,000	100,000	62,500	+12,500
China	Million phones	100	100	200	125	+25
	Trucks	25,000	25,000	0	37,500	+12,500

In this example we have simply assumed the post-trade consumption bundles of the two countries. In fact, the consumption choices of a country reflect both the preferences of its residents and the *relative prices*—the prices of one good in terms of another in international markets. Although we have not explicitly given the price of trucks in terms of phones, that price is implicit in our example: China sells the United States the 75 million phones the United States consumes in return for the 37,500 trucks China consumes, so 1 million phones are traded for 500 trucks. This tells us that the price of a truck on world markets must be equal to the price of 2,000 phones.

One requirement that the relative price must satisfy is that no country pays a relative price greater than its opportunity cost of obtaining the good in autarky. That is, the United States won't pay more than 1,000 trucks for 1 million phones from China, and China won't pay more than 4,000 phones for each truck from the United States. Once this requirement is satisfied, the actual relative price in international trade is determined by supply and demand; we'll turn to supply and demand in international trade in the next section. However, first let's look more deeply into the nature of the gains from trade.

PITFALLS

HOW TO CALCULATE RELATIVE PRICES

75 million phones sell for 37,500 trucks → so
75 million/37,500
= 1 million/500
= 2,000
= how many phones must be given up to purchase one truck
= price of truck in terms of phones

Comparative Advantage versus Absolute Advantage

It's easy to accept the idea that Vietnam and Thailand have a comparative advantage in shrimp production: they have a tropical climate that's better suited to shrimp farming than the climate of the United States, and they have a lot of usable coastal area. So the United States imports shrimp from Vietnam and Thailand.

But as we have seen in the case of cell phone assembly, the gains from trade depend on *comparative advantage*, rather than absolute advantage. Yes, it would take less labor to assemble a phone in the United States than in China. That is, the productivity of Chinese electronics workers is less than that of their U.S. counterparts. But what determines comparative advantage is not the amount of resources used to produce a good but the opportunity cost of that good—in this case, the quantity of other goods forgone to produce a phone. And the opportunity cost of phones is lower in China than in the United States.

Here's how it works: Chinese workers have low productivity compared with U.S. workers in the electronics industry. But Chinese workers have even lower productivity compared with U.S. workers in other industries. Because Chinese labor productivity in industries other than electronics is relatively very low, producing a phone in China, even though it takes a lot of labor, does not require forgoing the production of large quantities of other goods.

PORNCHAI KITTIWONGSAKUL/Getty Images

The tropical climates of Vietnam and Thailand give them a comparative advantage in shrimp production.

In the United States, the opposite is true: very high productivity in other industries (such as automobiles) means that assembling electronic products in the United States, even though it doesn't require much labor, requires sacrificing lots of other goods. Thus the opportunity cost of producing electronics is less in China than in the United States. Despite its lower labor productivity, China has a comparative advantage in the production of many consumer electronics, although the United States has an absolute advantage.

The source of China's comparative advantage in consumer electronics is reflected in global markets by the wages Chinese workers are paid. That's because a country's wage rates, in general, reflect its labor productivity. In countries where labor is highly productive in many industries, employers are willing to pay high wages to attract workers, so competition among employers leads to an overall high wage rate. In countries where labor is less productive, competition for workers is less intense and wage rates are correspondingly lower.

As the Global Comparison shows, there is indeed a strong relationship between overall levels of productivity and wage rates around the world. Because China has generally low productivity, it has a relatively low wage rate. Low wages, in turn, give China a cost advantage in producing goods when its productivity is only moderately low, such as consumer electronics. As a result, it's cheaper to produce these goods in China than in the United States.

Popular Misconceptions Arising from Misunderstanding Comparative Advantage

The kind of trade that takes place between low-wage, low-productivity economies like China and high-wage, high-productivity economies like the United States gives rise to two common misperceptions.

- *The pauper labor fallacy* is the belief that when a country with high wages imports goods produced by workers who are paid low wages, this must hurt the standard of living of workers in the importing country.
- *The sweatshop labor fallacy* is the belief that trade must be bad for workers in poor exporting countries because those workers are paid very low wages by our standards.

Both fallacies miss the nature of gains from trade: it's to the advantage of both countries if the poorer, lower-wage country exports goods in which it has a comparative advantage, even if its cost advantage in these goods depends on low wages. That is, both countries are able to achieve a higher standard of living through trade.

It's particularly important to understand that buying a good made by someone who is paid much lower wages than most U.S. workers doesn't necessarily imply that you're taking advantage of that person. It depends on the alternatives. Because workers in poor countries have low productivity across the board, they are offered low wages whether they produce goods exported to the United States or goods sold in local markets. A job that looks terrible by rich-country standards can be a step up for someone in a poor country.

International trade that depends on low-wage exports can nonetheless raise the exporting country's standard of living. This is especially true of very-low-wage nations. For example, Bangladesh and similar countries would be much poorer than they are—their citizens might even be starving—if they weren't able to export goods such as clothing based on their low wage rates.

Sources of Comparative Advantage

International trade is driven by comparative advantage, but where does comparative advantage come from? Economists who study international trade have found three main sources of comparative advantage: international differences in *climate*, international differences in *factor endowments*, and international differences in *technology*.

GLOBAL COMPARISON PRODUCTIVITY AND WAGES AROUND THE WORLD

Is it true that both the pauper labor argument and the sweatshop labor argument are fallacies? Yes, it is. The real explanation for low wages in low-income countries is low overall productivity.

The graph shows estimates of labor productivity, measured by the value of output (GDP) per worker, and wages, measured by the hourly compensation of the average worker, for several countries in 2018. Both productivity and wages are expressed as percentages of U.S. productivity and wages; for example, productivity and wages in Japan were 66% and 68%, respectively, of their U.S. levels. You can see the strong positive relationship between productivity and wages. The relationship isn't perfect, however. For example, Iceland has higher wages than its productivity might lead you to expect. But simple comparisons of wages also give a misleading sense of labor costs in low-income countries: their low wage advantage is mostly offset by low productivity.

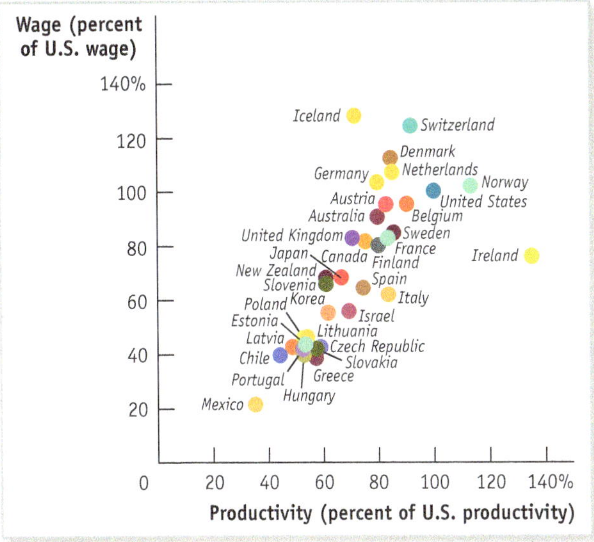

Data from: OECD and the World Bank, World Bank Development Indicators.

Differences in Climate One key reason the opportunity cost of producing shrimp in Vietnam and Thailand is less than in the United States is that shrimp need warm water—Vietnam has plenty of that, but the United States doesn't. In general, differences in climate play a significant role in international trade. Tropical countries export tropical products such as coffee, sugar, bananas, and shrimp. Countries in the temperate zones export crops such as wheat and corn. Some trade is even driven by the difference in seasons between the northern and southern hemispheres: winter deliveries of Chilean grapes have become commonplace in U.S. and European supermarkets.

Differences in Factor Endowments The United States trades more with Canada than with any other country (China comes in second). Among other things, Canada sells us a lot of forest products—lumber and products derived from lumber, such as pulp and paper. These exports don't reflect the special skill of Canadian lumberjacks. Canada has a comparative advantage in forest products because its forested area is much greater compared to the size of its labor force than is the ratio of forestland to the labor force in the United States.

Johner Images/Alamy

A greater endowment of forestland gives Canada a comparative advantage in forest products.

Forestland, like labor and capital, is a *factor of production:* an input used to produce goods and services. (Recall from Module 2 that the factors of production are land, labor, physical capital, and human capital.) Due to history and geography, the mix of available factors of production differs among countries, providing an important source of comparative advantage. The relationship between comparative advantage and factor availability is found in an influential model of international trade, the *Heckscher–Ohlin model,* described by two Swedish economists in the first half of the twentieth century.

Two key concepts in the model are *factor abundance* and *factor intensity.* Factor abundance refers to how large a country's supply of a factor is relative to its supply of other factors. **Factor intensity** refers to the ranking of

The **factor intensity** of a good is a measure of which factor is used in relatively greater quantities than other factors in production.

According to the **Heckscher–Ohlin model,** a country has a comparative advantage in a good whose production is intensive in the factors that are abundantly available in that country.

goods according to which factor is used in relatively greater quantities in production, compared to other factors. For instance, oil refining is a capital-intensive good because it tends to use a high ratio of capital to labor, while phone production is a labor-intensive good because it tends to use a high ratio of labor to capital.

According to the **Heckscher–Ohlin model,** *a country that has an abundant supply of a factor of production will have a comparative advantage in goods whose production is intensive in that factor.* Thus a country that has a relative abundance of capital will have a comparative advantage in capital-intensive industries such as oil refining, but a country that has a relative abundance of labor will have a comparative advantage in labor-intensive industries such as phone production.

The basic intuition behind this result is simple and based on opportunity cost.

- The opportunity cost of a given factor—the value that the factor would generate in alternative uses—is low for a country when it is relatively abundant in that factor.
- Relative to the United States, China has an abundance of low-skilled labor.
- As a result, the opportunity cost of the production of low-skilled, labor-intensive goods is lower in China than in the United States.

World trade in clothing is the most dramatic example of the validity of the Heckscher–Ohlin model in practice. Clothing production is a labor-intensive activity: it doesn't take much physical capital, nor does it require a lot of human capital in the form of highly educated workers. So you would expect labor-abundant countries such as China and Bangladesh to have a comparative advantage in clothing production. And they do.

The fact that international trade is the result of differences in factor endowments helps explain another fact: international specialization of production is often *incomplete.* That is, a country often maintains some domestic production of a good that it imports. A good example is U.S. trade in oil. Saudi Arabia exports oil to the United States because Saudi Arabia has an abundant supply of oil relative to its other factors of production. But the United States also produces some oil domestically because the size of its domestic oil reserves in Texas and Alaska (and now, increasingly, its oil shale reserves elsewhere) makes it economical to do so.

In our supply and demand analysis in the next section, we'll consider incomplete specialization by a country to be the norm. We should emphasize, however, that the fact that countries often incompletely specialize does not in any way change the conclusion that there are gains from trade.

Differences in Technology In the 1970s and 1980s, Japan became by far the world's largest exporter of automobiles, selling large numbers to the United States and the rest of the world. Japan's comparative advantage in automobiles wasn't the result of climate. Nor can it easily be attributed to differences in factor endowments: aside from a scarcity of land, Japan's mix of available factors is quite similar to that in other advanced countries. Instead, Japan's comparative advantage in automobiles was based on the superior production techniques developed by its manufacturers, which allowed them to produce more cars with a given amount of labor and capital than their American or European counterparts.

Japan's comparative advantage in automobiles was a case of comparative advantage caused by differences in technology—the techniques used in production.

The causes of differences in technology are somewhat mysterious. Sometimes they seem to be based on knowledge accumulated through experience—for example, Switzerland's comparative advantage in watches reflects a long tradition of watchmaking. Sometimes they are the result of a set of innovations that for some reason occur in one country but not in others.

Technological advantage, however, is often transitory. By adopting *lean production* (techniques designed to improve manufacturing productivity through increased efficiency), American auto manufacturers closed much of the gap in productivity with their Japanese competitors. Similarly, Europe's aircraft industry eventually closed a comparable gap with the U.S. aircraft industry. At any given point in time, however, differences in technology are a major source of comparative advantage.

ECONOMICS >> *in Action*

How Hong Kong Lost Its Shirts

The rise of Hong Kong was one of the most improbable-sounding economic success stories of the twentieth century. When a communist regime took over China in 1949, Hong Kong—which was at the time still a British colony—became in effect a city without a hinterland, largely cut off from economic relations with the territory just over the border. Until that point the people of Hong Kong had made a living largely by serving as a point of entry into China. However, after the city became cut off from China, you might have expected the city to languish. Instead, Hong Kong prospered, to such an extent that today the city—now returned to China, but governed as a special autonomous region—has a GDP per capita comparable to that of the United States.

Much of Hong Kong's ascent was the result of its clothing industry. In 1980, Hong Kong's garment and textile sectors employed almost 450,000 workers, close to 20% of total employment on the island. These workers overwhelmingly made apparel—shirts, trousers, dresses, and more—for export, especially to the United States.

More recently, however, the Hong Kong clothing industry has fallen sharply—in fact, it has almost disappeared, and along with it Hong Kong's apparel exports. Figure 15-4 shows Hong Kong's share of U.S. apparel imports since 1989, along with the share of a relative newcomer to the industry, Bangladesh. As you can see, Hong Kong has more or less dropped off the chart, while Bangladesh's share has risen significantly in recent years.

Why did Hong Kong lose its comparative advantage in making shirts, pants, and so on? It wasn't because the city's garment workers became less productive. Instead, it was because the city got better at other things. Apparel production is a labor-intensive, relatively low-tech industry; comparative advantage in that industry has historically always rested with poor, labor-abundant economies. Hong Kong no longer fits that description; Bangladesh does. Hong Kong's garment industry was a victim of the city's success.

FIGURE 15-4 Education, Skill Intensity, and Trade

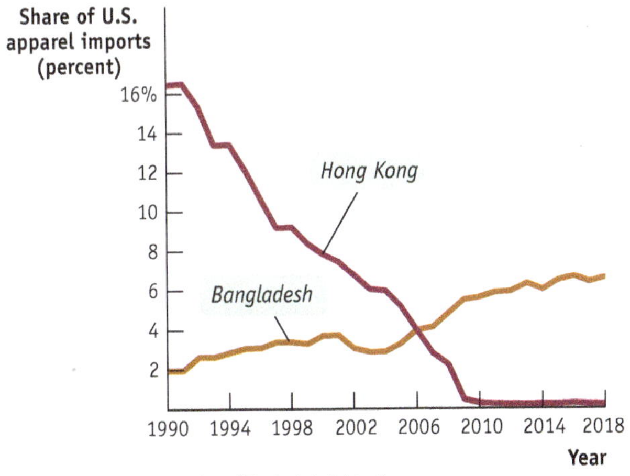

Data from: U.S. International Trade Administration.

>> *Quick Review*

- **Imports** and **exports** account for a growing share of the U.S. economy and the economies of many other countries.
- The growth of international trade and other international linkages is known as **globalization.** Extremely high levels of international trade are known as **hyperglobalization.**
- International trade is driven by comparative advantage. **The Ricardian model of international trade** shows that trade between two countries makes both countries better off than they would be in **autarky**—that is, there are gains from international trade.
- The main sources of comparative advantage are international differences in climate, factor endowments, and technology.
- The **Heckscher–Ohlin model** shows how comparative advantage can arise from differences in factor endowments: goods differ in their **factor intensity,** and countries tend to export goods that are intensive in the factors they have in abundance.

Check Your Understanding 15-1

1. In the United States, the opportunity cost of 1 ton of corn is 50 bicycles. In China, the opportunity cost of 1 bicycle is 0.01 ton of corn.
   a. Determine the pattern of comparative advantage.
   b. In autarky, the United States can produce 200,000 bicycles if no corn is produced, and China can produce 3,000 tons of corn if no bicycles are produced. Draw each country's production possibility frontier, assuming constant opportunity cost, with tons of corn on the vertical axis and bicycles on the horizontal axis.
   c. With trade, each country specializes its production. The United States consumes 1,000 tons of corn and 200,000 bicycles; China consumes 3,000 tons of corn and 100,000 bicycles. Indicate the production and consumption points on your diagrams, and use them to explain the gains from trade.
2. Explain the following patterns of trade using the Heckscher–Ohlin model.
   a. France exports wine to the United States, and the United States exports movies to France.
   b. Brazil exports shoes to the United States, and the United States exports shoe-making machinery to Brazil.

Solutions appear at back of book.

Supply, Demand, and International Trade

MODULE 16

WHAT YOU WILL LEARN

- Who gains and who loses from international trade?
- How do tariffs and quotas affect economic surplus?
- What are the arguments for and against trade protection policies?

16.1 Imports, Exports, and Wages

Glow Images/Superstock

Simple models of comparative advantage are helpful for understanding the fundamental causes of international trade. However, to analyze the effects of international trade at a more detailed level and to understand trade policy, it helps to return to the supply and demand model. We'll start by looking at the effects of imports on domestic producers and consumers, then turn to the effects of exports.

The Effects of Imports

Figure 16-1 shows the U.S. market for phones, ignoring international trade for a moment. It introduces a few new concepts: the *domestic demand curve,* the *domestic supply curve,* and the domestic or autarky price.

The **domestic demand curve** shows how the quantity of a good demanded by residents of a country depends on the price of that good. Why "domestic"? Because people living in other countries may demand the good, too. Once we introduce international trade, we need to distinguish between purchases of a good by domestic consumers and purchases by foreign consumers. So, the domestic demand curve reflects only the demand of residents of our own country.

Similarly, the **domestic supply curve** shows how the quantity of a good supplied by producers inside our own country depends on the price of that good. Once we introduce international trade, we need to distinguish between the supply of domestic producers and foreign supply—supply brought in from abroad.

In autarky, with no international trade in phones, the equilibrium in this market would be determined by the intersection of the domestic demand and domestic supply curves, point *A*. The equilibrium price of phones would be P_A, and the equilibrium quantity of phones produced and consumed would be Q_A. As always, both consumers and producers gain from the existence of the domestic market. In autarky, consumer surplus would be equal to the area of the blue-shaded triangle in

The **domestic demand curve** shows how the quantity of a good demanded by domestic consumers depends on the price of that good.

The **domestic supply curve** shows how the quantity of a good supplied by domestic producers depends on the price of that good.

FIGURE 16-1 Consumer and Producer Surplus in Autarky

In the absence of trade, the domestic price is P_A, the autarky price at which the domestic supply curve and the domestic demand curve intersect. The quantity produced and consumed domestically is Q_A. Consumer surplus is represented by the blue-shaded area, and producer surplus is represented by the red-shaded area.

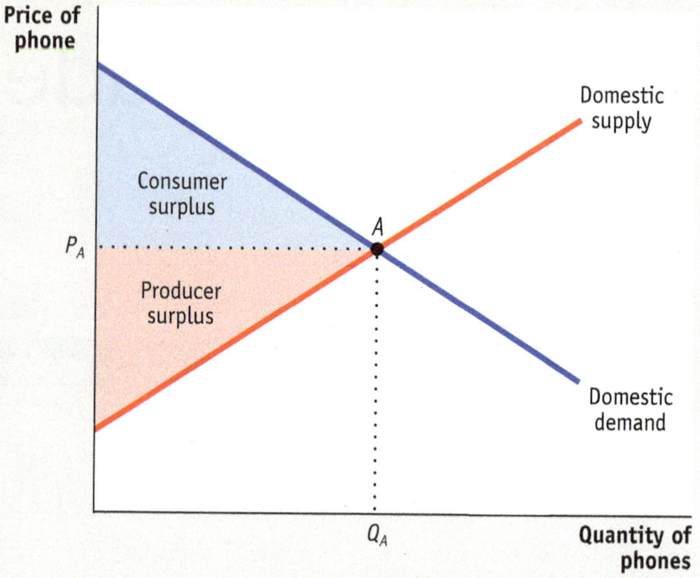

The **world price** of a good is the price at which that good can be bought or sold abroad.

Figure 16-1. Producer surplus would be equal to the area of the red-shaded triangle. And total surplus would be equal to the sum of these two shaded triangles.

Now let's imagine opening up this market to imports. To do this, we must make an assumption about the supply of imports. The simplest assumption, which we will adopt here, is that unlimited quantities of phones can be purchased from abroad at a fixed price, known as the world price of phones. Figure 16-2 shows a situation in which the **world price** of a phone, P_W, is lower than the phone price that would prevail in the domestic market in autarky, P_A.

FIGURE 16-2 The Domestic Market with Imports

Here the world price of phones, P_W, is below the autarky price, P_A. When the economy is opened to international trade, imports enter the domestic market, and the domestic price falls from the autarky price, P_A, to the world price, P_W. As the price falls, the domestic quantity demanded rises from Q_A to Q_D and the domestic quantity supplied falls from Q_A to Q_S. The difference between domestic quantity demanded and domestic quantity supplied at P_W, the quantity $Q_D - Q_S$, is filled by imports.

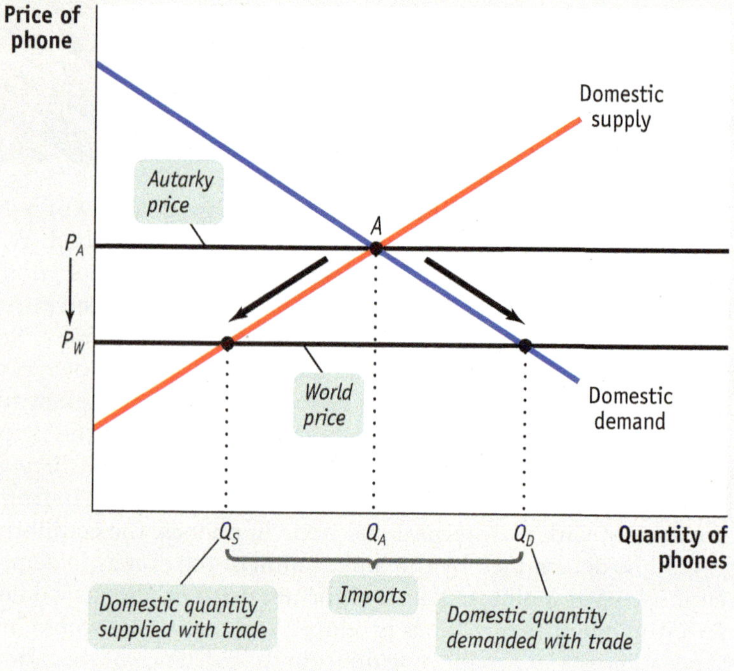

Given that the world price is below the domestic price of a phone, it is profitable for importers to buy phones abroad and resell them domestically. The imported phones increase the supply of phones in the domestic market, driving down the domestic market price. Phones will continue to be imported until the domestic price falls to a level equal to the world price.

The result is shown in Figure 16-2. Because of imports, the domestic price of a phone falls from P_A to P_W. The quantity of phones demanded by domestic consumers rises from Q_A to Q_D, and the quantity supplied by domestic producers falls from Q_A to Q_S. The difference between the domestic quantity demanded and the domestic quantity supplied, $Q_D - Q_S$, is filled by imports.

Now let's turn to the effects of imports on consumer surplus and producer surplus. Because imports of phones lead to a fall in their domestic price, consumer surplus rises and producer surplus falls. Figure 16-3 shows how this works. We label four areas: *W*, *X*, *Y*, and *Z*. The autarky consumer surplus we identified in Figure 16-1 corresponds to *W*, and the autarky producer surplus corresponds to the sum of *X* and *Y*. The fall in the domestic price to the world price leads to an increase in consumer surplus; it increases by *X* and *Z*, so consumer surplus now equals the sum of *W*, *X*, and *Z*. At the same time, producers lose *X* in surplus, so producer surplus now equals only *Y*.

The table in Figure 16-3 summarizes the changes in consumer and producer surplus when the phone market is opened to imports. Consumers gain surplus equal to the areas $X + Z$; producers lose surplus equal to *X*. So the sum of producer and consumer surplus—the total surplus generated in the phone market—increases by *Z*. As a result of trade, consumers gain and producers lose, but the gain to consumers exceeds the loss to producers.

This is an important result. We have just shown that opening up a market to imports leads to a net gain in total surplus, which is what we should

FIGURE 16-3 The Effects of Imports on Surplus

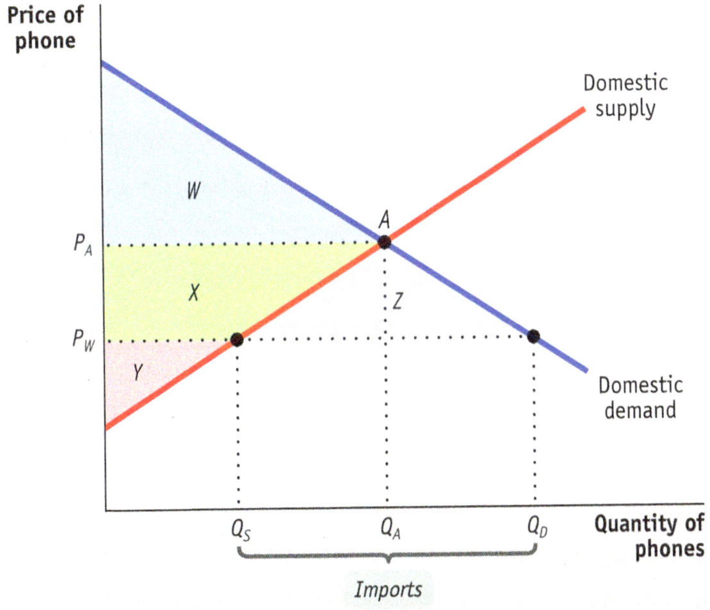

	Changes in surplus	
	Gain	**Loss**
Consumer surplus	$X + Z$	
Producer surplus		$-X$
Change in total surplus	$+Z$	

When the domestic price falls to P_W as a result of international trade, consumers gain additional surplus (areas $X + Z$) and producers lose surplus (area *X*). Because the gains to consumers outweigh the losses to producers, there is an increase in the total surplus in the economy as a whole (area *Z*).

have expected given the proposition that there are gains from international trade.

However, we have also learned that although the country as a whole gains, some groups—in this case, domestic producers of phones—lose as a result of international trade. As we'll see shortly, the fact that international trade typically creates losers as well as winners is crucial for understanding the politics of trade policy.

We turn next to the case in which a country exports a good.

The Effects of Exports

Figure 16-4 shows the effects on a country when it exports a good, in this case trucks. For this example, we assume that unlimited quantities of trucks can be sold abroad at a given world price, P_W, which is higher than the price that would prevail in the domestic market in autarky, P_A.

The higher world price makes it profitable for exporters to buy trucks domestically and sell them overseas. The purchases of domestic trucks drive the domestic price up until it is equal to the world price. As a result, the quantity demanded by domestic consumers falls from Q_A to Q_D and the quantity supplied by domestic producers rises from Q_A to Q_S. This difference between domestic production and domestic consumption, $Q_S - Q_D$, is exported.

Like imports, exports lead to an overall gain in total surplus for the exporting country, but they also create losers as well as winners. Figure 16-5 shows the effects of truck exports on producer and consumer surplus. In the absence of trade, the price of each truck would be P_A. Consumer surplus in the absence of trade is the sum of areas W and X, and producer surplus is area Y. As a result of trade, price rises from P_A to P_W, consumer surplus falls to W, and producer surplus rises to $Y + X + Z$. So producers gain $X + Z$, consumers lose X, and, as shown in the table accompanying the figure, the economy as a whole gains total surplus in the amount of Z.

We have learned, then, that imports of a particular good hurt domestic producers of that good but help domestic consumers, whereas exports of a particular good hurt domestic consumers of that good but help domestic producers. In each case, the gains are larger than the losses.

FIGURE 16-4 The Domestic Market with Exports

Here the world price, P_W, is greater than the autarky price, P_A. When the economy is opened to international trade, some of the domestic supply is now exported. The domestic price rises from the autarky price, P_A, to the world price, P_W. As the price rises, the domestic quantity demanded falls from Q_A to Q_D and the domestic quantity supplied rises from Q_A to Q_S. The portion of domestic production that is not consumed domestically, $Q_S - Q_D$, is exported.

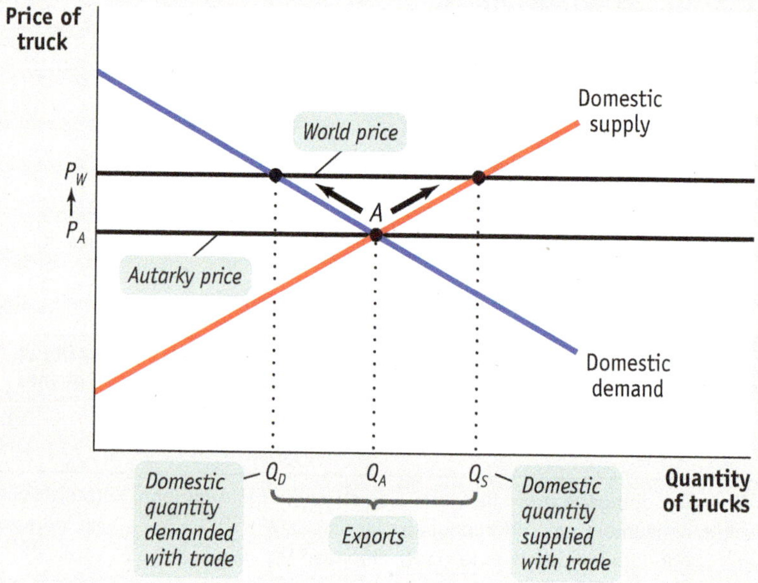

FIGURE 16-5 The Effects of Exports on Surplus

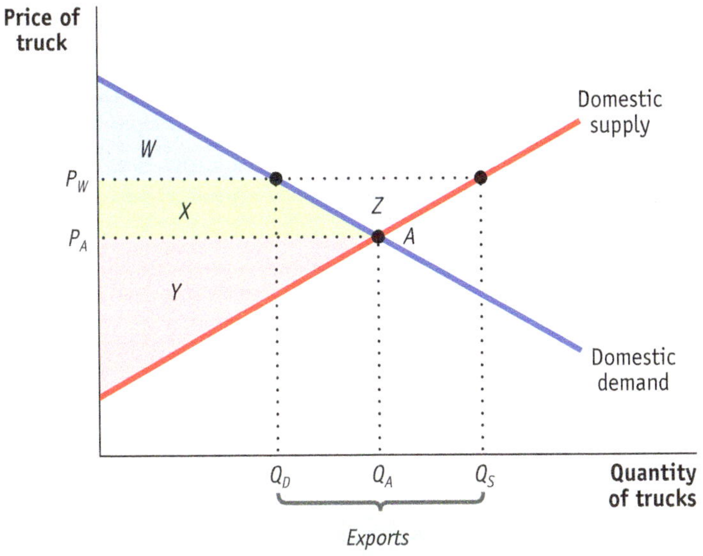

	Changes in surplus	
	Gain	Loss
Consumer surplus		− X
Producer surplus	X + Z	
Change in total surplus	+ Z	

When the domestic price rises to P_W as a result of trade, producers gain additional surplus (area $X + Z$) but consumers lose surplus (area X). Because the gains to producers outweigh the losses to consumers, there is an increase in the total surplus in the economy as a whole (area Z).

International Trade and Wages

So far we have focused on the effects of international trade on producers and consumers in a particular industry. For many purposes this is a very helpful approach. However, producers and consumers are not the only parts of society affected by trade—the owners of factors of production are also affected. In particular, the owners of labor, land, and capital employed in producing goods that are exported, or goods that compete with imported goods, can be deeply affected by trade.

Moreover, the effects of trade aren't limited to just those industries that export or compete with imports because *factors of production can often move between industries.* So now we turn our attention to the long-run effects of international trade on income distribution—how a country's total income is allocated among its various factors of production.

To begin our analysis, consider the position of Mia, who is initially employed as an accountant in an industry that is shrinking as a result of growing international trade. Suppose, for example, that she works in the U.S. apparel (clothing) industry, which formerly employed millions of people but has largely been displaced by imports from low-wage countries. Mia is likely to find a new job in another industry, such as health care, which has been expanding rapidly over time. How will the move affect her earnings?

The answer is, there probably won't be much effect. According to the U.S. Bureau of Labor Statistics, accountants earn roughly the same amount in health care that they do in what's left of the apparel industry—about $65,000 a year. So we shouldn't think of Mia as a producer of apparel who is hurt by competition from imports. Instead, we should think of her as a worker with particular skills who is affected by imports, mainly by the extent to which those imports change the wages of accountants in the economy as a whole.

The wage rate of accountants is a *factor price*—the price employers have to pay for the services of a factor of production. One key question about international

Exporting industries produce goods and services that are sold abroad.

Import-competing industries produce goods and services that are also imported.

trade is how it affects factor prices—not just narrowly defined factors of production like accountants, but broadly defined factors such as capital, unskilled labor, and college-educated labor.

Earlier in this section we described the Heckscher–Ohlin model of trade, which states that comparative advantage is determined by a country's factor endowment. This model also suggests how international trade affects factor prices in a country: compared to autarky, international trade tends to raise the prices of factors that are abundantly available and reduce the prices of factors that are scarce.

We won't work this out in detail, but the idea is simple. The prices of factors of production, like the prices of goods and services, are determined by supply and demand. If international trade increases the demand for a factor of production, that factor's price will rise; if international trade reduces the demand for a factor of production, that factor's price will fall.

Now think of a country's industries as consisting of both: **exporting industries,** which produce goods and services that are sold abroad, and **import-competing industries,** which produce goods and services that compete with goods and services that are imported from abroad. Compared with autarky, international trade leads to higher production in exporting industries and lower production in import-competing industries. This indirectly increases the demand for factors used by exporting industries and decreases the demand for factors used by import-competing industries.

In addition, the Heckscher–Ohlin model shows that a country tends to export goods that are intensive in its factors that are abundant in that country and to import goods that are intensive in factors that are scarce. *So international trade tends to increase the demand for factors that are more abundant in a country compared with other countries, and to decrease the demand for factors that are more scarce in a country compared with other countries. As international trade grows, the prices of abundant factors tend to rise, and the prices of scarce factors tend to fall.*

In other words, international trade tends to redistribute income toward a country's abundant factors and away from its less abundant factors.

U.S. exports tend to be human-capital-intensive (such as high-tech design and Hollywood movies), while U.S. imports tend to be unskilled-labor-intensive (such as phone assembly and clothing production). This suggests that the effect of international trade on the U.S. factor markets is to raise the wage rate of highly educated American workers and reduce the wage rate of unskilled American workers.

This effect has been a source of much concern in recent years. Wage inequality—the gap between the wages of high-paid and low-paid workers—has increased substantially over the last 40 years. Some economists believe that growing international trade is an important factor in that trend. If international trade has the effects predicted by the Heckscher–Ohlin model, its growth raises the wages of highly educated American workers, who already have relatively high wages, and lowers the wages of less educated American workers, who already have relatively low wages.

But keep in mind another phenomenon: trade reduces the income inequality between countries as poor countries improve their standard of living by exporting to rich countries.

How important are these effects? In some historical episodes, the impacts of international trade on factor prices have been very large. The opening of transatlantic trade in the late nineteenth century had a large negative impact on land rents in Europe, hurting landowners but helping workers and owners of capital.

The effects of trade on wages in the United States have generated considerable controversy in recent years. Most economists who have studied the issue agree that growing imports of labor-intensive products from newly industrializing economies, and the export of high-technology goods in return, have helped cause a widening wage gap between highly educated and less educated workers in this country. However, most economists believe that it is only one of several forces explaining the growth in American wage inequality.

Check Your Understanding 16-1

1. Due to a strike by truckers, trade in food between the United States and Mexico is halted. In autarky, the price of Mexican grapes is lower than that of U.S. grapes. Using a diagram of the U.S. domestic demand curve and the U.S. domestic supply curve for grapes, explain the effect of the strike on the following.
   a. U.S. grape consumers' surplus
   b. U.S. grape producers' surplus
   c. U.S. total surplus
2. What effect do you think the strike will have on Mexican grape producers? Mexican grape pickers? Mexican grape consumers? U.S. grape pickers?

Solutions appear at back of book.

>> Quick Review

- The intersection of the **domestic demand curve** and the **domestic supply curve** determines the domestic price of a good. When a market is opened to international trade, the domestic price is driven to equal the **world price.**
- If the world price is lower than the autarky price, trade leads to imports and the domestic price falls to the world price. There are overall gains from international trade because the gain in consumer surplus exceeds the loss in producer surplus.
- If the world price is higher than the autarky price, trade leads to exports and the domestic price rises to the world price. There are overall gains from international trade because the gain in producer surplus exceeds the loss in consumer surplus.
- Trade leads to an expansion of **exporting industries,** which increases demand for a country's abundant factors, and a contraction of **import-competing industries,** which decreases demand for its scarce factors.

16.2 The Effects of Trade Protection

Ever since David Ricardo laid out the principle of comparative advantage in the early nineteenth century, most economists have advocated **free trade.** That is, they have argued that government policy should not attempt either to reduce or to increase the levels of exports and imports that occur naturally as a result of supply and demand.

Despite the free-trade arguments of economists, however, many governments use taxes and other restrictions to limit imports. Less frequently, governments offer subsidies to encourage exports. Policies that limit imports, usually with the goal of protecting domestic producers in import-competing industries from foreign competition, are known as **trade protection** or simply as **protection.**

Let's look at the two most common protectionist policies, *tariffs* and *import quotas,* then turn to the reasons governments follow these policies.

The Effects of a Tariff

A **tariff** is a form of excise tax, levied only on sales of imported goods. For example, the U.S. government could declare that anyone bringing phones for sales into the country must pay a tariff of $100 per unit. In the distant past, tariffs were an important source of government revenue because they were relatively easy to collect. But in the modern world, tariffs are usually intended to discourage imports and protect import-competing domestic producers, and are not levied as a source of government revenue.

A tariff raises both the price received by domestic producers and the price paid by domestic consumers. Suppose, for example, that our country imports phones, and a phone costs $200 on the world market. As we saw earlier, under free trade the domestic price would also be $200. But if a tariff of $100 per unit is imposed, the domestic price will rise to $300, because it won't be profitable to import phones unless the price in the domestic market is high enough to compensate importers for the cost of paying the tariff.

Figure 16-6 illustrates the effects of a tariff on imports of phones. As before, we assume that P_W is the world price of a phone. Before the tariff is imposed, imports have driven the domestic price down to P_W, so that pre-tariff domestic production is Q_S, pre-tariff domestic consumption is Q_D, and pre-tariff imports are $Q_D - Q_S$.

Now suppose that the government imposes a tariff on each phone imported. As a consequence, it is no longer profitable to import phones unless the domestic

An economy has **free trade** when the government does not attempt either to reduce or to increase the levels of exports and imports that occur naturally as a result of supply and demand.

Policies that limit imports are known as **trade protection** or simply as **protection.**

A **tariff** is a tax levied on imports.

FIGURE 16-6 The Effect of a Tariff

A tariff raises the domestic price of the good from P_W to P_T. The domestic quantity demanded shrinks from Q_D to Q_{DT}, and the domestic quantity supplied increases from Q_S to Q_{ST}. As a result, imports—which had been $Q_D - Q_S$ before the tariff was imposed—shrink to $Q_{DT} - Q_{ST}$ after the tariff is imposed.

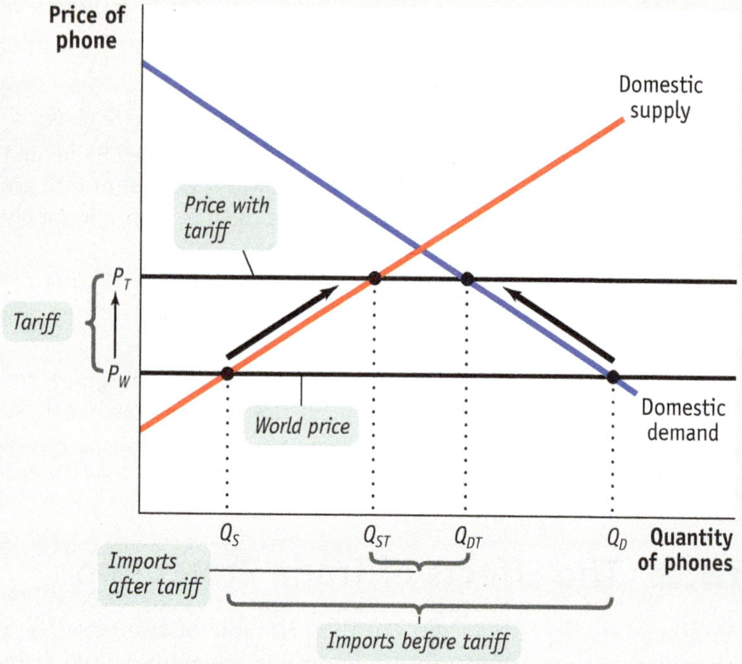

price received by the importer is greater than or equal to the world price plus the tariff. So the domestic price rises to P_T, which is equal to the world price, P_W, plus the tariff. Domestic production rises to Q_{ST}, domestic consumption falls to Q_{DT}, and imports fall to $Q_{DT} - Q_{ST}$.

A tariff, then, raises domestic prices, leading to increased domestic production and reduced domestic consumption compared to the situation under free trade. Figure 16-7 shows the effects on surplus. There are three effects:

1. The higher domestic price increases producer surplus, a gain equal to area *A*.
2. The higher domestic price reduces consumer surplus, a reduction equal to the sum of areas *A*, *B*, *C*, and *D*.
3. The tariff yields revenue to the government. How much revenue? The government collects the tariff—which, remember, is equal to the difference between P_T and P_W on each of the $Q_{DT} - Q_{ST}$ units imported. So total revenue is $(P_T - P_W) \times (Q_{DT} - Q_{ST})$. This is equal to area *C*.

The welfare effects of a tariff are summarized in the table in Figure 16-7. Producers gain, consumers lose, and the government gains. But consumer losses are greater than the sum of producer and government gains, leading to a net reduction in total surplus equal to areas $B + D$.

An excise tax creates inefficiency, or deadweight loss, because it prevents mutually beneficial trades from occurring. The same is true of a tariff, where the deadweight loss imposed on society is equal to the loss in total surplus represented by areas $B + D$.

Tariffs generate deadweight losses because they create inefficiencies in two ways:

1. Some mutually beneficial trades go unexploited: some consumers who are willing to pay more than the world price, P_W, do not purchase the good, even

FIGURE 16-7 A Tariff Reduces Total Surplus

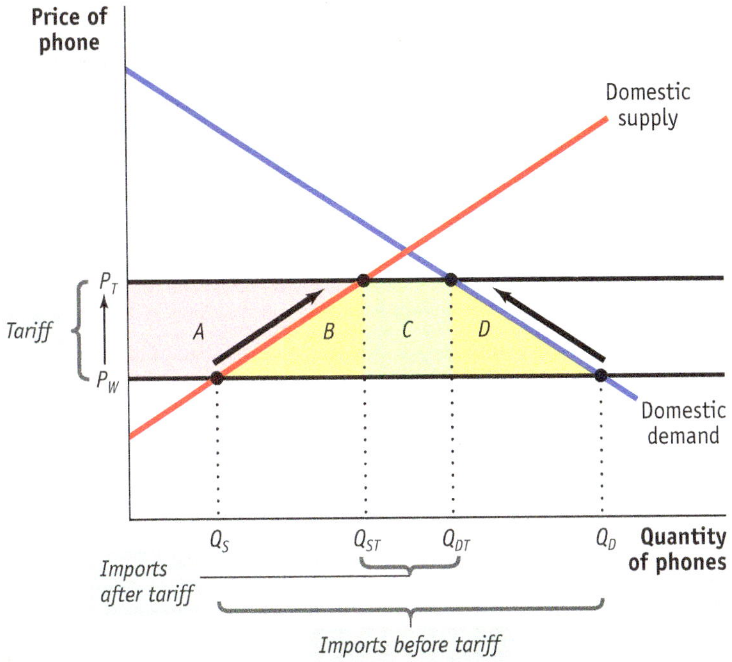

	Changes in surplus	
	Gain	**Loss**
Consumer surplus		$-(A + B + C + D)$
Producer surplus	A	
Government revenue	C	
Change in total surplus		$-(B + D)$

When the domestic price rises as a result of a tariff, producers gain additional surplus (area *A*), the government gains revenue (area *C*), and consumers lose surplus (areas *A* + *B* + *C* + *D*). Because the losses to consumers outweigh the gains to producers and the government, the economy as a whole loses surplus (areas *B* and *D*).

though P_W is the true cost of a unit of the good to the economy. The cost of this inefficiency is represented in Figure 16-7 by area *D*.

2. The economy's resources are wasted on inefficient production: some producers whose cost exceeds P_W produce the good, even though an additional unit of the good can be purchased abroad for P_W. The cost of this inefficiency is represented in Figure 16-7 by area *B*.

The Effects of an Import Quota

An **import quota,** another form of trade protection, is a legal limit on the quantity of a good that can be imported. For example, a U.S. import quota on Chinese phones might limit the quantity imported each year to 50 million units. Import quotas are usually administered through licenses: a number of licenses are issued, each giving the license-holder the right to import a limited quantity of the good each year.

A quota on sales has the same effect as an excise tax, with one difference: the money that would otherwise have accrued to the government as tax revenue under an excise tax becomes license-holders' revenue under a quota—also known as **quota rents.** Similarly, an import quota has the same effect as a tariff, with one difference: the money that would otherwise have been government revenue becomes quota rents to license-holders.

Look again at Figure 16-7. An import quota that limits imports to $Q_{DT} - Q_{ST}$ will raise the domestic price of phones by the same amount as the tariff we considered previously. That is, it will raise the domestic price from P_W to P_T. However, area *C* will now represent quota rents rather than government revenue.

An **import quota** is a legal limit on the quantity of a good that can be imported.

The difference between the demand and supply price at the quota amount is the **quota rent,** the earnings that accrue to the license-holder from ownership of the right to sell the good. It is equal to the market price of the license when the licenses are traded.

>> ***Quick Review***

- Most economists advocate **free trade,** although many governments engage in **trade protection** of import-competing industries. The two most common protectionist policies are tariffs and import quotas. Only in rare instances do governments subsidize exporting industries.
- A **tariff** is a tax on imports. It raises the domestic price above the world price, leading to a fall in trade and domestic consumption and a rise in domestic production. Domestic producers and the government gain, but domestic consumer losses more than offset this gain, leading to deadweight loss.
- An **import quota** is a legal quantity limit on imports. Its effect is like that of a tariff, except that revenues—the quota rents—accrue to the license-holder, not to the domestic government.

Who receives import licenses and so collects the quota rents? In the case of U.S. import protection, the answer may surprise you: the most important import licenses—mainly for clothing, and to a lesser extent for sugar—are granted to foreign governments.

Because the quota rents for most U.S. import quotas go to foreigners, the cost to the nation of such quotas is larger than that of a comparable tariff (a tariff that leads to the same level of imports). In Figure 16-7, the net loss to the United States from such an import quota would be equal to areas $B + C + D$, the difference between consumer losses and producer gains.

Check Your Understanding 16-2

1. Suppose the world price of butter is $0.50 per pound and the domestic price in autarky is $1.00 per pound. Use a diagram similar to Figure 16-6 to show the following.
   a. If there is free trade, domestic butter producers want the government to impose a tariff of no less than $0.50 per pound. Compare the outcome with a tariff of $0.25 per pound.
   b. What happens if a tariff greater than $0.50 per pound is imposed?
2. Suppose the government imposes an import quota rather than a tariff on butter. What quota limit would generate the same quantity of imports as a tariff of $0.50 per pound?

Solutions appear at back of book.

16.3 The Political Economy of Trade Protection

We have seen that international trade produces mutual benefits to the countries that engage in it. We have also seen that tariffs and import quotas, although they produce winners as well as losers, reduce total surplus. Yet many countries continue to impose tariffs and import quotas as well as to enact other protectionist measures.

To understand why trade protection takes place, we will first look at some common justifications for protection. Then we will look at the politics of trade protection. Finally, we will look at an important feature of trade protection in today's world: tariffs and import quotas are the subject of international negotiation and are policed by international organizations.

Arguments for Trade Protection

Advocates for tariffs and import quotas offer three common arguments:

1. The *national security* argument is based on the proposition that overseas sources of goods are vulnerable to disruption in times of international conflict. Therefore, a country should protect domestic suppliers of crucial goods with the aim to be self-sufficient in those goods. For example, during the coronavirus pandemic, 90% of medical masks used in the United States were produced overseas. As a result, masks were in extremely short supply and rose sharply in price as countries scrambled for supplies of this critical good.
2. The *job creation* argument points to the additional jobs created in import-competing industries as a result of trade protection. Economists argue that these jobs are offset by the jobs lost elsewhere, such as industries that use imported inputs and now face higher input costs. But noneconomists don't always find this argument persuasive.
3. The *infant industry* argument, often raised in newly industrializing countries, holds that new industries require a temporary period of trade protection to get established. For example, in the 1950s many countries in Latin America imposed tariffs and import quotas on manufactured goods, in an effort to

switch from their traditional role as exporters of raw materials to a new status as industrial countries.

In theory, the argument for infant industry protection can be compelling, particularly in high-tech industries that increase a country's overall skill level. Reality, however, is more complicated: it is most often industries that are politically influential that gain protection. In addition, governments tend to be poor predictors of the best emerging technologies. Finally, it is often very difficult to wean an industry from protection when it should be mature enough to stand on its own.

The Politics of Trade Protection

In reality, much trade protection has little to do with the arguments just described. Instead, it reflects the political influence of import-competing producers.

We've seen that a tariff or import quota leads to gains for import-competing producers and losses for consumers. Producers, however, usually have much more influence over trade policy decisions. The producers who compete with imports of a particular good are usually a smaller, more cohesive group than the consumers of that good.

For example, in 2018, the U.S. government imposed a 30% tariff on imports of solar panels, many of which come from China. While it helped U.S. producers, who employed about 2,000 workers, it hurt a much larger group, including tens of thousands of solar panel installers, whose business was hurt when panels became more expensive, leading to a decline in new installations. However, the voices of panel producers were heard much more clearly in Washington than the voices of concern from of those who buy panels or those who install them.

It would be nice to say that the main reason trade protection isn't more extensive is that economists have convinced governments of the virtues of free trade. A more important reason, however, is the role of *international trade agreements.*

International Trade Agreements and the World Trade Organization

When a country engages in trade protection, it hurts two groups. We've already addressed the adverse effect on domestic consumers, but protection also hurts foreign export industries. This means that countries care about each other's trade policies: the Canadian lumber industry, for example, has a strong interest in keeping U.S. tariffs on forest products low.

Because countries care about each other's trade policies, they enter into **international trade agreements:** treaties in which a country promises to engage in less trade protection against the exports of another country in return for a promise by the other country to do the same for its own exports. International trade agreements are especially important as a way to head off potential **trade wars,** in which countries engage in a series of escalating trade restrictions against one another in an attempt to force each other to make policy concessions. Most world trade is now governed by such agreements.

Some international trade agreements involve just two countries or a small group of countries. For example, in 1993 the United States, Canada, and Mexico were joined together in the **North American Free Trade Agreement,** or **NAFTA.** By 2008, NAFTA had removed most barriers to trade among the three nations. In 2018, the countries negotiated a revised agreement, the United States–Mexico–Canada Agreement or USMCA, which made some changes but kept the main structure of NAFTA intact. For accuracy's sake, we will refer to the current trade agreement as NAFTA–USMCA.

Most European countries are part of an even more comprehensive agreement, the **European Union,** or **EU.** Unlike members of NAFTA–USMCA, the 27 members of the EU agree to charge the same tariffs on goods imported from non-EU countries.

International trade agreements are treaties in which a country promises to engage in less trade protection against the exports of other countries in return for a promise by other countries to do the same for its own exports.

In a **trade war,** a pair of countries engage in a series of escalating trade restrictions against one another.

The **North American Free Trade Agreement,** or **NAFTA,** is a trade agreement among the United States, Canada, and Mexico.

The **European Union,** or **EU,** is a customs union among 28 European nations.

The **World Trade Organization,** or **WTO,** oversees international trade agreements and rules on disputes between countries over those agreements.

The EU also sets rules on policies other than trade, most notably requiring that each member nation freely accept migrants from any other member, while collecting fees from member nations to pay for things like agricultural subsidies. These rules and fees are often unpopular and controversial. In June 2016, Britain held a referendum on whether to leave the EU—a proposal popularly known as *Brexit* (short for "British exit"), which was approved by a narrow majority of voters. Negotiations over the details of Britain's exit from the EU reached an agreement in December 2020, and its formal approval was still in progress as this book went to press.

There are also global trade agreements covering most of the world. Such global agreements are overseen by the **World Trade Organization,** or **WTO,** an international organization composed of member countries—164 of them currently, accounting for the bulk of world trade. The WTO plays two roles:

1. It provides the framework for the massively complex negotiations involved in a major international trade agreement (the full text of the last major agreement, approved in 1994, was 24,000 pages long).
2. The WTO resolves disputes between its members that typically arise when one country claims that another country's policies violate its previous agreements.

An example of the WTO at work is the dispute between the United States and Brazil over American subsidies to its cotton farmers. These subsidies, in the amount of $3 billion to $4 billion a year, are illegal under WTO rules. Brazil argued that they artificially reduced the price of American cotton on world markets and hurt Brazilian cotton farmers. In 2005, the WTO ruled against the United States and in favor of Brazil, and the United States responded by cutting some export subsidies on cotton. However, in 2007, the WTO ruled that the United States had not done enough to fully comply, such as eliminating government loans to cotton farmers. In 2010, after Brazil threatened, in turn, to impose import tariffs on U.S.-manufactured goods, the two sides agreed to a framework for the solution to the cotton dispute.

The WTO rules do allow trade protection under certain circumstances. One such circumstance occurs when the foreign competition is "unfair" under certain technical criteria. Trade protection is also allowed as a temporary measure when a sudden surge of imports threatens to disrupt a domestic industry.

The WTO is sometimes, with great exaggeration, described as a world government. In fact, it has no army, no police, and no direct enforcement power. The grain of truth in that description is that when a country joins the WTO, it agrees to accept the organization's judgments—and these judgments apply not only to tariffs and import quotas but also to domestic policies that the organization considers trade protection disguised under another name. So in joining the WTO a country does give up some of its sovereignty.

16.4 Challenges to Globalization

The forward march of globalization over the past century is generally considered a major political and economic success because it has brought rising living standards to hundreds of millions of people. But it is also true that many people, including some economists and policy makers, are having second thoughts about globalization. These second thoughts arise largely from the decline of manufacturing in richer countries and offshore outsourcing that jeopardizes the jobs of non-manufacturing workers, once considered immune from foreign competition.

Greater Inequality Arising from Trade

We have seen that international trade has an effect on factor prices, particularly wages. Forty years ago, U.S. imports from low-income countries consisted mostly of raw materials and goods that depended upon the climate, such as bananas and coffee beans. So U.S. wages were relatively unaffected by international trade. But that is no longer the case. Today many of the manufactured goods consumed in the United States are imported from low-income countries. As a result, international trade now has a much larger effect on income inequality in the United States.

Trade with Asia has raised the greatest concerns among those who study the effect of international trade on wage levels in rich countries. China, despite its rapid economic growth and rising wages in recent years, is still a very low-wage country compared with the United States. Its hourly compensation in manufacturing is approximately 10% of the U.S. level. Other manufacturing exporters, such as India, Bangladesh, and Vietnam, have wage levels less than half of China's. As we discussed earlier in the section, it's clear that imports from these countries put downward pressure on the wages of less-skilled U.S. workers and contributed to income inequality.

One factor exacerbating the adverse effect of globalization on some workers is the fact that competition from imports sometimes hits particular communities very hard. In particular, there was a surge of U.S. imports from China between the late 1990s and the late 2000s—the "China shock"—that probably displaced around a million U.S. workers. That's actually not an enormous number in the economy as big as the United States, where 1.5 million workers are fired for one reason or another every month. But the jobs lost to Chinese corporations were concentrated in a relatively small number of towns and cities, like the furniture-manufacturing centers of North Carolina, and for those communities the impact was devastating.

Outsourcing

Chinese exports to the United States overwhelmingly consist of labor-intensive manufactured goods. However, some U.S. workers have also found themselves facing a new form of international competition. *Outsourcing,* in which a company hires another company to perform a task, such as running the corporate computer system, is a long-standing business practice. Until recently, however, outsourcing was normally done locally, with a company hiring another company in the same city or country.

Offshore outsourcing has the potential to disrupt the job prospects of millions of U.S. workers.

Now, modern telecommunications increasingly make it possible to engage in **offshore outsourcing,** in which businesses hire people in another country to perform various tasks. The classic example is call centers: the person answering the phone when you call a company's 1-800 help line may well be in India, which has taken the lead in attracting offshore outsourcing. Offshore outsourcing has also spread to fields such as software design and even health care: the radiologist examining your X-rays, like the person giving you computer help, may be on another continent.

The threat of offshore outsourcing differs from the threat posed by large-scale imports of manufactured goods from poorer countries. By and large, offshore outsourcing hits higher-skilled U.S. workers who imagined their jobs were safe from foreign competition. An example is U.S. computer programmers, many of whom have had their jobs outsourced to India or Eastern Europe. Although offshore outsourcing still accounts for a relatively small portion of international trade, some economists have warned that millions or even tens of millions of workers in rich countries may face unpleasant surprises in the not-too-distant future—workers such as bookkeepers, claims adjusters, and mortgage processors.

Offshore outsourcing takes place when businesses hire people in another country to perform various tasks.

Do these challenges of globalization undermine the argument that international trade is a good thing? The great majority of economists would argue that the gains from trade protection still exceed the losses. However, as international trade has grown and job losses in vulnerable sectors have mounted, the politics of international trade has become increasingly difficult and has led to calls for protectionist trade policies. In this debate it's important to understand that government programs, such as unemployment benefits, easily accessible health care, and retraining projects, can reduce the opposition to free trade by helping cushion the losses of those hurt by trade.

ECONOMICS >> *in Action*

Trade War, What Is It Good For?

James Ferguson/Financial Times

In 2019, the United States and China engaged in a classic trade war by levying tariffs on each other's exports.

Historically, the United States has been the global leader in promoting trade agreements and reducing tariffs—not just between it and its trading partners, but also around the world. The long-term trend of its tariff policy reflects this: in 1933, U.S. imports faced an average tariff rate of almost 20%; by 2016, that was down to just 1.5%.

That changed in 2017, when Donald Trump became president and moved to reverse decades of pro-trade policy. Starting in 2018, the United States began a series of tariff increases on imports from China, one of its largest trading partners, and China responded by raising its own tariffs on U.S. goods. As Figure 16-8 shows, the Trump trade war was serious: by the beginning of 2020, both countries were imposing average tariffs on the other's goods of about 21%.

What motivated the Trump administration to take a hard line on China? One fundamental concern was that China was not honoring its agreements as a member of the World Trade Organization, as many analysts had argued. In particular, China was widely accused of failing to respect "intellectual property rights" like patents and copyrights. In other words, it was accused of stealing valuable technology and original content from its trading partners. In addition, China was accused of subsidizing its high-technology industries, a violation of trade rules that gave them an unfair advantage against non-Chinese rivals.

However, President Trump also claimed that China had adopted an explicit policy of exporting much more to the United States than it imported in return, which led to big trade imbalances in China's favor and the loss of American jobs. Yet far fewer economists agreed with this second charge against China. Few economists agreed either that China's trade surplus was caused by unfair policies or that this surplus hurt overall U.S. employment. It's true that imports from China displaced some jobs. But these jobs were replaced by jobs elsewhere, including in sectors that export to China, like aircraft. Indeed, most economists argued that increased trade with China made the United States as a whole richer, even though this change created losers as well as winners (as mentioned in our 11th principle of economics).

In 2018 and 2019, the United States and China engaged in an escalating tit-for-tat tariff war that came to a temporary halt in early 2020, when China pledged to reduce its trade imbalance by buying more U.S. goods. Yet, as of late 2020, it appeared that China wasn't honoring this pledge.

What effect did the tariff war have on U.S. and Chinese trade? As of publication, that's a hard question to answer: both economics have been severely hurt by the COVID-19 pandemic, making it difficult to isolate the effects of the trade conflict. So far, it does not appear that the trade war led to a substantial return of manufacturing to the United States, but it did lead to losses for U.S. farmers, as China purchased more foodstuffs from Brazil and Australia. Instead of reshoring to the United States, the conflict induced some U.S. businesses with Chinese supply operations to move those operations to other locations, such as Vietnam.

Over the longer run, the mere fact that such a tariff war was possible may have a significant effect in reducing international trade, because it will make businesses more cautious about relying on overseas suppliers in general.

At the time of writing the future of the trade conflict was very much up in the air. In November 2020, Trump was defeated in his bid for reelection. It was unclear how much of his tariff policy would continue under his successor, Joe Biden, although one possibility was that U.S. pressure on China would refocus on alleged WTO violations.

Check Your Understanding 16-3

1. In 2017, the United States proposed a tariff on steel imports from China. Steel is an input in a large number and variety of U.S. industries. Explain why political lobbying to eliminate these tariffs is more likely to be effective than political lobbying to eliminate tariffs on consumer goods such as sugar or clothing.
2. Over the years, the WTO has increasingly found itself adjudicating trade disputes that involve not just tariffs or quota restrictions but also restrictions based on quality, health, and environmental considerations. Why do you think this has occurred? What method would you, as a WTO official, use to decide whether a quality, health, or environmental restriction is in violation of a free-trade agreement?

Solutions appear at back of book.

>> Quick Review

- The three major justifications for trade protection are national security, job creation, and protection of infant industries.
- Despite the deadweight losses, import protections are often imposed because groups representing import-competing industries are more influential than groups of consumers.
- To avoid **trade wars** and to further trade liberalization, countries engage in **international trade agreements.** Some agreements involve a small number of countries, such as the **North American Free Trade Agreement (NAFTA)** and the **European Union (EU).** The **World Trade Organization (WTO)** oversees global trade agreements and referees trade disputes between members.
- Resistance to globalization has emerged in response to a surge in imports from relatively poor countries and the **offshore outsourcing** of many jobs that had been considered safe from foreign competition.

BUSINESS CASE Li & Fung: From Guangzhou to You

Bloomberg/Getty Images

It's a very good bet that as you read this, you're wearing something manufactured in Asia. And if you are, it's also a good bet that the Hong Kong company Li & Fung was involved in getting your garment designed, produced, and shipped to your local store. From Levi's to Walmart, Li & Fung is a critical conduit in moving clothing produced in factories around the world to the shopping mall nearest you.

The company was founded in 1906 in Guangzhou, China. According to Victor Fung, the company's chairman, his grandfather's "value added" was that he spoke English, allowing him to serve as an interpreter in business deals between the Chinese and foreigners. When Mao's Communist Party seized control in mainland China, the company moved to Hong Kong. There, as Hong Kong's market economy took off during the 1960s and 1970s, Li & Fung grew as an export broker, bringing together Hong Kong manufacturers and foreign buyers.

However, the real transformation of the company came as Asian economies grew and changed. Hong Kong's rapid growth led to rising wages, making Li & Fung increasingly uncompetitive in garments, its main business. So the company reinvented itself: rather than being a simple broker, it became a "supply chain manager." It would not only allocate production of a good to a manufacturer, but would also break the allocation of the inputs down according to steps in the production process and then allocate final assembly of the good among its 12,000+ suppliers around the globe. Sometimes production would be done in sophisticated economies like those of Hong Kong or even Japan, where wages are high but so are quality and productivity. At other times production would be done in less advanced economies such as those of mainland China or Thailand, where labor is less productive but also cheaper.

For example, suppose you own a U.S. retail chain and want to sell garment-washed blue jeans. Rather than simply arrange for production of the jeans, Li & Fung will work with you on design, providing you with the latest production and style information such as which materials and colors are trendy. After the design has been finalized, Li & Fung will arrange for the creation of a prototype, find the most cost-effective way to manufacture it, and then place an order on your behalf. Li & Fung might secure fabric made in Korea and dyed in Taiwan, and then have the jeans assembled in Thailand or mainland China. And because production takes place in so many locations, Li & Fung provides transport logistics as well as quality control.

Li & Fung has been enormously successful. In 2019, the company had a market value of $13.2 billion, with offices and distribution centers in more than 50 countries.

You might ask, by the way, how Li & Fung has been affected by the U.S.–China trade war. The answer is that U.S. tariffs on Chinese exports hurt one important aspect of the company's business, but also opened other opportunities. Li & Fung has been helping U.S. customers shift to alternative sources, such as Vietnam and Bangladesh; it has also been helping customers in Europe and other locations take advantage of the low prices offered by Chinese suppliers shut out of U.S. markets.

QUESTIONS FOR THOUGHT

1. Why do you think it was profitable for Li & Fung to go beyond brokering exports to becoming a supply chain manager, breaking down the production process and sourcing the inputs from various suppliers across many countries?
2. What principle do you think underlies Li & Fung's decisions on how to allocate production of a good's inputs and its final assembly among various countries?
3. Why do you think a retailer prefers to have Li & Fung arrange international production of its jeans rather than purchase them directly from a jeans manufacturer in mainland China?
4. What is the source of Li & Fung's success? Is it based on human capital, on ownership of a natural resource, or on ownership of capital?

REVIEW

MODULE 15

1. International trade is of growing importance to the United States and of even greater importance to most other countries. International trade, like trade among individuals, arises from comparative advantage: the opportunity cost of producing an additional unit of a good is lower in some countries than in others. Goods and services purchased from abroad are **imports;** those sold abroad are **exports.** Foreign trade, like other economic linkages between countries, has been growing rapidly, a phenomenon called **globalization. Hyperglobalization,** the phenomenon of extremely high levels of international trade, has occurred as advances in communication and transportation technology have allowed supply chains of production to span the globe.
2. The **Ricardian model of international trade** assumes that opportunity costs are constant. It shows that there are gains from trade: two countries are better off with trade than in **autarky.**
3. In practice, comparative advantage reflects differences between countries in climate, factor endowments, and technology. The **Heckscher–Ohlin model** shows how differences in factor endowments determine comparative advantage: goods differ in **factor intensity,** and countries tend to export goods that are intensive in the factors they have in abundance.

MODULE 16

1. The **domestic demand curve** and the **domestic supply curve** determine the price of a good in autarky. When international trade occurs, the domestic price is driven to equality with the **world price,** the price at which the good is bought and sold abroad.
2. If the world price is below the autarky price, a good is imported. This leads to an increase in consumer surplus, a fall in producer surplus, and a gain in total surplus. If the world price is above the autarky price, a good is exported. This leads to an increase in producer surplus, a fall in consumer surplus, and a gain in total surplus.
3. International trade leads to expansion in **exporting industries** and contraction in **import-competing industries.** This raises the domestic demand for abundant factors of production, reduces the demand for scarce factors, and so affects factor prices, such as wages.
4. Most economists advocate **free trade,** but in practice many governments engage in **trade protection.** The two most common forms of **protection** are tariffs and quotas. On rare occasions, export industries are subsidized.
5. A **tariff** is a tax levied on imports. It raises the domestic price above the world price, hurting consumers, benefiting domestic producers, and generating government revenue. As a result, total surplus falls. An **import quota** is a legal limit on the quantity of a good that can be imported. It has the same effects as a tariff, except that the revenue goes not to the government but to those who receive import licenses.
6. Although several popular arguments have been made in favor of trade protection, in practice the main reason for protection is probably political: import-competing industries are well organized and well informed about how they gain from trade protection, while consumers are unaware of the costs they pay. Still, U.S. trade is fairly free, mainly because of the role of **international trade agreements,** in which countries agree to reduce trade protection against one another's exports. Trade agreements also help prevent **trade wars.** The **North American Free Trade Agreement (NAFTA), NAFTA–USCMA,** and the **European Union (EU)** cover a small number of countries. In contrast, the **World Trade Organization (WTO)** covers a much larger number of countries, accounting for the bulk of world trade. It oversees trade negotiations and adjudicates disputes among its members.
7. In the past few years, many concerns have been raised about the effects of globalization. One issue is the increase in income inequality due to the surge in imports from relatively poor countries over the past 20 years. Another concern is the increase in **offshore outsourcing,** as many jobs that were once considered safe from foreign competition have been moved abroad.

KEY TERMS

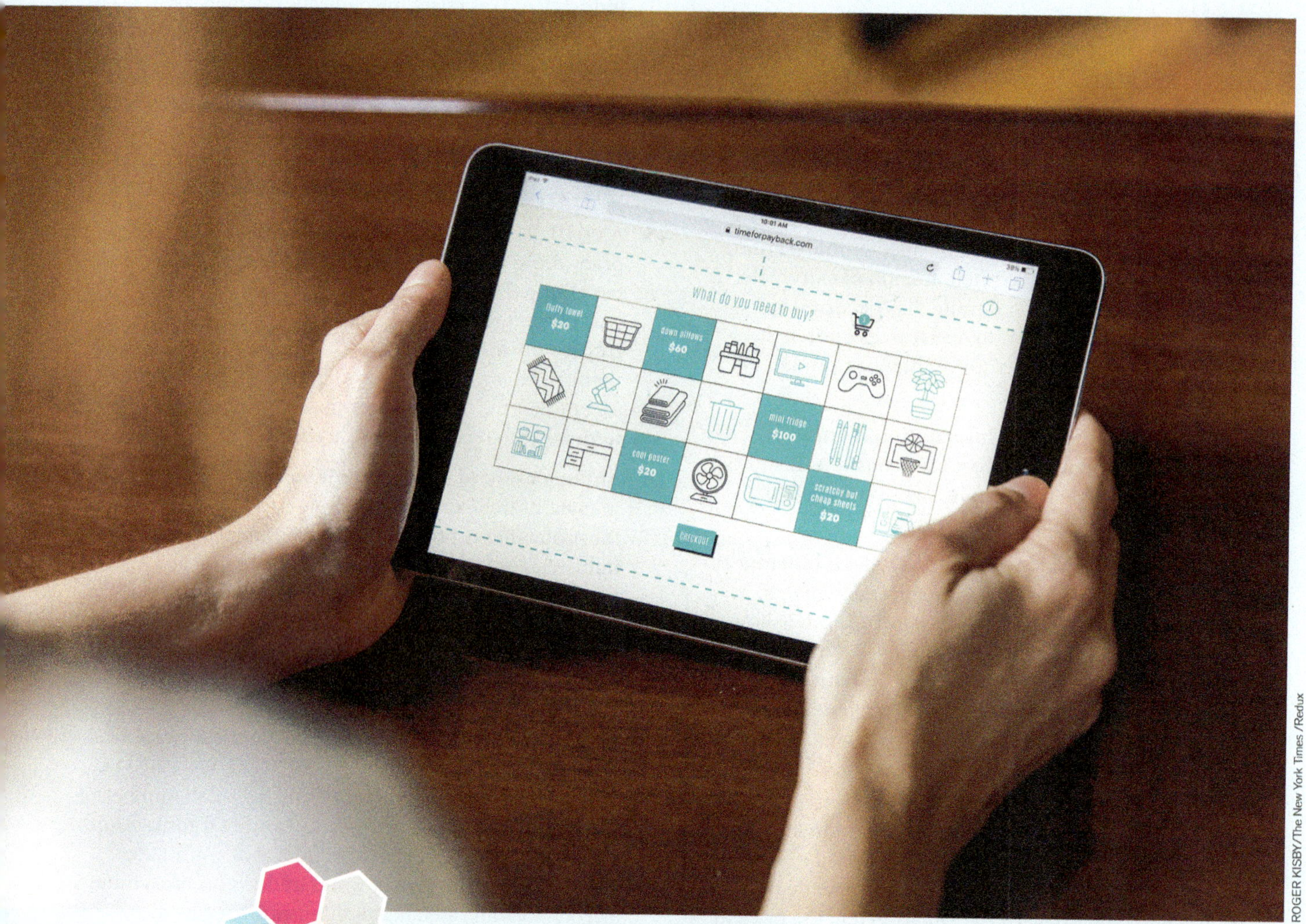

ROGER KISBY/The New York Times/Redux

Module 17 Making Decisions

Module 18 Behavioral Economics

Module 19 Maximizing Utility

SECTION 6

Economics and Decision Making

THE *PAYBACK* GAME SHOWS STUDENTS HOW TO MAKE GOOD DECISIONS

Tim Ranzetta and Jenny Nicholson, the co-creators of the free, interactive, web-based game *Payback*, are well versed in making decisions. As the fifth of six children in his family, Tim knew that he had to depend largely on himself to pay for college. In high school he began budgeting for his future college expenses. Even as a high school student, Tim understood that making the right economic decisions was critical to achieving his goals in life. So decades later, as a college loan consultant, he was well equipped to help college students and their families make decisions.

His co-creator, Jenny Nicholson, was also well versed in making decisions. The only member of her family to go to college, she grew up in difficult surroundings in Tennessee, often without running water or electricity. With her own decision-making skills she put herself through college and eventually built a career in advertising.

In creating *Payback*, Jenny and Tim emphasized the fact that college economic decisions weren't just about affording tuition and paying student loans, but they were also about *investment*. That is, they made it clear that college was an investment in human capital that generates a valuable payoff in the future. *Payback* emphasizes that every decision—from which college you attend (community college, state or private?), what activities you join (fraternity/sorority or student group?), what major you choose (Economics or Sociology?)—is about choosing between alternatives. More paid work or more leisure time? More study time or more sleep time? Go to graduate school or get a job? All are choices that rest upon understanding what the true cost of each option is and what the true payoffs are.

In this section we will follow up on those insights and undertake a deeper analysis of the economics of making decisions: how to make a decision that results in the best possible—often called *optimal*—economic outcome. Economists have formulated principles or methods of decision making that lead to optimal outcomes, regardless of whether the decision maker is an individual or a firm.

We'll start by examining the "decision problem" of an individual and learn about the three different types of economic decisions, each with a corresponding principle of decision making that leads to the best possible economic outcome. With this section we'll come to understand why economists consider decision making to be the very essence of microeconomics.

Despite the fact that people should use the principles of economic decision making to achieve optimal economic outcomes, they sometimes fail to do so. In other words, people are not always rational decision makers. For example, a shopper may knowingly spend more on gasoline in pursuit of a bargain than they save. Yet economists have discovered that people are *irrational in predictable ways*. In this section, we'll learn about these tendencies when we discuss behavioral economics, the branch of economics that studies predictably irrational economic behavior.

The section concludes with a discussion of utility, a measure of satisfaction from consumption, and how individuals make consumption decisions when faced with a limited budget.

MODULE 17

Making Decisions

WHAT YOU WILL LEARN

- Why does good decision making depend on accurately defining costs and benefits?
- What is the difference between **explicit** and **implicit** costs?
- What is the difference between **accounting profit** and **economic profit** and why is economic profit the correct basis for decisions?
- What are the three types of economic decisions?

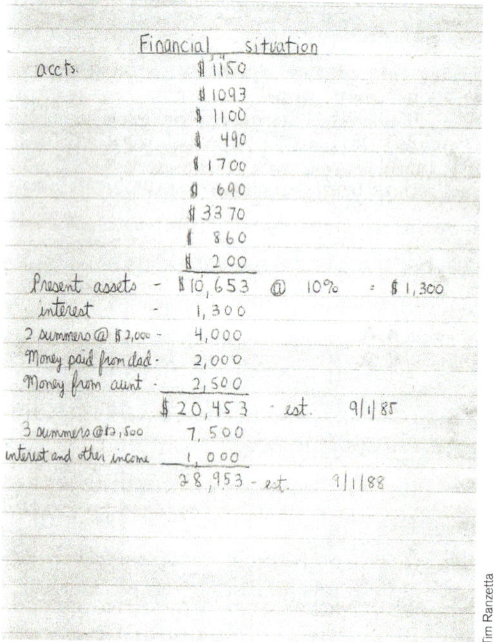

Tim Ranzetta

17.1 Costs, Benefits, and Profits

In making any type of decision, it's critical to define the costs and benefits of that decision accurately. If you don't know the costs and benefits, it is nearly impossible to make a good decision. So that is where we begin.

An important first step is to recognize the role of *opportunity cost,* a concept we first encountered in Module 1, where we learned that opportunity costs arise because *resources are scarce.* Because resources are scarce, the *true* cost of anything is what you must give up to get it—its opportunity cost.

When making decisions, it is crucial to think in terms of opportunity cost, because the opportunity cost of an action is often considerably more than the cost of any outlays of money.

Economists use the concepts of *explicit costs* and *implicit costs* to compare the relationship between opportunity costs and monetary outlays. We'll discuss these two concepts first. Then we'll define the concepts of *accounting profit* and *economic profit,* both of which are *ways of measuring whether the benefit of an action is greater than the cost.* Armed with these concepts for assessing costs and benefits, we will be in a position to consider our first principle of economic decision making: how to make "either–or" decisions.

Explicit versus Implicit Costs

Suppose that you face two choices upon graduation: take a less-than-ideal job or return to school for another year to get a graduate degree. To make that decision correctly, you need to know the cost of an additional year of school.

Here is where it is important to remember the concept of opportunity cost: the cost of the year spent getting an advanced degree includes what you forgo by not taking a job for that year. The opportunity cost of an additional year of school, like any cost, can be broken into two parts: the *explicit* cost of the year's schooling and the *implicit* cost.

An **explicit cost** is a cost that requires an outlay of money. For example, the explicit cost of the additional year of schooling includes tuition. An **implicit cost,**

An **explicit cost** is a cost that requires an outlay of money.

An **implicit cost** does not require an outlay of money. It is measured by the value, in dollar terms, of benefits that are forgone.

though, does not involve an outlay of money. Instead, it is measured by the *value,* in dollar terms, of the benefits that are forgone. For example, the implicit cost of the year spent in school includes the income you would have earned if you had taken a job instead.

TABLE 17-1 Opportunity Cost of an Additional Year of School

Explicit cost		Implicit cost	
Tuition	$10,000	Forgone salary	$50,000
Books and supplies	1,000		
Computer	1,500		
Total explicit cost	**$12,500**	**Total implicit cost**	**$50,000**
Total opportunity cost = Total explicit cost + Total implicit cost = $62,500			

A common mistake—both in economic analysis and in life, whether by an individual or by a business—is to ignore implicit costs and focus exclusively on explicit costs. But often the implicit cost of an activity is quite substantial—indeed, sometimes it is much larger than the explicit cost.

Table 17-1 gives a breakdown of hypothetical explicit and implicit costs associated with spending an additional year in school instead of taking a job. The explicit cost consists of tuition, books, supplies, and a computer for doing assignments—all of which require you to spend money. The implicit cost is the salary you would have earned if you had taken a job instead. As you can see, the total opportunity cost of attending an additional year of schooling is $62,500, the sum of the total implicit cost—$50,000 in forgone salary, and the total explicit cost—$12,500 in outlays on tuition, supplies, and computer. Because the implicit cost is four times as much as the explicit cost, ignoring the implicit cost could lead to a seriously misguided decision. This example illustrates a general principle: *The opportunity cost of any activity is equal to its explicit cost plus its implicit cost.*

A slightly different way of looking at the implicit cost in this example can deepen our understanding of opportunity cost:

- The forgone salary is the cost of using your own resources—your time—in going to school rather than working.
- The use of your time for more schooling, despite the fact that you don't have to spend any money on it, is still costly to you.

This explanation illustrates an important aspect of opportunity cost:

- In considering the cost of an activity, you should include the cost of using any of your own resources for that activity. You can calculate the cost of using your own resources by determining what they would have earned in their next-best use.

Accounting Profit versus Economic Profit

Let's return to Jenny Nicholson and imagine that she faces the choice of either completing a two-year full-time graduate program to become a pharmacist or spending two years working. We'll assume that to be certified as a pharmacist, she must complete the entire two-year graduate program. Which choice should she make?

To get started, let's consider what Jenny gains by getting the degree—what we might call her revenue from the pharmacology degree. Once she has completed the degree two years from now, she will receive earnings from the degree valued today at $600,000 over the rest of her lifetime. In contrast, if she doesn't get the degree and instead takes the job currently offered to her, two years from now her future lifetime earnings will be valued today at $500,000. The cost of the tuition for her pharmacology degree is $40,000, which she pays for with a student loan that costs her $4,000 in interest.

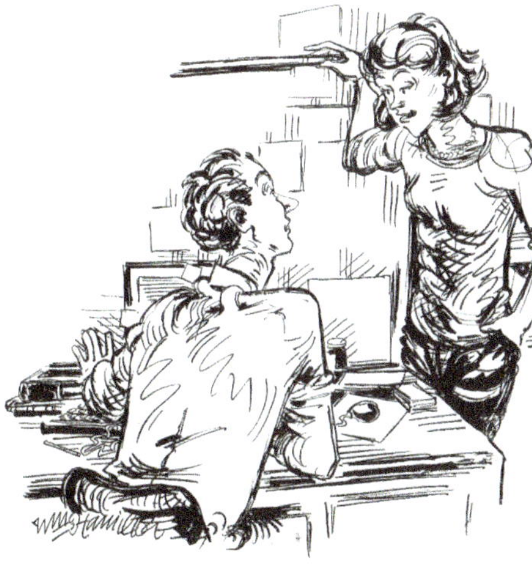

"I've done the numbers, and I will marry you."

At this point, what she should do might seem obvious: if she chooses the pharmacology degree, she gets a lifetime increase in the value of earnings of $600,000 − $500,000 = $100,000, and she pays $40,000 in tuition plus $4,000 in interest. That means she makes a profit of

Accounting profit is equal to revenue minus explicit cost.

Economic profit is equal to revenue minus the opportunity cost of resources used. It is usually less than the accounting profit.

Capital is the total value of assets owned by an individual or firm—physical assets plus financial assets.

The **implicit cost of capital** is the opportunity cost of the use of one's own capital—the income earned if the capital had been employed in its next-best alternative use.

$100,000 – $40,000 – $4,000 = $56,000 by getting her pharmacology degree. This $56,000 is Jenny's **accounting profit** from obtaining the degree: her revenue minus her explicit cost. In this example her explicit cost of getting the pharmacology degree is $44,000, the amount of her tuition plus student loan interest.

Although accounting profit is a useful measure, it would be misleading for Jenny to use only it in making her decision. To make the right decision, the one that leads to the best possible economic outcome for her, she needs to calculate her **economic profit**—the revenue she receives from the pharmacology degree minus her opportunity cost of staying in school (which is equal to her explicit cost *plus* her implicit cost of staying in school). In general, the economic profit of a given project will be less than the accounting profit because there are almost always implicit costs in addition to explicit costs.

When economists use the term *profit,* they are referring to *economic* profit, not *accounting* profit. This will be our convention in the rest of the book: when we use the term *profit,* we mean economic profit.

How does Jenny's economic profit from staying in school differ from her accounting profit? We've already encountered one source of the difference: her two years of forgone job earnings. This is an implicit cost of going to school full time for two years. We assume that the value today of Jenny's forgone earnings for the two years is $57,000.

Once we factor in Jenny's implicit costs and calculate her economic profit, we see that she is better off not getting a degree in pharmacology. You can see this in Table 17-2: her economic profit from getting the pharmacology degree is –$1,000. In other words, she incurs an *economic loss* of $1,000 if she gets the degree. Clearly, she is better off going to work now.

Let's consider a slightly different scenario to make sure that the concepts of opportunity costs and economic profit are well understood. Let's suppose that Jenny does not have to take out $40,000 in student loans to pay her tuition. Instead, she can pay for it with an inheritance from her grandmother. As a result, she doesn't have to pay $4,000 in interest. In this case, her accounting profit is $60,000 rather than $56,000. Would the right decision now be for her to get the pharmacology degree? Wouldn't the economic profit of the degree now be $60,000 – $57,000 = $3,000?

The answer is no, because in this scenario Jenny is using her own *capital* to finance her education, and the use of that capital has an opportunity cost even when she owns it.

Capital is the total value of the assets of an individual or a firm. An individual's capital usually consists of cash in the bank, stocks, bonds, and the ownership value of real estate such as a house. In the case of a business, capital also includes its equipment, its tools, and its inventory of unsold goods and used parts. (Economists like to distinguish between *financial assets,* such as cash, stocks, and bonds, and *physical assets,* such as buildings, equipment, tools, and inventory.)

The point is that even if Jenny owns the $40,000, using it to pay tuition incurs an opportunity cost—what she forgoes in the next-best use of that $40,000. If she hadn't used the money to pay her tuition, her next-best use of the money would have been to deposit it in a bank to earn interest.

To keep things simple, let's assume that she earns $4,000 on that $40,000 once it is deposited in a bank. Now, rather than pay $4,000 in explicit costs in the form of student loan interest, Jenny pays $4,000 in implicit costs from the forgone interest she could have earned.

This $4,000 in forgone interest earnings is what economists call the **implicit cost of capital**—the income the owner of the capital could have earned if the capital had

TABLE 17-2 Jenny's Economic Profit from Acquiring a Pharmacology Degree

Value of increase in lifetime earnings	$100,000
Explicit cost:	
Tuition	–40,000
Interest paid on student loan	–4,000
Accounting Profit	**56,000**
Implicit cost:	
Value of income forgone during 2 years spent in school	–57,000
Economic Profit	**–1,000**

been employed in its next-best alternative use. The net effect is that it makes no difference whether Jenny finances her tuition with a student loan or by using her own funds. This comparison reinforces how carefully you must keep track of opportunity costs when making a decision.

TABLE 17-3 "How Much" Decision versus "Either–Or" Decision

"Either–or" decisions	"How much" decisions
Tide or Cheer?	How many days before you do your laundry?
Buy a car or not?	How many miles do you go before an oil change in your car?
An order of nachos or a sandwich?	How many jalapeños on your nachos?
Run your own business or work for someone else?	How many workers should you hire in your company?
Prescribe drug A or drug B for your patients?	How much should a patient take of a drug that generates side effects?
Graduate school or not?	How many hours to study?

Making "Either–Or" Decisions

An "either–or" decision is one in which you must choose between two activities. That's in contrast to a "how much" decision, which requires you to choose how much of a given activity to undertake. For example, Jenny faced an "either–or" decision: to spend two years in graduate school to obtain a degree in pharmacology or to work. In contrast, a "how much" decision would be deciding how many hours to study or how many hours to work at a job. Table 17-3 contrasts a variety of "either–or" and "how much" decisions.

In making economic decisions, as we have already emphasized, it is vitally important to calculate opportunity costs correctly. The best way to make an "either–or" decision, the method that leads to the best possible economic outcome, is the straightforward **principle of "either–or" decision making.** According to this principle, *when making an "either–or" choice between two activities, choose the one with the positive economic profit.*

Let's examine Jenny's dilemma from a different angle to understand how this principle works:

- If she takes the job she is currently offered, the value of her total lifetime earnings is \$57,000 (the value today of her earnings over the next two years) + \$500,000 (the value today of her total lifetime earnings thereafter) = \$557,000.
- If she gets her pharmacology degree instead and works as a pharmacist, the value today of her total lifetime earnings is \$600,000 (value today of her lifetime earnings after two years in school) – \$40,000 (tuition) – \$4,000 (interest payments) = \$556,000. The economic profit from taking the job versus becoming a pharmacist is \$557,000 – \$556,000 = \$1,000.

So, the right choice for Jenny is to begin work immediately, which gives her an economic profit of \$1,000, rather than become a pharmacist, which would give her an economic profit of –\$1,000. In other words, by becoming a pharmacist she loses the \$1,000 economic profit she would have gained by starting work immediately.

In making "either–or" decisions, mistakes most commonly arise when people or businesses use their own assets in projects rather than rented or borrowed assets. That's because they fail to account for the implicit cost of using self-owned capital. This would have been true of Jenny, if she were to use her own savings to pay the tuition for pharmacology school. In contrast, when they rent or borrow assets, these rental or borrowing costs show up as explicit costs. If, for example, a restaurant owns its equipment and tools, it would have to compute its implicit cost of capital by calculating how much the equipment could be sold for and how much could be earned by using those funds in the next-best alternative project.

In addition, businesses run by the owner (an *entrepreneur*) often fail to calculate the opportunity cost of the owner's time in running the business. In that way, small businesses often underestimate their opportunity costs and overestimate their economic profit of staying in business.

According to the **principle of "either–or" decision making** when faced with an "either-or" choice between two activities, choose the one with the positive economic profit.

>> Quick Review

- All costs are opportunity costs. They can be divided into **explicit costs** and **implicit costs.**
- An activity's **accounting profit** is not necessarily equal to its **economic profit.**
- Due to the **implicit cost of capital**—the opportunity cost of using self-owned **capital**—and the opportunity cost of one's own time, economic profit is often substantially less than accounting profit.
- The **principle of "either–or" decision making** says that when making an "either–or" choice between two activities, choose the one with the positive economic profit.

Check Your Understanding 17-1

1. Karma and Don run a furniture-refinishing business from their home. Which of the following represents an explicit cost of the business and which represents an implicit cost?
   a. Supplies such as paint stripper, varnish, polish, sandpaper, and so on
   b. Basement space that has been converted into a workroom
   c. Wages paid to a part-time helper
   d. A van that they inherited and use only for transporting furniture
   e. The job at a larger furniture restorer that Karma gave up to run the business
2. Assume that Adam is considering entering a two-year apprenticeship program for skilled machinists that would, upon completion, make him a licensed machinist. During the apprenticeship, he earns a reduced salary of $15,000 per year. At the end of the apprenticeship, the value of his lifetime earnings is $725,000. What is Adam's best career choice?
3. Suppose you have three alternatives—A, B, and C—and you can undertake only one of them. In comparing A versus B, you find that B has an economic profit and A yields an economic loss. But in comparing A versus C, you find that C has an economic profit and A yields an economic loss. How do you decide what to do?

Solutions appear at back of book.

17.2 Making "How Much" Decisions: The Role of Marginal Analysis

Although many decisions in economics are "either–or," many others are "how much." Not many people will give up their cars if the price of gasoline goes up, but many people will drive less. How much less? A rise in corn prices won't persuade a lot of people to take up farming for the first time, but it will persuade farmers who were already growing corn to plant more. How much more?

Recall from our principles of microeconomics that "how much" is a decision at the margin. So, to understand "how much" decisions, we will use an approach known as *marginal analysis*. Marginal analysis involves comparing the benefit of doing a little bit more of some activity with the cost of doing a little bit more of that activity. The benefit of doing a little bit more of something is what economists call its *marginal benefit,* and the cost of doing a little bit more of something is what they call its *marginal cost.*

Why is this called "marginal" analysis? A margin is another name for an edge; what you do in marginal analysis is push out the edge a bit and see whether that is a good move. We will study marginal analysis by considering a hypothetical decision of how many years of school to complete. We'll consider the case of Alexa, who studies computer science in the hopes of becoming an app designer. Since there are a wide variety of topics that can be learned one year at a time (programming, applications, user interfaces), at the end of each year Alexa can decide whether to continue her studies or not.

Unlike Jenny, who faced an "either–or" decision of whether to get a pharmacology degree or not, Alexa faces a "how much" decision of how many years to study computer science. For example, she could study one more year, or five more years, or any number of years in between. We'll begin our analysis of Alexa's decision problem by defining Alexa's *marginal cost* of another year of study.

Marginal Cost

We'll assume that each additional year of schooling costs Alexa $10,000 in explicit costs—tuition, interest on a student loan, and so on. In addition to the explicit costs, she also has an implicit cost—the income forgone by spending one more year in school.

Unlike Alexa's explicit costs, which are constant (that is, the same each year), Alexa's implicit cost changes each year. That's because each year she spends in school leaves her better trained than the year before; and the better trained she is, the higher the salary she can command. Consequently, the income she forgoes by not working rises each additional year she stays in school. In other words, the greater the number of years Alexa has already spent in school, the higher her implicit cost of another year of school.

Table 17-4 contains the data on how Alexa's cost of an additional year of schooling changes as she completes more years. The second column shows how her total cost of schooling changes as the number of years she has completed increases. For example, Alexa's first year has a total cost of $30,000: $10,000 in explicit costs of tuition and the like as well as $20,000 in forgone salary.

The second column also shows that the total cost of attending two years is $70,000: $30,000 for her first year plus $40,000 for her second year. During her second year in school, her explicit costs have stayed the same ($10,000) but her implicit cost of forgone salary has gone up to $30,000. That's because she's a more valuable worker with one year of schooling under her belt than with no schooling.

Likewise, the total cost of three years of schooling is $130,000: $30,000 in explicit cost for three years of tuition plus $100,000 in implicit cost of three years of forgone salary. The total cost of attending four years is $220,000, and $350,000 for five years.

The change in Alexa's total cost of schooling when she goes to school an additional year is her *marginal cost* of the one-year increase in years of schooling. In general, the **marginal cost** of producing a good or service (in this case, producing one's own education) is the additional cost incurred by producing one more unit of that good or service. The arrows, which zigzag between the total costs in the second column and the marginal costs in the third column, are there to help you to see how marginal cost is calculated from total cost.

Similarly, total cost can be calculated from marginal cost: the total cost of a given quantity is the sum of the marginal costs of that quantity and of all of the previous ones. So the total cost of three years of schooling is $30,000 + $40,000 + $60,000 = $130,000; that is, the marginal cost of year 1 plus the marginal cost of year 2 plus the marginal cost of year 3.

As already mentioned, the third column of Table 17-4 shows Alexa's marginal costs of more years of schooling, which have a clear pattern: they are increasing. They go from $30,000, to $40,000, to $60,000, to $90,000, and finally to $130,000 for the fifth year of schooling. That's because each year of schooling would make Alexa a more valuable and highly paid employee if she were to work. As a result, forgoing a job becomes much more costly as she becomes more educated. This is an example of what economists call **increasing marginal cost,** which occurs when each unit of a good costs more to produce than the previous unit.

Figure 17-1 shows the **marginal cost curve,** a graphical representation of Alexa's marginal costs. The height of each shaded bar corresponds to the marginal cost of a given year of schooling. The red line connecting the dots at the midpoint of the top of each bar is Alexa's marginal cost curve. Alexa has an upward-sloping marginal cost curve because she has increasing marginal cost of additional years of schooling.

Although increasing marginal cost is a frequent phenomenon in real life, it's not the only possibility. **Constant marginal cost** occurs when the cost of

TABLE 17-4 Alexa's Marginal Cost of Additional Years in School

Quantity of schooling (years)	Total cost	Marginal cost
0	$0	
		$30,000
1	30,000	
		40,000
2	70,000	
		60,000
3	130,000	
		90,000
4	220,000	
		130,000
5	350,000	

The **marginal cost** of producing a good or service is the additional cost incurred by producing one more unit of that good or service.

Production of a good or service has **increasing marginal cost** when each additional unit costs more to produce than the previous one.

The **marginal cost curve** shows how the cost of producing one more unit depends on the quantity that has already been produced.

Production of a good or service has **constant marginal cost** when each additional unit costs the same to produce as the previous one.

FIGURE 17-1 Marginal Cost

The height of each shaded bar corresponds to Alexa's marginal cost of an additional year of schooling. The height of each bar is higher than the preceding one because each year of schooling costs more than the previous years. As a result, Alexa has increasing marginal cost and the marginal cost curve—the line connecting the midpoints at the top of each bar—is upward sloping.

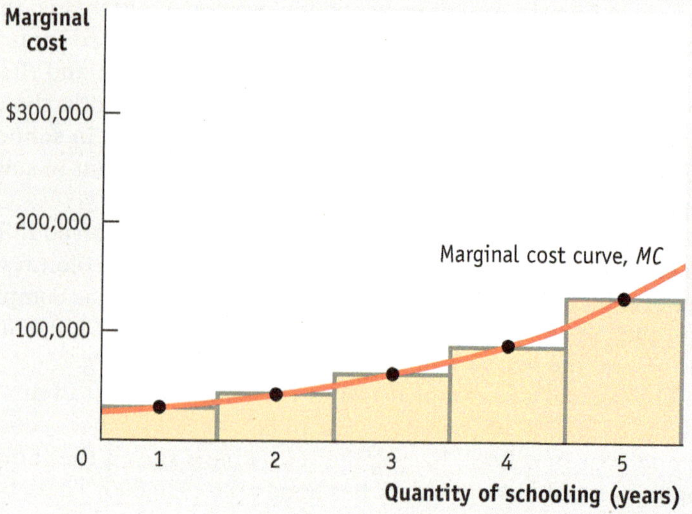

Production of a good or service has **decreasing marginal cost** when each additional unit costs less to produce than the previous one.

producing an additional unit is the same as the cost of producing the previous unit. Plant nurseries, for example, typically have constant marginal cost—the cost of growing one more plant is the same, regardless of how many plants have already been produced. With constant marginal cost, the marginal cost curve is a horizontal line.

There can also be **decreasing marginal cost,** which occurs when marginal cost falls as the number of units produced increases. With decreasing marginal cost, the marginal cost line is downward sloping. Decreasing marginal cost is often due to *learning effects* in production: for complicated tasks, such as assembling a new model of a car, workers are often slow and mistake-prone when assembling the earliest units, making for higher marginal cost on those units. But as workers gain experience, assembly time and the rate of mistakes fall, generating lower marginal cost for later units. As a result, overall production has decreasing marginal cost.

Finally, for the production of some goods and services the shape of the marginal cost curve changes as the number of units produced increases. For example, auto production is likely to have decreasing marginal costs for the first batch of

PITFALLS

TOTAL COST VERSUS MARGINAL COST

It can be easy to conclude that marginal cost and total cost must always move in the same direction. That is, if total cost is rising, then marginal cost must also be rising. Or if marginal cost is falling, then total cost must be falling as well. But the following example shows that this conclusion is wrong.

Let's consider the example of auto production, which is likely to involve learning effects. Suppose that for the first batch of cars of a new model, each car costs $10,000 to assemble. As workers gain experience with the new model, they become better at production. As a result, the per-car cost of assembly falls to $8,000 for the second batch. For the third batch, the per-car assembly cost falls again, to $6,500, as workers continue to gain expertise. For the fourth batch, the per-car cost of assembly falls to $5,000 and remains constant for the rest of the production run.

In this example, marginal cost is *decreasing* over batches one through four, falling from $10,000 to $5,000. However, it's important to note that total cost is still *increasing* over the entire production run because marginal cost is greater than zero.

To see this point, assume that each batch consists of 100 cars. Then the total cost of producing the first batch is 100 × $10,000 = 1,000,000. The total cost of producing the first and second batches of cars is $1,000,000 + (100 × $8,000) = $1,800,000. Likewise, the total cost of producing the first, second, and third batches is $1,800,000 + (100 × $6,500) = $2,450,000, and so on. As you can see, although marginal cost is decreasing over the first few batches of cars, total cost is increasing over the same batches.

This shows us that totals and marginals can sometimes move in opposite directions. So it is wrong to assert that they always move in the same direction. What we can assert is that *total cost increases whenever marginal cost is positive,* regardless of whether marginal cost is increasing or decreasing.

cars produced as workers iron out kinks and mistakes in production. Then production has constant marginal costs for the next batch of cars as workers settle into a predictable pace.

But at some point, as workers produce more cars, marginal cost begins to increase as they run out of factory floor space and the auto company incurs costly overtime wages. This gives rise to what we call a "swoosh"-shaped marginal cost curve—a topic we discuss in Section 7. For now, we'll stick to the simpler example of an increasing marginal cost curve.

TABLE 17-5 Alexa's Marginal Benefit of Additional Years in School

Quantity of schooling (years)	Total benefit	Marginal benefit
0	$0	
		$300,000
1	300,000	
		150,000
2	450,000	
		90,000
3	540,000	
		60,000
4	600,000	
		50,000
5	650,000	

Marginal Benefit

Alexa benefits from higher lifetime earnings as she completes more years of school. Exactly how much she benefits is shown in Table 17-5. Column 2 shows Alexa's total benefit according to the number of years of school completed, expressed as the value of her lifetime earnings. The third column shows Alexa's *marginal benefit* from an additional year of schooling. In general, the **marginal benefit** of producing a good or service is the additional benefit earned from producing one more unit.

As in Table 17-4, the data in the third column of Table 17-5 show a clear pattern. However, this time the numbers are decreasing rather than increasing. The first year of schooling gives Alexa a $300,000 increase in the value of her lifetime earnings. The second year also gives her a positive return, but the size of that return has fallen to $150,000; the third year's return is also positive, but its size has fallen yet again to $90,000; and so on. In other words, the more years of school that Alexa has already completed, the smaller the increase in the value of her lifetime earnings from attending one more year.

Alexa's schooling decision has what economists call **decreasing marginal benefit:** each additional year of school yields a smaller benefit than the previous year. Or, to put it slightly differently, with decreasing marginal benefit, the benefit from producing one more unit of the good or service falls as the quantity already produced rises.

Just as marginal cost can be represented by a marginal cost curve, marginal benefit can be represented by a **marginal benefit curve,** shown in blue in Figure 17-2.

The **marginal benefit** of a good or service is the additional benefit derived from producing one more unit of that good or service.

There is **decreasing marginal benefit** from an activity when each additional unit of the activity yields less benefit than the previous unit.

The **marginal benefit curve** shows how the benefit from producing one more unit depends on the quantity that has already been produced.

FIGURE 17-2 Marginal Benefit

The height of each shaded bar corresponds to Alexa's marginal benefit of an additional year of schooling. The height of each bar is lower than the one preceding it because an additional year of schooling has decreasing marginal benefit. As a result, Alexa's marginal benefit curve—the curve connecting the midpoints at the top of each bar—is downward sloping.

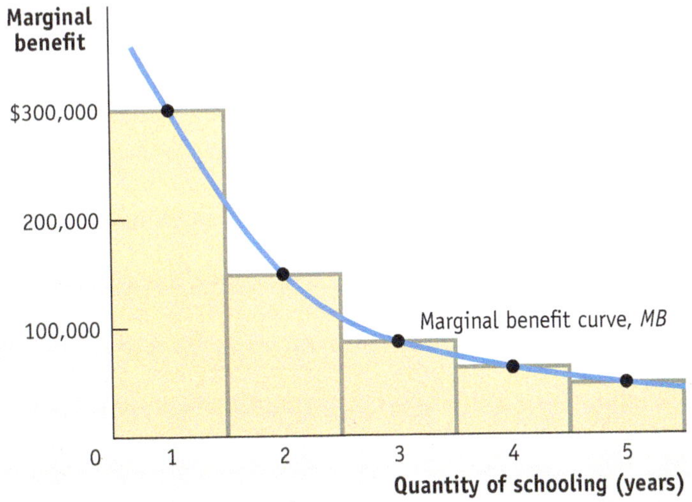

TABLE 17-6 Alexa's Profit from Additional Years of Schooling

Quantity of schooling (years)	Marginal benefit	Marginal cost	Additional profit	Decision
0				
	$300,000	$30,000	$270,000	Yes
1				
	150,000	40,000	110,000	Yes
2				
	90,000	60,000	30,000	Yes
3				
	60,000	90,000	−30,000	No
4				
	50,000	130,000	−80,000	No
5				

Alexa's marginal benefit curve slopes downward because she faces decreasing marginal benefit from additional years of schooling. Not all goods or activities exhibit decreasing marginal benefit.

Now we are ready to see how the concepts of marginal benefit and marginal cost are brought together to answer the question of how many years of additional schooling Alexa should undertake.

Marginal Analysis

Table 17-6 shows the marginal cost and marginal benefit numbers from Tables 17-4 and 17-5. It also adds an additional column: the additional profit to Alexa from staying in school one more year, equal to the difference between the marginal benefit and the marginal cost of that additional year in school. (Remember that it is Alexa's economic profit that we care about, not her accounting profit.) We can now use Table 17-6 to determine how many additional years of schooling Alexa should undertake to maximize her total profit.

First, imagine that Alexa chooses not to attend any additional years of school. We can see from column 4 that this is a mistake if Alexa wants to achieve the highest total profit from her schooling—the sum of the additional profits generated by another year of schooling. If she attends one additional year of school, she increases the value of her lifetime earnings by $270,000, the profit from the first additional year attended.

Now, let's consider whether Alexa should attend the second year of school. The additional profit from the second year is $110,000, so Alexa should attend the second year as well. What about the third year? The additional profit from that year is $30,000; so, yes, Alexa should attend the third year as well.

What about a fourth year? In this case, the additional profit is negative: it is –$30,000. Alexa loses $30,000 of the value of her lifetime earnings if she attends the fourth year. Clearly, Alexa is worse off by attending the fourth additional year rather than taking a job. And the same is true for the fifth year as well: it has a negative additional profit of –$80,000.

What have we learned? That Alexa should attend three additional years of school and stop at that point. Although the first, second, and third years of additional schooling increase the value of her lifetime earnings, the fourth and fifth years diminish it. So three years of additional schooling lead to the quantity that generates the maximum possible total profit. It is what economists call the **optimal quantity**—the quantity that generates the maximum possible total profit.

The **optimal quantity** is the quantity that generates the highest possible total profit.

Figure 17-3 shows how the optimal quantity can be determined graphically. Alexa's marginal benefit and marginal cost curves are shown together. If Alexa chooses fewer than three additional years (that is, years 0, 1, or 2), she will choose a level of schooling at which her marginal benefit curve lies *above* her marginal cost curve. She can make herself better off by staying in school.

If instead she chooses more than three additional years (years 4 or 5), she will choose a level of schooling at which her marginal benefit curve lies *below* her marginal cost curve. She can make herself better off by choosing not to attend the additional year of school and taking a job instead.

The table in Figure 17-3 confirms our result. The second column repeats information from Table 17-6, showing Alexa's marginal benefit minus marginal cost—the additional profit per additional year of schooling. The third column shows Alexa's total profit for different years of schooling. The total profit, for each

FIGURE 17-3 Alexa's Optimal Quantity of Years of Schooling

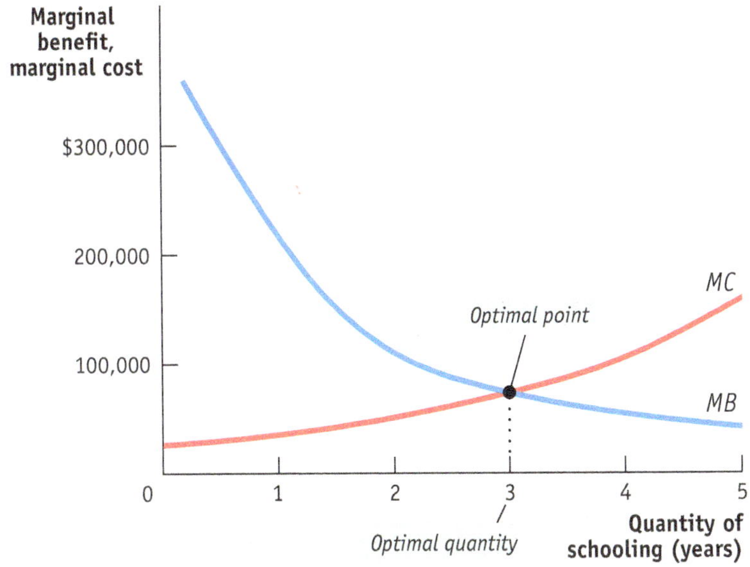

Quantity of schooling (years)	Additional profit	Total profit
0		$0
	$270,000	
1		270,000
	110,000	
2		380,000
	30,000	
3		410,000
	−30,000	
4		380,000
	−80,000	
5		300,000

The optimal quantity is the quantity that generates the highest possible total profit. It is the quantity at which marginal benefit is greater than or equal to marginal cost. Equivalently, it is the quantity at which the marginal benefit and marginal cost curves intersect. Here, they intersect at 3 additional years of schooling. The table confirms that 3 is indeed the optimal quantity: it leads to the maximum total profit of $410,000.

possible year of schooling is simply the sum of numbers in the second column up to and including that year.

For example, Alexa's profit from additional years of schooling is $270,000 for the first year and $110,000 for the second year. So the total profit for two additional years of schooling is $270,000 + $110,000 = $380,000. Similarly, the total profit for three additional years is $270,000 + $110,000 + $30,000 = $410,000. Our claim that three years is the optimal quantity for Alexa is confirmed by the data in the table in Figure 17-3: at three years of additional schooling, Alexa reaps the greatest total profit, $410,000.

Alexa's decision problem illustrates how you go about finding the optimal quantity when the choice involves a small number of quantities. (In this example, that is one through five years.) With small quantities, the rule for choosing the optimal quantity is: *Increase the quantity as long as the marginal benefit from one more unit is greater than the marginal cost, but stop before the marginal benefit becomes less than the marginal cost.*

In contrast, when a "how much" decision involves relatively large quantities, the rule for choosing the optimal quantity simplifies to this: *The optimal quantity is the quantity at which marginal benefit is equal to marginal cost.*

To see why this is so, consider the example of a farmer who finds that their optimal quantity of wheat produced is 5,000 bushels. Typically, they will find that in going from 4,999 to 5,000 bushels, their marginal benefit is only very slightly greater than their marginal cost—that is, the difference between marginal benefit and marginal cost is close to zero. Similarly, in going from 5,000 to 5,001 bushels, their marginal cost is only very slightly greater than their marginal benefit—again, the difference between marginal cost and marginal benefit is very close to zero.

So a simple rule for them in choosing the optimal quantity of wheat is to produce the quantity at which the difference between marginal benefit and marginal

PITFALLS

MUDDLED AT THE MARGIN

The idea of setting marginal benefit equal to marginal cost sometimes confuses people. Aren't we trying to maximize the *difference* between benefits and costs? Yes. And don't we wipe out our gains by setting benefits and costs equal to each other? Yes. But that is not what we are doing. Rather, what we are doing is setting *marginal,* not *total,* benefit and cost equal to each other.

Once again, the point is to maximize the total profit from an activity. If the marginal benefit from the activity is greater than the marginal cost, doing a bit more will increase that gain. If the marginal benefit is less than the marginal cost, doing a bit less will increase the total profit. *So only when the marginal benefit and marginal cost are equal is the difference between total benefit and total cost at a maximum.*

cost is approximately zero—that is, the quantity at which marginal benefit equals marginal cost.

Now we are ready to state the general rule for choosing the optimal quantity—one that applies for decisions involving either small quantities or large quantities. This general rule is known as the **profit-maximizing principle of marginal analysis:** *When making a profit-maximizing "how much" decision, the optimal quantity is the largest quantity at which marginal benefit is greater than or equal to marginal cost.*

Graphically, the optimal quantity is the quantity of an activity at which the marginal benefit curve intersects the marginal cost curve. For example, in Figure 17-3 the marginal benefit and marginal cost curves cross each other at three years—that is, marginal benefit equals marginal cost at the choice of three additional years of schooling, which we have already seen is Alexa's optimal quantity.

A straightforward application of marginal analysis explains why so many people went back to school in 2009 through 2011: in the depressed job market, the marginal cost of another year of school fell because the opportunity cost of forgone wages had fallen.

>> Quick Review

- A "how much" decision is made by using marginal analysis.
- The **marginal cost** of producing a good or service is represented graphically by the **marginal cost curve.** An upward-sloping marginal cost curve reflects **increasing marginal cost. Constant marginal cost** is represented by a horizontal marginal cost curve. A downward-sloping marginal cost curve reflects **decreasing marginal cost.**
- The **marginal benefit** of producing a good or service is represented by the **marginal benefit curve.** A downward-sloping marginal benefit curve reflects **decreasing marginal benefit.**
- The **optimal quantity,** the quantity which generates the highest possible total profit, is found by applying the **profit-maximizing principle of marginal analysis,** according to which the optimal quantity is the largest quantity at which marginal benefit is greater than or equal to marginal cost. Graphically, it is the quantity at which the marginal cost curve intersects the marginal benefit curve.

Check Your Understanding 17-2

1. For each of the "how much" decisions listed in Table 17-3, describe the nature of the marginal cost and of the marginal benefit.
2. Suppose that Alexa's school charges a fixed fee of \$70,000 for four years of schooling. If Alexa drops out before she finishes those four years, she still has to pay the \$70,000. Alexa's total cost for different years of schooling is now given by the data in the accompanying table. Assume that Alexa's total benefit and marginal benefit remain as reported in Table 17-5.

   Use this information to calculate (i) Alexa's new marginal cost, (ii) her new profit, and (iii) her new optimal years of schooling. What kind of marginal cost does Alexa now have—constant, increasing, or decreasing?

Quantity of schooling (years)	Total cost
0	\$0
1	90,000
2	120,000
3	170,000
4	250,000
5	370,000

Solutions appear at back of book.

17.3 Sunk Costs

According to the **profit-maximizing principle of marginal analysis,** when faced with a profit-maximizing "how much" decision, the optimal quantity is the largest quantity at which the marginal benefit is greater than or equal to marginal cost.

When making decisions, knowing what to ignore can be as important as what to include. Although we have devoted much attention in this module to costs that are important to take into account when making a decision, some costs should be ignored when doing so. We will now focus on the kinds of costs that people should ignore when making decisions—what economists call *sunk costs*—and why they should be ignored.

To gain some intuition, consider the following scenario. You own a car that is a few years old, and you have just replaced the brake pads at a cost of \$250. But then you find out that the entire brake system is defective and also must be replaced. This will cost you an additional \$1,500. Alternatively, you could sell the car and buy another of comparable quality, but with no brake defects, by spending an additional $1,600. What should you do: fix your old car, or sell it and buy another?

Some might say that you should take the latter option. After all, this line of reasoning goes, if you repair your car, you will end up having spent $1,750: $1,500 for the brake system and $250 for the brake pads. If instead you sell your old car and buy another one, you would spend only $1,600.

But this reasoning, although it sounds plausible, is wrong. It is wrong because it ignores the fact that you have *already* spent $250 on brake pads, and that $250 cannot be recovered. Therefore, it should be ignored and should have no effect on your decision whether or not to repair your car and keep it.

GeorgiNutsov/iStock/Getty Images

The $250 already spent on brake pads is irrelevant because it is a sunk cost.

From a rational viewpoint, the real cost, at this time, of repairing and keeping your car is $1,500, not $1,750. The correct decision, then, is to repair your car and keep it rather than spend $1,600 on a new car.

In this example, the $250 that has already been spent and cannot be recovered is what economists call a **sunk cost.** Sunk costs should be ignored in making decisions about future actions because they have no influence on their actual costs and benefits. Once something can't be recovered, it is irrelevant in making decisions about what to do in the future.

It is often psychologically hard to ignore sunk costs. And if, in fact, you haven't yet incurred the costs, then you should take them into consideration. That is, if you had known at the beginning that it would cost $1,750 to repair your car, then the right choice at that time would have been to buy a new car for $1,600. But once you have already paid the $250 for brake pads, you should no longer include it in your decision making about your next actions. It may be hard to accept that "bygones are bygones," but it is the right way to make a decision.

ECONOMICS >> *in Action*

The Cost of a Life

What's the marginal benefit to society of saving a human life? You might be tempted to answer that human life is infinitely precious. But in the real world, resources are scarce, so we must decide how much to spend on saving lives since we cannot spend infinite amounts. After all, we could surely reduce highway deaths by dropping the speed limit on interstates to 40 miles per hour, but the cost of a lower speed limit—in time and money—is more than most people are willing to pay.

Generally, people are reluctant to talk in a straightforward way about comparing the marginal cost of a life saved with the marginal benefit—it sounds too callous. Sometimes, however, the question becomes unavoidable.

For example, the cost of saving a life became an object of intense discussion in the United Kingdom after a horrible train crash near London's Paddington Station killed 31 people. There were accusations that the British government was spending too little on rail safety. However, the government estimated that improving rail safety would cost an additional $4.5 million per life saved. But if that amount was worth spending—that is, if the estimated marginal benefit of saving a life exceeded $4.5 million—then the implication was that the British government was spending far too little on traffic safety.

In contrast, the estimated marginal cost per life saved through highway improvements was only $1.5 million, making it a much better deal than saving lives through greater rail safety.

A **sunk cost** is a cost that has already been incurred and is nonrecoverable. A sunk cost should be ignored in decisions about future actions.

Check Your Understanding 17-3

1. You have decided to go into the ice-cream business and have bought a used ice-cream truck for $8,000. Now you are reconsidering. What is your sunk cost in the following scenarios?
   - **a.** The truck cannot be resold.
   - **b.** The truck can be resold, but only at a 50% discount.
2. You have gone through two years of medical school but are suddenly wondering whether you wouldn't be happier as a musician. Which of the following statements are potentially valid arguments and which are not?
   - **a.** "I can't give up now, after all the time and money I've put in."
   - **b.** "If I had thought about it from the beginning, I never would have gone to med school, so I should give it up now."
   - **c.** "I wasted two years, but never mind—let's start from here."
   - **d.** "My parents would kill me if I stopped now." (*Hint:* We're discussing your decision-making ability, not your parents'.)

Solutions appear at back of book.

>> Quick Review

- **Sunk costs** should be ignored in decisions regarding future actions. Because they have already been incurred and are nonrecoverable, they have no effect on future costs and benefits.

MODULE 18

Behavioral Economics

WHAT YOU WILL LEARN

- What do economists consider to be rational and irrational behavior?
- Why do people behave in irrational yet predictable ways sometimes?

18.1 How People Make Economic Choices

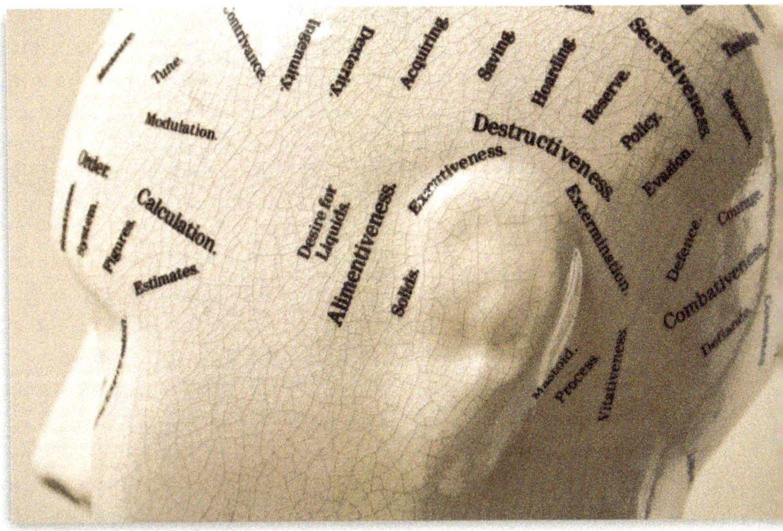

trenchcoates/Getty Images

Most economic models assume that people make choices based on achieving the best possible economic outcome for themselves. Human behavior, however, is often not so simple. Rather than acting like economic computing machines, people often make choices that fall short—sometimes far short—of the greatest possible economic outcome, or payoff.

Why people sometimes make less-than-perfect choices is the subject of behavioral economics, a branch of economics that combines economic modeling with insights from human psychology. Behavioral economics grew out of attempts by economists and psychologists to understand how people actually make—instead of theoretically make—economic choices.

It's well documented that people consistently engage in *irrational* behavior, choosing an option that leaves them worse off than other available options. Yet, as we'll soon learn, sometimes it's entirely *rational* for people to make a choice that is different from the one that generates the highest possible profit for themselves. For example, Alexa may decide to study computer science for two years rather than three years, the optimal number, because she wants to spend some time traveling.

The study of irrational economic behavior was largely pioneered by psychologists Daniel Kahneman and Amos Tversky. Kahneman won the 2002 Nobel Prize in economics for his work integrating insights from the psychology of human judgment and decision making into economics. Their work and the insights of others into why people often behave irrationally are having a significant influence on how economists analyze financial markets, labor markets, and other economic concerns.

Rational, but Human, Too

If you are **rational,** you will choose the available option that leads to the outcome you most prefer. But is the outcome you most prefer always the same as the one that gives you the best possible economic payoff? No. It can be entirely rational to choose an option that gives you a worse *economic* payoff because you care about something other than the size of that payoff. There are three principal

A **rational** decision maker chooses the available option that leads to the outcome they most prefer.

A decision maker operating with **bounded rationality** makes a choice that is close to but not exactly the one that leads to the best possible economic outcome.

Risk aversion is the willingness to sacrifice some economic payoff to avoid a potential loss.

An **irrational** decision maker chooses an option that leaves them worse off than choosing another available option.

reasons why people might prefer a worse economic payoff: concerns about fairness, bounded rationality, and risk aversion.

Concerns About Fairness In social situations, people often care about fairness as well as about the economic payoff to themselves. For example, no law requires you to tip a waiter or waitress. But concern for fairness leads most people to leave a tip (unless they've had outrageously bad service) because a tip is seen as fair compensation for good service, according to society's norms. Tippers are reducing their own economic payoff to be fair to waiters and waitresses.

Bounded Rationality Being an economic computing machine—choosing the option that gives you the best economic payoff—can require a fair amount of work: sizing up the options, computing the opportunity costs, calculating the marginal amounts, and so on. The mental effort required has its own opportunity cost. This realization led economists to the concept of **bounded rationality**—making a choice that is close to but not exactly the one that leads to the highest possible payoff, since the effort of finding the best payoff is too costly. In other words, bounded rationality is the "good enough" method of decision making.

Retailers are particularly good at exploiting their customers' tendency to engage in bounded rationality. For example, pricing items in units ending in 99¢ takes advantage of the tendency of shoppers to interpret an item that costs, say, $2.99 as significantly cheaper than one that costs $3.00. Bounded rationality leads them to give more weight to the $2 part of the price (the first number they see) than the 99¢ part.

Risk Aversion Because life is uncertain and the future unknown, sometimes a choice comes with significant risk. Although you may receive a high payoff if things turn out well, the possibility also exists that things may turn out badly and leave you worse off.

So even if you think a choice will give you the best payoff of all your available options, you may forgo it because you find the possibility that things could turn out badly too, well, risky. This is called **risk aversion**—the willingness to sacrifice some potential economic payoff to avoid a potential loss. Because risk makes most people uncomfortable, it's rational for them to give up some potential economic gain to avoid it.

Irrationality: An Economist's View

Sometimes, though, instead of being rational, people are **irrational**—they make choices that leave them worse off in terms of economic payoff *and* other considerations, such as fairness, than if they had chosen another available option. Is there anything systematic that economists and psychologists can say about economically irrational behavior? Yes, because most people are irrational in predictable ways. People's irrational behavior *typically* stems from six mistakes they make when thinking about economic decisions. The mistakes are listed in Table 18-1, and we will discuss each in turn.

TABLE 18-1 The Six Common Mistakes in Economic Decision Making

1. Misperceptions of opportunity cost
2. Overconfidence
3. Unrealistic expectations about future behavior
4. Counting dollars unequally
5. Loss aversion
6. Status quo bias

Misperceptions of Opportunity Costs As we discussed at the beginning of this section, people tend to ignore nonmonetary opportunity costs—opportunity costs that don't involve an outlay of cash. Likewise, a misperception of what exactly constitutes an opportunity cost (and what does not) is at the root of the tendency to count sunk costs in one's decision making. In this case, someone takes an opportunity cost into account when none actually exists.

Overconfidence It's a function of ego: we tend to think we know more than we actually do. And even if alerted to how widespread overconfidence is, people tend to think that it's someone else's problem, not theirs. (Certainly not yours or mine!)

Mental accounting is the habit of mentally assigning dollars to different accounts so that some dollars are worth more than others.

Loss aversion is an oversensitivity to loss, leading to unwillingness to recognize a loss and move on.

For example, one study asked students to estimate how long it would take them to complete their thesis "if everything went as well as it possibly could" and "if everything went as poorly as it possibly could." The results: the typical student thought it would take them 33.9 days to finish, with an average estimate of 27.4 days if everything went well and 48.6 days if everything went poorly. In fact, the average time it took to complete a thesis was much longer, 55.5 days. Students were, on average, from 14% to 102% more confident than they should have been about the time it would take to complete their thesis.

Overconfidence can cause problems with meeting deadlines. But it can cause far more trouble by having a strong adverse effect on people's financial health. Overconfidence often persuades people that they are in better financial shape than they actually are. It can also lead to bad investment and spending decisions. For example, nonprofessional investors who engage in a lot of speculative investing—such as quickly buying and selling stocks—on average have significantly worse results than professional brokers because of their misguided faith in their ability to spot a winner. Similarly, overconfidence can lead people to make a large spending decision, such as buying a car, without doing research on the pros and cons, relying instead on anecdotal evidence. Even worse, people tend to remain overconfident because they remember their successes, and explain away or forget their failures.

Unrealistic Expectations About Future Behavior Another form of overconfidence is being overly optimistic about your future behavior: tomorrow you'll study, tomorrow you'll give up ice cream, tomorrow you'll spend less and save more, and so on. Of course, as we all know, when tomorrow arrives, it's still just as hard to study or give up something that you like as it is right now.

Strategies that keep a person on the straight-and-narrow over time are often, at their root, ways to deal with the problem of unrealistic expectations about one's future behavior. Examples are automatic payroll deduction savings plans, diet plans with prepackaged foods, and mandatory attendance at study groups. By providing a way for someone to commit today to an action tomorrow, such plans counteract the habit of pushing difficult actions off into the future.

Counting Dollars Unequally If you tend to spend more when you pay with a credit card than when you pay with cash, particularly if you tend to splurge, then you are very likely engaging in **mental accounting.** This is the habit of mentally assigning dollars to different accounts, making some dollars worth more than others.

By spending more with a credit card, you are in effect treating dollars in your wallet as more valuable than dollars on your credit card balance, although in reality they count equally in your budget.

Credit card overuse is the most recognizable form of mental accounting. However, there are other forms as well, such as splurging after receiving a windfall, like an unexpected inheritance, or overspending at sales, buying something that seemed like a great bargain but that you later regretted. It's the failure to understand that, regardless of the form it comes in, a dollar is a dollar.

David Paul Morris/Bloomberg via Getty Images

A dollar is a dollar, whether it's in your wallet or on your credit card.

Loss Aversion **Loss aversion** is an oversensitivity to loss, leading to an unwillingness to recognize a loss and move on. In fact, in the lingo of the financial markets, "selling discipline"—being able and willing to quickly acknowledge when a stock you've bought is a loser and sell it—is a highly desirable trait to have.

Many investors, though, are reluctant to acknowledge that they've lost money on a stock and won't make it back. Although it's rational to sell the stock at that point and redeploy the remaining funds, most people find it so painful to admit a loss that they avoid selling for much longer than they should. According to Daniel Kahneman and Amos

The **status quo bias** is the tendency to avoid making a decision and sticking with the status quo.

Tversky, most people feel the misery of losing $100 about twice as keenly as they feel the pleasure of gaining $100.

Loss aversion can help explain why sunk costs are so hard to ignore: ignoring a sunk cost means recognizing that the money you spent is unrecoverable and therefore lost.

Status Quo Bias Another irrational behavior is **status quo bias,** the tendency to avoid making a decision altogether. A well-known example is the way that employees make decisions about investing in their employer-directed retirement accounts, known as 401(k)s. With a 401(k), employees can, through payroll deductions, set aside part of their salary tax-free, a practice that saves a significant amount of money every year in taxes. Some companies operate on an opt-in basis: employees have to actively choose to participate in a 401(k). Other companies operate on an opt-out basis: employees are automatically enrolled in a 401(k) unless they choose to opt out.

If everyone behaved rationally, then the proportion of employees enrolled in 401(k) accounts at opt-in companies would be roughly equal to the proportion enrolled at opt-out companies. In other words, your decision about whether to participate in a 401(k) should be independent of the default choice at your company. But, in reality, when companies switch to automatic enrollment and an opt-out system, employee enrollment rises dramatically. Clearly, people tend to just go with the status quo.

Why do people exhibit status quo bias? Some claim it's a form of "decision paralysis": when given many options, people find it harder to make a decision. Others claim it's due to loss aversion and the fear of regret, to thinking that "if I do nothing, then I won't have to regret my choice." Irrational, yes. But not altogether surprising. However, rational people know that, in the end, the act of not making a choice is still a choice.

Rational Models for Irrational People?

So why do economists still use models based on rational behavior when people are at times manifestly irrational? For one thing, models based on rational behavior still provide robust predictions about how people behave in most markets. For example, the great majority of farmers will use less fertilizer when it becomes more expensive—a result consistent with rational behavior.

Another explanation is that sometimes market forces can compel people to behave more rationally over time. For example, if you are a small-business owner who persistently exaggerates your abilities or refuses to acknowledge that your favorite line of items is a loser, then, sooner or later unless you learn to correct your mistakes, you will be out of business. As a result, it is reasonable to assume that when people are disciplined for their mistakes, as happens in most markets, rationality will win out over time.

Finally, economists depend on the assumption of rationality for the simple but fundamental reason that it makes modeling so much simpler. Remember that models are built on generalizations—it's much harder to extrapolate from messy, irrational behavior. Even behavioral economists, in their research, search for *predictably* irrational behavior in an attempt to build better models of how people behave. Clearly, there is an ongoing dialogue between behavioral economists and the rest of the economics profession, and economics itself has been irrevocably changed by it.

ECONOMICS >> *in Action*

In Praise of Hard Deadlines

Dan Ariely, a professor of psychology and behavioral economics, likes to do experiments with his students that help him explore the nature of irrationality. In his book *Predictably Irrational,* Ariely describes an experiment that gets to the heart of procrastination and ways to address it.

At the time, Ariely was teaching the same subject matter to three different classes, but he gave each class different assignment schedules. The grade in all three classes was based on three equally weighted papers.

Students in the first class were required to choose their own personal deadlines for submitting each paper. Once set, the deadlines could not be changed. Late papers would be penalized at the rate of 1% of the grade for each day late. Papers could be turned in early without penalty but also without any advantage, since Ariely would not grade papers until the end of the semester.

Students in the second class could turn in the three papers whenever they wanted, with no preset deadlines, as long as it was before the end of the term. Again, there would be no benefit for early submission.

Students in the third class faced what Ariely called the "dictatorial treatment." He established three hard deadlines at the fourth, eighth, and twelfth weeks.

So which classes do you think achieved the best and the worst grades? As it turned out, the class with the least flexible deadlines—the one that received the dictatorial treatment—got the best grades. The class with complete flexibility got the worst grades. And the class that got to choose its deadlines performed in the middle.

Ariely learned two simple things about overconfidence from these results. First—no surprise—students tend to procrastinate. Second, hard, equally spaced deadlines are the best cure for procrastination.

But the biggest revelation came from the class that set its own deadlines. The majority of those students spaced their deadlines far apart and got grades as good as those of the students under the dictatorial treatment. Some, however, did not space their deadlines far enough apart, and a few did not space them out at all. These last two groups did less well, putting the average of the entire class below the average of the class with the least flexibility. As Ariely notes, without well-spaced deadlines, students procrastinate and the quality of their work suffers.

This experiment provides two important insights:

1. People who acknowledge their tendency to procrastinate are more likely to use tools for committing to a path of action.
2. Providing those tools allows people to make themselves better off.

If you procrastinate, hard deadlines, as irksome as they may be, are truly for your own good.

Check Your Understanding 18-1

1. Which of the types of irrational behavior are suggested by each of the following events?
   - **a.** Although the housing market has fallen and Jenny wants to move, she refuses to sell her house for any amount less than what she paid for it.
   - **b.** Dan worked more overtime hours last week than he had expected. Although he is strapped for cash, he spends his unexpected overtime earnings on a weekend getaway rather than trying to pay down his student loan.
   - **c.** Carol has just started her first job and deliberately decided to opt out of the company's savings plan. Her reasoning is that she is very young and there is plenty of time in the future to start saving. Why not enjoy life now?
   - **d.** Jeremy's company requires employees to download and fill out a form if they want to participate in the company-sponsored savings plan. One year after starting the job, Jeremy had still not submitted the form needed to participate in the plan.
2. How would you determine whether a decision you made was rational or irrational?

Solutions appear at back of book.

>> Quick Review

- Behavioral economics combines economic modeling with insights from human psychology.
- **Rational** behavior leads to the outcome a person most prefers. **Bounded rationality, risk aversion,** and concerns about fairness are reasons why people might prefer outcomes with worse economic payoffs.
- **Irrational** behavior occurs because of misperceptions of opportunity costs, overconfidence, **mental accounting,** and unrealistic expectations about the future. **Loss aversion** and **status quo bias** can also lead to choices that leave people worse off than they would be if they chose another available option.

MODULE 19

Maximizing Utility

WHAT YOU WILL LEARN

- What factors determine how consumers spend their income?
- Why do economists use the concept of **utility** to describe people's tastes?
- Why does the **principle of diminishing marginal utility** accurately describe consumer behavior?
- What is the **optimum consumption bundle** and why do we use marginal analysis to determine it?

fullvalue/Getty Images

Earlier in this section we learned about principles for rational economic decision making that lead to the best possible outcomes. In this module, we will show how economists analyze the decisions of rational consumers, those who know what they want and make the most of available resources. We begin with the concept of utility—a measure of consumer satisfaction.

19.1 Utility: Getting Satisfaction

When analyzing consumer behavior, we're talking about people trying to get satisfaction—that is, about subjective feelings. Yet there is no simple way to measure subjective feelings. How much satisfaction do I get from my third egg roll? Is it less or more than yours? Does it even make sense to ask the question?

Luckily, we don't need to make comparisons between your feelings and mine. All that is required to analyze consumer behavior is to suppose that each individual is trying to maximize some personal measure of the satisfaction gained from consumption of goods and services. That measure is known as the consumer's **utility,** a concept we use to understand behavior but don't expect to measure in practice. Nonetheless, we'll see that the assumption that consumers maximize utility helps us think clearly about consumer choice.

The **utility** of a consumer is a measure of the satisfaction the consumer derives from consumption of goods and services.

An individual's **consumption bundle** is the collection of all the goods and services consumed by that individual.

An individual's **utility function** gives the total utility generated by their consumption bundle.

Utility and Consumption

An individual's utility depends on everything that individual consumes, from apples to Ziploc bags. The set of all the goods and services an individual consumes is known as the individual's **consumption bundle.** The relationship between an individual's consumption bundle and the total amount of utility it generates for that individual is known as the **utility function.** The utility function is a personal matter; two people with different tastes will have different utility functions. Someone who actually likes to consume 20 egg rolls in a sitting must have a utility function that looks different from that of someone who would rather stop at 3 egg rolls.

So we can think of consumers as using consumption to "produce" utility, much in the same way as in later modules we will think of producers as using inputs to produce output. However, it's obvious that people do not have a little computer in their heads that calculates the utility generated by their consumption choices. Nonetheless, people must make choices, and they usually base them on at least a rough attempt to decide which choice will give them greater satisfaction. I can have either a Coke or lemonade with my dinner. Which will I enjoy more? I can go backpacking through Europe this summer or save the money toward buying a car. Which will make me happier?

The concept of a utility function is just a way of representing the fact that when people consume, they take into account their preferences and tastes in a more or less rational way.

How do we measure utility? For the sake of simplicity, it is useful to suppose that we can measure utility in hypothetical units called—what else?—**utils.**

Figure 19-1 illustrates a utility function. It shows the total utility that Cassie, who likes egg rolls, gets from an all-you-can-eat Chinese buffet. We suppose that her consumption bundle consists of a Coke plus a number of egg rolls to be determined. The table that accompanies the figure shows how Cassie's total utility depends on the number of egg rolls; the curve in panel (a) of the figure shows that same information graphically.

Cassie's utility function slopes upward over most of the range shown, but it gets flatter as the number of egg rolls consumed increases. And in this example it eventually turns downward. According to the information in the table in Figure 19-1, total utility starts to decline after the eighth egg roll, making the ninth roll one egg roll too many. If she's rational, of course, Cassie will realize that and not consume the ninth egg roll.

So when Cassie is choosing how many egg rolls to consume, she will make this decision by taking into consideration the *change* in her total utility from consuming one more egg roll. This illustrates the general point: to maximize *total* utility, consumers must focus on *marginal* utility.

The Principle of Diminishing Marginal Utility

In addition to showing how Cassie's total utility depends on the number of egg rolls she consumes, the table in Figure 19-1 also shows the **marginal utility** generated by consuming each additional egg roll—that is, the *change* in total utility from consuming one additional egg roll. Panel (b) shows the implied **marginal utility curve.** Following our practice in Module 17 with the marginal benefit curve, the marginal utility curve is constructed by plotting points at the midpoint of the unit intervals.

The marginal utility curve slopes downward: each successive egg roll adds less to total utility than the previous one. This is reflected in the table: marginal utility falls from a high of 15 utils for the first egg roll consumed to −1 for the ninth one consumed. The fact that the ninth egg roll has negative marginal utility means that consuming it actually reduces total utility. (Restaurants that offer all-you-can-eat meals depend on the proposition that you can have too much of a good thing.) Not all marginal utility curves eventually become negative. But it is generally accepted that marginal utility curves do slope downward—that consumption of most goods and services is subject to *diminishing marginal utility.*

The basic idea behind the **principle of diminishing marginal utility** is that the additional satisfaction a consumer gets from one more unit of a good or service declines as the amount of that good or service consumed rises. Or, to put it

A **util** is a unit of utility.

The **marginal utility** of a good or service is the change in total utility generated by consuming one additional unit of that good or service.

The **marginal utility curve** shows how marginal utility depends on the quantity of a good or service consumed.

According to the **principle of diminishing marginal utility,** each successive unit of a good or service consumed adds less to total utility than the previous unit.

FIGURE 19-1 Cassie's Total Utility and Marginal Utility

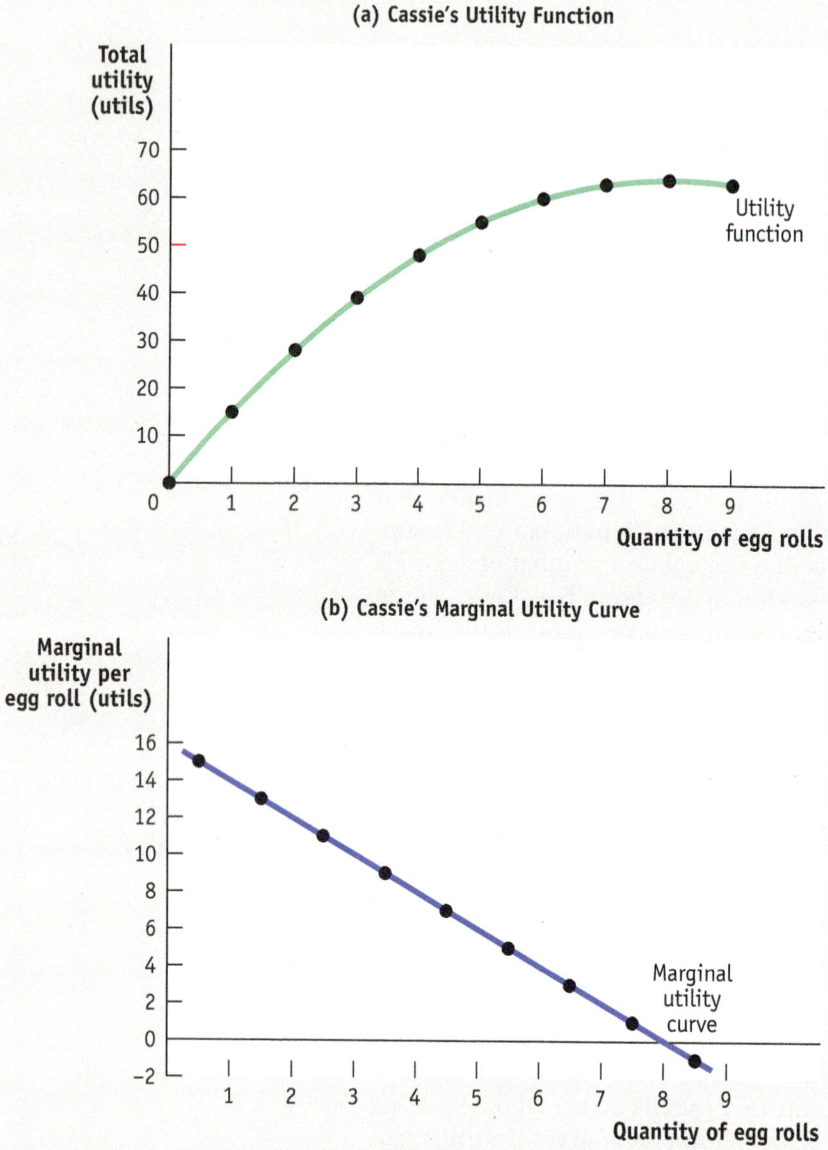

Quantity of egg rolls	Total utility (utils)	Marginal utility per egg roll (utils)
0	0	
		15
1	15	
		13
2	28	
		11
3	39	
		9
4	48	
		7
5	55	
		5
6	60	
		3
7	63	
		1
8	64	
		−1
9	63	

Panel (a) shows how Cassie's total utility depends on her consumption of egg rolls. It increases until it reaches its maximum utility level of 64 utils at 8 egg rolls consumed and decreases after that. Marginal utility is calculated in the table. Panel (b) shows the marginal utility curve, which slopes downward due to diminishing marginal utility. That is, each additional egg roll gives Cassie less additional utility than the previous egg roll.

slightly differently, the more of a good or service you consume, the closer you are to being *satiated*—reaching a point at which an additional unit of the good adds nothing to your satisfaction. For someone who almost never gets to eat a banana, the occasional banana is a marvelous treat. For someone who eats them all the time, a banana is just, well, a banana.

The principle of diminishing marginal utility isn't always true. But it is true in the great majority of cases, enough to serve as a foundation for our analysis of consumer behavior.

Check Your Understanding 19-1

1. Explain why a rational consumer who has diminishing marginal utility for a good would not consume an additional unit when it generates negative marginal utility, even when that unit is free.
2. Marta drinks three cups of coffee a day, for which she has diminishing marginal utility. Which of her three cups generates the greatest increase in total utility? Which generates the least?
3. In each of the following cases, determine if the consumer is experiencing diminishing marginal utility. Explain your answer.
   a. The more Mabel exercises, the more she enjoys each additional visit to the gym.
   b. Although Mei's iTunes music collection is huge, her enjoyment from buying another album has not changed as her collection has grown.
   c. When Dexter was a struggling student, his enjoyment from a good restaurant meal was greater than now, when he has them more frequently.

Solutions appear at back of book.

>> Quick Review

- **Utility** is a measure of a consumer's satisfaction from consumption, expressed in units of **utils.** Consumers try to maximize their utility. A consumer's **utility function** shows the relationship between the **consumption bundle** and the total utility it generates.
- To maximize utility, a consumer considers the **marginal utility** from consuming one more unit of a good or service, illustrated by the **marginal utility curve.**
- In the consumption of most goods and services, and for most people, the **principle of diminishing marginal utility** holds: each successive unit consumed adds less to total utility than the previous unit.

19.2 Budgets and Optimal Consumption

The principle of diminishing marginal utility explains why most people eventually reach a limit, even at an all-you-can-eat buffet where the cost of another egg roll is measured only in future indigestion. Under ordinary circumstances, however, it costs some additional resources to consume more of a good, and consumers must take that cost into account when making choices.

What do we mean by cost? As always, the fundamental measure of cost is *opportunity cost.* Because the amount of money a consumer can spend is limited, a decision to consume more of one good is also a decision to consume less of some other good.

Budget Constraints and Budget Lines

Consider Sammy, whose appetite is exclusively for egg rolls and Coke. He has a weekly income of $20 and since, given his appetite, more of either good is better than less, he spends all of it on egg rolls and Coke. We will assume that egg rolls cost $4 per roll and Coke costs $2 per bottle. What are his possible choices?

Whatever Sammy chooses, we know that the cost of his consumption bundle cannot exceed his income, the amount of money he has to spend. That is,

(19-1) Expenditure on egg rolls + Expenditure on Coke $\leq$ Total income

Consumers always have limited income, which constrains how much they can consume. So the requirement illustrated by Equation 19-1—that a consumer must choose a consumption bundle that costs no more than their income—is known as the consumer's **budget constraint.** It's a simple way of saying that a consumer can't spend more than the total amount of income available to them. In other words, consumption bundles are affordable when they obey the budget constraint. We call the set of all of Sammy's affordable consumption bundles his **consumption possibilities.** In general, whether or not a particular consumption bundle is included in a consumer's consumption possibilities depends on the consumer's income and the prices of goods and services.

A **budget constraint** requires that the cost of a consumer's consumption bundle be no more than the consumer's income.

A consumer's **consumption possibilities** is the set of all consumption bundles that can be consumed given the consumer's income and prevailing prices.

Figure 19-2 shows Sammy's consumption possibilities. The quantity of egg rolls in his consumption bundle is measured on the horizontal axis and the quantity of Cokes on the vertical axis. The downward-sloping line connecting points *A* through *F* shows which consumption bundles are affordable and which are not. Every bundle on or inside this line (the shaded area) is affordable; every bundle outside this line is unaffordable.

FIGURE 19-2 The Budget Line

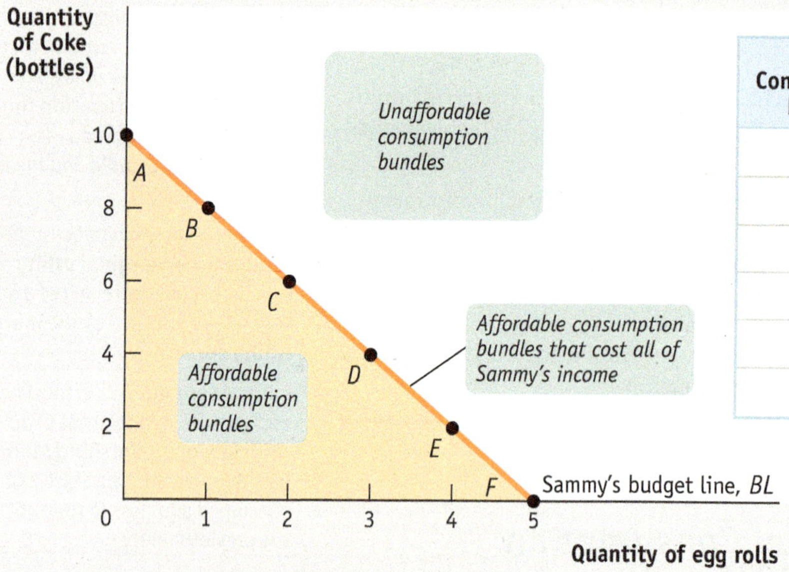

Consumption bundle	Quantity of egg rolls	Quantity of Coke (bottles)
A	0	10
B	1	8
C	2	6
D	3	4
E	4	2
F	5	0

The *budget line* represents the consumption bundles available to Sammy when he spends all of his income. Also, it is the boundary between the set of affordable consumption bundles (the *consumption possibilities*) and unaffordable ones. Given that egg rolls cost 2 per bottle, if Sammy spends all of his income on egg rolls (bundle *F*), he can purchase 5 egg rolls. If he spends all of his income on Cokes (bundle *A*), he can purchase 10 bottles of Coke.

As an example of one of the points, let's look at point *C*, representing 2 egg rolls and 6 Cokes, and check whether it satisfies Sammy's budget constraint. The cost of bundle *C* is 6 bottles of Coke × \$2 per bottle + 2 egg rolls × \$4 per roll = \$12 + \$8 = \$20. So bundle *C* does indeed satisfy Sammy's budget constraint: it costs no more than his weekly income of \$20. In fact, bundle *C* costs exactly as much as Sammy's income. By doing the arithmetic, you can check that all the other points lying on the downward-sloping line are also bundles at which Sammy spends all of his income.

The downward-sloping line has a special name, the **budget line.** It shows all the consumption bundles available to Sammy when he spends all of his income. It's downward sloping because when Sammy is consuming all of his income, say consuming at point *A* on the budget line, then to consume more egg rolls he must consume fewer Cokes—that is, he must move to a point like *B*. In other words, when Sammy chooses a consumption bundle that is on his budget line, the opportunity cost of consuming more egg rolls is consuming fewer Cokes, and vice versa. As Figure 19-2 indicates, any consumption bundle that lies above the budget line is unaffordable.

Do we need to consider the other bundles in Sammy's consumption possibilities, the ones that lie *within* the shaded region in Figure 19-2 bounded by the budget line? The answer is, for all practical situations, no: as long as Sammy continues to get positive marginal utility from consuming either good (in other words, Sammy doesn't get *satiated*)—and he doesn't get any utility from saving income rather than spending it, then he will always choose to consume a bundle that lies on his budget line and not within the shaded area.

Given his \$20 per week budget, which point on his budget line will Sammy choose?

A consumer's **budget line** shows the consumption bundles available to a consumer who spends all of their income.

Optimal Consumption Choice

Sammy will choose a consumption bundle that lies on his budget line. That's the best he can do given his budget constraint. We want to find the consumption bundle—the point on the budget line—that maximizes Sammy's total utility. This

TABLE 19-1 Sammy's Utility from Egg Roll and Coke Consumption

Utility from egg roll consumption		Utility from Coke consumption	
Quantity of egg rolls	Utility from egg rolls (utils)	Quantity of Coke (bottles)	Utility from Cokes (utils)
0	0	0	0
1	15	1	11.5
2	25	2	21.4
3	31	3	29.8
4	34	4	36.8
5	36	5	42.5
		6	47.0
		7	50.5
		8	53.2
		9	55.2
		10	56.7

bundle is Sammy's **optimal consumption bundle,** the consumption bundle that maximizes his total utility given the budget constraint.

A consumer's **optimal consumption bundle** is the consumption bundle that maximizes the consumer's total utility given their budget constraint.

Table 19-1 shows how much utility Sammy gets from consuming different amounts of egg rolls and Cokes. As you can see, Sammy has a healthy appetite; the more of either good he consumes, the higher his utility. (Although the quantities are not so large that an additional egg roll or Coke would give him *negative utility,* meaning they wouldn't be rational to consume.)

But because he has a limited budget, he must make a trade-off: the more egg rolls he consumes, the fewer bottles of Coke, and vice versa. That is, he must choose a point on his budget line.

Table 19-2 shows how Sammy's total utility varies for the different consumption bundles along his budget line. Each of the six possible consumption bundles, *A* through *F* from Figure 19-2, is listed in the first column. The second column shows the number of egg rolls consumed corresponding to each bundle. The third column shows the utility Sammy gets from consuming those egg rolls. The fourth column shows the quantity of Cokes Sammy can afford *given* the level of egg roll consumption. This quantity goes down as the number of egg rolls consumed goes up, because he is sliding down the budget line. The fifth column shows the utility he gets from consuming those Cokes. And the final column shows his *total utility.* In this example, Sammy's total utility is the sum of the utility he gets from egg rolls and the utility he gets from Cokes.

Figure 19-3 gives a visual representation of the data in Table 19-2. Panel (a) shows Sammy's budget line, to remind us that when he decides to consume more egg rolls he is also deciding to consume fewer Cokes. Panel (b) then shows how his total utility depends on that choice. The horizontal axis in panel (b) has two

TABLE 19-2 Sammy's Budget and Total Utility

Consumption bundle	Quantity of egg rolls	Utility from egg rolls (utils)	Quantity of Coke (bottles)	Utility from Cokes (utils)	Total utility (utils)
A	0	0	10	56.7	56.7
B	1	15	8	53.2	68.2
C	2	25	6	47.0	72.0
D	3	31	4	36.8	67.8
E	4	34	2	21.4	55.4
F	5	36	0	0	36.0

FIGURE 19-3 **Optimal Consumption Bundle**

Panel (a) shows Sammy's budget line and his six possible consumption bundles. Panel (b) shows how his total utility is affected by his consumption bundle, which must lie on his budget line. The quantity of egg rolls is measured from left to right on the horizontal axis, and the quantity of Cokes is measured from right to left. His total utility is maximized at bundle C, the highest point on his utility function, where he consumes 2 egg rolls and 6 bottles of Coke. This is Sammy's *optimal consumption bundle.*

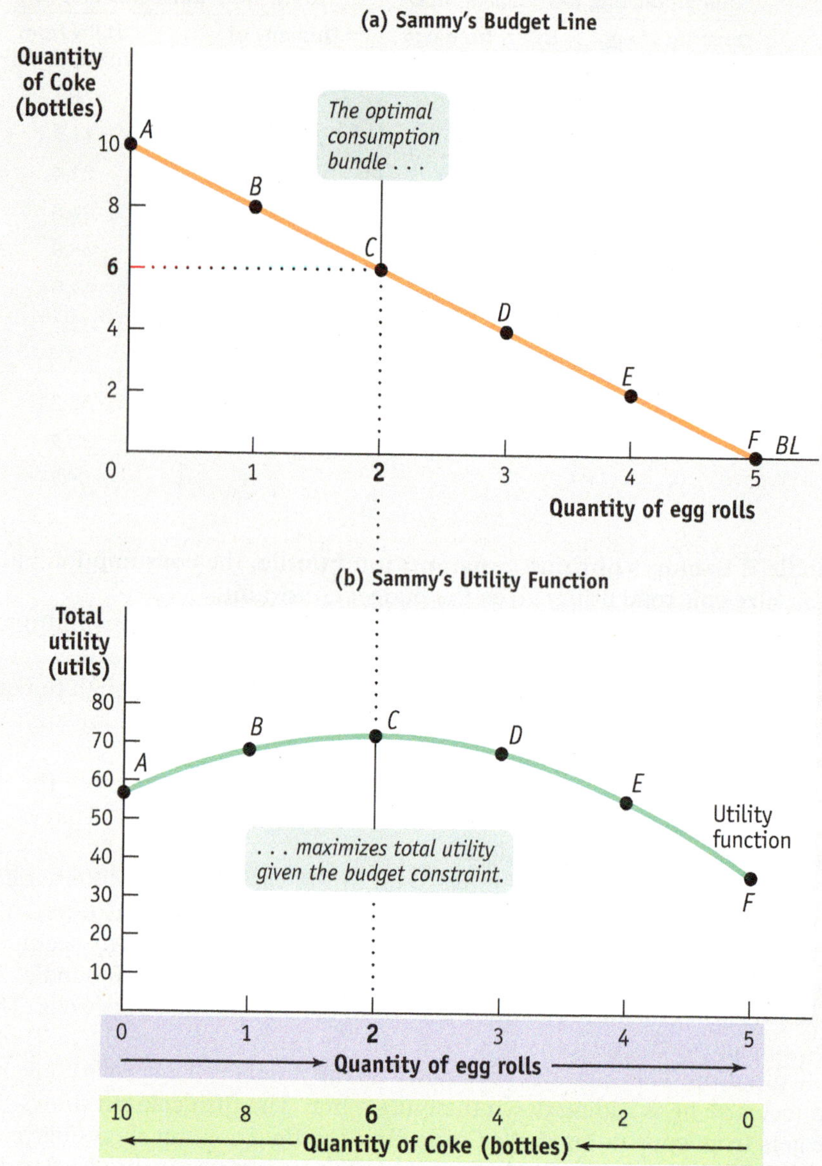

sets of labels: it shows both the quantity of egg rolls, increasing from left to right, and the quantity of Cokes, increasing from right to left.

The reason we can use the same axis to represent consumption of both goods is, of course, the budget line: the more egg rolls Sammy consumes, the fewer bottles of Coke he can afford, and vice versa.

Clearly, the consumption bundle that makes the best of the trade-off between egg roll consumption and Coke consumption, the optimal consumption bundle, is the one that maximizes Sammy's total utility. That is, Sammy's optimal consumption bundle puts him at the highest point of the total utility curve.

As always, we can find the highest point of the curve by direct observation. We can see from Figure 19-3 that Sammy's total utility is maximized at point *C*, his optimal consumption bundle, which contains 2 egg rolls and 6 bottles of Coke. Here we've solved Sammy's optimal consumption choice problem by calculating and comparing the utility generated by each bundle. But since it is a "how much" problem, marginal analysis will give us greater insight than direct calculation. So in the next section we turn to representing and solving the optimal consumption choice problem with marginal analysis.

Check Your Understanding 19-2

1. In the following two examples, find all the consumption bundles that lie on the consumer's budget line. Illustrate these consumption possibilities in a diagram and draw the budget line through them.
   a. The consumption bundle consists of movie tickets and buckets of popcorn. The price of each ticket is $10, the price of each bucket of popcorn is $5, and the consumer's income is $20. In your diagram, put movie tickets on the vertical axis and buckets of popcorn on the horizontal axis.
   b. The consumption bundle consists of underwear and socks. The price of each pair of underwear is $4, the price of each pair of socks is $2, and the consumer's income is $12. In your diagram, put pairs of socks on the vertical axis and pairs of underwear on the horizontal axis.

Solutions appear at back of book.

>> Quick Review

- The **budget constraint** requires that a consumer's total expenditure be no more than their income. The set of consumption bundles that satisfy the budget constraint is the consumer's **consumption possibilities.**
- A consumer who spends all of their income chooses a point on their **budget line.** The budget line slopes downward because on the budget line a consumer must consume less of one good to consume more of another.
- The consumption choice that maximizes total utility given the consumer's budget constraint is the **optimal consumption bundle.** It must lie on the consumer's budget line.

19.3 Spending the Marginal Dollar

As we've just seen, we can find Sammy's optimal consumption choice by finding the total utility he receives from each consumption bundle on his budget line and then choosing the bundle at which total utility is maximized. But we can also use marginal analysis instead, turning Sammy's problem of finding his optimal consumption choice into a "how much" problem.

To do this, think about choosing an optimal consumption bundle as a problem of *how much to spend on each good.* That is, to find the optimal consumption bundle with marginal analysis, ask whether Sammy can make himself better off by spending a little bit more of his income on egg rolls and less on Cokes, or by doing the opposite—spending a little bit more on Cokes and less on egg rolls. In other words, the marginal decision is a question of how to *spend the marginal dollar*—how to allocate an additional dollar between egg rolls and bottles of Coke in a way that maximizes utility.

Our first step in applying marginal analysis is to ask if Sammy is made better off by spending an additional dollar on either good; and if so, by how much is he better off. To answer this question we must calculate the **marginal utility per dollar** spent on either egg rolls or Cokes—how much additional utility Sammy gets from spending an additional dollar on either good.

Marginal Utility per Dollar

We've already introduced the concept of *marginal utility,* the additional utility a consumer gets from consuming one more unit of a good or service; now let's see how this concept can be used to derive the related measure of marginal utility per dollar.

Table 19-3 shows how to calculate the marginal utility per dollar spent on egg rolls and Cokes, respectively.

In panel (a) of the table, the first column shows different possible amounts of egg roll consumption. The second column shows the utility Sammy derives from each amount of egg roll consumption; the third column then shows the marginal utility, the increase in utility Sammy gets from consuming an additional egg roll. Panel (b) provides the same information for Cokes. The next step is to derive marginal utility *per dollar* for each good. To do this, we must divide the marginal utility of the good by its price in dollars.

To see why we must divide by the price, compare the third and fourth columns of panel (a). Consider what happens if Sammy increases his egg roll consumption from 2 rolls to 3 rolls. As we can see, this increase in egg roll consumption raises his total utility by 6 utils. But he must spend $4 for that additional roll, so the increase in his utility per additional dollar spent on egg rolls is 6 utils/$4 = 1.5 utils per dollar.

Similarly, if he increases his egg roll consumption from 3 rolls to 4 rolls, his marginal utility is 3 utils but his marginal utility per dollar is 3 utils/$4 = 0.75 util

The **marginal utility per dollar** spent on a good or service is the additional utility from spending one more dollar on that good or service.

TABLE 19-3 Sammy's Marginal Utility per Dollar

(a) Egg rolls (price = $4 per roll)

Quantity of egg rolls	utility from egg rolls (utils)	Marginal utility per roll (utils)	Marginal utility per dollar (utils/$)
0	0		
		15	3.75
1	15		
		10	2.50
2	25		
		6	1.50
3	31		
		3	0.75
4	34		
		2	0.50
5	36		

(b) Cokes (price = $2 per bottle)

Quantity of Coke (bottles)	utility from Cokes (utils)	Marginal utility per bottle of Coke (utils)	Marginal utility per dollar (utils/$)
0	0		
		11.5	5.75
1	11.5		
		9.9	4.95
2	21.4		
		8.4	4.20
3	29.8		
		7.0	3.50
4	36.8		
		5.7	2.85
5	42.5		
		4.5	2.25
6	47.0		
		3.5	1.75
7	50.5		
		2.7	1.35
8	53.2		
		2.0	1.00
9	55.2		
		1.5	0.75
10	56.7		

per dollar. Notice that because of diminishing marginal utility, Sammy's marginal utility per egg roll falls as the quantity of rolls he consumes rises. As a result, his marginal utility per dollar spent on egg rolls also falls as the quantity of rolls he consumes rises.

So the last column of panel (a) shows how Sammy's marginal utility per dollar spent on egg rolls depends on the quantity of rolls he consumes. Similarly, the last column of panel (b) shows how his marginal utility per dollar spent on Coke depends on the quantity of bottles of Coke he consumes. Again, marginal utility per dollar spent on each good declines as the quantity of that good consumed rises, due to diminishing marginal utility.

We will use the symbols MU_r and MU_c to represent the marginal utility per egg roll and bottle of Coke, respectively. And we will use the symbols P_r and P_c to represent the price of egg rolls (per roll) and the price of Coke (per bottle). Then the marginal utility per dollar spent on egg rolls is MU_r/P_r and the marginal utility per dollar spent on Cokes is MU_c/P_c. In general, the additional utility generated from an additional dollar spent on a good is equal to:

(19-2) Marginal utility per dollar spent on a good

= Marginal utility of one unit of the good/Price of one unit of the good

$= MU_{Good}/P_{Good}$

Now let's see how this concept helps us find the consumer's optimal consumption bundle using marginal analysis.

Optimal Consumption

Let's consider Figure 19-4. As in Figure 19-3, we can measure both the quantity of egg rolls and the quantity of bottles of Coke on the horizontal axis due to the budget constraint. Along the horizontal axis of Figure 19-4—also as in Figure 19-3—the quantity of egg rolls increases as you move from left to right, and the quantity

FIGURE 19-4 Marginal Utility per Dollar

Sammy's optimal consumption bundle is at point *C*, where his marginal utility per dollar spent on egg rolls, MU_r/P_r, is equal to his marginal utility per dollar spent on Cokes, MU_c/P_c. This illustrates the *utility-maximizing principle of marginal analysis:* at the optimal consumption bundle, the marginal utility per dollar spent on each good and service is the same. At any other consumption bundle on Sammy's budget line, such as bundle *B* in Figure 19-3, represented here by points B_r and B_c, consumption is not optimal: Sammy can increase his utility at no additional cost by reallocating his spending.

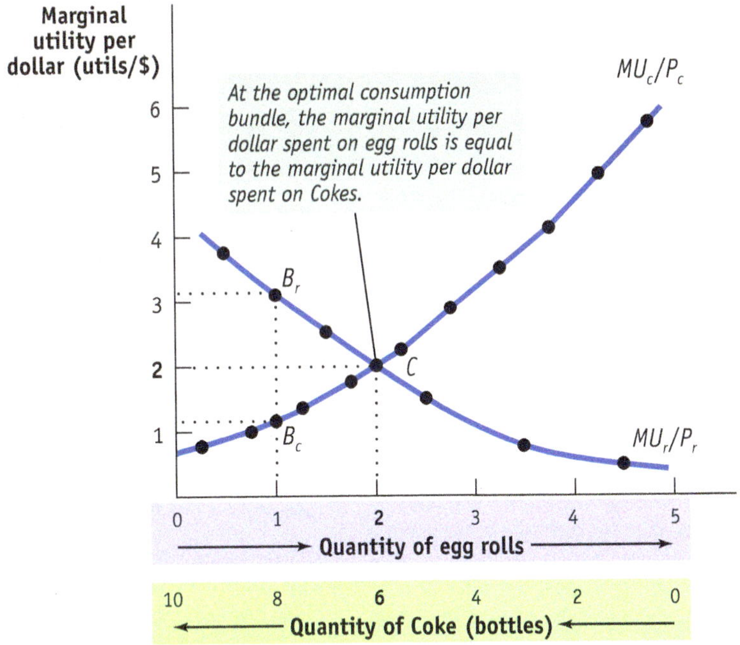

of Cokes increases as you move from right to left. The curve labeled MU_r/P_r in Figure 19-4 shows Sammy's marginal utility per dollar spent on egg rolls as derived in Table 19-3. Likewise, the curve labeled MU_c/P_c shows his marginal utility per dollar spent on Cokes. Notice that the two curves, MU_r/P_r and MU_c/P_c, cross at the optimal consumption bundle, point *C*, consisting of 2 egg rolls and 6 bottles of Coke.

Moreover, Figure 19-4 illustrates an important feature of Sammy's optimal consumption bundle: when Sammy consumes 2 egg rolls and 6 bottles of Coke, his marginal utility per dollar spent is the same, 2, for both goods. That is, at the optimal consumption bundle $MU_r/P_r = MU_c/P_c = 2$.

This isn't an accident. Consider another one of Sammy's possible consumption bundles—say, *B* in Figure 19-3, at which he consumes 1 egg roll and 8 bottles of Coke. The marginal utility per dollar spent on each good is shown by points B_r and B_c in Figure 19-4. At that consumption bundle, Sammy's marginal utility per dollar spent on egg rolls would be approximately 3, but his marginal utility per dollar spent on Cokes would be only approximately 1. This shows that he has made a mistake: he is consuming too many Cokes and not enough egg rolls.

How do we know this? If Sammy's marginal utility per dollar spent on egg rolls is higher than his marginal utility per dollar spent on Cokes, he has a simple way to make himself better off while staying within his budget: spend $1 less on Cokes and $1 more on egg rolls. We can illustrate this with points B_r and B_c in Figure 19-4. By spending an additional dollar on egg rolls, he gains the amount of utility given by B_r, about 3 utils. By spending $1 less on Cokes, he loses the amount of utility given by B_c, only about 1 util.

Because his marginal utility per dollar spent is higher for egg rolls than for Cokes, reallocating his spending toward egg rolls and away from Cokes would increase his total utility. But if his marginal utility per dollar spent on Cokes is higher, he can increase his utility by spending less on egg rolls and more on Cokes. So if Sammy has in fact chosen his optimal consumption bundle, his marginal utility per dollar spent on egg rolls and Cokes must be equal.

This is a general principle, which we call the **utility-maximizing principle of marginal analysis:** when a consumer maximizes utility in the face of a budget

According to the **utility-maximizing principle of marginal analysis,** the marginal utility per dollar spent must be the same for all goods and services in the optimal consumption bundle.

constraint, the marginal utility per dollar spent on each good or service in the consumption bundle is the same. That is, for any two goods r and c the optimal consumption rule says that at the optimal consumption bundle:

$$\text{(19-3)} \quad \frac{MU_r}{P_r} = \frac{MU_c}{P_c}$$

It's easiest to understand this rule using examples in which the consumption bundle contains only two goods, but it applies no matter how many goods or services a consumer buys: in the optimal consumption bundle, the marginal utilities per dollar spent for each and every good or service in that bundle are equal.

>> Quick Review

- According to the **utility-maximizing principle of marginal analysis,** the **marginal utility per dollar**—the marginal utility of a good divided by its price—is the same for all goods in the optimal consumption bundle.
- Whenever marginal utility per dollar is higher for one good than for another good, the consumer should spend $1 more on the good with the higher marginal utility per dollar and $1 less on the other. When he does, the consumer will move closer to his optimal consumption bundle. His optimal consumption bundle is achieved when the marginal utility per dollar is equal across all goods he consumes.

Check Your Understanding 19-3

1. In Table 19-3 you can see that marginal utility per dollar spent on egg rolls and marginal utility per dollar spent on Cokes are equal when Sammy increases his consumption of egg rolls from 3 to 4 rolls and his consumption of Cokes from 9 to 10 bottles. Explain why this is not Sammy's optimal consumption bundle. Illustrate your answer using the budget line in Figure 19-3.
2. Explain what is faulty about the following statement, using data from Table 19-3: "To maximize utility, Sammy should consume the bundle that gives him the maximum marginal utility per dollar for each good."

Solutions appear at back of book.

19.4 From Utility to the Demand Curve

We have now analyzed the optimal consumption choice of a consumer with a given amount of income who faces one particular set of prices—in our Sammy example, $20 of income per week, $4 per egg roll, and $2 per bottle of Coke.

But the main reason for studying consumer behavior is to go behind the market demand curve—to explain how the utility-maximizing behavior of individual consumers leads to the downward slope of the market demand curve.

Marginal Utility, the Substitution Effect, and the Law of Demand

Suppose that the price of egg rolls, P_r, rises. The price increase doesn't change the marginal utility a consumer gets from an additional egg roll, MU_r, at any given level of egg roll consumption. However, it does reduce the marginal utility *per dollar spent* on egg rolls, MU_r/P_r. And the decrease in marginal utility per dollar spent on egg rolls gives the consumer an incentive to consume fewer egg rolls when the price of egg rolls rises.

To see why, recall the utility-maximizing principle of marginal analysis: a utility-maximizing consumer chooses a consumption bundle for which the marginal utility per dollar spent on all goods is the same. If the marginal utility per dollar spent on egg rolls falls because the price of egg rolls rises, the consumer can increase their utility by purchasing fewer egg rolls and more of other goods.

The opposite happens if the price of egg rolls falls. In that case the marginal utility per dollar spent on egg rolls, MU_r/P_r, increases at any given level of egg roll consumption. As a result, a consumer can increase their utility by purchasing more egg rolls and less of other goods when the price of egg rolls falls.

So when the price of a good increases, an individual will normally consume less of that good and more of other goods. Correspondingly, when the price of a good decreases, an individual will normally consume more of that good and less of other goods. This explains why the individual demand curve, which relates an individual's consumption of a good to the price of that good, normally slopes downward—that is, it obeys the law of demand. And since—as we learned in Module 5—the market demand curve is the horizontal sum of all the individual demand curves of consumers, it, too, will slope downward.

An alternative way to think about why demand curves slope downward is to focus on opportunity costs. When the price of egg rolls decreases, an individual doesn't have to give up as many units of other goods to buy one more egg roll. So consuming egg rolls becomes more attractive. Conversely, when the price of a good increases, consuming that good becomes a less attractive use of resources, and the consumer buys less.

This effect of a price change on the quantity consumed is always present. It is known as the **substitution effect**—the change in the quantity consumed as the consumer substitutes other goods that are now relatively cheaper in place of the good that has become relatively more expensive. When a good absorbs only a small share of the consumer's spending, the substitution effect provides the complete explanation of why the consumer's individual demand curve slopes downward. Therefore, when a good absorbs only a small share of the average consumer's spending, the substitution effect provides the sole explanation of why the market demand curve slopes downward.

However, some goods, such as housing, absorb a large share of a typical consumer's spending. For such goods, the story behind the individual demand curve and the market demand curve becomes slightly more complicated.

The **substitution effect** of a change in the price of a good is the change in quantity of that good consumed as the consumer substitutes other goods that are now relatively cheaper in place of the good that has become relatively more expensive.

The **income effect** of a change in price of a good is the change in the quantity of a good consumed that results from a change in the consumer's overall purchasing power due to a change in the price of that good.

The Income Effect

For the vast majority of goods, the slopes of the individual and market demand curves are completely determined by the substitution effect. There are, however, some goods, like food or housing, that account for a substantial share of many consumers' spending. In such cases another effect, called the *income effect,* also comes into play.

Consider the case of a family that spends half its income on rental housing. Now suppose that the price of housing increases everywhere. This will have a substitution effect on the family's demand: other things equal, the family will have an incentive to consume less housing—say, by moving to a smaller apartment—and more of other goods. But the family will also, in a real sense, be made poorer by that higher housing price—its income will buy less housing than before.

The amount of income adjusted to reflect its true purchasing power is often termed "real income," in contrast to "money income" or "nominal income," which has not been adjusted. And this reduction in a consumer's real income will have an additional effect, beyond the substitution effect, on the family's consumption bundle, including its consumption of housing.

The change in the quantity of a good consumed that results from a change in the overall purchasing power of the consumer due to a change in the price of that good is known as the **income effect** of the price change. In this case, a change in the price of a good effectively changes a consumer's income because it alters the consumer's purchasing power. Along with the substitution effect, the income effect is another means by which changes in prices alter consumption choices.

1. For the great majority of goods and services, the income effect is not important and has no significant effect on individual consumption. Thus most market demand curves slope downward solely because of the substitution effect—end of story.
2. When it matters at all, the income effect usually reinforces the substitution effect. That is, when the price of a good that absorbs a substantial share of income rises, consumers of that good become a bit poorer because their purchasing power falls. As we learned in Module 5, the vast majority of goods are *normal goods,* goods for which demand decreases when income falls. So this effective reduction in income leads to a reduction in the quantity demanded and reinforces the substitution effect.

However, in the case of an *inferior good,* a good for which demand increases when income falls, the income and substitution effects work in opposite directions. Although the substitution effect tends to produce a decrease in the quantity of any good demanded as its price increases, in the case of an inferior good the income effect of a price increase tends to produce an *increase* in the quantity demanded. This makes sense because the price increase lowers the real income of the consumer, and as real income falls, the demand for an inferior good increases.

If a good were so inferior that the income effect exceeded the substitution effect, a price increase would lead to an increase in the quantity demanded. There is controversy over whether such goods, known as "Giffen goods," exist at all. If they do, they are very rare. You can generally assume that the income effect for an inferior good is smaller than the substitution effect, so a price increase will still lead to a decrease in the quantity demanded.

ECONOMICS >> *in Action*

Lower Gasoline Prices and the Urge to Splurge

For American consumers, 2015 was a year to indulge the urge to splurge, made possible by plunging gasoline prices. From early 2014 to early 2015, gas prices fell nearly 45%, according to a study by the JP Morgan Institute based upon data from millions of credit card and debit card users. This translated into a windfall of approximately $700 for the average American family.

Consumers spent about 80% of their windfall, saving the remaining 20%. Fast-food chains like McDonald's, Wendy's, or Taco Bell, often located near gas stations and which cater to lower-income consumers, were the biggest beneficiaries of this spending as people chose to eat out more frequently or added extras like bacon to their burgers.

This should come as no surprise as low-income households experienced the largest *income effect* from the fall in gas prices—gasoline purchases accounted for a significant share of household spending, especially for those earning less than $29,999 per year. Those households experienced a 1.6% increase in their average income from the fall in gas prices, while households earning $79,700 or more saw their average income increase by only 0.5%.

And data indicate that the *substitution effect*—lower gas prices leading to purchases of more gas and less of other goods—also affected consumers' choices. Not only did people buy more gasoline, they bought higher grades of gasoline. Predictably, sales of electric vehicles, which use much less gas per mile, dropped sharply in 2015 (about 15%) after rising sharply from 2011 to 2013, a period of high gas prices. Simultaneously, gas-guzzling SUVs saw an uptick in sales.

>> *Quick Review*

- Most goods absorb only a small fraction of a consumer's spending. For such goods, the **substitution effect** of a price change is the only important effect of the price change on consumption. It causes individual demand curves and the market demand curve to slope downward.
- When a good absorbs a large fraction of a consumer's spending, the **income effect** of a price change is present in addition to the substitution effect.
- For normal goods, demand rises when a consumer is richer and falls when a consumer is poorer, so that the income effect reinforces the substitution effect. For inferior goods, demand rises when a consumer is poorer and falls when a consumer is richer, so that the income and substitution effects move in opposite directions.

Check Your Understanding 19-4

1. In each of the following cases, state whether the income effect, the substitution effect, or both are significant. In which cases do they move in the same direction? In opposite directions? Why?
   a. Orange juice represents a small share of Clare's spending. She buys more lemonade and less orange juice when the price of orange juice goes up. She does not change her spending on other goods.
   b. Apartment rents have risen dramatically this year. Since rent absorbs a major part of her income, Delia moves to a smaller apartment. Assume that rental housing is a normal good.
   c. The cost of a semester-long meal ticket at the student cafeteria rises, representing a significant increase in living costs. Assume that cafeteria meals are an inferior good.
2. In the example described in Question 1c, how would you determine whether or not cafeteria meals are a Giffen good?

Solutions appear at back of book.

BUSINESS CASE

Beyond Impossible: McDonald's and Burger King's Beef-Free Battle

Geoff Robins/Getty Images

After decades of dependable growth, the fortunes of McDonald's have been on a roller coaster for the past several years. During the Great Recession, McDonald's had outperformed other fast-food restaurants and chain restaurants, such as TGI Friday's, as price-conscious customers were drawn to McDonald's "Dollar Menu." However, by 2013 the Dollar Menu was no longer profitable. When it was replaced with the "Dollar Menu and More," which included items costing up to $5, customer reaction was definitely not positive: from 2014 to 2015 revenue fell by 7.4% and, for the first time ever, McDonald's closed more restaurants than it opened in the United States. As Steve Easterbrook, CEO of McDonald's said at the time, "As we moved away from the Dollar Menu, we didn't replace it with offers of an equivalent form of value. And customers have voted with their feet."

McDonald's tried to lure back customers with its 2016 "McPick 2 Menu," which allowed customers to pick two items for $2. But as the economy slowly recovered, McDonald's found itself struggling to keep its price-conscious customers, while at the same time losing ground to the quickest growing segment of the restaurant industry: *fast-casual* restaurants that cater to customers with higher incomes. Fast-casual chains such as Chipotle and Panera offer a healthier menu using fresh ingredients, customizable, build-your-own selections, and a more comfortable dining environment. While the average McDonald's meal costs from $5 to $7, the typical Chipotle customer spends $12 for a meal. Despite their lower cost, McDonald's healthier menu options haven't sold particularly well because health-conscious customers tend to view McDonald's as the place to go for a quick burger and fries.

McDonald's also was caught flat-footed by the success of Burger King's plant-based Impossible Whopper burger in 2019. Costing $1 more than a regular beef burger, Impossible Burgers are completely meat-free, yet re-create the taste and feel of a beef burger. As the CEO of Restaurant Brands International, the parent company of Burger King, said, sales of the Impossible Whopper have been "highly incremental and have attracted new types of guests into our restaurant. We see a lot of millennial and Gen Z customers who tend to really connect with the message around sustainability." The strong demand for the Impossible Whopper lifted Burger's King sales by nearly 11% in late 2019 while McDonald's comparable sales grew by less than 5% over the same period.

McDonald's is now playing catch-up, rolling out its own plant-based Beyond Burger, called PLT, in selected markets. So the question in the minds of industry analysts is this: having succeeded in dominating the price-conscious but low-profitability segment of the food market, can McDonald's now transform itself in the minds of health-conscious and environmentally conscious customers who are willing to pay more for healthier and more sustainable food? Can it go beyond its identity as a place to buy a cheap beef burger and fries?

QUESTIONS FOR THOUGHT

1. How does the McPick 2 promotion resemble a consumer's optimal choice problem?
2. Give an example of a normal good and an inferior good mentioned in this case. Cite examples of income and substitution effects from the case.
3. Give an example of differences in consumer preferences illustrated by the case.

REVIEW

MODULE 17

1. All economic decisions involve the allocation of scarce resources. Some decisions are "either–or" decisions, in which the question is whether or not to do something. Other decisions are "how much" decisions, in which the question is how much of a resource to put into a given activity.

2. The cost of using a resource for a particular activity is the opportunity cost of that resource. Some opportunity costs are **explicit costs;** they involve a direct outlay of money. Other opportunity costs, however, are **implicit costs;** they involve no outlay of money but are measured by the dollar value of the benefits that are forgone. Both explicit and implicit costs should be taken into account in making decisions. Many decisions involve the use of **capital** and time, for both individuals and firms. So they should base decisions on **economic profit,** which takes into account implicit costs such as the opportunity cost of time and the **implicit cost of capital.** Making decisions based on **accounting profit** can be misleading. It is often considerably larger than economic profit because it includes only explicit costs and not implicit costs.

3. According to the **principle of "either–or" decision making,** when faced with an "either–or" choice between two activities, one should choose the activity with the positive economic profit.

4. A "how much" decision is made using marginal analysis, which involves comparing the benefit to the cost of doing an additional unit of an activity. The **marginal cost** of producing a good or service is the additional cost incurred by producing one more unit of that good or service. The **marginal benefit** of producing a good or service is the additional benefit earned by producing one more unit. The **marginal cost curve** is the graphical illustration of marginal cost, and the **marginal benefit curve** is the graphical illustration of marginal benefit.

5. In the case of **constant marginal cost,** each additional unit costs the same amount to produce as the previous unit. However, marginal cost and marginal benefit typically depend on how much of the activity has already been done. With **increasing marginal cost,** each unit costs more to produce than the previous unit and is represented by an upward-sloping marginal cost curve. With **decreasing marginal cost,** each unit costs less to produce than the previous unit, leading to a downward-sloping marginal cost curve. In the case of **decreasing marginal benefit,** each additional unit produces a smaller benefit than the unit before.

6. The **optimal quantity** is the quantity that generates the highest possible total profit. According to the **profit-maximizing principle of marginal analysis,** the optimal quantity is the quantity at which marginal benefit is greater than or equal to marginal cost. It is the quantity at which the marginal cost curve and the marginal benefit curve intersect.

7. A cost that has already been incurred and that is nonrecoverable is a **sunk cost.** Sunk costs should be ignored in decisions about future actions because they have no effect on future benefits and costs.

MODULE 18

1. With **rational** behavior, individuals will choose the available option that leads to the outcome they most prefer. **Bounded rationality** occurs because the effort needed to find the best economic payoff is costly. **Risk aversion** causes individuals to sacrifice some economic payoff to avoid a potential loss. People might also prefer outcomes with worse economic payoffs because they are concerned about fairness.

2. An **irrational** choice leaves someone worse off than if they had chosen another available option. It takes the form of misperceptions of opportunity cost; overconfidence; unrealistic expectations about future behavior; **mental accounting,** in which dollars are valued unequally; **loss aversion,** an oversensitivity to loss; and **status quo bias,** avoiding a decision by sticking with the status quo.

MODULE 19

1. Consumers maximize a measure of satisfaction called **utility.** Each consumer has a **utility function** that determines the level of total utility generated by their **consumption bundle,** the goods and services that are consumed. We measure utility in hypothetical units called **utils.**

2. A good's or service's **marginal utility** is the additional utility generated by consuming one more unit of the good or service. We usually assume that the **principle of diminishing marginal utility** holds: consumption of another unit of a good or service yields less additional utility than the previous unit. As a result, the **marginal utility curve** slopes downward.

3. A **budget constraint** limits a consumer's spending to no more than their income. It defines the consumer's **consumption possibilities,** the set of all affordable consumption bundles. A consumer who spends all of

their income will choose a consumption bundle on the **budget line.** An individual chooses the consumption bundle that maximizes total utility, the **optimal consumption bundle.**

4. We use marginal analysis to find the optimal consumption bundle by analyzing how to allocate the marginal dollar. According to the **utility-maximizing principle of marginal analysis,** at the optimal consumption bundle, the **marginal utility per dollar** spent on each good and service—the marginal utility of a good divided by its price—is the same.

5. Changes in the price of a good affect the quantity consumed in two possible ways: the **substitution effect** and the **income effect.** Most goods absorb only a small share of a consumer's spending; for these goods, only the substitution effect—buying less of the good that has become relatively more expensive and more of goods that are now relatively cheaper—is significant. It causes the individual and the market demand curves to slope downward. When a good absorbs a large fraction of spending, the income effect is also significant: an increase in a good's price makes a consumer poorer, but a decrease in price makes a consumer richer. This change in purchasing power makes consumers demand less or more of a good, depending on whether the good is normal or inferior. For normal goods, the substitution and income effects reinforce each other. For inferior goods, however, they work in opposite directions.

KEY TERMS

Terrance Klassen/AGE Fotostock

SECTION 7

Production and Costs

THE FARMER'S MARGIN

"O beautiful for spacious skies, for amber waves of grain." So begins the song "America the Beautiful." And those amber waves of grain are for real: although farmers now account for only a small minority of America's population, our agricultural industry is immensely productive and feeds much of the world.

If you look at agricultural statistics, however, something may seem rather surprising: when it comes to yield per acre, U.S. farmers are often nowhere near the top. Farmers in Western European countries grow much more—about three times as much wheat per acre as their U.S. counterparts. Are the Europeans better at growing wheat than we are?

No. European farmers are very skillful, but no more so than Americans. They produce more wheat per acre because they employ more inputs—more fertilizer and, especially, more labor—per acre. Of course, this means that European farmers have higher costs than their American counterparts. But because of government policies, European farmers receive a much higher price for their wheat than American farmers do. This gives them an incentive to use more inputs and to expend more effort at the margin to increase the crop yield per acre.

Notice our use of the phrase "at the margin." Like most decisions that involve a comparison of benefits and costs, decisions about inputs and production involve a comparison of marginal quantities—the marginal cost versus the marginal benefit of producing a bit more from each acre.

In Module 17, we considered the case of Alexa, who had to choose the number of years of schooling that maximized her profit from schooling. There we used the profit-maximizing principle of marginal analysis to find her optimal quantity of years of schooling. In this section, we will encounter producers who have to make similar "how much" decisions: choosing the quantity of output produced to maximize profit.

Here and in Section 8, we will show how marginal analysis can be used to understand these output decisions—decisions that lie behind the supply curve. The first step in this analysis is to show how the relationship between a firm's inputs and its output—its *production function*—determines its *cost curves*, the relationship between cost and quantity of output produced. That is what we will examine in this section. In Section 8, we will use our understanding of the firm's cost curves to derive the individual and the market supply curves.

MODULE 20

The Production Function

WHAT YOU WILL LEARN

- What is the firm's **production function?**
- Why is production often subject to **diminishing returns to inputs?**

Cultura Limited/Cultura Limited/Superstock

20.1 The Production Function

A *firm* is an organization that produces goods or services for sale. To do this, it must transform inputs into output. The quantity of output a firm produces depends on the quantity of inputs; this relationship is known as the firm's **production function.** As we'll see, a firm's production function underlies its *cost curves*. As a first step, let's look at the characteristics of a hypothetical production function.

Inputs and Output

To understand the concept of a production function, let's consider a farm that we assume, for the sake of simplicity, produces only one output, wheat, and uses only two inputs, land and labor. This particular farm is owned by a couple named Riley and Tyler. They hire workers to do the actual physical labor on the farm. Moreover, we will assume that all potential workers are of the same quality—they are all equally knowledgeable and capable of performing farmwork.

Riley and Tyler's farm sits on 10 acres of land. No more acres are available to them, and they are currently unable to either increase or decrease the size of their farm by selling, buying, or leasing acreage. Land here is what economists call a **fixed input**—an input whose quantity is fixed for a period of time and cannot be varied. Riley and Tyler are, however, free to decide how many workers to hire. The labor provided by these workers is called a **variable input**—an input whose quantity the firm can vary at any time.

In reality, whether the quantity of an input is really fixed depends on the time horizon. In the **long run**—that is, given that a long enough period of time has elapsed—firms can adjust the quantity of any input. For example, in the long run, Riley and Tyler can vary the amount of land they farm by buying or selling land. So there are no fixed inputs in the long run.

In contrast, the **short run** is defined as the time period during which at least one input is fixed. Later in this section, we'll look more carefully at the distinction between the short run and the long run. But for now, we will restrict our attention to the short run and assume that at least one input is fixed.

A **production function** is the relationship between the quantity of inputs a firm uses and the quantity of output it produces.

A **fixed input** is an input whose quantity is fixed for a period of time and cannot be varied.

A **variable input** is an input whose quantity the firm can vary at any time.

The **long run** is the time period in which all inputs can be varied.

The **short run** is the time period in which at least one input is fixed.

Riley and Tyler know that the quantity of wheat they produce depends on the number of workers they hire. Using modern farming techniques, one worker can cultivate the 10-acre farm, albeit not very intensively. When an additional worker is added, the land is divided equally among all the workers: each worker has 5 acres to cultivate when 2 workers are employed, each cultivates $3\frac{1}{3}$ acres when 3 are employed, and so on. So as additional workers are employed, the 10 acres of land are cultivated more intensively and more bushels of wheat are produced.

The **total product curve** shows how the quantity of output depends on the quantity of the variable input, for a given quantity of the fixed input.

The relationship between the quantity of labor and the quantity of output, for a given amount of the fixed input, constitutes the farm's production function. The production function for Riley and Tyler's farm, where land is the fixed input and labor is a variable input, is shown in the first two columns of the table in Figure 20-1; the diagram there shows the same information graphically. The curve in Figure 20-1 shows how the quantity of output depends on the quantity of the variable input, for a given quantity of the fixed input. It is called the farm's **total product curve.**

The physical quantity of output, bushels of wheat, is measured on the vertical axis; the quantity of the variable input, labor (that is, the number of workers employed), is measured on the horizontal axis. The total product curve here slopes upward, reflecting the fact that more bushels of wheat are produced as more workers are employed.

Although the total product curve in Figure 20-1 slopes upward along its entire length, the slope isn't constant: as you move up the curve to the right, it flattens out. To understand why the slope changes, look at the third column of the table in Figure 20-1, which shows the *change in the quantity of output* that is generated by adding one more worker. This is called the *marginal product* of labor, or *MPL:* the

FIGURE 20-1 Production Function and Total Product Curve for Riley and Tyler's Farm

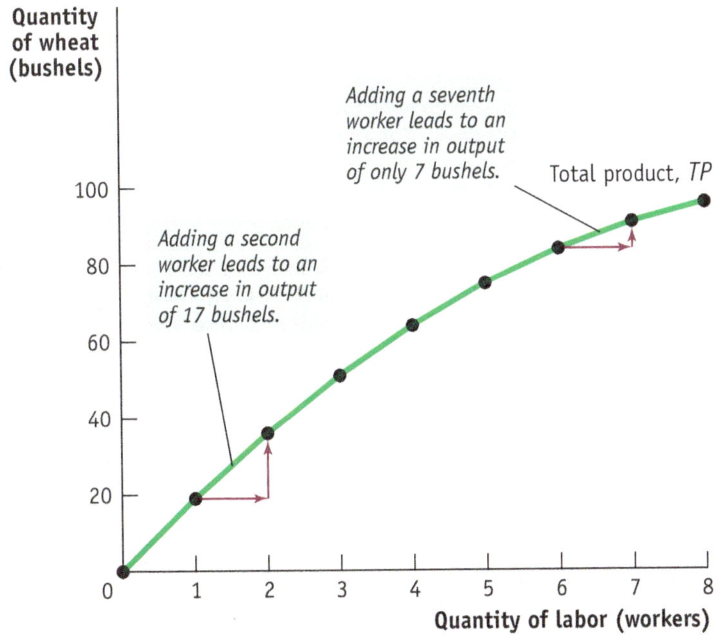

Quantity of labor *L* (workers)	Quantity of wheat *Q* (bushels)	Marginal product of labor $MPL = \Delta Q/\Delta L$ (bushels per worker)
0	0	
		19
1	19	
		17
2	36	
		15
3	51	
		13
4	64	
		11
5	75	
		9
6	84	
		7
7	91	
		5
8	96	

The table shows the production function, the relationship between the quantity of the variable input (labor, measured in number of workers) and the quantity of output (wheat, measured in bushels) for a given quantity of the fixed input. It also calculates the marginal product of labor on Riley and Tyler's farm. The total product curve shows the production function graphically. It slopes upward because more wheat is produced as more workers are employed. It also becomes flatter because the marginal product of labor declines as more and more workers are employed.

additional quantity of output from using one more unit of labor (where one unit of labor is equal to one worker). In general, the **marginal product** of an input is the additional quantity of output that is produced by using one more unit of that input.

In this example, we have data on changes in output at intervals of 1 worker. Sometimes data aren't available in increments of 1 unit—for example, you might have information only on the quantity of output when there are 40 workers and when there are 50 workers. In this case, we use the following equation to calculate the marginal product of labor:

$$\text{(20-1)}\quad \begin{array}{l}\text{Marginal}\\\text{product of}\\\text{labor}\end{array} = \begin{array}{l}\text{Change in quantity of}\\\text{output produced by one}\\\text{additional unit of output}\end{array} = \frac{\text{Change in quantity of output}}{\text{Change in quantity of labor}}$$

or

$$MPL = \frac{\Delta Q}{\Delta L}$$

PITFALLS

WHAT'S A UNIT?

The marginal product of labor (or any other input) is defined as the increase in the quantity of output when you increase the quantity of that input by one unit. But what do we mean by a "unit" of labor? Is it an additional hour of labor, an additional week, or a person-year?

The answer is that it doesn't matter, *as long as you are consistent.* One common source of error in economics is getting units confused—say, comparing the output added by an additional *hour* of labor with the cost of employing a worker for a *week.* Whatever units you use, be sure to use the same units throughout your analysis of any problem.

In this equation, Δ, the Greek uppercase delta, represents the change in a variable.

Now we can explain the significance of the slope of the total product curve: *it is equal to the marginal product of labor.* The slope of a line is equal to "rise" over "run" (explained in the Section 1 graph appendix). This implies that the slope of the total product curve is the change in the quantity of output (the "rise," ΔQ) divided by the change in the quantity of labor (the "run," ΔL). And this, as we can see from Equation 20-1, is simply the marginal product of labor. So, in Figure 20-1, the fact that the marginal product of the first worker is 19 also means that the slope of the total product curve in going from 0 to 1 worker is 19. Similarly, the slope of the total product curve in going from 1 to 2 workers is the same as the marginal product of the second worker, 17, and so on.

In this example, the marginal product of labor steadily declines as more workers are hired—that is, each successive worker adds less to output than the previous worker. So as employment increases, the total product curve gets flatter.

Figure 20-2 shows how the marginal product of labor depends on the number of workers employed on the farm. The marginal product of labor, *MPL,* is measured on the vertical axis in units of physical output—bushels of wheat—produced per additional worker, and the number of workers employed is measured on the horizontal axis. You can see from the table in Figure 20-1 that if 5 workers are employed instead of 4, output rises from 64 to 75 bushels; in this case, the marginal product of labor is 11 bushels—the same number found in Figure 20-2. To indicate that 11 bushels is the marginal product when employment rises from 4 to 5, we place the point corresponding to that information halfway between 4 and 5 workers.

In this example, the marginal product of labor falls as the number of workers increases. That is, there are *diminishing returns to labor* on Riley and Tyler's farm. In general, there are **diminishing returns to an input** when an increase in the quantity of that input, holding the quantity of all other inputs fixed, reduces that input's marginal product. Due to diminishing returns to labor, the *MPL* curve is negatively sloped.

The **marginal product** of an input is the additional quantity of output that is produced by using one more unit of that input.

There are **diminishing returns to an input** when an increase in the quantity of that input, holding the levels of all other inputs fixed, leads to a decline in the marginal product of that input.

To grasp why diminishing returns can occur, think about what happens as Riley and Tyler add more and more workers without increasing the number of acres of land. As the number of workers increases, the land is farmed more intensively and the number of bushels produced increases. But each additional worker is working with a smaller share of the 10 acres—the fixed input—than the previous worker. As a result, the additional worker cannot produce as much output as

FIGURE 20-2 Marginal Product of Labor Curve for Riley and Tyler's Farm

The marginal product of labor curve plots each worker's marginal product, the increase in the quantity of output generated by each additional worker. The change in the quantity of output is measured on the vertical axis and the number of workers employed on the horizontal axis. On Riley and Tyler's 10-acre farm, the first worker employed generates an increase in output of 19 bushels, the second worker generates an increase of 17 bushels, and so on. The curve slopes downward due to diminishing returns to labor.

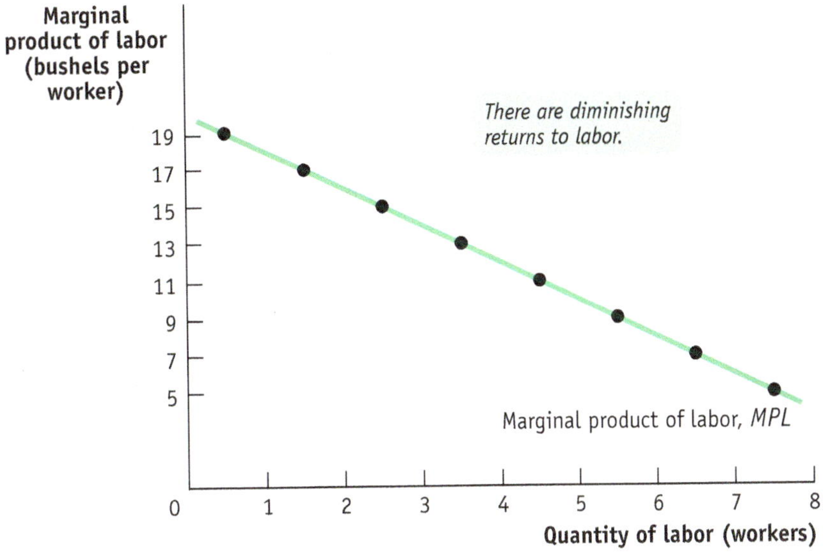

the previous worker. So it's not surprising that the marginal product of the additional worker falls.

The crucial point to emphasize about diminishing returns is that, like many propositions in economics, it is an "other things equal" proposition: each successive unit of an input will raise production by less than the last *if the quantity of all other inputs is held fixed.*

FIGURE 20-3 Total Product, Marginal Product, and the Fixed Input

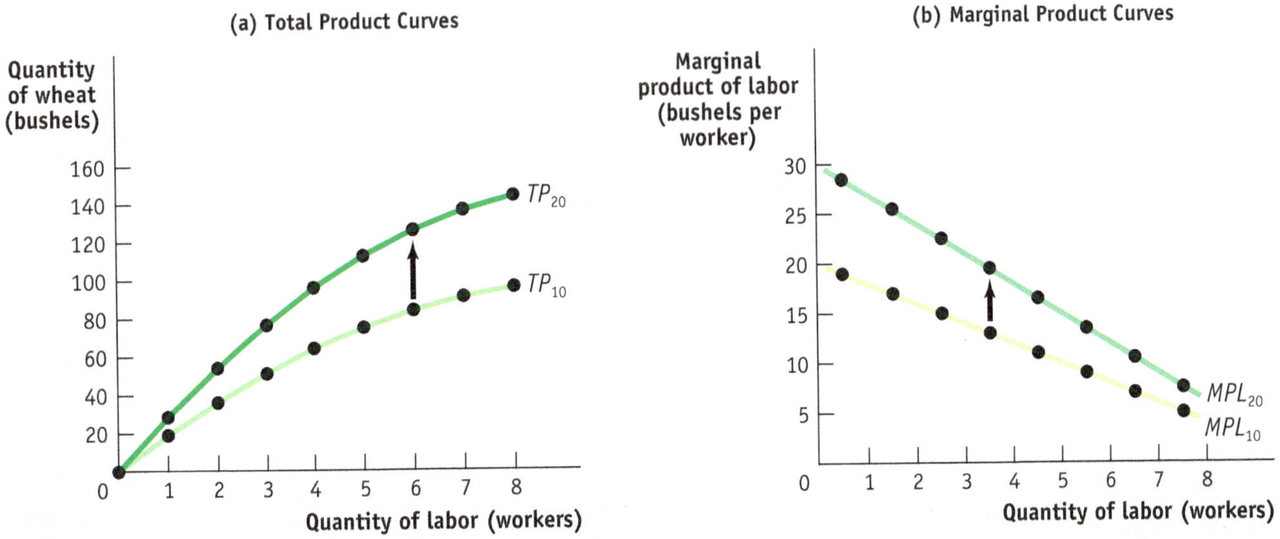

This figure shows how the quantity of output and the marginal product of labor depend on the level of the fixed input. Panel (a) shows two total product curves for Riley and Tyler's farm, TP_{10} when their farm is 10 acres and TP_{20} when it is 20 acres. With more land, each worker can produce more wheat. So, an increase in the fixed input shifts the total product curve up from TP_{10} to TP_{20}. This implies that the marginal product of each worker is higher when the farm is 20 acres than when it is 10 acres. Panel (b) shows the marginal product of labor curves. The increase in acreage also shifts the marginal product of labor curve up from MPL_{10} to MPL_{20}. Note that both marginal product of labor curves still slope downward due to diminishing returns to labor.

What would happen if the levels of other inputs were allowed to change? You can see the answer illustrated in Figure 20-3. Panel (a) shows two total product curves, TP_{10} and TP_{20}. TP_{10} is the farm's total product curve when its total area is 10 acres (the same curve as in Figure 20-1). TP_{20} is the total product curve when the farm has increased to 20 acres. Except when 0 workers are employed, TP_{20} lies everywhere above TP_{10} because with more acres available, any given number of workers produces more output. Panel (b) shows the corresponding marginal product of labor curves. MPL_{10} is the marginal product of labor curve given 10 acres to cultivate (the same curve as in Figure 20-2), and MPL_{20} is the marginal product of labor curve given 20 acres.

Both curves slope downward because, in each case, the amount of land is fixed, albeit at different levels. But MPL_{20} lies everywhere above MPL_{10}, reflecting the fact that the marginal product of the same worker is higher when they have more of the fixed input to work with.

Figure 20-3 demonstrates a general result: the position of the total product curve of a given input depends on the quantities of other inputs. If you change the quantity of the other inputs, both the total product curve and the marginal product curve of the remaining input will shift.

ECONOMICS >> *in Action*

Finding the Optimal Team Size

In both offices and learning environments, team projects are a favorite way of organizing work. According to one study, the most efficient team size is between 4 and 5 people (4.6 team members, to be exact). Yet researchers have found that project designers routinely create teams that are too large to be efficient. What are project designers failing to understand?

It's true that a larger team has access to more resources, specifically more labor and more human capital. But keep in mind that how large a team should be is a decision at the margin. And studies have shown that adding another person to a team of 5 generally *reduces* the marginal product of existing members. This result is due to a phenomenon called *social loafing:* as the size of the team increases, it's easier to hide individual lack of effort, and the connection between individual effort and reward weakens. As a result, the marginal product of the sixth member is equal to their personal contribution *minus* the loss due to social loafing that his presence inflicts on other team members.

A larger team also spends more time in coordination, which reduces each member's marginal product. So at some point, team losses from social loafing and coordination costs outweigh the individual contribution made by the sixth team member. This result is well documented among teams of software programmers: at some point, adding another team member reduces the output of the entire team.

This situation is illustrated in Figure 20-4. The top part of the figure shows how the value of the team project varies with the number of team members. Each additional member accomplishes less than the previous one, and beyond a certain point, an additional member is actually counterproductive. The bottom part of the figure shows the marginal product of each successive team member, which falls as more team members are employed and eventually becomes

FIGURE 20-4 Finding the Optimal Team Size

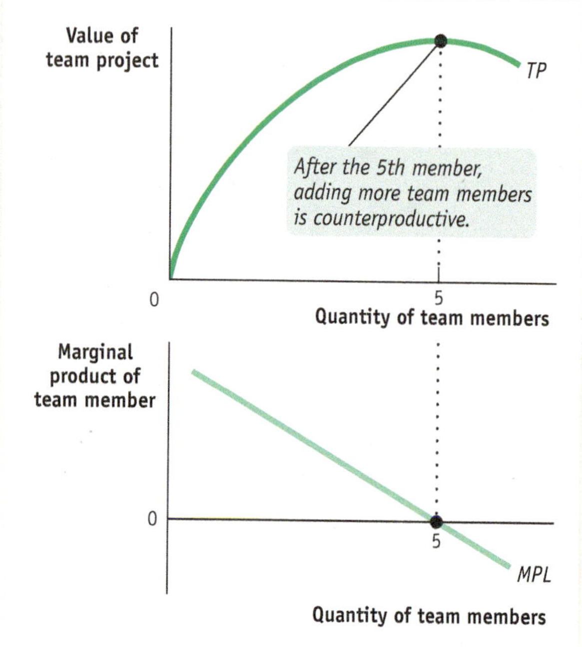

negative. In other words, the sixth team member has a negative marginal product.

It appears that project designers are creating teams that are too large by mistakenly focusing on the individual contribution of an additional team member rather than on the marginal product generated by the *entire* team when another person is added. So, instead of having one large project performed by a team of 10 people, it would be more efficient and productive to split the large project into two smaller projects performed by teams of 5 people. By thinking at the margin, we can understand why, in teamwork, 5 + 5 doesn't equal 10: two teams of 5 people will produce more than one team of 10 people.

Check Your Understanding 20-1

1. Bernie's ice-making company produces ice cubes using a 10-ton machine and electricity. The quantity of output, measured in terms of pounds of ice, is given in the accompanying table.

Quantity of electricity (kilowatts)	Quantity of ice (pounds)
0	0
1	1,000
2	1,800
3	2,400
4	2,800

   a. What is the fixed input? What is the variable input?

   b. Construct a table showing the marginal product of the variable input. Does it show diminishing returns?

   c. Suppose a 50% increase in the size of the fixed input increases output by 100% for any given amount of the variable input. What is the fixed input now? Construct a table showing the quantity of output and marginal product in this case.

Solutions appear at back of book.

>> Quick Review

- The firm's **production function** is the relationship between quantity of inputs and quantity of output. The **total product curve** shows how the quantity of output depends on the quantity of the **variable input** for a given quantity of the **fixed input,** and its slope is equal to the **marginal product** of the variable input. In the **short run,** the fixed input cannot be varied; in the **long run,** all inputs are variable.
- When the levels of all other inputs are fixed, **diminishing returns to an input** may arise, yielding a downward-sloping marginal product curve and a total product curve that becomes flatter as more output is produced.

MODULE

21

Firm Costs

WHAT YOU WILL LEARN

- What types of costs does a firm face?
- How does the firm generate its **marginal cost** and **average cost** curves?
- Why do a firm's costs differ in the **short run** and in the **long run?**

Ilene MacDonald/Alamy

21.1 From the Production Function to Cost Curves

Once Riley and Tyler know their production function, they know the relationship between inputs of labor and land and output of wheat. But if they want to maximize their profits, they need to translate this knowledge into information about the relationship between the quantity of output and cost. Let's see how they can do this.

To translate information about a firm's production function into information about its costs, we need to know how much the firm must pay for its inputs. We will assume Riley and Tyler face either an explicit or an implicit cost of $400 for the use of land. As we learned previously, it is irrelevant whether Riley and Tyler must rent the 10 acres of land for $400 from someone else or whether they own the land themselves and forgo earning $400 from renting it to someone else. Either way, they pay an opportunity cost of $400 by using the land to grow wheat. Moreover, since the land is a fixed input, the $400 Riley and Tyler pay for it is a **fixed cost,** denoted by *FC*—a cost that does not depend on the quanitity of output produced (in the short run). In business, fixed cost is often referred to as *overhead cost.*

We also assume that Riley and Tyler must pay each worker worker $200. Using their production function, Riley and Tyler know that the number of workers they must hire depends on the amount of wheat they intend to produce. So the cost of labor, which is equal to the number of workers multiplied by $200, is a **variable cost,** denoted by *VC*—a cost that depends on the quantity of output produced. It is variable because to produce more they have to employ more units of input.

Adding the fixed cost and the variable cost of a given quantity of output gives the **total cost,** or *TC,* of that quantity of output. We can express the relationship among fixed cost, variable cost, and total cost as an equation:

A **fixed cost** is a cost that does not depend on the quantity of output produced. It is the cost of the fixed input.

A **variable cost** is a cost that depends on the quantity of output produced. It is the cost of the variable input.

The **total cost** of producing a given quantity of output is the sum of the fixed cost and the variable cost of producing that quantity of output.

(21-1) Total cost = Fixed cost + Variable cost

or

$$TC = FC + VC$$

FIGURE 21-1 Total Cost Curve for Riley and Tyler's Farm

The table shows the variable cost, fixed cost, and total cost for various output quantities on Riley and Tyler's 10-acre farm. The total cost curve shows how total cost (measured on the vertical axis) depends on the quantity of output (measured on the horizontal axis). The labeled points on the curve correspond to the rows of the table. The total cost curve slopes upward because the number of workers employed, and hence total cost, increases as the quantity of output increases. The curve gets steeper as output increases due to diminishing returns to labor.

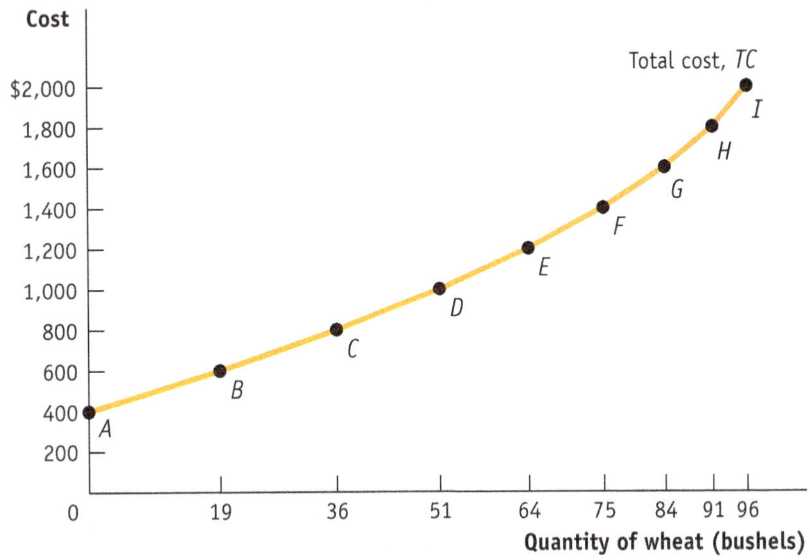

Point on graph	Quantity of labor L (workers)	Quantity of wheat Q (bushels)	Variable cost VC	Fixed cost FC	Total cost $TC = FC + VC$
A	0	0	$0	$400	$400
B	1	19	200	400	600
C	2	36	400	400	800
D	3	51	600	400	1,000
E	4	64	800	400	1,200
F	5	75	1,000	400	1,400
G	6	84	1,200	400	1,600
H	7	91	1,400	400	1,800
I	8	96	1,600	400	2,000

The table in Figure 21-1 shows how total cost is calculated for Riley and Tyler's farm. The second column shows the number of workers employed, *L*. The third column shows the corresponding level of output, *Q*, taken from the table in Figure 20-1. The fourth column shows the variable cost, *VC*, equal to the number of workers multiplied by $200, the cost per worker. The fifth column shows the fixed cost, *FC*, which is $400 regardless of how many workers are employed. The sixth column shows the total cost of output, *TC*, which is the variable cost plus the fixed cost.

The first column labels each row of the table with a letter, from *A* to *I*. These labels will be helpful in understanding our next step: drawing the **total cost curve,** a curve that shows how total cost depends on the quantity of output.

Riley and Tyler's total cost curve is shown in the diagram in Figure 21-1, where the horizontal axis measures the quantity of output in bushels of wheat and the vertical axis measures total cost in dollars. Each point on the curve corresponds to one row of the table in Figure 21-1. For example, point *A* shows the situation when 0 workers are employed: output is 0, and total cost is equal to fixed cost, $400. Similarly, point *B* shows the situation when 1 worker is employed: output is 19 bushels, and total cost is $600, equal to the sum of $400 in fixed cost and $200 in variable cost.

Like the total product curve, the total cost curve slopes upward: due to the variable cost, the more output produced, the higher the farm's total cost. But unlike the

The **total cost curve** shows how total cost depends on the quantity of output.

total product curve, which gets flatter as employment rises, the total cost curve gets *steeper.* That is, the slope of the total cost curve is greater as the amount of output produced increases. As we will soon see, the steepening of the total cost curve is also due to diminishing returns to the variable input. Before we can understand this, we must first look at the relationships among several useful measures of cost.

21.2 Two Key Concepts: Marginal Cost and Average Cost

Now that we've learned how to derive a firm's total cost curve from its production function, let's take a deeper look at total cost by deriving two extremely useful measures: *marginal cost* and *average cost.* As we'll see, these two measures of the cost of production have a somewhat surprising relationship to each other. Moreover, they will prove to be vitally important in Section 8, where we will use them to analyze the firm's output decision and the market supply curve.

Marginal Cost

We defined marginal cost in Module 17: it is the change in total cost generated by producing one more unit of output. We've already seen that the marginal product of an input is easiest to calculate if data on output are available in increments of one unit of that input. Similarly, marginal cost is easiest to calculate if data on total cost are available in increments of one unit of output. When the data come in less convenient increments, it's still possible to calculate marginal cost. But for the sake of simplicity, let's work with an example in which the data come in convenient one-unit increments.

Selena's Gourmet Salsas produces bottled salsa; Table 21-1 shows how its costs per day depend on the number of cases of salsa it produces per day. The firm has a fixed cost of $108 per day, shown in the second column, which represents the

TABLE 21-1 Costs at Selena's Gourmet Salsas

Quantity of salsa Q (cases)	Fixed cost FC	Variable cost VC	Total cost $TC = FC + VC$	Marginal cost of case $MC = \Delta TC/\Delta Q$
0	$108	$0	$108	
				$12
1	108	12	120	
				36
2	108	48	156	
				60
3	108	108	216	
				84
4	108	192	300	
				108
5	108	300	408	
				132
6	108	432	540	
				156
7	108	588	696	
				180
8	108	768	876	
				204
9	108	972	1,080	
				228
10	108	1,200	1,308	

daily cost of its food-preparation equipment. The third column shows the variable cost, and the fourth column shows the total cost. Panel (a) of Figure 21-2 plots the total cost curve. Like the total cost curve for Riley and Tyler's farm in Figure 21-1, this curve slopes upward, getting steeper as you move up it to the right.

The significance of the slope of the total cost curve is shown by the fifth column of Table 21-1, which calculates *marginal cost:* the additional cost of each additional unit. The general formula for marginal cost is:

(21-2) $$\text{Marginal cost} = \begin{array}{l}\text{Change in total cost}\\ \text{generated by one}\\ \text{additional unit of output}\end{array} = \frac{\text{Change in total cost}}{\text{Change in quantity of output}}$$

or

$$MC = \frac{\Delta TC}{\Delta Q}$$

As in the case of marginal product, marginal cost is equal to "rise" (the increase in total cost) divided by "run" (the increase in the quantity of output). So, just as marginal product is equal to the slope of the total product curve, marginal cost is equal to the slope of the total cost curve.

Now we can understand why the total cost curve gets steeper as we move it up to the right: as you can see in Table 21-1, marginal cost at Selena's Gourmet Salsas rises as output increases. Panel (b) of Figure 21-2 shows the marginal cost curve corresponding to the data in Table 21-1. Notice that, as in Figure 20-2, we plot the marginal cost for increasing output from 0 to 1 case of salsa halfway between 0 and 1, the marginal cost for increasing output from 1 to 2 cases of salsa halfway between 1 and 2, and so on.

Why does the marginal cost curve slope upward? Because there are diminishing returns to inputs in this example. As output increases, the marginal product of the variable input declines. This implies that more and more of the variable input must be used to produce each additional unit of output as the amount of output already produced rises. And since each unit of the variable input must be paid for, the additional cost per additional unit of output also rises.

FIGURE 21-2 Total Cost and Marginal Cost Curves for Selena's Gourmet Salsas

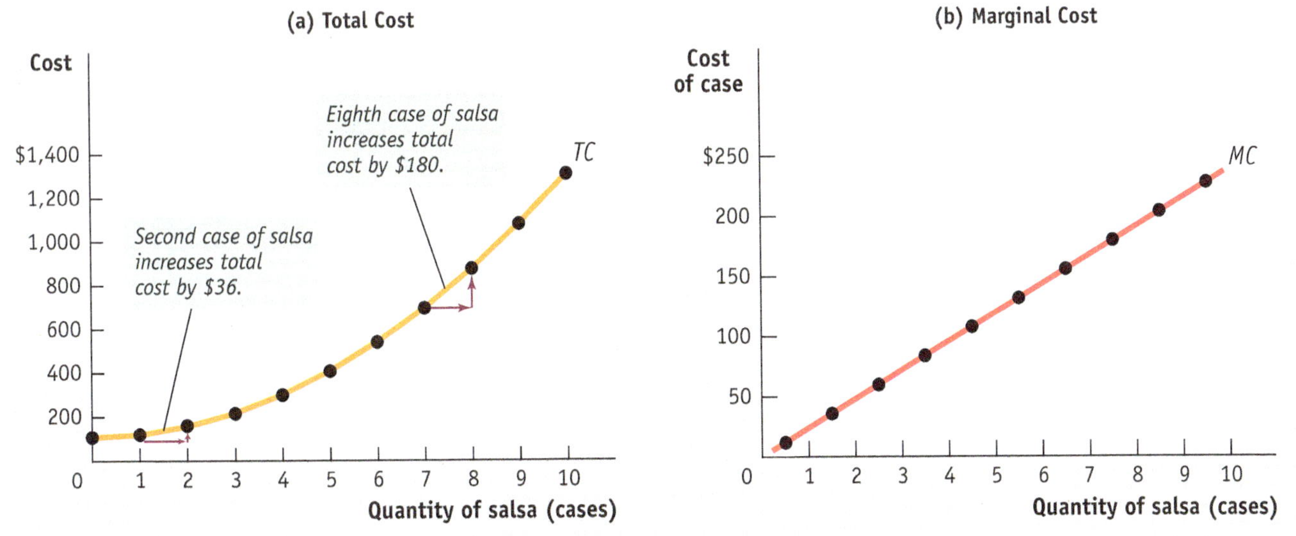

Panel (a) shows the total cost curve from Table 21-1. Like the total cost curve in Figure 21-1, it slopes upward and gets steeper as we move it up to the right. Panel (b) shows the marginal cost curve. It also slopes upward, reflecting diminishing returns to the variable input.

In addition, recall that the flattening of the total product curve is also due to diminishing returns: the marginal product of an input falls as more of that input is used if the quantities of other inputs are fixed. The flattening of the total product curve as output increases and the steepening of the total cost curve as output increases are just flip-sides of the same phenomenon. That is, as output increases, the marginal cost of output also increases because the marginal product of the variable input decreases.

We will return to marginal cost in Section 8, when we consider the firm's profit-maximizing output decision. Our next step is to introduce another measure of cost: *average cost.*

Average Total Cost

In addition to total cost and marginal cost, it's useful to calculate another measure, **average total cost,** often simply called **average cost.** The average total cost is total cost divided by the quantity of output produced; that is, it is equal to total cost per unit of output. If we let *ATC* denote average total cost, the equation looks like this:

$$\textbf{(21-3)}\quad ATC = \frac{\text{Total cost}}{\text{Quantity of output}} = \frac{TC}{Q}$$

Average total cost is important because it tells the producer how much the *average* or *typical* unit of output costs to produce. Marginal cost, meanwhile, tells the producer how much *one more* unit of output costs to produce. Although they may look very similar, these two measures of cost typically differ.

Table 21-2 uses data from Selena's Gourmet Salsas to calculate average total cost. For example, the total cost of producing 4 cases of salsa is $300, consisting of $108 in fixed cost and $192 in variable cost (from Table 21-1). So the average total cost of producing 4 cases of salsa is $300/4 = $75. You can see from Table 21-2 that as quantity of output increases, average total cost first falls and then rises.

Figure 21-3 plots that data to yield the *average total cost curve,* which shows how average total cost depends on output. As before, cost in dollars is measured on the vertical axis and quantity of output is measured on the horizontal axis. The average total cost curve has a distinctive U shape that corresponds to how average total cost first falls and then rises as output increases. Economists believe that such **U-shaped average total cost curves** are the norm for producers in many industries.

To help our understanding of why the average total cost curve is U-shaped, Table 21-2 breaks average total cost into its two underlying components, *average fixed cost* and *average variable cost.* **Average fixed cost,** or *AFC,* is fixed cost divided by the quantity of output, also known as the fixed cost per unit of output. For example, if Selena's Gourmet Salsas produces 4 cases of salsa, average fixed

Average total cost, often referred to simply as **average cost,** is total cost divided by quantity of output produced.

A **U-shaped average total cost curve** falls at low levels of output and then rises at higher levels.

Average fixed cost is the fixed cost per unit of output.

TABLE 21-2 Average Costs for Selena's Gourmet Salsas

Quantity of salsa *Q* (cases)	Total cost *TC*	Average total cost of case *ATC* = *TC*/*Q*	Average fixed cost of case *AFC* = *FC*/*Q*	Average variable cost of case *AVC* = *VC*/*Q*
1	$120	$120.00	$108.00	$12.00
2	156	78.00	54.00	24.00
3	216	72.00	36.00	36.00
4	300	75.00	27.00	48.00
5	408	81.60	21.60	60.00
6	540	90.00	18.00	72.00
7	696	99.43	15.43	84.00
8	876	109.50	13.50	96.00
9	1,080	120.00	12.00	108.00
10	1,308	130.80	10.80	120.00

FIGURE 21-3 Average Total Cost Curve for Selena's Gourmet Salsas

The average total cost curve for Selena's Gourmet Salsas is U-shaped. At low levels of output, average total cost falls because the *spreading effect* of falling average fixed cost dominates the *diminishing returns effect* of rising average variable cost. At higher levels of output, the opposite is true and average total cost rises. At point *M*, corresponding to an output of three cases of salsa per day, average total cost is at its minimum level, the minimum average total cost.

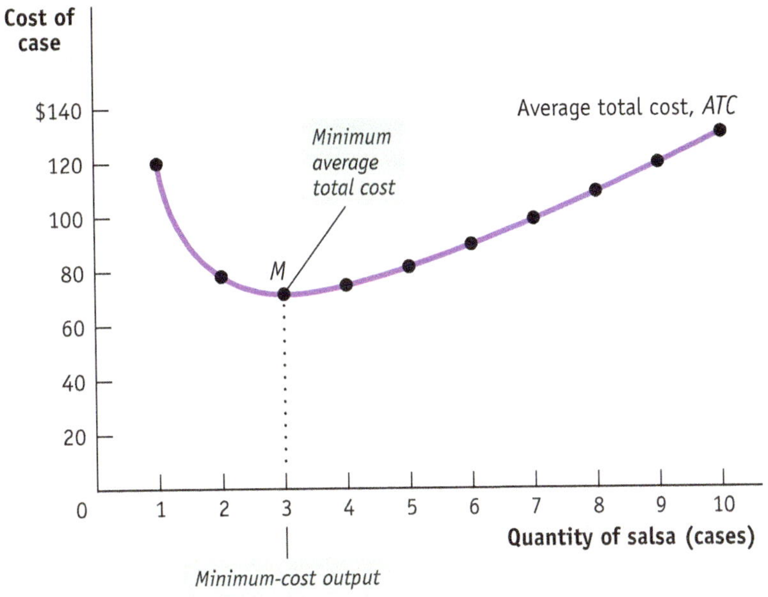

cost $108/4 = $27 per case. **Average variable cost,** or *AVC,* is variable cost divided by the quantity of output, also known as variable cost per unit of output. At an output of 4 cases, average variable cost is $192/4 = $48 per case.

Average variable cost is the variable cost per unit of output.

Writing these in the form of equations:

$$\text{(21-4)}\quad AFC = \frac{\text{Fixed cost}}{\text{Quantity of output}} = \frac{FC}{Q}$$

$$AVC = \frac{\text{Variable cost}}{\text{Quantity of output}} = \frac{VC}{Q}$$

Average total cost is the sum of average fixed cost and average variable cost. It has a U shape because these components move in opposite directions as output rises: *average fixed cost falls as more output is produced because the numerator (the fixed cost) is a fixed number but the denominator (the quantity of output) increases as more is produced.* Another way to think about this relationship is that, as more output is produced, the fixed cost is spread over more units of output; the end result is that the fixed cost *per unit of output*—the average fixed cost—falls. You can see this effect in the fourth column of Table 21-2: average fixed cost drops continuously as output increases.

Average variable cost, however, rises as output increases. As we've seen, this reflects diminishing returns to the variable input: each additional unit of output incurs more variable cost to produce than the previous unit. So variable cost rises at a faster rate than the quantity of output increases.

So increasing output has two opposing effects on average total cost:

1. *The spreading effect.* The larger the output, the greater the quantity of output over which fixed cost is spread, leading to lower average fixed cost.
2. *The diminishing returns effect.* The larger the output, the greater the amount of variable input required to produce additional units, leading to higher average variable cost.

At low levels of output, the spreading effect is very powerful because even small increases in output cause large reductions in average fixed cost. So at low levels of output, the spreading effect dominates the diminishing returns effect and

FIGURE 21-4 Marginal Cost and Average Cost Curves for Selena's Gourmet Salsas

Here we have the family of cost curves for Selena's Gourmet Salsas: the marginal cost curve (*MC*), the average total cost curve (*ATC*), the average variable cost curve (*AVC*), and the average fixed cost curve (*AFC*). Note that the average total cost curve is U-shaped and the marginal cost curve crosses the average total cost curve at the bottom of the U, point *M*, corresponding to the minimum average total cost from Table 21-2 and Figure 21-3.

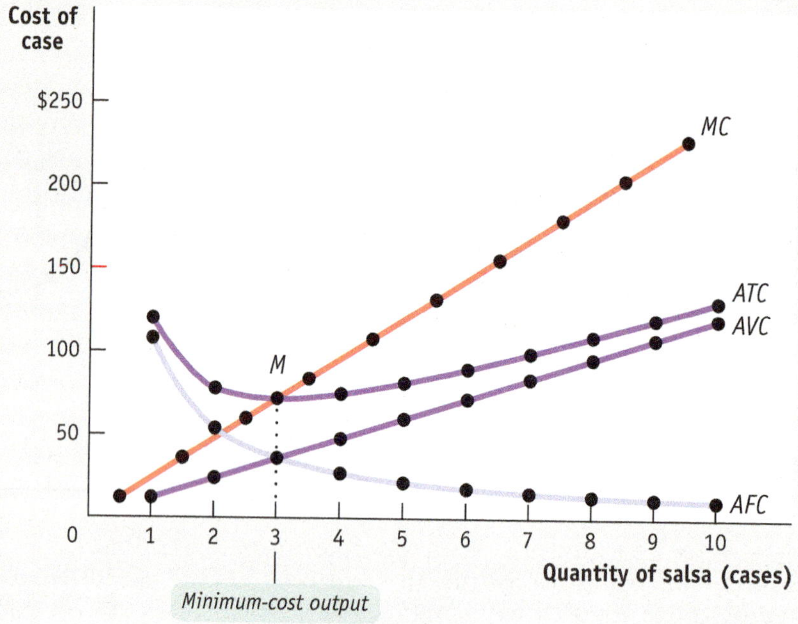

causes the average total cost curve to slope downward. But when output is large, average fixed cost is already quite small, so increasing output further has only a very small spreading effect.

Diminishing returns, however, usually grow increasingly important as output rises. As a result, when output is large, the diminishing returns effect dominates the spreading effect, causing the average total cost curve to slope upward. At the bottom of the U-shaped average total cost curve, point *M* in Figure 21-3, the two effects exactly balance each other. At this point, average total cost is at its minimum level, the minimum average total cost.

Figure 21-4 brings together in a single picture four members of the family of cost curves that we have derived from the total cost curve for Selena's Gourmet Salsas: the marginal cost curve (*MC*), the average total cost curve (*ATC*), the average variable cost curve (*AVC*), and the average fixed cost curve (*AFC*). All are based on the information in Tables 21-1 and 21-2. As before, cost is measured on the vertical axis and the quantity of output is measured on the horizontal axis.

Let's take a moment to note some features of the various cost curves.

- Marginal cost slopes upward—the result of diminishing returns that make an additional unit of output more costly to produce than the one before.
- Average variable cost also slopes upward—again, due to diminishing returns—but is flatter than the marginal cost curve. This is because the higher cost of an additional unit of output is averaged across all units, not just the additional units, in the average variable cost measure.
- Average fixed cost slopes downward because of the spreading effect.
- The marginal cost curve intersects the average total cost curve from below, crossing it at its lowest point, point *M* in Figure 21-4. This last feature is our next subject of study.

Minimum Average Total Cost

For a U-shaped average total cost curve, average total cost is at its minimum level at the bottom of the U. Economists call the quantity of output that corresponds to the minimum average total cost the **minimum-cost output.** In the case of Selena's Gourmet Salsas, the minimum-cost output is three cases of salsa per day.

The **minimum-cost output** is the quantity of output at which average total cost is lowest—the bottom of the U-shaped average total cost curve.

In Figure 21-4, the bottom of the U is at the level of output at which the marginal cost curve crosses the average total cost curve from below. Is this an accident? No—it reflects three general principles that are always true about a firm's marginal cost and average total cost curves:

1. At the minimum-cost output, average total cost *is equal to* marginal cost.
2. At output less than the minimum-cost output, marginal cost *is less than* average total cost and average total cost is falling.
3. At output greater than the minimum-cost output, marginal cost *is greater than* average total cost and average total cost is rising.

To understand these principles, think about how your grade in one course—say, a 3.0 in sociology—affects your overall grade point average. If your GPA before receiving that grade was higher than 3.0, the new grade lowers your average.

Similarly, if marginal cost—the cost of producing one more unit—is less than average total cost, producing that extra unit lowers average total cost. This is shown in Figure 21-5 by the movement from A_1 to A_2. In this case, the marginal cost of producing an additional unit of output is low, as indicated by the point MC_L on the marginal cost curve. When the cost of producing the next unit of output is less than average total cost, increasing production reduces average total cost. So, any quantity of output at which marginal cost is less than average total cost must be on the downward-sloping segment of the U.

But if your grade in sociology is higher than the average of your previous grades, this new grade raises your GPA. Similarly, if marginal cost is greater than average total cost, producing that extra unit raises average total cost. This is illustrated by the movement from B_1 to B_2 in Figure 21-5, where the marginal cost, MC_H, is higher than average total cost. So any quantity of output at which marginal cost is greater than average total cost must be on the upward-sloping segment of the U.

Finally, if your new grade is exactly equal to your previous GPA, the additional grade neither raises nor lowers that average—it stays the same. This corresponds

FIGURE 21-5 The Relationship Between the Average Total Cost and the Marginal Cost Curves

To see why the marginal cost curve (*MC*) must cut through the average total cost curve at the minimum average total cost (point *M*), corresponding to the minimum-cost output, we look at what happens if marginal cost is different from average total cost. If marginal cost is *less* than average total cost, an increase in output must reduce average total cost, as in the movement from A_1 to A_2. If marginal cost is *greater* than average total cost, an increase in output must increase average total cost, as in the movement from B_1 to B_2.

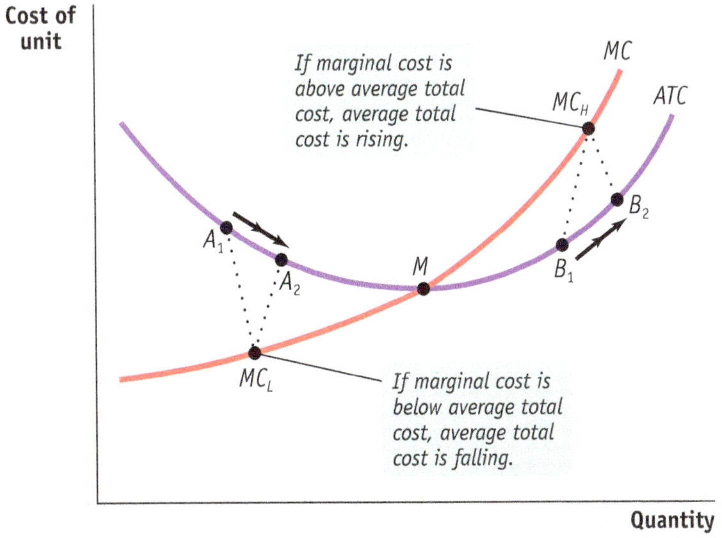

to point *M* in Figure 21-5: when marginal cost equals average total cost, we must be at the bottom of the U, because only at that point is average total cost neither falling nor rising.

Does the Marginal Cost Curve Always Slope Upward?

Up to this point, we have emphasized the importance of diminishing returns, which lead to a marginal product curve that always slopes downward and a marginal cost curve that always slopes upward. In practice, however, economists believe that marginal cost curves often slope *downward* as a firm increases its production from zero up to some low level, sloping upward only at higher levels of production: they look like the curve *MC* in Figure 21-6.

This initial downward slope occurs because a firm often finds that, when it starts with only a very small number of workers, employing more workers and expanding output allows its workers to specialize in various tasks. This, in turn, lowers the firm's marginal cost as it expands output. For example, one individual producing salsa would have to perform all the tasks involved: selecting and preparing the ingredients, mixing the salsa, bottling and labeling it, packing it into cases, and so on. As more workers are employed, they can divide the tasks, with each worker specializing in one or a few aspects of salsa-making.

This specialization leads to *increasing returns* from the hiring of additional workers and results in a marginal cost curve that initially slopes downward. But once there are enough workers to have completely exhausted the benefits of further specialization, diminishing returns to labor set in and the marginal cost curve changes direction and slopes upward. So typical marginal cost curves actually have the "swoosh" shape shown by *MC* in Figure 21-6. For the same reason, average variable cost curves typically look like *AVC* in Figure 21-6: they are U-shaped rather than strictly upward sloping.

However, as Figure 21-6 also shows, the key features we saw from the example of Selena's Gourmet Salsas remain true: the average total cost curve is U-shaped, and the marginal cost curve passes through the point of minimum average total cost.

FIGURE 21-6 More Realistic Cost Curves

A realistic marginal cost curve has a "swoosh" shape. Starting from a very low output level, marginal cost often falls as the firm increases output. That's because hiring additional workers allows greater specialization of their tasks and leads to increasing returns. Once specialization is achieved, however, diminishing returns to additional workers set in and marginal cost rises. The corresponding average variable cost curve is now U-shaped, like the average total cost curve.

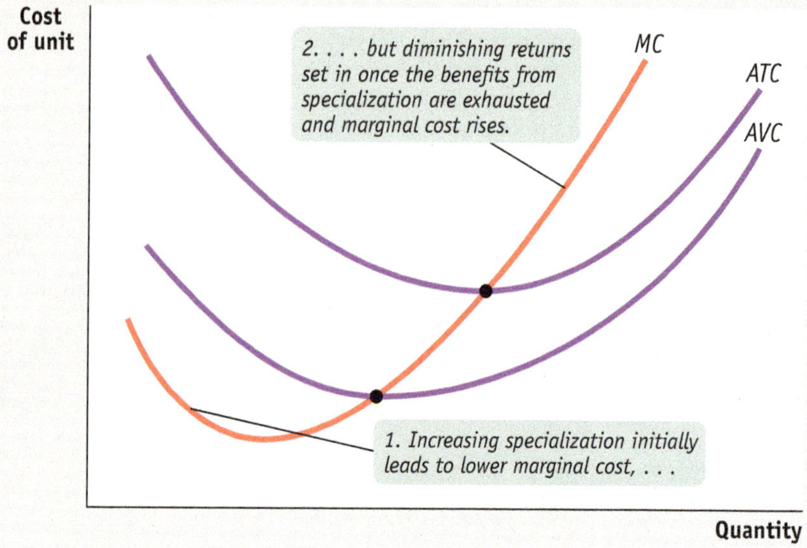

ECONOMICS >> *in Action*

Smart Grid Economics

If you like to listen to music, have to write term papers, or do laundry in the middle of the night, your local electricity grid would like to thank you. Why? Because you are using electricity when it is least costly to generate.

The problem is that energy cannot be stored efficiently on a large scale. So, power plant operators maintain both the main power stations that are designed to run continuously and the smaller power plants that operate only during periods of peak demand—such as during daytime working hours or periods of extreme outside temperatures.

These smaller power plants are more expensive to operate, incurring higher marginal cost per kilowatt generated than the average cost of generating a kilowatt (that is, cost averaged over kilowatts generated by the large and small plants). According to the U.S. Government Accountability Office, it can cost up to 10 times more to generate electricity during a summer afternoon (when air conditioners are running at maximum capacity) compared to nighttime.

But consumers typically aren't aware that the marginal cost of electricity varies over the course of a day or according to the weather. Instead, consumers see prices on their electric bills based on the average cost of electricity generation. As a result, electricity demand is inefficient—too high during high marginal cost periods and too low during low marginal cost periods. In the end, consumers end up paying more than they should for their electricity, as utility companies must eventually raise their prices to cover production costs.

To solve this inefficiency, utility companies, appliance manufacturers, and the federal government are working together to develop SMART Grid technologies—that help consumers adjust their usage according to the true marginal cost of a kilowatt in real time. "Smart" meters have been developed for home use, which allow the price to the consumer to vary according to the true marginal cost—which the consumer can see. And appliances such as dishwashers, refrigerators, dryers, and hot water heaters have been developed to run when electricity rates are lowest.

Studies have consistently shown that when consumers see the real marginal cost fluctuations and are asked to pay accordingly, they scale back their consumption during peak demand times. Clearly, SMART Grid technologies are just an application of smart economics.

Astro-O/Getty Images

With SMART Grid technology, consumers save money by basing their demand for electricity on marginal cost rather than average cost.

Check Your Understanding 21-1

1. Alicia's Apple Pies is a roadside business. Alicia must pay \$9.00 in rent each day. In addition, it costs her \$ 1.00 to produce the first pie of the day, and each subsequent pie costs 50% more to produce than the one before. For example, the second pie costs $\$1.00 \times 1.5 = \$ 1.50$ to produce, and so on.
   - **a.** Calculate Alicia's marginal cost, variable cost, average total cost, average variable cost, and average fixed cost as her daily pie output rises from 0 to 6. (*Hint:* The variable cost of two pies is just the marginal cost of the first pie, plus the marginal cost of the second pie, and so on.)
   - **b.** Indicate the range of pies for which the spreading effect dominates and the range for which the diminishing returns effect dominates.
   - **c.** What is Alicia's minimum-cost output? Explain why making one more pie lowers Alicia's average total cost when output is lower than the minimum-cost output. Similarly, explain why making one more pie raises Alicia's average total cost when output is greater than the minimum-cost output.

Solutions appear at back of book.

>> *Quick Review*

- The **total cost** of a given quantity of output equals the **fixed cost** plus the **variable cost** of that output. The **total cost curve** becomes steeper as more output is produced due to diminishing returns to the variable input.
- Marginal cost is equal to the slope of the total cost curve. Diminishing returns cause the marginal cost curve to slope upward.
- **Average total cost** (or **average cost**) is equal to the sum of **average fixed cost** and **average variable cost.** When the **U-shaped average total cost curve** slopes downward, the spreading effect dominates: fixed cost is spread over more units of output. When it slopes upward, the diminishing returns effect dominates: an additional unit of output requires more variable inputs.
- Marginal cost is equal to average total cost at the **minimum-cost output.** At higher output levels, marginal cost is greater than average total cost and average total cost is rising. At lower output levels, marginal cost is lower than average total cost and average total cost is falling.
- At low levels of output, there are often increasing returns to the variable input due to the benefits of specialization, making the marginal cost curve "swoosh"-shaped: initially sloping downward before sloping upward.

MODULE 22

Long-Run Costs and Economies of Scale

WHAT YOU WILL LEARN

- How do firms choose the optimal level of fixed cost?
- Why do costs differ in the long run compared to the short run?
- What are **returns to scale** and why do they matter?

Zvozdochka/Getty Images

22.1 Short-Run versus Long-Run Costs

Let's begin by supposing that Selena's Gourmet Salsas is considering whether to acquire additional food-preparation equipment. Acquiring additional machinery will affect its total cost in two ways. First, the firm will have to either rent or buy the additional equipment; either way, that will mean a higher fixed cost in the short run. Second, if the workers have more equipment, they will be more productive: fewer workers will be needed to produce any given output, so variable cost for any given output level will be reduced.

The table in Figure 22-1 shows how acquiring an additional machine affects costs. In our original example, we assumed that Selena's Gourmet Salsas had a fixed cost of $108. The left half of the table shows variable cost as well as total cost and average total cost assuming a fixed cost of $108. The average total cost curve for this level of fixed cost is given by ATC_1 in Figure 22-1. Let's compare that to a situation in which the firm buys additional food-preparation equipment, doubling its fixed cost to $216 but reducing its variable cost at any given level of output. The right half of the table shows the firm's variable cost, total cost, and average total cost with this higher level of fixed cost. The average total cost curve corresponding to $216 in fixed cost is given by ATC_2 in Figure 22-1.

From the figure you can see that when output is small, 4 cases of salsa per day or fewer, average total cost is smaller when Selena forgoes the additional equipment and maintains the lower fixed cost of $108: ATC_1 lies below ATC_2. For example, at 3 cases per day, average total cost is $72 without the additional machinery and $90 with the additional machinery. But as output increases beyond 4 cases

FIGURE 22-1 Choosing the Level of Fixed Cost for Selena's Gourmet Salsas

For any given level of output, there is a trade-off: a choice between lower fixed cost and higher variable cost, or higher fixed cost and lower variable cost. ATC_1 is the average total cost curve corresponding to a fixed cost of $108; it leads to lower fixed cost and higher variable cost. ATC_2 is the average total cost curve corresponding to a higher fixed cost of $216 but lower variable cost. At low output levels, at 4 or fewer cases of salsa per day, ATC_1 lies below ATC_2: average total cost is lower with only $108 in fixed cost. But as output goes up, average total cost is lower with the higher amount of fixed cost, $216: at more than 4 cases of salsa per day, ATC_2 lies below ATC_1.

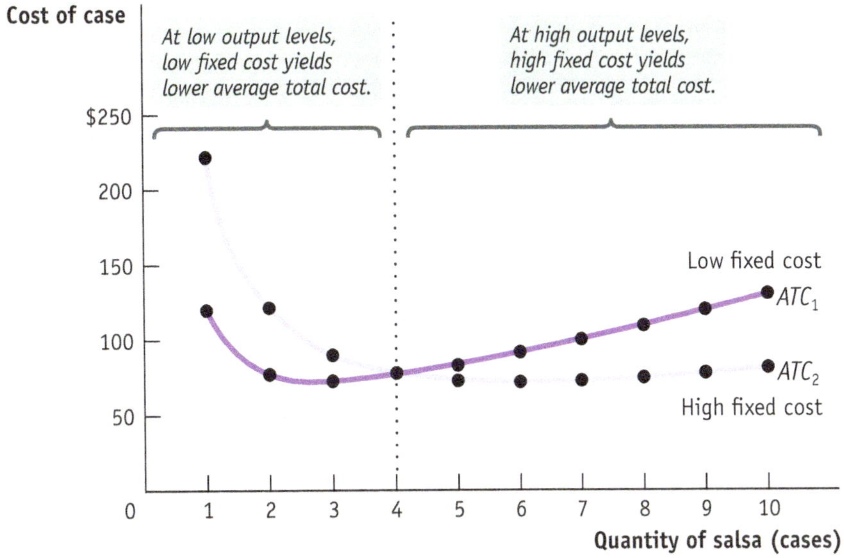

Quantity of salsa (cases)	Low fixed cost (FC = $108): High variable cost	Total cost	Average total cost of case ATC_1	High fixed cost (FC = $216): Low variable cost	Total cost	Average total cost of case ATC_2
1	$12	$120	$120.00	$6	$222	$222.00
2	48	156	78.00	24	240	120.00
3	108	216	72.00	54	270	90.00
4	192	300	75.00	96	312	78.00
5	300	408	81.60	150	366	73.20
6	432	540	90.00	216	432	72.00
7	588	696	99.43	294	510	72.86
8	768	876	109.50	384	600	75.00
9	972	1,080	120.00	486	702	78.00
10	1,200	1,308	130.80	600	816	81.60

per day, the firm's average total cost is lower if it acquires the additional equipment, raising its fixed cost to $216. So, at 9 cases of salsa per day, average total cost is $120 when fixed cost is $108 but only $78 when fixed cost is $216.

Why does average total cost change like this when fixed cost increases? When output is low, the increase in fixed cost from the additional equipment outweighs the reduction in variable cost from higher worker productivity—that is, there are too few units of output over which to spread the additional fixed cost. So, if Selena plans to produce 4 or fewer cases per day, she would be better off choosing the lower level of fixed cost, $108, to achieve a lower average total cost of production. When planned output is high, however, she should acquire the additional machinery.

In general, for each output level there is some choice of fixed cost that minimizes the firm's average total cost for that output level. So, when the firm has a desired output level that it expects to maintain over time, it should choose the level of fixed cost optimal for that level—that is, the level of fixed cost that minimizes its average total cost.

Now that we are studying a situation in which a fixed cost can change, we need to take time into account when discussing average total cost. All of the average

Joyce Marshall/Tribune News Service/FortWorth/TX/ USA/Newscom

To understand how firms operate over time, be sure to distinguish between short-run and long-run average costs.

total cost curves we have considered until now are defined for a given level of fixed cost—that is, they are defined for the short run, the period of time over which fixed cost doesn't vary. To reinforce that distinction, for the rest of this section, we will refer to these average total cost curves as *short-run average total cost curves.*

For most firms, it is realistic to assume that there are many possible choices of fixed cost, not just two. The implication: for such a firm, many possible short-run average total cost curves will exist, each corresponding to a different choice of fixed cost and so giving rise to what is called a firm's "family" of short-run average total cost curves.

At any given point in time, a firm will find itself on one of its short-run cost curves, the one corresponding to its current level of fixed cost; a change in output will cause it to move along that curve. If the firm expects that change in output level to be long-standing, then it is likely that the firm's current level of fixed cost is no longer optimal. Given sufficient time, it will want to adjust its fixed cost to a new level that minimizes average total cost for its new output level.

For example, if Selena had been producing 2 cases of salsa per day with a fixed cost of $108 but found herself increasing her output to 8 cases per day for the foreseeable future, then in the long run, she should purchase more equipment and increase her fixed cost to a level that minimizes average total cost at the 8-cases-per-day output level.

Suppose we do a thought experiment and calculate the lowest possible average total cost that can be achieved for each output level if the firm were to choose its fixed cost for each output level. Economists have given this thought experiment a name: the *long-run average total cost curve.* Specifically, the **long-run average total cost curve,** or *LRATC,* is the relationship between output and average total cost when fixed cost has been chosen to minimize average total cost *for each level of output.* If there are many possible choices of fixed cost, the long-run average total cost curve will have the familiar, smooth U shape, as shown by *LRATC* in Figure 22-2.

The **long-run average total cost curve** shows the relationship between output and average total cost when fixed cost has been chosen to minimize average total cost for each level of output.

We can now draw the distinction between the short run and the long run more fully. In the long run, when a producer has had time to choose the fixed cost appropriate for its desired level of output, that producer will be at some point on the long-run average total cost curve. But if the output level is altered, the firm will no

FIGURE 22-2 Short-Run and Long-Run Average Total Cost Curves

Short-run and long-run average total cost curves differ because a firm can choose its fixed cost in the long run. If Selena has chosen the level of fixed cost that minimizes short-run average total cost at an output of 6 cases, and she actually produces 6 cases, then she will be at point *C* on *LRATC* and ATC_6. But if she produces only 3 cases, she will move to point *B*. If she expects to produce only 3 cases for a long time, in the long run, she will reduce her fixed cost and move to point *A* on ATC_3. Likewise, if she produces 9 cases (putting her at point *Y*) and expects to continue this for a long time, she will increase her fixed cost in the long run and move to point *X* on ATC_9.

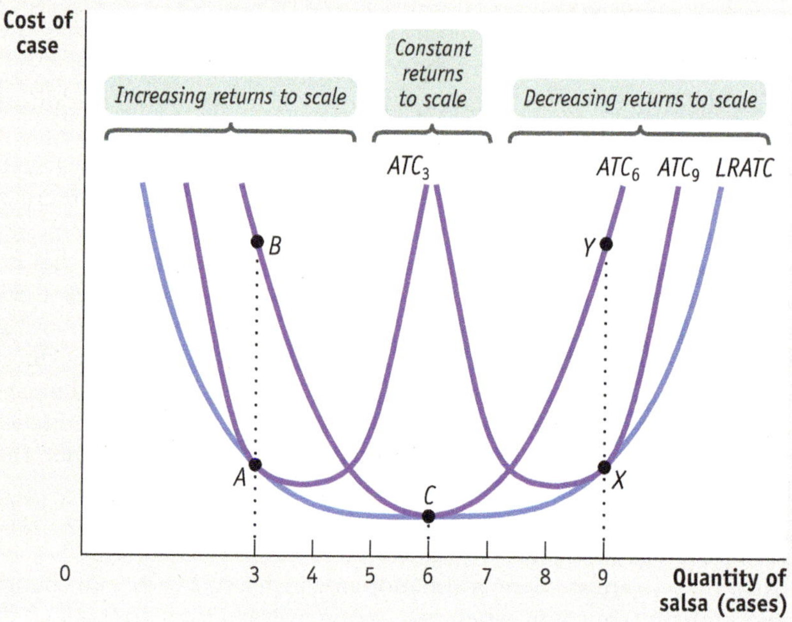

longer be on its long-run average total cost curve and will instead be moving along its current short-run average total cost curve. It will not be on its long-run average total cost curve again until it readjusts its fixed cost for its new output level.

Figure 22-2 illustrates this point. The curve ATC_3 shows short-run average total cost if Selena has chosen the level of fixed cost that minimizes average total cost at an output of 3 cases of salsa per day. This is confirmed by the fact that at 3 cases per day, ATC_3 touches *LRATC*, the long-run average total cost curve. Similarly, ATC_6 shows short-run average total cost if Selena has chosen the level of fixed cost that minimizes average total cost if her output is 6 cases per day. It touches *LRATC* at 6 cases per day. And ATC_9 shows short-run average total cost if Selena has chosen the level of fixed cost that minimizes average total cost if her output is 9 cases per day. It touches *LRATC* at 9 cases per day.

Suppose that Selena initially chose to be on ATC_6. If she actually produces 6 cases of salsa per day, her firm will be at point *C* on both its short-run and long-run average total cost curves. Suppose, however, that Selena ends up producing only 3 cases of salsa per day. In the short run, her average total cost is indicated by point *B* on ATC_6; it is no longer on *LRATC*. If Selena had known that she would be producing only 3 cases per day, she would have been better off choosing a lower level of fixed cost, the one corresponding to ATC_3, thereby achieving a lower average total cost. She could do this, for example, by selling her production plant and purchasing a smaller one. Then her firm would have found itself at point *A* on the long-run average total cost curve, which lies below point *B*.

Suppose, conversely, that Selena ends up producing 9 cases per day even though she initially chose to be on ATC_6. In the short run, her average total cost is indicated by point *Y* on ATC_6. But she would be better off purchasing more equipment and incurring a higher fixed cost to reduce her variable cost and move to ATC_9. This would allow her to reach point *X* on the long-run average total cost curve, which lies below *Y*.

The distinction between short-run and long-run average total costs is extremely important in making sense of how real firms operate over time. A company that has to increase output suddenly to meet a surge in demand will typically find that in the short run, its average total cost rises sharply because it is hard to get extra production out of existing facilities. But given time to build new factories or add machinery, short-run average total cost falls.

Returns to Scale

What determines the shape of the long-run average total cost curve? The answer is that *scale*, the size of a firm's operations, is often an important determinant of its long-run average total cost of production. Firms that experience scale effects in production find that their long-run average total cost changes substantially depending on the quantity of output they produce. There are **increasing returns to scale** (also known as *economies of scale*) when long-run average total cost declines as output increases.

As you can see in Figure 22-2, Selena's Gourmet Salsas experiences increasing returns to scale over output levels ranging from 0 up to 5 cases of salsa per day—the output levels over which the long-run average total cost curve is declining. In contrast, there are **decreasing returns to scale** (also known as *dis-economies of scale*) when long-run average total cost increases as output increases. For Selena's Gourmet Salsas, decreasing returns to scale occur at output levels greater than 7 cases, the output levels over which its long-run average total cost curve is rising.

There is also a third possible relationship between long-run average total cost and scale: firms experience **constant returns to scale** when long-run average total cost is constant as output increases. In this case, the firm's long-run average total cost curve is horizontal over the output levels for which there are constant returns to scale. As you see in Figure 22-2, Selena's Gourmet Salsas has constant returns to scale when it produces anywhere from 5 to 7 cases of salsa per day.

There are **increasing returns to scale** when long-run average total cost declines as output increases.

There are **decreasing returns to scale** when long-run average total cost increases as output increases.

There are **constant returns to scale** when long-run average total cost is constant as output increases.

TABLE 22-1 Concepts and Measures of Cost

	Measurement	Definition	Mathematical term
Short run	Fixed cost	Cost that does not depend on the quantity of output produced	*FC*
	Average fixed cost	Fixed cost per unit of output	$AFC = FC/Q$
Short run and long run	Variable cost	Cost that depends on the quantity of output produced	*VC*
	Average variable cost	Variable cost per unit of output	$AVC = VC/Q$
	Total cost	The sum of fixed cost (short run) and variable cost	$TC = FC$ (short run) $+ VC$
	Average total cost (Average cost)	Total cost per unit of output	$ATC = TC/Q$
	Marginal cost	The change in total cost generated by producing one more unit of output	$MC = \Delta TC/\Delta Q$
Long run	Long-run average total cost	Average total cost when fixed cost has been chosen to minimize average total cost for each level of output	*LRATC*

What explains these scale effects in production? The answer ultimately lies in the firm's technology of production. Increasing returns often arise from the increased *specialization* that larger output levels allow—a larger scale of operation means that individual workers can limit themselves to more specialized tasks, becoming more skilled and efficient at doing them.

Another source of increasing returns is a very large initial setup cost; in some industries—such as auto manufacturing, electricity generating, or petroleum refining—incurring a high fixed cost in the form of plant and equipment is necessary to produce any output.

A third source of increasing returns, found in certain high-tech industries such as software development, is that the value of a good or service to an individual increases when a large number of others own or use the same good or service (known as *network externalities*). As we'll see in Section 9, where we study monopoly, increasing returns have very important implications for how firms and industries interact and behave.

Decreasing returns—the opposite scenario—typically arise in large firms due to problems of coordination and communication: as the firm grows in size, it becomes ever more difficult and thus more costly to communicate and to organize its activities. Although increasing returns induce firms to get larger, decreasing returns tend to limit their size. And when there are constant returns to scale, scale has no effect on a firm's long-run average total cost: it is the same regardless of whether the firm produces 1 unit or 100,000 units.

Summing Up Costs: The Short and Long of It

If a firm is to make the best decisions about how much to produce, it has to understand how its costs relate to the quantity of output it chooses to produce. Table 22-1 provides a quick summary of the concepts and measures of cost you have learned about.

ECONOMICS >> *in Action*

How the Sharing Economy Reduces Fixed Cost

The *sharing economy* is a relatively new phenomenon in which technology allows unrelated parties (firms and individuals) to share assets like office space, homes, computing capacity, software, cars, small jets, machinery, financial capital, books, and even clothes. Uber and Airbnb are probably the most prominent examples of how the sharing economy works: their web platforms allow both drivers with cars and homeowners with rooms to spare to share their assets with others. But even the Cloud itself, the vast digital network into which you upload your photos and team-project term papers to share with others, is a feature of the sharing economy because it allows firms and individuals to rent computing capacity, storage, and software.

So, what does the sharing have to do with fixed cost? A lot. If the use of an asset can be obtained only when needed, then it goes from incurring a fixed cost to incurring a variable cost. Take, for example, a company jet. Instead of incurring the fixed cost of owning and maintaining a company jet full time (one which might sit on the runway for a significant amount of time), a company can now purchase, through NetJets or similar firms, the services of a jet on an as-needed basis. In effect, by turning the fixed cost of ownership and operation into a variable cost, the sharing economy might allow smaller companies to operate in markets that would have previously been unprofitable for them. Likewise, sharing allows individuals to afford assets (a car, a home, a designer handbag) that were previously unaffordable because the assets can now be used to generate income.

And the sharing economy marketplace makes for a more efficient use of society's resources overall, as it improves the allocation of resources to those who can make the best use of them.

Smith Collection/Gado/Getty Images

Firms in the sharing economy, like Turo, help convert fixed costs to variable costs and allow for a more efficient use of resources.

Check Your Understanding 22-1

1. The accompanying table shows three possible combinations of fixed cost and average variable cost. Average variable cost is constant in this example (it does not vary with the quantity of output produced).

Choice	Fixed cost	Average variable cost
1	$8,000	$1.00
2	12,000	0.75
3	24,000	0.25

   a. For each of the three choices, calculate the average total cost of producing 12,000, 22,000, and 30,000 units. For each of these quantities, which choice results in the lowest average total cost?

   b. Suppose that the firm, which has historically produced 12,000 units, experiences a sharp, permanent increase in demand that leads it to produce 22,000 units. Explain how its average total cost will change in the short run and in the long run.

   c. Explain what the firm should do instead if it believes the change in demand is temporary.

2. In each of the following cases, explain what kind of scale effects you think the firm will experience and why.

   a. A telemarketing firm in which employees make sales calls using computers and telephones

   b. An interior design firm in which design projects are based on the expertise of the firm's owner

   c. A diamond-mining company

3. Draw a graph like Figure 22-2, and insert a short-run average total cost curve corresponding to a long-run output choice of 5 cases of salsa per day. Use the graph to show why Selena should change her fixed cost if she expects to produce only 4 cases per day for a long period of time.

Solutions appear at back of book.

>> Quick Review

- In the long run, firms choose fixed cost according to expected output. Higher fixed cost reduces average total cost when output is high. Lower fixed cost reduces average total cost when output is low.
- There are many possible short-run average total cost curves, each corresponding to a different level of fixed cost. The **long-run average total cost curve,** *LRATC,* shows average total cost over the long run, when the firm has chosen fixed cost to minimize average total cost for each level of output.
- A firm that has fully adjusted its fixed cost for its output level will operate at a point that lies on both its current short-run and long-run average total cost curves. A change in output moves the firm along its current short-run average total cost curve. Once it has readjusted its fixed cost, the firm will operate on a new short-run average total cost curve and on the long-run average total cost curve.
- Scale effects arise from the technology of production. **Increasing returns to scale** tend to make firms larger. **Decreasing returns to scale** tend to limit their size. With **constant returns to scale,** scale has no effect.

BUSINESS CASE

The Rise of the Machine at Amazon

Justin Sullivan/Getty Images

One of the main pillars of Amazon's success is its promise of speedy delivery. For the majority of Prime-eligible items, customers receive their orders within two business days. Even better, in select zip codes Amazon can now deliver within 24 hours. And if you happen to live in a major city, odds are that you can receive your delivery in one to two hours. None of its competitors comes close to matching Amazon's speed. What accounts for Amazon's prodigious delivery abilities?

The answer: robots. Visit an Amazon fulfillment center, and you will see hundreds of them swarming an 125,000-square-foot area, engaged in a finely coordinated dance. They haul shelves of merchandise, weighing up to 700 pounds, and deliver them to human "pickers" who assemble orders and to human "stockers" who sort incoming inventory.

As of 2019, Amazon had more than 100,000 robots working in its 175 fulfillment centers, which collectively shipped out more than 5 billion orders. Before the arrival of robots, human employees did this tedious work, often walking 10 to 15 miles daily, carrying heavy loads. By eliminating the need for humans to walk miles carting merchandise, warehouse operations have become much more efficient. In addition, because robots don't need aisles between shelves like people do, there's more room for merchandise storage in Amazon's fulfillment centers.

Over the past 20 years, Amazon has invested an enormous amount of money in perfecting its warehouse management and order fulfillment operations to satisfy customers' desire to receive their items quickly. The company's spokesperson, Phil Hardin, explains the widespread use of robots this way: "It's an investment that has implications for a lot of elements of our cost structure. It has been a great innovation for us, . . . and we think it makes our warehouses more productive." Indeed, some estimates show that, by embracing automation, Amazon has cut the cost of order fulfillment nearly in half.

Amazon's competitors have taken notice. Walmart, for example, also uses robotic systems to speed up delivery times. Robotics companies like 6 River Systems have been working with warehouse management companies such as Flowspace to provide order fulfillment services for non-Amazon sellers. However, with Amazon's huge scale advantage, it remains to be seen whether other retailers can ever catch up.

QUESTIONS FOR THOUGHT

1. Describe the shift in Amazon's cost structure based on the concepts from this section. Is Amazon on a short-run or long-run cost curve? What are the relevant returns to scale in Amazon's operations?
2. What are the pros and cons of Amazon's strategy?
3. What advantage does a robotic system give Amazon over its rivals? How likely is it that they will catch up with Amazon? What market factors does it depend upon?

REVIEW

MODULE 20

1. The relationship between inputs and output is a producer's **production function.** In the short run, the quantity of a fixed input cannot be varied but the quantity of a **variable input** can. In the **long run,** the quantities of all inputs can be varied. For a given amount of the fixed input, the **total product curve** shows how the quantity of output changes as the quantity of the variable input changes. We may also calculate the **marginal product** of an input, the increase in output from using one more unit of that input.
2. There are **diminishing returns to an input** when its marginal product declines as more of the input is used, holding the quantity of all other inputs fixed.

MODULE 21

1. **Total cost,** represented by the **total cost curve,** is equal to the sum of **fixed cost,** which does not depend on output, and **variable cost,** which does depend on output. Due to diminishing returns, marginal cost—the increase in total cost generated by producing one more unit of output—normally increases as output increases.
2. **Average total cost** (also known as **average cost**), calculated total cost divided by quantity of output, is the cost of the average unit of output, and marginal cost is the cost of one more unit produced. Economists believe that **U-shaped average total cost curves** are typical, because average total cost consists of two parts: average fixed cost, which falls when output increases (the spreading effect), and **average variable cost,** which rises with output (the diminishing returns effect).
3. When average total cost is U-shaped, the bottom of the U is the level of output at which average total cost is minimized, the point of **minimum-cost output.** This is also the point at which the marginal cost curve crosses the average total cost curve from below. Due to gains from specialization, the marginal cost curve may slope downward initially before sloping upward, giving it a "swoosh" shape.

MODULE 22

1. In the long run, a producer can change its fixed input and its level of fixed cost. By accepting a higher fixed cost, a firm can lower its variable cost for any given output level, and vice versa. The **long-run average total cost curve** shows the relationship between output and average total cost when fixed cost has been chosen to minimize average total cost at each level of output. A firm moves along its short-run average total cost curve as it changes the quantity of output, and it returns to a point on both its short-run and long-run average total cost curves once it has adjusted fixed cost to its new output level.
2. As output increases, there are **increasing returns to scale** if long-run average total cost declines, **decreasing returns to scale** if it increases, and **constant returns to scale** if it remains constant. Scale effects depend on the technology of production.

KEY TERMS

Production function p. 236
Fixed input p. 236
Variable input p. 236
Long run p. 236
Short run p. 236
Total product curve p. 237
Marginal product p. 238
Diminishing returns to an input p. 238
Fixed cost p. 242
Variable cost p. 242
Total cost p. 242
Total cost curve p. 243
Average total cost p. 246
Average cost p. 246
U-shaped average total cost curve p. 246
Average fixed cost p. 246
Average variable cost p. 247
Minimum-cost output p. 249
Long-run average total cost curve p. 254
Increasing returns to scale p. 255
Decreasing returns to scale p. 255
Constant returns to scale p. 255

Richard Levine/Corbis via Getty Images

SECTION 8

Market Structure and Perfect Competition

DECK THE HALLS

One sure sign it's the holiday season is the sudden appearance of Christmas tree sellers setting up shop in vacant lots, parking lots, and garden centers all across the country. Until the 1950s, virtually all Christmas trees were obtained by individuals going to local forests to cut down their own. However, by the 1950s, increased demand from population growth and diminished supply from the loss of forests created a market opportunity. Seeing an ability to profit by growing and selling Christmas trees, farmers responded to the demand.

So rather than venturing into the forest to cut your own tree, you now have a wide range of tree sizes and varieties to choose from—and they are available close to home. In 2018, nearly 33 million farmed trees were sold in the United States, for a total of over $2 billion.

Note that the supply of Christmas trees is relatively price inelastic for two reasons: it takes time to acquire land for planting, and it takes time for the trees to grow. However, these limits apply only in the short run. Over time, farms that are already in operation can increase their capacity and new tree farmers can enter the business. And, over time, the trees will mature and be ready to harvest. So, the increase in the quantity supplied in response to an increase in price will be much larger in the long run than in the short run.

Where does the supply curve come from? Why is there a difference between the short-run and the long-run supply curve? In this section, we will use our understanding of costs, developed in Section 7, as the basis for an analysis of the supply curve. As we'll see, this will require that we understand the behavior both of individual firms and of an entire industry, composed of these many individual firms.

Our analysis in this section assumes that the industry in question is characterized by *perfect competition*. We begin by explaining the concept of perfect competition, providing a brief introduction to the conditions that give rise to a perfectly competitive industry. We then show how a producer under perfect competition decides how much to produce. Finally, we use the cost curves of the individual producers to derive the *industry supply curve* under perfect competition.

By analyzing the way a competitive industry evolves over time, we will come to understand the distinction between the short-run and long-run effects of changes in demand on a competitive industry—for example, the effect of America's preference for readily available trees for the holidays on the Christmas tree farming industry. We will conclude with a deeper discussion of the conditions necessary for an industry to be perfectly competitive.

MODULE 23

Introduction to Market Structure

WHAT YOU WILL LEARN

- What is the meaning of market structure?
- What are the four principal types of market structure?

Richard Levine/Alamy

To discuss how firms determine what price to set and what quantity to produce, we need to identify the type of market we are looking at. In this module, we will learn about the basic characteristics of the four major types of markets in the economy.

23.1 Types of Market Structure

The real world holds a mind-boggling array of different markets. We observe widely different behavior patterns by producers across markets: in some markets, firms are extremely competitive; in others, they seem somehow to coordinate their actions to avoid competing with one another; and some markets are monopolies in which there is no competition at all.

To develop principles and make predictions about markets and how producers will behave in them, economists have developed four primary models of market structure: *perfect competition, monopoly, oligopoly,* and *monopolistic competition.* This system of market structure is based on two dimensions:

1. The number of firms in the market (one, few, or many)
2. Whether the goods offered are identical or differentiated

Differentiated goods are goods that are different but considered at least somewhat substitutable by consumers (think Coke versus Pepsi).

Figure 23-1 provides a simple visual summary of the types of market structure classified according to the two dimensions. In *perfect competition,* many firms each sell an identical product. In *monopoly,* a single firm sells a single, undifferentiated product. In *oligopoly,* a few firms—more than one but not a large number—sell products that may be either identical or differentiated. And in *monopolistic competition,* many firms each sell a differentiated product—think of producers of economics textbooks.

FIGURE 23-1 Types of Market Structure

The behavior of any given firm and the market it occupies are analyzed using one of four models of market structure—monopoly, oligopoly, perfect competition, or monopolistic competition. This system for categorizing market structure is based on two dimensions: (1) whether products are differentiated or identical and (2) the number of producers in the industry—one, a few, or many.

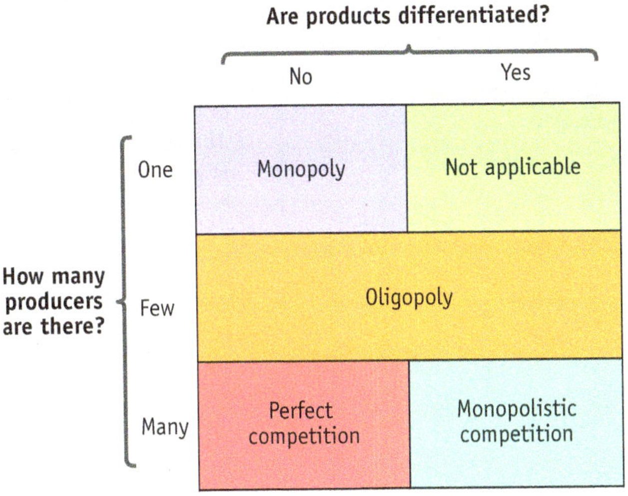

23.2 Perfect Competition

Suppose that Yves and Zoe are neighboring farmers, both of whom grow Christmas trees. And because both sell their output to the same set of Christmas tree consumers, in a real sense, Yves and Zoe compete with each other.

Does this mean that Yves should try to stop Zoe from growing Christmas trees or that Yves and Zoe should form an agreement to grow fewer trees? Almost certainly not: there are thousands of Christmas tree farmers, and Yves and Zoe are competing with all those other growers as well as with each other. Because so many farmers sell Christmas trees, if any one of them produced more or less, there would be no measurable effect on market prices.

When people talk about business competition, the image they often have in mind is a situation in which two or three rival firms are intensely struggling for advantage. But economists know that when an industry consists of only a few main competitors, it's actually a sign that competition is fairly limited. As the example of Christmas trees suggests, when there is enough competition, it doesn't even make sense to identify your rivals: there are so many competitors that you cannot single out any one of them as a rival.

We can put it another way: Yves and Zoe are **price-taking producers.** A producer is a price-taker when its actions cannot affect the market price of the good or service it sells. As a result, a price-taking producer considers the market price as given. When there is enough competition—when competition is what economists call "perfect"—then every producer is a price-taker.

And there is a similar definition for consumers: a **price-taking consumer** is a consumer who cannot influence the market price of the good or service by his or her actions. That is, the market price is unaffected by how much or how little of the good the consumer buys.

A **price-taking producer** is a producer whose actions have no effect on the market price of the good or service it sells.

A **price-taking consumer** is a consumer whose actions have no effect on the market price of the good or service they buy.

A **perfectly competitive market** is a market in which all market participants are price-takers.

Defining Perfect Competition

In a **perfectly competitive market,** all market participants, both consumers and producers, are price-takers. That is, neither consumption decisions by individual consumers nor production decisions by individual producers affect the market price of the good.

A **perfectly competitive industry** is an industry in which producers are price-takers.

A producer's **market share** is the fraction of the total industry output accounted for by that producer's output.

A good is a **standardized product,** also known as a **commodity,** when consumers regard the products of different producers as the same good.

The supply and demand model, which we introduced in Section 2 and have used repeatedly since then, is a model of a perfectly competitive market. It depends fundamentally on the assumption that no individual buyer or seller of a good, such as coffee beans or Christmas trees, can affect the price at which they can buy or sell the good.

As a general rule, consumers are indeed price-takers. Instances in which consumers are able to affect the prices they pay are rare. It is, however, quite common for producers to have a significant ability to affect the prices they receive. When producers can affect prices, they are no longer price-takers. Monopoly, oligopoly, and monopolistic competitively producers are all non-price-takers.

Thus, the model of perfect competition is appropriate for some but not all markets. An industry in which producers are price-takers is called a **perfectly competitive industry.** Under what circumstances will all producers be price-takers? In the next section, we will find that there are two necessary conditions for a perfectly competitive industry, and that a third condition is often present as well.

Conditions That Lead to Perfect Competition

The markets for major grains, like wheat and corn, are perfectly competitive: individual wheat and corn farmers, as well as individual buyers of wheat and corn, take market prices as given. In contrast, the markets for some of the food items made from these grains—in particular, breakfast cereals—are by no means perfectly competitive. There is intense competition among cereal brands but not *perfect* competition. To understand the difference between the market for wheat and the market for shredded wheat cereal is to understand the importance of the two necessary conditions for perfect competition.

1. **Many Producers** *For an industry to be perfectly competitive, it must contain many producers, none of whom has a large* **market share.** A producer's market share is the fraction of the total industry output accounted for by that producer's output. The distribution of market share constitutes a major difference between the grain industry and the breakfast cereal industry.

   In the market for wheat, there are thousands of producers—wheat farmers—none of whom accounts for more than a tiny fraction of total wheat sales. In contrast, the breakfast cereal industry is dominated by four producers: Kellogg's, General Mills, Post Foods, and the Quaker Oats Company. Kellogg's and General Mills alone account for 65% of all cereal sales in the United States. Kellogg's executives know that if they try to sell more cornflakes, they are likely to drive down the market price of cornflakes. That is, they know that their actions influence market prices, simply because they are such a large part of the market, and that changes in their production will significantly affect the overall quantity supplied. It makes sense to assume that producers are price-takers only when an industry does *not* contain any large producers like Kellogg's.

2. **Standardized Product** *An industry can be perfectly competitive only if every firm produces a* **standardized product.** A standardized product is a product that consumers regard as the same good even when it comes from different producers and is sometimes known as a **commodity.** Because wheat is a standardized product, consumers regard the output of one wheat producer as a perfect substitute for that of another producer. This clearly isn't true in the breakfast cereal market: consumers don't consider Cap'n Crunch to be a good substitute for Wheaties.

Because wheat is a standardized product, one farmer cannot increase the price for their wheat without losing all sales to other wheat farmers.

The Photo Works

The market for wheat and other major grains is perfectly competitive. The market for breakfast cereals made from wheat and other grains is not.

In contrast, the maker of Wheaties has some ability to increase its price without fear that it will lose all its customers to the maker of Cap'n Crunch. So the second necessary condition for a competitive industry is that the industry output is a standardized product.

3. **Free Entry and Exit** Economists refer to the arrival of new firms into an industry as *entry;* they refer to the departure of firms from an industry as *exit.* When there are no obstacles to entry into or exit from an industry, we say that the industry has **free entry and exit.**

Free entry and exit is not strictly necessary for perfect competition. However, it ensures that the number of firms in an industry can adjust to changing market conditions. And, in particular, it ensures that firms in an industry cannot act to keep other firms out. Free entry and exit arises when there are no obstacles, such as government regulations or limited access to key resources, that prevent new producers from entering the market. And, no additional costs are associated with shutting down the firm and exiting the industry.

An industry has **free entry and exit** when new producers can easily enter into an industry and existing producers can easily leave that industry.

>> Quick Review

- Neither the actions of a **price-taking producer** nor those of a **price-taking consumer** can influence the market price of a good.
- In a **perfectly competitive market,** all producers and consumers are price-takers. Consumers are almost always price-takers, but this is often not true of producers. An industry in which producers are price-takers is a **perfectly competitive industry.**
- Two necessary conditions for a perfectly competitive industry is that it contains many producers, each of which produces a **standardized product** (also known as a **commodity**), but none of those producers has a large **market share.**
- Although not a necessary condition, most perfectly competitive industries are also characterized by **free entry and exit.**

Check Your Understanding 23-1

1. In each of the following situations, do you think the industry described will be perfectly competitive or not? Explain your answer.
   a. There are three producers of aluminum, a good sold in many places, in the world.
   b. The price of natural gas is determined by global supply and demand. A small share of that global supply is produced by a handful of companies located in the North Sea.
   c. Dozens of designers sell high-fashion clothes. Each designer has a distinctive style and a loyal clientele.
   d. There are many baseball teams in the United States, one or two in each major city and each selling tickets to its hometown events.

Solutions appear at back of book.

23.3 Monopoly

The De Beers monopoly was created in South Africa in the 1880s by Cecil Rhodes, a British imperialist and businessman. At that time, South Africa was the largest single source of diamonds, and South African mines dominated the world's supply of diamonds. There were, however, many mining companies, all competing with each other. Rhodes bought the great majority of those mines and consolidated them into a single company, De Beers. By 1889, De Beers controlled almost all of the world's diamond production. De Beers, in other words, became a *monopolist.*

Defining Monopoly

A producer is a **monopolist** if it is the sole supplier of a good that has no close substitutes. When a firm is a monopolist, the industry is a **monopoly.** Monopoly is the most extreme departure from perfect competition.

In practice, true monopolies are hard to find in the modern American economy, partly because of legal obstacles. A contemporary entrepreneur who tried to consolidate all the firms in an industry the way that Rhodes did would soon land in court, accused of breaking *antitrust* laws, which are intended to prevent monopolies from emerging. Monopolies do, however, play an important role in some sectors of the economy.

The ability of a monopolist to raise its price above the competitive level by reducing output is known as **market power.** And market power is what monopoly

A **monopolist** is the only producer of a good that has no close substitutes. An industry controlled by a monopolist is known as a **monopoly.**

Market power is the ability of a firm to raise prices.

To earn economic profits, a monopolist must be protected by a **barrier to entry**—something that prevents other firms from entering the industry.

A **natural monopoly** exists when economies of scale provide a large cost advantage to a single firm that produces all of an industry's output.

is all about. A wheat farmer who is 1 of 100,000 wheat farmers has no market power: they must sell wheat at the going market price. Your local water utility company, though, does have market power: it can raise prices and still keep many (though not all) of its customers, because they have nowhere else to go. In short, it's a monopolist.

Why Do Monopolies Exist?

A monopolist making profits will not go unnoticed by others. (Recall that we mean "economic profit," revenue over and above the opportunity costs of the firm's resources.) But won't other firms crash the party, grab a piece of the action, and drive down prices and profits in the long run?

For a profitable monopoly to persist, something must keep others from going into the same business; that "something" is known as a **barrier to entry.** There are five principal types of barriers to entry: control of a scarce resource or input, increasing returns to scale, technological superiority, a network externality, and a government-created barrier to entry.

1. **Control of a Scarce Resource or Input** A monopolist that controls a resource or input crucial to an industry can prevent other firms from entering its market. Cecil Rhodes created the De Beers monopoly by establishing control over the mines that produced the bulk of the world's diamonds.
2. **Increasing Returns to Scale** Many Americans have natural gas piped into their homes for cooking and heating. Invariably, the local gas company is a monopolist. But why don't rival companies compete to provide gas?

In the early nineteenth century, when the natural gas industry was just starting up, companies did compete for local customers. But this competition didn't last long; soon local gas companies became a monopoly in almost every town because of the large fixed cost of providing a town with gas lines. The cost of laying gas lines didn't depend on how much gas a company sold, so a firm with a larger volume of sales had a cost advantage: because it was able to spread the fixed cost over a larger volume, it had a lower average total cost than smaller firms.

Local gas supply is an industry in which average total cost falls as output increases. As we learned earlier, the phenomenon is called *increasing returns to scale,* which results in economies of scale. Economies of scale will encourage firms to grow larger. In an industry characterized by economies of scale, larger firms are more profitable and drive out smaller ones. For the same reason, established firms have a cost advantage over any potential entrant—a potent barrier to entry. So increasing returns to scale—economies of scale—can both give rise to and sustain a monopoly.

A monopoly created and sustained by increasing returns is called a **natural monopoly.** The defining characteristic of a natural monopoly is that it possesses increasing returns to scale over the range of output that is relevant for the industry. The source of this condition is large fixed costs: when large fixed costs are required to operate, a given quantity of output is produced at lower average total cost by one large firm than by two or more smaller firms.

The most visible natural monopolies in the modern economy are local utilities—water, gas, power generation, and fiber-optic cable. As we'll see later, natural monopolies pose a special challenge to public policy.

3. **Technological Superiority** A firm that maintains a consistent technological advantage over potential competitors can establish itself as a monopolist. For example, from the 1970s through the 1990s, the semiconductor chip manufacturer Intel was able to maintain a consistent advantage over potential competitors in both the design and production of microprocessors, the chips that run computers. But technological superiority is typically not a barrier to entry over the longer term: over time competitors will invest in upgrading their technology

to match that of the technology leader. In fact, in later years Intel found its technological superiority eroded by a competitor, Advanced Micro Devices (also known as AMD), which was able to produce chips approximately as fast and as powerful as Intel chips.

In the digital economy, an increasingly important source of monopoly power is *network externalities.*

alexsl/Getty Images

Top social media sites like Facebook and Instagram have an advantage over their competition in attracting new users.

4. **Network Externalities** If you were the only person in the world with an internet connection, what would that connection be worth to you? The answer, of course, is nothing. Your internet connection is valuable only because other people are also connected. And, in general, the more people who are connected, the more valuable your connection is. This phenomenon, whereby the value of a good or service to an individual is greater when many others use the same good or service, is called a **network externality**—its value derives from enabling its users to participate in a network of other users.

The earliest form of network externalities arose in transportation, when the value of a road or airport increased as the number of people who had access to it rose. But network externalities are especially prevalent in the technology and communications sectors of the economy.

The classic case is computer operating systems. Worldwide, most personal computers run on Microsoft Windows. Although many believe that Apple has a superior operating system, the wider use of Windows in the early days of personal computers attracted more software development and technical support, giving it a lasting dominance. More recent examples of firms that came to dominate their industries through network externalities are eBay, Facebook, Amazon, Netflix, Google, PayPal, and Snapchat.

When a network externality exists, the firm with the largest network of customers using its product has an advantage in attracting new customers, one that may allow it to become a monopolist. At a minimum, the dominant firm can charge a higher price and so earn higher profits than its competitors. Moreover, a network externality gives an advantage to the firm with the deepest pockets. Companies with the most money on hand can sell the most goods at a loss, with the expectation that doing so will give them the largest customer base.

In practice, a network externality behaves a lot like a case of increasing returns to scale: for the larger firm, the cost of obtaining a new customer is less than for a smaller firm. Like a natural monopoly, network externalities present a difficult problem for public policy makers. We will examine these issues in more detail later in this section.

5. **Government-Created Barriers** The pharmaceutical company Merck introduced Propecia, a drug effective against baldness, in 1998. Although Propecia was very profitable and other drug companies had the know-how to produce it, no other firms challenged Merck's monopoly. That's because the U.S. government had given Merck the sole legal right to produce the drug in the United States. Propecia is an example of a monopoly protected by government-created barriers.

A **network externality** exists when the value of a good or service to an individual is greater when many other people use the same good or service.

The most important legally created monopolies today arise from *patents* and *copyrights.* A **patent** gives an inventor the sole right to make, use, or sell that invention for a period that in most countries lasts between 16 and 20 years. Patents are given to the creators of new products, such as drugs or mechanical devices. Similarly, a **copyright** gives the creator of a literary or artistic work the sole right to profit from that work, usually for a period equal to the creator's lifetime plus 70 years.

A **patent** gives an inventor a temporary monopoly in the use or sale of an invention.

A **copyright** gives the creator of a literary or artistic work the sole right to profit from that work.

The justification for patents and copyrights is a matter of incentives. If inventors were not protected by patents, they would gain little reward from their efforts: as soon as a valuable invention was made public, others would copy it and sell products based on it. And if inventors could not expect to profit from their inventions, then there would be no incentive to incur the costs of invention in the first place. The same is true for the creators of literary or artistic works. The law thus allows a monopoly to exist temporarily by granting property rights that encourage invention and creation.

Patents and copyrights are temporary because the law strikes a compromise. The higher price for the good that holds while the legal protection is in effect compensates inventors for the cost of invention; conversely, the lower price that results once the legal protection lapses benefits consumers.

Because the lifetime of the temporary monopoly cannot be tailored to specific cases, this system is imperfect and leads to some missed opportunities. In some cases, there can even be significant welfare issues. For example, the violation of U.S. drug patents by pharmaceutical companies in low-income countries has been a major source of controversy, pitting the needs of low-income patients who cannot afford to pay retail drug prices against the interests of the drug manufacturers who have incurred high research costs to discover these drugs.

To solve this problem, some U.S. drug companies and low-income countries have negotiated deals in which the patents are honored, but the U.S. companies sell their drugs at deeply discounted prices.

>> Quick Review

- In a **monopoly,** a single firm uses its market power to charge higher prices and produce less output than a competitive industry, generating profits in the short and long run.
- Profits will not persist in the long run unless there is a **barrier to entry** such as control of natural resources, increasing returns to scale, technological superiority, network externalities, or government-created barriers.
- A **natural monopoly** arises when average total cost is declining over the output range relevant for the industry. This creates a barrier to entry because an established monopolist has lower average total cost than an entrant.
- In certain technology and communications sectors of the economy, a **network externality** enables a firm with the largest number of customers to become a monopolist.
- **Patents** and **copyrights,** government-created barriers, are a source of temporary monopoly that attempt to balance the need for higher prices, as compensation to an inventor for the cost of invention, against the increase in consumer surplus from lower prices and greater efficiency.

Check Your Understanding 23-2

1. Currently, Texas Tea Oil Co. is the only local supplier of home heating oil in Frigid, Alaska. This winter residents were shocked that the price of a gallon of heating oil had doubled and believed that they were the victims of market power. Explain which of the following pieces of evidence support or contradict that conclusion.
   a. There is a national shortage of heating oil, and Texas Tea could procure only a limited amount.
   b. Last year, Texas Tea and several other competing local oil-supply firms merged into a single firm.
   c. The cost to Texas Tea of purchasing heating oil from refineries has gone up significantly.
   d. Recently, some nonlocal firms have begun to offer heating oil to Texas Tea's regular customers at a price much lower than Texas Tea's.
   e. Texas Tea has acquired an exclusive government license to draw oil from the only heating oil pipeline in the state.
2. Suppose the government is considering extending the length of a patent from 20 years to 30 years. How would this change each of the following?
   a. The incentive to invent new products
   b. The length of time during which consumers have to pay higher prices
3. Explain the nature of the network externality in each of the following cases.
   a. A new type of web-based payment system called PayMo
   b. A new type of car engine, which runs on solar cells
   c. A website for trading locally provided goods and services

Solutions appear at back of book.

23.4 Oligopoly

Many familiar goods and services are supplied by only a few competing sellers, which means the industries in question are oligopolies. For example, Google has a market share of 62.5% in the American search engine market, while

Bing/Microsoft and Yahoo/Verizon Media have a combined share of 36.6%. In the U.S. smartphone market, Apple and Samsung have market shares of 56% and 27%, respectively. In the American toothpaste market, Colgate-Palmolive accounts for 48% of the market, while Crest and Sensodyne account for 29% and 22%, respectively. Verizon, AT&T, and T-Mobile collectively account for about 88% of the American wireless telephone subscriptions, and most domestic airline routes are covered by only two to three carriers. The breakfast cereal industry, which we discussed earlier, is also an example of oligopoly. The list could go on for several more pages.

Colin Underhill/Alamy

Oligopolies supply familiar goods and services in a market with only a few competing sellers.

Defining Oligopoly

An industry with only a few firms is known as an **oligopoly;** a producer in such an industry is known as an **oligopolist.** Oligopolists compete with each other for sales. But oligopolists aren't like price-taking producers in a perfectly competitive industry. Because there are only a few firms in an oligopoly, oligopolists know that how much they produce will affect the market price. That is, like monopolists, oligopolists have some market power.

Economists refer to a situation in which firms compete but also possess market power—which enables them to affect market prices—as **imperfect competition.** There are two important forms of imperfect competition: oligopoly and *monopolistic competition*. Of these, oligopoly is probably the more important in practice.

It's important to realize that an oligopoly isn't necessarily made up of large firms. What matters isn't size per se; the question is how many competitors there are. When a small town has only two grocery stores, grocery service there is just as much an oligopoly as air shuttle service between New York and Washington, D.C.

Why are oligopolies so prevalent? Essentially, an oligopoly is the result of the same factors that sometimes produce a monopoly, but in somewhat weaker form. Probably the most important source of oligopolies is the existence of increasing returns to scale, which give bigger producers a cost advantage over smaller ones. When these effects are very strong, they lead to a monopoly; when they are not that strong, they lead to an industry with a small number of firms.

For example, larger grocery stores typically have lower costs than smaller stores. But the advantages of large scale taper off once grocery stores are reasonably large, which is why two or three stores often survive in small towns.

Oligopoly and the Potential for Collusion

In addition to its prevalence, another aspect of oligopoly makes it of special interest: the potential for *collusion* among the producers. Sellers engage in **collusion** when they cooperate to raise their joint profits rather than compete with one another. The potential for collusion arises because the small number of producers makes the profits of oligopolists *interdependent:* what one producer does significantly affects the profits earned by other producers in the industry. This gives oligopolists an incentive to try to cooperate. In contrast, in perfect competition, or in monopolistic competition (as we will discuss shortly), there are simply too many sellers to allow effective cooperation.

An **oligopoly** is an industry with only a small number of firms. A producer in such an industry is known as an **oligopolist.**

When no one firm has a monopoly, but producers nonetheless realize that they can affect market prices, an industry is characterized by **imperfect competition.**

Sellers engage in **collusion** when they cooperate to raise their joint profits.

Is It an Oligopoly or Not?

In practice, it is not always easy to determine an industry's market structure just by looking at the number of producers. Take the U.S. market for beer, for example: although there are hundreds of beer brewers, many of them are small niche

FIGURE 23-2 Market Share in U.S. Beer Market in 2018

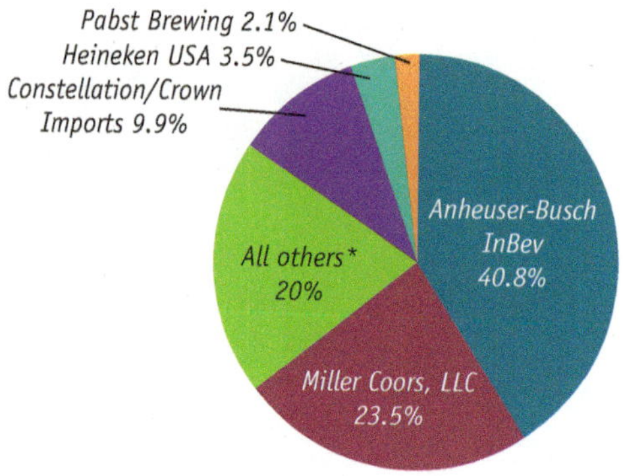

Data from: America's Beer Distributors.

producers (makers of craft beer), leaving the overall market dominated by two very large brewers. Anheuser-Busch InBev and MillerCoors account for 40.8% and 23.5%, respectively, of American beer sales. You can see the distribution of brewers in Figure 23-2.

Economists often use a measure called the **Herfindahl–Hirschman Index,** or HHI. The HHI for an industry is the square of each firm's market share summed over the firms in the industry. The HHI takes into account the distribution of market share among the top firms by squaring each firm's market share, thereby giving more weight to larger firms. For example, if an industry contains only three firms and their market shares are 60%, 25%, and 15%, then the HHI for the industry is:

$$\text{HHI} = 60^2 + 25^2 + 15^2 = 4{,}450$$

By squaring each market share, the HHI calculation produces numbers that are much larger when a larger share of an industry output is dominated by fewer firms. Thus, it's a better measure of just how concentrated the industry is. In Figure 23-2, we can see the HHI is 2,598 for the beer industry. It's a relatively highly concentrated industry and therefore much more likely that the producers in the industry behave like oligopolists.

>> Quick Review

- In addition to perfect competition and monopoly, oligopoly and monopolistic competition are important types of market structure. They are forms of **imperfect competition.**
- **Oligopoly** is a common market structure, one in which there are only a few firms, called **oligopolists,** in the industry. It arises from the same forces that lead to monopoly, except in weaker form.
- Unlike perfect competition or monopolistic competition, the small number of producers in oligopoly leads to interdependence between the producers and the potential for **collusion.**
- The **Herfindahl–Hirschman index,** the sum of the squares of the market shares of each firm in the industry, is a widely used measure of industry concentration.

Check Your Understanding 23-3

1. Explain why each of the following industries is an oligopoly, not a perfectly competitive industry.
   a. The world oil industry, where a few countries near the Persian Gulf control much of the world's oil reserves.
   b. The microprocessor industry, where two firms, Intel and its bitter rival AMD, dominate the technology.
   c. The wide-body passenger jet industry, composed of the American firm Boeing and the European firm Airbus, where production is characterized by extremely large fixed cost.

Solutions appear at back of book.

23.5 Monopolistic Competition

Leo owns the Wonderful Wok stand in the food court of a big shopping mall. He offers the only dim sum and fried rice there, but there are also more than a dozen alternatives, from Bodacious Burgers to Pizza Paradise. When deciding what to charge for a meal, Leo knows that he must take those alternatives into account: even people who normally prefer fried rice won't order a $15 lunch from Leo when they can get a burger, fries, and a drink for $6.

But Leo also knows that he won't lose all his business even if his lunches cost a bit more than the alternatives. Dim sum and fried rice aren't the same thing as burgers or pizza. Some people will really be in the mood for fried rice that day, and they will buy from Leo even if they could dine more cheaply on burgers. Of course, the reverse is also true: even if Chinese food is a bit cheaper, some people will choose burgers instead. In other words, Leo does have some market power: he has *some limited* ability to set his own price.

So how would you describe Leo's situation? He definitely isn't a price-taker, so he isn't in a situation of perfect competition. But you wouldn't exactly call him a

Herfindahl-Hirschman Index, or HHI, is the square of each firm's share of market sales summed over the industry. It gives a picture of the industry market structure.

monopolist, either. Although he's the only seller of Chinese food in that food court, he does face competition from other food vendors. And he's definitely not an oligopolist because there are far too many other food court vendors in the shopping mall to make collusion possible.

Monopolistic competition is a market structure in which there are many competing firms in an industry, each firm sells a differentiated product, and there is free entry into and exit from the industry in the long run.

Defining Monopolistic Competition

Economists describe Leo's situation as one of **monopolistic competition.** Monopolistic competition is particularly common in service industries like restaurants and gas stations, but it also exists in some manufacturing industries. It involves three necessary conditions: large numbers of competing producers, differentiated products, and free entry into and exit from the industry in the long run.

In a monopolistically competitive industry, each producer has some ability to set the price of their differentiated product. But exactly how high they can set it is limited by the competition they face from other existing and potential producers that produce close, but not identical, products.

1. **Large Numbers** In a monopolistically competitive industry, there are many firms. Such an industry does not look either like a monopoly, where the firm faces no competition, or like an oligopoly, where each firm has only a few rivals. Instead, each seller has many competitors. For example, there are many vendors in a big food court, many gas stations along a major highway, and many hotels at a popular beach resort.
2. **Differentiated Products** In a monopolistically competitive industry, each firm has a product that consumers view as somewhat distinct from the products of competing firms. Such product differentiation can come in the form of different styles or types, different locations, or different levels of quality. At the same time, though, consumers see these competing products as close substitutes. If Leo's food court contained 15 vendors selling exactly the same kind and quality of food, there would be perfect competition: any seller who tried to charge a higher price would have no customers. But suppose that Wonderful Wok is the only Chinese food vendor, Bodacious Burgers is the only hamburger stand, and so on. The result of this differentiation is that each vendor has some ability to set his or her own price: each firm has some—albeit limited—market power.
3. **Free Entry and Exit in the Long Run** In monopolistically competitive industries, new producers, with their own distinct products, can enter the industry freely in the long run. For example, other food vendors would open outlets in the food court if they thought it would be profitable to do so. In addition, firms will exit the industry if they find they are not covering their costs in the long run.

Monopolistic competition, then, differs from the three market structures we have examined so far. It's not the same as perfect competition: firms have some power to set prices. It's not pure monopoly: firms face some competition. And it's not the same as oligopoly: there are many firms and free entry, which eliminates the potential for collusion that is so important in oligopoly. As we'll see in a later section, competition among the sellers of differentiated products is the key to understanding how monopolistic competition works.

Lynne Sutherland/Alamy

You'll find monopolistic competition in any food court, where restaurants vie for your food dollar.

Now that we have introduced the idea of market structure and presented the four principal models of market structure, we can proceed to explain and predict firm behavior (e.g., price and quantity determination) and analyze individual markets.

ECONOMICS >> *in Action*

The Monopoly That Wasn't: China and the Market for Rare Earths

A quiver of panic shot through the U.S. high-technology and military sectors in 2010. Rare earths, a group of 17 elements that are critical in the manufacturing of high-tech products like smartphones and military jet components, had suddenly become much harder to obtain.

China controlled 85% to 95% of the global supply of rare earths and, until 2009, made them relatively abundant and cheap on world markets. However, in 2010, China adopted an export quota—a limit on the amount of rare earths that could be exported, severely restricting supply on the world market and leading to sharply higher prices. For example, the rare earth dysprosium went from $166 per kilo in 2010 to nearly $1,000 per kilo in 2011, a nearly fivefold increase.

But the panic proved to be temporary. China's dominance in rare earths was due to its low cost of production, and not to a monopoly position. In fact, only about a third of the world's rare earth reserves are found in China. Rare earths mines in Australia and the United States, which had been mothballed during the period of low prices, were reopened in response to the sharply higher prices. In addition, other sources emerged, such as the recovery of rare earths from discarded computer equipment.

This episode revealed to government and business leaders outside of China how vulnerable they were to disruptions in the supply of Chinese rare earths. As a result, they committed to keeping the alternative sources operating, even if prices should fall. And China's leaders learned that without control over the global sources of rare earths, what looked like a monopoly position, in fact, wasn't.

Check Your Understanding 23-4

1. Each of the following goods and services is a differentiated product. Which are differentiated as a result of monopolistic competition and which are not? Explain your answers.
   a. Ladders
   b. Soft drinks
   c. Department stores
   d. Steel

2. You must determine which of two types of market structure better describes an industry, but you are allowed to ask only one question about the industry. What question should you ask to determine if an industry is:
   a. Perfectly competitive or monopolistically competitive?
   b. A monopoly or monopolistically competitive?

Solutions appear at back of book.

>> *Quick Review*

- In **monopolistic competition,** there are many competing producers, each with a differentiated product, and free entry and exit in the long run.

Perfect Competition

MODULE
24

WHAT YOU WILL LEARN

- What is perfect competition, and why do economists consider it an important benchmark?
- What factors make a firm or an industry perfectly competitive?
- How does a **perfectly competitive industry** determine the profit-maximizing output level?
- What determines if a firm is profitable or unprofitable?

24.1 Production and Profits

Consider Noelle, who runs a Christmas tree farm. Suppose that the market price of Christmas trees is $72 per tree and that Noelle is a price-taker—she can sell as many as she wants at that price. Then we can use the data in Table 24-1 to find her profit-maximizing level of output by direct calculation.

The first column shows the quantity of output in number of trees, and the second column shows Noelle's total revenue from her output: the market value of trees she produced. Total revenue, *TR*, is equal to the market price multiplied by the quantity of output:

(24-1) $TR = P \times Q$

In this example, total revenue is equal to $72 per tree times the quantity of output in trees.

The third column of Table 24-1 shows Noelle's total cost. The fourth column shows her profit, equal to total revenue minus total cost:

(24-2) Profit $= TR - TC$

As indicated by the numbers in the table, profit is maximized at an output of 50 trees, where profit is equal to $720. But we can gain more insight into the profit-maximizing choice of output by viewing it as a problem of marginal analysis, a task we'll do next.

The Optimal Output Rule

Recall the *profit-maximizing principle of marginal analysis: the optimal amount of an activity is the level at which marginal benefit is equal to marginal cost.* To apply this principle, consider the effect on a producer's profit of increasing output by

Marginal revenue is the change in total revenue generated by an additional unit of output.

According to the **optimal output rule,** profit is maximized by producing the quantity of output at which the marginal revenue of the last unit produced is equal to its marginal cost.

TABLE 24-1 Profit for Noelle's Farm When Market Price Is $72

Quantity of trees *Q*	Total Revenue *TR*	Total cost *TC*	Profit *TR* – *TC*
0	$0	$560	–$560
10	720	1,200	–480
20	1,440	1,440	0
30	2,160	1,760	400
40	2,880	2,240	640
50	3,600	2,880	720
60	4,320	3,680	640
70	5,040	4,640	400

one unit. The marginal benefit of that unit is the additional revenue generated by selling it. This measure has a name—it is called the **marginal revenue** of that unit of output. The general formula for marginal revenue is:

(24-3) $$\text{Marginal revenue} = \begin{matrix}\text{Change in total revenue}\\ \text{generated by one}\\ \text{additional unit of output}\end{matrix} = \frac{\text{Change in total revenue}}{\text{Change in quantity of output}}$$

or

$$MR = \frac{\Delta TR}{\Delta Q}$$

In this equation, the Greek uppercase delta (the triangular symbol) represents the change in a variable.

So, Noelle maximizes her profit by producing trees up to the point at which the marginal revenue is equal to marginal cost. We can summarize this as the producer's **optimal output rule:** *profit is maximized by producing the quantity at which the marginal revenue of the last unit produced is equal to its marginal cost. That is, $MR = MC$ at the optimal quantity of output.*

We can learn how to apply the optimal output rule with the help of Table 24-2, which provides various short-run cost measures for Noelle's farm. The second column contains the farm's variable cost, and the third column shows its total cost of output based on the assumption that the farm incurs a fixed cost of $560. The fourth column shows marginal cost. Notice that, in this example, the marginal

TABLE 24-2 Short-Run Costs for Noelle's Farm

Quantity of trees *Q*	Variable cost *VC*	Total cost *TC*	Marginal cost of tree *MC* = Δ*TC*/Δ*Q*	Marginal revenue of tree *MR*	Net gain of tree = *MR* – *MC*
0	$0	$560			
			$64	$72	$8
10	640	1,200			
			24	72	48
20	880	1,440			
			32	72	40
30	1,200	1,760			
			48	72	24
40	1,680	2,240			
			64	72	8
50	2,320	2,880			
			80	72	–8
60	3,120	3,680			
			96	72	–24
70	4,080	4,640			

cost initially falls but then rises as output increases. This gives the marginal cost curve the "swoosh" shape described in Module 21. It will shortly become clear that this shape has important implications for short-run production decisions.

The fifth column contains the farm's marginal revenue, which has an important feature: Noelle's marginal revenue equal to price is constant at $72 for every output level. The sixth and final column shows the calculation of the net gain per tree, which is equal to marginal revenue minus marginal cost—or, equivalently in this case, market price minus marginal cost. As you can see, it is positive for the 1st through 50th trees; producing each of these trees raises Noelle's profit. For the 51st through 70th trees, however, net gain is negative: producing them would decrease, not increase, profit. So, to maximize profits, Noelle will produce up to the point at which the marginal revenue of the last unit produced is greater than or equal to the marginal cost of the last unit produced; any more reduces her profit. Hence, 50 trees is Noelle's profit-maximizing output.

The **marginal revenue curve** shows how marginal revenue varies as output varies.

The Optimal Output Rule for a Price-Taking Firm

Because Noelle receives $72 for every tree produced, we know that her farm is a price-taking firm. A price-taking firm cannot influence the market price by its actions. It always takes the market price as given because it cannot lower the market price by selling more or raise the market price by selling less. So, for a price-taking firm, the additional revenue generated by producing one more unit is always the market price.

Be sure to keep this fact in mind in future sections, where we will learn that marginal revenue is not equal to the market price if the industry is not perfectly competitive. As a result, firms are not price-takers when an industry is not perfectly competitive. For the remainder of this section, we will assume that the industry in question is like Christmas tree farming, perfectly competitive.

Figure 24-1 shows that Noelle's profit-maximizing quantity of output is, indeed, 50 trees. The figure shows the marginal cost curve, *MC*, drawn from the data in the fourth column of Table 24-2. As in Section 7, we plot the marginal cost of increasing output from 10 to 20 trees halfway between 10 and 20, and so on. The *MC* curve is smooth, allowing us to see how *MC* changes as one more tree is produced. The horizontal line at $72 is Noelle's **marginal revenue curve.**

FIGURE 24-1 The Price-Taking Firm's Profit-Maximizing Quantity of Output

At the profit-maximizing quantity of output, the market price is equal to marginal cost. It is located at the point at which the marginal cost curve crosses the marginal revenue curve, which is a horizontal line at the market price. Here, the profit-maximizing point is at an output of 50 trees, the output quantity at point *E*.

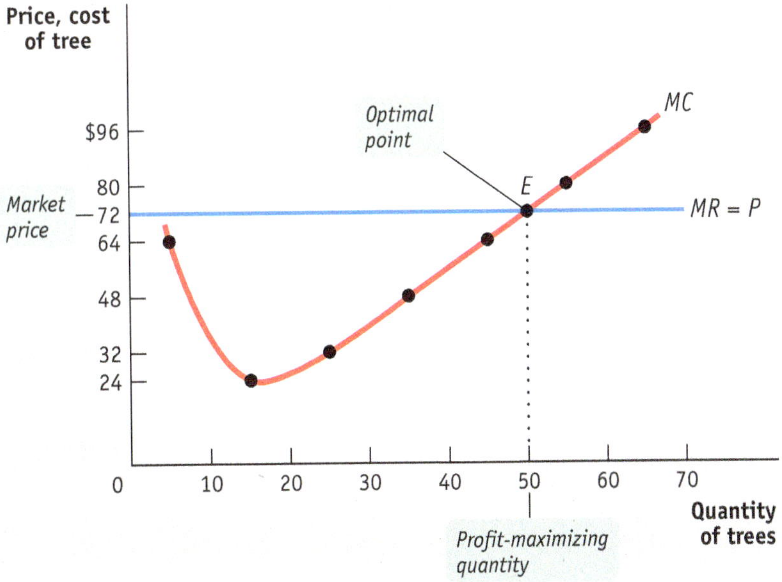

According to the **price-taking firm's optimal output rule,** a price-taking firm's profit is maximized by producing the quantity of output at which the market price is equal to the marginal cost of the last unit produced.

Note that whenever a firm is a price-taker, its marginal revenue curve is a horizontal line at the market price: it can sell as much as it likes at the market price. Regardless of whether the firm sells more or less, the market price is unaffected. In effect, the individual firm faces a horizontal, perfectly elastic demand curve for its output. The marginal cost curve crosses the marginal revenue curve at point E, where $MC = MR$. Sure enough, the quantity of output at E is 50 trees.

So we can refine the optimal output rule to apply to the case of a perfectly competitive firm. The **price-taking firm's optimal output rule** says that a price-taking firm's profit is maximized by producing the quantity of output up to the point at which the market price is equal to the marginal cost of the last unit produced. That is, $P = MC$ at the price-taking firm's optimal quantity of output. In fact, the price-taking firm's optimal output rule is just an application of the optimal output rule to the particular case of a price-taking firm. Why? Because in the case of a price-taking firm, marginal revenue is equal to the market price.

Does this mean that the price-taking firm's production decision can be entirely summed up as "produce up to the point where the marginal cost of production is equal to the price"? No, not quite. Before applying the profit-maximizing principle of marginal analysis to determine how much to produce, a potential producer must as a first step answer an "either–or" question: should it produce at all? If the answer to that question is yes, it then proceeds to the second step—a "how much" decision: maximizing profit by choosing the quantity of output at which marginal cost is equal to price.

To understand why the first step in the production decision involves an "either–or" question, we need to ask how we determine whether it is profitable or unprofitable to produce at all. That is, we need to determine whether the firm should produce or shut down.

Produce or Shut Down?

Recall from Section 6 that a firm's decision whether to stay in a given business depends on its *economic profit*—the measure of profit based on the opportunity cost of resources used in the business. To put it a slightly different way: in the calculation of economic profit, a firm's total cost incorporates the implicit cost—the benefits forgone in the next best use of the firm's resources—as well as the explicit cost in the form of actual cash outlays.

In contrast, *accounting profit* is profit calculated using only the explicit costs incurred by the firm. This means that economic profit incorporates the opportunity cost of resources owned by the firm and used in the production of output, while accounting profit does not.

A firm may make positive accounting profit while making zero or even negative economic profit. It's important to understand clearly that a firm's decision to produce or not, to stay in business or to close down permanently, should be based on economic profit, not accounting profit. We will assume, as we always do, that the cost numbers given in Tables 24-1 and 24-2 include all costs, implicit as well as explicit, and that the profit numbers in Table 24-1 are therefore economic profit.

So, what determines whether Noelle's farm earns a profit or generates a loss? The answer is that, *given the farm's cost curves, whether or not it is profitable depends on the market price of trees—specifically, whether the market price is more or less than the farm's minimum average total cost.*

In Table 24-3, we calculate short-run average variable cost and short-run average total cost for Noelle's farm. These are short-run values because we take fixed cost as given. (We'll turn to the effects of changing fixed cost shortly.) The short-run average total cost curve, ATC, is shown in Figure 24-2, along with the marginal cost curve, MC, from Figure 24-1. As you can see, average total cost is minimized at point C, corresponding to an output of 40 trees—the *minimum-cost output*—and an average total cost of $56 per tree.

TABLE 24-3 Short-Run Average Costs for Noelle's Farm

Quantity of trees *Q*	Variable cost *VC*	Total cost *TC*	Short-run average variable cost of tree *AVC* = *VC/Q*	Short-run average tost cost of tree *ATC* = *TC/Q*
10	$640.00	$1,200.00	$64.00	$120.00
20	880.00	1,440.00	44.00	72.00
30	1,200.00	1,760.00	40.00	58.67
40	1,680.00	2,240.00	42.00	56.00
50	2,320.00	2,880.00	46.40	57.60
60	3,120.00	3,680.00	52.00	61.33
70	4,080.00	4,640.00	58.29	66.29

To see how these curves can be used to decide whether production is profitable or unprofitable, recall that profit is equal to total revenue minus total cost, $TR - TC$. This means:

- If the firm produces a quantity at which $TR > TC$, the firm is profitable.
- If the firm produces a quantity at which $TR = TC$, the firm breaks even.
- If the firm produces a quantity at which $TR < TC$, the firm incurs a loss.

We can also express this idea in terms of revenue and cost per unit of output. If we divide profit by the number of units of output, Q, we obtain the following expression for profit per unit of output:

(24-4) $\text{Profit}/Q = TR/Q - TC/Q$

TR/Q is average revenue, which is the market price. TC/Q is average total cost. So, a firm is profitable if the market price for its product is more than the average

FIGURE 24-2 Costs and Production in the Short Run

This figure shows the marginal cost curve, *MC*, and the short-run average total cost curve, *ATC*. When the market price is $14, output will be 40 trees (the minimum-cost output), represented by point *C*. The price of $14, equal to the firm's minimum average total cost, is the firm's *break-even price.*

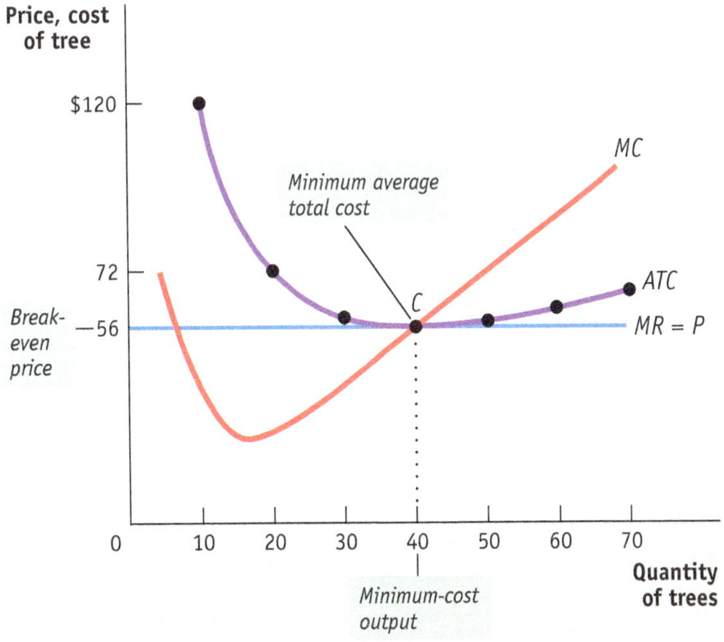

total cost of the quantity the firm produces; a firm loses money if the market price is less than average total cost of the quantity the firm produces. This means:

- If the firm produces a quantity at which $P > ATC$, the firm is profitable.
- If the firm produces a quantity at which $P = ATC$, the firm breaks even.
- If the firm produces a quantity at which $P < ATC$, the firm incurs a loss.

In summary, in the short run a firm will maximize profit by producing the quantity of output at which $MC = MR$. A perfectly competitive firm is a price-taker, so it can sell as many units of output as it would like at the market price. For a perfectly competitive firm then, it is always true that $MR = P$. The firm is profitable, or breaks even, as long as the market price is greater than, or equal to, average total cost.

In the next module, we develop the perfect competition model using graphs to analyze the firm's level of profit.

Check Your Understanding 24-1

1. Refer to the graph provided to answer the questions that follow.

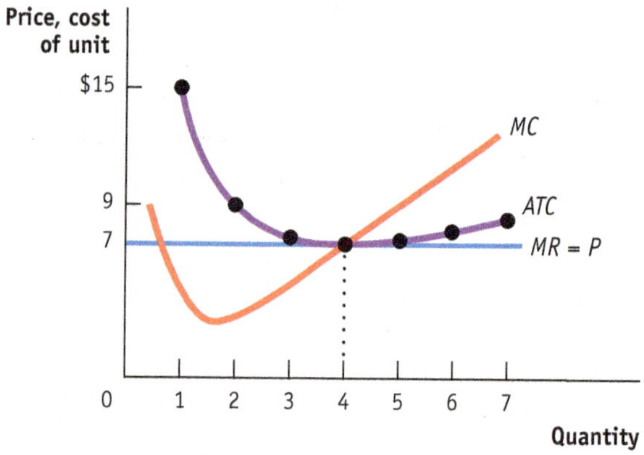

a. At what level of output does the firm maximize profit? Explain.
b. At the profit-maximizing quantity of output, is the firm profitable, does it break even, or does it earn a loss? Explain.

2. If a firm has a total cost of $500 at a quantity of 50 units, and it is at that quantity that average total cost is minimized for the firm, what is the lowest price that would allow the firm to break even? Explain.

Solutions appear at back of book.

>> Quick Review

- A producer chooses output according to the **optimal output rule.** For a price-taking firm, **marginal revenue** is equal to price and it chooses output according to the **price-taking firm's optimal output rule** $P = MC$.

Graphing Perfect Competition

MODULE 25

WHAT YOU WILL LEARN

- How do we use graphs to determine a perfectly competitive firm's production decision?
- What determines a perfect competitor's economic profit or loss?
- When should a perfectly competitive firm shut down in the short run?

In the previous module, we learned about the firm's optimal output rule. We also learned how to compare market price and average total cost to determine whether or not a competitive firm is profitable. Now we can evaluate the profitability of perfectly competitive firms in a variety of situations.

Duncan Selby/Alamy

25.1 Graphing Perfect Competition

Figure 25-1 illustrates this result, showing how the market price determines whether a firm is profitable. It also shows how profits are depicted graphically. Each panel shows the marginal cost curve, *MC*, and the short-run average total cost curve, *ATC*. Average total cost is minimized at point *C*. Panel (a) shows the case we have already analyzed, in which the market price of trees is \$72 per tree. Panel (b) shows the case in which the market price of trees is lower, \$10 per tree.

In panel (a), we see that at a price of \$72 per tree the profit-maximizing quantity of output is 50 trees, indicated by point *E*, where the marginal cost curve, *MC*, intersects the marginal revenue curve—which for a price-taking firm is a horizontal line at the market price. At that quantity of output, average total cost is \$57.60 per tree, indicated by point *Z*. Since the price per tree exceeds average total cost per tree, Noelle's farm is profitable.

Noelle's total profit when the market price is \$72 is represented by the area of the shaded rectangle in panel (a). To see why, notice that total profit can be expressed in terms of profit per unit:

(25-1) $\text{Profit} = TR - TC = (TR/Q - TC/Q) \times Q$

or, equivalently,

$$\text{Profit} = (P - ATC) \times Q$$

FIGURE 25-1 Profitability and the Market Price

In panel (a), the market price is \$72. The farm is profitable because price exceeds minimum average total cost, the break-even price, \$56. The farm's optimal output choice is indicated by point *E*, corresponding to an output of 50 trees. The average total cost of producing 50 trees is indicated by point *Z* on the *ATC* curve, corresponding to an amount of \$57.60. The vertical distance between *E* and *Z* corresponds to the farm's per-unit profit, \$72.00 – \$57.60 = \$14.40. Total profit is given by the area of the shaded rectangle, 50 × \$14.40 = \$720.00. In panel (b), the market price is \$40; the farm is unprofitable because the price falls below the minimum average total cost, \$56. The farm's optimal output choice when producing is indicated by point *A*, corresponding to an output of 30 trees. The farm's per-unit loss, \$58.67 – \$40.00 = \$18.67, is represented by the vertical distance between *A* and *Y*. The farm's total loss is represented by the shaded rectangle, 30 × \$18.67 = \$560.00 (adjusted for rounding error).

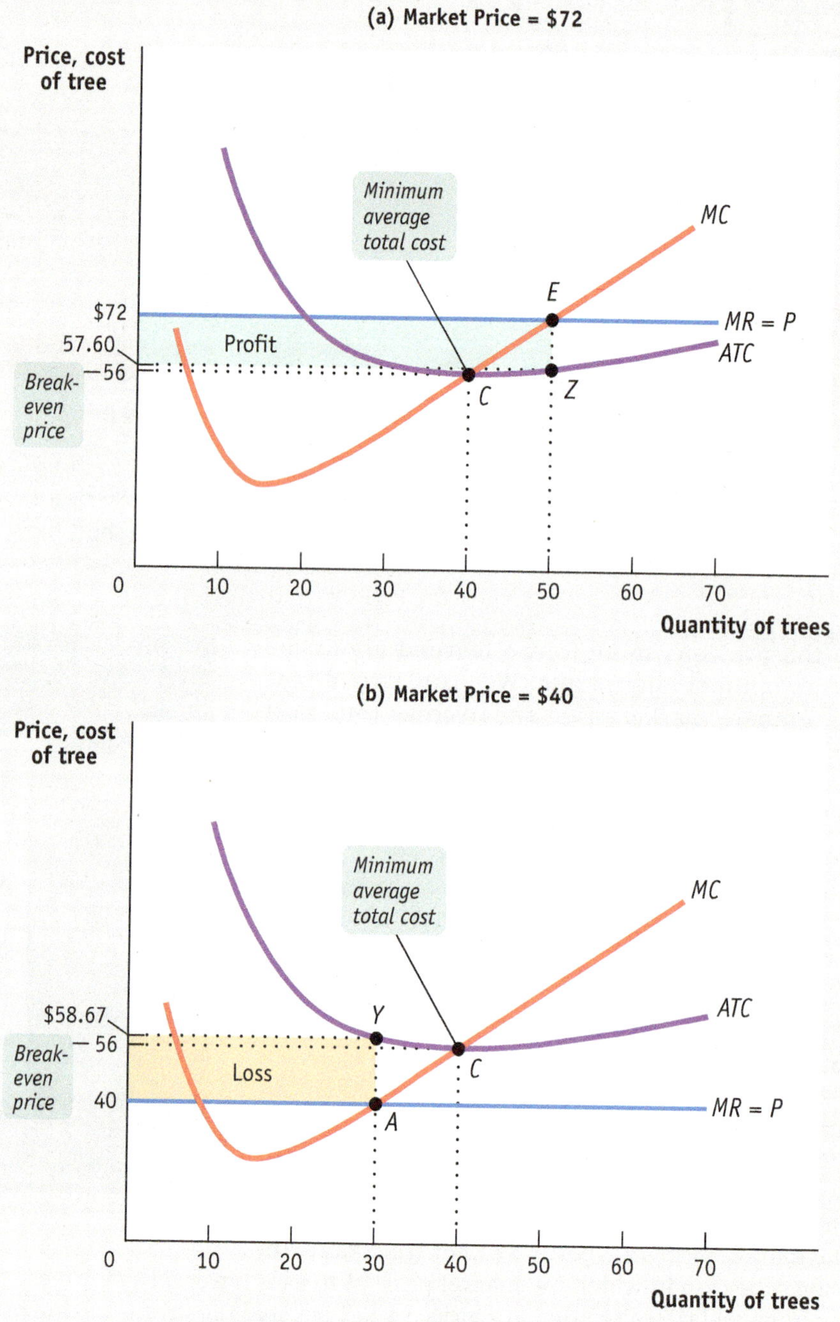

since *P* is equal to *TR*/*Q* and *ATC* is equal to *TC*/*Q*. The height of the shaded rectangle in panel (a) corresponds to the vertical distance between points *E* and *Z*. It is equal to *P* – *ATC* = \$72 – \$57.60 = \$14.40 per tree. The shaded rectangle has a width equal to the output: *Q* = 50 trees. The area of that rectangle is thus equal to Noelle's profit: 50 trees × \$14.40 profit per tree = \$720.00.

What about the situation illustrated in panel (b)? Here the market price of trees is \$40 per tree. Setting price equal to marginal cost leads to a profit-maximizing output of 30 trees, indicated by point *A*. At this output, Noelle has an average total cost of \$58.67 per tree, indicated by point *Y*. At the profit-maximizing output quantity—30 trees—average total cost exceeds the market price. This means that Noelle's farm generates a loss, not a profit.

How much does she lose by producing when the market price is \$40? On each tree she loses $ATC - P$ = \$58.67 – \$40.00 = \$18.67, an amount corresponding to the vertical distance between points *A* and *Y*. And she would produce 30 trees, which corresponds to the width of the shaded rectangle. So, the total value of the losses is \$18.67 × 30 = \$560.00 (adjusted for rounding error), an amount that corresponds to the area of the shaded rectangle in panel (b).

But how does a producer know, in general, whether or not its business will be profitable? It turns out that the crucial test lies in a comparison of the market price to the producer's *minimum average total cost*. On Noelle's farm, minimum average total cost, which is equal to \$56, occurs at an output quantity of 40 trees, indicated by point *C*.

Whenever the market price exceeds minimum average total cost, the producer can find some output level for which the average total cost is less than the market price. In other words, the producer can find a level of output at which the firm makes a profit. Thus, Noelle's farm will be profitable whenever the market price exceeds \$56. And she will achieve the highest possible profit by producing the quantity at which marginal cost equals the market price.

Conversely, if the market price is less than minimum average total cost, there is no output level at which price exceeds average total cost. As a result, the firm will be unprofitable at any quantity of output. As we saw, at a price of \$40—an amount less than minimum average total cost—Noelle did indeed lose money. By producing the quantity at which marginal cost equals the market price, Noelle did the best she could, but the best that she could do was a loss of \$560. Any other quantity would have increased the size of her loss.

The minimum average total cost of a price-taking firm is called its **break-even price,** the price at which it earns zero profit. (Recall that's *economic profit*.) A firm will earn positive profit when the market price is above the break-even price, and it will suffer losses when the market price is below the break-even price. Noelle's break-even price of \$56 is the price at point *C* in Figures 24-2 and 25-1.

The **profit determination rule** allows us to determine whether a producer is profitable by comparing the market price of the good to the producer's break-even price—its minimum average total cost:

- Whenever the market price exceeds minimum average total cost, the producer is profitable.
- Whenever the market price equals minimum average total cost, the producer breaks even.
- Whenever the market price is less than minimum average total cost, the producer is unprofitable.

The Short-Run Production Decision

You might be tempted to say that if a firm is unprofitable because the market price is below its minimum average total cost, it shouldn't produce any output. In the short run, however, this conclusion isn't the right one.

In the short run, sometimes the firm should produce even if price falls below minimum average total cost. The reason is that total cost includes *fixed cost*—cost that does not depend on the amount of output produced and can only be altered in the long run.

In the short run, fixed cost must still be paid, regardless of whether or not a firm produces. For example, if Noelle rents a refrigerated truck for the year, she has to pay the rent on the truck regardless of whether she produces any trees. *Since it cannot be changed in the short run, her fixed cost is irrelevant to her decision about whether to produce or shut down in the short run.*

The **break-even price** of a price-taking firm is the market price at which it earns zero profit.

According to the **profit determination rule,** whether a producer is profitable depends on a comparison of the market price of the good to the producer's break-even price—its minimum average total cost.

FIGURE 25-2 The Short-Run Individual Supply Curve

When the market price equals or exceeds Noelle's *shut-down price* of $40, the minimum average variable cost indicated by point *A*, she will produce the output quantity at which marginal cost is equal to price. So at any price equal to or above the minimum average *variable* cost, the short-run individual supply curve is the firm's marginal cost curve; this corresponds to the upward-sloping segment of the individual supply curve. When market price falls below minimum average variable cost, the firm ceases operation in the short run. This corresponds to the vertical segment of the individual supply curve along the vertical axis.

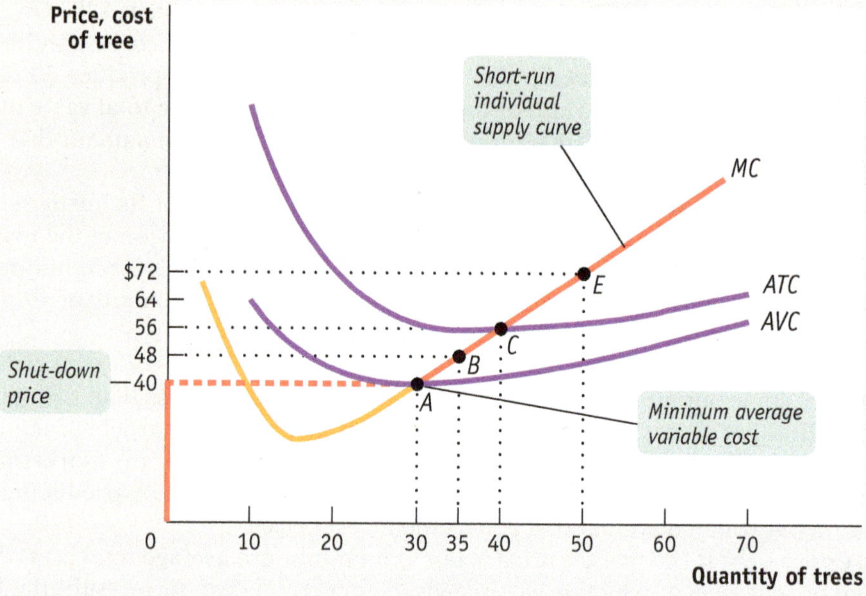

Although fixed cost should play no role in the decision about whether to produce in the short run, other costs—variable costs—do matter. An example of variable costs is the wages of workers who must be hired to help with planting and harvesting. Since variable costs can be saved by *not* producing, they should play a role in determining whether or not to produce in the short run.

Let's turn to Figure 25-2, which shows both the short-run average total cost curve, *ATC*, and the short-run average variable cost curve, *AVC*, drawn from the information in Table 24-3. Recall that the difference between the two curves—the vertical distance between them—represents average fixed cost, the fixed cost per unit of output, *FC/Q*.

Because the marginal cost curve has a "swoosh" shape—falling at first before rising—the short-run average variable cost curve is U-shaped: the initial fall in marginal cost causes average variable cost to fall as well, before rising marginal cost eventually pulls it up again. The short-run average variable cost curve reaches its minimum value of $40 at point *A*, at an output of 30 trees.

We are now prepared to fully analyze the optimal production decision in the short run. We need to consider two cases:

Case 1: When the market price is below minimum average *variable* cost

Case 2: When the market price is greater than or equal to minimum average *variable* cost

A firm will cease production in the short run if the market price falls below the **shut-down price,** which is equal to minimum average variable cost.

According to the **shut-down rule,** the firm should cease production when price falls below the shut-down price, equal to the minimum average variable cost.

Case 1: The Shut-Down Decision

When the market price is below minimum average variable cost, the price the firm receives per unit is not covering its variable cost per unit. A firm in this situation should cease production immediately. Why? Because there is no level of output at which the firm's total revenue covers its variable costs—the costs it can avoid by not operating.

In this case, the firm maximizes its profits by not producing at all—by, in effect, minimizing its losses. It will still incur a fixed cost in the short run, but it will no longer incur any variable cost. This means that the minimum average variable cost is equal to the **shut-down price,** the price at which the firm ceases production in the short run. This gives us the firm's **shut-down rule:** when price falls below the shut-down price—minimum average variable cost—the firm should cease production. In the example of Noelle's tree farm, the shut-down rule says that she will cease production in the short run by laying off workers and halting all planting and harvesting of trees.

Case 2: The Short-Run Decision to Produce When price is greater than minimum average variable cost, however, the firm should produce in the short run. In this case, the firm maximizes profit—or minimizes loss—by choosing the output quantity at which its marginal cost is equal to the market price. For example, if the market price of each tree is $72, Noelle should produce at point *E* in Figure 25-2, corresponding to an output of 50 trees. Note that point *C* in Figure 25-2 corresponds to the farm's break-even price of $56 per tree. Since *E* lies above *C*, Noelle's farm will be profitable; she will generate a per-tree profit of $72 – $57.60 = $14.40 when the market price is $72.

But what if the market price lies between the shut-down price and the break-even price—that is, between minimum average *variable* cost and minimum average *total* cost? In the case of Noelle's farm, this corresponds to prices anywhere between $40 and $56—say, a market price of $48. At $48, Noelle's farm is not profitable; since the market price is below minimum average total cost, the farm is losing the difference between price and average total cost per unit produced.

Yet even if it isn't covering its total cost per unit, it is covering its variable cost per unit and some—but not all—of the fixed cost per unit. If a firm in this situation shuts down, it would incur no variable cost but would still incur the *full* fixed cost. As a result, shutting down generates an even greater loss than continuing to operate.

This means that whenever price lies between minimum average total cost and minimum average variable cost, the firm is better off producing some output in the short run. The reason is that by producing, it can cover its variable cost per unit and at least some of its fixed cost, even though it is incurring a loss. We call this decision the **interim production decision rule.** In this case, the firm maximizes profit—that is, minimizes loss—by choosing the quantity of output at which its marginal cost is equal to the market price. So, if Noelle faces a market price of $48 per tree, her profit-maximizing output is given by point *B* in Figure 25-2, corresponding to an output of 35 trees.

It's worth noting that the decision to produce when the firm is covering its variable costs but not all of its fixed cost is similar to the decision to ignore *sunk costs*. You may recall from Section 6 that a sunk cost is a cost that has already been incurred and cannot be recouped, and because it cannot be changed, it should have no effect on any current decision.

In the short-run production decision, fixed cost is, in effect, like a sunk cost—it has been spent, and it can't be recovered in the short run. This comparison also illustrates why variable cost does indeed matter in the short run: it can be avoided by not producing.

And what happens if market price is exactly equal to the shut-down price, minimum average variable cost? In this instance, the firm is indifferent between producing 30 units or 0 units. As we'll see shortly, this is an important point when looking at the behavior of an industry as a whole. For the sake of clarity, we'll assume that the firm, although indifferent, does indeed produce output when price is equal to the shut-down price.

Putting everything together, we can now draw the **short-run individual supply curve** of Noelle's farm, the red line in Figure 25-2; it shows how the profit-maximizing quantity of output in the short run depends on the price. As you can see, the curve is in two segments. The upward-sloping red segment starting at point *A* shows the short-run profit-maximizing output when market price is equal to or above the shut-down price of $40 per tree.

As long as the market price is equal to or above the shut-down price, Noelle produces the quantity of output at which marginal cost is equal to the market price. That is, at market prices equal to or above the shut-down price, the firm's short-run supply curve corresponds to its marginal cost curve. But at any market price below minimum average variable cost—in this case, $40 per tree—the firm shuts down and output drops to zero in the short run. This corresponds to the vertical segment of the curve that lies on top of the vertical axis.

According to the **interim production decision rule,** when price lies between minimum average total cost (break-even price) and minimum average variable cost (shut-down price), the firm produces in the short run to minimize loss.

The **short-run individual supply curve** shows how an individual producer's profit-maximizing output quantity depends on the market price, taking fixed cost as given.

Do firms really shut down temporarily without going out of business? Yes. In fact, in some businesses, temporary shut-downs are routine. The most common examples are industries in which demand is highly seasonal, like outdoor amusement parks in climates with cold winters. Such parks would have to offer very low prices to entice customers during the colder months—prices so low that the owners would not cover their variable costs (principally wages and electricity). The wiser choice economically is to shut down until warm weather brings enough customers who are willing to pay a higher price.

The Long Run: Changing Fixed Cost, Entry and Exit

Although fixed cost cannot be altered in the short run, in the long run, firms can acquire or get rid of machines, buildings, and so on. In the long run, the level of fixed cost is a matter of choice. A firm will choose the level of fixed cost that minimizes the average total cost for its desired output quantity. Now we will focus on an even bigger question facing a firm when choosing its fixed cost: whether to incur *any* fixed cost at all by remaining in its current business.

istockphoto/Thinkstock

Buying or selling equipment allows a firm to change its fixed cost.

In the long run, a producer can always eliminate fixed cost by selling off its plant and equipment. If it does so, it can't produce: it has exited the industry. In contrast, a potential producer can take on some fixed cost by acquiring machines and other resources, which enables it to produce: it can enter the industry.

This means that in a perfectly competitive industry, *the number of producers is fixed in the short run.* In contrast, *because fixed cost can be changed in the long run, exit and entry can occur and the number of producers can change.*

Consider Noelle's farm once again. To simplify our analysis, we will sidestep the problem of choosing among several possible levels of fixed cost. Instead, we will assume from now on that Noelle has only one possible choice of fixed cost if she operates, the amount of $560. Alternatively, she can choose a fixed cost of zero if she exits the industry. It is changes in fixed cost that cause short-run average total cost curves to differ from long-run average total cost curves. With this assumption, Noelle's short-run and long-run average total cost curves are one and the same.

Suppose that the market price of trees is consistently less than $56 over an extended period of time. In that case, Noelle never fully covers her fixed cost: her business runs at a persistent loss. In the long run, then, she can do better by closing her business and leaving the industry. In other words, *in the long run,* firms will exit an industry if the market price is consistently less than their break-even price—their minimum average total cost.

Conversely, suppose that the price of Christmas trees is consistently above the break-even price,$56, for an extended period of time. Because her farm is profitable, Noelle will remain in the industry and continue producing.

But things won't stop there. The perfectly competitive Christmas tree industry meets the criterion of *free entry:* there are many potential tree producers because the necessary inputs are easy to obtain. And the cost curves of those potential producers are likely to be similar to Noelle's, since the technology used by other producers is likely to be very similar to what Noelle uses. If the price is high enough to generate profits for existing producers, it will also attract some of these potential producers into the industry. *In the long run*, then, a price in excess of $56 should lead to entry: new producers will come into the Christmas tree industry.

As we will see in the next module, exit and entry lead to an important distinction between the *short-run industry supply curve* and the *long-run industry supply curve.*

Summing Up: The Perfectly Competitive Firm's Profitability and Production Conditions

In this module, we've studied where the supply curve for a perfectly competitive, price-taking firm comes from. Every perfectly competitive firm makes its production decisions by maximizing profit, and these decisions determine the supply curve. Table 25-1 summarizes the perfectly competitive firm's profitability and production conditions. It also relates them to entry into and exit from the industry.

TABLE 25-1 Summary of the Perfectly Competitive Firm's Profitability and Production Conditions

Profitability condition (minimum *ATC* = break-even price)	Result
$P >$ minimum *ATC*	Firm profitable. Entry into industry in the long run.
$P =$ minimum *ATC*	Firm breaks even. No entry into or exit from industry in the long run.
$P <$ minimum *ATC*	Firm unprofitable. Exit from industry in the long run.
Production condition (minimum *AVC* = shut-down price)	**Result**
$P >$ minimum *AVC*	If $P <$ minimum *ATC*, the interim production decision rule applies: firm produces in the short run.
	If $P >$ minimum *ATC*, firm covers all variable cost and fixed cost. It is profitable. Entry into industry in the long run.
$P =$ minimum *AVC*	Firm indifferent between producing in the short run or not. Just covers variable cost.
$P <$ minimum *AVC*	Firm does not cover variable cost. The shut-down rule applies. Firm will shut down in the short run.

ECONOMICS >> *in Action*

Farmers Know How

If there is one profession that requires a firm understanding of profit maximization, it's farming. Farmers must respond to constantly fluctuating prices for their output, as well as constantly changing input prices. Furthermore, the farming industry satisfies the condition of a competitive market because it is composed of thousands of individual price-taking farmers.

For a good illustration of farmers' economic acumen, we can examine American crop prices over the past two decades, a period marked by boom and then retrenchment. From 2003 to 2013, prices for corn and soybeans rose to all-time highs, increasing by 300% and 250%, respectively.

This impressive rise in prices from 2003 to 2013 was mainly due to two demand-based factors. First, corn prices benefited from a congressional mandate to increase the use of corn-based ethanol, a biofuel that is blended into gasoline, as a means of reducing American dependency on imported oil. Second, crop prices were pushed upward by rapidly rising exports to China and other developing countries.

Being smart profit-maximizers, farmers responded by farming their land more intensively—using more fertilizer, for example—and by increasing their acreage. By 2013, fertilizer prices had doubled compared to 2005. And over the decade

R. Hamilton Smith/Getty Images

Farmers show their economic acumen by moving up and down their supply curves as crop prices change.

from 2003 to 2013, the average price of farmland tripled, with some farmland selling for 10 times its 2003 price.

Each of these strategies made complete economic sense, as each farmer moved up their individual supply curve. And because the individual supply curve is the marginal cost curve, each farmer's costs also went up as more inputs were employed to produce more output.

However, things changed dramatically in 2014, when farmland prices plunged nearly 9%. By 2019, prices were down 23% on an inflation-adjusted basis from their 2013 peak. Various factors contributed to this fall. On the demand side, the boom in shale oil production, a substitute for ethanol, pushed down the price of ethanol, while a strong U.S. dollar reduced the demand by foreign buyers for American crops. More recently, retaliation by the Chinese government against U.S. tariffs imposed in 2018 and 2019 significantly reduced demand for American agricultural products. On the supply side, bumper harvests also sharply depressed crop prices.

Thinking like economists, farmers responded by moving back down their supply curve, withdrawing from production the most expensive land to cultivate, and reducing their demand for additional acreage. As a result, the average price of farmland has trended downward. And, unsurprisingly, from 2012 to 2019, the price of fertilizer fell significantly, nearly 50%, from its highs. So if you want to see profit maximization in action, watch a farmer.

>> Quick Review

- A producer chooses output according to the **optimal output rule.** For a price-taking firm, **marginal revenue** is equal to price and it chooses output according to the **price-taking firm's optimal output rule** $P = MC$.
- According to the **profit determination rule,** profitability is determined by comparing price to the firm's **break-even price,** equal to the minimum average total cost. When price is above it, the firm is profitable; when price falls below, the firm is unprofitable; it breaks even when price is equal to the break-even price.
- Fixed cost is irrelevant to the firm's optimal short-run production decision. When price exceeds its **shut-down price,** which is equal to minimum average variable cost, the price-taking firm produces the quantity of output at which marginal cost equals price. When price falls below the shut-down price, the **shut-down rule** applies and the firm should cease production.
- When price lies between minimum average total cost (break-even price) and minimum average variable cost (shut-down price), the **interim production decision rule** applies: the firm produces in the short run to minimize loss. This defines the firm's **short-run individual supply curve.**
- In the long run, fixed cost can be changed. If price consistently falls below minimum average total cost, a firm will set its fixed cost equal to zero and exit the industry. If price exceeds minimum average total cost, the firm is profitable and will remain in the industry; other firms will enter the industry in the long run.

Check Your Understanding 25-1

1. Draw a short-run diagram showing a U-shaped average total cost curve, a U-shaped average variable cost curve, and a "swoosh"-shaped marginal cost curve. On it, indicate the range of output and the range of price for which the following actions are optimal.
   a. The firm shuts down immediately.
   b. The firm operates in the short run despite sustaining a loss.
   c. The firm operates while making a profit.
2. Maine has a very active lobster industry, which harvests lobsters during the summer months. The rest of the year lobsters can be obtained from other parts of the world, but at a much higher price. Maine is also full of "lobster shacks," roadside restaurants serving lobster dishes that are open only during the summer. Explain why it is optimal for lobster shacks to operate only in the summer.

Solutions appear at back of book

Long-Run Outcomes in Perfect Competition

MODULE 26

WHAT YOU WILL LEARN

- Why does it make sense for a firm to behave differently in the short run versus the long run?
- How does the **short-run industry supply curve** differ from the **long-run industry supply curve?**

In this module, we examine the long run in a perfectly competitive market. We will see that perfect competition leads to a desirable market outcome. In upcoming sections, we will contrast it with the outcomes in the three alternative market structures: monopoly, oligopoly, and monopolistic competition.

RyanJLane/Getty Images

26.1 The Perfectly Competitive Industry Supply Curve

Why will an increase in the demand for Christmas trees lead to a large price increase at first but a much smaller increase in the long run? The answer lies in the behavior of the **industry supply curve**—the relationship between the price and the total output of an industry as a whole. The industry supply curve is what we referred to in earlier sections as the supply curve or the market supply curve. But here we take some extra care to distinguish between the individual supply curve of a single firm and the supply curve of the industry as a whole.

As you might guess from the previous module, the industry supply curve must be analyzed in somewhat different ways for the short run and the long run. Let's start with the short run.

The Short-Run Industry Supply Curve

Recall that in the short run, the number of producers in an industry is fixed—there is no entry or exit. And you may also remember from Module 6 that the market supply curve is the horizontal sum of the individual supply curves of all producers—you find it by summing the total output across all suppliers at every given price. We will do that exercise here under the assumption that all the producers are

The **industry supply curve** shows the relationship between the price of a good and the total output of the industry as a whole.

FIGURE 26-1 The Short-Run Market Equilibrium

The short-run industry supply curve, *S*, is the industry supply curve taking the number of producers—here, 100—as given. It is generated by adding together the individual supply curves of the 100 producers. Below the shut-down price of $40, no producer wants to produce in the short run. Above $40, the short-run industry supply curve slopes upward, as each producer increases output as price increases. It intersects the demand curve, *D*, at point E_{MKT}, the point of short-run market equilibrium, corresponding to a market price of $72 and a quantity of 5,000 trees.

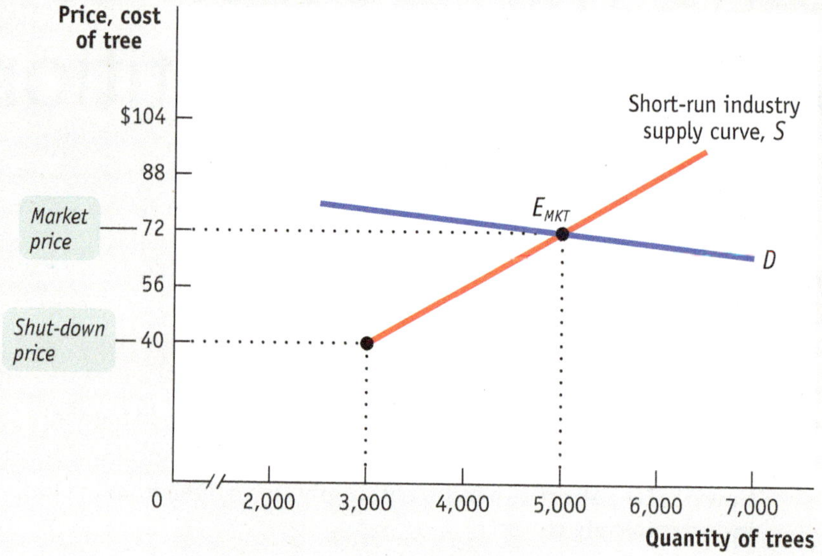

alike—an assumption that makes the derivation particularly simple. Let's assume there are 100 Christmas tree farms, each with the same costs as Noelle's farm.

Each of these 100 farms will have an individual short-run supply curve like the one in Figure 25-2 from the previous module. At a price below $40, no farms will produce. At a price of $40 or more, each farm will produce the quantity of output at which its marginal cost is equal to the market price. As you can see from Figure 25-2, this will lead each farm to produce 40 trees if the price is $56 per tree, 50 trees if the price is $72, and so on. If there are 100 tree farms and the price of Christmas trees is $72 per tree, the industry as a whole will produce 5,000 trees, corresponding to 100 farms × 50 trees per farm, and so on. The result is the **short-run industry supply curve,** shown as *S* in Figure 26-1. This curve shows the quantity that producers will supply at each price, *taking the number of producers as given.*

The demand curve *D* in Figure 26-1 crosses the short-run industry supply curve at E_{MKT}, corresponding to a price of $72 and a quantity of 5,000 trees. Point Z_{MKT} is a **short-run market equilibrium:** the quantity supplied equals the quantity demanded, taking the number of producers as given. But the long run may look quite different, because in the long run farms may enter or exit the industry.

The **short-run industry supply curve** shows how the quantity supplied by an industry depends on the market price, given a fixed number of producers.

There is a **short-run market equilibrium** when the quantity supplied equals the quantity demanded, taking the number of producers as given.

The Long-Run Market Equilibrium

Suppose that in addition to the 100 farms currently in the Christmas tree business, there are many other potential producers. Suppose also that each of these potential producers would have the same cost curves as existing producers like Noelle if it entered the industry.

When will additional producers enter the industry? Whenever existing producers are making a profit—that is, whenever the market price is above the break-even price of $56 per tree, the minimum average total cost of production. For example, at a price of $72 per tree, new firms will enter the industry.

What will happen as additional producers enter the industry? Clearly, the quantity supplied at any given price will increase. The short-run industry supply curve will shift to the right. This will, in turn, alter the market equilibrium and result in a lower market price. Existing firms will respond to the lower market price by reducing their output, but the total industry output will increase because of the larger number of firms in the industry.

FIGURE 26-2 The Long-Run Market Equilibrium

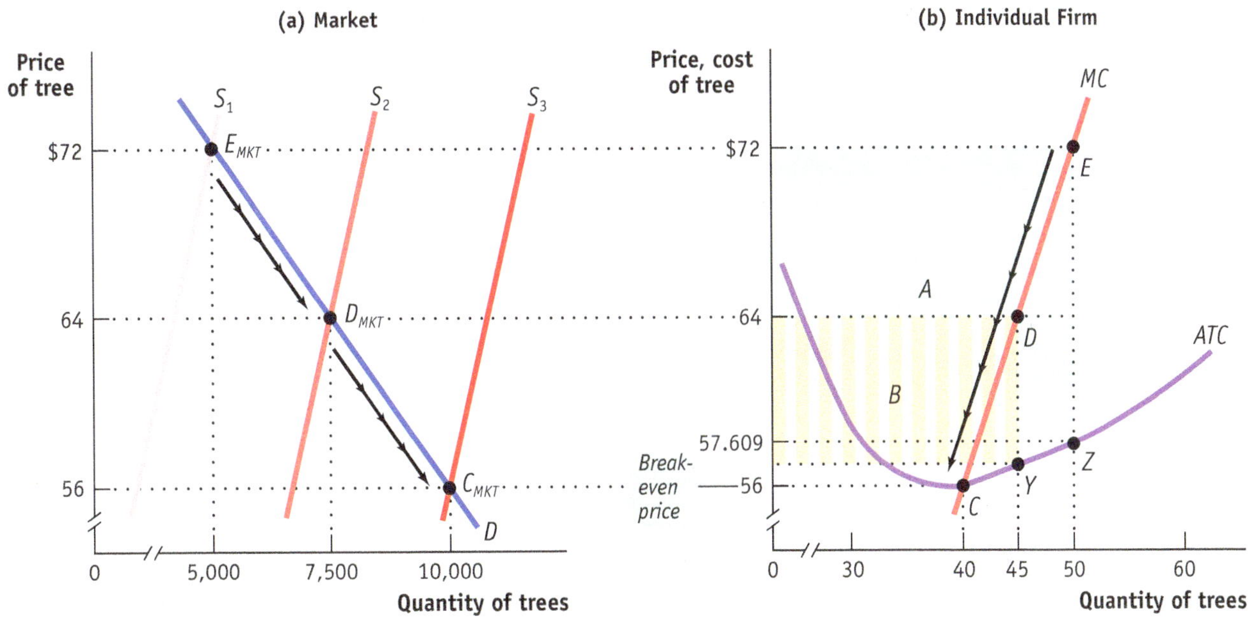

Point E_{MKT} of panel (a) shows the initial short-run market equilibrium. Each of the 100 existing producers makes an economic profit, illustrated in panel (b) by the green rectangle labeled *A*, the profit of an existing firm. Profits induce entry by additional producers, shifting the short-run industry supply curve outward from S_1 to S_2 in panel (a), resulting in a new short-run equilibrium at point D_{MKT}, at a lower market price of $64 and higher industry output. Existing firms reduce output and profit falls to the area given by the striped rectangle labeled *B* in panel (b). Entry continues to shift out the short-run industry supply curve, as price falls and industry output increases yet again. Entry of new firms ceases at point C_{MKT} on supply curve S_3 in panel (a). Here market price is equal to the break-even price; existing producers make zero economic profits, and there is no incentive for entry or exit. So C_{MKT} is also a long-run market equilibrium.

Figure 26-2 illustrates the effects of this chain of events on an existing firm and on the market; panel (a) shows how the market responds to entry, and panel (b) shows how an individual existing firm responds to entry. (Note that these two graphs have been rescaled in comparison to Figures 25-2 and 26-1 to better illustrate how profit changes in response to price.) In panel (a), S_1 is the initial short-run industry supply curve, based on the existence of 100 producers. The initial short-run market equilibrium is at E_{MKT}, with an equilibrium market price of $72 and a quantity of 5,000 trees. At this price, existing producers are profitable, which is reflected in panel (b): an existing firm makes a total profit represented by the green-shaded rectangle labeled *A* when market price is $72.

These profits will induce new producers to enter the industry, shifting the short-run industry supply curve to the right. For example, the short-run industry supply curve when the number of producers has increased to 167 is S_2. Corresponding to this supply curve is a new short-run market equilibrium labeled D_{MKT}, with a market price of $64 and a quantity of 7,500 trees. At $64, each firm produces 45 trees, so that industry output is $167 \times 45 = 7{,}500$ trees (rounded).

From panel (b), you can see the effect of the entry of 67 new producers on an existing firm: the fall in price causes it to reduce its output, and its profit falls to the area represented by the striped rectangle labeled *B*.

Although diminished, the profit of existing firms at D_{MKT} means that entry will continue and the number of firms will continue to rise. If the number of producers rises to 250, the short-run industry supply curve shifts out again to S_3, and the market equilibrium is at C_{MKT}, with a quantity supplied and demanded of 10,000 trees and a market price of $56 per tree.

A market is in **long-run market equilibrium** when the quantity supplied equals the quantity demanded, given that sufficient time has elapsed for entry into and exit from the industry to occur.

Like E_{MKT} and D_{MKT}, C_{MKT} is a short-run equilibrium. But it is also something more. Because the price of $56 is each firm's break-even price, an existing producer makes zero economic profit—neither a profit nor a loss, earning only the opportunity cost of the resources used in production—when producing its profit-maximizing output of 40 trees.

At this price there is no incentive either for potential producers to enter or for existing producers to exit the industry. So C_{MKT} corresponds to a **long-run market equilibrium**—a situation in which the quantity supplied equals the quantity demanded given that sufficient time has elapsed for producers to either enter or exit the industry. *In a long-run market equilibrium, all existing and potential producers have fully adjusted to their optimal long-run choices; as a result, all entry and exit ceases, and each firm makes zero economic profit.*

The Long-Run Industry Supply Curve To explore further the significance of the difference between short-run and long-run equilibrium, consider the effect of an increase in demand on an industry with free entry that is initially in long-run equilibrium. Panel (b) in Figure 26-3 shows the market adjustment; panels (a) and (c) show how an existing individual firm behaves during the process.

FIGURE 26-3 Comparing the Short-Run and Long-Run Industry Supply Curves

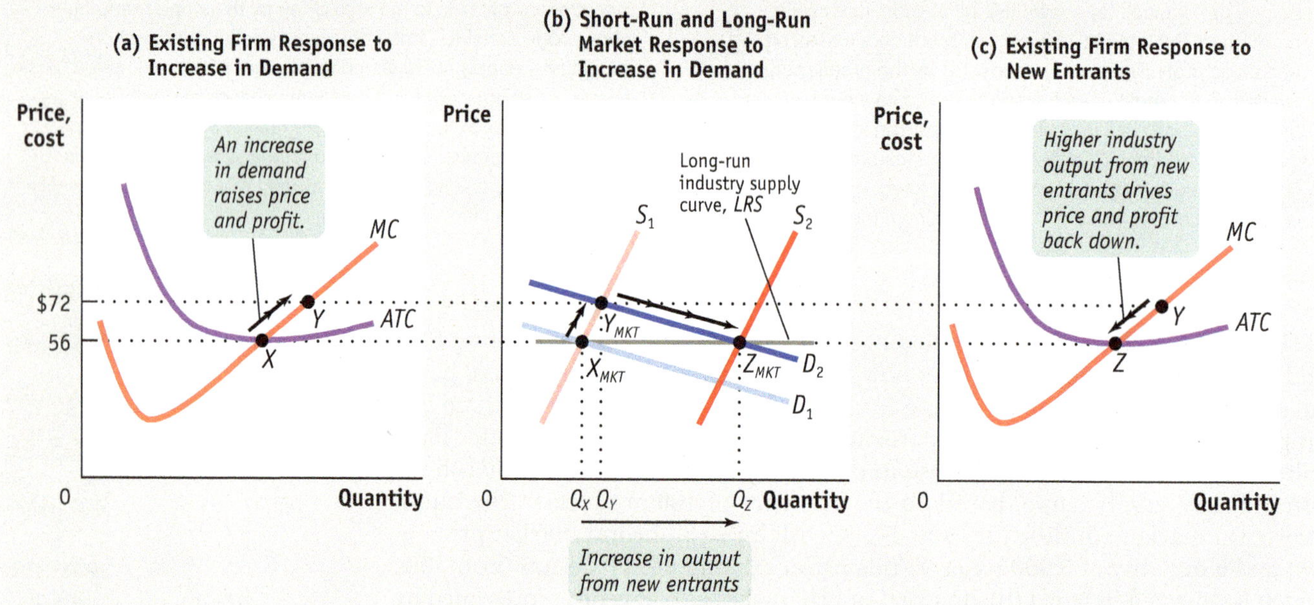

Panel (b) shows how an industry adjusts in the short and long run to an increase in demand; panels (a) and (c) show the corresponding adjustments by an existing firm. Initially the market is at point X_{MKT} in panel (b), a short-run and long-run equilibrium at a price of $56 and industry output of Q_X. An existing firm makes zero economic profit, operating at point X in panel (a) at minimum average total cost. Demand increases as D_1 shifts rightward to D_2 in panel (b), raising the market price to $72. Existing firms increase their output, and industry output moves along the short-run industry supply curve S_1 to a short-run equilibrium at Y_{MKT}. Correspondingly, the existing firm in panel (a) moves from point X to point Y. But at a price of $72, existing firms are profitable. As shown in panel (b), in the long run, new entrants arrive and the short-run industry supply curve shifts rightward, from S_1 to S_2. There is a new equilibrium at point Z_{MKT}, at a lower price of $56 and higher industry output of Q_Z. An existing firm responds by moving from Y to Z in panel (c), returning to its initial output level and zero economic profit. Production by new entrants accounts for the total increase in industry output, $Q_Z - Q_X$. Like X_{MKT}, Z_{MKT} is also a short-run and long-run equilibrium: with existing firms earning zero economic profit, there is no incentive for any firms to enter or exit the industry. The horizontal line passing through X_{MKT} and Z_{MKT}, LRS, is the long-run industry supply curve: at the break-even price of $56, producers will produce any amount that consumers demand in the long run.

In panel (b) of Figure 26-3, D_1 is the initial demand curve and S_1 is the initial short-run industry supply curve. Their intersection at point X_{MKT} is both a short-run and a long-run market equilibrium because the equilibrium price of $56 leads to zero economic profit—and therefore neither entry nor exit. It corresponds to point X in panel (a), where an individual existing firm is operating at the minimum of its average total cost curve.

Now suppose that the demand curve shifts out for some reason to D_2. As shown in panel (b), in the short run, industry output moves along the short-run industry supply curve S_1 to the new short-run market equilibrium at Z_{MKT}, the intersection of S_1 and D_2. The market price rises to $72 per tree, and industry output increases from to Q_X to Q_Y. This corresponds to an existing firm's movement from X to Y in panel (a) as the firm increases its output in response to the rise in the market price.

But we know that Y_{MKT} is not a long-run equilibrium, because $72 is higher than minimum average total cost, and thus existing producers are making economic profits. This will lead additional firms to enter the industry.

Over time entry will cause the short-run industry supply curve to shift to the right. In the long run, the short-run industry supply curve will have shifted out to S_2, and the equilibrium will be at Z_{MKT}—with the price falling back to $56 per tree and industry output increasing yet again, from to Q_Y to Q_Z. Like X_{MKT} before the increase in demand, Z_{MKT} is both a short-run and a long-run market equilibrium.

The effect of entry on an existing firm is illustrated in panel (c), in the movement from Y to Z along the firm's individual supply curve. The firm reduces its output in response to the fall in the market price, ultimately arriving back at its original output quantity, corresponding to the minimum of its average total cost curve. In fact, every firm that is now in the industry—the initial set of firms and the new entrants—will operate at the minimum of its average total cost curve, at point Z. This means that the entire increase in industry output, from Q_X to Q_Z, comes from production by new entrants.

The line *LRS* that passes through X_{MKT} and Z_{MKT} in panel (b) is the **long-run industry supply curve.** It shows how the quantity supplied by an industry responds to the price, given that producers have had time to enter or exit the industry.

In this particular case, the long-run industry supply curve is horizontal at $56. In other words, in this industry, supply is *perfectly elastic* in the long run: given time to enter or exit, producers will supply any quantity that consumers demand at a price of $56. Perfectly elastic long-run supply is actually a good assumption for many industries. In this case we speak of there being *constant costs across the industry:* each firm, regardless of whether it is an incumbent or a new entrant, faces the same cost structure (that is, each firm has the same cost curves). Industries that satisfy this condition are those in which there is a perfectly elastic supply of inputs—industries such as agriculture and bakeries.

In other industries, however, even the long-run industry supply curve slopes upward. The usual reason for this is that producers must use some input that is in limited supply (that is, inelastically supplied). As the industry expands, the price of that input is driven up. Consequently, later entrants in the industry find that they have a higher cost structure than early entrants. An example is beachfront resort hotels, which must compete for a limited quantity of prime beachfront property. Industries that behave like this are said to have *increasing costs across the industry.*

It is possible for the long-run industry supply curve to slope downward. This can occur when an industry faces increasing returns to scale, with average costs falling as output rises. Notice that we said that the *industry* faces increasing returns. However, when increasing returns apply at the level of the individual firm, the industry usually ends up dominated by a small number of firms (an oligopoly) or a single firm (a monopoly).

In some cases, the advantages of large scale for an entire industry accrue to all firms in that industry. For example, the costs of new technologies such as solar

The **long-run industry supply curve** shows how the quantity supplied responds to the price once producers have had time to enter or exit the industry.

FIGURE 26-4 Comparing the Short-Run and Long-Run Industry Supply Curves

The long-run industry supply curve may slope upward, but it is always flatter—more elastic—than the short-run industry supply curve. This is because of entry and exit: a higher price attracts new entrants in the long run, resulting in a rise in industry output and a fall in price; a lower price induces existing producers to exit in the long run, generating a fall in industry output and an eventual rise in price.

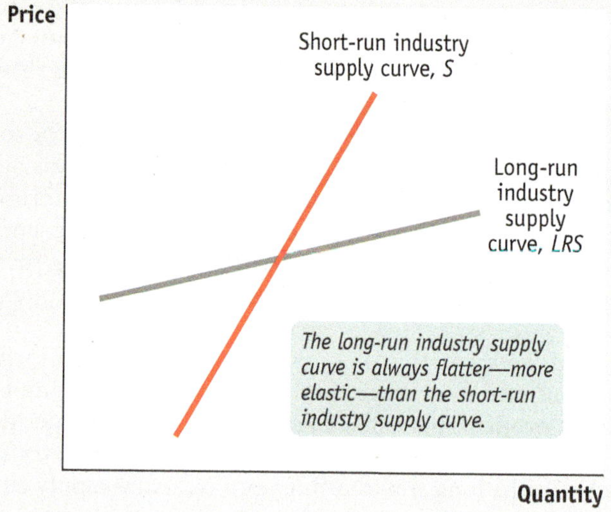

panels tend to fall as the industry grows because that growth leads to improved knowledge, a larger pool of workers with the right skills, and so on.

Regardless of whether the long-run industry supply curve is horizontal or upward sloping or even downward sloping, the long-run price elasticity of supply is *higher* than the short-run price elasticity whenever there is free entry and exit. As shown in Figure 26-4, the long-run industry supply curve is always flatter than the short-run industry supply curve. The reason is entry and exit: a high price caused by an increase in demand attracts entry by new producers, resulting in a rise in industry output and an eventual fall in price; a low price caused by a decrease in demand induces existing firms to exit, leading to a fall in industry output and an eventual increase in price.

The distinction between the short-run industry supply curve and the long-run industry supply curve is very important in practice. We often see a sequence of events like that shown in Figure 26-3: an increase in demand initially leads to a large price increase, but prices return to their initial level once new firms have entered the industry. Or we see the sequence in reverse: a fall in demand reduces prices in the short run, but they return to their initial level as producers exit the industry.

The Cost of Production and Efficiency in Long-Run Equilibrium

Our analysis leads us to three conclusions about the cost of production and efficiency in the long-run equilibrium of a perfectly competitive industry. These results will be important in our discussion in Section 9 when we consider how monopoly gives rise to inefficiency.

1. ***In a perfectly competitive industry in equilibrium, the value of marginal cost is the same for all firms.*** That's because all firms produce the quantity of output at which marginal cost equals the market price, and as price-takers they all face the same market price.
2. ***In a perfectly competitive industry with free entry and exit, each firm will have zero economic profit in long-run equilibrium.*** Each firm produces the quantity of output that minimizes its average total cost—corresponding to point *Z* in panel (c) of Figure 26-4. So the total cost of production of the industry's output is minimized in a perfectly competitive industry.

The exception is an industry with increasing costs across the industry. Given a sufficiently high market price, early entrants make positive economic profits, but the last entrants do not as the market price falls. Costs are minimized for later entrants, as the industry reaches long-run equilibrium, but not necessarily for the early ones.

3. ***The long-run market equilibrium of a perfectly competitive industry is efficient: no mutually beneficial transactions go unexploited.*** To understand this, recall a fundamental requirement for efficiency: all consumers who have a willingness to pay greater than or equal to sellers' costs actually get the good. In addition, when a market is efficient (except under certain, well-defined conditions), the market price matches all consumers with a willingness to pay greater than or equal to the market price to all sellers who have a cost of producing the good less than or equal to the market price.

So, in the long-run equilibrium of a perfectly competitive industry, production is efficient: costs are minimized and no resources are wasted. In addition, the allocation of goods to consumers is efficient: every consumer willing to pay the cost of producing a unit of the good gets it. Indeed, no mutually beneficial transaction is left unexploited. Moreover, this condition tends to persist over time as the environment changes: the force of competition makes producers responsive to changes in consumers' desires and to changes in technology.

ECONOMICS >> *in Action*

A Global Pork Shortage Hits Chinese Diners Hard

REUTERS/Jason Lee

A reduction in the supply of Chinese pork—combined with hefty taxes on pork from the United States—meant a boon for pork producers in other countries.

Powered by rapidly rising incomes, Chinese consumers have been eating more meat, and their meat of preference has definitely been pork. In the past 20 years, pork consumption per capita in China has nearly doubled. In 2020, the average Chinese consumer ate an estimated 66 pounds of pork per year, compared to 53 pounds for the average American.

However, the market for pork in China hit a devastating supply shock—a leftward shift of the supply curve—in 2018, when African swine fever, a deadly and rapidly spreading disease, first appeared in Chinese pig stocks. Because there was no vaccine against the disease, animals exposed to the disease had to be destroyed immediately to stop the spread. By late 2019, some 40% of Chinese pigs—equivalent to hundreds of millions of animal—had been lost. As a result, China has experienced a chronic shortage of pork and skyrocketing pork prices. The producer price of pork in China—the price at the farm—has more than doubled, rising by 125%.

The demand and supply reverberations have spread globally. As the world's largest consumer of pork, China "has a major influence on the price and availability of pork worldwide," according to a study commissioned by the U.S. National Pork Board. In 2019, there was a global surge in pork and bacon prices, registering the steepest rise seen in 15 years. As one market observer commented, "It doesn't matter where you are in the world at the moment, pork prices are up."

Reduction in the supply of Chinese-produced pork has been a boon to pork producers in other countries. Pork producers in Brazil, Australia, and the European Union have entered the Chinese market on a large scale. (Due to the Trump administration's tariffs against China, U.S. pork producers have benefited less.) By late 2019, imports of foreign pork into China had surged by 150%. The import surge increased the supply curve for Chinese consumers relative to the right, dampening the rise in pork prices.

Yet, the gain to non-Chinese pork producers may be short-lived. Fifty percent of China's domestically produced pork comes from small-scale farms—farms that are typically too small to effectively fight against a disease like African swine fever. Decimated by the epidemic, small-scale pork farms are being forced to exit the market, and modern, large-scale pork farms are expanding their share of total output. By modernizing its methods of pork production, China hopes never to be hit with a devastating pork shortage like this again.

>> Quick Review

- The **industry supply curve** corresponds to the supply curve of earlier sections. In the short run, the time period over which the number of producers is fixed, the **short-run market equilibrium** is given by the intersection of the **short-run industry supply curve** and the demand curve. In the long run, the time period over which producers can enter or exit the industry, the **long-run market equilibrium** is given by the intersection of the **long-run industry supply curve** and the demand curve. In the long-run market equilibrium, no producer has an incentive to enter or exit the industry.
- The long-run industry supply curve is often horizontal, although it may slope upward when a necessary input is in limited supply. It is always more elastic than the short-run industry supply curve.
- In the long-run market equilibrium of a perfectly competitive industry, each firm produces at the same marginal cost, which is equal to the market price, and the total cost of production of the industry's output is minimized. It is also efficient.

Check Your Understanding 26-1

1. Which of the following events will induce firms to enter an industry? Which will induce firms to exit? When will entry or exit cease? Explain your answer.
   a. A technological advance lowers the fixed cost of production of every firm in the industry.
   b. The wages paid to workers in the industry go up for an extended period of time.
   c. A permanent change in consumer tastes increases demand for the good.
   d. The price of a key input rises due to a long-term shortage of that input.
2. Assume that the egg industry is perfectly competitive and is in long-run equilibrium with a perfectly elastic long-run industry supply curve. Health concerns about cholesterol then lead to a decrease in demand. Construct a figure similar to Figure 26-4, showing the short-run behavior of the industry and how long-run equilibrium is reestablished.

Solutions appear at back of book

BUSINESS CASE

Retail Wars: Big Box Stores in the Age of Amazon

AP Images/Gerry Broome

The large number of defunct or dying shopping malls littered across the United States confirms that the brick-and-mortar retail industry has undergone what Robin Lewis, author of *The New Rules of Retail*, describes as "a period that would only be paralleled by the Industrial Revolution." Online shopping has decimated many long-established retailers such as Sears and J.C. Penney, and even newer ones such as Circuit City and Toys "R" Us.

But in the last few years, several brick-and-mortar retailers such as Walmart and Target have put up a vigorous fight. To combat consumers' penchant for showrooming—visiting a brick-and-mortar store to inspect the merchandise, and then buying it with a mobile shopping app on their smartphone at a cheaper price—Target stocks products that manufacturers have slightly modified as Target exclusives, making it harder to find an online comparison. Both Target and Walmart have beefed up their online retail presence, and they send discount alerts and coupons directly to customers' phones. Both stores leveraged their existing infrastructure by pairing digital commerce with brick-and-mortar convenience, allowing customers to order online and pick up (and return) merchandise in stores, a challenge to Amazon's warehouse and delivery model. Walmart also instituted a price-match guarantee, in which customers receive Walmart gift cards for the value of any price difference.

Yet the most innovative counter-assault is the brainchild of Hubert Joly, the CEO of Best Buy. In 2012, by all appearances Best Buy was soon to follow its rival, electronics superstore Circuit City, into bankruptcy. However, by 2019, Best Buy was consistently beating its Wall Street earnings forecasts. How did Joly deliver? The first and perhaps most necessary strategy was price-matching: "Until I match Amazon's prices, the customers are ours to lose," Mr. Joly said. Second, Best Buy distinguished itself in an area that couldn't be captured by using robots or fast delivery: customer service. To keep its sales associates well-informed and happy, Joly reinstated a much-loved employee discount and instituted an ambitious training program to ensure that employees could answer questions about entirely new categories such as virtual reality headsets. Third, Joly transformed Best Buy's delivery infrastructure so that it could ship its items nearly as fast as Amazon could. In the end, Joly has found a way to change showroomers into customers.

For brick-and-mortar retailers, today's retail environment is a race for survival. As one analyst said, "Only a couple of retailers can play the lowest-price game. This is going to accelerate the demise of retailers who do not have either competitive pricing or standout store experience."

QUESTIONS FOR THOUGHT

1. From the evidence in the case, what can you infer about whether or not the retail market for electronics satisfied the conditions for perfect competition before the advent of comparison price shopping via mobile app? What was the most important impediment to competition?
2. What effect is the introduction of shopping apps having on competition in the retail market for electronics? On the profitability of brick-and-mortar retailers like Best Buy? What, on average, will be the effect on the consumer surplus of purchasers of these items?
3. Why are some retailers responding by having manufacturers make slightly modified or exclusive versions of products for them? Is this trend likely to increase or diminish?

REVIEW

MODULE 23

1. There are four main types of market structure based on the number of firms in the industry and product differentiation: perfect competition, monopoly, oligopoly, and monopolistic competition.
2. In a **perfectly competitive market,** all producers are **price-taking producers** and all consumers are **price-taking consumers**—no one's actions can influence the market price. Consumers are normally price-takers, but producers often are not. In a **perfectly competitive industry,** all producers are price-takers.
3. There are two necessary conditions for a perfectly competitive industry: there are many producers, none of whom have a large **market share,** and the industry produces a **standardized product** or **commodity**—goods that consumers regard as equivalent. A third condition is often satisfied as well: **free entry and exit** into and from the industry.
4. A **monopolist** is a producer who is the sole supplier of a good without close substitutes. An industry controlled by a monopolist is a **monopoly.** The ability of a monopoly to raise its price above the competitive level by reducing output is known as **market power.** And market power is what monopoly is all about.
5. To persist, a monopoly must be protected by a **barrier to entry.** This can take the form of control of a natural resource or input, increasing returns to scale that give rise to a **natural monopoly,** technological superiority, **network externality,** or government rules that prevent entry by other firms, such as **patents** or **copyrights.**
6. Many industries are **oligopolies:** there are only a few producers, called **oligopolists.** Oligopolies exist for more or less the same reasons that monopolies exist, but in weaker form. They are characterized by **imperfect competition:** firms compete but possess some market power. The small number of firms leads to the potential for **collusion** to raise joint profits.
7. **Monopolistic competition** is a market structure in which there are many competing firms, each producing a differentiated product, and there is free entry and exit in the long run. Product differentiation takes three main forms: by style or type, by location, and by quality. The extent of imperfect competition can be measured by the **Herfindahl–Hirschman Index.**

MODULE 24

1. A producer chooses output according to the **optimal output rule:** produce the quantity at which **marginal revenue** equals marginal cost. For a price-taking firm, marginal revenue is equal to price and its **marginal revenue curve** is a horizontal line at the market price. It chooses output according to the **price-taking firm's optimal output rule:** produce the quantity at which price equals marginal cost. However, a firm that produces the optimal quantity may not be profitable.

MODULE 25

1. According to the **profit determination rule,** whether a producer is profitable depends on a comparison of the market price of the good to the producer's **break-even price**—its minimum average total cost. If market price exceeds the break-even price, the firm is profitable; if it is less, the firm is unprofitable; if it is equal, the firm breaks even. When profitable, the firm's per-unit profit is $P - ATC$; when unprofitable, its per-unit loss is $ATC - P$.
2. Fixed cost is irrelevant to the firm's optimal short-run production decision, which depends on its **shut-down price**—its minimum average variable cost—and the market price. When the market price is equal to or exceeds the shut-down price, the firm produces the output quantity where marginal cost equals the market price. When price falls below the shut-down price, the **shut-down rule** applies and the firm should cease production. When price lies between minimum average total cost (break-even price) and minimum average variable cost (shut-down price), the **interim production decision rule** applies: the firm produces in the short run to minimize loss. This defines the firm's **short-run individual supply curve.**
3. Fixed cost matters over time. If the market price is below minimum average total cost for an extended period of time, firms will exit the industry in the long run. If it is above this cost, existing firms are profitable and new firms will enter the industry in the long run.

MODULE 26

1. The **industry supply curve** depends on the time period. The **short-run industry supply curve** is the industry supply curve given that the number of firms is fixed. The **short-run market equilibrium** is given by the intersection of the short-run industry supply curve and the demand curve.
2. The **long-run industry supply curve** is the industry supply curve given sufficient time for entry into and exit from the industry. In the **long-run market equilibrium**—given by the intersection of the long-run industry supply curve and the demand curve—no producer has an incentive to enter or exit. The long-run industry supply curve is often horizontal. It may slope upward if there is limited supply of an input,

resulting in increasing costs across the industry. It may even slope downward, in the case of decreasing costs across the industry. But it is always more elastic than the short-run industry supply curve.

3. In the long-run market equilibrium of a competitive industry, profit maximization leads each firm to produce at the same marginal cost, which is equal to market price. Free entry and exit means that each firm earns zero economic profit—producing the output corresponding to its minimum average total cost. So, the total cost of production of an industry's output is minimized. The outcome is efficient because every consumer with a willingness to pay greater than or equal to marginal cost gets the good.

KEY TERMS

ANGELA WEISS/Getty Images

Module 27 Monopoly in Practice

Module 28 Monopoly, Government Policy, and Social Welfare

Module 29 Price Discrimination

SECTION 9

Monopoly

"SHINE BRIGHT LIKE A DIAMOND"

Rihanna, the superstar singer, fashion icon, and makeup mogul, is well known for her association with diamond gemstones. Her 2012 hit song "Diamonds" topped the charts in over 20 countries. In 2018, she became the brand ambassador for one of the oldest and most exclusive purveyors of diamond jewelry, Chopard of Paris. Her annual Diamond Ball raises millions of dollars for charity.

But why does Rihanna focus on diamonds? Diamonds are a symbol of luxury, valued not only for their appearance but also for their perceived rarity.

Yet, as geologists will tell you, diamonds aren't actually all that rare. In fact, according to the *Dow Jones–Irwin Guide to Fine Gems and Jewelry*, diamonds are "more common than any other gem-quality colored stone. They only seem rarer."

Why do diamonds seem more precious and rare than rubies, emeralds, and other stones? Part of the answer is a brilliant marketing campaign. But the main reason diamonds seem to be rare is the legacy of a company named De Beers, which *made* them rare. For 100 years, the company controlled most of the world's diamond mines, allowing it to limit the quantity of diamonds supplied to the market.

In the previous section, we concentrated exclusively on perfectly competitive markets—those in which there are many producers. But the diamond market has historically been very different. At the height of its power, De Beers controlled the global diamond market and was unlike the producers we've studied so far. It was a *monopolist,* the sole (or almost sole) producer of a good. Monopolists behave differently from producers in perfectly competitive industries: whereas perfect competitors take the price at which they can sell their output as given, monopolists know that their actions affect market prices and take that into account when deciding how much to produce.

In this section, we examine not only how monopolies function but also how they differ from industries in perfect competition. We'll also look at the policies governments adopt in response to monopoly behavior. We conclude with a discussion of how monopolists use *price discrimination*—charging different types of consumers different prices for the same good—to increase profits.

MODULE

27 Monopoly in Practice

WHAT YOU WILL LEARN

- What is the significance of **monopoly,** a type of industry in which only one producer, a **monopolist,** operates?
- How does being a monopolist affect a firm's price and output decisions?

mevans/iStockphoto

In this module, we turn to monopoly, the market structure at the opposite end of the spectrum from perfect competition. We will now learn how a monopolist, De Beers, for instance, increases its profit by reducing output. And we will see the crucial role that market demand plays in leading a monopolist to behave differently from a perfectly competitive industry. (Remember that profit here is economic profit, not accounting profit.)

27.1 The Monopolist's Demand Curve and Marginal Revenue

Recall the firm's *optimal output rule:* a profit-maximizing firm produces the quantity of output at which the marginal cost of producing the last unit of output equals marginal revenue—the change in total revenue generated by that last unit of output. That is, $MR = MC$ at the profit-maximizing quantity of output.

Although the optimal output rule holds for all firms, we will see shortly that its application leads to different profit-maximizing output levels for a monopolist compared to a firm in a perfectly competitive industry—that is, a price-taking firm. We can see the difference by comparing the demand curve faced by a monopolist to the demand curve faced by an individual perfectly competitive firm.

Comparing Demand Curves

Recall that each of the firms in a perfectly competitive industry faces a *perfectly elastic* demand curve that is horizontal at the market price, like D_C in panel (a) of Figure 27-1. A perfectly competitive firm can sell as much as it likes at the market price, yet will lose all its sales if it attempts to charge more.

Therefore, the marginal revenue of a perfectly competitive producer is simply the market price. As a result, the price-taking firm's optimal output rule is to produce the output level at which the marginal cost of the last unit produced is equal to the market price.

FIGURE 27-1 Comparing the Demand Curves of a Perfectly Competitive Producer and a Monopolist

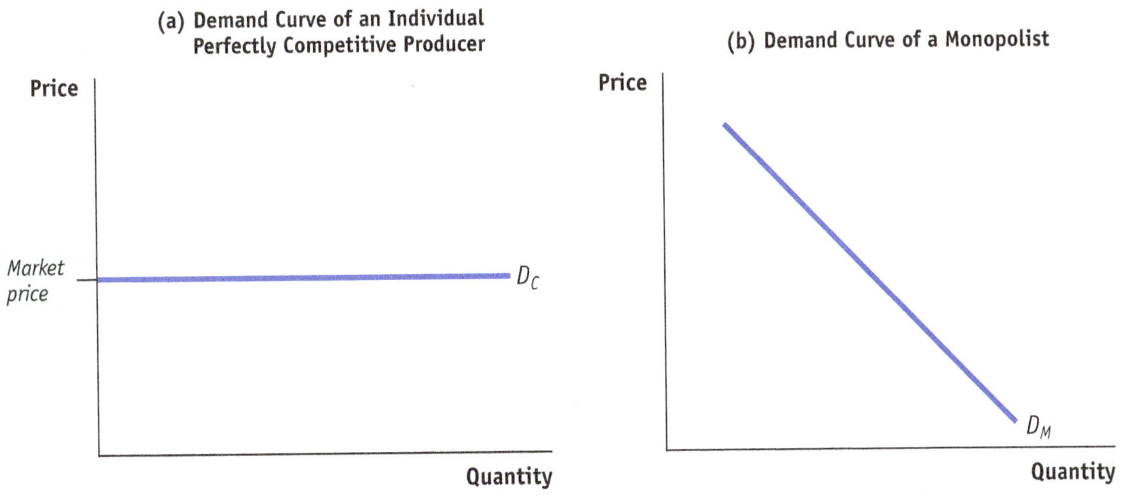

Because an individual perfectly competitive producer cannot affect the market price of a good, it faces the horizontal demand curve D_C, as shown in panel (a), allowing it to sell as much as it wants at the market price. A monopolist, though, can affect the price. Because it is the sole supplier in the industry, it faces the market demand curve D_M, as shown in panel (b). To sell more output, it must lower the price; by reducing output, it raises the price.

In contrast, a monopolist is the sole supplier of its good. So its demand curve is simply the market demand curve. Like virtually all market demand curves, it slopes downward, like D_M in panel (b) of Figure 27-1. As a result, a monopolist must cut its price to sell more. *This downward slope creates a difference—a "wedge"—between the price of the good and the marginal revenue received by the monopolist for that good.*

Table 27-1 shows this wedge between price and marginal revenue for a monopolist, by calculating the monopolist's total revenue and marginal revenue schedules from its demand schedule.

Comparing Marginal Revenue and Price

Now let's examine how the wedge between the monopolist's marginal revenue and price changes according to the quantity of output. The first two columns of Table 27-1 show a hypothetical demand schedule for De Beers diamonds, and we will assume that all diamonds are exactly alike. The demand curve implied by this schedule is shown in panel (a) of Figure 27-2. The third column of Table 27-1 shows De Beers's total revenue from selling each quantity of diamonds—the price per diamond multiplied by the number of diamonds sold. The last column calculates marginal revenue, the change in total revenue from producing and selling another diamond.

Why Marginal Revenue Differs from Price for a Monopolist

After the first diamond, the marginal revenue a monopolist receives from selling one more unit is less than the price at which that unit is sold. For example, if De Beers sells 10 diamonds, the price at which the 10th diamond is sold is \$500. But the marginal revenue—the change in total revenue in going from 9 to 10 diamonds—is only \$50.

TABLE 27-1 Demand, Total Revenue, and Marginal Revenue for the De Beers Monopoly

Price of diamond *P*	Quantity of diamonds *Q*	Total revenue $TR = P \times Q$	Marginal revenue $MR = \Delta TR/\Delta Q$
$1,000	0	$0	
			$950
950	1	950	
			850
900	2	1,800	
			750
850	3	2,550	
			650
800	4	3,200	
			550
750	5	3,750	
			450
700	6	4,200	
			350
650	7	4,550	
			250
600	8	4,800	
			150
550	9	4,950	
			50
500	10	5,000	
			−50
450	11	4,950	
			−150
400	12	4,800	
			−250
350	13	4,550	
			−350
300	14	4,200	
			−450
250	15	3,750	
			−550
200	16	3,200	
			−650
150	17	2,550	
			−750
100	18	1,800	
			−850
50	19	950	
			−950
0	20	0	

The marginal revenue from that 10th diamond is less than the price because an increase in production by a monopolist has two opposing effects on revenue:

1. *A quantity effect.* One more unit is sold, increasing total revenue by the price at which the unit is sold (in this case, +$500).
2. *A price effect.* To sell the last unit, the monopolist must cut the market price on *all* units sold. This decreases total revenue (in this case, by 9 × −$50 = −$450).

The quantity effect and the price effect when the monopolist goes from selling 9 diamonds to 10 diamonds are illustrated by the two shaded areas in panel (a) of Figure 27-2. Increasing diamond sales from 9 to 10 means moving down the demand curve from *A* to *B*, reducing the price per diamond from $550 to $500. The green-shaded area represents the quantity effect: De Beers sells the 10th diamond at a price of $500. This is offset, however, by the price effect, represented by the yellow-shaded area. To sell that 10th diamond, De Beers must reduce the price on all its diamonds from $550 to $500. So it loses 9 × $50 = $450 in revenue, the yellow-shaded area. As point *C* indicates, the total effect on revenue of selling one more diamond—the marginal revenue—derived from an increase in diamond sales from 9 to 10 is only $50.

Point *C* lies on the monopolist's marginal revenue curve, labeled *MR* in panel (a) of Figure 27-2 and taken from the last column of Table 27-1. The crucial point about the monopolist's marginal revenue curve is that it is always *below* the demand curve. That's because of the price effect: a monopolist's marginal revenue from selling an additional unit is always less than the price the monopolist receives for the previous unit. It is the price effect that creates the wedge between the monopolist's marginal revenue curve and the demand curve: to sell an additional diamond, De Beers must cut the market price on all units sold.

In fact, this wedge exists for any firm that possesses market power, such as an oligopolist as well as a monopolist. Having market power means that the firm faces a downward-sloping demand curve. As a result, there will always be a price effect from an increase in its output. So, *for a firm with market power, the marginal revenue curve always lies below its demand curve.*

Take a moment to compare the monopolist's marginal revenue curve with the marginal revenue curve for a perfectly competitive firm, one without market power. For such a firm, there is no price effect from an increase in output: its marginal revenue curve is simply its horizontal demand curve. For a perfectly competitive firm, then, market price and marginal revenue are always equal.

To emphasize how the quantity and price effects offset each other for a firm with market power, De Beers's total revenue curve is shown in panel (b) of Figure 27-2. Notice that it is hill-shaped: as output rises from 0 to 10 diamonds, total revenue increases. This reflects the fact that at *low levels of output, the quantity effect is stronger than the price effect:* as the monopolist sells more, it has to lower the price on only very few units, so the price effect is small. As output rises

FIGURE 27-2 A Monopolist's Demand, Total Revenue, and Marginal Revenue Curves

Panel (a) shows the monopolist's demand and marginal revenue curves for diamonds from Table 27-1. The marginal revenue curve lies below the demand curve. To see why, consider point *A* on the demand curve, where 9 diamonds are sold at $550 each, generating total revenue of $4,950. To sell a 10th diamond, the price on all 10 diamonds must be cut to $500, as shown by point *B*. As a result, total revenue increases by the green area (the quantity effect: +$500) but decreases by the yellow area (the price effect: –$450). So, the marginal revenue from the 10th diamond is $50 (the difference between the green and yellow areas), which is much lower than its price, $500. Panel (b) shows the monopolist's total revenue curve for diamonds. As output goes from 0 to 10 diamonds, total revenue increases. It reaches its maximum at 10 diamonds—the level at which marginal revenue is equal to 0—and declines thereafter. The quantity effect dominates the price effect when total revenue is rising; the price effect dominates the quantity effect when total revenue is falling.

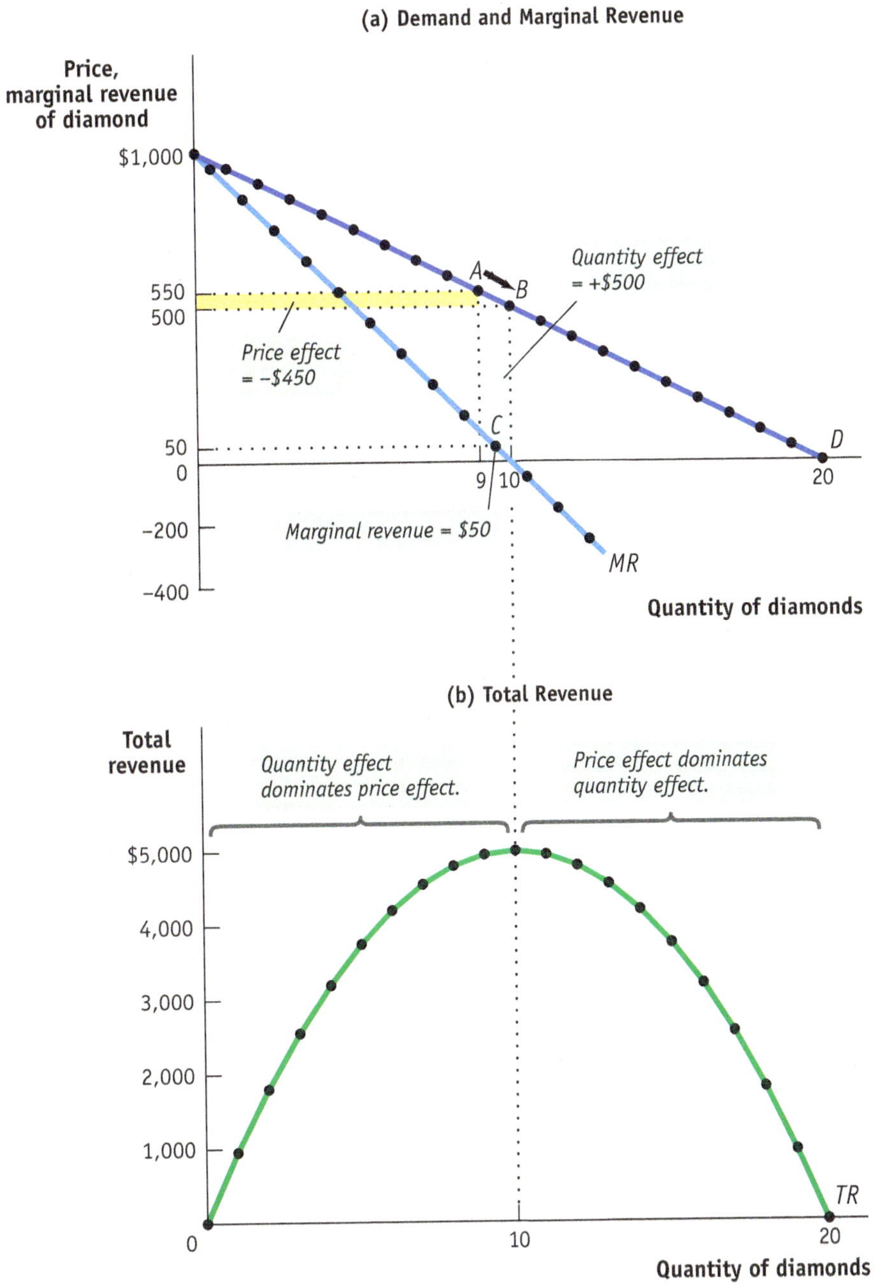

beyond 10 diamonds, total revenue actually falls. This reflects the fact that *at high levels of output, the price effect is stronger than the quantity effect:* as the monopolist sells more, it now has to lower the price on many units of output, making the price effect very large.

Correspondingly, the marginal revenue curve lies below 0 at output levels above 10 diamonds. For example, an increase in diamond production from 11 to 12 yields only $400 for the 12th diamond, the revenue is reduced from the price effect of selling diamonds 1 through 11 by $550 ($50 × 11) and only increased by $400 from the quantity effect. As a result, the marginal revenue of the 12th diamond is –$150 ($400 – $550).

27.2 The Monopolist's Profit-Maximizing Output and Price

To complete the story of how a monopolist maximizes profit, we now bring in the monopolist's marginal cost. Let's assume that there is no fixed cost of production; we'll also assume that the marginal cost of producing an additional diamond is constant at $200, no matter how many diamonds De Beers produces. Then marginal cost will always equal average total cost, and the marginal cost curve (and the average total cost curve) is a horizontal line at $200, as shown in Figure 27-3.

To maximize profit, the monopolist compares marginal cost with marginal revenue. If marginal revenue exceeds marginal cost, De Beers increases profit by producing more; if marginal revenue is less than marginal cost, De Beers increases profit by producing less. So, the monopolist maximizes its profit by using the optimal output rule:

(27-1) $MR = MC$ at the monopolist's profit-maximizing quantity of output

The monopolist's optimal point is shown in Figure 27-3. At *A*, the marginal cost curve, *MC*, crosses the marginal revenue curve, *MR*. The corresponding output level, 8 diamonds, is the monopolist's profit-maximizing quantity of output, Q_M. The price at which consumers demand 8 diamonds is $600, so the monopolist's price, P_M, is $600—corresponding to point *B*. The average total cost of producing each diamond is $200, so the monopolist earns a profit of $600 – $200 = $400 per diamond, and total profit is 8 × $400 = $3,200 as indicated by the shaded area.

27.3 Monopoly versus Perfect Competition

When Cecil Rhodes consolidated many independent diamond producers into De Beers, he converted a perfectly competitive industry into a monopoly. We can now use our analysis to see the effects of such a consolidation.

FIGURE 27-3 The Monopolist's Profit-Maximizing Output and Price

This figure shows the demand, marginal revenue, and marginal cost curves. Marginal cost per diamond is constant at $200, so the marginal cost curve is horizontal at $200. According to the optimal output rule, the profit-maximizing quantity of output for the monopolist is at *MR* = *MC*, shown by point *A*, where the marginal cost and marginal revenue curves cross at an output of 8 diamonds. The price De Beers can charge per diamond is found by going to the point on the demand curve directly above point *A*, which is point *B* here—a price of $600 per diamond. It makes a profit of $400 × 8 = $3,200. A perfectly competitive industry produces the output level at which *P* = *MC*, given by point *C*, where the demand curve and the marginal cost curve cross. So, a competitive industry produces 16 diamonds, sells at a price of $200, and makes zero profit.

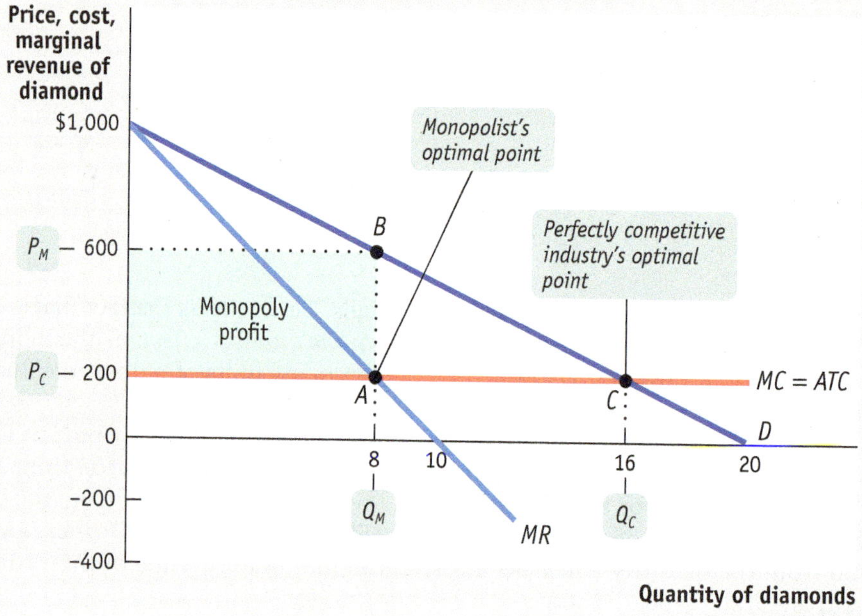

Let's look again at Figure 27-3 and ask how this same market would work if, instead of being a monopoly, the industry were perfectly competitive. We will continue to assume that there is no fixed cost and that marginal cost (MC) is constant, so average total cost (ATC) and marginal cost are equal.

If the diamond industry consists of many perfectly competitive firms, each of those producers takes the market price as given. For each firm, marginal revenue is equal to the market price. So, each firm within the industry uses the price-taking firm's optimal output rule:

(27-2) $P = MC$ at the perfectly competitive firm's profit-maximizing quantity of output

In Figure 27-3, this corresponds to producing at point *C*, where the price per diamond, P_C, is \$200, equal to the marginal cost of production. So, the profit-maximizing output of an industry under perfect competition, Q_C, is 16 diamonds.

But does the perfectly competitive industry earn any profits at point *C*? No, the price of \$200 is equal to the average total cost per diamond. So there are no economic profits for this industry when it produces at the perfectly competitive output level.

We've already seen that once the industry is consolidated into a monopoly, the result is very different. The monopolist's calculation of marginal revenue takes the price effect into account so that marginal revenue is less than the price. That is,

(27-3) $P > MR = MC$ at the monopolist's profit-maximizing quantity of output

We've also seen that the monopolist produces less than the competitive industry—8 diamonds rather than 16. The price under monopoly is \$600, compared with only \$200 under perfect competition. The monopolist earns a positive profit, but the competitive firm does not.

As suggested earlier, compared with a competitive industry, a monopolist does the following:

- Produces a smaller quantity: $Q_M < Q_C$
- Charges a higher price: $P_M > P_C$
- Earns a profit

PITFALLS

IS THERE A MONOPOLY SUPPLY CURVE?

Given how a monopolist applies its optimal output rule, you might be tempted to ask what this implies for the supply curve of a monopolist. But this is a meaningless question: *monopolists don't have supply curves.*

Remember that a supply curve shows the quantity that producers are willing to supply for any given market price. A monopolist, however, does not take the price as given; it chooses a profit-maximizing quantity, taking into account its own ability to influence the price.

27.4 Monopoly: The General Picture

Figure 27-3 involved specific numbers and assumed that marginal cost was constant, that there was no fixed cost, and, therefore, that the average total cost curve was a horizontal line. Figure 27-4 shows a more general picture of monopoly in action: *D* is the market demand curve; *MR*, the marginal revenue curve; *MC*, the marginal cost curve; and *ATC*, the average total cost curve. Here we return to the usual assumption that the marginal cost curve has a "swoosh" shape and the average total cost curve is U-shaped.

Applying the optimal output rule, we see that the profit-maximizing level of output is the output at which marginal revenue equals marginal cost, indicated by point *A*. The profit-maximizing quantity of output is Q_M, and the price charged by the monopolist is P_M. At the profit-maximizing level of output, the monopolist's average total cost is ATC_M, shown by point *C*.

Profit is equal to the difference between total revenue and total cost. So, we have:

(27-4)
$$\begin{aligned} \text{Profit} &= TR - TC \\ &= (P_M \times Q_M) - (ATC_M \times Q_M) \\ &= (P_M - ATC_M) \times Q_M \end{aligned}$$

FIGURE 27-4 The Monopolist's Profit

In this case, the marginal cost curve has a "swoosh" shape and the average total cost curve is U-shaped. The monopolist maximizes profit by producing the level of output at which $MR = MC$, given by point A, generating quantity Q_M. It finds its monopoly price, P_M, from the point on the demand curve directly above point A, point B here. The average total cost of Q_M is shown by point C. Profit is given by the area of the shaded rectangle.

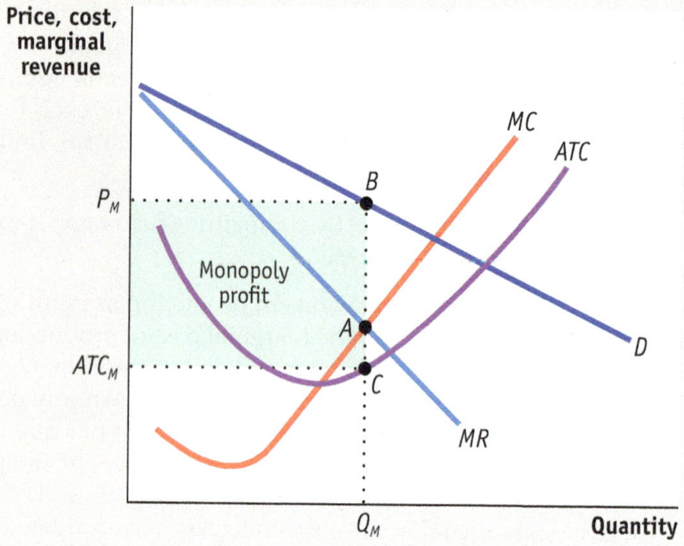

Profit is equal to the area of the shaded rectangle in Figure 27-4, with a height of $P_M - ATC_M$ and a width of Q_M.

From Section 8 we know that a perfectly competitive industry can have profits in the *short run but not in the long run*. In the short run, price can exceed average total cost, allowing a perfectly competitive firm to make a profit. But we also know that this cannot persist.

In the long run, any profit in a perfectly competitive industry will be "competed away" as new firms enter the market. In contrast, barriers to entry allow a monopolist to make profits in *both the short run and the long run*.

ECONOMICS >> *in Action*

Shocked by the High Price of Electricity

Steve Allen/Getty Images

Although electric utilities were deregulated in the 1990s, there's been a trend toward reregulating them.

Historically, electric utilities in the United States were recognized as natural monopolies. A utility serviced a defined geographic area and owned both the plants that generated electricity and the transmission lines that delivered it to retail customers. The rates charged to customers were regulated by the government and were set at a level to cover the utility's cost of operation plus a modest return on capital to its shareholders.

Beginning in the late 1990s, however, there was a move toward deregulation, based on the belief that competition would deliver lower retail electricity prices. Competition occurs at two junctures in the channel from power generation to retail customers: (1) distributors compete to sell electricity to retail customers, and (2) power generators compete to supply power to distributors.

That was the theory, at least. By 2018, only 16 states had instituted some form of electricity deregulation, while 7 had started but then suspended deregulation: leaving 27 states to continue with a regulated monopoly electricity provider. Why did so few states actually follow through on electricity deregulation?

One major obstacle is the lack of choice in power generators, the bulk of which still entail large up-front fixed costs. In many markets, there is only one power generator. Although consumers appear to have a choice in their electricity distributor, the choice is illusory, since everyone must get their electricity from the same source in the end. Even when there is choice in power generators, there is frequently no choice in transmission, which is controlled by monopoly power-line companies.

In fact, deregulation can make consumers worse off when there is only one power generator. Unfettered by regulations that set consumer prices, a monopoly power generator can engage in market manipulation. And that is exactly what happened in California during 2000 and 2001. After California deregulated its electricity market, an "energy crisis" suddenly occurred that brought blackouts and billions of dollars in electricity surcharges to homes and businesses. It turned out that a monopoly power generator intentionally reduced the amount of power supplied to consumers to drive up prices. After an investigation, regulators discovered audiotapes on which executives could be heard discussing plans to shut down power plants during times of peak energy demand, joking about how they were "stealing" more than $1 million a day from California's electricity consumers.

Another problem associated with deregulation of energy markets is that it tends to lead to insufficient investment in new power plants. Without regulation, power generators are no longer guaranteed a market price that gives them a profitable rate of return on new power plants. As a result, in many states power generators have refused to invest in new plants. This has led to a shortfall in capacity as electricity demand has grown. For example, Texas, a deregulated state, has experienced massive blackouts due to insufficient capacity, and in New Jersey and Maryland, regulators have intervened to compel producers to build more power plants.

Lastly, consumers in deregulated states have been subject to big spikes in their electricity bills, often paying much more than consumers in regulated states. Angry customers and exasperated regulators have prompted many states to shift into reverse, with Illinois, Montana, and Virginia moving to regulate their industries. California and Montana have gone so far as to mandate that their electricity distributors reacquire power plants that were sold off during deregulation. In addition, regulators have been on the prowl, fining utilities in Texas, New York, and Illinois for market manipulation.

Check Your Understanding 27-1

1. Use the accompanying total revenue schedule of Emerald, Inc., a monopoly producer of 10-carat emeralds, to calculate the answers to parts a–d. Then answer part e.
   a. The demand schedule
   b. The marginal revenue schedule
   c. The quantity effect component of marginal revenue per output level
   d. The price effect component of marginal revenue per output level
   e. What additional information is needed to determine Emerald, Inc.'s profit-maximizing output?

Quantity of emeralds demanded	Total revenue
1	$100
2	186
3	252
4	280
5	250

2. Use Figure 27-3 to show what happens to the following items when the marginal cost of diamond production rises from $200 to $400.
   - Marginal cost curve
   - Profit-maximizing price and quantity
   - Profit of the monopolist
   - Perfectly competitive industry profits

Solutions appear at back of book.

>> Quick Review

- The crucial difference between a firm with market power, such as a monopolist, and a firm in a perfectly competitive industry is that perfectly competitive firms are price-takers that face horizontal demand curves, but a firm with market power faces a downward-sloping demand curve.
- Due to the price effect of an increase in output, the marginal revenue curve of a firm with market power always lies below its demand curve. So, a profit-maximizing monopolist chooses the output level at which marginal cost is equal to marginal revenue—*not* to price.
- As a result, the monopolist produces less and sells its output at a higher price than a perfectly competitive industry would. It earns profits in the short run and the long run.

MODULE

28

Monopoly, Government Policy, and Social Welfare

WHAT YOU WILL LEARN

- Why does the presence of monopoly typically reduce social welfare?
- What tools do policy makers use to address the problem of monopoly?
- How do digital giants like Amazon, Google, and Facebook fit into our model of monopoly and what special challenges do they present?

Yury Zap/Shutterstock

It's profitable to be a monopolist, but it's not so beneficial to be a monopolist's customer. A monopolist, by reducing output and raising prices, benefits at the expense of consumers. But buyers and sellers always have conflicting interests: buyers want lower prices while sellers want higher prices. Is the conflict under monopoly any different than it is under perfect competition?

The answer is yes, because *monopoly is a source of inefficiency: the losses to consumers from monopoly behavior are larger than the gains to the monopolist.* Because monopoly leads to net losses to society's welfare, governments often try either to prevent the emergence of monopolies or to limit their effects. In this module, we will see why monopoly leads to inefficiency and examine the policies governments adopt in an attempt to prevent this inefficiency.

28.1 Welfare Effects of Monopoly

By restricting output below the level at which marginal cost is equal to the market price, a monopolist increases its profit but hurts consumers. When comparing the monopolist's gain in profit to the loss in consumer surplus, we learn that the loss in consumer surplus is larger than the monopolist's gain. As a result, monopoly causes a net loss for society.

To see why, let's return to the case where the marginal cost curve is horizontal, as shown in the two panels of Figure 28-1. Here the marginal cost curve is *MC,* the demand curve is *D,* and, in panel (b), the marginal revenue curve is *MR.*

FIGURE 28-1 Monopoly Causes Inefficiency

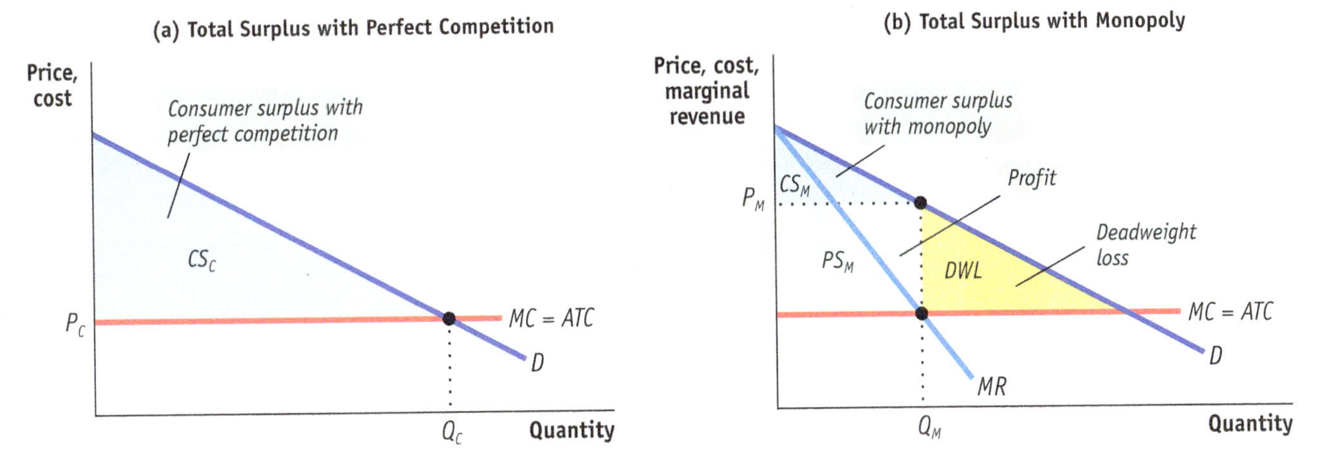

Panel (a) depicts a perfectly competitive industry: output is Q_C, and market price, P_C, is equal to *MC*. Since price is exactly equal to each producer's average total cost of production per unit, there is no profit and no producer surplus. So total surplus is equal to consumer surplus, the entire shaded area. Panel (b) depicts the industry under monopoly: the monopolist decreases output to Q_M and charges P_M. Consumer surplus (blue area) has shrunk: a portion of it has been captured as profit (green area), and a portion of it has been lost to deadweight loss (yellow area), the value of mutually beneficial transactions that do not occur because of monopoly behavior. As a result, total surplus falls.

Panel (a) shows what happens if this industry is perfectly competitive. Equilibrium output is Q_C; the price of the good, P_C, is equal to marginal cost, and marginal cost is also equal to average total cost because there is no fixed cost and marginal cost is constant. Each firm is earning exactly its average total cost per unit of output, so there is no profit and no producer surplus in this equilibrium.

The consumer surplus generated by the market is equal to the area of the blue-shaded triangle CS_C shown in panel (a). Since there is no producer surplus when the industry is perfectly competitive, CS_C also represents the total surplus.

Panel (b) shows the results for the same market, but this time, assuming that the industry is a monopoly. The monopolist produces the level of output Q_M, at which marginal cost is equal to marginal revenue, and it charges the price P_M. The industry now earns profit—which is also the producer surplus—equal to the area of the green rectangle, PS_M. Note that this profit is surplus captured from consumers as consumer surplus shrinks to the area of the blue triangle, CS_M.

By comparing panels (a) and (b), we see that in addition to the redistribution of surplus from consumers to the monopolist, another important change has occurred: the sum of profit and consumer surplus—total surplus—is *smaller* under monopoly than under perfect competition. That is, the sum of CS_M and PS_M in panel (b) is less than the area CS_C in panel (a). The total surplus shrinks by the yellow triangle *DWL* as the market goes from perfect competition to monopoly. So monopoly produces a net loss for society equal to the area *DWL*.

This net loss arises because some mutually beneficial transactions do not occur. There are people for whom an additional unit of the good is worth more than the marginal cost of producing it but who don't consume it because they are not willing to pay P_M. The wedge between price and marginal cost created by monopoly operates much like the wedge created by a tax, which we learned about in Module 14. In other words, monopoly acts much like a tax on consumers and produces the same kind of inefficiency.

So monopoly hurts the welfare of society as a whole and is a source of market failure. Is there anything government policy can do about it?

28.2 Government Policy Toward Monopoly

Monopoly reduces society's welfare and is a source of market failure. Therefore, the optimal government policy is to prevent monopoly from occurring. Prevention, however, is not always feasible or may carry large costs. In those cases, the best policy is to permit the monopoly to operate and to mitigate its adverse effects on society's welfare. To craft government policy toward a monopolist requires an understanding of the source of its monopoly power. Here we give a list of optimal policy responses according to the source of monopoly power.

1. **Control of a Scare Resource or Input:** The policy prescription is straightforward: break up the monopoly by compelling the monopolist to share the scarce resource or input with rivals. For example, in the case of De Beers, modern regulators would have forced Cecil Rhodes to break up the De Beers monopoly by selling its mines to rivals. Moreover, regulators today actively seek to prevent the creation of monopoly by disallowing mergers between rivals when their combined market share would give them substantial market power. For example, in 2018, the FTC disallowed a merger between the owners of Crisco and Wesson cooking oils that would have given them 70% of the retail cooking oil market. The scarce input in this case was the control of the supply and distribution chain from farms to grocery shelves.
2. **Technological Superiority:** The policy prescription is to do nothing as, over time, rivals will innovate to overcome the monopolist's technological advantage. For example, in the 1960s and 1970s, the market for computers was dominated by IBM's mainframe computers. Over time, IBM's market power melted away as innovation led to the creation of personal computers, smartphones, and cloud computing.
3. **Government-Created Barriers such as Patents:** The optimal policy is to do nothing. The government itself has created the monopoly for a limited time as a reward for innovation.
4. **Network Externalities:** A single, dominant firm arising from network externalities, such as Facebook, is typically aware that if it tries to raise price or degrade quality (such as by running lots of ads), a rival network can quickly emerge. Network externality monopolists are usually limited in the harm they can inflict on consumers, so government policy has generally been to do nothing.
5. **Natural Monopoly:** The optimal government policy is to allow the monopoly to operate, but to mitigate its adverse effects, usually by *public ownership* or *regulation*. Government policy toward natural monopoly involves making trade-offs, and there may be no single "right" answer depending upon the circumstances.

28.3 Dealing with Natural Monopoly

Recall from Module 23 that natural monopoly arises from increasing returns to scale: the lowest average cost is achieved when there is only one producer in the industry. As a result, policies to encourage rivals to enter the market will lead to higher average total cost across the industry. Yet even in the case of a natural monopoly, a profit-maximizing monopolist acts in a way that causes inefficiency—it charges consumers a price that is higher than marginal cost and, by doing so, prevents some potentially beneficial transactions. Also, it can seem unfair that a firm that has managed to establish a monopoly position earns a large profit at the expense of consumers.

As we mentioned earlier, there are two main policy tools for dealing with natural monopoly.

1. Public Ownership

Instead of allowing a private monopolist to control an industry, the government establishes a public agency to provide the good and protect consumers' interests. Well-known examples are the U.S. Postal Service and Amtrak for passenger rail service. Municipal airports are another example of publicly owned monopolies.

The advantage of **public ownership,** in principle, is that it can set prices based on the criterion of efficiency rather than profit maximization. Experience suggests, however, that public ownership as a solution to the problem of natural monopoly often works badly in practice. One reason is that publicly owned firms have less incentive than private companies to keep costs down or offer high-quality products. (If you have ever eaten food served on an Amtrak train, you will know what we mean.)

Richard Elliot/AA Travel/Topfoto/The Image Works

Amtrak, a public company, has provided train service, at a loss, to destinations that attract few passengers.

2. Regulation

In the United States, the more common policy tool used to address natural monopoly has been to leave the industry in private hands but subject it to regulation. For example, most local utilities like cable, electricity, and natural gas are covered by **price regulation** that limits the prices they can charge.

Figure 28-2 shows an example of price regulation of a natural monopoly—a highly simplified version of a local gas company. The company faces a demand

In **public ownership** of a monopoly, the good is supplied by the government or by a firm owned by the government.

Price regulation limits the price that a monopolist is allowed to charge.

FIGURE 28-2 Unregulated and Regulated Natural Monopoly

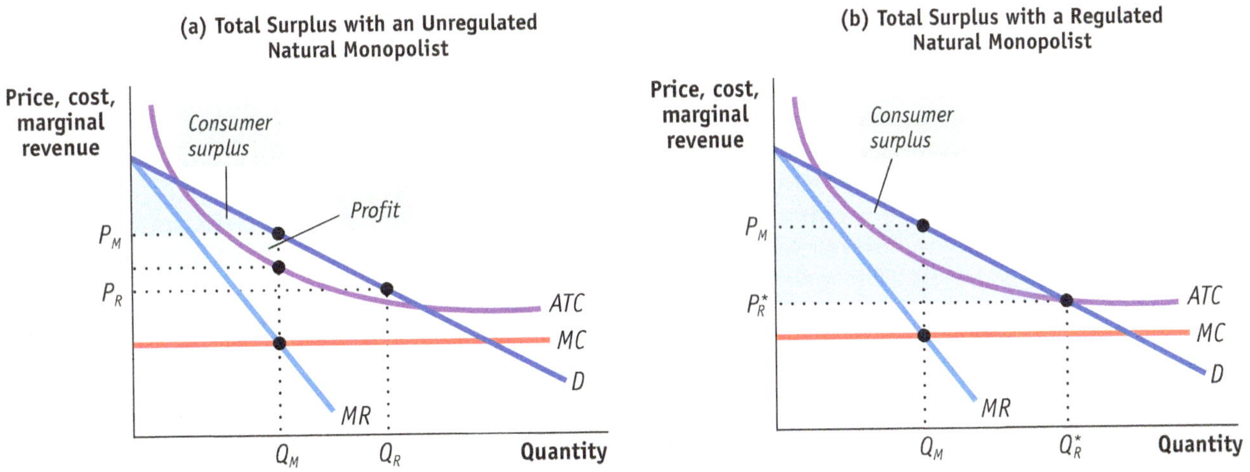

This figure shows the case of a natural monopolist. In panel (a), if the monopolist is allowed to charge P_M, it makes a profit, shown by the green area; consumer surplus is shown by the blue area. If it is regulated and must charge the lower price P_R, output increases from Q_M to Q_R and consumer surplus increases. Panel (b) shows what happens when the monopolist must charge a price equal to average total cost, the price P_R^*. Output expands to Q_R^*, and consumer surplus is now the entire blue area. The monopolist makes zero profit. This is the greatest total surplus possible when the monopolist is allowed to at least break even, making P_R^* the best regulated price.

curve *D*, with an associated marginal revenue curve *MR*. For simplicity, we assume that the firm's total costs consist of two parts: a fixed cost and variable costs that are incurred at a constant proportion to output. In this case, marginal cost is constant, and the marginal cost curve (which here is also the average variable cost curve) is the horizontal line *MC*.

The average total cost curve is the downward-sloping curve *ATC;* it slopes downward because the higher the output, the lower the average fixed cost (the fixed cost per unit of output). Because average total cost slopes downward over the range of output relevant for market demand, this is a natural monopoly.

Panel (a) illustrates a case of natural monopoly without regulation. The unregulated natural monopolist chooses the monopoly output Q_M and charges the price P_M. Since the monopolist receives a price greater than its average total cost, it earns a profit. This profit is exactly equal to the producer surplus in this market, represented by the green-shaded rectangle. Consumer surplus is given by the blue-shaded triangle.

Now suppose that regulators impose a price ceiling on local gas deliveries—one that falls below the monopoly price P_M but above *ATC*, say, at P_R in panel (a). At that price, the quantity demanded is Q_R.

Does the company have an incentive to produce that quantity? Yes. If the price at which the monopolist can sell its product is fixed at P_R by regulators, the firm's output no longer affects the market price. The monopolist ignores the *MR* curve and is willing to expand output to meet the quantity demanded as long as the price it receives for the next unit is greater than marginal cost and the monopolist at least breaks even on total output. Thus, with price regulation, the monopolist produces more, at a lower price.

Of course, the monopolist will not be willing to produce at all if the imposed price means producing at a loss. That is, the price ceiling has to be set high enough to allow the firm to cover its average total cost. Panel (b) shows a situation in which regulators have pushed the price down as far as possible, at the level where the average total cost curve crosses the demand curve. At any lower price, the firm loses money. The price here, P_R^*, is the best regulated price: the monopolist is just willing to operate and produces Q_R^*, the quantity demanded at that price. Consumers and society gain as a result.

The welfare effects of this regulation can be seen by comparing the shaded areas in the two panels of Figure 28-2. Consumer surplus is increased by the regulation, with the gains coming from two sources. First, profits are eliminated and added instead to consumer surplus. Second, the larger output and lower price lead to an overall welfare gain—an increase in total surplus. In fact, panel (b) illustrates the largest total surplus possible.

This all looks terrific: consumers are better off, profits are eliminated, and overall welfare increases. Unfortunately, things are rarely that easy in practice. The main problem is that regulators don't have the information required to set the price exactly at the level at which the demand curve crosses the average total cost curve. Sometimes they set it too low, creating shortages; at other times, they set it too high. Also, regulated monopolies, like publicly owned firms, tend to exaggerate their costs to regulators and to provide inferior quality to consumers. However, as the Economics in Action, "Shocked by the High Price of Electricity," shows, some level of regulation is generally better than none.

28.4 Network Externalities and Dominant Firms: A New Generation of Market Power

The topic of monopoly and antitrust regulation has recently become one of the hottest topics of economic discussion in recent years. Why? It's due to the rise of the digital economy and the network externalities that it creates. Companies such as Facebook, Microsoft, Apple, Google, eBay, Twitter, and PayPal have transformed the economy. They represent the fastest growing and among the most profitable firms in the economy. Network externalities provide a number of ways of gaining market power and, potentially, of becoming a monopolist (or very close to one). However, since network externalities benefit consumers, the market power they generate presents a unique set of problems to regulators.

As we learned earlier, increasing returns to scale and network externalities share the critical feature that "bigger is better": the firm with the largest network is preferred by consumers to firms with smaller networks. Hence, the biggest firm in the industry gets bigger while smaller firms shrink. Eventually, the biggest firm—the *dominant* firm—will become large enough relative to any rivals to exert market power and behave like a monopolist.

As in standard monopoly, the dominant firm in a network externalities industry creates a deadweight loss to society if it raises price and reduces output in order to capture surplus from consumers. And in fast-moving digital industries, there's another potential inefficiency caused by market power: *stifling innovation*. The dominant firm, by using its size advantage to deter rivals from entering the market or using their network, stifles the innovation that they can bring.

Microsoft is the best example of a network externalities firm that used its size to vanquish rivals and stifle innovation. The source of Microsoft's network externality is its Windows operating system. A federal court found Microsoft guilty of engaging in "monopolization": using its market dominance in the PC operating systems market to harm Netscape, a rival to Microsoft's Internet Explorer, as well as crushing companies with superior technology who tried to develop Windows-based applications software.

Rather than breaking Microsoft up into smaller companies, the court mandated that Microsoft open up its operating-system software to rival applications software companies. However, Microsoft's position was by then so dominant that rival software companies were never able to establish a significant market share. A case in point: after having an initial market share of 90% share of the internet browser market, Netscape eventually disappeared. Not surprisingly, Microsoft's software division remains highly profitable, reporting profits of nearly $13 billion in 2019.

ECONOMICS >> *in Action*

A New Generation of Market Power

The digital giants, Amazon, Facebook, and Google, are the quintessential firms of the digital economy. Amazon, which began as an online retailer of books, has grown into a corporate behemoth: a general retailer, a marketing platform, a provider of delivery and logistical services, a payment service, a credit lender, an auction house, a major book publisher, a producer of television and films, a hardware manufacturer, a fashion creator, and a leading provider of cloud services and computing power.

Facebook is the world's dominant social platform, with nearly 2.3 billion active users as of 2018. Google accounts for 92% of global search engine activity. Together, Facebook and Google account for 73% of digital advertising in the United States. In 2018, Amazon reported annual revenue of over $142 billion, Facebook reported nearly $56 billion, and Google reported over $136 billion. (This data was found using Google, written on a computer purchased on Amazon, while not looking at any open Facebook pages.)

Economists have noted a striking feature of these three companies: each one has relied on practices that, in previous eras, were found to be either anti-competitive or had created critical large-scale infrastructure that warranted regulation as a natural monopoly.

imageBROKER/Alamy Stock Photo

The digital giants, Google, Facebook, and Amazon, have presented difficult regulatory challenges for antitrust policy makers.

For example, all three firms have taken actions to eliminate rivals. Amazon has purchased a myriad of e-retailing companies—such as Audible, Diapers.com, and Zappos—to maintain its dominance as the one-stop shopping website. Likewise, Facebook has bought rival social-networking platforms, such as Friendster, Instagram, and WhatsApp. According to EU antitrust authorities, Google has harmed competitors by requiring equipment manufacturers to install its search engine on their products.

Amazon's massive warehouse system of over 100 warehouses across the country, manned by fleets of robots, enables it to provide superfast delivery. And the volume discounts it receives from delivery companies like UPS aren't available to smaller rivals. So third-party suppliers, like Eveready Batteries, find it necessary to list their products on Amazon Marketplace. Yet, this enables Amazon to gather finely detailed data on customers' shopping habits, which they then can use to create their own "Amazon Basics" brand, which directly competes against the third-party suppliers.

Until recently, U.S. regulators have chosen not to intervene. One explanation for the years of regulatory inaction is that policy makers understood that, like natural monopoly, there was no easy fix to the problem of market dominance arising from network externalities.

However, there's been a mighty change in the past few years. In 2019, regulators opened investigations into all three firms. In 2020, regulators accused Facebook of illegally quashing competition by buying up rivals and called for the acquisitions to be unwound by selling them off; launched an investigation of Amazon's treatment of third-party sellers; and accused Google of using its market power to fend off rivals. In addition, consumers and independent app developers sued Apple, claiming that it captured higher fees by requiring app purchases to be transacted using Apple's App store.

What appears to have caused the shift is growing concerns that the tech giants were harming suppliers, squashing rivals and impeding innovation. Moreover, some have voiced the concern that the enormous economic weight of the digital giants will translate into outsized political power, making it harder to check their dominance and their exercise of market power. This echoes one of the primary concerns that led to the creation of U.S. antitrust law in the 1890s. Regulators have, in recent years, moved beyond simply looking at consumer price and quantity to assess harm from market power; now they are taking a longer view, looking at the effects on suppliers, innovation and political influence.

Will these antitrust actions have any real effect? It depends upon the nature of the network externality. Regulators are likely to have more success against Apple, Amazon, and Facebook because, while these firms benefit from network externalities generally, the allegedly illegal actions they have taken are not ones that arise from a network externality. For example, while Amazon itself benefits from the network externality that consumers and suppliers like one dominant marketing platform, there's no network externality that makes it better to buy an Amazon-branded battery than an Eveready battery on that platform. Likewise, Twitter is not any easier to use if owned by Facebook.

In contrast, in the case of Google, the network externality is very strong: a firm wants to advertise on the search engine platform that has the highest number of hits. So many industry observers think that while Apple, Amazon, and Facebook are at risk of serious antitrust remedies, Google will probably be able to pay a fine and keep chugging along, much as Microsoft has done.

Check Your Understanding 28-1

1. What policy should the government adopt in the following cases? Explain.
   a. Internet service in Anytown, Ohio, is provided by cable. Customers feel they are being overcharged, but the cable company claims it must charge prices that allow it to recover the costs of laying cable.
   b. The only two airlines that currently fly to Alaska need government approval to merge. Other airlines wish to fly to Alaska but need government-allocated landing slots to do so.
2. True or false? Explain your answer.
   a. Society's welfare is lower under monopoly because some consumer surplus is transformed into profit for the monopolist.
   b. A monopolist causes inefficiency because there are consumers who are willing to pay a price greater than or equal to marginal cost but less than the monopoly price.
3. Suppose a monopolist mistakenly believes that its marginal revenue is always equal to the market price. Assuming constant marginal cost and no fixed cost, draw a diagram comparing the level of profit, consumer surplus, total surplus, and deadweight loss for this misguided monopolist compared to a smart monopolist. Explain your findings.
4. Some social media industry observers claim that Facebook is so dominant in the social media market that is now like a utility, such as a water utility. What have you learned about monopoly that might validate this claim? What evidence might invalidate this claim?

Solutions appear at back of book.

>> Quick Review

- The choice of government policy toward monopoly depends upon the source of market power: preventing or breaking up a monopoly (scarce resources), doing nothing (technological superiority or government-created barriers), or living with it and mitigating the harm (natural monopoly and network externality market power).
- Two methods of managing natural monopoly are public ownership and price regulation. Both policies have drawbacks: firms tend to be poorly run and don't invest in lowering costs. Under price regulation, too low a price ceiling can create shortages. A drawback of public ownership is that publicly owned companies are often poorly run.
- Dealing with market power arising from network externalities is a challenge for policy makers because "bigger is better" for consumers. Yet the dominant firm can exploit its market power to rise prices and create deadweight loss, as well as stifling innovation by driving rivals out of business. But if a digital giant is broken up, another dominant firm is likely to reemerge.

MODULE 29

Price Discrimination

WHAT YOU WILL LEARN

- What is **price discrimination** and why is it so prevalent in certain industries?

Vincenzo Lombardo/Exactostock-1672/Superstock

Up to this point, we have considered only the case of a monopolist who charges all consumers the same price. However, monopolists want to maximize their profits, and often they do so by charging different prices for the same product. In this module, we look at how monopolists increase their profits by engaging in *price discrimination.*

29.1 Price Discrimination Defined

A monopolist who charges everyone the same price is known as a **single-price monopolist.** As the term suggests, not all monopolists do this. In fact, many, if not most, monopolists find that they can increase their profits by charging different customers different prices for the same good: they engage in **price discrimination.**

One of the most striking examples of price discrimination involves airline tickets. Although there are a number of airlines, most air routes in the United States are serviced by only one or two carriers. As a result, these carriers have market power and can set prices. So any regular airline passenger quickly becomes aware that the question "How much will it cost me to fly there?" rarely has a simple answer.

If you are willing to buy a nonrefundable ticket a month in advance and happen to purchase the ticket on Tuesday or Wednesday evening, the round trip may cost only $150. But if you have to go on a business trip tomorrow, which happens to be a Tuesday, and come back on Wednesday, the same round trip might cost $550. Yet the business traveler and the visiting grandparent receive the same product—the same cramped seat, the same awful food (if indeed any food is served).

You might argue that airlines are not usually monopolists—that in most flight markets, the airline industry is an oligopoly because there is more than one firm offering flights to most destinations. In fact, price discrimination takes place under oligopoly and monopolistic competition as well as monopoly because these firms have some market power and can therefore influence prices. But it doesn't happen under perfect competition, where firms have no ability to influence prices. And once we've seen why monopolists sometimes price-discriminate, we'll be in a good position to understand why it happens in oligopoly and monopolistic competition, too.

A **single-price monopolist** offers its product to all consumers at the same price.

Sellers engage in **price discrimination** when they charge different prices to different consumers for the same good.

29.2 The Logic of Price Discrimination

Let's begin by looking at why price discrimination might be more profitable than charging all consumers the same price. Imagine that Air Sunshine offers the only nonstop flights between Bismarck, North Dakota, and Fort Lauderdale, Florida. Assume that there are no capacity problems—the airline can fly as many planes as the number of passengers warrants. Also assume that there is no fixed cost. The marginal cost to the airline of providing a seat is \$125, however many passengers it carries.

Further assume that the airline knows there are two kinds of potential passengers: 2,000 business travelers who want to travel between these destinations each week and 2,000 students who want to do the same.

Will potential passengers take the flight? It depends on the price. The business travelers, it turns out, really need to fly; they will take the plane as long as the price is no more than \$550. Since they are flying purely for business, we assume that cutting the price below \$550 will not lead to any increase in business travel. The students, however, have less money and more time; if the price goes above \$150, they will take the bus. The implied demand curve is shown in Figure 29-1.

So what should the airline do? If it has to charge everyone the same price, its options are limited. It could charge \$550; that way it would get as much as possible out of the business travelers but lose the student market. Or it could charge only \$150; that way it would get both types of travelers but would make significantly less money from sales to business travelers.

We can quickly calculate the profits from each of these alternatives. If the airline charged \$550, it would sell 2,000 tickets to business travelers, earning total revenue of 2,000 × \$550 = \$1.1 million and incurring costs of 2,000 × \$125 = \$250,000; so its profit would be \$850,000, illustrated by the shaded area *B* in Figure 29-1.

If the airline charged only \$150, it would sell 4,000 tickets, receiving revenue of \$4,000 × \$150 = \$600,000 and incurring costs of \$4,000 × \$125 = \$500,000; in this case, its profit would be \$100,000. If the airline must charge everyone the same price, charging the higher price and forgoing sales to students are clearly more profitable.

FIGURE 29-1 Two Types of Airline Customers

Air Sunshine has two types of customers, business travelers willing to pay at most \$550 per ticket and students willing to pay at most \$150 per ticket. There are 2,000 of each kind of customer. Air Sunshine has a constant marginal cost of \$125 per seat. If Air Sunshine could charge these two types of customers different prices, it would maximize its profit by charging business travelers \$550 and students \$150 per ticket. It would capture all of the consumer surplus as profit.

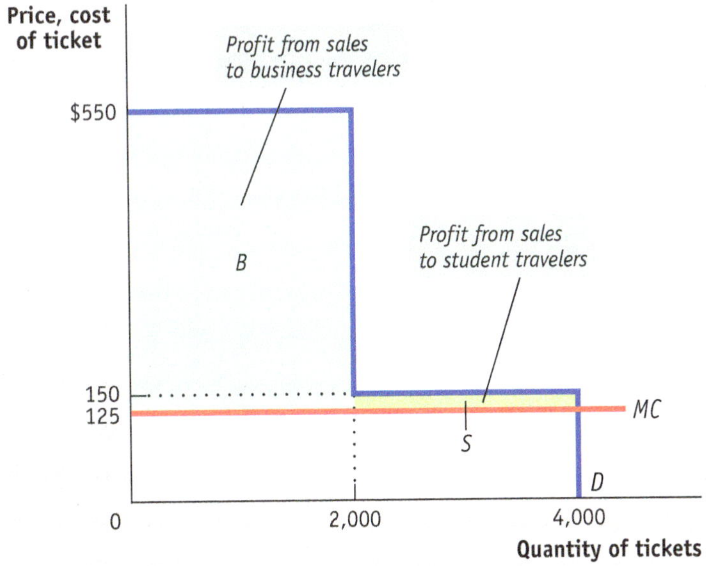

On many airline routes, the fare you pay depends on the type of traveler you are.

What the airline would really like to do, however, is charge the business travelers the full $550 but offer $150 tickets to the students. That's a lot less than the price paid by business travelers, but it's still above marginal cost; so if the airline could sell those extra 2,000 tickets to students, it would make an additional $50,000 in profit. That is, it would make a profit equal to the areas *B* plus *S* in Figure 29-1.

It would be more realistic to suppose that there is some "give" in each group's demand: at a price below $550, there would be some increase in business travel, and at a price above $150, some students would still purchase tickets. But this, it turns out, does not do away with the argument for price discrimination.

The important point is that the two groups of consumers differ in their *sensitivity to price*—that a high price has a larger effect in discouraging purchases by students than purchases by business travelers. As long as different groups of customers respond differently to the price, a monopolist will find that it can capture more consumer surplus and increase its profit by charging them different prices.

29.3 Price Discrimination and Elasticity

A more realistic description of the demand that airlines face would not specify particular prices at which different types of travelers would choose to fly. Instead, it would distinguish between the groups on the basis of their sensitivity to the price—their price elasticity of demand.

Suppose that a company sells its product to two easily identifiable groups of people—business travelers and students. It just so happens that business travelers are very insensitive to the price: there is a certain amount of the product they just have to have whatever the price, but they cannot be persuaded to buy much more than that no matter how cheap it is. Students, though, are more flexible: offer a good enough price and they will buy quite a lot, but raise the price too high and they will switch to something else. What should the company do?

The answer is the one already suggested by our simplified example: the company should charge business travelers, who have a low price elasticity of demand, a higher price than it charges students, who have a high price elasticity of demand.

The actual situation of the airlines is very much like this hypothetical example. Business travelers typically place a high priority on being at the right place at the right time and are not very sensitive to the price. But nonbusiness travelers are fairly sensitive to the price: faced with a high price, they might take the bus, drive to another airport to get a lower fare, or skip the trip altogether.

So why doesn't an airline simply announce different prices for business and nonbusiness customers? First, this would probably be illegal because U.S. law places some limits on the ability of companies to practice open price discrimination. Second, even if it were legal, it would be a hard policy to enforce: business travelers might be willing to wear casual clothing and claim they were visiting family in Fort Lauderdale in order to save $400.

So what the airlines do—quite successfully—is impose rules that indirectly have the effect of charging business and nonbusiness travelers different fares. Business travelers usually travel during the week and want to be home on the weekend, so the round-trip fare is much higher if you don't stay over a Saturday night. The requirement of a weekend stay for a cheap ticket effectively separates business from nonbusiness travelers.

Similarly, business travelers often visit several cities in succession rather than make a simple round trip, so round-trip fares are much lower than twice the one-way fare. Many business trips are scheduled on short notice, so fares are much lower if you book far in advance. Fares are also lower if you purchase a last-minute ticket, taking your chances on whether you actually get a seat—business travelers have to make it to that meeting; people visiting their relatives don't.

Because customers must show their ID at check-in, airlines make sure there are no resales of tickets between the two groups that would undermine their ability to price-discriminate—students can't buy cheap tickets and resell them to business travelers. Look at the rules that govern ticket-pricing, and you will see an ingenious implementation of profit-maximizing price discrimination.

29.4 Perfect Price Discrimination

Let's return to the example of business travelers and students traveling between Bismarck and Fort Lauderdale, illustrated in Figure 29-1, and ask what would happen if the airline could distinguish between the two groups of customers to charge each a different price.

Clearly, the airline would charge each group its willingness to pay—that is, the maximum that each group is willing to pay. For business travelers, the willingness to pay is \$550; for students, it is \$150. As we have assumed, the marginal cost is \$125 and does not depend on output, making the marginal cost curve a horizontal line. As we noted earlier, we can easily determine the airline's profit: it is the sum of the areas of the rectangle *B* and the rectangle *S*.

In this case, the consumers do not get any consumer surplus! The entire surplus is captured by the monopolist in the form of profit. When a monopolist is able to capture the entire surplus in this way, we say that it achieves **perfect price discrimination.**

In general, the greater the number of different prices a monopolist is able to charge, the closer it can get to perfect price discrimination. Figure 29-2 shows a monopolist facing a downward-sloping demand curve, a monopolist who we assume is able to charge different prices to different groups of consumers, with the consumers who are willing to pay the most being charged the most.

In panel (a), the monopolist charges two different prices; in panel (b), the monopolist charges three different prices. Two things are apparent here:

1. *The greater the number of prices the monopolist charges, the lower the lowest price—that is, some consumers will pay prices that approach marginal cost.*
2. *The greater the number of prices the monopolist charges, the more money it extracts from consumers.*

With a very large number of different prices, the picture would look like panel (c), a case of perfect price discrimination. Here, consumers least willing to buy the good pay marginal cost, and the entire consumer surplus is extracted as profit.

Both our airline example and the example in Figure 29-2 can be used to make another point: a monopolist that can engage in perfect price discrimination doesn't cause any inefficiency! The source of inefficiency is eliminated: all potential consumers who are willing to purchase the good at a price equal to or above marginal cost are able to do so. The perfectly price-discriminating monopolist manages to scoop up all consumers by offering some of them lower prices than it charges others.

In practice, monopolists find it nearly impossible to perfectly price-discriminate. That's because a monopolist is not able to know the true willingness to pay of every consumer. While each consumer knows their true willingness to pay, the monopolist does not. Thus, the consumer's information advantage allows them to disguise their true willingness to pay. For example, a business flyer who uses a senior citizen discount when purchasing their ticket is able to disguise that they have a true willingness to pay equal to the \$550 business-class fare.

Due to its information disadvantage, the price-discriminating monopolist is forced to offer only a limited number of different prices [as in panel (b) of Figure 29-2]—prices that correspond to the willingness to pay of the different types of consumers that the monopolist can identify.

Perfect price discrimination takes place when a monopolist charges each consumer their willingness to pay—the maximum that the consumer is willing to pay.

FIGURE 29-2 Price Discrimination

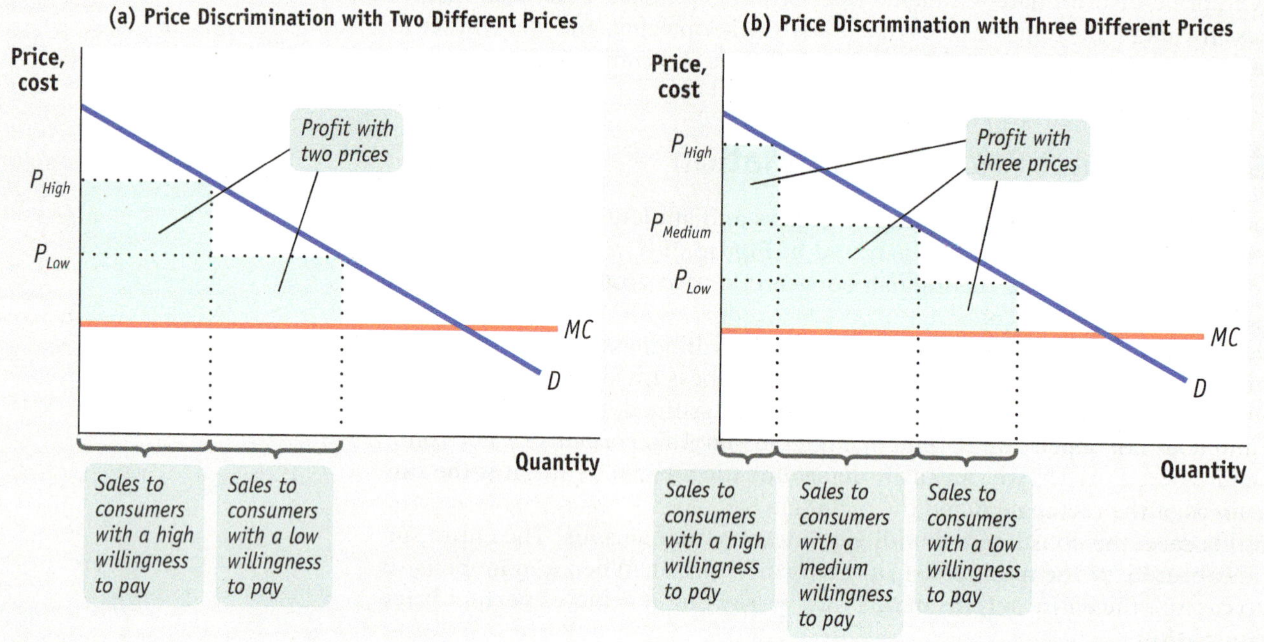

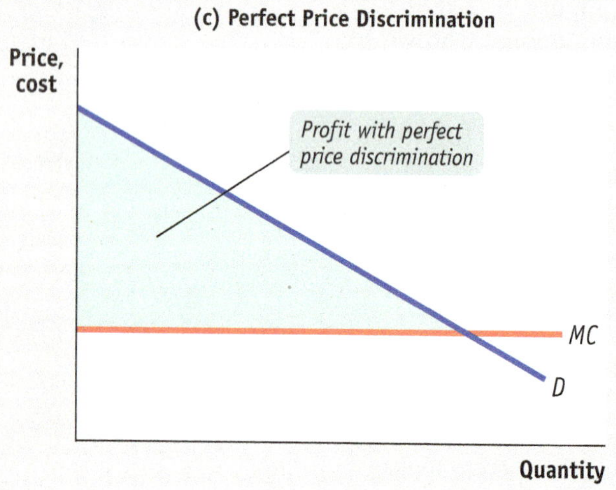

Panel (a) shows a monopolist that charges two different prices; its profit is shown by the shaded area. Panel (b) shows a monopolist that charges three different prices; its profit, too, is shown by the shaded area. It is able to capture more of the consumer surplus and to increase its profit. That is, by increasing the number of different prices charged, the monopolist captures more of the consumer surplus and makes a larger profit. Panel (c) shows the case of perfect price discrimination, where a monopolist charges each consumer their willingness to pay; the monopolist's profit is given by the shaded triangle.

Historically, monopolists have used a number of pricing strategies to try to identify different types of consumers in order to move closer to perfect price discrimination. Examples are:

- *Advance purchase restrictions.* Prices are lower for consumers who purchase well in advance (or in some cases for those who purchase at the last minute). This identifies those who have a higher sensitivity to price and are therefore willing to plan far in advance to get a cheaper price.
- *Volume discounts.* Often the price is lower if you buy a large quantity. For a consumer who plans to consume a lot of a good, the cost of the last unit—the marginal cost to the consumer—is considerably less than the average price. This identifies those who plan to buy a lot and so are likely to be more sensitive to price from those who don't.
- *Two-part tariffs.* With a two-part tariff, a customer pays a flat fee up-front and then a per-unit fee on each item purchased. The cost of the first item you buy

is in effect much higher than that of subsequent items, making the two-part tariff behave like a volume discount. For example, an Amazon Prime membership, which gives free shipping on a vast selection of items at a cost of $119 per year, is a type of two-part tariff.

- *Sales and outlet stores.* Holding regular sales, such as Black Friday sales, Labor Day sales, Memorial Day sales, and so on, is a way to identify those consumers who have a higher sensitivity to price and are therefore willing to wait to get a lower price. Likewise, building an outlet store at a distance from the center of the city allows the monopolist to establish a separate market for those customers who have a higher sensitivity to price and are therefore willing to drive a distance to get a lower price.
- *Digital personalized pricing.* The fastest-growing method of price discrimination is digital personalized pricing. By gathering personal data on shoppers' online choices and characteristics, online retailers can greatly reduce the information advantages that shoppers have about their true willingness to pay. For example, the online travel agency Orbitz discovered that Mac computer users spend as much as 30% more a night on hotels. So it shows them a fancier and costlier menu of hotels than it shows to PC users. Digital personalized pricing has the potential to achieve a closer approximation to perfect price discrimination than any other method because of its ability to collect and analyze very precise information about shoppers.

Compared to a single-price monopolist, price discrimination—even when it is not perfect—can increase the efficiency of the market. For example, with price discrimination, firms can sell to consumers who were formerly priced out of the market. Those who are now able to purchase the good at a lower price generate enough surplus to offset the loss in surplus to those now facing a higher price and no longer buying the good. In this way total surplus increases when price discrimination is introduced. This explanation of price discrimination also helps explain why government policies on monopoly typically focus on preventing deadweight losses, not preventing price discrimination—unless it causes serious issues of equity.

Suppose a drug is disproportionately prescribed to senior citizens, who are often on fixed incomes and so are very sensitive to price. A policy that allows a drug company to charge senior citizens a low price and everyone else a high price may indeed increase total surplus. But price discrimination that creates serious concerns about equity is likely to be prohibited—for example, an ambulance service that charges patients based on the severity of their emergency.

Check Your Understanding 29-1

1. True or false? Explain your answer.
   a. A single-price monopolist sells to some customers to whom a price-discriminating monopolist refuses to sell.
   b. A price-discriminating monopolist creates more inefficiency than a single-price monopolist because it captures more of the consumer surplus.
   c. Under price discrimination, a customer with highly elastic demand will pay a lower price than a customer with inelastic demand.
2. Which of the following are cases of price discrimination and which are not? In the cases of price discrimination, identify those consumers with high and those with low price elasticity of demand.
   a. Damaged merchandise is marked down.
   b. Restaurants have senior citizen discounts.
   c. Food manufacturers place discount coupons for their merchandise in newspapers.
   d. Airline tickets cost more during the summer peak flying season.

Solutions appear at back of book.

>> Quick Review

- Not every monopolist is a **single-price monopolist.** Many monopolists, as well as oligopolists and monopolistic competitors, engage in **price discrimination.**
- Price discrimination is profitable when consumers differ in their sensitivity to the price. A price-discriminating monopolist charges higher prices to low-elasticity consumers and lower prices to high-elasticity ones. The most widely used techniques are advance purchase restrictions, volume discounts, two-part tariffs, sales and outlet stores, and digital personalized pricing. Compared to a single-price monopoly, price discrimination reduces deadweight loss.
- Digital personalized pricing comes the closest to achieving **perfect price discrimination,** in which each consumer pays a price equal to their willingness to pay. This allows the monopolist to capture the total surplus in the market. No deadweight loss is incurred because all mutually beneficial transactions occur. Unless it causes serious equity issues, governments tend to focus on preventing deadweight loss and not on preventing price discrimination.

BUSINESS CASE

Amazon and Hachette Go to War

Horacio Villalobos/Getty Images

In May 2014, all-out war broke out between Amazon, the third-largest U.S. book retailer, and Hachette, the fourth-largest book publisher. Suddenly Amazon took weeks to deliver Hachette publications (paper and e-books), including best-sellers from authors like Stephen Colbert, Dan Brown, and J. D. Salinger, meanwhile at the same time offering shoppers suggestions for non-Hachette books as alternatives. In addition, pre-order options for forthcoming Hachette books—including one by J. K. Rowling of Harry Potter fame—disappeared from Amazon's website, along with many other Hachette books. These same books were readily available, often at lower prices, at rival book retailers, such as Barnes and Noble.

All publishers pay retailers a share of sales prices. In this case, hostilities were set off by Amazon's demand that Hachette raise that share from 30% to 50%. This was a familiar story: Amazon demanded ever-larger percentages during yearly contract negotiations. Since it won't carry a publisher's books without an agreement, a protracted disagreement and the resulting loss of sales are disastrous for publishers. This time, however, Hachette refused to give in and went public with Amazon's demands.

Amazon claimed that the publisher could pay more out of its profit margin—around 75% on e-books, 60% on paperbacks, and 40% on hardcovers. Indeed, Amazon openly admitted that its long-term objective was to displace publishers altogether and deal directly with authors itself. This model has been popularized by companies like Netflix that are now producing their own media content. Amazon has already received support from some famous authors, including Dean Koontz and Michael Lewis. Ironically, publishers countered that Amazon's calculations ignored the costs of editing, marketing, advertising, and at times supporting struggling writers until they became successful; yet recently, Amazon has found success in publishing as many large publishers have cut their marketing and editing budgets. Amazon, they claimed, would eventually destroy the book industry, and now the publishing industry.

In the conflict, Amazon faced some very angry authors. Douglas Preston, a best-selling Hachette author of thrillers, saw his sales drop by at least 60%. Speaking of the comfortable lifestyle that his writing supported, Preston observed that if Amazon decided not to sell his books at all, "All this goes away." In the end, the conflict became a public relations disaster for Amazon as writers and even some readers turned against them. So, Amazon eventually capitulated and agreed to allow Hachette to set the price of its e-books. However, given Amazon's size and influence, authors remain wary about the future.

In fact, a few years later Amazon became the largest U.S. book retailer. This is largely due to Amazon's costly investments in its website and its vast warehouse and speedy delivery system, despite sometimes charging higher prices than rival websites. These upgrades have been funded by Amazon investors, who waited patiently for 20 years, incurring billions of dollars in losses. But 2015 was a turning point for Amazon. That year, the company made a small profit, and each year since, it has experienced increased profitability. In 2018, Amazon made over $10 billion. The wait for its investors finally paid off. Over the same time period, Amazon's share price increased by nearly 500%.

QUESTIONS FOR THOUGHT

1. What is the source of surplus in this industry? Who generates it? How is it divided among the various agents (authors, publishers, and retailers)?
2. What are the various sources of market power here? What is at risk for the various parties?

REVIEW

MODULE 27

1. The key difference between a monopoly and a perfectly competitive industry is that a single perfectly competitive firm faces a horizontal demand curve, but a monopolist faces a downward-sloping demand curve. This gives the monopolist **market power**—the ability to raise the market price by reducing output—compared to a perfectly competitive firm.
2. The marginal revenue of a monopolist is composed of a quantity effect (the price received from the additional unit) and a price effect (the reduction in the price at which all units are sold). Because of the price effect, a monopolist's marginal revenue is always less than the market price, and the marginal revenue curve lies below the demand curve.
3. At the monopolist's profit-maximizing output level, marginal cost equals marginal revenue, which is less than market price. At the perfectly competitive firm's profit-maximizing output level, marginal cost equals the market price. So in comparison to perfectly competitive industries, monopolies produce less, charge higher prices, and earn profits in both the short run and the long run.

MODULE 28

1. A monopoly creates deadweight losses by charging a price above marginal cost: the loss in consumer surplus exceeds the monopolist's profit. The government should intervene to prevent the formation of monopolies that are created to exploit monopoly power and earn monopoly profits. If they already exist, the government should break them up. Monopolies based on government-created barriers and technological superiority will disappear over time. However, breaking up a natural monopoly will raise costs and reduce welfare.
2. Natural monopolies can still cause deadweight losses. To limit these losses, governments sometimes impose **public ownership** and at other times impose **price regulation.** They may also choose to do nothing. A price ceiling on a monopolist, as opposed to a perfectly competitive industry, need not cause shortages and can increase total surplus.
3. Market power arising from network externalities poses a difficult policy problem because consumers benefit from bigger networks. On the one hand, market power imposes deadweight loss and stifles innovation in fast-moving digital industries. On the other hand, the digital giants innovate as well and are successful because consumers have preferred them. Moreover, given the dynamics of network externalities, if the digital giant is broken up, dominant firms with market power are likely to reemerge.

MODULE 29

1. Not all monopolists are **single-price monopolists.** Monopolists, as well as oligopolists and monopolistic competitors, often engage in **price discrimination** to make higher profits, using various techniques to differentiate consumers based on their sensitivity to price, charging those with less elastic demand higher prices. Compared to a single-price monopoly, price discrimination reduces deadweight loss. The most widely used techniques are advance purchase restrictions, volume discounts, two-part tariffs, sales and outlet stores, and digital personalized pricing.
2. Digital personalized pricing comes the closest to achieving **perfect price discrimination,** in which each consumer pays a price equal to their willingness to pay. While the monopolist captures the total surplus in the market, no deadweight loss is incurred because all mutually beneficial transactions occur. Unless it causes serious equity issues, governments tend to focus on preventing deadweight loss and not preventing price discrimination.

KEY TERMS

Public ownership p. 311
Price regulation p. 311
Single-price monopolist p. 316
Price discrimination p. 316
Perfect price discrimination p. 319

UKraft/Alamy Stock Photo

Module 30 Oligopoly

Module 31 Game Theory

Module 32 Monopolistic Competition

Module 33 Product Differentiation and Advertising

SECTION 10

Oligopoly and Monopolistic Competition

REGULATORS GIVE BRIDGESTONE A FLAT TIRE

With sales of over $33 billion in 2019, Bridgestone is the largest tire company by sales in the United States. But only 5 years earlier it suffered a particularly humiliating turn of events, courtesy of the U.S. Justice Department. In 2014, Bridgestone admitted that for several years it had met with competitors like Hitachi Automotive and Mitsubishi Electric. To set prices and split up the market for rubber automotive parts, behavior called *price-fixing*. In all, 26 companies pled guilty to price-fixing for rubber automotive parts, 32 people were indicted, and a total of more than $2 billion in fines were assessed by the U.S. government.

What Bridgestone and their co-conspirators were doing was illegal. According to the indictment issued by the Justice Department, their actions were undertaken to "suppress and eliminate competition." The effect was to raise the price of auto parts to auto manufacturers throughout the country—from General Motors to Toyota to Chrysler.

The case brought against Bridgestone and its co-conspirators illustrates the issues posed by *oligopoly*—a type of market structure in which there are only a few producers. When there are only a few producers in an industry, *strategic behavior* arises because each firm understands that its behavior affects how rival firms will respond. As a result, they are tempted to *collude* to raise profits, as Bridgestone and its rivals did. The potential for anti-competitive behavior keeps regulators very busy engaging in *antitrust policy:* investigating and often intervening in oligopolistic industries to protect consumers.

After analyzing oligopoly, we will turn to our last category of market structure—*monopolistic competition*. In monopolistically competitive industries, there are too many producers to permit collusion, but not enough to lead to perfect competition. Therefore, monopolistic competitors try to soften the competition between themselves by engaging in *product differentiation* and advertising, as a way of increasing and protecting their market shares.

Both oligopoly and monopolistic competition are highly prevalent in today's economy—far more than either perfect competition or monopoly. So when you are choosing between eating at Chipotle or Red Lobster, understand that you are enjoying the variety that product differentiation by monopolistic competitors creates. And when you notice that airlines always seem to raise and lower fares within a few days of one another, understand that you are observing oligopoly strategic behavior in action.

MODULE 30

Oligopoly

WHAT YOU WILL LEARN

- What is oligopoly and why does it occur?
- Why do oligopolists benefit from collusion and how are consumers hurt by it?
- Why is **antitrust policy,** policy that is aimed at preventing collusion among oligopolists, a critical function of government?

Martin Barraud/Getty Images

Recall that oligopoly arises because barriers to entry exist that limit the number of firms in the industry, barriers that are weaker than those that lead to monopoly. Oligopolists are tempted to engage in the kind of behavior that got Bridgestone, Hitachi Automotive, and Mitsubishi Electric into trouble because they understand that their profits are *interdependent:* what one firm does affects the profits of its rivals. As a result, the study of oligopoly introduces us to the topic of strategic behavior and the various types of "games" that oligopolists play.

30.1 Understanding Oligopoly

Oligopolists can behave very differently than firms in other types of market structure because they operate in a state of **interdependence.** This means that pricing and production decisions of one firm significantly affect the profits of its rivals. To begin to understand how oligopolists think and behave, we will start with an example.

A Duopoly Example

We'll now examine the simplest version of oligopoly, an industry in which there are only two producing firms—a **duopoly—**and each is known as a **duopolist.**

When a firm's decision significantly affects the profits of other firms in the industry, the firms are in a situation of **interdependence.**

An oligopoly consisting of only two firms is a **duopoly.** Each firm is known as a **duopolist.**

Going back to our opening story, imagine that there are only two producers of auto tires, Bridgestone and Hitachi. To make things simpler, suppose that once a company has incurred the fixed cost needed to produce tires, the marginal cost of producing another tire is zero. So the companies are concerned only with the revenue they receive from sales and not with their costs.

Table 30-1 shows a hypothetical demand schedule for tires and the total revenue of the industry at each price–quantity combination.

TABLE 30-1	**Demand Schedule for Tires**	
Price of tire	**Quantity of tires demanded (millions)**	**Total revenue (millions)**
$12	0	$0
11	10	110
10	20	200
9	30	270
8	40	320
7	50	350
6	60	360
5	70	350
4	80	320
3	90	270
2	100	200
1	110	110
0	120	0

If this were a perfectly competitive industry, each firm would have an incentive to produce more as long as the market price was above marginal cost. Since the marginal cost is assumed to be zero, this would mean that at equilibrium tires would be provided free. Firms would produce until price equals zero, yielding a total output of 120 million tires and zero revenue for both firms.

Yet, surely the firms would not be that stupid. With only two firms in the industry, each would realize that by producing more, it drives down the market price. So each firm would, like a monopolist, realize that profits would be higher if it and its rival limited their production.

So how much will the two firms produce?

One possibility is that the two companies will engage in *collusion*—they will cooperate to raise their joint profits. The strongest form of collusion is a **cartel,** an arrangement between producers that determines how much each is allowed to produce. The world's most famous cartel is the Organization of Petroleum Exporting Countries (OPEC), described in an Economics in Action in Module 31.

As its name indicates, OPEC is actually an agreement among governments rather than firms. There's a reason this cartel is an agreement among governments: cartels among firms are illegal in the United States and many other jurisdictions. But let's ignore the law for a moment (which is, of course, what Bridgestone did in real life—to its detriment).

Let's illustrate with an example of a cartel formed by only two firms, Bridgestone and Hitachi. We'll assume that this particular cartel decided to act as if it were a monopolist, maximizing total industry profits. It's obvious from Table 30-1 that to maximize the combined profits of the two firms, the cartel should set total industry output at 60 million tires, which would sell at a price of $6 per tire, leading to revenue of $360 million, the maximum possible.

Then the only question would be how much of that 60 million tires each firm gets to produce. A fair solution might be for each firm to produce 30 million tires with revenues for each firm of $180 million.

But even if the two firms agreed on such a deal, they might have a problem: each of the firms would have an incentive to break its word and produce more than the agreed-upon quantity.

Collusion and Competition

Suppose that the presidents of Bridgestone and Hitachi were to agree that each would produce 30 million tires over the next year. Both would understand that this plan maximizes their combined profits. And both would have an incentive to cheat.

To see why, consider what would happen if Hitachi honored its agreement, producing only 30 million tires, but Bridgestone ignored its promise and produced 40 million tires. This increase in total output would drive the price down from $6 to $5 per tire, the price at which 70 million tires are demanded. The industry's total revenue would fall from $360 million ($6 × 60 million tires) to $350 million ($5 × 70 million tires). However, Bridgestone's revenue would *rise,* from $180 million ($6 × 30 million tires) to $200 million ($5 × 40 million tires). Since we are assuming a marginal cost of zero, this would mean a $20 million increase in Bridgestone's profits.

But Hitachi's president might make exactly the same calculation. And if both firms were to produce 40 million tires, the price would drop to $4 per tire; thus, each firm's profits would fall, from $180 million to $160 million.

A **cartel** is an agreement among several producers to obey output restrictions to increase their joint profits.

Why do individual firms have an incentive to produce more than the quantity that maximizes their joint profits? Because neither firm has as strong an incentive to limit its output as a true monopolist would.

Let's go back for a minute to the theory of monopoly. We know that a profit-maximizing monopolist sets marginal cost (which in this case is zero) equal to marginal revenue. But what is marginal revenue? Recall that, under monopoly, producing an additional unit of a good has two effects:

1. A positive *quantity* effect: one more unit is sold, increasing total revenue by the price at which that unit is sold.
2. A negative *price* effect: to sell one more unit, the monopolist must cut the market price on *all* units sold.

The negative price effect is the reason marginal revenue for a monopolist is less than the market price. In the case of oligopoly, when considering the effect of increasing production, a firm is concerned only with the price effect on its *own* units of output, not those of its fellow oligopolists. Both Bridgestone and Hitachi suffer a negative price effect if Bridgestone decides to produce extra tires and so drives down the price. But Bridgestone cares only about the negative price effect on the units it produces, not about the loss to Hitachi.

This tells us that an individual firm in an oligopolistic industry faces a smaller price effect from an additional unit of output than does a monopolist; therefore, the marginal revenue that such a firm calculates is higher. So, it will seem to be profitable for any one company in an oligopoly to increase production, even if that increase reduces the profits of the industry as a whole. But if everyone thinks that way, the result is that everyone earns a lower profit!

Until now, we have been able to analyze producer behavior by asking what a producer should do to maximize profits. But even if Bridgestone and Hitachi are both trying to maximize profits, what does this predict about their behavior? Will they engage in collusion, reaching and holding to an agreement that maximizes their combined profits? Or will they engage in **noncooperative behavior,** with each firm acting in its own self-interest, even though this has the effect of driving down everyone's profits? Both strategies sound like profit maximization. Which will actually describe their behavior?

Now you see why oligopoly presents the potential for strategic behavior: there are only a small number of players, making collusion a real possibility. If there were dozens or hundreds of firms, it would be safe to assume they would behave noncooperatively. However, for reasons we will cite shortly, oligopolists are often unable to collude.

Since collusion is ultimately more profitable than noncooperative behavior, firms do have an incentive to collude if they can. One way for oligopolists to achieve collusion is to formalize it—sign an agreement (maybe even make a legal contract) or establish some financial incentives for the companies to set their prices high. But in the United States and many other nations, you can't do that—at least not legally. Companies cannot make a legal contract to keep prices high: not only is the contract unenforceable but writing it is a one-way ticket to jail. Neither can they sign an informal agreement, which lacks the force of law but perhaps rests on threats of retaliation—that's illegal, too.

In fact, executives from rival companies rarely meet without lawyers present, who make sure that the conversation does not stray into inappropriate territory. Even hinting at how nice it would be if prices were higher can bring you an unwelcome interview with the Justice Department or the Federal Trade Commission.

For example, in an emblematic 2013 case, the Justice Department launched a price-fixing case against Monsanto and other large producers of genetically modified seed. The Justice Department was alerted by a series of meetings held between Monsanto and Pioneer Hi-Bred International, two companies that account for 60% of the U.S. market in corn and soybean seed. The two companies, parties to

When firms ignore the effects of their actions on each others' profits, they engage in **noncooperative behavior.**

a licensing agreement involving genetically modified seed, claimed that no illegal discussions of price-fixing occurred in those meetings. But the fact that the two firms discussed prices as part of the licensing agreement was enough to trigger action by the Justice Department.

Sometimes, as we've seen, oligopolistic firms just ignore the rules. But more often they find ways to achieve collusion without a formal agreement, as we'll soon see.

Check Your Understanding 30-1

1. Which of the following factors increase the likelihood that an oligopolist will collude with other firms in the industry? Which increase the likelihood that an oligopolist will act noncooperatively and raise output? Explain your answers.
   a. The firm's initial market share is small. (*Hint:* Think about the price effect.)
   b. The firm has a cost advantage over its rivals.
   c. The firm's customers face additional costs when they switch from the use of one firm's product to another firm's product.
   d. The oligopolist has a lot of unused production capacity but knows that its rivals are operating at their maximum production capacity and cannot increase the amount they produce.

Solutions appear at back of book.

>> Quick Review

- Oligopolies operate in a state of **interdependence,** in which a firm's pricing and production decisions directly affect the other firm(s) in the industry.
- Some of the key issues in oligopoly can be understood by looking at the simplest case, a **duopoly**—an industry containing only two firms, called **duopolists.**
- By acting as if they were a single monopolist, oligopolists can maximize their combined profits. So there is an incentive to form a **cartel.**
- However, each firm has an incentive to cheat—to produce more than it is supposed to under the cartel agreement. So there are two principal outcomes: successful collusion or behaving **noncooperatively** by cheating.

30.2 Oligopoly in Practice

How do oligopolies usually work in practice? The answer depends both on the legal framework that limits what firms can do and on the underlying ability of firms in a given industry to cooperate without formal agreements.

The Legal Framework

To understand oligopoly pricing in practice, we must be familiar with the legal constraints under which oligopolistic firms operate. In the United States, oligopoly first became an issue during the second half of the nineteenth century, when the growth of railroads—themselves an oligopolistic industry—created a national market for many goods.

Large firms that were producing oil, steel, and many other products soon emerged. The industrialists quickly realized that profits would be higher if they could limit price competition. So, many industries formed cartels—that is, they signed formal agreements to limit production and raise prices. Until 1890, when the first federal legislation against such cartels was passed, this was perfectly legal.

However, although these cartels were legal, they weren't legally *enforceable*—members of a cartel couldn't ask the courts to force a firm that was violating its agreement to reduce its production. And firms often did violate their agreements, for the reason already suggested by our duopoly example: there is always a temptation for each firm in a cartel to produce more than it is supposed to.

In 1881, clever lawyers at John D. Rockefeller's Standard Oil Company came up with a solution—the so-called trust. In a trust, shareholders of all the major companies in an industry placed their shares in the hands of a board of trustees who controlled the companies. This, in effect, merged the companies into a single firm that could then engage in monopoly pricing. In this way, the Standard Oil Trust established what was essentially a monopoly of the oil industry, and it was soon followed by sugar, whiskey, lead, cottonseed oil, and linseed oil trusts.

Eventually there was a public backlash, driven partly by concern about the economic effects of the trust movement, partly by fear that the owners of the trusts

Sidney Harris/Cartoonstock.com

"Frankly, I'm dubious about amalgamated smelting and refining pleading innocent to their anti-trust violation due to insanity."

were simply becoming too powerful. The result was the Sherman Antitrust Act of 1890, which was intended both to prevent the creation of more monopolies and to break up existing ones. At first this law went largely unenforced, but over the decades that followed, the federal government became increasingly committed to making it difficult for oligopolistic industries either to become monopolies or to behave like them. Such efforts are known to this day as **antitrust policy.**

Among advanced countries, the United States is unique in its long tradition of antitrust policy. Until recently, other advanced countries did not have policies against price-fixing, and some had even supported the creation of cartels, believing that it would help their own firms against foreign rivals. But the situation has changed radically over the past 30 years, as the European Union (EU)—a supranational body tasked with enforcing antitrust policy for its member countries—has moved toward U.S. practices. Today, EU and U.S. regulators often target the same firms because price-fixing has "gone global" as international trade has expanded.

During the early 1990s, the United States instituted an amnesty program in which a price-fixer receives a much-reduced penalty if it informs on its co-conspirators. In addition, Congress increased the maximum fines levied upon conviction. These two new policies clearly made informing on your cartel partners a dominant strategy, and it has paid off because executives from Belgium, Britain, Canada, France, Germany, Italy, Mexico, the Netherlands, South Korea, and Switzerland, as well as from the United States, have been convicted of cartel crimes in U.S. courts. As one lawyer commented, "you get a race to the courthouse" as each conspirator seeks to be the first to come clean.

Life has gotten much tougher over the past few years if you want to operate a cartel.

Tacit Collusion and Price Wars

If a real industry were as simple as our tire example, it probably wouldn't be necessary for the company presidents to meet or do anything that could land them in jail. Both firms would realize that it was in their mutual interest to restrict output to 30 million tires each and that any short-term gains to either firm from producing more would be much less than the later losses as the other firm retaliated. So even without any explicit agreement, the firms would probably achieve the tacit collusion needed to maximize their combined profits.

Firms are said to be engaged in **tacit collusion** when, as in our example, they restrict output in a way that raises the profits of another firm and expect the favor to be returned even without an enforceable agreement—although they act "as if" they had such an agreement and are in legal jeopardy if they even discuss prices.

Real industries are nowhere near that simple. Nonetheless, in most oligopolistic industries, most of the time, the sellers do appear to succeed in keeping prices above their noncooperative level. Tacit collusion, in other words, is the normal state of oligopoly.

Although tacit collusion is common, it rarely allows an industry to push prices all the way up to their monopoly level; collusion is usually far from perfect. As we discuss next, there are four factors that make it hard for an industry to coordinate on high prices.

Antitrust policy consists of efforts undertaken by the government to prevent oligopolistic industries from becoming or behaving like monopolies.

When firms limit production and raise prices in a way that raises one anothers' profits, even though they have not made any formal agreement, they are engaged in **tacit collusion.**

1. Less Concentration In a less concentrated industry, the typical firm will have a smaller market share than in a more concentrated industry. This tilts firms toward noncooperative behavior because when a smaller firm cheats and increases its output, it gains for itself all of the profit from the higher output. And if its rivals retaliate by increasing their output, the firm's losses are limited because of its relatively modest market share. A less concentrated industry is often an indication that there are low barriers to entry.

2. Complex Products and Pricing Schemes In our tire example the two firms produce only one product. In reality, however, oligopolists often sell thousands or even tens of thousands of different products. Under these circumstances, keeping track of what other firms are producing and the prices they are charging is difficult. This makes it hard to determine whether a firm is cheating on the tacit agreement.

3. Differences in Interests In the tire example, a tacit agreement for the firms to split the market equally is a natural outcome, probably acceptable to both firms. In real industries, however, firms often differ both in their perceptions about what is fair and in their real interests.

For example, suppose that Hitachi was a long-established tire producer and Bridgestone a more recent entrant to the industry. Hitachi might feel that it deserved to continue producing more than Bridgestone, but Bridgestone might feel that it was entitled to 50% of the business.

Alternatively, suppose that Bridgestone's marginal costs were lower than Hitachi's. Even if they could agree on market shares, they would then disagree about the profit-maximizing level of output.

4. Bargaining Power of Buyers Often oligopolists sell not to individual consumers but to large buyers—other industrial enterprises, nationwide chains of stores, and so on. These large buyers are in a position to bargain for lower prices from the oligopolists: they can ask for a discount from an oligopolist and warn that they will go to a competitor if they don't get it. An important reason that large retailers like Walmart are able to offer lower prices to customers than small retailers is precisely their ability to use their size to extract lower prices from their suppliers.

These difficulties in enforcing tacit collusion have sometimes led companies to defy the law and create illegal cartels. We've already examined the case of the tire industry and in the upcoming Economics in Action, we'll look at the chocolate industry.

Because tacit collusion is often hard to achieve, most oligopolies charge prices that are well below what the same industry would charge if it were controlled by a monopolist—or what they would charge if they were able to collude explicitly. In addition, sometimes collusion breaks down and there is a **price war.** A price war sometimes simply involves a collapse of prices to their noncooperative level. Sometimes they even go *below* that level, as sellers try to put each other out of business or at least punish what they regard as cheating.

A **price war** occurs when tacit collusion breaks down and prices collapse.

ECONOMICS >> *in Action*

The Case Against Chocolate Producers Melts

In the Bridgestone case, company executives admitted to price-fixing, giving investigators indisputable evidence of collusion that was used to prosecute the company. However, without solid evidence, the prosecution of price-fixing can be a tricky business. The differing outcomes of price-fixing allegations in the U.S. and Canadian chocolate industry make that point abundantly clear.

In late 2015, an 8-year-long probe into collusion by the major Canadian chocolate makers finally ended. It started when Cadbury Canada disclosed that

Daniel Acker/Bloomberg via Getty Images

Are chocolate makers engaging in price-fixing?

it had colluded with Hershey Canada, Nestlé Canada, and Mars Canada. In the ensuing court case, 13 Cadbury Canada executives revealed their contacts with the other companies, including one episode in which a Nestlé Canada executive handed over details about a forthcoming price hike to Cadbury Canada. According to court documents, top executives of Hershey Canada, Nestlé Canada, and Mars Canada secretly met to set prices. After protracted litigation, all four producers settled the case and paid fines totaling more than $23 million that were then distributed among consumers.

South of the border, several of the largest U.S. grocery chains and snack retailers were convinced that they, too, had been victims of collusion by chocolate makers. In 2010, one of these stores, SuperValu, filed a lawsuit against the U.S. divisions of the four chocolate makers. In contrast to Canada, where the big four controlled a little less than 50% of the market, in the U.S. market, they controlled over 75%. SuperValu claimed that the U.S. companies had been fixing prices since 2002, regularly increasing prices by mid-single-digit to double-digit amounts within a few days of one another.

Indeed, over that period the price of chocolate candy in the United States had soared, climbing by 17% from 2008 to 2010, far in excess of the rate of inflation. U.S. chocolate makers, however, defended their actions, contending that they were simply passing on the higher costs of cocoa beans, dairy products, and sugar. And as antitrust experts pointed out, without solid evidence such as conversations or written agreements between companies, price-fixing can be very difficult to prove because it is not illegal for producers to raise prices at the same time.

In 2014, a U.S. judge threw out the collusion case against the U.S. chocolate producers, stating that closely timed price increases were not sufficient proof of collusion and that there was no evidence that U.S. producers knew of the collusion between the Canadian counterparts. Federal judge Christopher Conner concluded that the companies engaged in "rational, competitive behavior" when they increased prices to counter anticipated cost increases. In 2015, Canadian regulators finally closed their books on the case, deciding against bringing further criminal charges against the four companies.

>> *Quick Review*

- Oligopolies operate under legal restrictions in the form of **antitrust policy.** But many succeed in achieving **tacit collusion,** which occurs when firms, without any formal agreement, limit production and raise prices in a way that raises one another's profits.
- Tacit collusion is limited by a number of factors, including large numbers of firms, complex products and pricing, differences in interests among firms, and the bargaining power of buyers. When collusion breaks down, there is a **price war.**

Check Your Understanding 30-2

1. Which of the following factors are likely to support the conclusion that there is tacit collusion in this industry? Which are not? Explain.
   a. For many years the price in the industry has changed infrequently, and all the firms in the industry charge the same price. The largest firm publishes a catalog containing a "suggested" retail price. Changes in price coincide with changes in the catalog.
   b. There has been considerable variation in the market shares of the firms in the industry over time.
   c. Firms in the industry build unnecessary features into their products to make it hard for consumers to switch from one company's products to another company's products.
   d. Firms meet yearly to discuss their annual sales forecasts.
   e. Firms tend to adjust their prices upward at the same times.

Solutions appear at back of book

Game Theory

MODULE
31

WHAT YOU WILL LEARN

- How do the insights gained from **game theory** help us understand the strategic behavior of oligopolists?
- Why are oligopolists often able to maintain profits in the long run without formal collusion?

31.1 Games Oligopolists Play

photosindia/Getty Images

In our duopoly example and in real life, each oligopolistic firm realizes both that its profit depends on what its competitor does and that its competitor's profit depends on what it does. Each firm's decisions, then, will significantly affect the profit of the other firm (or firms, in the case of more than two).

In effect, the two firms are playing a game in which the profit of each player depends not only on its own actions but also on those of the other player (or players). To understand more fully how oligopolists behave, economists, along with mathematicians, developed the area of study of such games, known as **game theory.** It has many applications, not just to economics but also to military strategy, politics, and other social sciences.

Let's see how game theory helps us understand oligopoly.

The Prisoners' Dilemma

Game theory deals with any situation in which the reward to any one player—the **payoff**—depends not only on their own actions but also on those of other players in the game. In the case of oligopolistic firms, the payoff is simply the firm's profit.

When there are only two players, as in a duopoly, the interdependence between the players can be represented with a **payoff matrix** like that shown in Figure 31-1. Each row corresponds to an action by one player (in this case, Bridgestone); each column corresponds to an action by the other (in this case, Hitachi). For simplicity, let's assume that Bridgestone can pick only one of two alternatives: produce 30 million tires or produce 40 million tires. Hitachi has the same pair of choices.

The matrix contains four boxes, each divided by a diagonal line. Each box shows the payoff to the two firms that results from a pair of choices: the number below the diagonal shows Bridgestone's profits; the number above the diagonal shows Hitachi's profits.

The study of behavior in situations of interdependence is known as **game theory.**

The reward received by a player in a game, such as the profit earned by an oligopolist, is that player's **payoff.**

A **payoff matrix** shows how the payoff to each of the participants in a two-player game depends on the actions of both. Such a matrix helps us analyze situations of interdependence.

FIGURE 31-1 A Payoff Matrix

Two firms, Bridgestone and Hitachi, must decide how many tires to produce. The profits of the two firms are *interdependent:* each firm's profit depends not only on its own decision but also on the other firm's decision. Each row represents an action by Bridgestone; each column an action by Hitachi. Both firms will be better off if they both choose the lower output, but it is in each firm's individual interest to choose the higher output.

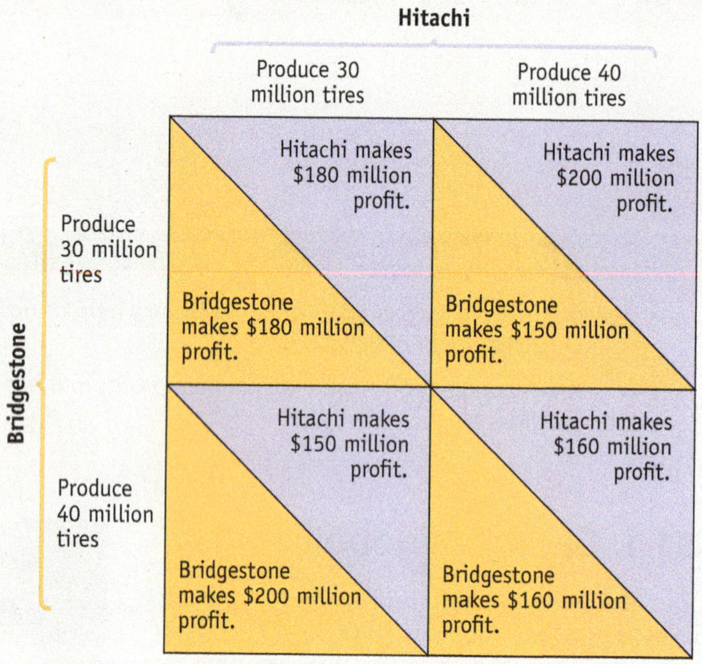

These payoffs show what we concluded from our earlier analysis: the combined profit of the two firms is maximized if they each produce 30 million tires. Either firm can, however, increase its own profits by producing 40 million tires while the other produces only 30 million tires. But if both produce the larger quantity, both will have lower profits than if they had both held their output down.

The particular situation shown here is a version of a famous—and seemingly paradoxical—case of interdependence that appears in many contexts. Known as the **prisoners' dilemma,** it is a type of game in which the payoff matrix implies the following:

- Each player has an incentive, regardless of what the other player does, to cheat—to take an action that benefits it at the other's expense.
- When both players cheat, both are worse off than they would have been if neither had cheated.

The original illustration of the prisoners' dilemma occurred in a fictional story about two accomplices in crime—let's call them Thelma and Louise—who have been caught by the police. The police have enough evidence to put them behind bars for 5 years. They also know that the pair have committed a more serious crime, one that carries a 20-year sentence; unfortunately, they don't have enough evidence to convict the women on that charge. To do so, they would need each of the prisoners to implicate the other in the second crime.

Prisoners' dilemma is a game based on two premises: (1) Each player has an incentive to choose an action that benefits itself at the other player's expense; (2) when both players act in this way, both are worse off than if they had acted cooperatively.

So the police put the miscreants in separate cells and say the following to each: "Here's the deal: if neither of you confesses, you know that we'll send you to jail for 5 years. If you confess and implicate your partner, and she doesn't do the same, we'll reduce your sentence from 5 years to 2. But if your partner confesses and you don't, you'll get the maximum 20 years. And if both of you confess, we'll give you both 15 years."

Figure 31-2 shows the payoffs that face the prisoners, depending on the decision of each to remain silent or to confess. (Usually the payoff matrix reflects the

FIGURE 31-2 The Prisoners' Dilemma

Each of two prisoners, held in separate cells, is offered a deal by the police—a light sentence if she confesses and implicates her accomplice but her accomplice does not do the same, a heavy sentence if she does not confess but her accomplice does, and so on. It is in the joint interest of both prisoners not to confess; it is in each one's individual interest to confess.

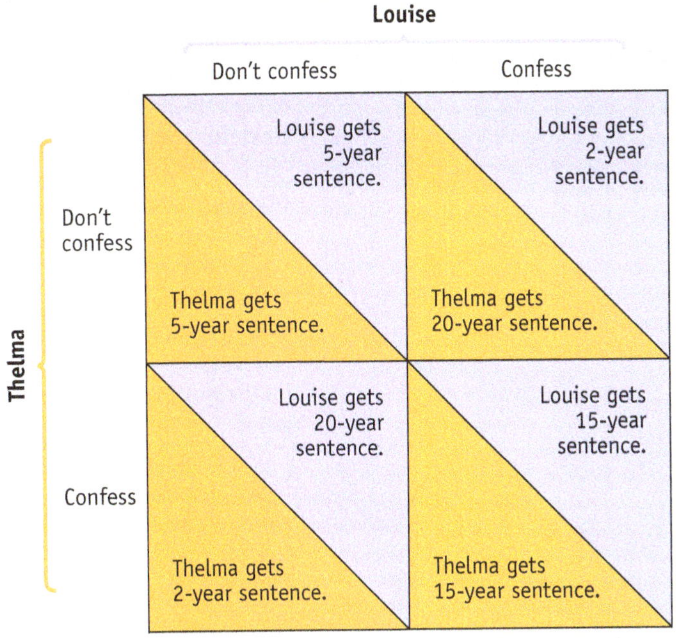

players' payoffs, and higher payoffs are better than lower payoffs. This case is an exception: a higher number of years in prison is bad, not good!) Let's assume that the prisoners have no way to communicate and that they have not sworn an oath not to harm each other or anything of that sort. So each acts in her own self-interest. What will they do?

The answer is clear: both will confess. Look at it first from Thelma's point of view: she is better off confessing, regardless of what Louise does. If Louise doesn't confess, Thelma's confession reduces her own sentence from 5 years to 2. If Louise *does* confess, Thelma's confession reduces her sentence from 20 to 15 years. Either way, it's clearly in Thelma's interest to confess. And because she faces the same incentives, it's clearly in Louise's interest to confess, too. To confess in this situation is a type of action that economists call a *dominant strategy*. An action is a **dominant strategy** when it is the player's best action regardless of the action taken by the other player.

It's important to note that not all games have a dominant strategy—it depends on the structure of payoffs in the game. But in the case of Thelma and Louise, it is clearly in the interest of the police to structure the payoffs so that confessing is a dominant strategy for each person. As long as the two prisoners have no way to make an enforceable agreement that neither will confess (something they can't do if they can't communicate, and the police certainly won't allow them to do so because the police want to compel each one to confess), however, Thelma and Louise will each act in a way that hurts the other.

So if each prisoner acts rationally in her own interest, both will confess. Yet if neither of them had confessed, both would have received a much lighter sentence! In a prisoners' dilemma, each player has a clear incentive to act in a way that hurts the other player—but when both make that choice, it leaves both of them worse off.

When Thelma and Louise both confess, they reach an *equilibrium* of the game. We have used this concept of equilibrium many times; it is an outcome in which no individual or firm has any incentive to change his or her action.

An action is a **dominant strategy** when it is a player's best action regardless of the action taken by the other player.

In game theory, this kind of equilibrium—in which each player takes the action that is best for them given the actions taken by other players, and vice versa—is known as a **Nash equilibrium,** after the mathematician and Nobel laureate John Nash. (Nash's life was chronicled in the best-selling biography *A Beautiful Mind,* which was made into a movie.) Because the players in a Nash equilibrium do not take into account the effect of their actions on others, this is also known as a **noncooperative equilibrium.**

Now look back at Figure 31-1: Bridgestone and Hitachi are in the same situation as Thelma and Louise. Each firm is better off producing the higher output, regardless of what the other firm does. Yet if both produce 40 million tires, both are worse off than if they had followed their agreement and produced only 30 million tires. In both cases, then, the pursuit of individual self-interest—the effort to maximize profits or to minimize jail time—has the perverse effect of hurting both players.

Prisoners' dilemmas appear in many situations. Clearly, the players in any prisoners' dilemma would be better off if they had some way of enforcing cooperative behavior—if Thelma and Louise had both sworn to a code of silence or if Bridgestone and Hitachi had signed an enforceable agreement not to produce more than 30 million tires. In the United States, however, an agreement setting the output levels of two oligopolists isn't just unenforceable; it's illegal. So, then, it seems that a noncooperative equilibrium is the only possible outcome. Or is it?

Overcoming the Prisoners' Dilemma: Repeated Interaction and Tacit Collusion

Thelma and Louise in their cells are playing what is known as a *one-shot* game—that is, they play the game with each other only once. They get to choose once and for all whether to confess or hang tough, and that's it. However, most of the games that oligopolists play aren't one-shot; instead, they expect to play the game repeatedly with the same rivals.

An oligopolist usually expects to be in business for many years, and it knows that its decision today about whether to cheat is likely to affect the way other firms treat it in the future. So a smart oligopolist doesn't decide what to do just based on the effect on profit in the short run. Instead, it engages in **strategic behavior,** taking account of the effects of the action it chooses today on the future actions of other players in the game. And under some conditions, oligopolists that behave strategically can manage to behave as if they had a formal agreement to collude.

Suppose that Bridgestone and Hitachi expect to be in the tire business for many years and therefore expect to play the game of cheat versus collude shown in Figure 31-1 many times. Would they really betray each other time and again?

Probably not. Suppose that Bridgestone considers two strategies. In one strategy, it always cheats, producing 40 million tires each year, regardless of what Hitachi does. In the other strategy, it starts with good behavior, producing only 30 million tires in the first year, and watches to see what its rival does. If Hitachi also keeps its production down, Bridgestone will stay cooperative, producing 30 million tires again for the next year. But if Hitachi produces 40 million tires, Bridgestone will take the gloves off and also produce 40 million tires the next year. This latter strategy—start by behaving cooperatively, but thereafter do whatever the other player did in the previous period—is generally known as **tit for tat.**

Tit for tat is a form of strategic behavior, which we have just defined as behavior intended to influence the future actions of other players. Tit for tat offers a reward to the other player for cooperative behavior—if you behave cooperatively, so will I. It also provides a punishment for cheating—if you cheat, don't expect me to be nice in the future.

A **Nash equilibrium,** also known as a **noncooperative equilibrium,** results when each player in a game chooses the action that maximizes their payoff given the actions of other players, ignoring the effects of their action on the payoffs received by those other players.

A firm engages in **strategic behavior** when it attempts to influence the future behavior of other firms.

A strategy of **tit for tat** involves playing cooperatively at first and then doing whatever the other player did in the previous period.

The payoff to Bridgestone of each of these strategies would depend on which strategy Hitachi chooses. Consider the four possibilities, as shown in Figure 31-3:

1. If Bridgestone plays tit for tat and so does Hitachi, both firms will make a profit of $180 million each year.
2. If Bridgestone plays always cheat but Hitachi plays tit for tat, Bridgestone makes a profit of $200 million the first year but only $160 million per year thereafter.
3. If Bridgestone plays tit for tat but Hitachi plays always cheat, Bridgestone makes a profit of only $150 million in the first year but $160 million per year thereafter.
4. If Bridgestone plays always cheat and Hitachi does the same, both firms will make a profit of $160 million each year.

Which strategy is better? In the first year, Bridgestone does better playing always cheat, whatever its rival's strategy: it assures itself that it will get either $200 million or $160 million (which of the two payoffs it actually receives depends on whether Hitachi plays tit for tat or always cheat). This is better than what it would get in the first year if it played tit for tat: either $180 million or $150 million. But by the second year, a strategy of always cheat gains Bridgestone only $160 million per year for the second and all subsequent years, regardless of Hitachi's actions.

Over time, the total amount gained by Bridgestone by playing always cheat is less than the amount it would gain by playing tit for tat: for the second and all subsequent years, it would never get any less than $160 million and would get as much as $180 million if Hitachi played tit for tat as well. Which strategy, always cheat or tit for tat, is more profitable depends on two things: how many years Bridgestone expects to play the game and what strategy its rival follows.

If Bridgestone expects the tire business to end in the near future, it is in effect playing a one-shot game. So it might as well cheat and grab what it can. Even

FIGURE 31-3 How Repeated Interaction Can Support Collusion

A strategy of tit for tat involves playing cooperatively at first and then following the other player's move. This rewards good behavior and punishes bad behavior. If the other player cheats, playing tit for tat will lead to only a short-term loss in comparison to playing always cheat. But if the other player plays tit for tat, also playing tit for tat leads to a long-term gain. So, a firm that expects other firms to play tit for tat may well choose to do the same, leading to successful tacit collusion.

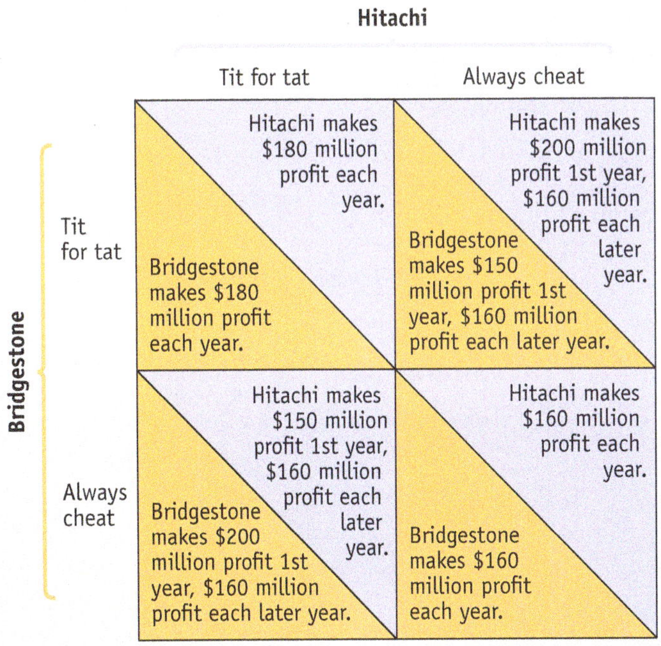

if Bridgestone expects to remain in the tire business for many years (therefore, to find itself repeatedly playing this game with Hitachi) and, for some reason, expects Hitachi always to cheat, it should also always cheat. That is, Bridgestone should follow the old rule "Do unto others before they do unto you."

But if Bridgestone expects to be in the business for a long time and thinks Hitachi is likely to play tit for tat, it will make more profits over the long run by playing tit for tat, too. It could have made some extra short-term profits by cheating at the beginning, but this would provoke Hitachi into cheating, too, and would, in the end, mean lower profits.

The lesson of this story is that when oligopolists expect to compete with one another over an extended period of time, each individual firm will often conclude that it is in its own best interest to be helpful to the other firms in the industry. So, it will restrict its output in a way that raises the profits of the other firms, expecting them to return the favor, and without a formal agreement. In other words, the firms engage in tacit collusion.

ECONOMICS >> *in Action*

The Demise of OPEC

OPEC—composed of the 17 countries of Algeria, Angola, Austria, Cameroon, Ecuador, Gabon, Iran, Iraq, Kuwait, Libya, Nigeria, Qatar, Republic of Congo, Saudi Arabia, Syria, the United Arab Emirates, and Venezuela—is a cartel that controlled 44% of global crude oil output in 2019. The cartel accounts for 72% of proven crude oil reserves and generates 60% of global crude oil exports. Unlike corporations that are legally prohibited from forming cartels, national governments can do whatever they like in setting prices.

For many years OPEC was the largest, most successful, and most economically important cartel in the world. Its members met regularly to set the price and production quotas for oil.

Figure 31-4 shows the price of oil (in constant dollars) since 1947. OPEC first demonstrated its muscle in 1973: in the aftermath of the Yom Kippur War in the Middle East, OPEC producers limited their output—and they liked the resulting price increase so much that they decided to continue the practice. Following a second wave of turmoil from the Iran–Iraq War in 1979, output quotas fell further and prices shot even higher.

Higher oil prices spurred more exploration and production. By the mid-1980s, a growing glut of oil on world markets and cheating by cash-strapped OPEC members led to a price collapse. But in the late 1990s, OPEC emerged successful once again as Saudi Arabia, the largest producer by far, began acting as the "swing producer": allowing other members to produce as much as they wanted and then adjusting its own output to meet the overall production limit. By 2008, the price of oil had soared to $145 per barrel.

Yet, by late 2015, OPEC was nearly dead as a successful cartel as the price of oil had dropped to under $55 per barrel.

In fact, few industry observers believe that OPEC (or OPEC plus Russia) will ever regain its glory days, with a consensus of $60 per barrel

FIGURE 31-4 Crude Oil Prices, 1947–2019 (in Constant 2019 Dollars)

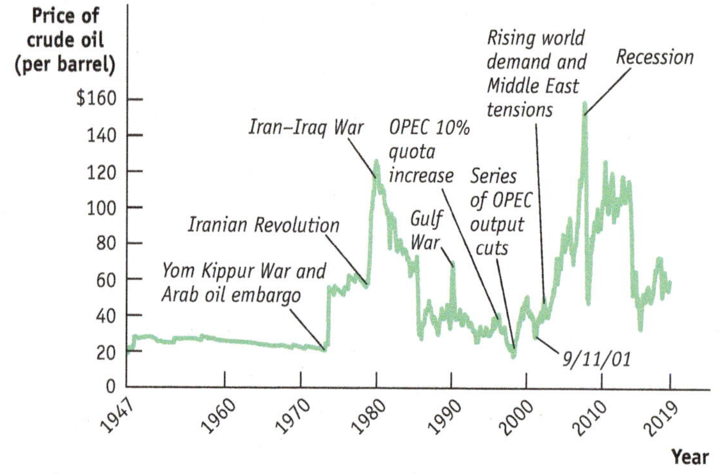

Data from: Energy Information Administration, FRED.

as the most likely maximum price for the near future. One important factor is the rising popularity of renewables as more and more countries shift their economies toward green technology and away from fossil fuels like oil. But the most important near-term factor dampening the rise in oil prices is the vast expansion of oil supply from the United States arising from new fracking technologies. Within five years, the United States is expected to overtake Saudi Arabia as the world's largest oil producer. As one analyst said, "U.S. shale is a huge game changer for OPEC. If prices rise to $60 and a large volume of oil can come back quickly, that's a very significant constraint on the ability of OPEC to manage the oil market." And, unlike Russia, it is virtually impossible that U.S. producers (of whom there are thousands) will ever agree to a voluntary output limitation.

Check Your Understanding 31-1

1. Find the Nash (noncooperative) equilibrium actions for the following payoff matrix. Which actions maximize the total payoff of Nikita and Margaret? Why is it unlikely that they will choose those actions without some communication?

		Nikita: Build missile	Nikita: Don't build missile
Margaret	Build missile	−10 / −10	−20 / 8
	Don't build missile	8 / −20	0 / 0

2. Which of the following factors make it more likely that oligopolists will play noncooperatively? Which make it more likely that they will engage in tacit collusion? Explain.
   a. Each oligopolist expects several new firms to enter the market in the future.
   b. It is very difficult for a firm to detect whether another firm has raised output.
   c. The firms have coexisted while maintaining high prices for a long time.

Solutions appear at back of book

>> Quick Review

- Economists use **game theory** to study firms' behavior when there is interdependence between their **payoffs.** The game can be represented with a **payoff matrix.** Depending on the payoffs, a player may or may not have a **dominant strategy.**
- When each firm has an incentive to cheat, but both are worse off if both cheat, the situation is known as a **prisoners' dilemma.**
- Players who don't take their interdependence into account arrive at a **Nash,** or **noncooperative, equilibrium.** But if a game is played repeatedly, players may engage in **strategic behavior,** sacrificing short-run profit to influence future behavior.
- In repeated prisoners' dilemma games, **tit for tat** is often a good strategy, leading to successful tacit collusion.

MODULE 32

Monopolistic Competition

WHAT YOU WILL LEARN

- What is **monopolistic competition** and why does it occur?
- How are prices and profits determined in monopolistic competition in the short run and the long run?
- How can monopolistic competition lead to not only inefficiency and excess capacity but also more product diversity?

© Lauri Patterson/iStockphoto

Dehooks/Dreamstime.com

stocksolutions/Shutterstock

Brent Hofacker/Shutterstock

Like oligopoly, monopolistic competition is a very common type of market structure. For example, along any major street in any town across America, monopolistic competition is on display as Chipotle, McDonald's, Panera, Red Lobster, and many more brands of food outlets compete for your tastebuds. In this module, we'll examine how a monopolistically competitive industry behaves and why they combine some features of perfect competitition with those of monopoly.

32.1 Understanding Monopolistic Competition

As the term *monopolistic competition* suggests, this market structure combines some features typical of monopoly but with others typical of perfect competition. Because each firm is offering a distinct product, it is in a way like a monopolist: it faces a downward-sloping demand curve and has some market power—the ability within limits to determine the price of its product. However, unlike a pure monopolist, a monopolistically competitive firm does face competition: the amount of its product it can sell depends on the prices and products offered by other firms in the industry.

The same, of course, is true of an oligopoly. In a monopolistically competitive industry, however, there are *many* producers and no barriers to entry. This means that collusion is impossible in monopolistically competitive industries. So in situations of monopolistic competition, we can safely assume that firms behave noncooperatively and ignore the potential for collusion. What they do, instead, is product differentiate.

Monopolistic Competition in the Short Run

Recall the distinction between short-run and long-run equilibrium. The short-run equilibrium of an industry takes the number of firms as given. The long-run equilibrium, by contrast, is reached only after enough time has elapsed for firms to enter or exit the industry. To analyze monopolistic competition, we focus first on the short run and then on how an industry moves from the short run to the long run.

Panels (a) and (b) of Figure 32-1 show two possible situations that a typical firm in a monopolistically competitive industry might face in the short run. In each case, the firm looks like any monopolist: it faces a downward-sloping demand curve, which implies a downward-sloping marginal revenue curve.

We assume that every firm has an upward-sloping marginal cost curve but that it also faces some fixed costs so that its average total cost curve is U-shaped. This assumption doesn't matter in the short run, but, as we'll see shortly, it is crucial to understanding the long-run equilibrium.

In each case, the firm, to maximize profit, sets marginal revenue equal to marginal cost. So how do these two figures differ? In panel (a), the firm is profitable; in panel (b), it is unprofitable. (Recall that we are referring always to economic profit, not accounting profit—that is, a profit given that all factors of production are earning their opportunity costs.)

In panel (a), the firm faces the demand curve D_P and the marginal revenue curve MR_P. It produces the profit-maximizing output Q_P, the quantity at which marginal revenue is equal to marginal cost, and sells it at the price P_P. This price is

FIGURE 32-1 The Monopolistically Competitive Firm in the Short Run

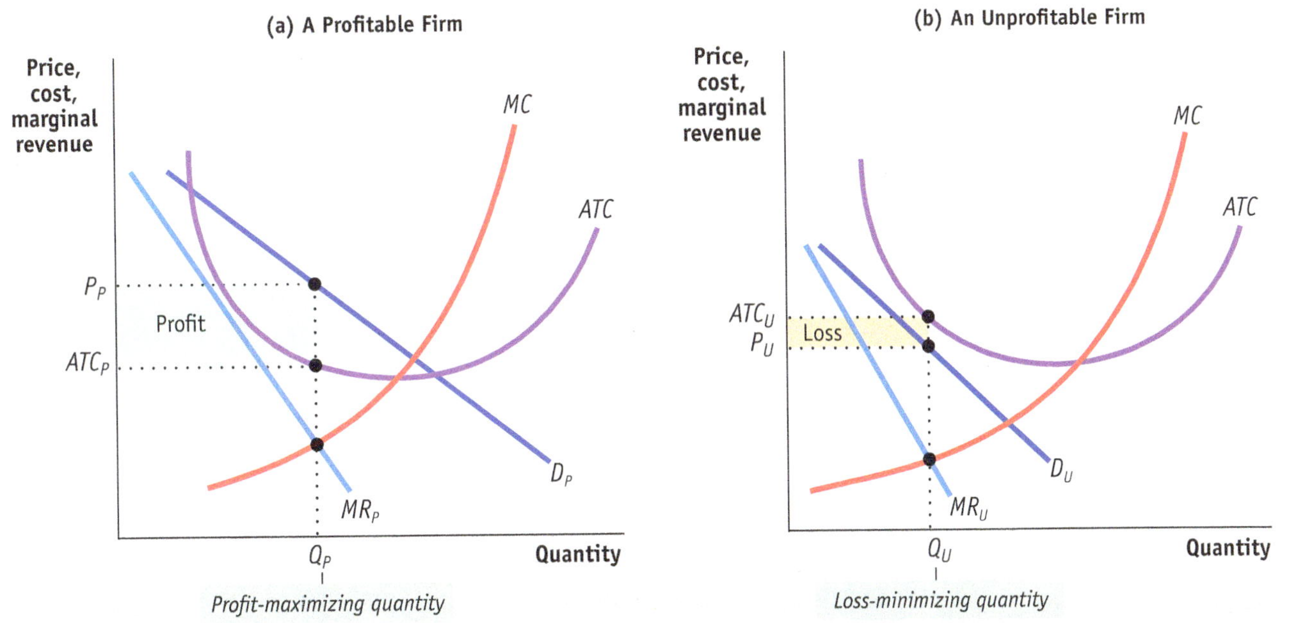

The firm in panel (a) can be profitable for some output quantities: the quantities for which its average total cost curve, *ATC*, lies below its demand curve, *Dp*. The profit-maximizing output quantity is *Qp*, the output at which marginal revenue, *MRp*, is equal to marginal cost, *MC*. The firm charges price *Pp* and earns a profit, represented by the area of the green-shaded rectangle. The firm in panel (b), however, can never be profitable because its average total cost curve lies above its demand curve, D_U, for every output quantity. The best that it can do if it produces at all is to produce quantity Q_U and charge price P_U. This generates a loss, indicated by the area of the yellow-shaded rectangle. Any other output quantity results in a greater loss.

above the average total cost at this output, ATC_P. The firm's profit is indicated by the area of the green-shaded rectangle.

In panel (b), the firm faces the demand curve D_U and the marginal revenue curve MR_U. It chooses the quantity Q_U at which marginal revenue is equal to marginal cost. However, in this case, the price P_U is *below* the average total cost ATC_U; so at this quantity the firm loses money. Its loss is equal to the area of the yellow-shaded rectangle. Since Q_U is the profit-maximizing quantity—which means, in this case, the loss-minimizing quantity—there is no way for a firm in this situation to make a profit.

We can confirm this by noting that at *any* quantity of output, the average total cost curve in panel (b) lies above the demand curve D_U. Because $ATC > P$ at all quantities of output, this firm always suffers a loss.

As this comparison suggests, the key to whether a firm with market power is profitable or unprofitable in the short run lies in the relationship between its demand curve and its average total cost curve. In panel (a), the demand curve D_P crosses the average total cost curve, meaning that some of the demand curve lies above the average total cost curve. So there are some price–quantity combinations available at which price is higher than average total cost, indicating that the firm can choose a quantity at which it makes positive profit.

In panel (b), by contrast, the demand curve D_U does not cross the average total cost curve—it always lies below it. So the price corresponding to each quantity demanded is always less than the average total cost of producing that quantity. There is no quantity at which the firm can avoid losing money.

These figures, showing firms facing downward-sloping demand curves and their associated marginal revenue curves, look just like ordinary monopoly analysis. The "competition" aspect of monopolistic competition comes into play, however, when we move from the short run to the long run.

Monopolistic Competition in the Long Run

Obviously, an industry in which existing firms are losing money, like the one in panel (b) of Figure 32-1, is not in long-run equilibrium. When existing firms are losing money, some firms will *exit* the industry. The industry will not be in long-run equilibrium until the persistent losses have been eliminated by the exit of some firms.

It may be less obvious that an industry in which existing firms *are* earning profits, like the one in panel (a) of Figure 32-1, is also not in long-run equilibrium. Given that there is *free entry* into the industry, persistent profits earned by the existing firms will lead to the entry of additional producers. The industry will not be in long-run equilibrium until the persistent profits have been eliminated by the entry of new producers.

How will entry or exit by other firms affect the profits of a typical existing firm? Because the differentiated products offered by firms in a monopolistically competitive industry compete for the same set of customers, entry or exit by other firms will affect the demand curve facing every existing producer. If new gas stations open along a highway, each of the existing gas stations will no longer be able to sell as much gas as they did before at any given price. So, as illustrated in panel (a) of Figure 32-2, entry of additional producers into a monopolistically competitive industry will lead to a *leftward* shift of the demand curve and the marginal revenue curve facing a typical existing producer. (Remember: The demand curve will shift left as firms lose buyers. New firms entering the market will take some buyers away from existing firms causing demand for older firms to decrease.)

Conversely, suppose that some of the gas stations along the highway close. Then each of the remaining stations will be able to sell more gasoline at any given price. Thus, as illustrated in panel (b), exit of firms from an industry will lead to a

FIGURE 32-2 Entry and Exit Shift Existing Firm's Demand Curve and Marginal Revenue Curve

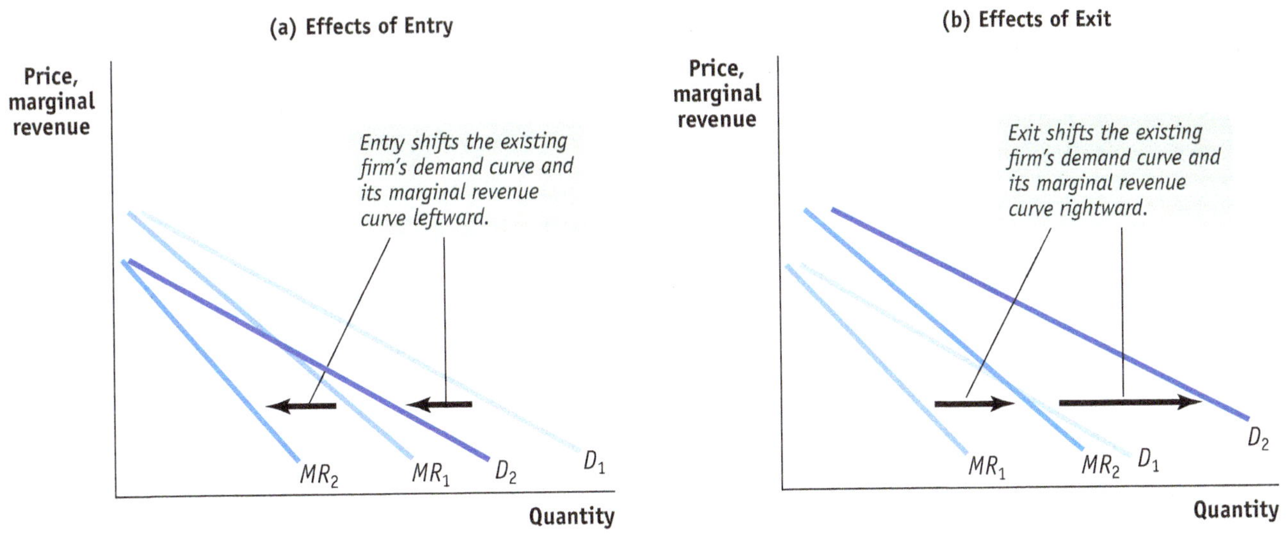

Entry will occur in the long run when existing firms are profitable. In panel (a), entry causes each existing firm's demand curve and marginal revenue curve to shift to the left. The firm receives a lower price for every unit it sells, and its profit falls. Entry will cease when firms make zero profit. Exit will occur in the long run when existing firms are unprofitable. In panel (b), exit from the industry shifts each remaining firm's demand curve and marginal revenue curve to the right. The firm receives a higher price for each unit it sells, and profit rises. Exit will cease when the remaining firms make zero profit.

rightward shift of the demand curve and marginal revenue curve facing a typical remaining producer.

The industry will be in long-run equilibrium when there is neither entry nor exit. This will occur only when every firm earns zero profit. So, in the long run, a monopolistically competitive industry will end up in **zero-profit equilibrium,** in which firms just manage to cover their costs at their profit-maximizing output quantities. (The app industry offers an example of this principle, as you will see in the upcoming Economics in Action.)

We have seen that a firm facing a downward-sloping demand curve will earn positive profits if any part of that demand curve lies above its average total cost curve; it will incur a loss if its demand curve lies everywhere below its average total cost curve. So, in zero-profit equilibrium, the firm must be in a borderline position between these two cases; its demand curve must just touch its average total cost curve. That is, it must be just *tangent* to it at the firm's profit-maximizing output quantity—the output quantity at which marginal revenue equals marginal cost.

If this is not the case, the firm operating at its profit-maximizing quantity will find itself making either profit or loss, as illustrated in the panels of Figure 32-1. But we also know that free entry and exit means that this cannot be a long-run equilibrium. Why? In the case of a profit, new firms will enter the industry, shifting the demand curve of every existing firm leftward until all profits are extinguished. In the case of a loss, some existing firms will exit and so shift the demand curve of every remaining firm to the right until all losses are extinguished. All entry and exit ceases only when every existing firm makes zero profit at its profit-maximizing quantity of output.

In the long run, a monopolistically competitive industry ends up in **zero-profit equilibrium:** each firm makes zero profit at its profit-maximizing quantity.

Figure 32-3 shows a typical monopolistically competitive firm in such a zero-profit equilibrium. The firm produces Q_{MC}, the output at which $MR_{MC} = MC$, and charges price P_{MC}. At this price and quantity, represented by point *Z*, the

FIGURE 32-3 The Long-Run Zero-Profit Equilibrium

If existing firms are profitable, entry will occur and shift each existing firm's demand curve leftward. If existing firms are unprofitable, each remaining firm's demand curve shifts rightward as some firms exit the industry. Entry and exit will cease when every existing firm makes zero profit at its profit-maximizing quantity. So, in long-run zero-profit equilibrium, the demand curve of each firm is tangent to its average total cost curve at its profit-maximizing quantity: at the profit-maximizing Q_{MC}, price, P_{MC}, equals average total cost, ATC_{MC}. A monopolistically competitive firm is like a monopolist without monopoly profits.

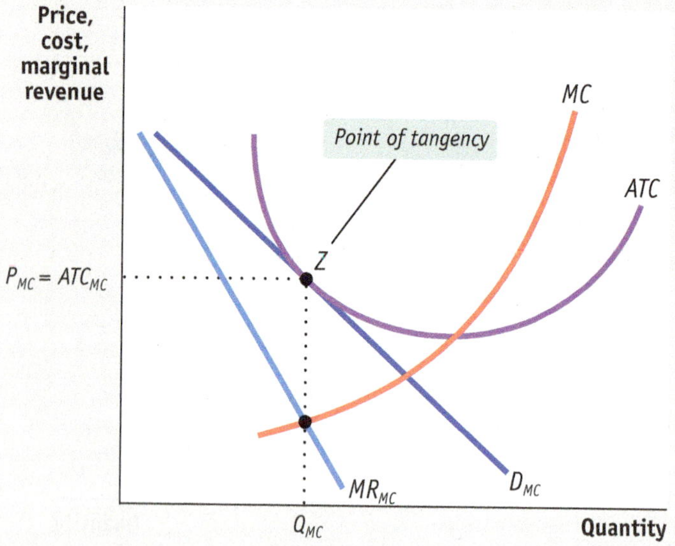

demand curve is just tangent to its average total cost curve. The firm earns zero profit because price, P_{MC}, is equal to average total cost, ATC_{MC}.

The normal long-run condition of a monopolistically competitive industry, then, is that each producer is in the situation shown in Figure 32-3. Each producer acts like a monopolist, facing a downward-sloping demand curve and setting marginal cost equal to marginal revenue so as to maximize profits. But this is just enough to achieve zero economic profit. The producers in the industry are like monopolists without monopoly profits.

>> Quick Review

- Like a monopolist, each firm in a monopolistically competitive industry faces a downward-sloping demand curve and marginal revenue curve. In the short run, it may earn a profit or incur a loss at its profit-maximizing quantity.
- If the typical firm earns positive profit, new firms will enter the industry in the long run, shifting each existing firm's demand curve to the left. If the typical firm incurs a loss, some existing firms will exit the industry in the long run, shifting the demand curve of each remaining firm to the right.
- The long-run equilibrium of a monopolistically competitive industry is a **zero-profit equilibrium** in which firms just break even. The typical firm's demand curve is tangent to its average total cost curve at its profit-maximizing quantity.

Check Your Understanding 32-1

1. Currently a monopolistically competitive industry, composed of firms with U-shaped average total cost curves, is in long-run equilibrium. Describe how the industry adjusts, in both the short and long run, in each of the following situations.
   a. A technological change that increases fixed cost for every firm in the industry
   b. A technological change that decreases marginal cost for every firm in the industry
2. Why, in the long run, is it impossible for firms in a monopolistically competitive industry to create a monopoly by joining together to form a single firm?

Solutions appear at back of book

32.2 Monopolistic Competition versus Perfect Competition

In a way, long-run equilibrium in a monopolistically competitive industry looks a lot like long-run equilibrium in a perfectly competitive industry. In both cases, there are many firms; in both cases, profits have been competed away; in both cases, the price received by every firm is equal to the average total cost of production.

However, the two versions of long-run equilibrium are different—in ways that are economically significant.

Price, Marginal Cost, and Average Total Cost

Figure 32-4 compares the long-run equilibrium of a typical firm in a perfectly competitive industry with that of a typical firm in a monopolistically competitive industry. Panel (a) shows a perfectly competitive firm facing a market price equal to its minimum average total cost; panel (b) reproduces Figure 32-3. Comparing the panels, we see two important differences.

First, in the case of the perfectly competitive firm shown in panel (a), the price, P_{PC}, received by the firm at the profit-maximizing quantity, Q_{PC}, is equal to the firm's marginal cost of production, MC_{PC}, at that quantity of output. By contrast, at the profit-maximizing quantity chosen by the monopolistically competitive firm in panel (b), Q_{MC}, the price, P_{MC}, is *higher* than the marginal cost of production, MC_{MC}.

This difference translates into a difference in the attitude of firms toward consumers. A wheat farmer, who can sell as much wheat as he likes at the going market price, would not get particularly excited if you offered to buy some more wheat at the market price. Since he has no desire to produce more at that price and can sell the wheat to someone else, you are not doing him a favor.

But if you decide to fill up your tank at Jamil's gas station rather than at Katy's, you are doing Jamil a favor. He is not willing to cut his price to get more customers—he's already made the best of that trade-off. But if he gets a few more customers than he expected at the *posted* price, that's good news: an additional sale at the posted price increases his revenue more than it increases his costs because the posted price exceeds marginal cost.

The fact that monopolistic competitors, unlike perfect competitors, want to sell more at the going price is crucial to understanding why they engage in activities like advertising that help increase sales.

FIGURE 32-4 Comparing Long-Run Equilibrium in Perfect Competition and Monopolistic Competition

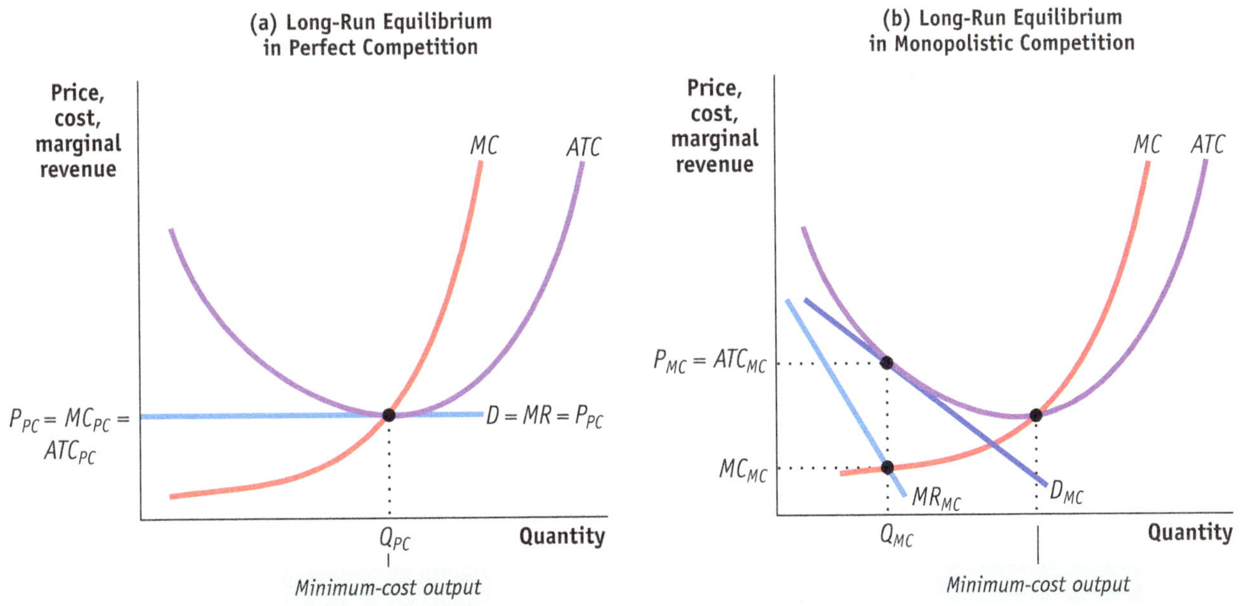

Panel (a) shows the situation of the typical firm in long-run equilibrium in a perfectly competitive industry. The firm operates at the minimum-cost output Q_{PC}, sells at the competitive market price P_{PC}, and makes zero profit. It is indifferent to selling another unit of output because P_{PC} is equal to its marginal cost, MC_{PC}. Panel (b) shows the situation of the typical firm in long-run equilibrium in a monopolistically competitive industry. At Q_{MC} it makes zero profit because its price, P_{MC}, just equals average total cost, ATC_{MC}. At Q_{MC} the firm would like to sell another unit at price P_{MC} since P_{MC} exceeds marginal cost, MC_{MC}. But it is unwilling to lower price to make more sales. It therefore operates to the left of the minimum-cost output level and has excess capacity.

Firms in a monopolistically competitive industry have **excess capacity:** they produce less than the output at which average total cost is minimized.

The other difference between monopolistic competition and perfect competition that is visible in Figure 32-4 involves the position of each firm on its average total cost curve. In panel (a), the perfectly competitive firm produces at point Q_{PC}, at the bottom of the U-shaped *ATC* curve. That is, each firm produces the quantity at which average total cost is minimized—the *minimum-cost output.* As a consequence, the total cost of industry output is also minimized.

Under monopolistic competition, in panel (b), the firm produces at Q_{MC}, on the *downward-sloping* part of the U-shaped *ATC* curve: it produces less than the quantity that would minimize average total cost. This failure to produce enough to minimize average total cost is sometimes described as the **excess capacity** issue. The typical vendor in a food court or gas station along a road is not big enough to take maximum advantage of available cost savings. So the total cost of industry output is not minimized in the case of a monopolistically competitive industry. Correspondingly, the market price under monopolistic competition is higher than in perfect competition.

Some people have argued that, because every monopolistic competitor has excess capacity and higher prices, monopolistically competitive industries are inefficient. But the issue of efficiency under monopolistic competition turns out to be a subtle one that does not have a clear answer.

Is Monopolistic Competition Inefficient?

A monopolistic competitor, like a monopolist, charges a price that is above marginal cost. As a result, some people who are willing to pay at least as much for an egg roll at Wonderful Wok as it costs to produce it are deterred from doing so. In monopolistic competition, some mutually beneficial transactions go unexploited.

Furthermore, it is often argued that monopolistic competition is subject to a further kind of inefficiency: that the excess capacity of every monopolistic competitor implies *wasteful duplication* because monopolistically competitive industries offer too many varieties. According to this argument, it would be better if there were only two or three vendors in the food court, not six or seven. If there were fewer vendors, they would each have lower average total costs and so could offer food more cheaply.

Is this argument against monopolistic competition right—that it lowers total surplus by causing inefficiency? Not necessarily. It's true that if there were fewer gas stations along a highway, each gas station would sell more gasoline and so would have lower costs per gallon. But there is a drawback: motorists would be inconvenienced because gas stations would be farther apart. The point is that the diversity of products offered in a monopolistically competitive industry is beneficial to consumers. So the higher price consumers pay because of excess capacity is offset to some extent by the value they receive from greater diversity.

There is, in other words, a trade-off: more producers means not only higher average total costs but also greater product diversity. Does a monopolistically competitive industry arrive at the socially optimal point on this trade-off? Probably not—but it is hard to say whether there are too many firms or too few! Most economists now believe that duplication of effort and excess capacity in monopolistically competitive industries are not important issues in practice.

ECONOMICS >> *in Action*

Hits and Flops in the App Store

There's no denying that some apps have been extremely lucrative creations. King Digital Entertainment, the company that created the wildly popular game app Candy Crush, was purchased by Activision, owners of Call of Duty, Guitar Hero, and Skylanders, for nearly $6 billion in 2016. That same year, Uber, the ride-sharing app, was valued at an astounding $66 billion. Spurred by these success stories, an unprecedented number of people have rushed to develop mobile apps. But lost in the rush is the fact that the vast majority of apps have flopped or are barely alive.

Although a few apps have been extraordinarily profitable, the app industry can't escape the zero-profit equilibrium.

The app industry looks a lot like an example of monopolistic competition. First, there is free entry in app design. And second, apps are differentiated products. They are differentiated by platform: the iOS (Apple) platform, the Android (Google) platform, or the Microsoft platform. They are also differentiated by function: sharing photos, digital coloring books, a virtual koi pond, travel pricing and reservations, personal finance management, and so on. And within each functional subgroup of apps there are variations, each trying to capture a larger share of the market. In 2019, the iOS platform had 2.2 million available apps, slightly less than the 2.6 million apps available from Google Play. The two platforms generated close to 105 billion downloads in 2019. But as one industry observer, Frank Bi, commented, ". . . the easy money is gone."

Hundreds of thousands of apps now languish in obscurity for every breakout hit like TikTok, Snapchat, or Clash of Clans. The original App Store model of selling apps for a dollar or two per download is outdated. Today most apps are downloaded for free or at a minimum expense. In 2011, 63% of apps were paid downloads at an average price of $3.64; by 2019, that figure dropped to less than 7% with an average price of $1.01. It's estimated that in 75% of downloads, the app is used once and never again.

At this point, many app developers are struggling to survive, unable to generate enough download revenue to continue operations. In other words, the app creation industry has reached the zero-profit equilibrium state that characterizes monopolistic competition. So, in the end, this cutting-edge, high-tech industry cannot escape the consequences of the economics of monopolistic competition.

Check Your Understanding 32-2

1. True or false? Explain your answers.
   a. Like a firm in a perfectly competitive industry, a firm in a monopolistically competitive industry is willing to sell a good at any price that equals or exceeds marginal cost.
   b. Suppose there is a monopolistically competitive industry in long-run equilibrium that possesses excess capacity. All the firms in the industry would be better off if they merged into a single firm and produced a single product, but whether consumers are made better off by this is ambiguous.
   c. Fads and fashions are more likely to arise in monopolistic competition or oligopoly than in monopoly or perfect competition.

Solutions appear at back of book

>> Quick Review

- In the long-run equilibrium of a monopolistically competitive industry, there are many firms, each earning zero profit.
- Price exceeds marginal cost, so some mutually beneficial trades are unexploited.
- Monopolistically competitive firms have **excess capacity** because they do not minimize average total cost. But it is not clear that this is actually a source of inefficiency since consumers gain from product diversity.

MODULE 33

Product Differentiation and Advertising

WHAT YOU WILL LEARN

- What is the purpose of **production differentiation?**
- What are the various ways in which products can be differentiated?
- Why do firms advertise and create **brand names?**

Richard Levine/Alamy Stock Photo

Product differentiation often plays an important role in oligopolistic industries. For example, Arm & Hammer laundry detergent may get your clothes cleaner, but Proctor & Gamble's Gain laundry detergent comes in a lavender fragrance. In oligopoly, product differentiation reduces the intensity of competition between firms when tacit collusion cannot be achieved.

Product differentiation plays an even more important role in monopolistically competitive industries. Because tacit collusion is virtually impossible when there are many producers, product differentiation is the only way monopolistically competitive firms can acquire some market power.

In this module, we learn how firms differentiate their products to earn profits.

33.1 How Firms Differentiate Their Products

How do firms in the same industry—such as fast-food vendors, gas stations, or chocolate makers—differentiate their products? Sometimes the difference is mainly in the minds of consumers rather than in the products. We'll discuss the role of advertising and the importance of brand names in achieving this kind of product differentiation later in the module. But, in general, firms differentiate their products by—surprise!—actually making them different.

The key to product differentiation is that consumers have different preferences and are willing to pay somewhat more to satisfy those preferences. Each producer can carve out a market niche by producing something that caters to the particular preferences of some group of consumers better than the products of other firms.

There are three important forms of **product differentiation:**

1. By style or type
2. By location
3. By quality

Product differentiation is the attempt by a firm to convince buyers that its product is different from other products in the industry. It takes three main forms: by style or type, by location, or by quality.

Differentiation by Style or Type

The sellers in Leo's food court offer different types of fast food: hamburgers, pizza, tacos, and so on. Each consumer arrives at the food court with some preference for one or another of these offerings. This preference may depend on the consumer's mood, their diet, or what they have already eaten that day. These preferences will not make consumers indifferent to price: if Wonderful Wok were to charge $15 for an egg roll, everybody would go to Bodacious Burgers or Pizza Paradise instead. But some people will choose a more expensive meal if that type of food is closer to their preference. So the products of the different vendors are substitutes, but they aren't *perfect* substitutes—they are *imperfect substitutes*.

Vendors in a food court aren't the only sellers that differentiate their offerings by type. Clothing stores concentrate on business or casual clothes, on trendy or classic styles, and so on. Auto manufacturers offer sedans, minivans, sport-utility vehicles, and sports cars, each type aimed at drivers with different needs and tastes.

Books offer yet another example of differentiation by type and style. Mysteries are differentiated from romances; among mysteries, we can differentiate among hard-boiled detective stories, whodunits, and police procedurals. And no two writers of horror and fantasy are exactly alike: Stephen King and George R. R. Martin each have their devoted fans.

In fact, product differentiation is characteristic of most consumer goods. As long as people differ in their tastes, producers find it possible and profitable to produce a range of varieties.

Differentiation by Location

Gas stations along a road offer differentiated products. True, the gas may be exactly the same. But the location of the stations is different, and location matters to consumers: it's more convenient to stop for gas near your home, near your workplace, or near wherever you are when the gas gauge shows you are low on fuel.

In fact, many monopolistically competitive industries supply goods differentiated by location. This is especially true in service industries, from car mechanics to drugstores, when customers often choose the seller who is closest rather than cheapest.

For industries that differentiate by location, proximity is everything.

Differentiation by Quality

Do you have a craving for chocolate? How much are you willing to spend on it? You see, there's chocolate and then there's chocolate: although ordinary chocolate may not be very expensive, gourmet chocolate can cost several dollars per bite.

With chocolate, as with many goods, there is a range of possible qualities. Likewise, you can get a usable bicycle for less than $100; you can get a much fancier bicycle for 10 times as much. It all depends on how much the additional quality matters to you and how much you will miss the other things you could have purchased with that money.

Because consumers vary in what they are willing to pay for higher quality, producers can differentiate their products by quality—some offering lower-quality, inexpensive products and others offering higher-quality products at a higher price.

Product Differentiation: In Sum

Product differentiation, then, can take several forms. Whatever form it takes, however, there are two important features of industries with differentiated products: *competition among sellers* and *value in variety.*

Competition among sellers means that even though sellers of differentiated products are not offering identical goods, they are to some extent competing for a limited market. If more businesses enter the market, each will find that it sells less quantity at any given price. For example, if a new gas station opens along a road, each of the existing gas stations will sell a bit less.

Value in variety refers to the gain to consumers from the proliferation of differentiated products. A food court with eight vendors makes consumers happier than one with only six vendors, even if the prices are the same, because some customers will get a meal that is closer to what they had in mind. A road on which there is a gas station every two miles is more convenient for motorists than a road where gas stations are five miles apart.

When a product is available in many different qualities, fewer people are forced to pay for more quality than they need or to settle for lower quality than they want. There are, in other words, benefits to consumers from a greater variety of available products.

>> Quick Review

- **Product differentiation** can occur in oligopolies that fail to achieve tacit collusion as well as in monopolistic competition. It takes three main forms: by style or type, by location, or by quality. The products of competing sellers are considered imperfect substitutes.
- Producers compete for the same market, so entry by more producers reduces the quantity each existing producer sells at any given price. In addition, consumers gain from the increased variety of products.

Check Your Understanding 33-1

1. Each of the following goods and services is a differentiated product. Which are differentiated as a result of monopolistic competition and which are not? Explain your answers.
   a. Ladders
   b. Soft drinks
   c. Clothing stores
   d. Steel
2. You must determine which of two types of market structure better describes an industry, but you are allowed to ask only one question about the industry. What question should you ask to determine if an industry is:
   a. Perfectly competitive or monopolistically competitive?
   b. A monopoly or monopolistically competitive?

Solutions appear at back of book

33.2 Controversies About Product Differentiation

Up to this point, we have assumed that products are differentiated in a way that corresponds to some real desire of consumers. For example, there is real convenience in having a gas station nearby. Likewise, your taste buds know that Chinese and Mexican cuisines are different from one another.

In the real world, however, some instances of product differentiation can seem puzzling if you think about them. What is the real difference between Crest and Colgate toothpaste? Between Energizer and Duracell batteries? Or a Marriott and a Hilton hotel room? Most people would be hard-pressed to answer any questions about differences. Yet the producers of these goods make considerable efforts to convince consumers that their products are different from and better than those of their competitors.

No discussion of product differentiation is complete without spending at least a bit of time on the two related issues—and puzzles—of *advertising* and *brand names.*

The Role of Advertising

Wheat farmers don't advertise their wares on TV, but car dealers do. That's not because farmers are shy and car dealers are outgoing; it's because advertising is worthwhile only in industries in which firms have at least some market power.

The purpose of advertisements is to convince people to buy more of a seller's product at the going price. A perfectly competitive firm, which can sell as much as it likes at the going market price, has no incentive to spend money convincing consumers to buy more. Only monopolists, oligopolists, and monopolistic competitors—firms that have some market power and therefore charge a price above marginal cost—can gain from advertising. Industries that are more or less perfectly competitive, like the milk industry, do advertise—but these ads are sponsored by an association on behalf of the industry as a whole, not on behalf of the milk that comes from the cows on a particular farm.

Given that advertising works, it's not hard to see why firms with market power would spend money on it. But the big question about advertising is *why* it works. A related question is whether advertising is, from society's point of view, a waste of resources.

Not all advertising poses a puzzle. Much of it is straightforward: it's a way for sellers to inform potential buyers about what they have to offer (or, occasionally, for buyers to inform potential sellers about what they want). Nor is there much controversy about the economic usefulness of ads that provide information: the real estate ad that declares "sunny, charming, 2 br, 1 ba, a/c" tells you things you need to know (even if a few euphemisms are involved—"charming," of course, means "small").

But what information is being conveyed when Jay-Z touts Samsung cell phones or when Gigi Hadid promotes a BMW? Surely nobody believes that Jay-Z is personally responsible for the superior operating system of a Samsung phone or that Gigi Hadid's engineering know-how led her to choose a BMW over a rival car. Yet companies believe, with good reason, that money spent on such promotions increases their sales—and that they would be in big trouble if they stopped advertising but their competitors continued to do so.

Why are consumers influenced by ads that do not really provide any information about the product? One answer is that consumers are not as rational as economists typically assume. Perhaps consumers' judgments, or even their tastes, can be influenced by things that economists think ought to be irrelevant, such as which company has hired the most charismatic celebrity to endorse its product. And there is surely some truth to this. Consumer rationality is a useful working assumption; it is not an absolute truth.

However, another answer is that consumer response to advertising is not entirely irrational because ads can serve as indirect signals in a world where consumers don't have good information about products. Suppose, to take a common example, that you need to avail yourself of some service that you don't use regularly—finding a dentist or a furniture mover. Using a search engine, you will see firms with sponsored listings pop up at top or with larger displays. You know that these listings appear as they do because the firms paid extra for them; still, it may be quite rational to call one of the firms with a big display ad. After all, the big ad probably means that it's a relatively large, successful company—otherwise, the company wouldn't have found it worth spending the money for the larger ad.

Barbara Smaller/CartoonStock

"The active ingredient is marketing."

A **brand name** is a name owned by a particular firm that distinguishes that firm's products from those of other firms.

The same principle may partly explain why ads feature celebrities. You don't really believe that Justin Bieber prefers one brand of underwear over another. But the fact that Calvin Klein is willing and able to pay him nearly $70 million to put his name on his product tells you that it is a major company that is likely to stand behind its product. According to this reasoning, an expensive advertisement serves to establish the quality of a firm's products in the eyes of consumers.

The possibility that it is rational for consumers to respond to advertising also has some bearing on the question of whether advertising is a waste of resources. If ads only work by manipulating the weak-minded, the hundreds of billions of dollars that U.S. businesses spend annually will have been an economic waste—except to the extent that ads sometimes provide entertainment. To the extent that advertising conveys important information, however, it is an economically productive activity after all.

Brand Names

You've been driving all day, and you decide that it's time to find a place to sleep. On your right, you see a sign for the Bates Motel; on your left, you see a sign for a Motel 6, or a Best Western, or some other national chain. Which one do you choose?

Unless they were familiar with the area, most people would head for the chain. In fact, most motels in the United States are members of major chains; the same is true of most fast-food restaurants and many, if not most, stores in shopping malls.

Jonathan Larsen/Diadem Images/Alamy

Advertising and brand names that provide useful information can be valuable to consumers.

Motel chains and fast-food restaurants are only one aspect of a broader phenomenon: the role of **brand names,** names owned by particular companies that differentiate their products in the minds of consumers. In many cases, a company's brand name is the most important asset it possesses: clearly, McDonald's is worth far more than the sum of the deep-fat fryers and hamburger grills the company owns.

In fact, companies often go to considerable lengths to defend their brand names, suing anyone else who uses them without permission. You may talk about blowing your nose on a kleenex or using scotch tape to wrap gifts, but unless the product in question comes from Kleenex or Scotch, legally the seller must describe it as a facial tissue or adhesive tape.

As with advertising, with which they are closely linked, the social usefulness of brand names is a source of dispute. Does the preference of consumers for known brands reflect consumer irrationality? Or do brand names convey real information? That is, do brand names create unnecessary market power, or do they serve a real purpose?

As in the case of advertising, the answer is probably some of both. On one side, brand names often do create unjustified market power. Many consumers will pay more for brand-name goods in the supermarket even though consumer experts assure us that the cheaper store brands are equally good. Similarly, many common medicines, like aspirin, are cheaper—with no loss of quality—in their generic form.

On the other side, for many products the brand name does convey information. A traveler arriving in a strange town can be sure of what awaits in a Holiday Inn or a McDonald's; a tired and hungry traveler may find this preferable to trying an independent hotel or restaurant that might be better—but might be worse.

In addition, brand names offer some assurance that the seller is engaged in repeated interaction with its customers and so has a reputation to protect. If a traveler eats a bad meal at a restaurant in a tourist trap and vows never to eat there again, the restaurant owner may not care, since the chance is small that the traveler will be in the same area again in the future. But if that traveler eats a bad meal at McDonald's and vows never to eat there again, that matters to the company. This gives McDonald's an incentive to provide consistent quality, thereby assuring travelers that quality controls are in place. Not surprisingly, branding has become a feature of peer-to-peer e-commerce as companies recognize that many customers will pay extra for assurances of quality and safety in anonymous, online transactions. Hence, Uber created its Premium class of ride that uses luxury cars driven by drivers with high ratings. Likewise Airbnb created the category of Plus properties, accommodations that are vetted by Airbnb staff and have a record of great reviews.

ECONOMICS >> *in Action*

The Perfume Industry: Leading Consumers by the Nose

The perfume industry has remarkably few barriers to entry: to make a fragrance, it is easy to purchase ingredients, mix them, and bottle the result. Even if you don't think you have a very good "nose," consultants are readily available to help you create something special (or even copy someone else's fragrance). So how is it possible that a successful perfume can generate a profit rate of almost 100%? Why don't rivals enter and compete away those profits?

A clue to the answer is that the most successful perfumes these days are heavily promoted by celebrities. Rihanna, Beyonce, Taylor Swift, and Zendaya all have perfumes that are marketed by them. Britney Spears has 28! In fact, the cost of producing what is in the bottle is minuscule compared to the total cost of selling a successful perfume—only about 3% of the production cost and less than 1% of the retail price. The remaining 97% of the production cost goes into packaging, marketing, and advertising.

The extravagant bottles that modern perfumes come in—some shaped like spaceships or encrusted with rhinestones—incur a cost of four to six times that of the perfume inside. Top bottle designers earn well over $100,000 for a single design. Add on to that the cost of advertising, in-store employees who spritz and hawk, and the commissions to salespeople.

Finally, include the cost of celebrity endorsements that run into the millions of dollars. For example, Beyonce reportedly has earned more than $40 million dollars on her fragrance, Heat. Moreover, in comparison to older fragrances that have been around for decades like Chanel or Dior, modern fragrances are made with much cheaper synthetic ingredients. So while a scent like Chanel would last 24 hours, modern fragrances last only a few hours at best.

As one celebrated "nose," Roja Dora, commented, "Studies show that people will say that a particular perfume is one of their favorites, but in a blind test they hate it. The trouble is that most people buy scent for their ego, after seeing an image in an advert and wanting to identify themselves in a certain way."

So here's a metaphysical question: even if perfume buyers really hate a fragrance in a blind test, but advertising convinces them that it smells wonderful, who are we to say that they are wrong to buy it? Isn't the attractiveness of a scent in the mind of the beholder?

The Advertising Archives/Alamy Stock Photo

In the perfume industry, it's packaging and advertising that generate profits.

>> Quick Review

- In industries with product differentiation, firms advertise to increase the demand for their products.
- Advertising is not a waste of resources when it gives consumers useful information about products.
- Advertising that simply touts a product is harder to explain. Either consumers are irrational or expensive advertising communicates that the firm's products are of high quality.
- Some firms create **brand names.** As with advertising, the economic value of brand names can be ambiguous. They convey real information when they assure consumers of product quality.

Check Your Understanding 33-2

1. In which of the following cases is advertising likely to be economically useful? Economically wasteful? Explain your answer.

  a. Advertisements on the benefits of aspirin
  b. Advertisements for Bayer aspirin
  c. Advertisements on the benefits of drinking orange juice
  d. Advertisements for Tropicana orange juice
  e. Advertisements that state how long a plumber or an electrician has been in business

2. Some industry analysts have stated that a successful brand name is like a barrier to entry. Explain the reasoning behind this statement.

Solutions appear at back of book

BUSINESS CASE

Virgin Atlantic Blows the Whistle . . . or Blows It?

Ian Waldie/Getty Images

The United Kingdom is home to two long-haul airline carriers (carriers that fly between continents): British Airways and its rival, Virgin Atlantic. Although British Airways is the dominant company, with a market share generally between 50% and 100% on routes between London and various American cities, Virgin has been a tenacious competitor.

The rivalry between the two has ranged from relatively peaceable to openly hostile over the years. In the 1990s, British Airways lost a court case alleging it had engaged in "dirty tricks" to drive Virgin out of business. In April 2010, however, British Airways may well have wondered if the tables had been turned.

It all began in mid-July 2004, when oil prices were rising. British prosecutors alleged that the two airlines had plotted to levy fuel surcharges on passengers. For the next two years, according to the prosecutors, the rivals had established a cartel through which they coordinated increases in surcharges. British Airways first introduced a £5 ($8.25) surcharge on long-haul flights when a barrel of oil traded at about $38. It increased the surcharge six times so that by 2006, when oil was trading at about $69 a barrel, the surcharge was £70 ($115). At the same time, Virgin Atlantic also levied a £70 fee. These surcharges increased within days of each other.

Eventually, three Virgin executives decided to blow the whistle in exchange for immunity from prosecution. British Airways immediately suspended its executives under suspicion and paid fines of nearly $500 million to U.S. and U.K. authorities. And in 2010, four British Airways executives were prosecuted by British authorities for their alleged role in the conspiracy.

The lawyers for the executives argued that although the two airlines had swapped information, this was not proof of a criminal conspiracy. In fact, they argued, Virgin was so fearful of American regulators that it had admitted to criminal behavior before confirming that it had indeed committed an offense.

One of the defense lawyers, Clare Montgomery, argued that because U.S. laws against anti-competitive behavior are much tougher than those in the United Kingdom, companies may be compelled to blow the whistle to avoid investigation. "It's a race," she said. "If you don't get to them and confess first, you can't get immunity. The only way to protect yourself is to go to the authorities, even if you haven't [done anything]." The result was that the Virgin executives were given immunity in both the United States and the United Kingdom, but the British Airways executives were subject to prosecution (and possible multiyear jail terms) in both countries.

In late 2011, the case came to a shocking end for Virgin Atlantic and U.K. authorities. Citing e-mails that Virgin was forced to turn over by the court, the judge found insufficient evidence that there was ever a conspiracy between the two airlines. The court was incensed enough to threaten to rescind the immunity granted to the three Virgin executives.

QUESTIONS FOR THOUGHT

1. Explain why Virgin Atlantic and British Airways might collude in response to increased oil prices. Was the market conducive to collusion or not?
2. How would you determine whether illegal behavior actually occurred? What might explain these events other than illegal behavior?
3. Explain the dilemma facing the two airlines as well as their individual executives.

REVIEW

MODULE 30

1. Because there are only a few sellers in oligopoly, they operate in a state of **interdependence:** the actions by one firm have a significant effect on the profits of its rivals. An oliopoly with only two sellers is a **duopoly.** Like monopoly, oligopoly arises from barriers to entry but in weaker form.
2. Because of their interdependence, there is a potential for oligopolists to engage in strategic behavior. The firms in an oligopoly could maximize their combined profits by colluding and acting as a **cartel,** setting output levels for each firm as if they were a single monopolist. But each individual firm has an incentive to produce more than it would in such an arrangement—to engage in **noncooperative behavior.**
3. To limit the ability of oligopolists to collude and act like monopolists, most governments pursue an **antitrust policy** designed to make collusion more difficult. In practice, however, **tacit collusion** is widespread.
4. A variety of factors make tacit collusion difficult: large numbers of firms, complex products and pricing, differences in interests, and the bargaining power of buyers. When tacit collusion breaks down, there is a **price war.**

MODULE 31

1. Economists use **game theory** to analyze strategic behavior. In the case of a game with two players, the **payoff** of each player depends both on its own actions and on the actions of the other; this interdependence can be represented as a **payoff matrix.** Depending on the structure of payoffs in the payoff matrix, a player may have a **dominant strategy**—an action that is always the best regardless of the other player's actions.
2. **Duopolists** face a particular type of game known as a **prisoners' dilemma;** if each acts independently in its own interest, the resulting **Nash equilibrium** or **noncooperative equilibrium** will be bad for both. However, firms that expect to play a game repeatedly tend to engage in **strategic behavior,** trying to influence each other's future actions. A particular strategy that seems to work well in maintaining tactic collusion is **tit for tat.**

MODULE 32

1. Monopolistic competition is a market structure in which there are many competing producers, each producing a differentiated product, and there is free entry and exit in the long run.
2. Short-run profits will attract entry of new firms in the long run. This reduces the quantity each existing producer sells at any given price and shifts its demand curve to the left. Short-run losses will induce exit by some firms in the long run. This shifts the demand curve of each remaining firm to the right.
3. In the long run, a monopolistically competitive industry is in **zero-profit equilibrium:** at its profit-maximizing quantity, the demand curve for each existing firm is tangent to its average total cost curve. There are zero profits in the industry and no entry or exit.
4. In long-run equilibrium, firms in a monopolistically competitive industry sell at a price greater than marginal cost. They also have **excess capacity** because they produce less than the minimum-cost output; as a result, they have higher costs than firms in a perfectly competitive industry. Whether or not monopolistic competition is inefficient is ambiguous because consumers value the variety of products that it creates.

MODULE 33

1. **Product differentiation** is undertaken by both oligopolists and monopolistic competitors. It is the attempt by a firm to convince buyers that its product is different from other products in the industry. It takes three main forms: by style or type, by location, or by quality.
2. A firm with market power—a monopolist, an oligopolist, or a monopolistic competitor—will always prefer to make an additional sale at the going price, so it will engage in advertising to increase demand for its product and enhance its market power. Advertising and **brand names** that provide useful information to consumers are economically valuable. But they are economically wasteful when their only purpose is to create market power. In reality, advertising and brand names are likely to be some of both economically valuable and economically wasteful.

KEY TERMS

Interdependence p. 326
Duopoly p. 326
Duopolist p. 326
Cartel p. 327
Noncooperative behavior p. 328
Antitrust policy p. 330
Tacit collusion p. 330
Price war p. 331
Game theory p. 333
Payoff p. 333
Payoff matrix p. 333
Prisoners' dilemma p. 334
Dominant strategy p. 335
Nash equilibrium p. 336
Noncooperative equilibrium p. 336
Strategic behavior p. 336
Tit for tat p. 336
Zero-profit equilibrium p. 343
Excess capacity p. 346
Product differentiation p. 349
Brand name p. 352

Ariel Skelley/DigitalVision/Getty Images; Wichita Eagle/Getty Images

SECTION 11

Market Failure and the Role of Government

TROUBLE UNDERFOOT

When researchers at Duke University published a paper with an unassuming title, "Increased stray gas abundance in a subset of drinking water wells near Marcellus shale gas extraction," the effects of that publication were anything but restrained. While its results are not definitive, the paper presented evidence that fracking—the extraction of natural gas by fracturing underground shale deposits with chemical-laden pressurized jets of water—at the Marcellus gas field in Pennsylvania contaminated underground drinking water supplies with ethane and propane.

The Duke paper provided support to some critics of fracking who claim that it poses an intolerable pollution threat to drinking water supplies. It also helped fuel an increasingly polarized debate over the costs and benefits of fracking.

You may recall from our discussion in Section 2 that fracking has dramatically reduced the cost of energy in the United States, leading to lower heating bills for homeowners and lower production costs for suppliers. And fracking has the potential to significantly reduce air pollution as consumers and industries move from dirtier-burning gasoline and coal to cleaner-burning natural gas.

However, as anticipated in Section 2, the environmental benefits of cleaner air from cheaper natural gas have been challenged by the specter of polluted drinking water from fracking. A key question in assessing the trade-off is the role of government: should regulators do more to protect groundwater supplies? Would more regulatory oversight of how fracking wells are drilled reduce groundwater contamination? What amount of contamination would regulators find acceptable? And how would they enforce it?

The dilemma posed by fracking is just one example of the dilemmas that are caused by *externalities*. An externality occurs when individuals impose costs or deliver benefits to others but don't have an economic incentive to take those costs or benefits into account when making decisions. In Section 1, we stated that one of the principal sources of market failure is actions that create side effects that are not properly taken into account—that is, actions that create externalities.

In this section, we'll examine the economics of externalities, seeing how they can get in the way of market efficiency and lead to market failure, why they provide a reason for government intervention in markets, and how economic analysis can be used to guide government policy. We will also introduce *climate change*—the most extreme form of externality ever created and arguably the most pressing concern to the planet today.

This section ends with an analysis of two additional areas where markets often fail: *public goods* and *common resources*. So, like externalities, public goods and common resources provide a reason for governments to intervene in markets to improve society's welfare.

MODULE 34

Externalities

WHAT YOU WILL LEARN

- What are **externalities** and why do they lead to inefficiency?
- How do **negative externalities** and **positive externalities** differ?

iStockphoto/Thinkstock

When individuals or firms take actions that impose costs on or provide benefits for others but don't have an economic incentive to take those costs or benefits into account, economists say that *externalities* are generated.

Externalities, then, arise from the side effects of actions. We begin this module by looking at the case of pollution, which generates a *negative externality*—a side effect that imposes costs on others. Next, we will analyze activities that generate *positive externalities,* side effects that generate benefits for others. For example, getting a flu shot helps protect others from catching the flu and generates a positive externality.

In the case of positive and negative externalities, achieving the optimal solution takes place at the margin, setting the benefit of doing a little bit more of something equal to the cost of doing that something a little bit more, as we'll see.

34.1 The Economics of a Negative Externality: Pollution

Pollution is a bad thing. Yet most pollution is a side effect of activities that provide us with good things: our air is polluted by power plants generating the electricity that lights our cities, and our rivers are damaged by fertilizer runoff from farms that grow our food. And groundwater contamination may occur from fracking, which also produces cleaner-burning fuel. Why shouldn't we accept a certain amount of pollution as the cost of a good life?

Actually, we do. Even highly committed environmentalists don't think that we can or should completely eliminate pollution—even an environmentally conscious society would accept *some* pollution as the cost of producing useful goods and services. What environmentalists argue is that unless there is a strong and effective environmental policy, our society will generate *too much* pollution—too much of a bad thing. And the great majority of economists agree.

To see why, we need a framework that lets us think about how much pollution a society *should* have. We'll then be able to see why a market economy, left to itself, will produce more pollution than it should. We'll start by adopting the simplest framework to study the problem—assuming that the amount of pollution emitted by a polluter is directly observable and controllable.

The Costs and Benefits of Pollution

How much pollution should society allow? We learned previously that "how much" decisions always involve comparing the marginal benefit from an additional unit of something with the marginal cost of that additional unit. The same is true of pollution.

The **marginal social cost of pollution** is the additional cost imposed on society as a whole by an additional unit of pollution.

For example, sulfur dioxide from coal-fired power plants mixes with rainwater to form acid rain, which damages fisheries, crops, and forests, while groundwater contamination, which may be a side effect of fracking, damages health. Typically, the marginal social cost of pollution is increasing—each additional unit of pollution emitted causes a greater level of damage than the unit before. That's because nature can often safely handle low levels of pollution but is increasingly harmed as pollution reaches higher levels.

The **marginal social benefit of pollution** is the benefit to society from an additional unit of pollution. This may seem like a confusing concept—how can there be any benefit to society from pollution? The answer lies in the understanding that pollution can be reduced—but at a cost. For example, air pollution from coal-fired power plants can be reduced by using more expensive coal and expensive scrubbing technology; contamination of drinking water due to fracking can be limited with more-expensive drilling techniques; wastewater contamination of rivers and oceans can be reduced by building water treatment facilities.

All these methods of reducing pollution have an opportunity cost. That is, avoiding pollution requires using scarce resources that could have been employed to produce other goods and services. So the marginal social benefit of pollution is the goods and services that could be had by society if it tolerated another unit of pollution.

Comparisons between the pollution levels tolerated in high-income and low-income countries illustrate the importance of the level of the marginal social benefit of pollution in deciding how much pollution a society wishes to tolerate. Because low-income countries have a higher opportunity cost of resources spent on reducing pollution than higher-income countries, they tolerate higher levels of pollution. For example, the World Health Organization has estimated that 3.8 million people in low-income countries die prematurely from breathing polluted indoor air caused by burning dirty fuels like wood, dung, and coal to heat and cook—a situation that residents of high-income countries can afford to avoid.

Using hypothetical numbers, Figure 34-1 shows how we can determine the **socially optimal quantity of pollution**—the quantity of pollution that society would choose if all the social costs and benefits were fully accounted for. The upward-sloping marginal social cost curve, *MSC*, shows how the marginal cost to society of an additional unit of pollution varies with the quantity of pollution. It is typically upward sloping because the harm inflicted by a unit of pollution typically increases as more pollution has already been emitted. In contrast, the marginal social benefit curve, *MSB*, is downward sloping. At high levels of pollution, the cost of achieving a reduction in pollution is fairly small. However, as pollution levels drop, it becomes progressively more costly to engineer a further fall in pollution as more expensive techniques must be used, so the *MSB* is higher at lower levels of pollution.

As we can see from Figure 34-1, the socially optimal quantity of pollution in this example isn't zero. It's Q_{OPT}, the quantity corresponding to point *O*, where *MSB* crosses *MSC*. At Q_{OPT}, the marginal social benefit from an additional unit of pollution and its marginal social cost are equalized at $200.

The **marginal social cost of pollution** is the additional cost imposed on society as a whole by an additional unit of pollution.

The **marginal social benefit of pollution** is the additional gain to society as a whole from an additional unit of pollution.

The **socially optimal quantity of pollution** is the quantity of pollution that society would choose if all the costs and benefits of pollution were fully accounted for.

FIGURE 34-1 The Socially Optimal Quantity of Pollution

Pollution yields both costs and benefits. Here the curve *MSC* shows how the marginal cost to society as a whole from emitting one more unit of pollution emissions depends on the quantity of emissions. The *MSC* curve is upward sloping, so the marginal social cost increases as pollution increases. The curve *MSB* shows how the marginal benefit to society as a whole of emitting an additional unit of pollution emissions depends on the quantity of pollution emissions. The *MSB* curve is downward sloping, so the marginal social benefit falls as pollution increases. The socially optimal quantity of pollution is Q_{OPT}. At that quantity, the marginal social benefit of pollution is equal to the marginal social cost, corresponding to $200.

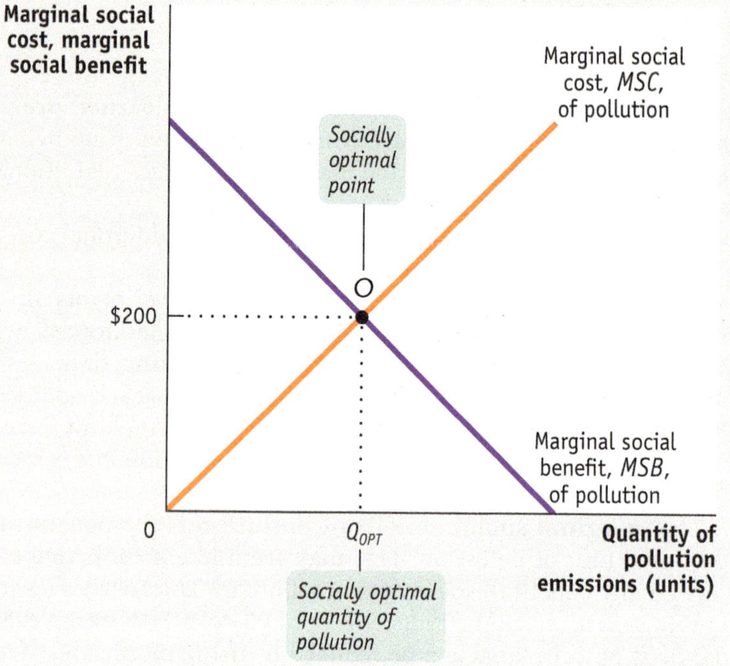

But will a market economy, left to itself, arrive at the socially optimal quantity of pollution? No, it won't. Let's see why.

Why a Market Economy Produces Too Much Pollution

While pollution yields both benefits and costs to society, in a market economy without government intervention, too much pollution will be produced. In that case, polluters alone—owners of power plants or gas-drilling companies, for example—decide how much pollution occurs. And they have no incentive to take into account the cost that pollution inflicts on others. Instead, the companies' incentives are determined by the private monetary costs and benefits of generating power, such as the price of coal, the price earned for a kilowatt of energy, and so on.

Figure 34-2 shows the result of this asymmetry between who reaps the benefits and who pays the costs. In a market economy without government intervention, since polluters are the only ones making the decisions, only the private benefits of pollution are taken into account when choosing how much pollution to produce rather than the costs to society. So instead of producing the socially optimal quantity, Q_{OPT}, the market economy will generate the amount Q_{MKT}. At Q_{MKT}, the marginal social benefit of an additional unit of pollution is zero, while the marginal social cost of an additional unit is much higher—$400.

A **negative externality** is an uncompensated cost that an individual or firm imposes on others.

A **positive externality** is a benefit that an individual or firm confers on others without receiving compensation.

The environmental costs of pollution are the best-known and most important example of a **negative externality**—an uncompensated cost that an individual or firm imposes on others. In a modern economy, there are many examples of external costs besides pollution. A very familiar one is the external cost of traffic congestion: an individual who chooses to drive during rush hour increases congestion and has no incentive to take into account the inconvenience inflicted on other drivers. Another familiar example is the cost created by people who text while driving, increasing the risk of accidents that will harm others as well as themselves.

We'll see later in this module that there are also important examples of **positive externalities,** benefits that individuals or firms confer on others without

FIGURE 34-2 Why a Market Economy Produces Too Much Pollution

In the absence of government intervention, the quantity of pollution will be Q_{MKT}, the level at which the marginal social benefit of pollution is zero. This is an inefficiently high quantity of pollution: the marginal social cost, $400, greatly exceeds the marginal social benefit, $0. An optimal Pigouvian tax* of $200, the value of the marginal social cost of pollution when it equals the marginal social benefit of pollution, can move the market to the socially optimal quantity of pollution, Q_{OPT}.

*Pigouvian taxes are covered in the next module on pollution policy.

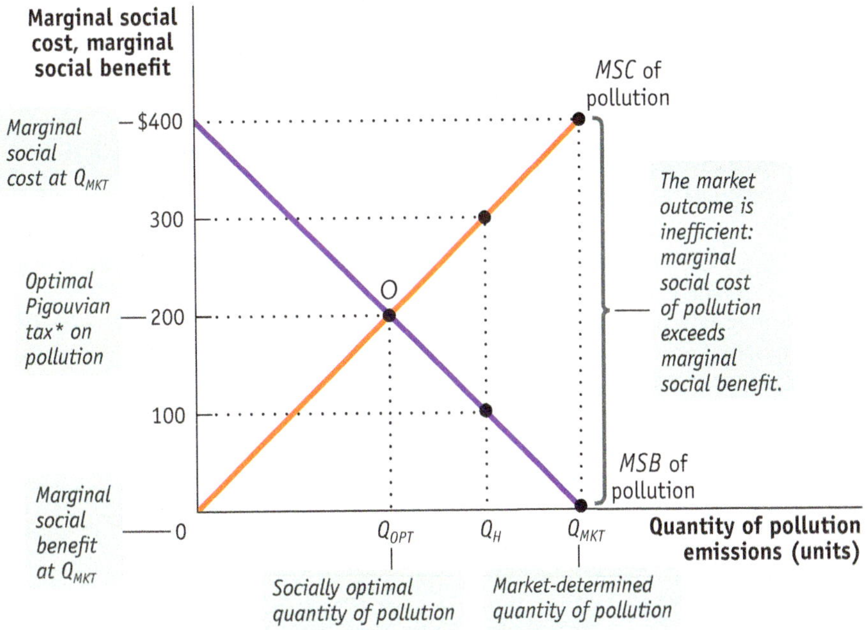

receiving compensation. For example, when you get a flu shot, you are less likely to pass on the flu virus to your roommates. Yet you alone incur the monetary cost of the vaccination and the painful jab.

Externalities can lead to private decisions—that is, decisions by individuals or firms—that are not optimal for society as a whole. Let's take a closer look at why, focusing on the case of pollution.

The Inefficiency of Excess Pollution

We have just shown that in the absence of government action, the quantity of pollution will be inefficient: polluters will pollute up until the point at which the marginal social benefit of pollution is zero, as shown by quantity Q_{MKT} in Figure 34-2. Recall that an outcome is inefficient if someone could be made better off without someone else being made worse off. We have already seen why the equilibrium quantity in a perfectly competitive market with no externalities is the efficient quantity of the good, the quantity that maximizes total surplus. Here, we can use a variation of that analysis to show how the presence of a negative externality upsets the result.

Because the marginal social benefit of pollution is zero at Q_{MKT}, reducing the quantity of pollution by one ton would subtract very little from the total social benefit from pollution. In other words, the benefit to polluters from that last unit of pollution is very low—virtually zero. Meanwhile, the marginal social cost imposed on the rest of society of that last ton of pollution at Q_{MKT} is quite high—$400. So by reducing the quantity of pollution at Q_{MKT} by one unit, the total social cost of pollution falls by $400 but the total social benefit falls by virtually zero. So total surplus rises by approximately $400 if the quantity of pollution at Q_{MKT} is reduced by one unit.

If the quantity of pollution is reduced further, there will be more gains in total surplus, though they will be smaller. For example, if the quantity of pollution is Q_H in Figure 34-2, the marginal social benefit of a unit of pollution is $100, but the marginal social cost is still much higher at $300. This means that reducing the quantity of pollution by one ton leads to a net gain in total surplus of approximately $300 – $100 = $200. Thus, Q_H is still an inefficiently high quantity of pollution. Only if the quantity of pollution is reduced to Q_{OPT}, where the marginal social cost and the marginal social benefit of an additional unit of pollution are both $200, is the outcome efficient.

>> Quick Review

- There are costs as well as benefits to reducing pollution, so the optimal quantity of pollution isn't zero. Instead, the **socially optimal quantity of pollution** is the quantity at which the **marginal social cost of pollution** is equal to the **marginal social benefit of pollution.**
- External costs and benefits are known as **externalities.** Pollution is an example of an **external cost,** or **negative externality;** in contrast, some activities can give rise to **external benefits,** or **positive externalities.**
- Left to itself, a market economy will typically generate an inefficiently high level of pollution because polluters have no incentive to take into account the costs they impose on others.

Check Your Understanding 34-1

1. Wastewater runoff from large poultry farms adversely affects their neighbors. Explain the following:
   a. The nature of the externality imposed
   b. The outcome in the absence of government intervention or a private deal
   c. The socially optimal outcome
2. According to Yasmin, any student who borrows a book from the university library and fails to return it on time imposes a negative externality on other students. She claims that rather than charging a modest fine for late returns, the library should charge a huge fine so that borrowers will never return a book late. Is Yasmin's economic reasoning correct?

Solutions appear at back of book.

34.2 The Economics of Positive Externalities

New Jersey is the most densely populated state in the United States, lying along the northeastern corridor, an area of almost continuous development stretching from Washington, D.C., to Boston. Yet a drive through New Jersey reveals a surprising feature: acre upon acre of farmland, growing everything from corn to pumpkins to the famous Jersey tomatoes. This is no accident: starting in 1961, New Jerseyans have voted in a series of measures that subsidize farmers to permanently preserve their farmland rather than sell it to developers. By 2020, the Green Acres Program, administered by the state, had preserved over 1.2 million acres of open space.

Why have New Jersey citizens voted to raise their own taxes to subsidize the preservation of farmland? Because they believe that preserved farmland in an already heavily developed state provides benefits, such as natural beauty, access to fresh food, and the conservation of wild bird populations. In addition, preservation alleviates the negative externalities that come with more development, such as pressure on roads, water supplies, and municipal services—and, inevitably, more pollution. The Trust for Public Land estimated that every $1 invested in state preservation programs returns $10 in economic value by diminishing local pollution, enhancing the natural environment, and reducing flood risk. Not surprisingly, the average value of nearby homes increased by 16%.

In this section, we'll explore the topics of positive externalities. They are, in many ways, the mirror images of negative externalities. Left to its own, the market will produce too little of a good (in this case, preserved New Jersey farmland) that generates benefits for others. But society as a whole is better off when policies are adopted that increase the supply of such a good.

Preserved Farmland: A Positive Externality

Preserved farmland yields both benefits and costs to society. In the absence of government intervention, the farmer who wants to sell their land incurs all the costs of preservation—namely, the forgone profit to be made from selling the farmland to a developer. But the benefits of preserved farmland accrue not to the farmer but to neighboring residents, who have no right to influence how the farmland is disposed of.

Figure 34-3 illustrates society's problem. The marginal social cost of preserved farmland, shown by the *MSC* curve, is the additional cost imposed on society by an additional acre of such farmland. This represents the forgone profits that would have accrued to farmers if they had sold their land to developers. The line is upward sloping because when very few acres are preserved and there is plenty of land available for development, the profit that could be made from selling an acre to a developer is small. But as the number of preserved acres increases and few are left for development, the amount a developer is willing to pay for them, and therefore the forgone profit, increases as well.

Lijuan Guo/Shutterstock

New Jerseyans understand that preserving local farmland makes them better off.

The *MSB* curve represents the marginal social benefit of preserved farmland. It is the additional benefit that accrues to society—in this case, the farmer's neighbors—when an additional acre of farmland is preserved. The curve is downward sloping because as more farmland is preserved, the benefit to society of preserving another acre falls.

As Figure 34-3 shows, the socially optimal point, *O*, occurs when the marginal social cost and the marginal social benefit are equalized—here, at a price of $10,000 per acre. At the socially optimal point, Q_{OPT} acres of farmland are preserved.

The market alone will not provide Q_{OPT} acres of preserved farmland. Instead, in the market outcome, no acres will be preserved; the level of preserved farmland, Q_{MKT}, is equal to zero. That's because farmers will set the marginal social cost of preservation—their forgone profits—at zero and sell all their acres to developers. Because farmers bear the entire cost of preservation but gain none of the benefits, an inefficiently low quantity of acres will be preserved in the market outcome.

This is clearly inefficient because at zero acres preserved, the marginal social benefit of preserving an acre of farmland is $20,000. So how can the economy be induced to produce Q_{OPT} acres of preserved farmland, the socially optimal level? The answer is a **Pigouvian subsidy:** a payment designed to encourage activities that generate positive externalities. The optimal Pigouvian subsidy, as shown in Figure 34-3, is equal to the marginal social benefit of preserved farmland at the socially optimal level, Q_{OPT}—that is, $10,000 per acre.

So New Jersey voters are indeed implementing the right policy to raise their social welfare—taxing themselves in order to provide subsidies for farmland preservation.

Positive Externalities in Today's Economy

In the overall U.S. economy, the single most important source of positive externalities is the creation of knowledge. In industries such as programming, app design, robotics, artificial intelligence, green technology, and bioengineering, innovations by one firm are quickly emulated and improved upon by rival firms. Such spreading of knowledge across individuals and firms is known as a **technology spillover.** In today's economy, the greatest sources of technology spillovers are major universities and research institutes.

A **Pigouvian subsidy** is a payment designed to encourage activities that yield external benefits.

A **technology spillover** is an external benefit that results when knowledge spreads among individuals and firms.

In technologically advanced countries such as the United States, Japan, the United Kingdom, Germany, France, and Israel, there is an ongoing exchange of people and ideas among private industries, major universities, and research institutes located in close proximity. The dynamic interplay that occurs in these *research clusters* spurs innovation and competition, theoretical advances, and

FIGURE 34-3 Why a Market Economy Preserves Too Little Farmland

Without government intervention, the quantity of preserved farmland will be zero, the level at which the marginal social cost of preservation is zero. This is an inefficiently low quantity of preserved farmland: the marginal social benefit is $20,000, but the marginal social cost is zero. An optimal Pigouvian subsidy of $10,000, the value of the marginal social benefit of preservation when it equals the marginal social cost, can move the market to the socially optimal level of preservation, Q_{OPT}.

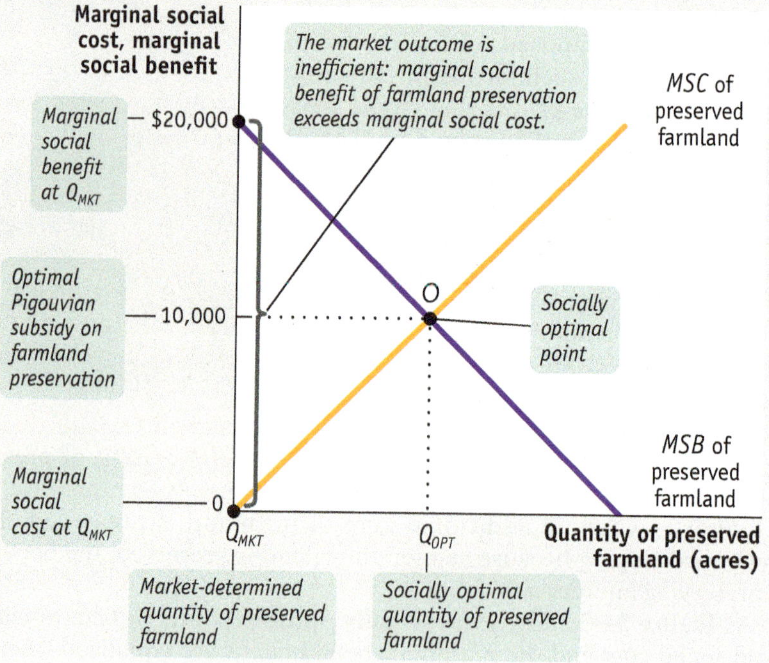

practical applications. One of the best-known and most successful research clusters is the Research Triangle in North Carolina, anchored by Duke University, North Carolina State University, and the University of North Carolina at Chapel Hill, several other universities and hospitals, and companies such as IBM, Pfizer, and Qualcomm. Ultimately, the areas of technology spillover increase the economy's productivity and raise living standards.

But research clusters don't appear out of thin air. Except in a few instances in which firms have funded basic research on a long-term basis, research clusters have grown up around major universities. And like farmland preservation in New Jersey, major universities and their research activities are subsidized by government. In fact, government policy makers in advanced countries have long understood that the external benefits generated by knowledge, stemming from basic education to high-tech research, are key to the economy's growth over time.

ECONOMICS >> *in Action*

Texting and Driving

Why is that person in the car in front of you driving so erratically? Is the driver drunk? No, the driver is texting or using their cell phone to check social media or make calls.

Traffic safety experts take the risks posed by driving while using a cell phone very seriously: a driver is 23 times more likely to have an accident while texting. The National Safety Council has estimated that approximately one in four traffic accidents is attributable to the use of cell phones while driving.

Car crashes are the leading cause of teen deaths, and texting and driving is a large, contributing factor. In 2017, there were nearly 275 teenager deaths attributed to distracted driving.

Using hands-free, voice-activated devices to make a call doesn't seem to help much because the main danger is distraction. As one traffic consultant put it, "It's not where your eyes are; it's where your head is."

The National Safety Council urges people not to use cell phones while driving. Most states have some restrictions on cell phone use while driving. But in response to a growing number of accidents, several states have banned cell phone use behind the wheel altogether. In 48 states and the District of Columbia, Puerto Rico, Guam, and the U.S. Virgin Islands, it is illegal to text and drive. Cell phone use while driving is illegal in many other countries as well, including Japan and Israel.

Why not leave the decision up to the driver? Because the risk posed by driving while using a cell phone isn't just a risk to the driver; it's also a safety risk to others—to a driver's passengers, to pedestrians, and to people in other cars. Even if you decide that the benefit to you of using your cell phone while driving is worth the cost, you aren't taking into account the cost to other people. Driving while using a cell phone, in other words, generates a serious—and sometimes fatal—negative externality.

Andrey_Popov/Shutterstock

Using a cell phone while driving makes you a danger to others as well as to yourself.

Check Your Understanding 34-2

1. In 2019, the U.S. Department of Education spent almost $120 billion on college student aid. Explain why this can be an optimal policy to encourage the creation of knowledge.
2. In each of the following cases, determine whether an external cost or an external benefit is imposed and what an appropriate policy response would be.
   a. Trees planted in urban areas improve air quality and lower summer temperatures.
   b. Water-saving toilets reduce the need to pump water from rivers and aquifers. The cost of a gallon of water to homeowners is virtually zero.
   c. Bottled drinks are packaged in plastic that does not decompose when discarded. As a result, they take up vast amounts of landfill space or must be burned, releasing pollutants.

Solutions appear at back of book.

>> Quick Review

- When there are positive externalities, or external benefits, a market economy, left to itself, will typically produce too little of the good or activity. The socially optimal quantity of the good or activity can be achieved by an optimal **Pigouvian subsidy.**
- The most important example of positive externalities in the economy is the creation of knowledge through **technology spillover.**

MODULE

35

Pollution, Government Policy, and the Great Energy Transition

WHAT YOU WILL LEARN

- What are the various ways governments intervene to address pollution?
- Why are some policies more efficient than others?

Accent Alaska.com/Alamy

By the 1960s, vast tracts of ghostly, withered trees in the northeastern United States and southeastern Canada revealed an ominous truth: these great forests were dying. Moreover, the lakes and streams within them were dying, too, as the stock of fish and other aquatic life plummeted.

The culprit was *acid rain,* a phenomenon that occurs when rain mixes with airborne sulfur dioxide pollutants from coal-burning power plants. The result is highly acidic rain that poisons trees and aquatic life. Before 1970, there were no rules governing the amount of sulfur dioxide that coal-burning power plants in the United States could emit.

In 1970, Congress adopted the Clean Air Act, which set rules forcing power plants to reduce their emissions. And it worked—the acidity of rainfall declined significantly. Economists, however, argued that a more flexible system of rules that exploits the effectiveness of markets could reduce pollution at a lower cost. In 1990, this theory was put into effect with a modified version of the Clean Air Act. And guess what? The economists were right!

In this module, we'll look at the three types of policies governments typically use to deal with pollution: environmental standards, emissions taxes, and tradable emissions permits.

We will also see how economic analysis has been used to improve those policies. And we will look at the issue of climate change and how government policy can be used to address it.

35.1 Government Policies to Address Pollution

Environmental Standards

Among the most serious negative externalities we face today are those associated with actions that damage the environment—air pollution, water pollution, habitat destruction, and so on. Protection of the environment has become a major role of government in all advanced nations. In the United States, the Environmental Protection Agency is the principal enforcer of environmental policies at the national level, supported by the actions of state and local governments.

How does a country protect its environment? At present the main policy tools are **environmental standards,** rules that protect the environment by specifying actions by producers and consumers. A familiar example is the law that requires almost all vehicles to have catalytic converters, which reduce the emission of toxic gases and other pollutants that cause smog and lead to health problems. Other rules require communities to treat their sewage or factories to avoid or limit certain kinds of pollution. For example, environmental standards were put in place in 2014, compelling new coal- and gas-fired power plants to adopt cleaner-burning technologies.

Mischa Richter/The New Yorker Collection/The Cartoon Bank

"They have very strict anti-pollution laws in this state."

Environmental standards came into widespread use in the 1960s and 1970s, and they have had considerable success in reducing pollution. For example, since the United States passed the Clean Air Act in 1970, overall emission of pollutants into the air has fallen by more than a third, even though the population has grown by a third and the size of the economy has more than doubled.

Emissions Taxes versus Environmental Standards

Another policy tool to address pollution directly is to charge polluters an **emissions tax.** Emissions taxes depend on the amount of pollution a firm emits. As we learned in Section 4, a tax imposed on an activity will reduce the level of that activity.

Recall that without government intervention, polluters have an incentive to increase pollution beyond the socially optimal quantity of pollution. In fact, polluters will push pollution up to the quantity, shown in Figure 34-2, the point at which marginal social benefit equals zero.

As shown in that figure, if the marginal social benefit and marginal social cost of an additional unit of pollution are equal at $200 (as shown in Figure 34-2 in the previous module), a tax on polluters of $200 per units of pollution will induce them to reduce their emissions to the socially optimal quantity.

This illustrates a general result: an emissions tax equal to the marginal social cost at the socially optimal quantity of pollution induces polluters to internalize the externality—to take into account the true cost to society of their actions.

An emissions tax is also a more efficient way (that is, a cost-minimizing way) to reduce pollution than environmental standards because the tax ensures that the marginal benefit of pollution is equal for all sources of pollution. Environmental standards, by contrast, treat all polluters the same, when they actually differ according to their costs of pollution reduction.

Environmental standards are rules that protect the environment by specifying actions by producers and consumers.

An **emissions tax** is a tax that depends on the amount of pollution a firm produces.

Taxes designed to reduce the costs imposed on society from a negative externality are known as **Pigouvian taxes.**

Tradable emissions permits are licenses to emit limited quantities of pollutants that can be bought and sold by polluters.

The term *emissions tax* may convey the misleading impression that taxes are a solution to only one kind of negative externality, pollution. In fact, taxes can be used to discourage any activity that generates negative externalities, such as driving (which inflicts environmental damage greater than the cost of producing gasoline) or smoking (which inflicts health costs on society far greater than the cost of making a cigarette).

In general, taxes designed to reduce the costs imposed on society from a negative externality are known as **Pigouvian taxes,** after the economist A. C. Pigou, who emphasized their usefulness in his classic 1920 book, *The Economics of Welfare*. In our example, the optimal Pigouvian tax is $200, which sets the marginal social cost of pollution equal to the social optimal quantity.

Are there any problems with emissions taxes? The main concern is that in practice, government officials usually aren't sure how high the tax should be set. If they set it too low, there won't be sufficient reduction in pollution; if they set it too high, emissions will be reduced by more than is efficient. This uncertainty around the optimal level of the emissions tax can't be eliminated, but the nature of the risks can be changed by using an alternative policy, issuing tradable emissions permits.

Tradable Emissions Permits

Tradable emissions permits are licenses to emit limited quantities of pollutants that can be bought and sold by polluters. They are usually issued to polluting firms according to some formula reflecting their history. For example, each power plant might be issued permits equal to 50% of its emissions before the system went into effect. The more important point, however, is that these permits are *tradable*.

Under this system, a market in permits to pollute will emerge. Firms that pollute typically have different costs of reducing pollution. Polluters who place a higher value on the right to pollute—those with older technology, making it more costly to reduce pollution—will purchase permits from polluters who place a lower value on the right to pollute—those with newer technology that have a lower cost of reducing pollution. As a result, a polluter with a higher value for a unit of emissions will pollute more than a polluter with a lower value.

In the end, those with the lowest cost of reducing pollution will reduce their pollution the most, while those with the highest cost of reducing pollution will reduce their pollution the least. The total effect is to allocate pollution reduction efficiently—that is, in the least costly way.

Just like emissions taxes, tradable emissions permits provide polluters with an incentive to take the marginal social cost of pollution into account. To see why, suppose that the market price of a permit to emit one unit of pollution is $200. Every polluter now has an incentive to limit its emissions to the point where its marginal benefit of one unit of pollution is $200. Why?

If the marginal benefit of one more unit of pollution is greater than $200, then it is cheaper to pollute more than to pollute less. In that case, the polluter will buy a permit and emit another unit. And if the marginal benefit of one more unit of pollution is less than $200, then it is cheaper to reduce pollution than to pollute more. In that scenario, the polluter will reduce pollution rather than buy the $200 permit.

From this example we can see how an emissions permit leads to the same outcome as an emissions tax when they are the same amount: a polluter who pays $200 for the right to emit one unit faces the same incentives as a polluter who faces an emissions tax of $200 per unit. And it's equally true for polluters who have received more permits from regulators than they plan to use: by not emitting one unit of pollution, a polluter frees up a permit that it can sell for $200. In other words, the opportunity cost of a unit of pollution to this firm is $200, regardless of whether it is used.

Recall that when using emissions taxes to arrive at the optimal level of pollution, the problem arises of finding the right amount of the tax: if the tax is too low, too much pollution is emitted; if the tax is too high, too little pollution is emitted (in other words, too many resources are spent reducing pollution). A similar problem with tradable emissions permits is getting the quantity of permits right, which is much like the flip side of getting the level of the tax right.

Because it is difficult to determine the optimal quantity of pollution, regulators can find themselves either issuing too many permits, so that there is insufficient pollution reduction, or issuing too few, so that there is too much pollution reduction.

In the case of sulfur dioxide pollution, the U.S. government first relied on environmental standards but then turned to a system of tradable emissions permits. Currently, the largest emissions permit trading system is the European Union system for controlling emissions of carbon dioxide.

>> Quick Review

- Governments often limit pollution with **environmental standards.** Generally, such standards are an inefficient way to reduce pollution because they are inflexible.
- Environmental goals can be achieved efficiently in two ways: **emissions taxes** and **tradable emissions permits.** These methods are efficient because they are flexible, allocating more pollution reduction to those who can do it more cheaply. They also motivate polluters to adopt new pollution-reducing technology. An emissions tax is a form of **Pigouvian tax.** The optimal Pigouvian tax is equal to the marginal social cost of pollution at the socially optimal quantity of pollution.

Check Your Understanding 35-1

1. Some opponents of tradable emissions permits object to them on the grounds that polluters that sell their permits benefit monetarily from their contribution to polluting the environment. Assess this argument.
2. Explain the following.
   a. Why an emissions tax smaller than or greater than the marginal social cost at Q_{OPT} leads to a smaller total surplus compared to the total surplus generated if the emissions tax had been set optimally?
   b. Why a system of tradable emissions permits that sets the total quantity of allowable pollution higher or lower than Q_{OPT} leads to a smaller total surplus compared to the total surplus generated if the number of permits had been set optimally?
   c. How a carbon tax, which is a tax on carbon emissions, would encourage consumers to use more renewable energy sources?

Solutions appear at back of book.

35.2 The Economics of Climate Change and the Great Energy Transition

It is safe to say that one of the most challenging problems that the world will face during your lifetime is **climate change.** Science has conclusively shown that emissions of *greenhouse gases* are changing Earth's climate. On a global scale, **greenhouse gases** trap heat in Earth's atmosphere, leading to extreme weather patterns around the world—drought, flooding, extreme temperatures, destructive storm activity, and rising sea levels. Climate change inflicts huge costs and suffering, as crops fail, homes are washed away, tropical diseases spread, animal species are lost, and areas become uninhabitable. Moreover, the burden of this cost will fall more heavily on lower-income countries, which have fewer resources to cope with the change.

In 2018, a scientific report by 13 federal agencies warned that unmitigated climate change could lower U.S. GDP by 10% by 2100. One study estimated that 20% of world GDP would be lost under the same conditions. Economists and scientists widely recognize that the direct cost of fossil-fuel consumption greatly underestimates the social cost. In a World Bank study, Nobel prize–winning economist Joseph Stiglitz and Nicholas Stern estimated that the true environmental cost of carbon emissions ranged from $50 to $100 per ton as of 2017 and may climb as high as $400 by 2050. According to industry observers, the plunge in national electricity demand caused by the pandemic of 2020 is likely to hasten the permanent closure of many coal plants.

An accumulation of greenhouse gases caused by the use of fossil fuels has led to changes in Earth's climate, known as **climate change.**

Greenhouse gases are gas emissions that trap heat in Earth's atmosphere.

Fossil fuels such as coal, oil, and natural gas are fuels derived from fossil sources.

Renewable energy sources such as solar and wind power are inexhaustible sources of energy (unlike fossil fuel sources, which are exhaustible).

Clean energy sources are those that do not emit greenhouse gases. Renewable energy sources are also clean energy sources.

The Cause of Climate Change

The rise in Earth's temperature began in the first half of the nineteenth century and has accelerated since the 1980s, as Figure 35-1 shows. The source of the vast majority of greenhouse gases is human activity—specifically, the burning of **fossil fuels** such as coal, oil, and natural gas, which are derived from fossil sources and are used to generate electricity or power vehicles. Burning fossil fuels releases carbon into the atmosphere, which turns into greenhouse gases. While fossil fuels are in limited supply, **renewable energy sources** are inexhaustible. Examples are solar and wind-generated power. Unlike fossil fuels, renewables are **clean energy sources** because they do not emit greenhouse gases.

Over the past decade, government subsidies, environmental regulation, and the threat of emissions taxes have spurred huge investments in clean energy sources, leading to dramatic cost reductions for renewables. While coal (the most polluting fossil fuel) was once the energy source of choice in the United States, accounting for nearly 60% of power generation, environmental restrictions and technological innovations have rendered it more costly than natural gas or renewables. By 2019, the use of coal as a power source had fallen to 20%, which is even lower than the 23% share accounted for by renewables. In fact, in many instances, prices for industrial-scale solar power and wind power have become even cheaper than cleaner-burning natural gas power, as Figure 35-2 shows.

Despite these advances, world energy consumption remains overwhelmingly dependent upon fossil fuels. In 2018, they accounted for approximately 85% of total consumption, while renewables accounted for only 10.8%. (Nuclear energy accounts for the difference of approximately 4%.) Why? It's dollars and cents. Historically, fossil fuels have been a cheaper source of energy than renewables. In much of the world, energy is generated by aging power plants that run on coal. This is true of both China and India, where 70% or more of the electricity is generated by coal.

FIGURE 35-1 Global Mean Surface Temperature Anomaly

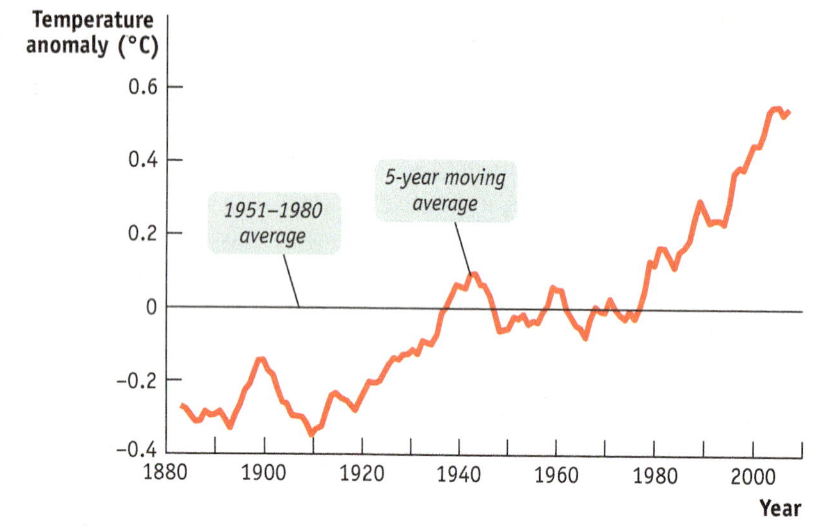

FIGURE 35-2 The Average Cost of Energy in North America, 2009–2017

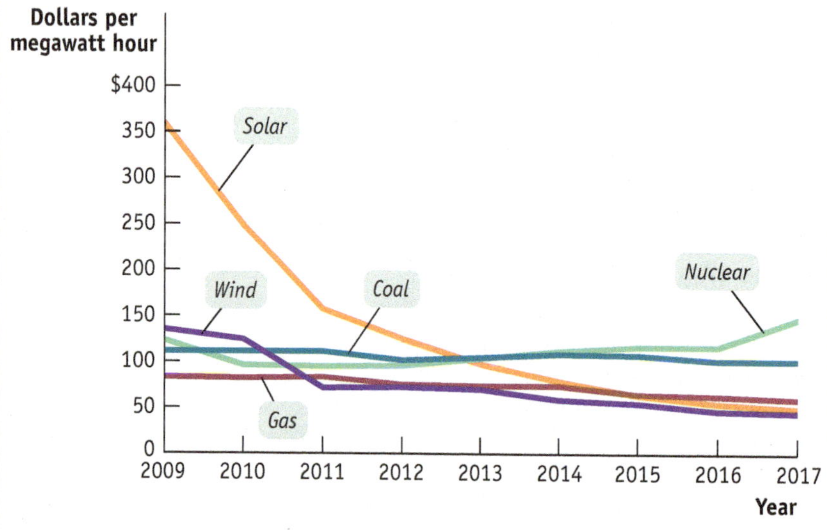

Policies to Address Climate Change

Earlier in this section, we learned about government policies aimed at achieving an efficient level of greenhouse gas emissions. These included regulations or mandates, emissions taxes, and cap-and-trade systems.

However, history has shown that to solve a complex and global negative externality problem like greenhouse gas emissions, other policies are needed. These include both government subsidies to research and development (R&D) and multilateral agreements.

Jim Morin, Morintoons Syndicate

Government Subsidies to R&D Since the 1980s, the U.S. government has provided billions of dollars in subsidies for R&D dedicated to lowering the cost of clean energy sources. These subsidies were critical in kick-starting innovation in the clean energy sector that has become increasingly cost competitive with the fossil-fuel industry. According to the Energy Information Administration, since 2016, the federal government has spent almost $7 billion on subsidies for renewable energy. These subsidies have the advantage of allowing the government to encourage energy innovation while avoiding imposing taxes on fossil fuels or regulating them—both less popular policies that have the potential to provoke a political backlash.

Multilateral Agreements Most countries would be disinclined to undertake costly policies to reduce greenhouse gas emissions if other countries refuse to do the same. To encourage cooperation, multilateral agreements set common objectives and allocate burden-sharing across countries, significantly increasing the chances of success in tackling climate change. In 2015, 196 countries came together under the **Paris Agreement**, committing to reduce emissions of greenhouse gases, with a common goal of limiting the increase in Earth's temperature to 2° Centigrade, the level beyond which the effects of climate change are considered to be catastrophic and irreversible. Another example of a successful multilateral agreement was the Montreal Protocol of 1987. By setting limits on the production of ozone-depleting chemicals around the world, this agreement is credited with saving Earth's ozone layer, the part of the upper atmosphere that protects Earth from the harmful effects of ultraviolet radiation coming from the sun.

Incentives for Individual Choices Incentives aimed at individual choices have an important role to play in addressing climate change. For example, through smart-metering, individuals are motivated to conserve energy, a fast and cost-effective way to reduce greenhouse gases. Higher gasoline taxes and wider availability of charging stations can motivate drivers to switch to electrically powered cars. Individuals can also privately alter their choices, such as using less air conditioning, taking public transportation, or eating less meat (an emissions-heavy source of nutrition).

Climate Change Mitigation: Costs and Benefits

Reducing greenhouse gas emissions to sustainable levels requires a major structural shift in the economy that will inevitably affect growth rates and consumption. Consequently, some have claimed that attempts to mitigate climate change should be abandoned because the costs to consumers are too high.

However, that argument fails under a cost-benefit analysis. In a review of the latest scientific evidence, the Intergovernmental Panel on Climate Change concluded that meeting the Paris Agreement goals would mean that global consumption would shrink by 3–11% by 2100 compared to the status quo. But this number is quite a modest loss given that the world economy will continue growing, with an average growth rate of around 3% over the last several years. And as mentioned earlier, global losses by 2100 from runaway climate change are estimated at 20% of GDP.

Moreover, when the direct health costs from fossil-fuel air pollution are taken into account, the losses from runaway climate change climb significantly.

The **Paris Agreement** is an international agreement by 196 countries to reduce their greenhouse gas emissions.

The World Health Organization estimates that 4.6 million people die annually from air pollution caused by burning fossil fuels.

Nearly 1.25 million "excess" deaths are estimated to occur each year in China alone, from fossil fuel–fouled air. The health benefits of switching to clean energy are estimated to be as much as 5% of global GDP. In addition, the estimates of the costs of mitigating climate change don't incorporate the rapidly dropping price of clean energy sources as technology advances.

So claims that the costs of addressing climate change are too high don't withstand scrutiny. That's why, as the next Economics in Action describes, over 3,500 economists have advocated for a carbon tax to combat climate change.

ECONOMICS >> *in Action*

Over 3,500 Economists Agree: Tax Greenhouse Gas Emissions

In 2019, 3,558 economists from across the ideological spectrum—4 former chairs of the Federal Reserve System, 27 Nobel laureates, 15 former chairs of the Council of Economic Advisers, and 2 former secretaries of the Department of Treasury—signed a joint statement calling for a tax on greenhouse gas emissions to fight climate change, with the proceeds of the tax to be distributed to American consumers. In their words, "Global climate change is a serious problem calling for immediate national action." Published in the *Wall Street Journal,* it was the largest public statement by economists in history.

According to the statement, an emissions tax is needed to quickly reduce emissions, and it should be raised every year until emissions reductions goals are set. A tax, they argue, is more efficient than regulations. By distributing the tax revenues to American consumers in the form of a "carbon dividend," they also believe that this system is politically more viable and more equitable than a cap-and-trade system. Finally, they argue that imports from abroad should also be taxed according to their true environmental cost so that U.S. firms aren't put at a cost disadvantage relative to foreign firms. For the economics profession, it was an indisputable show of support for the validity of the economics of climate change.

But, as of writing, political considerations make the adoption of a carbon tax difficult. Newly elected president Joe Biden has committed to urgent action through a program of subsidies, green infrastructure projects, and increased government regulation. The "social cost of carbon," the cost figure of greenhouse gas damage inflicted used when assessing government projects (such as coal mining on federal land), was raised significantly. The Biden administration has set a goal of making the United States carbon neutral (no net emissions of carbon) by 2050. To achieve this requires a wholesale shift toward renewable energy, electric cars, and zero-emissions mass transit, as well as adopting policies that remove greenhouse gases such as large-scale reforestation.

>> *Quick Review*

- **Climate change** is the result of burning fossil fuels that release **greenhouse gases** into the atmosphere. Climate change inflicts huge costs and suffering, especially on residents of lower-income countries. Under unmitigated climate change, a federal report estimates losses as high as 10% of U.S. GDP in 2100; another study estimates losses as high as 20% of world GDP.
- Unlike fossil fuels (coal, oil, and natural gas), **renewable energy sources,** such as solar and wind power, are inexhaustible. They are **clean energy sources** because they do not emit greenhouse gases. In the United States, environmental restrictions and subsidies have combined to spur innovation in clean energy sources, which are now cheaper than fossil fuels in many applications.
- World energy consumption is currently highly dependent on fossil fuels, a legacy of fossil fuels' historically lower cost compared to clean energy resources. However, economists and scientists estimate that the true cost of greenhouse gas emissions is far higher than the current market price.
- In addition to the standard set of tools for achieving the efficient level of greenhouse gas emissions (mandates, emissions tax, or cap-and-trade system), other policies can be of critical importance for addressing climate change. They include government subsidies to R&D in clean energy sources, multilateral agreements such as the **Paris Agreement,** and incentives to individual choice, particularly energy conservation.
- While addressing climate change will require a structural shift in the economy away from fossil fuels and toward clean energy sources, claims that addressing climate change is too costly fail under a cost-benefit analysis.

Check Your Understanding 35-2

1. What are the types of fossil fuels? What are the main clean energy sources? What are their relationships to climate change?
2. What market failure led to climate change? What are the estimated losses to GDP from unmitigated climate change?
3. Why are government subsidies an important policy tool in addressing climate change? Multilateral agreements? Incentives to individual choice?
4. How would you respond to the argument that the structural change to the economy required to address climate change is too costly?

Solutions appear at back of book.

MODULE 36

Public Goods and Common Resources

WHAT YOU WILL LEARN

- What is a **public good** and how is it different from a **private good?**
- What is a **common resource** and why is it overused?
- What is an **artificially scarce good** and why is it underconsumed?

In this module, we will take a somewhat different approach to the question of why markets sometimes fail. Here we focus on how *the characteristics of goods often determine whether markets can deliver them efficiently.* When goods have the "wrong" characteristics, the resulting market failures resemble those associated with externalities or market power.

This alternative way of looking at sources of inefficiency deepens our understanding of why markets sometimes don't work well and how government can take actions that increase society's welfare.

Telekhovskyi/Shutterstock

36.1 Private Goods—and Others

What's the difference between installing a new bathroom in a house and building a municipal sewage system? What's the difference between growing wheat and fishing in the open ocean?

These aren't trick questions. In each case, there is a basic difference in the characteristics of the goods involved. Bathroom fixtures and wheat have the characteristics necessary to allow markets to work efficiently. Public sewage systems and fish in the sea do not.

Let's look at these crucial characteristics and why they matter.

Characteristics of Goods

Goods like bathroom fixtures or wheat have two characteristics that, as we'll soon see, are essential if a good is to be efficiently provided by a market economy.

- They are **excludable:** suppliers of the good can prevent people who don't pay from consuming it.

A good is **excludable** if the supplier of that good can prevent people who do not pay for it from consuming it.

FIGURE 36-1 Four Types of Goods

There are four types of goods. The type of a good depends on (1) whether or not it is excludable—whether a producer can prevent someone from consuming it; and (2) whether or not it is rival in consumption—whether it is impossible for the same unit of a good to be consumed by more than one person at the same time.

	Rival in consumption	Nonrival in consumption
Excludable	**Private goods** • Wheat • Bathroom fixtures	**Artificially scarce goods** • On-demand movies • Computer software
Non excludable	**Common resources** • Clean water • Biodiversity	**Public goods** • Public sanitation • National defense

- They are **rival in consumption:** the same unit of the good cannot be consumed by more than one person at the same time.

When a good is both excludable and rival in consumption, it is called a **private good.** Wheat is an example of a private good. It is *excludable:* the farmer can sell a bushel to one consumer without having to provide wheat to everyone in the county. And it is *rival in consumption:* if you eat bread baked with a farmer's wheat, that wheat cannot be consumed by someone else.

But not all goods possess these two characteristics. Some goods are **nonexcludable—**the supplier cannot prevent consumption of the good by people who do not pay for it. Fire protection is one example: a fire department that puts out fires before they spread protects the whole city, not just people who have made contributions to the Firemen's Benevolent Association. An improved environment is another: the city of London couldn't have ended the Great Stink for some residents while leaving the River Thames foul for others.

Nor are all goods rival in consumption. Goods are **nonrival in consumption** if more than one person can consume the same unit of the good at the same time. TV shows are nonrival in consumption: your decision to watch a show does not prevent other people from watching the same show.

Because goods can be either excludable or nonexcludable, rival or nonrival in consumption, there are four types of goods, illustrated by the matrix in Figure 36-1:

- *Private goods,* which are excludable and rival in consumption, like wheat
- *Public goods,* which are nonexcludable and nonrival in consumption, like a public sewer system
- *Common resources,* which are nonexcludable but rival in consumption, like clean water in a river
- *Artificially scarce goods,* which are excludable but nonrival in consumption, like on-demand movies on Amazon Prime

There are, of course, many other characteristics that can be used to distinguish between types of goods—necessities versus luxuries, normal versus inferior, and so on. Why focus on whether goods are excludable and rival in consumption?

Why Markets Can Supply Only Private Goods Efficiently

As we learned in earlier modules, markets are typically the best means for a society to deliver goods and services to its members; that is, markets are efficient except in the case of the well-defined problems of market power, externalities, or other instances of market failure. But there is yet another condition that must be met, one rooted in the nature of the good itself: markets cannot supply goods

A good is **rival in consumption** if the same unit of the good cannot be consumed by more than one person at the same time.

A good that is both excludable and rival in consumption is a **private good.**

When a good is **nonexcludable,** the supplier cannot prevent consumption by people who do not pay for it.

A good is **nonrival in consumption** if more than one person can consume the same unit of the good at the same time.

and services efficiently unless they are private goods—excludable and rival in consumption.

To see why excludability is crucial, suppose that a farmer had only two choices: either produce no wheat or provide a bushel of wheat to every resident of the county who wants it, whether or not that resident pays for it. It seems unlikely that anyone would grow wheat under those conditions.

Yet the operator of a municipal sewage system faces pretty much the same problem as our hypothetical farmer. A sewage system makes the whole city cleaner and healthier—but that benefit accrues to all the city's residents, whether or not they pay the system operator. That's why no private entrepreneur came forward with a plan to end London's Great Stink.

The general point is that if a good is nonexcludable, self-interested consumers won't be willing to pay for it—they will take a "free ride" on anyone who *does* pay. So there is a **free-rider problem.** Examples of the free-rider problem are familiar from daily life. One you may have encountered is when students are required to do a group project. There is often a tendency for some group members to shirk, relying on others in the group to get the work done. The shirkers *free-ride* on someone else's effort.

Goods that are nonexcludable suffer from the **free-rider problem:** many individuals are unwilling to pay for their own consumption and instead will take a "free ride" on anyone who does pay.

Because of the free-rider problem, the forces of self-interest alone do not lead to an efficient level of production for a nonexcludable good. Even though consumers would benefit from increased production of the good, no one individual is willing to pay for more, and so no producer is willing to supply it. The result is that nonexcludable goods suffer from *inefficiently low production*. That is, they are undersupplied in a market economy. In fact, in the face of the free-rider problem, self-interest may not ensure that any amount of the good—let alone the efficient quantity—is produced.

Goods that are excludable and nonrival in consumption, like on-demand movies, suffer from a different kind of inefficiency. As long as a good is excludable, it is possible to earn a profit by making it available only to those who pay. Therefore, producers are willing to supply an excludable good. But the marginal cost of letting an additional viewer watch an on-demand movie is zero because it is nonrival in consumption. So the efficient price to the consumer is also zero—or, to put it another way, individuals should watch movies up to the point where their marginal benefit is zero.

But if Amazon actually charges viewers $4 for on-demand movies, viewers will consume the good only up to the point at which their marginal benefit is $4. When consumers must pay a price greater than zero for a good that is nonrival in consumption, the price they pay is higher than the marginal cost of allowing them to consume that good, which is zero. So, in a market economy, goods that are nonrival in consumption suffer from *inefficiently low consumption*—they are underconsumed.

Now we can see why private goods are the only goods that can be efficiently produced and consumed in a competitive market. (That is, a private good will be efficiently produced and consumed in a market free of market power, externalities, or other instances of market failure.) Because private goods are excludable, producers can charge for them and so have an incentive to produce them. And because they are also rival in consumption, it is efficient for consumers to pay a positive price—a price equal to the marginal cost of production. If one or both of these characteristics are lacking, a market economy will not lead to efficient production and consumption of the good.

Fortunately for the market system, most goods are private goods. Food, clothing, shelter, and most other desirable things in life are excludable and rival in consumption, so markets can provide us with most things. Yet there are crucial goods that don't meet these criteria—and in most cases, that means that the government must step in.

>> Quick Review

- Goods can be classified according to two attributes: whether they are **excludable** and whether they are **rival in consumption.**
- Goods that are both excludable and rival in consumption are **private goods.** Private goods can be efficiently produced and consumed in a competitive market.
- When goods are **nonexcludable,** there is a **free-rider problem:** consumers will not pay producers, leading to inefficiently low production.
- When goods are **nonrival in consumption,** the efficient price for consumption is zero. But if a positive price is charged to compensate producers for the cost of production, the result is inefficiently low consumption.

Check Your Understanding 36-1

1. Classify each of the following goods according to whether they are excludable and whether they are rival in consumption. What kind of good is each?
   a. Use of a public space such as a park
   b. A cheese burrito
   c. Information from a password-protected website
   d. Publicly announced information on the path of an incoming hurricane
2. Which of the goods in Question 1 will be provided by a competitive market? Which will not be? Explain your answer.

Solutions appear at back of book.

36.2 Public Goods

A **public good** is the exact opposite of a private good: it is a good that is both nonexcludable and nonrival in consumption. A public sewer system is an example of a public good: you can't keep a river clean without making it clean for everyone who lives near its banks, and my protection from great stinks does not come at my neighbor's expense.

Here are some other examples of public goods:

- *Disease prevention.* When doctors act to stamp out an epidemic before it can spread, they protect people around the world.
- *National defense.* A strong military protects all citizens.
- *Scientific research.* More knowledge benefits everyone.

Because these goods are nonexcludable, they suffer from the free-rider problem, so no private firm would be willing to produce them. And because they are nonrival in consumption, it would be inefficient to charge people for consuming them. As a result, society must find nonmarket methods for providing these goods.

Providing Public Goods

Public goods are provided through a variety of means. The government doesn't always get involved—in many cases, a nongovernmental solution has been found for the free-rider problem. But these solutions are usually imperfect in some way.

Some public goods are supplied through voluntary contributions. For example, private donations support a considerable amount of scientific research. But they are insufficient to finance huge, socially important projects like basic medical research.

Some public goods are supplied by self-interested individuals or firms because those producing the goods are able to make money in an indirect way. The classic example is broadcast television, which in the United States is supported entirely by advertising. The downside of such indirect funding is that it skews the nature and quantity of the public goods that are supplied, as well as imposing additional costs on consumers. TV stations show the programs that yield the most advertising revenue (that is, programs best suited for selling prescription drugs, weight-loss remedies, and the like to the segment of the population that buys them), which are not necessarily the programs people most want to see. And viewers must also endure many commercials.

Some potentially public goods are deliberately made excludable and therefore subject to charge, like on-demand movies. In the United Kingdom, where most television programming is paid for by a yearly license fee assessed on every television owner (£154.50, or about $200 in 2019), television viewing is made artificially excludable by the use of television detection vans that roam neighborhoods in an attempt to locate televisions in nonlicensed households and fine the

A **public good** is both nonexcludable and nonrival in consumption.

residents. However, as noted earlier, when suppliers charge a price greater than zero for a nonrival good, consumers will consume an inefficiently low quantity of that good.

In small communities, a high level of social encouragement or pressure can be brought to bear on people to contribute money or time to provide the efficient level of a public good. Volunteer fire departments, which depend both on the volunteered services of the firefighters themselves and on contributions from local residents, are a good example. But as communities grow larger and more anonymous, social pressure is increasingly difficult to apply, compelling larger towns and cities to tax residents to provide salaried firefighters for fire protection services.

As this last example suggests, when these other solutions fail, it is up to the government to provide public goods. Indeed, the most important public goods—national defense, the legal system, disease control, fire protection in municipalities, and so on—are provided by government and paid for by taxes. Economic theory tells us that the provision of public goods is one of the crucial roles of government.

Getmilitaryphotos/Shutterstock

RichLegg/Getty Images

Government provides public goods like national defense and the legal system.

How Much of a Public Good Should Be Provided?

In some cases, provision of a public good is an "either–or" decision: London would either have a sewage system—or not. But in most cases, governments must decide not only whether to provide a public good but also *how much* of that public good to provide. For example, street cleaning is a public good—but how often should the streets be cleaned? Once a month? Twice a month? Every other day?

Imagine a city in which there are only two residents, Theo and Abby. Assume that the public good in question is street cleaning and that Theo and Abby truthfully tell the government how much they value a unit of the public good, where a unit is equal to one street cleaning per month. Specifically, each of them tells the government *their willingness to pay for another unit of the public good supplied*—an amount that corresponds to that *individual's marginal benefit* of another unit of the public good.

Using this information plus information on the cost of providing the good, the government can use marginal analysis to find the efficient level of providing the public good: the level at which the marginal social benefit of the public good is equal to the marginal cost of producing it. Recall from Module 35 that the *marginal social benefit* of a good is the benefit that accrues to society as a whole from the consumption of one additional unit of the good.

But what is the marginal social benefit of another unit of a public good—a unit that generates utility for *all* consumers, not just one consumer, because it is nonexcludable and nonrival in consumption? This question leads us to an important principle: *in the special case of a public good, the marginal social benefit of a unit of the good is equal to the sum of the individual marginal benefits that are enjoyed by all consumers of that unit.*

Because people can all simultaneously consume the same unit of a public good, the marginal social benefit of an additional unit of that good is the *sum* of

Telekhovskyi/Shutterstock

We all benefit when someone does the cleaning up.

the individual marginal benefits of all who enjoy the public good. And the efficient quantity of a public good is the quantity at which the marginal social benefit is equal to the marginal cost of providing it.

We can show this result with the following equation, where MB_T and MB_A are Theo and Abby's marginal benefit of another unit of street cleaning, respectively. MC is the marginal cost of providing it. So at the efficient quantity of the public good:

$$MB_T + MB_A = M_C$$

One basic rationale for the existence of government is that it provides a way for citizens to tax themselves in order to provide public goods—particularly a vital public good like national defense.

Of course, if society really consisted of only two individuals, they would probably manage to strike a deal to provide the good. But imagine a city with a million residents, each of whose individual marginal benefit from provision of the good is only a tiny fraction of the marginal social benefit. It would be impossible for people to reach a voluntary agreement to pay for the efficient level of street cleaning—the potential for free-riding makes it too difficult to make and enforce an agreement among so many people. But they could and would vote to tax themselves to pay for a citywide sanitation department.

Check Your Understanding 36-2

1. The town of Centreville, population 16, has two types of residents, Homebodies and Revelers. Using the accompanying table, the town must decide how much to spend on its New Year's Eve party. No individual resident expects to directly bear the cost of the party.

Money spent on party	Individual marginal benefit of additional $1 spent on party	
	Homebody	Reveler
$0		
	$0.05	$0.13
1		
	0.04	0.11
2		
	0.03	0.09
3		
	0.02	0.07
4		

a. Suppose there are 10 Homebodies and 6 Revelers. Determine the marginal social benefit schedule of money spent on the party. What is the efficient level of spending?

b. Suppose there are 6 Homebodies and 10 Revelers. How do your answers to part a change? Explain.

c. Suppose that the individual marginal benefit schedules are known but no one knows the true proportion of Homebodies versus Revelers. Individuals are asked their preferences. What is the likely outcome if each person assumes that others will pay for any additional amount of the public good? Why is it likely to result in an inefficiently high level of spending? Explain.

Solutions appear at back of book.

>> Quick Review

- A **public good** is both nonexcludable and nonrival in consumption.
- Because most forms of public-good provision by the private sector have serious defects, they are typically provided by the government and paid for with taxes.
- The marginal social benefit of an additional unit of a public good is equal to the sum of each consumer's individual marginal benefit from that unit. At the efficient quantity, the marginal social benefit equals the marginal cost of providing the good.
- No individual has an incentive to pay for providing the efficient quantity of a public good because each individual's marginal benefit is less than the marginal social benefit. This is a primary justification for the existence of government.

A **common resource** is nonexcludable and rival in consumption: you can't stop me from consuming the good, and more consumption by me means less of the good available for you.

36.3 Common Resources

A **common resource** is a good that is nonexcludable but is rival in consumption. An example is the stock of fish in a limited fishing area, like the fisheries off the coast of New England. Traditionally, anyone who had a boat could go out to sea and catch fish—fish in the sea were a nonexcludable good. Yet because the total number of fish is limited, the fish that one person catches are no longer available to be caught by someone else. So, fish in the sea are rival in consumption.

Other examples of common resources are clean air and water as well as the diversity of animal and plant species on the planet (biodiversity). In each of these cases, the fact that the good, though rival in consumption, is nonexcludable poses a serious problem.

Common resources left to the market suffer from **overuse:** individuals ignore the fact that their use depletes the amount of the resource remaining for others.

The Problem of Overuse

Because common resources are nonexcludable, individuals cannot be charged for their use. Yet because they are rival in consumption, an individual who uses a unit depletes the resource by making that unit unavailable to others. As a result, a common resource is subject to **overuse:** an individual will continue to use it until their marginal benefit of its use is equal to their own individual marginal cost, ignoring the cost that this action inflicts on society as a whole.

Fishing is a classic example of a common resource. In heavily fished waters, my fishing imposes a cost on others by reducing the fish population and making it harder for others to catch fish. But I have no personal incentive to take this cost into account, since I cannot be charged for fishing. As a result, from society's point of view, I catch too many fish.

Traffic congestion is another example of overuse of a common resource. A major highway during rush hour can accommodate only a certain number of vehicles per hour. If I decide to drive to work alone rather than carpool or work at home, I make the commute of many other people a bit longer—but I have no incentive to take these consequences into account.

In the case of a common resource, the *marginal social cost* of my use of that resource is higher than my *individual marginal cost,* the cost to me of using an additional unit of the good.

Figure 36-2 illustrates this point. It shows the demand curve for fish, which measures the marginal benefit of fish—the benefit to consumers when an additional unit of fish is caught and consumed. It also shows the supply curve for fish, which measures the marginal cost of production of the fishing industry. We know that the industry supply curve is the horizontal sum of each individual fisherman's

FIGURE 36-2 A Common Resource

The supply curve *S*, which shows the marginal cost of production of the fishing industry, is composed of the individual supply curves of the individual fishermen. But each fisherman's individual marginal cost does not include the cost that their actions impose on others: the depletion of the common resource. As a result, the marginal social cost curve, *MSC*, lies above the supply curve; in an unregulated market, the quantity of the common resource used, Q_{MKT}, exceeds the efficient quantity of use, Q_{OPT}.

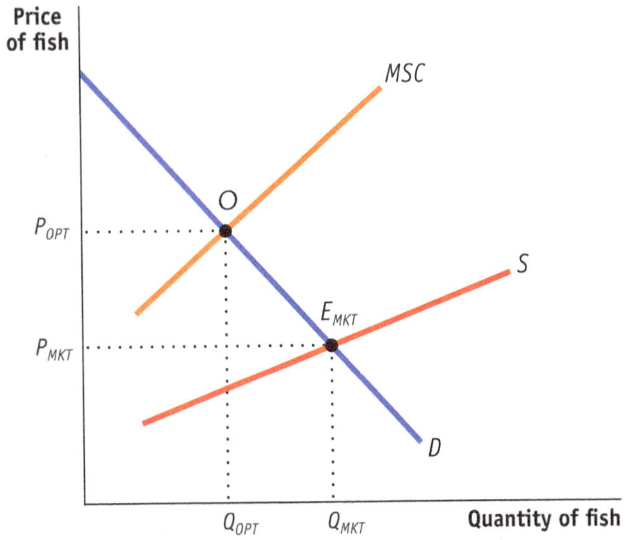

supply curve—equivalent to their individual marginal cost curve. The fishing industry supplies the quantity where its marginal cost is equal to the price, the quantity Q_{MKT}.

But the efficient outcome is to catch the quantity Q_{OPT}, the quantity of output that equates the marginal benefit to the marginal social cost, not to the fishing industry's marginal cost of production. The market outcome results in overuse of the common resource.

As we noted, there is a close parallel between the problem of managing a common resource and the problem posed by negative externalities. In the case of an activity that generates a negative externality, the marginal social cost of production is greater than the industry's marginal cost of production, the difference being the marginal external cost imposed on society. Here, the loss to society arising from a fisherman's depletion of the common resource plays the same role as the external cost plays when there is a negative externality. In fact, many negative externalities (such as pollution) can be thought of as involving common resources (such as clean air).

The Efficient Use and Maintenance of a Common Resource

Because common resources pose problems similar to those created by negative externalities, the solutions are also similar. To ensure efficient use of a common resource, society must find a way of getting individual users of the resource to take into account the costs they impose on other users. This is basically the same principle as that of getting individuals to internalize a negative externality that arises from their actions.

There are three fundamental ways to induce people who use common resources to internalize the costs they impose on others:

1. Tax or otherwise regulate the use of the common resource
2. Create a system of tradable licenses for the right to use the common resource
3. Make the common resource excludable and assign property rights to some individuals

alptraum/Thinkstock

If it weren't for fees and restrictions, some common resources would be overrun.

Tax and Regulate Like activities that generate negative externalities, use of a common resource can be reduced to the efficient quantity by imposing a Pigouvian tax. For example, some countries have imposed "congestion charges" on those who drive during rush hour, in effect charging them for use of the common resource of city streets. Likewise, visitors to national parks must pay a fee, and the number of visitors to any one park is restricted.

Create a System of Tradable Licenses A second way to correct the problem of overuse is to create a system of tradable licenses for the use of the common resource, much like the systems designed to address negative externalities. The policy maker issues the number of licenses that corresponds to the efficient level of use of the good. Making the licenses tradable ensures that the right to use the good is allocated efficiently—that is, those who end up using the good (those willing to pay the most for a license) are those who gain the most from its use.

Assign Property Rights But when it comes to common resources, often the most natural solution is simply to assign property rights. At a fundamental level, common resources are subject to overuse because *nobody owns them*. The essence of ownership of a good—the *property right* over the good—is that you can limit who can and cannot use the good as well as how much of it can be used.

When a good is nonexcludable, in a very real sense, no one owns it because a property right cannot be enforced—and consequently no one has an incentive to use it efficiently. So one way to correct the problem of overuse is to make the good excludable and assign property rights over it to someone. The good then has an owner who has an incentive to protect the value of the good—to use it efficiently rather than overuse it.

>> Quick Review

- A **common resource** is rival in consumption but nonexcludable.
- The problem with common resources is **overuse:** a user depletes the amount of the common resource available to others but does not take this cost into account when deciding how much to use the common resource.
- Like negative externalities, a common resource can be efficiently managed by Pigouvian taxes, by the creation of a system of tradable licenses for its use, or by making it excludable and assigning property rights.

Check Your Understanding 36-3

1. Rocky Mountain Forest is a government-owned forest in which private citizens were allowed in the past to harvest as much timber as they wanted free of charge. State in economic terms why this is problematic from society's point of view.
2. You are the new forest service commissioner and have been instructed to come up with ways to preserve the forest for the general public. Name three different methods you could use to maintain the efficient level of tree harvesting and explain how each would work. For each method, what information would you need to know to achieve an efficient outcome?

Solutions appear at back of book.

36.4 Artificially Scarce Goods

An **artificially scarce good** is a good that is excludable but nonrival in consumption. As we've already seen, on-demand movies are a familiar example. The marginal cost to society of allowing an individual to watch the movie is zero, because one person's viewing doesn't interfere with other people's viewing. Yet Amazon and companies like it prevent individuals from seeing on-demand movies if they haven't paid. Goods like software, video games, and digital books, which are valued for the information they embody (and are sometimes called *information goods*), are also artificially scarce.

As we've already seen, markets will supply artificially scarce goods: because they are excludable, the producers can charge people for consuming them.

But artificially scarce goods are nonrival in consumption, which means that the marginal cost of an individual's consumption is zero. So the price that the supplier of an artificially scarce good charges exceeds marginal cost. Because the efficient price is equal to the marginal cost of zero, the good is "artificially scarce," and consumption of the good is inefficiently low. However, unless the producer can somehow earn revenue for producing and selling the good, the producer will be unwilling to produce at all—an outcome that leaves society even worse off than it would otherwise be with positive but inefficiently low consumption.

We have seen that, in the cases of public goods, common resources, and artificially scarce goods, a market economy will not provide adequate incentives for efficient levels of production and consumption. Fortunately for the sake of market efficiency, most goods are private goods. Food, clothing, shelter, and most other desirable things in life are excludable and rival in consumption, so the types of market failure discussed in this module are important exceptions rather than the norm.

An **artificially scarce good** is excludable but nonrival in consumption.

heshphoto/AGE Fotostock

Intellectual property goods, like video games, must be made artificially scarce, which creates an incentive to pirate them.

ECONOMICS >> *in Action*

Twenty-First-Century Piracy

Intellectual property piracy, or IPP, is the illegal copying, distribution, or use of intellectual property. Intellectual property has accounted for a larger and larger share of the U.S. economy: as of 2019, patented intellectual property accounted for 74% of U.S. exports. Hence, the extent of IPP is carefully monitored, with the FBI devoting substantial resources to fighting it.

The most common forms of IPP include the piracy of software, sophisticated digital hardware, counterfeit goods, movies, music, and games. Piracy is a global industry that cost the owners of intellectual property rights—musicians, actors, movie studios, software companies, and creators of software and games—over $1 trillion in 2019. For example, Torrentfreak.com, a website that tracks illegal downloads, found that the final episode of *Game of Thrones* was illegally downloaded 1.5 million times within eight hours of its airing. Moreover, the Business Software Alliance estimates that 36% of all software in use is pirated.

Authorities have stepped up their efforts to combat IPP. In Canada, internet service providers (ISPs) now keep track of illegal downloads, with fines up to $5,000 per illegal download. The FBI has now teamed up with Interpol, the international crime-fighting agency, to find, charge, and extradite to the United States individuals who run large-scale pirating operations abroad.

What is the connection to artificially scarce goods? It stems from the fact that, once an intellectual property good is created, the marginal cost to deliver another unit to a consumer is virtually zero—it involves only a few seconds-long internet download. And because intellectual property goods are nonrival in consumption, my consumption of a bootleg version of the movie *Avengers: Endgame* or a computer game doesn't impede or reduce your consumption of them.

However, if movie and game creators are unable to charge people for the right to use their products, they won't produce them in the first place. (This explains why free versions of software or games are knock-offs of commercial versions and are of inferior quality.) So, intellectual property goods must be made artificially scarce. However, this creates the incentive to pirate them. So you can be sure that law enforcement agencies are engaged in their own version of the game whack-a-mole in their efforts to stop intellectual property piracy.

>> *Quick Review*

- An **artificially scarce good** is excludable but nonrival in consumption.
- Because the good is nonrival in consumption, the efficient price to consumers is zero. However, because it is excludable, sellers charge a positive price, which leads to inefficiently low consumption.

BUSINESS CASE Xcel Energy Goes for a Win-Win

iurii/Shutterstock

Historically, renewables have been more expensive than fossil fuels, and federal subsidies to the renewable energy industry have been critical in bringing costs to consumers down as well as in funding innovation. However, over the years, those subsidies have frequently been at risk. For example, from 2012 to 2013, newly installed wind capacity plunged by 93% from when federal subsidies ended. In 2014 and 2015, wind capacity revived when those subsidies were restored. But in 2017, a new pattern appeared: when federal subsidies for renewable energy were again at risk as Congress debated whether to cut them, the percentage of newly installed power capacity that was accounted for by renewables fell only modestly—from nearly 50% in 2017 to 48% in 2018. In 2020, the future of the subsidies was again unclear: without congressional action, they will largely expire at the end of 2021. However, by 2020, renewables were projected to account for 78% of newly installed power capacity. Will the threat to end subsidies stall their meteoric rise?

Benjamin Fowke, the CEO of Xcel Energy of Colorado, is undeterred. He is trained in finance and accounting, so it's safe to say that he is no starry-eyed dreamer. Xcel Energy has announced that across its eight-state system, 60% of its energy will be generated by renewables and its carbon emissions will be reduced by 80% by 2030.

Fowke is positioning Xcel Energy to take advantage of the *learning curve* associated with the cost of renewable energy. This term is used to describe the dramatic fall in costs that is often achieved after a new technology is introduced. Adoption of new technology spreads because scientists, innovators, and manufacturers get better and better at exploiting it. A virtuous cycle is generated as costs fall and adoption of the new technology increases, spurring further investment and further reducing cost.

An example is solar energy: the price to consumers of a watt of solar energy has dropped by nearly 75% since 1998. The learning curve has been steepest in the last decade, with solar prices dropping by 60%. In the case of wind energy, prices have dropped 90% since 1980.

According to Fowke, it is now cheaper to build new wind turbines than to operate its lowest-cost existing coal plants. For example, in 2017, Xcel purchased wind energy at a cost of $15 to $20 per megawatt-hour, compared to $25 to $35 for natural gas-generated power, the main energy source in competition with renewables.

Unsurprisingly, competition with conventional fossil-fuel producers encourages the solar and wind industries, along with producers of other renewables, to keep improving their product and prices to stay ahead of the competition.

QUESTIONS FOR THOUGHT

1. Explain how subsidies affect the future adoption of a new technology that are subject to steep learning curve effects. Relate this to the role of government intervention when externalities are present.
2. Is Fowke right or wrong to persist in the adoption of renewables when federal subsidies are under threat? Analyze the investment decision that a CEO like Fowke must make in deciding whether and when to invest more capacity in renewables versus fossil fuel sources.
3. How does this case illustrate the way in which business and government can work together in a market economy?

REVIEW

MODULE 34

1. When pollution can be directly observed and controlled, government policies should be geared directly toward producing the **socially optimal quantity of pollution,** the quantity at which the **marginal social cost of pollution** is equal to the **marginal social benefit of pollution.** In the absence of government intervention, a market produces too much pollution because polluters take only their benefit from polluting into account, not the costs imposed on others.
2. Pollution is an example of a **negative externality,** an action that inflicts an uncompensated cost on others. In contrast, a **positive externality,** such as a flu shot, confers an uncompensated benefit on others.

MODULE 35

1. Governments often deal with pollution by imposing **environmental standards,** a method, economists argue, that is usually an inefficient way to reduce pollution. Two efficient (cost-minimizing) methods for reducing pollution are **emissions taxes,** a form of **Pigouvian tax,** and **tradable emissions permits.** The optimal Pigouvian tax on pollution is equal to its marginal social cost at the socially optimal quantity of pollution. These methods also provide incentives for the creation and adoption of production technologies that cause less pollution.
2. When a good or activity generates positive externalities, such as **technology spillovers,** an optimal **Pigouvian subsidy** to producers moves the market to the socially optimal quantity of production.
3. A history of heavy reliance on **fossil fuels,** which emit **greenhouse gases,** has led to problems created by **climate change.** Unlike fossil fuels, **renewable energy sources** are inexhaustible. Policies such as taxes, tax credits, subsidies, and mandates, as well as consumer use of smart metering and industrial commitments, can help ensure a wide-scale shift toward renewable **clean energy sources.** Multilateral agreements such as the **Paris Agreement** commit many countries to common objectives and allocate burden-sharing across countries in order to tackle climate change.

MODULE 36

1. Goods may be classified according to whether or not they are **excludable** and whether or not they are **rival in consumption.**
2. Free markets can deliver efficient levels of production and consumption for **private goods,** which are both excludable and rival in consumption. When goods are nonexcludable or nonrival in consumption, or both, free markets cannot achieve efficient outcomes.
3. When goods are **nonexcludable,** there is a **free-rider problem:** some consumers will not pay for the good, consuming what others have paid for and leading to inefficiently low production. When goods are **nonrival in consumption,** they should be free, and any positive price leads to inefficiently low consumption.
4. A **public good** is nonexcludable and nonrival in consumption. In most cases, a public good must be supplied by the government. The marginal social benefit of a public good is equal to the sum of the individual marginal benefits to each consumer. The efficient quantity of a public good is the quantity at which marginal social benefit equals the marginal cost of providing the good. Like a positive externality, marginal social benefit is greater than any one individual's marginal benefit, so no individual is willing to provide the efficient quantity.
5. A **common resource** is rival in consumption but nonexcludable. It is subject to **overuse,** because an individual does not take into account the fact that their use depletes the amount available for others. This is similar to the problem of a negative externality: the marginal social cost of an individual's use of a common resource is always higher than their individual marginal cost. Pigouvian taxes, the creation of a system of tradable licenses, and the assignment of property rights are possible solutions.
6. **Artificially scarce goods** are excludable but nonrival in consumption. Because no marginal cost arises from allowing another individual to consume the good, the efficient price is zero. A positive price compensates the producer for the cost of production but leads to inefficiently low consumption.

KEY TERMS

Marginal social cost of pollution p. 361
Marginal social benefit of pollution p. 361
Socially optimal quantity of pollution p. 361
Negative externality p. 362
Positive externalities p. 362
Pigouvian subsidy p. 365
Technology spillover p. 365
Environmental standards p. 369
Emissions tax p. 369
Pigouvian taxes p. 370
Tradable emissions permits p. 370
Climate change p. 371
Greenhouse gases p. 371
Fossil fuels p. 372
Renewable energy sources p. 372
Clean energy sources p. 372
Paris Agreement p. 373
Excludable p. 375
Rival in consumption p. 376
Private good p. 376
Nonexcludable p. 376
Nonrival in consumption p. 376
Free-rider problem p. 377
Public good p. 378
Common resource p. 380
Overuse p. 381
Artificially scarce good p. 383

Monika Graff/The Image Works

SECTION 12

Factor Markets and the Distribution of Income

THE VALUE OF A DEGREE

Does higher education pay? Yes, it does: in the modern economy, employers are willing to pay a premium for workers with more education. And the size of that premium has increased a lot over the last few decades. In 2019, Americans with four-year college degrees made 85% more per week on average than those without a degree. That percentage is up from 71% in 2017 and 45% in the early 1980s. In fact, according to David Autor, a professor of economics at MIT, the true cost of a college degree is approximately *negative* $500,000. That is, a college degree is cheaper than free.

In other words, not getting a college degree will cost you about half a million dollars over your lifetime. That's roughly double what the negative cost was 35 years ago. And because having a bachelor's degree is so valuable, more Americans than ever are getting one: in 2019, 35% of those aged 25 to 29 had at least a bachelor's degree, compared to 24.7% in 1995.

Who decided that the wages of workers with a four-year college degree would be so much more than for workers without one? The answer, of course, is that nobody decided it. Wage rates are prices, the prices of different kinds of labor, and they are decided, like other prices, by supply and demand.

Still, there is a qualitative difference between the wage rate of high school grads and the price of used textbooks: the wage rate isn't the price of a *good*, it's the price of a *factor of production*. And although markets for factors of production are in many ways similar to those for goods, there are also some important differences.

In this section, we examine *factor markets*, the markets in which the factors of production such as labor, land, and capital are traded. Factor markets, like markets for goods and services, play a crucial role in the economy: they allocate productive resources to producers and help ensure that those resources are used efficiently.

We begin by describing the major factors of production and the demand for factors of production, which leads to a crucial insight: the *marginal productivity theory of income distribution*. We then consider some challenges to the marginal productivity theory followed by a discussion of the supply of the most important factor, labor. The section concludes by analyzing how government can take actions that reduce economic insecurity, address income inequality, and increase society's welfare.

MODULE 37

Factor Markets

WHAT YOU WILL LEARN

- What are the economy's factors of production?
- How are factors like land, labor, **physical capital,** and **human capital** traded in factor markets?
- How do factor markets determine the **factor distribution of income?**

czbalazs/Getty Images

Jupiterimages/Getty Images

istockphoto/Thinkstock

Goodluz/Thinkstock/Getty Images

You may recall that we have already defined a factor of production in the context of the circular-flow diagram of the economy: it is any resource that is used by firms to produce goods and services for consumption by households. Factors of production are bought and sold in *factor markets,* and the prices in factor markets are known as *factor prices.* What are these factors of production, and why do factor prices matter?

37.1 The Economy's Factors of Production

Economists divide factors of production into four principal classes: land, labor, *physical capital,* and *human capital.* Land is a resource provided by nature; labor is the work done by human beings. Capital is the value of the assets that are used by a firm in producing its output. There are two broad types of capital.

Physical capital—often referred to simply as *capital*—consists of manufactured resources such as equipment, buildings, tools, and machines. In the modern economy, **human capital,** the improvement in labor created by education and knowledge, and embodied in the workforce, is at least equally significant. The importance of human capital has increased greatly because of the progress of technology, which has made a high level of technical knowledge essential to many jobs. This is one cause of the increased premium paid for workers with advanced degrees.

Physical capital—often referred to simply as *capital*—consists of manufactured productive resources such as equipment, buildings, tools, and machines.

Human capital is the improvement in labor created by education and knowledge that is embodied in the workforce.

Why Factor Prices Matter

Factor markets and factor prices play a key role in one of the most important processes that must take place in any market economy: *the allocation of resources among producers*. As we will see, it is through the allocation of resources that an economy decides what and how much to produce.

To see how factor markets operate in the real-life allocation of an economy's resources, consider Midland, Texas, which is at the heart of the new Texas oil boom. During the oil boom of 2016 to 2019, employment in Midland rose 24%, six times the growth in America as a whole, led by surging employment in the oil fields.

What ensured that workers came to Midland? The factor market: the high demand for workers drove up wages, not just for those directly employed in the oil fields but also for those providing services to those workers, like barbers. In fact, by 2019, barbers willing to move to Midland could earn as much as $180,000 a year. In other words, the markets for factors of production—oil field workers and barbers in this example—allocate the factors of production to where they are needed. In this sense, factor markets are similar to goods markets, which allocate goods among consumers.

But there are two features that make factor markets special. The first is that demand in a factor market is called *derived demand;* that is, demand for the factor is derived from a firm's output choice. The second feature is that factor markets are where most of us get the largest shares of our income (government transfers being the next largest source of income in the economy).

Factor Incomes and the Distribution of Income

Most American families get most of their income in the form of wages and salaries—that is, they get their income by selling their own labor. Some people, however, get most of their income from physical capital: when you own stock in a company, what you really own is a share of that company's physical capital. And some people get much of their income from rents earned on land they own.

As a consequence, the prices of factors of production have a major impact on how the economic pie is sliced among different groups. For example, a higher wage rate, other things equal, means that a larger proportion of the economy's total income goes to people who derive their income from labor, and less goes to those who derive their income from capital or land. Economists refer to how the economic pie is sliced as the *distribution of income*. Specifically, factor prices determine the **factor distribution of income**—how the total income of the economy is divided among labor, land, and capital.

Check Your Understanding 37-1

1. Suppose that the government places price controls on the market for college professors, imposing a wage that is lower than the market wage. Describe the effect of this policy on the production of college degrees. What sectors of the economy do you think will be adversely affected by this policy? What sectors of the economy might benefit?

Solutions appear at back of book.

>> Quick Review

- Economists usually divide the economy's factors of production into four principal categories: labor, land, **physical capital,** and **human capital.**
- Through factor markets, the economy's factors of production are allocated to the producers who need them most.
- The demand for a factor is a derived demand. Factor prices, which are set in factor markets, determine the **factor distribution of income**—how the economy's total income is divided among labor, land, and capital.

37.2 Marginal Productivity and Factor Demand

In this section, we will learn how the demand for a factor of production arises from decisions by producers. Let's begin by assuming that both the labor market and the goods market are perfectly competitive. That is, workers selling their labor are price-takers, and the firms that employ them are price-takers in the goods market.

The **factor distribution of income** is the division of total income among labor, land, and capital.

FIGURE 37-1 The Production Function and Marginal Product of Labor Curve for Riley and Tyler's Farm

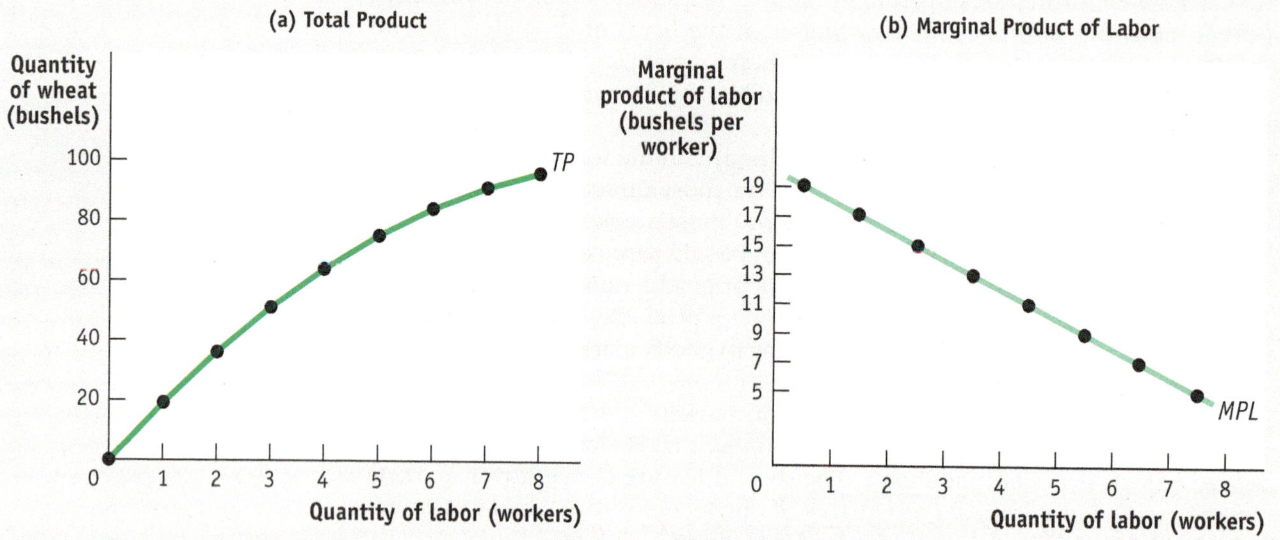

Panel (a) shows how the quantity of output of wheat on Riley and Tyler's farm depends on the number of workers employed. Panel (b) shows how the marginal product of labor depends on the number of workers employed.

All economic decisions are based on comparing costs to benefits—usually a comparison of marginal costs to benefits. So what is the employer's marginal cost of hiring another worker? It is simply the worker's wage rate. But what is the marginal benefit of that worker? To answer that question, we return to the *production function,* which illustrates how inputs are transformed by the production process into output.

Value of the Marginal Product

Figure 37-1 reproduces Figures 20-1 and 20-2, which showed the production function for wheat on Riley and Tyler's farm. Panel (a) uses the total product (*TP*) curve to show how total wheat production depends on the number of workers employed on the farm; panel (b) shows how the *marginal product* of labor (*MPL*), the increase in output from employing one more worker, depends on the number of workers employed. Table 37-1, which reproduces the table in Figure 20-1, shows the numbers behind the figure.

TABLE 37-1 Employment and Output for Riley and Tyler's Farm

Quantity of labor L (workers)	Quantity of wheat Q (bushels)	Marginal product of labor $MPL = \frac{\Delta Q}{\Delta L}$ (bushels per worker)
0	0	
		19
1	19	
		17
2	36	
		15
3	51	
		13
4	64	
		11
5	75	
		9
6	84	
		7
7	91	
		5
8	96	

Assume that workers must be paid \$200 each and that the price of wheat is \$20 per bushel. We'll now show Riley and Tyler use marginal analysis to determine the optimal numbers of workers to hire.

To see how this alternative approach works, let's suppose that Riley and Tyler are considering whether or not to employ an additional worker. At each level of employment, they would compare the cost to the benefit of hiring an additional worker. The increase in *cost* from employing that additional worker is the wage rate, *W*. The *benefit* to Riley and Tyler from employing that extra worker is the value of the extra output that worker can produce. What is this value? It is the marginal product of labor, *MPL*, multiplied by the price per unit of output, *P*. This amount—the extra value of output that is generated by employing one more unit of labor—is known as the **value of the marginal product** of labor, or *VMPL*:

(37-1) Value of the marginal product of labor = $VMPL = P \times MPL$

So should Riley and Tyler hire that extra worker? The answer is yes if the value of the extra output is more than the cost of the worker—that is, if $VMPL > W$. Otherwise, they shouldn't hire that worker.

So the decision to hire labor is a marginal decision, in which the marginal benefit to the producer from hiring an additional worker (*VMPL*) should be compared with the marginal cost to the producer (*W*). And as with any marginal decision, the optimal choice is where marginal benefit is just equal to marginal cost. That is, to maximize profit, Riley and Tyler will employ workers up to the point at which, for the last worker employed:

(37-2) $VMPL = W$ *at the optimal level of employment*

This rule doesn't apply only to labor; it applies to any factor of production. The value of the marginal product of any factor is its marginal product times the price of the good it produces. Applying this rule to all factors of production gives us the **price-taking producer's optimal employment rule:** *a price-taking producer employs each factor of production up to the level at which the value of the marginal product is equal to that factor's price.*

It's important to realize that this rule doesn't conflict with our analysis in Section 8. There we saw that a profit-maximizing producer of a good chooses the level of output at which the price of that good is equal to the marginal cost of production. It's just a different way of looking at the same rule. If the level of output is chosen so that price equals marginal cost, then it is also true that at that output level, the value of the marginal product of labor will equal the wage rate.

Now let's look more closely at why choosing the level of employment at which the value of the marginal product of the last worker employed is equal to the wage rate is the right method, and how it helps us understand factor demand.

The **value of the marginal product** of a factor is the value of the additional output generated by employing one more unit of that factor.

The **price-taking producer's optimal employment rule** says that a price-taking producer's profit is maximized by employing each factor of production up to the level at which the value of the marginal product is equal to the factor's price.

The **value of the marginal product curve** of a factor shows how the value of the marginal product of that factor depends on the quantity of the factor employed.

Value of the Marginal Product and Factor Demand

Table 37-2 calculates the value of the marginal product of labor on Riley and Tyler's farm, on the assumption that the price of wheat is $20 per bushel. In Figure 37-2, the horizontal axis shows the number of workers employed; the vertical axis measures the value of the marginal product of labor *and* the wage rate. The curve shown is the **value of the marginal product curve** of labor. This curve, like the marginal product of labor curve, slopes downward because of diminishing returns to labor in production. That is, the value of the marginal product of each worker is less than that of the preceding worker, because the marginal product of each worker is less than that of the preceding worker.

Figure 37-2 illustrates the price-taking firm's optimal employment rule for the example of Riley and Tyler's farm. At market wage rate of $200, Riley and Tyler will maximize their profits by employing five workers because, at 5 workers, the value of marginal product of labor equals $200. This outcome is shown as point *A*.

If the wage rate were higher than $200, we would simply move up the curve and reduce the number of workers employed; if the wage rate were lower

TABLE 37-2 Value of the Marginal Product of Labor for Riley and Tyler's Farm

Quantity of labor *L* (workers)	Marginal product of labor *MPL* (bushels per worker)	Value of the marginal product of labor $VMPL = P \times MPL$
0		
	19	$380
1		
	17	340
2		
	15	300
3		
	13	260
4		
	11	220
5		
	9	180
6		
	7	140
7		
	5	100
8		

FIGURE 37-2 The Value of the Marginal Product Curve

This curve shows how the value of the marginal product of labor depends on the number of workers employed. It slopes downward because of diminishing returns to labor in production. To maximize profit, Riley and Tyler choose the level of employment at which the value of the marginal product of labor is equal to the market wage rate. For example, at a wage rate of $200, the profit-maximizing level of employment is 5 workers, shown by point *A*. The value of the marginal product curve of a factor is the producer's individual demand curve for that factor.

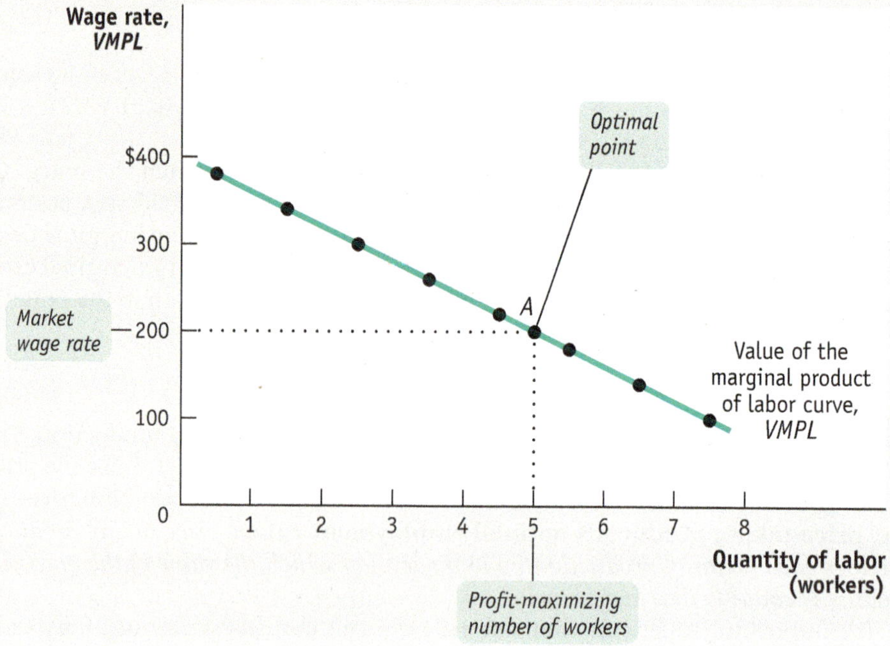

than $200, we would move down the curve and increase the number of workers employed.

We can briefly examine what would happen if Riley and Tyler employ fewer than 5 workers—say only 3 workers. At 3 workers, we can see from Table 37-2 that the value of the marginal product of labor is $260, Since $260 – $200 = $60, so Riley and Tyler will increase their profit by $60 by hiring 1 more worker. And if they should hire 8 workers instead of the optimal number, 5, Table 37-2 shows that the value of the marginal product of labor is only $100, greater than the wage rate of $200. So by reducing employment by 1 worker, Riley and Tyler can increase their profit by $200 – $100 = $100. Using this method we can see from Table 37-2 that whenever Riley and Tyler don't employ the optimal number of workers, 5, they can always increase their profit by changing the number of workers. More than 5 workers, profit increases by reducing the number of workers; less than 5 workers, profit increases by increasing the number of workers. When the value of the marginal product of the last worker hired equals the wage rate, then the firm has reached its optimal employment level.

This means that the value of the marginal product of labor curve is the individual producer's labor demand curve. And, in general, a producer's value of the marginal product curve for any factor of production is that producer's individual demand curve for that factor of production.

Ilene MacDonald/Alamy

Firms continue to hire workers until the value of the marginal product of the last worker hired equals the wage rate.

Shifts of the Factor Demand Curve

As in the case of ordinary demand curves, it is important to distinguish between movements along the factor demand curve and shifts of the factor demand curve. What causes factor demand curves to shift? There are three main causes:

1. Changes in the price of output
2. Changes in the supply of other factors
3. Changes in technology

Let's look at each in detail.

1. Changes in the Price of Output Remember that factor demand is derived demand: if the price of a good that is produced with a factor changes, so will the value of the marginal product of the factor that is employed to produce that good. That is, in the case of labor demand, if *P* changes, $VMPL = P \times MPL$ will change at any given level of employment.

Figure 37-3 illustrates the effects of changes in the price of wheat, assuming that $200 is the current wage rate. Panel (a) shows the effect of an *increase* in the price of wheat. This shifts the value of the marginal product of labor curve upward, because *VMPL* rises at any given level of employment. If the wage rate remains unchanged at $200, the optimal point moves from point *A* to point *B*: the profit-maximizing level of employment rises.

Panel (b) shows the effect of a *decrease* in the price of wheat. This shifts the value of the marginal product of labor curve downward. If the wage rate remains unchanged at $200, the optimal point moves from point *A* to point *C*: the profit-maximizing level of employment falls.

2. Changes in the Supply of Other Factors Suppose that Riley and Tyler acquire more land to cultivate—say, by clearing a woodland on their property. Each worker now produces more wheat because each one has more land to work with. As a result, the marginal product of labor on the farm rises at any given level of employment. This has the same effect as an increase in the price of wheat,

FIGURE 37-3 Shifts of the Value of the Marginal Product Curve

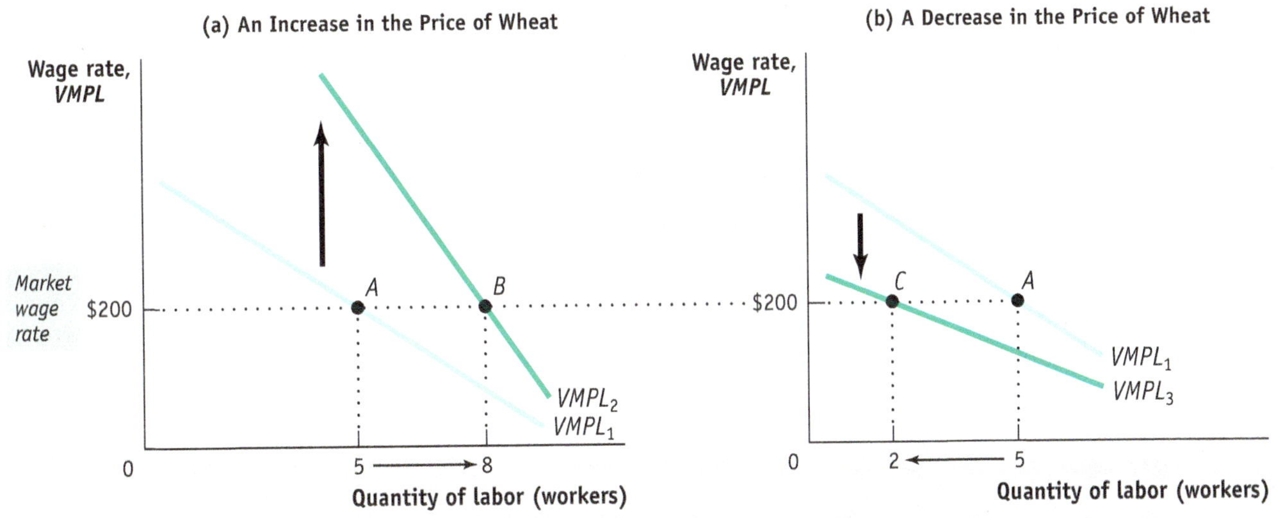

Panel (a) shows the effect of an increase in the price of wheat on Riley and Tyler's demand for labor. The value of the marginal product of labor curve shifts upward, from $VMPL_1$ to $VMPL_2$. If the market wage rate remains at $200, profit-maximizing employment rises from 5 workers to 8 workers, shown by the movement from point *A* to point *B*. Panel (b) shows the effect of a decrease in the price of wheat. The value of the marginal product of labor curve shifts downward, from $VMPL_1$ to $VMPL_3$. At the market wage rate of $200, profit-maximizing employment falls from 5 workers to 2 workers, shown by the movement from point *A* to point *C*.

which is illustrated in panel (a) of Figure 37-3: the value of the marginal product of labor curve shifts upward, and at any given wage rate, the profit-maximizing level of employment rises.

In contrast, suppose Riley and Tyler cultivate less land. This leads to a fall in the marginal product of labor at any given employment level. Each worker produces less wheat because each has less land to work with. As a result, the value of the marginal product of labor curve shifts downward—as in panel (b) of Figure 37-3—and the profit-maximizing level of employment falls.

3. Changes in Technology In general, the effect of technological progress on the demand for any given factor can go either way: improved technology can either increase or reduce the demand for a given factor of production. And, frequently, a decrease in one factor leads to an increase in another.

How can technological progress reduce factor demand? Consider horses, which were once an important factor of production. The development of substitutes for horse power, such as cars and tractors, greatly reduced the demand for horses. At the same time, however, demand increased for other factors such as drivers, manufacturers, and skilled auto mechanics.

In today's economy, the expanding use of automation and robots as a substitute for human labor has some analysts predicting that the factor demand for human workers will decrease in certain industries in the coming decades. Robots can collect goods from warehouse shelves and lay bricks at construction sites, eliminating the need for humans to perform these tasks. And, as you might predict, at the same time, the demand for other factors such as software developers and robotics engineers will increase. The usual effect of technological progress is to increase the demand for a given factor by raising its productivity. So despite persistent fears that machinery and automation would reduce the demand for labor, over the long term, the U.S. economy has seen both large wage increases and large increases in employment. That's because technological progress has raised labor productivity, and as a result, increased the demand for labor.

ECONOMICS >> *in Action*

The Factor Distribution of Income in the United States

When we talk about the factor distribution of income, what are we talking about in practice?

In the United States, as in all advanced economies, payments to labor account for most of the economy's total income. Figure 37-4 shows the factor distribution of income in the United States in 2019: in that year, 68.9% of total income in the economy took the form of *compensation of employees*—a number that includes both wages and benefits such as health insurance. This number is somewhat low by historical standards (it was 72.1% in 1972 and 70.2% in 2007). It reflects the slow recovery after the Great Recession when unemployment and wage rates took more than five years to return to pre-recession levels.

However, measured wages and benefits don't capture the full income of "labor" because a significant fraction of total income in the United States (usually 7% to 10%) is *proprietors' income*—the earnings of people who own their own businesses. Part of that income should be considered wages these business owners pay themselves. So, the true share of labor in the economy is probably a few percentage points higher than the reported "compensation of employees" share.

But much of what we call compensation of employees is really a return on human capital. A surgeon isn't just supplying the services of a pair of ordinary hands (at least the patient hopes not!): that

FIGURE 37-4 Factor Distribution of Income in the United States in 2019

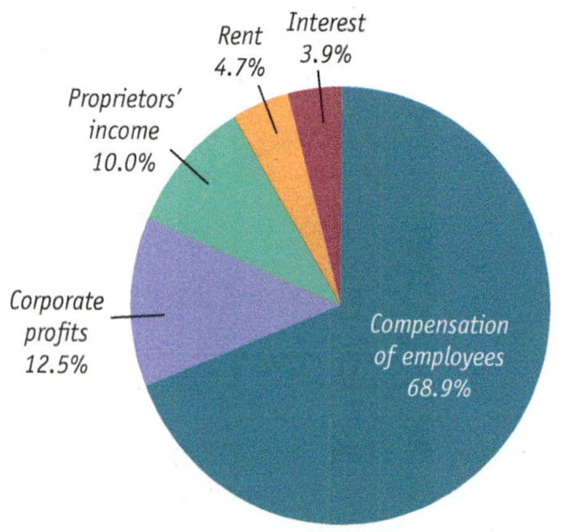

Data from: Bureau of Economic Analysis.

individual is also supplying the result of many years and hundreds of thousands of dollars invested in training and experience. We can't directly measure what fraction of wages is really a payment for education and training, but many economists believe that human capital has become *the* most important factor of production in modern economies.

Check Your Understanding 37-2

1. In the following cases, state the direction of the shift of the demand curve for labor and what will happen, other things equal, to the market equilibrium wage rate and quantity of labor employed as a result.
   a. Service industries, such as retailing and banking, experience an increase in demand. These industries use relatively more labor than nonservice industries.
   b. Due to overfishing, there is a fall in the amount of fish caught per day by commercial fishers; this decrease affects their demand for workers.
2. Explain the following statement: "When firms in different industries all compete for the same workers, then the value of the marginal product of the last worker hired will be equal across all firms regardless of whether they are in different industries."

Solutions appear at back of book.

>> Quick Review

- In a perfectly competitive market economy, the price of the good multiplied by the marginal product of labor is equal to the **value of the marginal product** of labor: $VMPL = P \times MPL$. A profit-maximizing producer hires labor up to the point at which the value of the marginal product of labor is equal to the wage rate: $VMPL = W$. The **value of the marginal product curve** of labor slopes downward due to diminishing returns to labor in production.
- The market demand curve for labor is the horizontal sum of all the individual demand curves of producers in that market. It shifts for three reasons: changes in the output price, changes in the supply of other factors, and technological progress.

MODULE 38

Marginal Productivity Theory and the Economy's Distribution of Income

WHAT YOU WILL LEARN

- What is the **marginal productivity theory of income distribution?**
- Why is it a key measure of the efficiency of the economy and how its benefits are distributed?
- Why does it sometimes fail to hold and what factors account for the divergences, such as workplace discrimination?

Yuri_Arcurs/E+/Getty Images

What does microeconomics have to say about how the economy's total income is divided among the various factors of production—workers (labor), landowners (land), firms (physical capital), and professional workers (human capital)? In this module, we will address that question.

First we will examine the "benchmark" case, called the *marginal productivity theory of income distribution*. It is the income distribution that arises if all factors are paid their value of marginal product when markets are in perfectly competitive equilibrium. The extent to which the distribution of income reflects this benchmark case is an important indicator of the overall level of efficiency of the economy. However, it is also important to understand that while the marginal productivity theory of income distribution is a measure of efficiency, it isn't a measure of equity or fairness. In fact, an economy that satisfies the benchmark case may leave a significant number of people with unsatisfactory standards of living without some form of government intervention. An example is the condition of the *working poor*, a group we will examine in more detail in Module 40.

In real life, the marginal productivity theory of income distribution *mostly* explains the actual income distribution among American factors of production. In other words, factors in the U.S. economy are *mostly* paid according to their value of marginal product. Here we will take a detailed look at the labor market, allowing us to see why the theory explains most of the actual wage differences in the economy. But we will also address the fact that not *all* of actual wage differences are accounted for by the theory, and are likely to reflect other factors, such as discrimination or market power.

According to the **marginal productivity theory of income distribution,** every factor of production is paid its equilibrium value of the marginal product.

The **equilibrium value of the marginal product** of a factor is the additional value produced by the last unit of that factor employed in the factor market as a whole.

38.1 The Marginal Productivity Theory of Income Distribution

The **marginal productivity theory of income distribution** sums up what we have learned about payments to factors when goods markets and factor markets are perfectly competitive. According to this theory, each factor is paid the value of the output generated by the last unit of that factor employed in the factor market as a whole—its **equilibrium value of the marginal product.**

To understand why the marginal productivity theory of income distribution is important, look back at Figure 37-4, which shows the factor distribution of income in the United States, and ask yourself this question: Who or what decided that labor would get 68% of total U.S. income? Why not 90% or 50%?

The answer, according to the marginal productivity theory of income distribution, is that the division of income among the economy's factors of production isn't arbitrary: it is determined by each factor's marginal productivity at the economy's equilibrium. The wage rate earned by *all* workers in the economy is equal to the increase in the value of output generated by the last worker employed in the economy-wide labor market.

So far we have treated factor markets as if every unit of each factor were identical. That is, as if all land were identical, all labor were identical, and all capital were identical. But in reality, factors differ considerably with respect to productivity. For example, workers have different skills and abilities.

Rather than thinking of one land market for all land resources in an economy, and similarly one capital market and one labor market, we can instead think of different markets for different types of land, physical capital, human capital, and labor. For example, the market for computer programmers is different from the market for pastry chefs.

When we consider that there are separate factor markets for different types of factors, we can still apply the marginal productivity of income distribution. That is, when the labor market for computer programmers is in equilibrium, the theory says that the wage rate earned by all computer programmers is equal to the market's equilibrium value of the marginal product—the value of the marginal product of the last computer programmer hired in that market.

The marginal productivity theory of income distribution rests on the assumption that factor markets as well as goods and services markets are perfectly competitive. And as we know from earlier modules, many markets don't satisfy that criterion. So it is useful as a benchmark but not as an exact representation of the real world.

And it's important to note that to the extent marginal productivity theory of income distribution works, it's an explanation of what markets do, not a statement about what is fair or right. That is, it doesn't tell us what the income distribution "ought" to be. Rather, the marginal productivity theory of income distribution can serve as a benchmark to help society decide what is the right trade-off of equity versus efficiency for its members.

38.2 Is the Marginal Productivity Theory of Income Distribution Really True?

As we said in the introduction to this module, the marginal productivity theory of income distribution explains most but not all of the actual distribution of income. But what accounts for the divergence? To answer this question, economists have

Compensating differentials are higher wages that arise from the greater difficulty of a job.

done vast amounts of empirical research, focusing mainly on labor markets because they are the source of most of the divergence. From that research, several widely accepted causes for the divergence between theory and reality have emerged.

Wage Disparities in Practice

Wage rates in the United States cover a very wide range. In 2019, nearly two million workers received the legal federal minimum of $7.25 per hour. At the other extreme, the chief executives of several companies were paid more than $100 million, which works out to $20,000 per hour even if they worked 100-hour weeks. Even leaving out these extremes, there is a huge range of wage rates. Are people really that different in their marginal productivities?

A particular source of concern is the existence of systematic wage differences across gender and race. Figure 38-1 compares annual median earnings in 2018 of full-time workers aged 25 or older classified by gender and race. As a group, White males had the highest earnings. Other data show that women (averaging across all races) earned only about 79% as much; Black or African American workers (male and female combined), only 70% as much; Hispanic workers (again, male and female combined), only 67% as much. Do marginal productivity differences really explain these persistent differences across gender and race?

Wage Disparities Explained by Marginal Productivity Theory

Differences in marginal productivity can indeed explain a signifcant portion of wage disparities. There are four main factors that lead to differences in marginal productivity among workers.

1. Compensating Differentials Across different jobs, whether wages are higher or lower often depends on how attractive or unattractive the job is. These wage differences are known as **compensating differentials.** Workers with unpleasant or dangerous jobs demand a higher wage than workers with jobs that require the same skill and effort but lack the unpleasant or dangerous qualities. For example, truckers who haul hazardous loads are paid more than truckers who haul

FIGURE 38-1 Median Earnings by Gender and Race, 2018

The U.S. labor market continues to show large differences across workers according to gender and race. Women are paid substantially less than men; Black or African-American and Hispanic workers are paid substantially less than White male workers.

Data from: Federal Reserve Bank of St. Louis and U.S. Census Bureau.

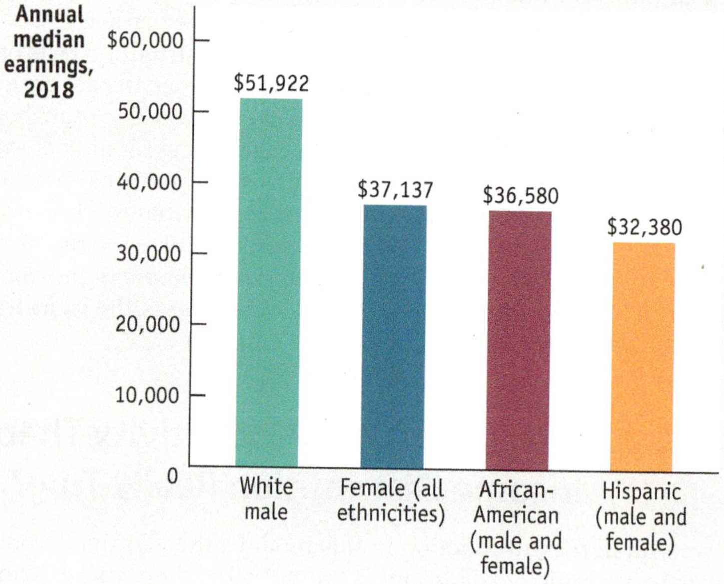

nonhazardous loads. During the height of the coronavirus pandemic, retailers like Amazon and Kroger gave their in-store and warehouse workers extra pay to compensate for the hazard of catching the virus. But for any *given* job, the marginal productivity theory of income distribution generally holds true. So hazardous-load truckers are paid a wage equal to the equilibrium value of the marginal product of the last person employed in the labor market for hazardous-load truckers.

2. Differences in Ability Differences in ability generate differences in wages that are consistent with marginal productivity theory. A person with higher abilities produces a better product that commands a higher price compared to a person with lower abilities. The person with higher abilties also generates a higher value of the marginal product, and this difference in the value of the marginal product translates into differences in earning potential. Professional sports is a good example: practice is important, but most of the population just doesn't have what it takes to throw passes like Tom Brady or hit tennis balls like Serena Williams. The same is true in other fields of endeavor.

3. Differences in Human Capital Recall that human capital—education and training—is at least as important in the modern economy as physical capital in the form of buildings and machines. Different people embody quite different quantities of human capital, and a person with a higher quantity of human capital typically generates a higher value of the marginal product by producing a product that commands a higher price. So, differences in human capital account for substantial differences in wages.

The most direct way to see the effect of human capital on wages is to look at the relationship between educational levels and earnings. Figure 38-2 shows earnings differentials by gender, ethnicity, and three educational levels for people aged 25 or older in 2018. As you can see, regardless of gender or ethnicity, higher education is associated with higher median earnings. For example, in 2018, White females with 9 to 12 years of schooling but without a high school diploma had median earnings 32% less than those with a high school diploma and 63% less than those with a college degree—and similar patterns exist for the other five groups. Because even now men typically have had more years of education than women and Whites more years than African Americans and Hispanics, differences

FIGURE 38-2 Earnings Differentials by Education, Gender, and Ethnicity, 2018

It is clear that, regardless of gender or ethnicity, education pays: those with a high school diploma earn more than those without one, and those with a college degree earn substantially more than those with only a high school diploma. Other patterns are evident as well: for any given education level, White males earn more than every other group, and males earn more than females for any given ethnic group.

Data from: U.S. Census Bureau.

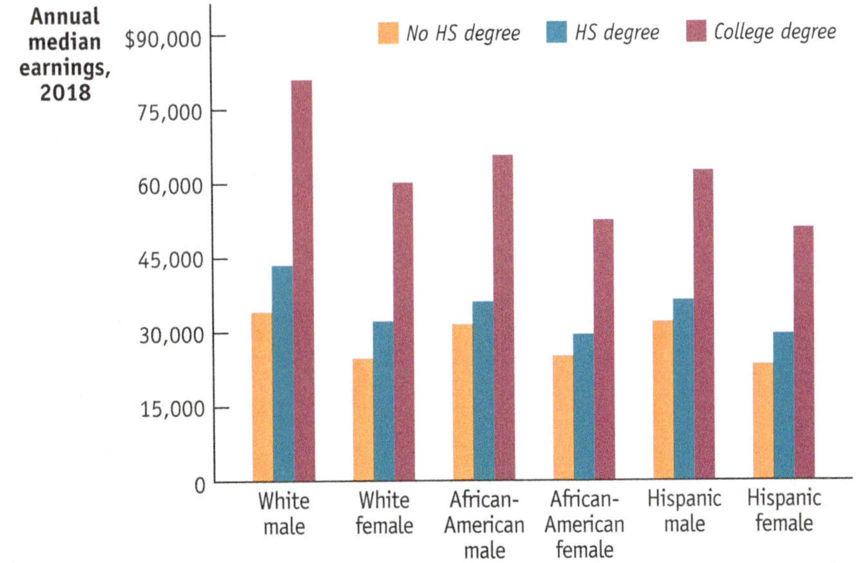

in level of education are part of the explanation for the earnings differences shown in Figure 38-2.

4. Differences in Job Tenure Differences in job tenure also lead to differences in wages that are consistent with marginal productivity theory. Workers with longer job tenure tend to have more work experience, a form of human capital, and therefore higher wages.

5. The Gender Gap: An Exercise in Applying Marginal Productivity Theory A good illustration of these factors is found in research on the *gender-wage gap,* the persistent difference in the earnings of men compared to women. In the U.S. labor market, researchers have found that the gender gap is largely explained by differences in:

- human capital (women tend to have lower levels of it than men)
- choice of occupation (women have tended to choose occupations such as nursing and teaching, in which they earn less)
- career interruptions (women move in and out of the labor force more frequently)
- part-time status (women are more likely to work part-time rather than of full-time)
- overtime status (women are less likely to work overtime)

For example, a recent U.S. Department of Labor study indicates that the gender-wage gap fell from 20.4% to 5.0% once the preceding factors were accounted for. Moreover, over the past 37 years, even the unadjusted gender-wage gap has fallen significantly, from 37.7% in 1979 to 18.9% in 2018, as women have begun to close in on men in terms of these five factors.

But it's also important to emphasize that earnings differences arising from these factors are not necessarily fair. The United States lags behind other advanced countries in providing government or legal support for child care. As a result, American women face more career interruptions than men and are also less able to work full time than men. Similarly, a society in which people of color typically receive a poor education because they live in underfunded school districts, then go on to earn low wages because they are poorly educated, may have labor markets that are well described by marginal productivity theory (and would be consistent with the earnings differences across racial and ethnic groups and between the genders shown in Figure 38-2). Yet many people would still consider the resulting distribution of income unfair.

38.3 Wage Disparities Unexplained by Marginal Productivity Theory

While marginal productivity theory can explain a significant portion of income distribution, it cannot explain all of it. Now we will turn to factors that are unexplained by marginal productivity theory, yet play a role in determining that actual distribution of income.

Market Power

The marginal productivity theory of income distribution is based on the assumption that factor markets are perfectly competitive. But when market power is present, that assumption is violated and the theory no longer applies. In fact, depending upon the source of the market power, workers may be paid more or less than the equilibrium value of their marginal product.

Unions are a source of market power in factor markets. **Unions** are organizations of workers that try to raise wages and improve working conditions for their members. Through collective bargaining, unions can achieve better wage deals than workers could achieve by bargaining individually with employers. As a result, wages for unionized workers tend to exceed the equilibrium value of the marginal product. In 2019, the median weekly earnings of union members in the United States were $1,082, compared to $892 for workers not represented by unions—more than a 20% difference. Studies have shown that unionization helps reduce the wage differences between White men and women, as well as between White and non-White workers.

Unions are organizations of workers that try to raise wages and improve working conditions for their members by bargaining collectively with employers.

According to the **efficiency-wage model,** it may be economically rational for an employer to pay a wage greater than the market equilibrium level as an incentive for better performance.

Just as unionized workers can extract higher wages than they would otherwise receive, if an employer is large enough in the labor market, it can lower wages below the competitive level. Recent research has highlighted how a wave of consolidations within industries over the past 20 years has depressed wages and employment as workers are left with fewer employment alternatives. When firms exercise market power in labor markets, workers are paid less than their value of marginal product. Many economists now believe that, in the United States, the market power exercised by employers outweighs the market power exercised by unions.

For example, in 2015, Uber slashed fares in over 100 cities—some by as much as 45%—to undercut rivals like Lyft. Uber drivers saw their incomes plummet. Although Uber drivers are not employees but independent contractors, Uber's size gave it the market power to lower the hourly returns to its drivers, who generally responded by working more hours.

Efficiency Wages

Another source of wage differentials is the phenomenon of *efficiency wages*—a type of incentive scheme used by employers to motivate workers to work hard and to reduce worker turnover. Suppose a worker performs a job that is extremely important but that the employer can observe how well the job is being performed only at infrequent intervals—say, serving as a caregiver for the employer's child. Then it makes sense for the employer to pay more than the worker could earn in an alternative job—that is, more than the equilibrium wage. Why? Because earning a premium makes losing this job quite costly for the worker.

The **efficiency-wage model** states that when it is difficult to observe a worker's performance, it may be economically rational for an employer to pay a wage greater than the market equilibrium level as an incentive for better performance. The threat of losing a job that pays a premium motivates the worker to perform well and avoid being fired. Likewise, paying a premium also reduces worker turnover—the frequency with which an employee leaves a job voluntarily. Despite the fact that it may take no more effort and skill to be a child's caregiver than to be a hospital care aide, efficiency wages show why it often makes economic sense for a parent to pay a caregiver more than the equilibrium wage of hospital care aides.

Like the price floors and, in particular, much like the minimum wage—efficiency wages lead to a surplus of labor in labor markets where they are used. This surplus of labor translates into unemployment—some workers are actively searching for a high-paying efficiency-wage job but are unable to get one, and other more fortunate but no more deserving workers are able to acquire one.

As a result, two workers with exactly the same profile—the same skills and same job history—may earn unequal wages: the worker who is lucky enough to get an efficiency-wage job earns more than the worker who gets a standard job (or who remains unemployed while searching for a higher-paying job).

Discrimination

Discrimination occurs when someone is denied opportunities based upon their personal characteristics, characteristics that have no impact on their economic performance. As we noted in Module 9, discrimination is a type of market failure because mutually beneficial transactions are forgone and makes society worse off. Moreover, the lack of fairness hurts individuals and their families. Thus, policies to counteract and eliminate discrimination make society, as well as individuals and their families, better off in the long run.

During the history of the United States, formal workplace discrimination on the basis of race, gender, ethnicity, disability, religion, sexual orientation, or gender identification was legal for longer than it was illegal. Fortunately for us, those days are over and the overall level of discrimination in the economy has fallen significantly since the 1960s, when Civil Rights legislation was first adopted.

However, that does not mean that discrimination has been eliminated. While it is illegal to adopt a formal policy of discrimination, a significant amount of informal discrimination exists. For example, researchers found that when they submitted fictitious job applications using identical résumés but with ethnically identifiable names, White-identified applicants received 36% more call-backs than Black-identified applicants and 24% more than Latino-identified applicants.

It's important to undertand that discrimination is *not* a natural consequence of market competition. On the contrary, market forces tend to work against discrimination. To see why, consider the incentives that would exist if social convention dictated that women be paid 30% less than men with equivalent qualifications and experience. Companies would be able to reduce their costs by hiring women rather than men. The result would be to create an excess demand for female workers, which would eventually drive up their wages.

But if market competition works against discrimination, how is it that so much discrimination has taken place? The answer is twofold.

First, when labor markets don't work well, employers may have the ability to discriminate without hurting their profits. For example, the presence of monopoly profits (such as arising from natural monopoly), market interferences (such as unions or minimum-wage laws), or market failures (such as efficiency wages) can lead an employer to offer wages that are above the equilibrium level in a competitive labor market. As a result, there are more job applicants than there are jobs, leaving employers free to discriminate among applicants.

Second, a significant share of discriminatory outcomes arise as the result of past discrimination that became institutionalized or systemic. Often this was the direct result of government policies. For example, until the 1960s, state and local governments in many parts of the country barred Blacks from attending "Whites-only" public schools and universities. Instead they were forced to attend inferior schools or were restricted to a very small number of places in historically Black colleges. Discriminatory housing and mortgage lending practices forced Black families to live in neighborhoods that lacked good schools or adequate transportation to jobs. And informal discrimination created a pattern of "last hired, first fired" over the business cycle for many Black workers. As a result, many generations of Black households stayed mired in poverty with limited employment prospects, preventing them from gaining the skills or human capital required for well-paying jobs. So even though formal discrimination has disappeared, the market economy can lead to discriminatory outcomes based upon past discrimination.

ECONOMICS >> *in Action*

Marginal Productivity and the Minimum-Wage Puzzle

The U.S. government, like many other governments, puts a floor under wages: nationally, employers aren't allowed to pay workers less than $7.25 an hour. However, many states and some cities impose their own minimum wages, in some cases well above the national standard. For example, Arizona requires that employers pay at least $12.00 an hour. Seattle requires payment of $16.39 an hour.

Labor economists have devoted a lot of attention to state and local minimum wages, both because they affect millions of workers and because they serve as "natural experiments": by looking at what happens when a state increases its minimum wage, and especially by comparing the results with developments in neighboring states, economists can gather important information about how labor markets actually work in the real world.

The results of such an experiment may seem readily apparent: a state that increases its minimum wage, say from $7.25 to $16.39, raises the cost of labor. Minimum-wage workers, like employees at fast-food restaurants, are now more expensive to hire. Wouldn't these higher costs lead employers to reduce employment and workers to lose their jobs? But that's not what seems to happen, according to many labor economists (although there are some dissenters). Instead, even significant minimum-wage hikes, while they do raise wages for many workers, appear to have no effect on employment. How is this possible?

The answer, suggest some of the economists who have pioneered this line of research, is monopsony: because large employers use their market power to hold down wages, paying workers less than their marginal product, moderate increases in the minimum wage do not discourage hiring because even the new higher wage is still below labor's marginal product, so employing workers is still profitable. If correct, this analysis has implications well beyond minimum-wage policy, because it casts doubt on how well the marginal productivity theory of income distribution works for the economy as a whole.

Check Your Understanding 38-1

1. Assess each of the following statements. Do you think they are true, false, or ambiguous? Explain.
   a. The marginal productivity theory of income distribution is inconsistent with the presence of income disparities associated with gender, race, or ethnicity.
   b. Companies that engage in workplace discrimination but whose competitors do not are likely to have lower profits as a result of their actions.
   c. Workers who are paid less because they have less experience are not the victims of discrimination.

Solutions appear at back of book.

>> Quick Review

- According to the **marginal productivity theory of income distribution,** in a perfectly competitive economy, each factor of production is paid its **equilibrium value of the marginal product.**
- **Compensating differentials,** as well as differences in ability, human capital, and job tenure, account for a significant proportion of actual wage disparities. These factors are consistent with marginal productivity theory.
- Wage disparities that are not consistent with marginal productivity theory arise from the use of market power, efficiency wages, and discrimination. **Unions** exert market power through collective bargaining for workers, raising their pay and living standards. In contrast, firms in consolidated industries can exert market power to hold down employment and wages.
- According to the **efficiency-wage model,** employers are willing to pay workers an above-equilibrium wage to induce better performance when it is difficult to observe performance. It also results in lower worker turnover.
- Discrimination has historically been a major factor in wage disparities. Market competition tends to work against discrimination. But discrimination can leave a long-lasting legacy of diminished human capital acquisition.

MODULE 39

The Market for Labor

WHAT YOU WILL LEARN

- How do decisions about **time allocation** determine labor supply?
- Why may workers work fewer hours when wages go up?
- What factors shift the supply of labor?

NickyLloyd/Getty Images

Marginal productivity theory tells us about the demand for factors of production. But what about the supply of factors? In this module, we focus exclusively on the supply of labor. Labor is the most important factor of production in the modern U.S. economy, accounting for most of factor income. We will look at how labor supply arises from a worker's decision about time allocation and explore the determination of equilibrium wage and quantity in the labor market.

39.1 The Supply of Labor

Up to this point, we have focused on the demand for factors, which determines the quantities demanded of labor, capital, or land by producers as a function of their factor prices. What about the supply of factors?

Work versus Leisure

In the labor market, the roles of firms and households are the reverse of what they are in markets for goods and services. A good such as wheat or smartphones is supplied by firms and demanded by households; labor, though, is demanded by firms and supplied by households. How do people decide how much labor to supply?

As a practical matter, most people have limited control over their work hours: either you take a job that involves working a set number of hours per week or you don't get the job at all. To understand the logic of labor supply, however, it helps to put realism to one side for a bit and imagine an individual who can choose to work as many or as few hours as that individual likes.

Why wouldn't such an individual work as many hours as possible? Because workers are human beings, too, and have other uses for their time. An hour spent on the job is an hour not spent on other, presumably more pleasant, activities. So the decision about how much labor to supply involves making a decision about **time allocation**—how many hours to spend on different activities.

Decisions about labor supply result from decisions about **time allocation:** how many hours to spend on different activities.

By working, people earn income that they can use to buy goods. The more hours an individual works, the more goods they can afford to buy. But this increased purchasing power comes at the expense of a reduction in **leisure,** the time spent not working. (Leisure doesn't necessarily mean time spent goofing off. It could mean time spent with one's family, pursuing hobbies, exercising, and so on.) And though purchased goods yield utility, so does leisure. Indeed, we can think of leisure itself as a normal good, which most people would like to consume more of as their incomes increase.

Kevin Kozicki/Image Source/Getty Images

Every worker faces a trade-off between leisure and work.

How does a rational individual decide how much leisure to consume? By making a marginal comparison, of course. In analyzing consumer choice, we asked how a utility-maximizing consumer uses a marginal *dollar*. In analyzing labor supply, we ask how an individual uses a marginal *hour*.

Consider Jaden, an individual who likes both leisure and the goods money can buy. Suppose that his wage rate is $10 per hour. In deciding how many hours he wants to work, he must compare the marginal utility of an additional hour of leisure with the additional utility he gets from $10 worth of goods. If $10 worth of goods adds more to his total utility than an additional hour of leisure, he can increase his total utility by giving up an hour of leisure to work an additional hour. If an extra hour of leisure adds more to his total utility than $10 worth of goods, he can increase his total utility by working one fewer hour in order to gain an hour of leisure.

At Jaden's optimal labor supply choice, then, his marginal utility of one hour of leisure is equal to the marginal utility he gets from the goods that his hourly wage can purchase. This is very similar to the *optimal consumption rule* except that it is a rule about time rather than money.

Our next step is to ask how Jaden's decision about time allocation is affected when his wage rate changes.

Wages and Labor Supply

Suppose that Jaden's wage rate doubles, from $10 to $20 per hour. How will he change his time allocation?

You could argue that Jaden will work longer hours, because his incentive to work has increased: by giving up an hour of leisure, he can now gain twice as much money as before. But you could equally well argue that he will work less, because he doesn't need to work as many hours to generate the income to pay for the goods he wants.

As these opposing arguments suggest, the quantity of labor Jaden supplies can either rise or fall when his wage rate rises. To understand why, let's recall the distinction between *substitution effects* and *income effects*. We saw there that a price change affects consumer choice in two ways: by changing the opportunity cost of a good in terms of other goods (the substitution effect) and by making the consumer richer or poorer (the income effect).

Now think about how a rise in Jaden's wage rate affects his demand for leisure. The opportunity cost of leisure—the amount of money he gives up by taking an hour off instead of working—rises. That substitution effect gives him an incentive, other things equal, to consume *less* leisure and work *longer* hours. Conversely, a higher wage rate makes Jaden richer—and this income effect leads him, other things equal, to want to consume *more* leisure and work *fewer* hours, because leisure is a normal good.

So, in the case of labor supply, the substitution effect and the income effect work in opposite directions. If the substitution effect is so powerful that it dominates the income effect, an increase in Jaden's wage rate leads him to supply *more* hours of labor. If the income effect is so powerful that it dominates the

Leisure is time available for purposes other than just earning money to buy marketed goods.

The **individual labor supply curve** shows how the quantity of labor supplied by an individual depends on that individual's wage rate.

substitution effect, an increase in the wage rate leads him to supply *fewer* hours of labor.

We see, then, that the **individual labor supply curve**—the relationship between the wage rate and the number of hours of labor supplied by an individual worker—does not necessarily slope upward. If the income effect dominates, a higher wage rate will reduce the quantity of labor supplied.

Figure 39-1 illustrates the two possibilities for labor supply. If the substitution effect dominates the income effect, the individual labor supply curve slopes upward; panel (a) shows an increase in the wage rate from $10 to $20 per hour leading to a *rise* in the number of hours worked from 40 to 50. However, if the income effect dominates, the quantity of labor supplied goes down when the wage rate increases. Panel (b) shows the same rise in the wage rate leading to a *fall* in the number of hours worked from 40 to 30.

Economists refer to an individual labor supply curve that contains both upward-sloping and downward-sloping segments as a "backward-bending labor supply curve." At lower wage rates, the substitution effect dominates the income effect. At higher wage rates, the income effect eventually dominates the substitution effect.

Is a negative response of the quantity of labor supplied to the wage rate a real possibility? Yes: many labor economists believe that income effects on the supply of labor may be somewhat stronger than substitution effects.

The most compelling piece of evidence for this belief comes from Americans' increasing consumption of leisure over the past century. At the end of the nineteenth century, wages adjusted for inflation were only about one-eighth what they are today; the typical workweek was 70 hours, and very few workers retired at age 65. Today the typical workweek is less than 40 hours, and most people retire at age 65 or earlier. So it seems that Americans have chosen to take advantage of higher wages in part by consuming more leisure.

FIGURE 39-1 The Individual Labor Supply Curve

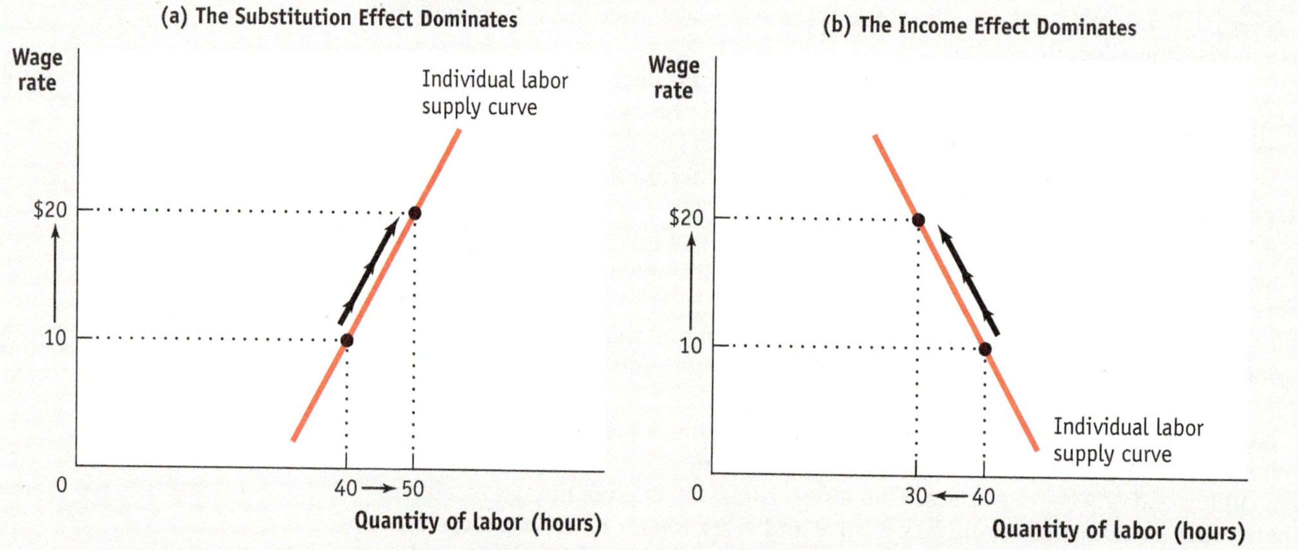

When the substitution effect of a wage increase dominates the income effect, the individual labor supply curve slopes upward, as in panel (a). Here a rise in the wage rate from $10 to $20 per hour increases the number of hours worked from 40 to 50. But when the income effect of a wage increase dominates the substitution effect, the individual labor supply curve slopes downward, as in panel (b). Here the same rise in the wage rate reduces the number of hours worked from 40 to 30. The individual labor supply curve shows how the quantity of labor supplied by an individual depends on that individual's wage rate.

Shifts of the Labor Supply Curve

Now that we have examined how income and substitution effects shape the individual labor supply curve, we can turn to the market labor supply curve. In any labor market, the market supply curve is the horizontal sum of the individual labor supply curves of all workers in that market. A change in any factor *other than the wage* that alters workers' willingness to supply labor causes a shift of the labor supply curve. A variety of factors can lead to such shifts, including changes in preferences and social norms, changes in population, changes in opportunities, and changes in wealth.

Changes in Preferences and Social Norms Changes in preferences and social norms can lead workers to increase or decrease their willingness to work at any given wage. A striking example of this phenomenon is the large increase in the number of employed women—particularly married, employed women—that has occurred in the United States since the 1960s. Until that time, women who could afford to largely avoided working outside the home. Changes in preferences and norms in post–World War II America (helped along by the invention of labor-saving home appliances such as washing machines, increasing urbanization of the population, and higher female education levels) have induced large numbers of American women to join the workforce—a phenomenon often repeated in other countries that experience similar social and technological forces.

Changes in Population Changes in the population size generally lead to shifts of the labor supply curve. A larger population tends to shift the labor supply curve rightward as more workers are available at any given wage; a smaller population tends to shift the labor supply curve leftward. From 1990 to 2020, the U.S. labor force has grown approximately 1% per year, generated by immigration and a relatively high birth rate. As a result, from 1990 to 2020, the U.S. labor market had a rightward-shifting labor supply curve. However, while the population continued to grow after 2008, from 2008 through 2011, the size of the labor force temporarily shrank as workers disillusioned by bad job prospects left the labor force. As a result, the U.S. labor supply curve shifted leftward during this period.

Changes in Opportunities At one time, teaching was the only occupation considered suitable for well-educated women. However, as opportunities in other professions opened up to women starting in the 1960s, many women left teaching and potential female teachers chose other careers. This generated a leftward shift of the supply curve for teachers, reflecting a fall in the willingness to work at any given wage and forcing school districts to pay more to maintain an adequate teaching staff. These events illustrate a general result: when superior alternatives arise for workers in another labor market, the supply curve in the original labor market shifts leftward as workers move to the new opportunities. Similarly, when opportunities diminish in one labor market—say, layoffs in the manufacturing industry due to increased foreign competition—the supply in alternative labor markets increases as workers move to these other markets.

Changes in Wealth A person whose wealth increases will buy more normal goods, including leisure. So when a class of workers experiences a general rise in their wealth levels—say, due to a stock market boom—the income effect from the wealth increase will shift the labor supply curve associated with those workers leftward as workers consume more leisure and work less. Note that *the income effect caused by a change in wealth shifts the labor supply curve*, but *the income effect from a wage rate increase*—as we discussed in the case of the individual labor supply curve—*is a movement along the labor supply curve.*

Belinda Howell/Getty Images

The high costs of child care in the United States depress American women's labor supply in comparison to other high-income countries.

ECONOMICS >> *in Action*

The Real Housewives of the United States

If you watch old TV shows, you might think that the United States in the 1950s was a land of traditional families, with a male breadwinner and a stay-at-home housewife. The reality wasn't that stark: even in 1960, more than 40% of women in their prime working years (ages 25–54) were in the paid labor force. But that compared with 97% labor force participation for men in the same age group.

Over the 35 years that followed, women moved in large numbers into jobs outside the home: by the mid-1990s, more than 75% of prime-working-age women were in the paid workforce. But over the next few decades women's employment stagnated, or even declined a bit.

The funny thing is that this didn't happen in other wealthy countries, where women's employment continued to rise. By 2019, around 85% of prime-working-age women in northern European countries and Canada were in the workforce, while the United States was still at 75%. Even Japan, which used to be famous for blatant gender discrimination, had higher female employment than the United States.

Why did the United States diverge? The most likely explanation is public policy that affects labor supply decisions. Most other wealthy countries either directly provide day care for children of working mothers or subsidize and regulate private day care. The United States doesn't have a comparable policy, so the costs of going to work are much higher for U.S. women with children than for their counterparts abroad.

One implication of this explanation is that changing policy could have large implications for labor supply. Some U.S. politicians are now advocating creation of a national program that subsidizes child care. They argue that such a program would partly (but not completely) pay for itself, because more women would take paying jobs and would, as a result, pay higher taxes. The logic of labor supply says that these claims are probably right.

>> *Quick Review*

- The choice of how much labor to supply is a problem of **time allocation:** a choice between work and **leisure.**
- A rise in the wage rate causes both an income and a substitution effect on an individual's labor supply. The substitution effect of a higher wage rate induces more hours of work supplied, other things equal. This is countered by the income effect: higher income leads to a higher demand for leisure, a normal good. If the income effect dominates, a rise in the wage rate can actually cause the individual labor supply curve to slope the "wrong" way: downward.
- The market labor supply curve is the horizontal sum of the individual labor supply curves of all workers in that market. It shifts for four main reasons: changes in preferences and social norms, changes in population, changes in opportunities, and changes in wealth.

Check Your Understanding 39-1

1. Formerly, Jaden was free to work as many or as few hours per week as he wanted. But a new law limits the maximum number of hours he can work per week to 35. Explain under what circumstances, if any, he is made:
   - **a.** Worse off
   - **b.** Equally as well off
   - **c.** Better off
2. Explain in terms of the income and substitution effects how a fall in Jaden's wage rate can induce him to work more hours than before.

Solutions appear at back of book.

The Economics of the Welfare State

MODULE 40

WHAT YOU WILL LEARN

- What is the **welfare state** and how does it benefit society?
- What are the causes and consequences of poverty?
- How has income inequality in the United States changed over time?
- What are the special concerns about **private health insurance** and how have governments acted to address them?

40.1 Poverty, Inequality, and Public Policy

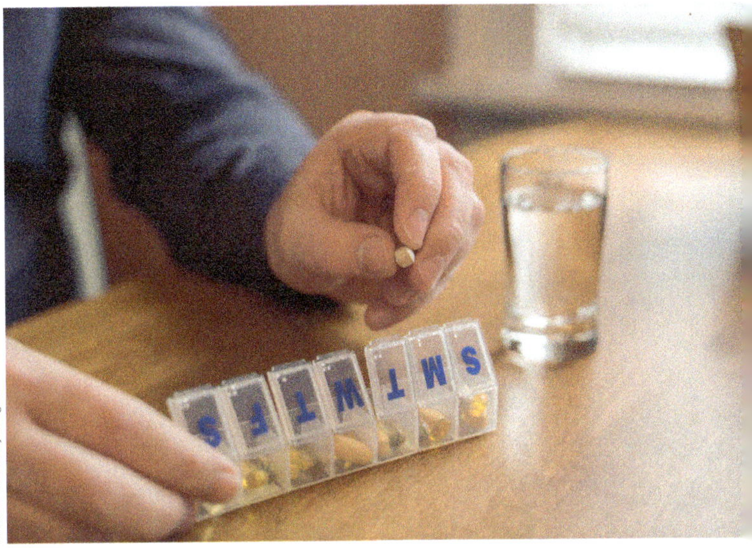

Kristen Prahl/Getty Images

The term **welfare state** has come to refer to the collection of government programs that are designed to alleviate economic hardship. A large share of the government spending of all wealthy countries consists of **government transfers**—payments by the government to individuals and families—that provide financial aid to people experiencing poverty, assistance to unemployed workers, guaranteed income for the elderly, and assistance in paying medical bills for those with large health care expenses.

In this module, we discuss the underlying rationale for welfare state programs. We'll look at the two main kinds of programs operating in the United States: income support programs, of which Social Security is by far the largest, and health care programs, dominated by Medicare and Medicaid. We conclude by evaluating the effectiveness of these programs.

The Logic of the Welfare State

There are three major economic rationales for the creation of the welfare state. We'll now turn to a discussion of each.

The **welfare state** is the collection of government programs designed to alleviate economic hardship.

A **government transfer** is a government payment to an individual or a family.

1. Alleviating Income Inequality Suppose that the Taylor family, which has an income of only $15,000 a year, receives a government check for $1500, which might help them afford things that significantly improve their quality of life, such as a better place to live or a more nutritious diet. Also suppose that the Fisher family, which has an income of $300,000 a year, faces an extra tax of $1,500. This

A **poverty program** is a government program designed to aid the poor.

A **social insurance program** is a government program designed to provide protection against unpredictable financial distress.

The **poverty threshold** is the annual income below which a family is officially considered poor.

The **poverty rate** is the percentage of the population living below the poverty threshold.

probably wouldn't make much difference to their quality of life; at worst, they might have to give up a few minor luxuries.

This hypothetical exchange illustrates the first major rationale for the welfare state: *alleviating income inequality*. Because a marginal dollar is worth more to a poor person than to a rich one, modest transfers from the rich to the poor will do the rich little harm but benefit the poor a lot. So, according to this argument, a government that plays Robin Hood, taking modest amounts from the rich to give to the poor, does more good than harm. As long as the amounts are relatively modest, the inefficiencies created by the transfers (which we learned about in Module 14 on taxation) will be outweighed by the benefits to society. Programs that are designed to aid the poor are known as **poverty programs.**

2. Alleviating Economic Insecurity The second major rationale for the welfare state is *alleviating economic insecurity*. When bad things happen, such as a flood or an illness, they almost always happen to a limited number of people. For example, during the devastating floods that hit Texas in 2017, millions of Texans were rendered homeless. But the floods also left the rest of the United States unscathed.

Now suppose there's a government program that provides aid to families in distress, paying for that aid by taxing families that are having a good year. Arguably, this program will make all the families better off, because even families that don't currently receive aid from the program might need it at some point in the future. Each family will therefore feel safer knowing that the government stands ready to help when disaster strikes. Programs designed to provide protection against unpredictable financial distress are known as **social insurance programs.**

3. Reducing Poverty and Providing Access to Health Care The third and final major rationale for the welfare state involves the *social benefits of poverty reduction and access to health care*, especially when applied to children of low-income households. Researchers have documented that such children, on average, suffer lifelong disadvantages. Even after adjusting for ability, children from economically disadvantaged backgrounds are more likely to be underemployed or unemployed, engage in crime, and suffer chronic health problems—all of which impose significant social costs. So, according to the evidence, programs that help to alleviate poverty and provide access to health care generate external benefits to society.

The Problem of Poverty

What, exactly, do we mean by poverty? Any definition is somewhat arbitrary. Since 1965, however, the U.S. government has maintained an official definition of the **poverty threshold,** a minimum annual income that is considered adequate to purchase the necessities of life. Families whose incomes fall below the poverty threshold are considered poor.

The official poverty threshold depends on the size and composition of a family and is adjusted every year to reflect changes in the cost of living. In 2019, the poverty threshold for an adult living alone was $12,140; for a household consisting of two adults and two children, it was $25,100.

Trends in Poverty Although the United States as a whole has grown far more prosperous over the past several decades, the official U.S. **poverty rate,** the percentage of the U.S. population living below the poverty threshold, has not declined.

The orange line in Figure 40-1 shows the poverty rate from 1967 to 2018. As you can see, since 1967, poverty has fluctuated up and down, with no clear trend over the long run. In 2018, the poverty rate was approximately the same as it had been during the 1960s, even though the United States as a whole was far richer.

In response to this surprising result, researchers have identified a number of limitations to the official poverty measure, of which the most important is that

FIGURE 40-1 Trends in the U.S. Poverty Rate, 1967–2018

The official poverty rate has shown no clear trend since the late 1960s. However, an alternative measure, known as the supplemental poverty measure, or SPM, which most experts consider to be more accurate, has declined modestly.

Data from: U.S. Census Bureau; Fox, Liana, et al., NBER Report No. w19789.

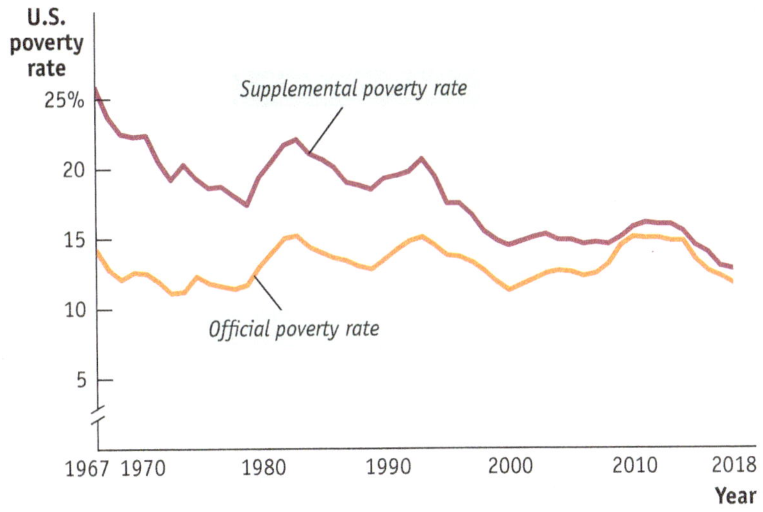

the definition of income doesn't actually include many forms of government aid. For example, it excludes the monetary value of food stamps. So the U.S. Census Bureau now releases a Supplemental Poverty Measure that includes income from government aid, a measure that experts consider to be more accurate.

The burgundy line in Figure 40-1 shows how the rate of poverty according to this measure has changed over time. While it shows more progress than the standard measure, the change is still surprisingly little considering that total real income in the United States has risen by more than 250%.

Who Are the Poor? There's a widely held image of poverty in the United States: a Black or Hispanic family with no husband present and the female head of the household unemployed at least part of the time. This picture isn't completely off-base: poverty is disproportionately high among Blacks and Hispanics as well as among female-headed households. But a majority of those in poverty don't fit the stereotype.

In 2018, 38.1 million Americans were in poverty—11.8% of the population, or slightly more than one in seven persons. Of those in poverty, the single largest group is Whites, making up 41% of the total. Hispanics follow, representing 28% of those in poverty; then Blacks at 23% and Asians at 5%. However, African Americans, Hispanics, and Asians are more likely to be poor than Whites. And one-third of all people in poverty are children, and about one in six children in the United States lives in poverty.

There is also a correlation between family makeup and poverty. Female-headed families with no spouse present have a very high poverty rate: 24.9%. Married couples are much less likely to be poor, with a poverty rate of only 4.7%; still, about 39% of families in poverty were in married households with both spouses present.

What really stands out in the data, however, is the association between poverty and inadequate employment. Adults who work full time are very unlikely to be poor: only 2.3% of full-time workers were poor in 2018. Many industries, particularly in the retail and service sectors, now rely primarily on part-time workers who typically lack benefits such as health plans, paid vacation days, and retirement benefits. These jobs also usually pay a lower hourly wage than comparable full-time work. As a result, many of the poor are members of what analysts call the *working poor:* workers whose incomes fall at or below the poverty threshold.

The coronavirus pandemic illustrated many of the challenges that the working poor face: for financial reasons, choosing to work while sick or choosing to forgo medical care.

What Causes Poverty? Poverty is often blamed on lack of education, and educational attainment clearly has a strong positive effect on income level—those with more education earn, on average, higher incomes than those with less education. For example, in 1979, the median weekly wage of men with a college degree was 29% higher than that of men with only a high school diploma; by 2017, the "college premium" had increased to 86%.

Lack of proficiency in English is also a barrier to higher income. For example, Mexican-born male workers in the United States—two-thirds of whom have not graduated from high school and many of whom have poor English skills—earn less than half of what native-born men earn.

And it's important not to overlook the role of racial and gender discrimination; although less pervasive today than 60 years ago, discrimination still erects formidable barriers to advancement for many Americans. Non-Whites earn less and are less likely to be employed than Whites with comparable levels of education. Studies find that Black males suffer persistent discrimination by employers in favor of Whites, Black women, and Hispanic immigrants. Women earn lower incomes than men with similar qualifications.

In addition, one important source of poverty that should not be overlooked is bad luck. Many families find themselves impoverished when a wage-earner loses a job, a family business fails, or a family member falls seriously ill.

Some of the bad luck that leads to poverty afflicts groups of people rather than individuals. In particular, there are high concentrations of poor Americans in geographic regions that have been left behind by economic change. Consider, for example, Harlan County, Kentucky, a former coal-mining center that has been left behind by changes in markets and technology. More than 40% of the county's residents—who are 96% White—are below the poverty line.

Consequences of Poverty The consequences of poverty are often severe and long-lasting, particularly for children. In 2016, nearly 20% of children in the United States lived in poverty. Poverty is often associated with lack of access to health care, which can lead to health problems that erode the ability to attend school and work later in life. Affordable housing is also frequently a problem, leading poor families to move often, disrupting school and work schedules.

Recent medical studies have shown that children raised in severe poverty tend to suffer from lifelong learning disabilities. As a result, American children growing up in or near poverty tend to be at a disadvantage throughout their lives. Even talented children who come from poor families are unlikely to finish college.

Other studies have shown that the environment in which a poor child grows up also makes a difference. Poor children who grow up in highly segregated, inner-city neighborhoods are much less likely to be employed as adults than those who are equally poor but grow up in areas that are economically diverse and less segregated.

Economists Raj Chetty, John Friedman, and Nathaniel Hendren, of the Opportunity Insights Project of Harvard University, found that the geographic concentration of poverty is especially deleterious. Children who grow up in poor neighborhoods that have higher rates of unstable family structures have a much more difficult time escaping

The United States has a high poverty rate compared to other rich countries.

poverty. Neighborhoods with more stable family structures (lower divorce rates and higher marriage rates) tend to have higher levels of upward mobility regardless of whether a child is from a single-parent or two-parent family. In other words, the average family structure of the neighborhood counts more than the child's own family structure. In addition, neighborhoods with stronger support structures and role models of upward mobility have higher rates of escape from poverty. As a result, according to the researchers, when poor children move to neighborhoods with more stable family structures, stronger support networks, and more role models, they are more likely to graduate from school and earn higher incomes. As Chetty comments, "One of the strongest patterns that emerges is that what you are exposed to as a child—in terms of career pathways, crime, marriage, etc.—impacts how you grow up."

Mean household income is the average income across all households.

Median household income is the income of the household lying at the exact middle of the income distribution.

Economic Inequality

The United States is a rich country. The average household income in 2018 was $90,021. How is it possible, then, that so many Americans still live in poverty? The answer is that income is unequally distributed, with many households earning much less than the average and others earning much more.

Table 40-1 shows the distribution of pre-tax income—income before federal income taxes are paid—among U.S. families in 2018, as estimated by the Census Bureau. Households are grouped into *quintiles*, each containing 20%, or one-fifth, of the population. The first, or bottom, quintile contains households whose income put them below the 20th percentile in income, the second quintile contains households whose income put them between the 20th and 40th percentiles, and so on.

For each group, Table 40-1 shows three numbers. The second column shows the income ranges that define the group. For example, in 2018, the bottom quintile consisted of households with annual incomes of less than $25,601, the next quintile of households had incomes between $25,601 and $50,000, and so on. The third columns shows the average income group, ranging from $13,775 for the bottom fifth to $416,520 for the top 5%. The fourth column shows the percentage of total U.S. income received by each group.

Mean versus Median Household Income

At the bottom of Table 40-1 are two useful numbers for thinking about the incomes of American households. **Mean household income,** also called average household income, is the total income of all U.S. households divided by the number of households. **Median household income** is the income of a household in the exact middle of the income distribution—the level of income at which half of all households have lower income and

TABLE 40-1 U.S. Income Distribution in 2018

Income group	Income range	Average income	Percent of total income
Bottom quintile	$25,600 and under	$13,775	3.1%
Second quintile	$25,601 to $50,000	37,293	8.3
Third quintile	$50,001 to $79,542	63,572	14.1
Fourth quintile	$79,543 to $130,000	101,570	22.6
Top quintile	$130,001 and over	233,895	52.0
Top 5%	$248,728 and over	416,520	23.1
Mean income = $90,021		**Median income = $63,179**	

Data from: U.S. Census Bureau.

half have higher income. It's very important to realize that these two numbers do not measure the same thing.

Economists often illustrate the difference by asking people to first imagine a room containing several dozen more or less ordinary wage-earners and then to think about what happens to the mean and median incomes of the people in the room if a Silicon Valley billionaire walks in. The mean income soars, because the billionaire's income pulls up the average, but the median income hardly rises at all.

This example explains why economists regard median income as a better guide to the economic status of typical American families than mean income: mean income is strongly affected by the incomes of a relatively small number of very-high-income Americans, who are not representative of the population as a whole; median income is not.

What we learn from Table 40-1 is that income in the United States is quite unequally distributed. The average income of the poorest fifth, those in the bottom quintile, of families is less than a quarter of the average income of families in the middle, and the richest fifth, those in the top quintile, have an average income more than three times that of families in the middle. The incomes of the richest fifth of the population are, on average, about 15 times as high as those of the poorest fifth.

It's important to note that the data in Table 40-1 overstate the true degree of inequality in America to some degree. Two reasons account for that:

- Household incomes vary from year to year. In any given year, many households at the bottom of the income distribution are having a particularly bad year, just as many at the top are having a particularly good year. Over time, their incomes will revert to a more normal level and thereby reduce the level of measured inequality.
- Household incomes vary over the lifetime. Young people, and retired people, on average, have lower incomes than people in their prime working years. So data that mixes people of different ages will show more income inequality than data that makes comparisons among people of similar ages.

Despite those qualifications, there is a considerable amount of genuine income inequality in the United States, and income has become considerably more unequal since 1980.

International Comparisons of Inequality A good way to gain some perspective on the level of income inequality in the United States is to compare it to levels in other countries. To do that, economists created the *Gini coefficient,* a measure of income inequality based on the type of data found in Table 40-1. Mathematically, a country's Gini coefficient can range from 0, indicating a perfectly equal distribution of income, to 1, indicating the most unequal distribution of income possible—one in which all the income goes to a single person.

Figure 40-2 shows recent estimates of the Gini coefficient for many of the world's countries. Countries with a high degree of income inequality have a Gini coefficient close to 0.5. Aside from a few countries in Africa, the highest levels of income inequality are found in Latin America, especially Brazil. Countries with a very equal income distribution have Gini coefficients around 0.25. The most equal distributions of income are in Europe, especially in Scandinavia. According to the most recent data, the United States has a Gini coefficient of 0.41. So, compared to other wealthy countries, the United States has unusually high inequality, though it isn't as unequal as Latin America. In 2016, the top 1% income bracket in the United States ($390,000 and up) garnered 20% of national income, compared to 6% in Denmark and 14% in Canada.

When Is Inequality a Problem? Some level of income inequality in an economy is desirable. In a market-based economy, a significant share of the observed

FIGURE 40-2 **Income Inequality Around the World**

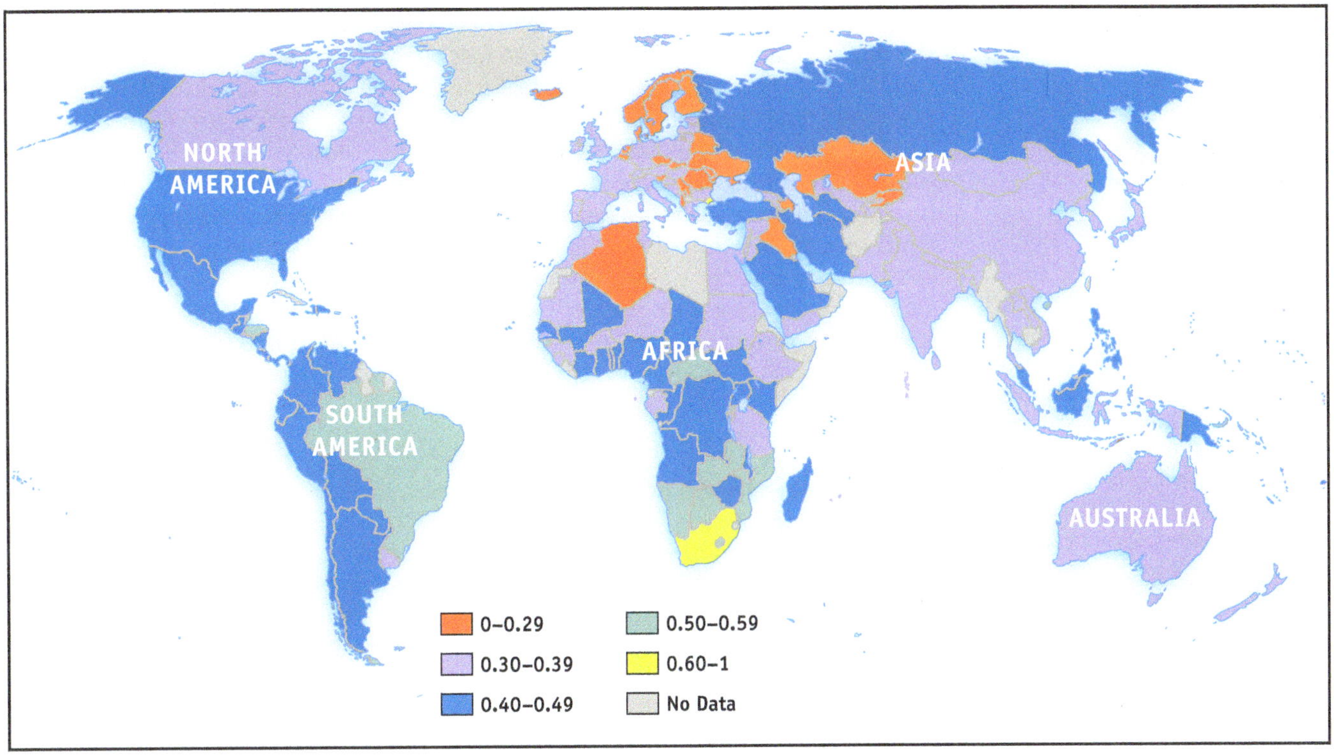

The highest levels of income inequality are found in Africa and Latin America. The most equal distributions of income are in Europe, especially in Scandinavia. Compared to other wealthy countries, the United States, with a Gini coefficient of 0.41, has unusually high inequality. (Gini coefficients are from 2008 to 2017.)
Data from: World Bank, *World Development Indicators*, 2019.

inequality will be the economic rewards of skill, effort, innovation, and education. Without those contributions, the economy and living standards would stagnate.

Yet, high income inequality is a problem because it means that a significant share of a country's population is not sharing in the country's overall prosperity. In the United States, inequality has been rising for 40 years; it is the reason the poverty rate has not fallen even though the United States has become considerably richer. A further concern is how high inequality extends across generations. The children of poor parents are much more likely to be poor than the children of affluent parents—a correlation that is stronger in the United States than in other rich countries. In the United States, concerns over the long-term rise in inequality have become a significant political issue in recent years.

Extreme inequality can hurt a nation's long-term economic prospects if, as is often the case, it limits opportunities. Those born into low-income families may fail to receive adequate nutrition and health care, limiting their productivity as adults; they may also lack access to education and job opportunities, limiting their ability to make contributions to economic growth. In some cases, high inequality also contributes to social and political instability, which further damages nation's economic performance.

Economic Insecurity

As we stated earlier, although the rationale for the welfare state rests in part on the social benefits of reducing poverty and inequality, it also rests in part on the benefits of reducing economic insecurity, which afflicts even relatively well-off families.

One form economic insecurity takes is the risk of a sudden loss of income, which usually happens when a family member loses a job and either spends an extended period without work or is forced to take a new job that pays considerably less. For example, in the wake of the coronavirus pandemic in the spring of 2020, the unemployment rate jumped from less than 5% to nearly 15%. And economic inequality sharply increased as 40% of low-income Americans (those with incomes below $40,000) reported a job loss, while only 13% of households with incomes over $100,000 reported a job loss. Moreover, a third of those who lost their jobs or had their wages cut said they couldn't cover their monthly expenses.

Even if a family doesn't face a loss in income, it can face a surge in expenses. Until implementation of the Affordable Care Act in 2014, the most common reason for such a surge was a medical problem that required expensive treatment, such as heart disease or cancer. Estimates show that 60% of personal bankruptcies in the United States in 2009 were due to medical expenses.

>> Quick Review

- **Welfare state** programs, which include **government transfers,** absorb a large share of government spending in wealthy countries.
- The ability-to-pay principle explains one rationale for the welfare state: alleviating income inequality. **Poverty programs** do this by aiding the poor. **Social insurance programs** address a second rationale: alleviating economic insecurity. The external benefits to society of poverty reduction and access to health care, especially for children, are a third rationale for the welfare state.
- The official U.S. **poverty threshold** is adjusted yearly to reflect changes in the cost of living but not in the average standard of living. But even though average income has risen significantly, the U.S. **poverty rate** is no lower than it was 50 years ago.
- The causes of poverty can include lack of education, the legacy of racial and gender discrimination, and bad luck. The consequences of poverty are dire for children.
- **Median household income** is a better indicator of typical household income than **mean household income.** A comparison across countries shows that the United States has less income inequality than poor countries but has more than all other rich countries.

Check Your Understanding 40-1

1. Indicate whether each of the following programs is a poverty program or a social insurance program.

a. A pension guarantee program, which provides pensions for retirees if they have lost their employment-based pension due to their employer's bankruptcy

b. The federal program known as SCHIP, which provides health care for children in families that are above the poverty threshold but still have relatively low income

c. The Section 8 housing program, which provides housing subsidies for low-income households

d. The federal flood program, which provides financial help to communities hit by major floods

2. Recall that the poverty threshold is not adjusted to reflect changes in the standard of living. As a result, is the poverty threshold a relative or an absolute measure of poverty? That is, does it define poverty according to how poor someone is relative to others or according to some fixed measure that doesn't change over time? Explain.

3. The accompanying table gives the distribution of income for a very small economy of five people.

a. What is the mean income? What is the median income? Which measure is more representative of the income of the average person in the economy? Why?

b. What income range defines the first quintile? The third quintile?

	Income
Sephora	$39,000
Kelly	17,500
Raul	900,000
Vijay	15,000
Oskar	28,000

Solutions appear at back of book.

40.2 The U.S. Welfare State

In 2019, the U.S. welfare state consisted of three huge programs (Social Security, Medicare, and Medicaid); several other fairly big programs, including the Affordable Care Act, Temporary Assistance for Needy Families, food stamps, and the Earned Income Tax Credit; and a number of smaller programs. Table 40-2 shows one useful way to categorize the programs existing in 2019, along with spending on each listed program.

A **means-tested** program is a program available only to individuals or families whose incomes fall below a certain level.

First, the table distinguishes between programs that are **means-tested** and those that are not. In means-tested programs, benefits are available only to families or individuals whose income or wealth falls below some minimum. Basically, means-tested programs are poverty programs designed to help only those with

TABLE 40-2 Major U.S. Welfare State Programs, 2019

	Monetary transfers	In-kind
Means-tested	Temporary Assistance for Needy Families: $20.7 billion Supplemental Security Income: $53.0 billion Earned Income Tax Credit: $60.6 billion	Food stamps: $71.2 billion Medicaid: $418.7 billion Affordable Care Act: $48.9 billion
Not means-tested	Social Security: $1,041.2 billion Unemployment insurance: $26.8 billion	Medicare: $644.9 billion

Data from: Office of Management and Budget and Congressional Budget Office; all data are the projected amount for 2019.

An **in-kind benefit** is a benefit given in the form of goods or services.

A **negative income tax** is a program that supplements the income of low-income working families.

low incomes. By contrast, non-means-tested programs provide their benefits to everyone, although, as we'll see, they tend in practice to reduce income inequality.

Second, the table distinguishes between programs that provide monetary transfers that beneficiaries can spend as they choose and those that provide **in-kind benefits,** which are given in the form of goods or services rather than money. As the numbers suggest, in-kind benefits are dominated by Medicare and Medicaid, which pay for health care. We'll discuss health care in the next section of this module. For now, let's examine the other major programs.

Finally, economists use the term **negative income tax** to describe a program that supplements the earnings of low-income working families. The United States has a program known as the Earned Income Tax Credit (EITC), which provides additional income to millions of workers. It has become more generous as traditional welfare has become less generous. Only workers who earn income are eligible for the EITC. Over a certain range of incomes, the more a worker earns, the higher the amount of EITC received. That is, the EITC acts as a negative income tax for low-wage workers. In 2019, married couples with two children would receive a tax credit equal to 40% of their income up to $14,550. For 2019, the EITC was capped at $5,828. (Payments were slightly lower for single-parent families or workers without children.) The EITC starts to phase out at incomes over $24,800. As of 2019, the payment ceased at an income of $52,483 for married couples with two children.

Social Security and Unemployment Insurance

Social Security, the largest program in the U.S. welfare state, is a non-means-tested program that guarantees retirement income to qualifying older Americans. It also provides benefits to workers who become disabled and "survivor benefits" to family members of workers who die.

Social Security is supported by a dedicated tax on wages: the Social Security portion of the payroll tax pays for Social Security benefits. The benefits workers receive on retirement depend on their taxable earnings during their working years: the more you earn up to the maximum amount subject to Social Security taxes ($132,900 in 2019), the more you receive in retirement. Benefits are not, however, strictly proportional to earnings. Instead, they're determined by a formula that gives high earners more than low earners, but with a sliding scale, that makes the program relatively more generous for low earners.

UniversalImagesGroup/Getty Images

President Franklin D. Roosevelt signed the Social Security Act in 1935, creating the modern welfare state.

Because most seniors don't receive pensions from their former employers and most don't own enough assets to provide them with a living, Social Security benefits are an enormously important source of income for them. At least 50% of married couples and 70% of unmarried persons 65 and older rely on Social

Security for more than half their income. Social Security accounts for at least 90% of income for 21% of married couples and 45% of unmarried persons over 60. In most cases, these people have no income at all except for Social Security.

Unemployment insurance, although normally a much smaller amount of government transfers than Social Security, is another key social insurance program. It provides workers who lose their jobs with about 35% of their previous salary until they find a new job or until 26 weeks have passed. Like Social Security, unemployment insurance is not means-tested.

The Effects of the Welfare State on Poverty and Inequality

The U.S. welfare state redistributes income from those with higher incomes and wealth to those with less. Government statistics show that this redistribution significantly reduces the U.S. poverty rate. However, statistics show only the direct effect of taxes and transfers, not the indirect effect, such as changes in behavior. For example, we know that many older Americans who are now retired would instead be working if they didn't receive Social Security checks. Yet, the statistics can't capture this effect. As a result, statistics reveal only a partial indicator of the effects of the welfare state. Nonetheless, the results are striking.

Table 40-3 shows how a number of government programs affected the poverty rate, as measured by the Supplemental Poverty Measure, for the population as a whole and for different age groups in 2012 (the most current data available). For each program it shows the amount, in percentage points, by which that group's poverty rate was reduced by the program. For example, it says that without Social Security, the poverty rate among older Americans would have been almost 40 percentage points higher than it was.

Table 40-4 shows a Congressional Budget Office estimate of the effect of taxes and transfers on the share of aggregate income going to each quintile of the income distribution in 2016 (the latest available data). The effect of government programs was to increase the share of income going to the poorest 80% of the population, especially the share going to the poorest 20%, while reducing the share of income going to the richest 20%.

In early 2021, the U.S. government enacted a new piece of legislation, the American Rescue Plan, that provided major new benefits to many families. Many of these benefits were designed to be temporary, a response to the economic slump caused by the coronavirus pandemic. However, although the bill's provisions will expire within two years unless extended, its framers hoped that some of the benefits will be made permanent.

TABLE 40-3 Effects of Government Programs on Reducing the Rate of Poverty, 2012

	All People	Children	Nonelderly adults	65 years and older
Social Security	8.56%	1.97%	4.08%	39.86%
Refundable Tax Credits	3.02	6.66	2.25	0.20
SNAP (Food Stamps)	1.62	3.01	1.27	0.76
Unemployment Insurance	0.79	0.82	0.88	0.31
Supplemental Security Income	1.07	0.84	1.12	1.21
Housing Subsidies	0.91	1.39	0.66	1.12
School Lunches	0.38	0.91	0.25	0.03
Temporary Assistance for Needy Families	0.21	0.46	0.14	0.05
WIC (supplemental nutrition program for women, infants, and children)	0.13	0.29	0.09	0.00

Data from: Council of Economic Advisers.

TABLE 40-4 Effects of Taxes and Transfers on Income Distribution, 2016

Quintiles	Share of aggregate income without taxes and transfers	Share of aggregate income with taxes and transfers
Bottom quintile	3.8%	7.7%
Second quintile	8.9	11.1
Third quintile	13.6	14.7
Fourth quintile	20.5	20.3
81st–99th percentiles	38.5	35.1
Top 1%	15.8	12.5

Data from: Congressional Budget Office.

The most important of these benefits is a new program giving every family with less than $75,000 in income a cash grant of $3,600 a year for each child under 6 and $3,000 for each child between 6 and 17. This will have large effects. Independent estimates suggest that the new benefit will cut child poverty in half.

Check Your Understanding 40-2

1. Explain how the negative income tax avoids the disincentive to work that characterizes poverty programs that simply give benefits based on low income.
2. According to Table 40-3, what effect does the U.S. welfare state have on the overall poverty rate? On the poverty rate for those aged 65 and over?

Solutions appear at back of book.

>> Quick Review

- **Means-tested** programs are designed to reduce poverty, but non-means-tested programs do so as well. Programs are classified according to whether they provide monetary or **in-kind benefits.**
- The **negative income tax** addresses these concerns: it supplements the incomes of only low-income working families.
- Social Security, the largest program in the U.S. welfare state, is a non-means-tested program that provides retirement income for the elderly. Unemployment insurance is also a key social insurance program that is not means-tested.
- Overall, the American welfare state is redistributive. It increases the share of income going to the poorest 80% while reducing the share going to the richest 20%.

40.3 Health Care and the Welfare State

A large part of the welfare state, in both the United States and other wealthy countries, is devoted to paying for health care. In most wealthy countries, the government pays between 70% and 80% of all medical costs. The private sector plays a larger role in the U.S. health care system. Yet even in the United States, the government pays roughly half of all health care costs; furthermore, it indirectly subsidizes private health insurance through the federal tax code.

Figure 40-3 shows who paid for U.S. health care in 2018. Only 12% of health care consumption spending (all spending on health care except investment in health care buildings and facilities) was expenses "out of pocket"—that is, paid directly by individuals. Most health care spending, 88%, was paid for by some kind of insurance. Of this 88%, considerably less than half was private insurance; the rest was some kind of government insurance, mainly Medicare and Medicaid. To understand why, we need to examine the special economics of health insurance.

FIGURE 40-3 Who Paid for U.S. Health Care in 2018?

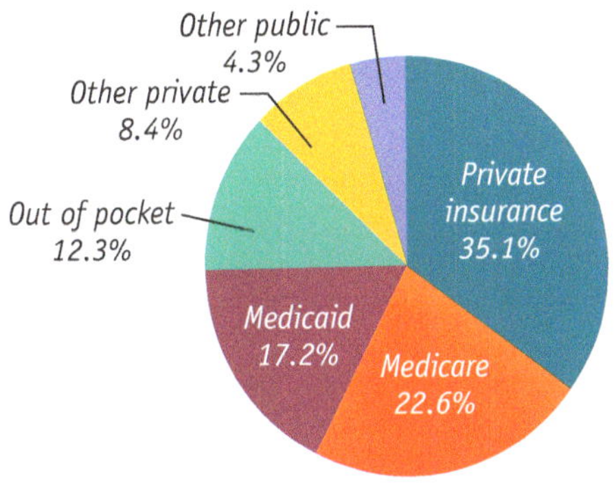

In the United States in 2018, insurance paid for 88% of health care consumption costs: the sum of 35.1% (private insurance), 22.6% (Medicare), 17.2% (Medicaid), 8.4% (other private), and 4.3% (other public). The percentage paid for by private insurance, 35.1%, was a uniquely high number among advanced countries. Even so, substantially more U.S. health care was paid for by Medicare, Medicaid, and other government programs than by other means. (Total may not add up to 100 due to rounding.)

Data from: Department of Health and Human Services Centers for Medicare and Medicaid Services.

The Economics of Health Insurance

In 2018, U.S. personal health care expenses were $11,121 per person—17.8% of gross domestic product. This did not, however, mean that the typical American spent $10,000 on medical treatment. In fact, in any given year, half the population incurs only

Under **private health insurance,** each member of a large pool of individuals pays a fixed amount annually to a private company that agrees to pay most of the medical expenses of the pool's members.

minor medical expenses. But a small percentage of the population faces huge medical bills, with 10% of the population typically accounting for almost two-thirds of medical costs.

Is it possible to predict who will have high medical costs? To a limited extent, yes: there are broad patterns to illness. For example, the elderly are more likely to need expensive surgery or drugs than the young. But the fact is that anyone can suddenly need very expensive medical treatment, costing many thousands of dollars in a very short time—far beyond what most families can easily afford. Yet nobody wants to be unable to afford such treatment if it becomes necessary. As a result, most people would like to be covered by *health insurance*—insurance that covers the costs of medical bills.

The Problem with Private Health Insurance Under **private health insurance,** each member of a large pool of individuals agrees to pay a fixed amount annually (called a *premium*) into a common fund that is managed by a private company, which then pays most of the medical expenses of the pool's members. The problem with private health insurance is that it is subject to market failure. Let's examine why.

People typically don't want to purchase health insurance until they are already sick, to avoid paying premiums when they are healthy. But as a result, the average person who purchases a private health insurance policy is sicker and has higher medical expenses than the average person who does not. Premiums have to be raised to account for the higher medical expenses, which in turn leads more of the relatively healthy insured people to stop buying insurance and leave the pool. Without some type of intervention, this dynamic continues for more rounds until only extremely sick people are left in the pool. In some cases, this means that the private insurance company collapses, unable to charge high enough premiums to cover its medical cost outlays. Economists call this phenomenon the *private health insurance market death spiral.*

Private health insurers employ several methods to counteract the death spiral: refusing insurance to anyone who had any sign of a preexisting medical condition, dropping those who did develop an illness while insured, and refusing to cover some procedures such as delivering a baby. As a result, private health insurance markets have left a significant number of people uninsured—particularly those with preexisting conditions, who need it most.

So how *do* people get health insurance when private insurance markets perform so poorly? There are three principal ways: employment-based health insurance, government health insurance, and government intervention in the market through the Affordable Care Act.

Employment-Based Health Insurance Private insurers can avoid the death spiral by selling insurance indirectly to peoples' employers rather than to individuals. The advantage of *employment-based health insurance* is that employees are likely to contain a representative mix of healthy and less healthy people rather than a group of people who want insurance because they expect to incur high medical bills. This is especially true if the employer is a large company with thousands of workers. Employers require their employees to participate in the company health insurance plan because allowing employees to opt out (which healthier ones will be tempted to do) raises the cost of providing insurance for everyone else.

There's another reason employment-based insurance is widespread in the United States: it gets special, favorable tax treatment. Workers pay taxes on their paychecks, but workers who receive health insurance from their employers don't pay taxes on the value of the benefit. So, employment-based health insurance is, in effect, subsidized by the U.S. tax system.

However, many working Americans don't receive employment-based health insurance. Those who aren't covered include mostly older Americans, because relatively few employers offer workers insurance that continues after they retire, the many workers whose employers don't offer coverage (especially part-time workers), and the unemployed.

Government Health Insurance

Table 40-5 shows the breakdown of health insurance coverage across the U.S. population in 2018. A majority of Americans, 178 million people, received health insurance through their employers. The majority of those who didn't have private insurance were covered by two government programs, Medicare and Medicaid. (The numbers don't add up because some people have more than one form of coverage. For example, many recipients of Medicare also have supplemental coverage through either Medicaid or private policies.)

TABLE 40-5 Number of Americans Covered by Health Insurance, 2018 (millions)

Covered by private health insurance	**217.8**
Employment-based	178.4
Direct purchase	34.9
Covered by government	**111.3**
Medicaid	57.7
Medicare	57.8
Military health care	11.4
Uninsured/not covered	**27.5**

Data from: U.S. Census Bureau.

Medicare, financed by payroll taxes, is available to all Americans 65 and older, regardless of their income and wealth. You can get an idea of how much difference Medicare makes to the finances of elderly Americans by comparing the median income per person of Americans 65 and older—$43,696—with average annual Medicare payments per recipient, which were more than $13,000 in 2018. As with health care spending in general, however, the average can be misleading: in a given year, about 7% of Medicare recipients account for 50% of the costs.

Unlike Medicare, Medicaid is a means-tested program, paid for with federal and state government revenues. There's no simple way to summarize the criteria for eligibility because Medicaid is partly paid for by state governments and each state sets its own rules. Of the nearly 57.7 million Americans covered by Medicaid in 2018, 35 million were children under 18 and many of the rest were parents of children under 18. Most of the cost of Medicaid, however, is accounted for by a small number of older Americans, especially those needing long-term care.

More than 11.4 million Americans receive health insurance as a consequence of military service. Unlike Medicare and Medicaid, which pay medical bills but don't deliver health care directly, the Veterans Health Administration, which has more than 9 million clients, runs hospitals and clinics around the country.

Frank Cotham The New Yorker Collection/The Cartoon Bank

"For me, crime pays for what Medicare doesn't cover."

The Affordable Care Act

In 2010, Congress passed the Affordable Care Act (ACA), which went fully into effect in 2014. At the time, the U.S. health care system was clearly in trouble. One source of the trouble was the rapid growth in the uninsured. The percentage of working-age Americans without health insurance grew from 1997 to 2010, peaking with almost a quarter of working-age Americans uninsured. Most of the uninsured were low-wage workers, employed at jobs that lacked health insurance benefits, and unable to afford private insurance on their own.

Meanwhile, health care spending was rising rapidly, leading to sharply higher insurance premiums. In fact, health care spending has tripled as a share of U.S. income since 1965. The source of this higher spending is medical progress: as medical science progresses, more illnesses are treatable but at greater cost.

The ACA was the largest expansion of the American welfare state since the creation of Medicare and Medicaid in 1965. It had two major objectives: covering the uninsured and controlling costs. Let's look at each in turn.

1. Covering the Uninsured The ACA moved to cover the uninsured in two ways. First, it expanded eligibility for Medicaid, covering most of the expense for states that were willing to expand Medicaid to cover everyone up to 133% of the poverty line. (As of 2019, 37 states including the District of Columbia had expanded Medicaid.)

Second, the ACA moved to make private insurance available to more Americans. On one side, insurance companies were prohibited from denying insurance or charging higher premiums to people with preexisting medical conditions. On the other, many lower- and middle-income households were given subsidies to make insurance more affordable.

2. Cost Control Before the ACA, private insurers had high operating costs due to the amounts they spent on marketing and weeding out high-cost applicants. But because the ACA eliminated insurers' ability to spend resources on weeding out applicants, it has the potential to increase efficiency.

The ACA contained a number of additional measures, many of them involving Medicare, intended to help control health care costs. Health care providers were encouraged to band together to form "accountable care organizations," coordinating care in ways that save money; organizations that did so would receive a share of the savings. Hospitals were encouraged to provide effective care by rules that reduced payments to hospitals whose patients tend to be readmitted at high rates. Special taxes on "Cadillac" health insurance—extremely generous plans—aimed to discourage excessive treatment. And the ACA eliminated copayments for preventive care, in the hope that patients would be encouraged to take care of medical issues before they required expensive treatment.

As it turns out, the rate at which health costs were rising slowed sharply around 2010, just as the ACA was passed. It's unclear how much of this cost slowdown was caused by the law's provisions.

Effects of the ACA

Although the ACA was passed in 2010, its most important provisions didn't take effect until the beginning of 2014. By 2017, however, its main effects were clear.

FIGURE 40-4 Uninsured Working-Age Americans, 1997–2018

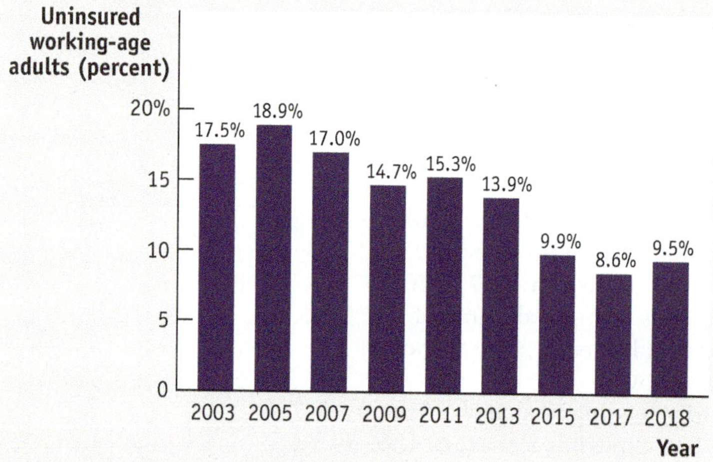

Before the ACA was implemented, the share of uninsured working-age adults was rising dramatically. Since the ACA's implementation, that share has fallen sharply.

Data from: U.S. Census.

The first effect can be seen in Figure 40-4, which shows the uninsured percentage of the working-age population. This percentage began dropping after 2010, partly because of a recovering economy but also because some provisions of the ACA went into effect, notably a rule allowing Americans under the age of 26 to remain on their parents' policies. And after 2013, with the law in full effect, the number of uninsured fell sharply. By 2017, the percent of working-age adults without health insurance had been cut almost in half.

Yet a sizable number of people remain uninsured. The law does not cover undocumented immigrants, and a significant number of states have chosen not to accept the federally funded expansion of Medicaid, leaving several million people in a *gap* where they receive neither Medicaid nor subsidies to buy private insurance. So progress toward covering the uninsured has been substantial but incomplete.

Furthermore, in 2017, Republicans in Congress succeeded in repealing one important provision in the ACA, the requirement that all legal residents have insurance, although the rest of the law remained intact. This change is generally believed to have driven up premiums, because fewer healthy people signed up, although many beneficiaries were insulated from this premium increase, thanks to the subsidies mandated by the law. Some states, like New Jersey, imposed their own requirements that residents have coverage and saw premiums drop noticeably. But in states that didn't do this, the move probably led to a significant fall in the number of insured Americans, seen in the slight uptick for uninsured rates in 2018.

ECONOMICS >> *in Action*

Long-Term Trends in Income Inequality in the United States

Does inequality tend to rise, fall, or stay the same over time? The answer is yes—all three. Over the course of the past century, the United States has gone through periods characterized by all three trends: an era of falling inequality during the 1930s and 1940s, an era of stable inequality for about 35 years after World War II, and an era of rising inequality over the past 40 years.

Detailed U.S. data on income by quintiles, as shown in Table 40-1, are available starting from 1947. Panel (a) of Figure 40-5 shows the annual rate of growth of income, adjusted for inflation, for each quintile over two periods: from 1947 to 1980 and from 1980 to 2018. There's a clear difference between the two periods. In the first period, income within each group grew at about the same rate—that is, there wasn't much change in the inequality of income, just growing incomes across the board.

After 1980, however, incomes grew much more quickly at the top than in the middle and more quickly in the middle than at the bottom. So inequality has increased substantially since 1980. Overall, inflation-adjusted income for families in the top quintile rose 83% between 1980 and 2018 while actually falling slightly for families in the bottom quintile.

Although detailed data on income distribution aren't available before 1947, economists have used other information, such as income tax data, to estimate the share of income going to the top 10% of the population all the way back to 1917. Panel (b) of Figure 40-5 shows this measure from 1917 to 2018. These data, like the more detailed data available since 1947, show that American inequality was more or less stable between 1947 and the late 1970s but has risen substantially since.

As we've already seen, inequality has increased substantially since the 1970s. In fact, pre-tax income appears to be as unequally distributed in America today as it was in the

FIGURE 40-5 Trends in U.S. Income Inequality

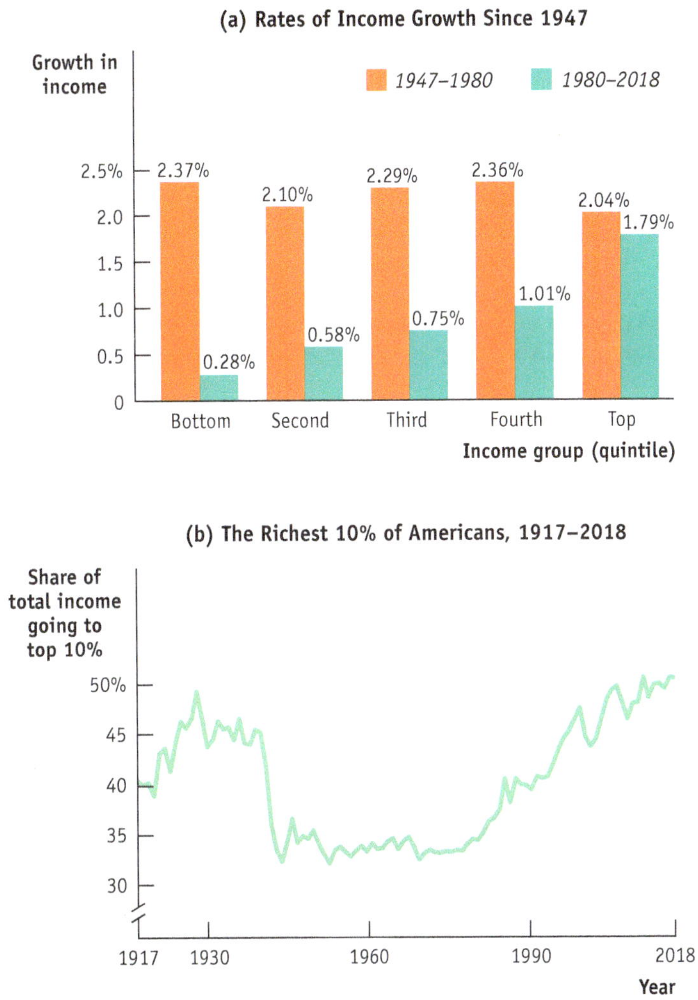

Data from: U.S. Census Bureau [panel (a)]. Emmanuel Saez, "Striking It Richer: The Evolution of Top Incomes in the United States." University of California, Berkeley, discussion paper, 2008 (updated 2019) [panel (b)].

1920s, prompting many commentators to describe the current state of the nation as a new Gilded Age—albeit one in which the effects of inequality are moderated by taxes and the existence of the welfare state.

There is intense debate among economists about the causes of this widening inequality. The most popular explanation is rapid technological change, which has increased the demand for highly skilled or talented workers more rapidly than the demand for other workers, leading to a rise in the wage gap between the highly skilled and other workers. Growing international trade may also have contributed by allowing the United States to import labor-intensive products from low-wage countries rather than making them domestically, reducing the demand for less-skilled American workers and depressing their wages. Rising immigration may be yet another source. On average, immigrants have lower education levels than native-born workers and increase the supply of low-skilled labor while depressing low-skilled wages.

However, these explanations fail to account for one key feature: much of the rise in inequality doesn't reflect a rising gap between highly educated workers and those with less education but rather growing differences among highly educated workers themselves. For example, schoolteachers and top business executives have similarly high levels of education, but executive paychecks have risen dramatically and teachers' salaries have not. For some reason, a few superstars—a group that includes literal superstars in the entertainment world but also such groups as Wall Street traders and top corporate executives—now earn much higher incomes than was the case a generation ago. It's still unclear what caused the change.

>> *Quick Review*

- Health insurance satisfies an important need because expensive medical treatment is unaffordable for most families. **Private health insurance** has an inherent problem: those who buy insurance are disproportionately sicker than the average person, which drives up costs and premiums, leading healthier people to forgo insurance, further driving up costs and premiums and ultimately leading private insurance companies to fail.
- The majority of Americans not covered by private insurance are covered by Medicare, which is a non-means-tested single-payer system for those over 65, and Medicaid, which is means-tested.
- Health care costs everywhere are increasing rapidly due to medical progress. The 2010 ACA legislation was designed to address the large and growing share of uninsured Americans, to reduce inefficiency in the health care insurance market, and to exercise cost control in health care spending.

Check Your Understanding 40-3

1. If you are enrolled in a four-year degree program, it is likely that you are required to enroll in a health insurance program run by your school unless you can show proof of existing insurance coverage.

- **a.** Explain how you and your parents benefit from this health insurance program even though, given your age, it is unlikely that you will need expensive medical treatment.
- **b.** Explain how your school's health insurance program avoids the problem of the adverse selection death spiral faced by private insurance.

2. According to its critics, what accounts for the higher costs of the U.S. health care system compared to those of other wealthy countries?

Solutions appear at back of book.

BUSINESS CASE Walmart Revolutionizes Its Labor Practices

AP Images/David J. Phillip

With 2.2 million employees in 2019—roughly 1.5% of the country's working population—Walmart is America's largest private employer. The big-box retail chain is so large that Walmart's employee policies are considered a barometer of the current state of the labor market for retail workers.

Yet in the 1990s and early to mid-2000s, Walmart was considered a notoriously bad place to work. It was known for failing to provide workers with consistent schedules, for offering few benefits, and for paying wages so low that some employees qualified for food stamps and other antipoverty programs. During this period, Walmart was hit with several lawsuits alleging overtime violations, sexual harassment by managers, and gender discrimination.

Not only were Walmart employees unsatisfied—customers were too. They complained of dirty bathrooms, empty shelves, endless checkout lines, and impossible-to-find sales help. "Walmart's relentless focus on costs does seem to have taken some toll on in-store conditions and stock levels," an analyst explained, adding, "If an item is not on the shelf, then you cannot sell it." As of 2015, only 16% of Walmart stores were meeting the company's own customer service goals.

But in 2015, Walmart suddenly began to overhaul its labor practices. At first the changes were fairly modest: higher wages and more consistent work scheduling. By 2016, Walmart's average pay for a nonmanagerial full-time worker was $13.69 per hour, up 16% from 2014 (but still below Costco's hourly rate of nearly $20 per hour).

The changes produced clear results. Customer feedback improved markedly: by 2016, 75% of Walmart stores were hitting their customer service targets. Walmart sales, which had been sliding relative to those of competitors, rose.

The changes didn't stop there. In 2018, in the midst of a strong economy, the company raised starting pay, introduced a year-end bonus to employees, and added 10 weeks of fully paid maternity leave for full-time employees. As one market observer said, "Those are 'sticky benefits'—the kind that might keep you from leaving Walmart just to earn 50 cents or $1 an hour more, or might woo you to Walmart in the first place."

At the same time, in order to counter the threat from rival retailer Amazon, Walmart has been investing more in worker training while investing heavily in its own e-commerce capabilities. Now customers can "click and collect" in their local Walmart store. When an item isn't on the shelf, customers can order it online. If necessary, a Walmart sales associate will walk a customer through that process. The company has created "Walmart Academies," located in the back of stores, where associates can expand their skills by learning about management responsibilities and mobile shopping apps.

Yes, indeed, a revolution is under way in Aisle 6.

QUESTIONS FOR THOUGHT

1. Use the marginal productivity theory of income distribution to explain how companies like Walmart can pay workers so little that they fall below the poverty line.
2. Use the case to explain how similar workers in the same labor market can end up being paid different wages in equilibrium. Also explain why Walmart believed it could improve its profitability by raising its labor costs.
3. Some politicians want to encourage more companies to adopt a high-wage strategy. What are the possible positive and negative effects of such a policy?
4. When an employer introduces "sticky benefits," such as generous child-care benefits, what does that imply about the costs of worker turnover to the employer?
5. What factors do you think compelled Walmart to change its labor practices? Be specific.

REVIEW

MODULE 37

1. Just as there are markets for goods and services, there are markets for factors of production, including labor, land, and both **physical capital** and **human capital.** These markets determine the **factor distribution of income.**

2. According to the **price-taking producer's optimal employment rule,** a price-taking producer's profit is maximized by employing each factor of production up to the level at which its **value of the marginal product** is equal to the factor's price. The value of the marginal product of a factor is equal to its marginal product multiplied by the price of the output it produces. The **value of the marginal product curve** is therefore the individual price-taking producer's demand curve for a factor.

3. The market demand curve for labor is the horizontal sum of the individual demand curves of producers in that market. It shifts for three main reasons: changes in output price, changes in the supply of other factors, and technological changes.

MODULE 38

1. When a competitive labor market is in equilibrium, the market wage is equal to the **equilibrium value of the marginal product** of labor, the additional value produced by the last worker hired in the labor market as a whole. This insight leads to the **marginal productivity theory of income distribution,** according to which each factor is paid the value of the marginal product of the last unit of that factor employed in the factor market as a whole.

2. The marginal productivity theory of income distribution assumes that factor markets and goods markets are perfectly competitive, so it serves as a benchmark rather than an accurate representation of reality. However, it does explain most but not all of the observed income distribution in the economy. Most wage disparities can be explained by factors that are consistent with marginal productivity theory: **compensating differentials,** and differences in ability, human capital, and job tenure.

3. Economists believe that market power, discrimination, and efficiency wages account for most wage disparities not explained by marginal productivity theory. Market power can be exercised by workers, in the form of **unions,** and it can be exercised by employers that are large playersin the labor market. Unions raise wages and improve working conditions; market power exercised by employers lowers wages and employment. Free markets tend to diminish discrimination, but discrimination remains a real source of wage disparity, especially through its effects on human capital acquisition. Discrimination is typically maintained either through problems in labor markets or (historically) through institutionalization in government policies.

4. According to the **efficiency-wage model,** employers will pay above-equilibrium wages to elicit better performance from workers when workers' performance is hard to observe. Efficiency wages also reduce worker turnover. Because both unions and efficiency wages result in wages above the equilibrium level, they will lead to an excess supply of workers in the labor market.

MODULE 39

1. Labor supply is the result of decisions about **time allocation,** where each worker faces a trade-off between **leisure** and work. An increase in the hourly wage rate tends to increase work hours via the substitution effect but to reduce work hours via the income effect. If the net result is that a worker increases the quantity of labor supplied in response to a higher wage, the **individual labor supply curve** slopes upward. If the net result is that a worker reduces work hours, the individual labor supply curve—unlike supply curves for goods and services—slopes downward.

2. The market labor supply curve is the horizontal sum of the individual labor supply curves of all workers in that market. It shifts for four main reasons: changes in preferences and social norms, changes in population, changes in opportunities, and changes in wealth.

MODULE 40

1. The **welfare state** absorbs a large share of government spending in all wealthy countries. **Government transfers** are the payments made by the government to individuals and families. **Poverty programs** alleviate income inequality by helping the poor; **social insurance programs** alleviate economic insecurity. Welfare state programs also deliver external benefits to society through poverty reduction and improved access to health care, particularly for children.

2. Despite the fact that the **poverty threshold** is adjusted according to the cost of living but not according to the standard of living, and that the average American income has risen substantially over the last 30 years, the **poverty rate,** the percentage of the population with an income below the poverty threshold, is no lower than it was 30 years ago. There are various causes of poverty: lack of education, the legacy of discrimination, and bad luck. The consequences of

poverty are particularly harmful for children, resulting in more chronic disease, lower lifetime earnings, and higher rates of criminality.

3. **Median household income,** the income of a family at the center of the income distribution, is a better indicator of the income of the typical household than **mean household income** because it is not distorted by the inclusion of a small number of very wealthy households. International comparisons show that the United States has significantly higher income inequality than other advanced countries, but not as much as countries in Latin America. While some inequality is desirable, too much inequality limits opportunities and can persist across generations. High inequality can reduce a country's economic growth, as well as leading to political and economic strife.

4. Both **means-tested** and non-means-tested programs reduce poverty. The major **in-kind benefits** programs are Medicare and Medicaid, which pay for medical care. Due to concerns about the effects on incentives to work and on family cohesion, aid to poor families has become significantly less generous even as the **negative income tax** has become more generous. Social Security, the largest U.S. welfare state program, has significantly reduced poverty among the elderly. Unemployment insurance is also a key social insurance program.

5. Health insurance satisfies an important need because most families cannot afford expensive medical treatment. **Private health insurance,** unless it is employment-based or carefully screens applicants, has the potential to fall into an adverse selection death spiral. Most Americans are covered by employment-based private health insurance; the majority of the rest are covered by Medicare (a single-payer system for those 65 and over in which the government pays for most medical bills from tax revenue) or Medicaid (for those with low incomes).

6. Compared to other countries, the United States relies more heavily on private health insurance and has substantially higher health care costs per person without clearly providing better care. Health care costs are rising, largely due to advances in technology. The rising number of uninsured and the financial distress caused by lack of insurance prompted the passage in 2010 of the Affordable Care Act, or ACA. Its objective is to reduce the number of uninsured, reduce inefficiency in the health insurance market, and reduce the rate of growth of health care costs. By 2016, the percentage of uninsured among the working-age adult population had been cut in half.

KEY TERMS

Solutions to *Check Your Understanding* Questions

This section offers suggested answers to the *Check Your Understanding* questions found within modules.

MODULE 1

1-1 Check Your Understanding

1. **a.** This is an example of a command economy since King George is making the decisions about what each of his subjects should consume.

   b. This is an example of a market economy transaction: George makes his own consumption decisions and is not subject to a central authority decreeing what he will get.

   c. This is an example of a market economy transaction: without Hillary's direction the market economy produces those goods and services that she demands.

2. Market failure occurs when the benefit from an activity is not equal to the cost of that activity. In this case it must be that the benefit that Ruth gets from driving to work is less than the cost incurred by society from her driving and contributing to traffic congestion.

3. **a.** This is a scenario of an economic recession: when unemployment rises this implies that less labor is being hired and therefore the level of production in the economy is falling. This is a recession.

   b. An economic boom occurs when the unemployment rate falls to unusually low levels.

   c. This is a description of economic growth.

1-2 Check Your Understanding

1. **a.** This illustrates the concept of opportunity cost. Given that a person can only eat so much at one sitting, having a slice of chocolate cake requires that you forgo eating something else, such as a slice of coconut cream pie.

   b. This illustrates the concept that resources are scarce. Even if there were more resources in the world, the total amount of those resources would be limited. As a result, scarcity would still arise. For there to be no scarcity, there would have to be unlimited amounts of everything (including unlimited time in a human life), which is clearly impossible.

   c. This illustrates the concept that people usually exploit opportunities to make themselves better off. Students will seek to make themselves better off by signing up for the tutorials of teaching assistants with good reputations and avoiding those teaching assistants with poor reputations. It also illustrates the concept that resources are scarce. If there were unlimited spaces in tutorials with good teaching assistants, they would not fill up.

   d. This illustrates the concept of marginal analysis. Your decision about allocating your time is a "how much" decision: how much time spent exercising versus how much time spent studying. You make your decision by comparing the benefit of an additional hour of exercising to its cost, the effect on your grades of one fewer hour spent studying.

2. **a.** Yes. The increased time spent commuting is a cost you will incur if you accept the new job. That additional time spent commuting—or equivalently, the benefit you would get from spending that time doing something else—is an opportunity cost of the new job.

   b. Yes. One of the benefits of the new job is that you will be making $50,000. But if you take the new job, you will have to give up your current job; that is, you have to give up your current salary of $45,000. So $45,000 is one of the opportunity costs of taking the new job.

   c. No. A more spacious office is an additional benefit of your new job and does not involve forgoing something else. So it is not an opportunity cost.

1-3 Check Your Understanding

1. **a.** This illustrates the concept that markets usually lead to efficiency. Any seller who wants to sell a book for at least $30 does indeed sell to someone who is willing to buy a book for $30. As a result, there is no way to change how used textbooks are distributed among buyers and sellers in a way that would make one person better off without making someone else worse off.

   b. This illustrates the concept that there are gains from trade. Students trade tutoring services based on their different abilities in academic subjects.

   c. This illustrates the concept that when markets don't achieve efficiency, government intervention can improve society's welfare. In this case the market, left alone, will permit bars and nightclubs to impose costs on their neighbors in the form of loud music, costs that the bars and nightclubs have no incentive to take into account. This is an inefficient outcome because society as a whole can be made better off if bars and nightclubs are induced to reduce their noise.

   d. This illustrates the concept that resources should be used as efficiently as possible to achieve society's goals. By closing neighborhood clinics and shifting funds to the main hospital, better health care can be provided at a lower cost.

   e. This illustrates the concept that markets move toward equilibrium. Here, because books with the same amount of wear and tear sell for about the same price, no buyer or seller can be made better off by engaging in a different trade than they undertook. This means that the market for used textbooks has moved to an equilibrium.

2. **a.** This does not describe an equilibrium situation. Many students should want to change their behavior and switch to eating at the restaurants. Therefore, the situation described is not an equilibrium. An equilibrium will be established when students are equally as well off eating at the restaurants as eating at the dining

hall—which would happen if, say, prices at the dining hall were higher than at the restaurants.

b. This does describe an equilibrium situation. By changing your behavior and riding the bus, you would not be made better off. Therefore, you have no incentive to change your behavior.

1-4 Check Your Understanding

1. a. This illustrates the principle that increases in the economy's potential lead to economic growth over time. Cheaper solar panels will lower the cost of energy, increasing the economy's potential and economic growth. Solar panel manufacturers will be better off but firms producing competing energy will be worse off.

b. This illustrates the principle that overall spending sometimes gets out of line with the economy's productive capacity; when it does, government policy can change spending. The tax cut would increase people's after-tax incomes, leading to higher consumer spending.

c. This illustrates the principle that one person's spending is another person's income. As oil companies decrease their spending on labor by laying off workers and paying remaining workers lower wage, those workers' incomes fall. In turn, those workers decrease their consumer spending, causing restaurants and other businesses to lose income.

MODULE 2

2-1 Check Your Understanding

1. a. False. An increase in the resources available to Boeing for use in producing Dreamliners and small jets changes the production possibility frontier (PPF) by shifting it outward. This is because Boeing can now produce more small jets and Dreamliners than before. In the accompanying figure, the line labeled "Boeing's original *PPF*" represents Boeing's original production possibility frontier, and the line labeled "Boeing's new *PPF*" represents the new production possibility frontier that results from an increase in resources available to Boeing.

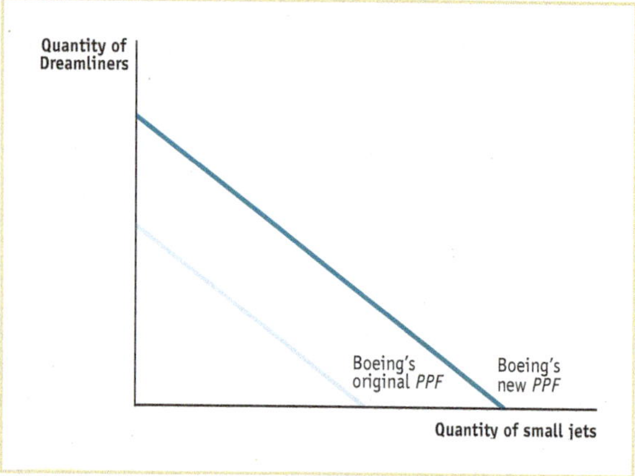

b. True. A technological change that allows Boeing to build more small jets for any amount of Dreamliners built results in a change in its production possibility frontier (PPF). This is illustrated in the accompanying figure: the new production possibility frontier is represented by the line labeled "Boeing's new *PPF*," and the original production frontier is represented by the line labeled "Boeing's original *PPF*." Since the maximum quantity of Dreamliners that Boeing can build is the same as before, the new production possibility frontier intersects the vertical axis at the same point as the original frontier. But since the maximum possible quantity of small jets is now greater than before, the new frontier intersects the horizontal axis to the right of the original frontier.

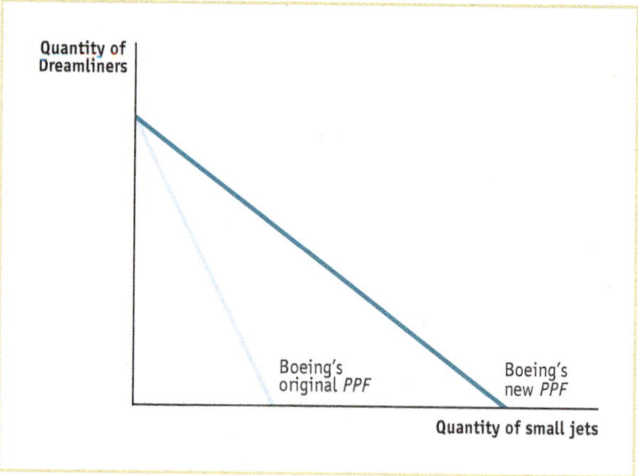

c. False. The production possibility frontier illustrates how much of one good an economy must give up to get more of another good only when resources are used efficiently in production. If an economy is producing inefficiently—that is, inside the frontier—then it does not have to give up a unit of one good to get another unit of the other good. Instead, by becoming more efficient in production, this economy can have more of both goods.

MODULE 3

3-1 Check Your Understanding

1. a. The United States has an absolute advantage in automobile production because it takes fewer Americans (6) to produce a car in one day than Italians (8). The United States also has an absolute advantage in washing machine production because it takes fewer Americans (2) to produce a washing machine in one day than Italians (3).

b. In Italy the opportunity cost of a washing machine in terms of an automobile is $\frac{3}{8}$: $\frac{3}{8}$ of a car can be produced with the same number of workers and in the same time it takes to produce 1 washing machine. In the United States the opportunity cost of a washing machine in terms of an automobile is $\frac{2}{6} = \frac{1}{3}$: $\frac{1}{3}$ of a car can be produced with the same number of workers and in the same time it takes to produce 1 washing machine. Since $\frac{1}{3} < \frac{3}{8}$, the United States has a comparative advantage in the production of washing machines: to produce a washing machine, only $\frac{1}{3}$ of a car must be given up in the United States but $\frac{3}{8}$ of a car must be given up in Italy. This means that Italy has a comparative advantage in automobiles. This can be checked as follows. The opportunity cost of an automobile in terms of a washing machine in Italy is $\frac{8}{3}$, equal to $2\frac{2}{3}$: $2\frac{2}{3}$ washing machines can be produced with the same number of workers and in the time it takes to produce 1 car in Italy. And the opportunity cost of an automobile in terms of a washing machine in the United States is $2\frac{2}{3}:2\frac{2}{3}$, equal to 3: 3 washing machines can be produced with the same number of workers and in the time it takes to produce 1 car in the United States. Since $2\frac{2}{3} < 3$, Italy has a comparative advantage in producing automobiles.

c. The greatest gains are realized when each country specializes in producing the good for which it has a comparative advantage. Therefore, the United States should specialize in washing machines and Italy should specialize in automobiles.

2. At a trade of 10 U.S. large jets for 15 Brazilian small jets, Brazil gives up less for a large jet than it would if it were building large jets itself. Without trade, Brazil gives up 3 small jets for each large jet it produces. With trade, Brazil gives up only 1.5 small jets for each large jet from the United States. Likewise, the United States gives up less for a small jet than it would if it were producing small jets itself. Without trade, the United States gives up $\frac{3}{4}$ of a large jet for each small jet. With trade, the United States gives up only $\frac{2}{3}$ of a large jet for each small jet from Brazil.

MODULE 4

4-1 Check Your Understanding

1. An increase in the amount of money spent by households results in an increase in the flow of goods to households. This, in turn, generates an increase in demand for factors of production by firms. So, there is an increase in the number of jobs in the economy.

4-2 Check Your Understanding

1. a. This is a normative statement because it stipulates what should be done. In addition, it may have no "right" answer. That is, should people be prevented from all dangerous personal behavior if they enjoy that behavior—like skydiving? Your answer will depend on your point of view.

b. This is a positive statement because it is a description of fact.

MODULE 5

5-1 Check Your Understanding

1. a. The quantity of umbrellas demanded is higher at any given price on a rainy day than on a dry day. This is a rightward *shift of* the demand curve, since at any given price the quantity demanded rises. This implies that any specific quantity can now be sold at a higher price.

b. The quantity of summer Caribbean cruises demanded rises in response to a price reduction. This is a *movement along* the demand curve for summer Caribbean cruises.

c. The demand for roses increases the week of Valentine's Day. This is a rightward *shift of* the demand curve.

d. The quantity of gasoline demanded falls in response to a rise in price. This is a *movement along* the demand curve.

MODULE 6

6-1 Check Your Understanding

1. a. The quantity of houses supplied rises as a result of an increase in prices. This is a *movement along* the supply curve.

b. The quantity of strawberries supplied is higher at any given price. This is a rightward *shift of* the supply curve.

c. The quantity of labor supplied is lower at any given wage. This is a leftward *shift of* the supply curve compared to the supply curve during school vacation. So, to attract workers, fast-food chains have to offer higher wages.

d. The quantity of labor supplied rises in response to a rise in wages. This is a *movement along* the supply curve.

e. The quantity of cabins supplied is higher at any given price. This is a rightward *shift of* the supply curve.

6-2 Check Your Understanding

1. a. The supply curve shifts rightward. At the original equilibrium price of the year before, the quantity of grapes supplied exceeds the quantity demanded. This is a case of surplus. The price of grapes will fall.

b. The demand curve shifts leftward. At the original equilibrium price, the quantity of hotel rooms supplied exceeds the quantity demanded. This is a case of surplus. The rates for hotel rooms will fall.

c. The demand curve for second-hand snowblowers shifts rightward. At the original equilibrium price, the quantity of second-hand snowblowers demanded exceeds the quantity supplied. This is a case of shortage. The equilibrium price of second-hand snowblowers will rise.

MODULE 7

7-1 Check Your Understanding

1. a. The market for large cars: this is a rightward shift in demand caused by a decrease in the price of a complement, gasoline. As a result of the shift, the equilibrium price of large cars will rise and the equilibrium quantity of large cars bought and sold will also rise.

b. The market for fresh paper made from recycled stock: this is a rightward shift in supply due to a technological innovation. As a result of this shift, the equilibrium price of fresh paper made from recycled stock will fall and the equilibrium quantity bought and sold will rise.

c. The market for movies at a local movie theater: this is a leftward shift in demand caused by a fall in the price of a substitute, on-demand films from the cable company. As a result of this shift, the equilibrium price of movie tickets will fall and the equilibrium number of people who go to the movies will also fall.

2. Upon the announcement of the new chip, the demand curve for computers using the earlier chip shifts leftward, as demand decreases, and the supply curve for these computers shifts rightward, as supply increases.

a. If demand decreases relatively more than supply increases, then the equilibrium quantity falls, as shown here:

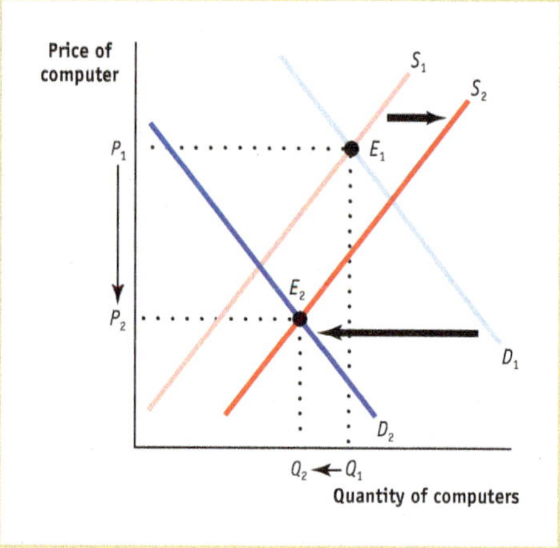

If supply increases relatively more than demand decreases, then the equilibrium quantity rises, as shown here:

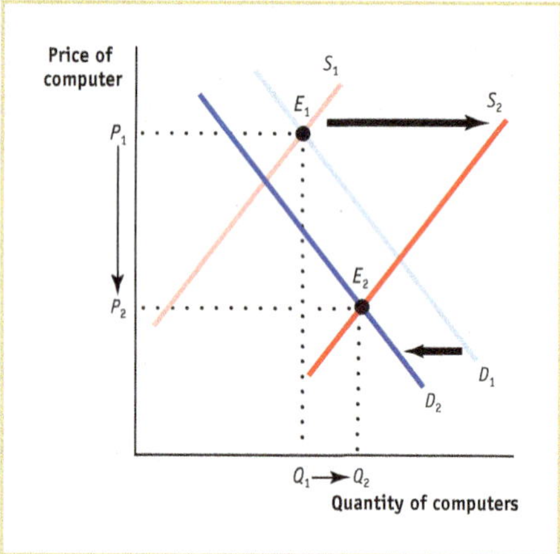

b. In both cases, the equilibrium price falls.

3. a. The increased price of labor causes the supply curve for bicycles to shift to the left since it is now more expensive to produce bicycles. Suppliers respond to this wage increase by producing a lower quantity of the good at every price. But, if at the same time, incomes rise and bicycles are a normal good, we also have the demand curve shifting to the right. Since both curves are shifting and we do not know the magnitude of these shifts, we should expect that we have a situation of indeterminancy. With certainty, the new equilibrium price will be greater than the initial equilibrium price. The new equilibrium quantity may be equal to, greater than, or less than the initial equilibrium quantity.

b. The medical report will cause the demand curve for bicycles to shift to the right as people decide to consume a greater quantity of bicycles at every price due to a change in their tastes and preferences (which are influenced by the medical report). At the same time the supply curve is also shifting to the right due to the entry of new firms, implying that at every price more bicycles can be supplied. Since both curves are shifting we can anticipate a situation of indeterminancy; we know with certainty that the new equilibrium quantity is greater than the initial equilibrium quantity, but we cannot determine whether the new equilibrium price has increased, decreased, or remained the same relative to the initial equilibrium price.

MODULE 8

8-1 Check Your Understanding

1. A consumer buys each pepper if the price is less than (or just equal to) the consumer's willingness to pay for that pepper. The demand schedule is constructed by asking how many peppers will be demanded at any given price. The accompanying table illustrates the demand schedule.

Price of pepper	Quantity of peppers demanded	Quantity of peppers demanded by Casey	Quantity of peppers demanded by Josey
$0.90	1	1	0
0.80	2	1	1
0.70	3	2	1
0.60	4	2	2
0.50	5	3	2
0.40	6	3	3
0.30	8	4	4
0.20	8	4	4
0.10	8	4	4
0.00	8	4	4

When the price is $0.40, Casey's consumer surplus from the first pepper is $0.50, from his second pepper $0.30, from his third pepper $0.10, and he does not buy any more peppers. Casey's individual consumer surplus is therefore $0.90. Josey's consumer surplus from her first pepper is $0.40, from her second pepper $0.20, from her third pepper $0.00 (since the price is exactly equal to her willingness to pay, she buys the third pepper but receives no consumer surplus from it), and she does not buy any more peppers. Josey's individual consumer surplus is therefore $0.60. Total consumer surplus at a price of $0.40 is therefore $0.90 + $0.60 = $1.50.

8-2 Check Your Understanding

1. a. A producer supplies each pepper if the price is greater than (or just equal to) the producer's cost of producing that pepper. The supply schedule is constructed by asking how many peppers will be supplied at any price. The accompanying table illustrates the supply schedule.

b. When the price is $0.70, Cara's producer surplus from the first pepper is $0.60, from her second pepper $0.60, from her third pepper $0.30, from her fourth pepper $0.10, and she does not supply any more peppers. Cara's individual producer surplus is therefore $1.60. Jamie's producer surplus from his first pepper is $0.40, from his second pepper $0.20, from his third pepper $0.00 (since the price is exactly equal to his cost, he sells the third pepper but receives no producer surplus from it), and he does not supply any more peppers. Jamie's individual producer surplus is therefore $0.60. Total producer surplus at a price of $0.70 is therefore $1.60 + $0.60 = $2.20.

Price of pepper	Quantity of peppers supplied	Quantity of peppers supplied by Cara	Quantity of peppers supplied by Jamie
$0.90	8	4	4
0.80	7	4	3
0.70	7	4	3
0.60	6	4	2
0.50	5	3	2
0.40	4	3	1
0.30	3	2	1
0.20	2	2	0
0.10	2	2	0
0.00	0	0	0

MODULE 9

9-1 Check Your Understanding

1. The quantity demanded equals the quantity supplied at a price of $0.50, the equilibrium price. At that price, a total quantity of five peppers will be bought and sold. Casey will buy three peppers and receive consumer surplus of $0.40 on his first, $0.20 on his second, and $0.00 on his third pepper. Josey will buy two peppers and receive consumer surplus of $0.30 on her first and $0.10 on her second pepper. Total consumer surplus is therefore $1.00. Cara will supply three peppers and receive producer surplus of $0.40 on her first, $0.40 on her second, and $0.10 on her third pepper. Jamie will supply two peppers and receive producer surplus of $0.20 on his first and $0.00 on his second pepper. Total producer surplus is therefore $1.10. Total surplus in this market is therefore $1.00 + $1.10 = $2.10.

2. **a.** If Josey consumes one fewer pepper, she loses $0.60 (her willingness to pay for her second pepper); if Casey consumes one more pepper, he gains $0.30 (his willingness to pay for his fourth pepper). This results in an overall loss of consumer surplus of $0.60 – $0.30 = $0.30.

   b. Cara's cost of the last pepper she supplied (the third pepper) is $0.40, and Jamie's cost of producing one more (his third pepper) is $0.70. Total producer surplus therefore falls by $0.70 – $0.40 = $0.30.

   c. Josey's willingness to pay for her second pepper is $0.60; this is what she would lose if she were to consume one fewer pepper. Cara's cost of producing her third pepper is $0.40; this is what she would save if she were to produce one fewer pepper. If we therefore reduced quantity by one pepper, we would lose $0.60 – $0.40 = $0.20 of total surplus.

3. The new guideline is likely to reduce the total life span of kidney recipients because younger recipients (those with small children) are more likely to get a kidney compared to the original guideline. As a result, total surplus is likely to fall. However, this new policy can be justified as an acceptable sacrifice of efficiency for fairness because it's a desirable goal to reduce the chance of a small child losing a parent.

9-2 Check Your Understanding

1. When these rights are separated, someone who owns both the above-ground and the mineral rights can sell each of these separately in the market for above-ground rights and the market for mineral rights. And each of these markets will achieve efficiency: If the market price for above-ground rights is higher than the seller's cost, the seller will sell that right and total surplus increases. If the market price for mineral rights is higher than the seller's cost, the seller will sell that right and total surplus increases. If the two rights, however, cannot be sold separately, a seller can only sell both rights or none at all. Imagine a situation in which the seller values the mineral right highly (that is, has a high cost of selling it) but values the above-ground right much less. If the two rights are separate, the owner may sell the above-ground right (increasing total surplus) but not the mineral right. If, however, the two rights cannot be sold separately, and the owner values the mineral right sufficiently highly, she may not sell either of the two rights. In this case, surplus could have been created through the sale of the above-ground right but goes unrealized because the two rights could not be sold separately.

2. There will be many sellers willing to sell their books but only a few buyers who want to buy books at that price. As a result, only a few transactions will actually occur, and many transactions that would have been mutually beneficial will not take place. This, of course, is inefficient.

3. Markets, alas, do not always lead to efficiency. When there is market failure, the market outcome may be inefficient. This can occur for three main reasons. Markets can fail when, in an attempt to capture more surplus, one party—a monopolist, for instance—prevents mutually beneficial trades from occurring. Markets can also fail when one individual's actions have side effects—externalities—on the welfare of others. Finally, markets can fail when the goods themselves—such as goods about which some relevant information is private—are unsuited for efficient management by markets. When markets don't achieve efficiency, government intervention can improve society's welfare.

MODULE 10

10-1 Check Your Understanding

1. **a.** Fewer homeowners are willing to rent out their driveways because the price ceiling has reduced the payment they receive. This is an example of a fall in price leading to a fall in the quantity supplied. It is shown in the accompanying diagram by the movement from point *E* to point *A* along the supply curve, a reduction in quantity of 400 parking spaces.

   b. The quantity demanded increases by 400 spaces as the price decreases. At a lower price, more fans are willing to drive and rent a parking space. It is shown in the diagram by the movement from point *E* to point *B* along the demand curve.

c. Under a price ceiling, the quantity demanded exceeds the quantity supplied; as a result, shortages arise. In this case, there will be a shortage of 800 parking spaces. It is shown by the horizontal distance between points *A* and *B*.

d. Price ceilings result in wasted resources. The additional time fans spend to guarantee a parking space is wasted time.

e. Price ceilings lead to inefficient allocation of a good—here, the parking spaces—to consumers.

f. Price ceilings lead to black markets.

2. a. False. By lowering the price that producers receive, a price ceiling leads to a decrease in the quantity supplied.

b. True. A price ceiling leads to a lower quantity supplied than in an efficient, unregulated market. As a result, some people who would have been willing to pay the market price, and so would have gotten the good in an unregulated market, are unable to obtain it when a price ceiling is imposed.

c. True. Those producers who still sell the product now receive less for it and are therefore worse off. Other producers will no longer find it worthwhile to sell the product at all and so will also be made worse off.

3. a. Since the apartment is rented quickly at the same price, there is no change (either gain or loss) in producer surplus. So any change in total surplus comes from changes in consumer surplus. When you are evicted, the amount of consumer surplus you lose is equal to the difference between your willingness to pay for the apartment and the rent-controlled price. When the apartment is rented to someone else at the same price, the amount of consumer surplus the new renter gains is equal to the difference between their willingness to pay and the rent-controlled price. So this will be a pure transfer of surplus from one person to another only if both your willingness to pay and the new renter's willingness to pay are the same. Since, under rent control, apartments are not always allocated to those who have the highest willingness to pay, the new renter's willingness to pay may be equal to, lower than, or higher than your willingness to pay. If the new renter's willingness to pay is lower than yours, this will create additional deadweight loss: there is some additional consumer surplus that is lost. However, if the new renter's willingness to pay is higher than yours, this will create an increase in total surplus, as the new renter gains more consumer surplus than you lost.

b. This creates deadweight loss: if you were able to give the ticket away, someone else would be able to obtain consumer surplus, equal to their willingness to pay for the ticket. You neither gain nor lose any surplus, since you cannot go to the concert whether or not you give the ticket away. If you were able to sell the ticket, the buyer would obtain consumer surplus equal to the difference between their willingness to pay for the ticket and the price at which you sell the ticket. In addition, you would obtain producer surplus equal to the difference between the price at which you sell the ticket and your cost of selling the ticket (which, since you won the ticket, is presumably zero). Since the restriction to neither sell nor give away the ticket means that this surplus cannot be obtained by anybody, it creates deadweight loss. If you could give the ticket away, as described above, there would be consumer surplus that accrues to the recipient of the ticket; and if you give the ticket to the person with the highest willingness to pay, there would be no deadweight loss.

c. This creates deadweight loss. If students buy ice cream on campus, they obtain consumer surplus: their willingness to pay must be higher than the price of the ice cream. Your college obtains producer surplus: the price is higher than your college's cost of selling the ice cream. Prohibiting the sale of ice cream on campus means that these two sources of total surplus are lost: there is deadweight loss.

d. Given that your dog values ice cream equally as much as you do, this is a pure transfer of surplus. As you lose consumer surplus, your dog gains equally as much consumer surplus.

10-2 Check Your Understanding

1. a. Some gas station owners will benefit from getting a higher price. Q_F indicates the sales made by these owners. But some will lose; there are those who make sales at the market equilibrium price of P_E but do not make sales at the regulated price of P_F. These missed sales are indicated on the graph by the fall in the quantity demanded along the demand curve, from point *E* to point *A*.

b. Those who buy gas at the higher price of P_F will probably receive better service; this is an example of *inefficiently high quality* caused by a price floor as gas station owners compete on quality rather than price. But opponents are correct to claim that consumers are generally worse off—those who buy at P_F would have been happy to buy at P_E, and many who were willing to buy at a price between P_E and P_F are now unwilling to buy. This is indicated on the graph by the fall in the quantity demanded along the demand curve, from point *E* to point *A*.

c. Proponents are wrong because consumers and some gas station owners are hurt by the price floor, which creates "missed opportunities"—desirable transactions between consumers and station owners that never take place. The deadweight loss, the amount of total surplus lost because of missed opportunities, is indicated by the shaded area in the accompanying figure. Moreover, the inefficiency of wasted resources arises as consumers spend time and money driving to other states. The price floor also tempts people to engage in black market activity. With the price floor, only Q_F units are sold. But at prices between P_E and P_F, there are drivers who cumulatively want to buy more than Q_F and owners who are willing to sell to them, a situation likely to lead to illegal activity.

MODULE 11

11-1 Check Your Understanding

1. By the midpoint method, the percent change in the price of strawberries is

$$\frac{\$1.00 - \$1.50}{(\$1.50 + \$1.00)/2} \times 100 = \frac{-\$0.50}{\$1.25} \times 100 = -40\%$$

Similarly, the percent change in the quantity of strawberries demanded is

$$\frac{200{,}000 - 100{,}000}{(100{,}000 + 200{,}000)/2} \times 100 = \frac{100{,}000}{150{,}000} \times 100 = 67\%$$

Dropping the minus sign, the price elasticity of demand using the midpoint method is 67%/40% = 1.7.

2. By the midpoint method, the percent change in the quantity of movie tickets demanded in going from 4,000 tickets to 5,000 tickets is

$$\frac{5{,}000 - 4{,}000}{(4{,}000 + 5{,}000)/2} \times 100 = \frac{1{,}000}{4{,}500} \times 100 = 22\%$$

Since the price elasticity of demand is 1 at the current consumption level, it will take a 22% reduction in the price of movie tickets to generate a 22% increase in quantity demanded.

3. Since price rises, we know that quantity demanded must fall. Given the current price of \$0.50, a \$0.05 increase in price represents a 10% change, using the method in Equation 11-2. So the price elasticity of demand is

$$\frac{\text{Change in quantity demanded}}{10\%} = 1.2$$

so that the change in quantity demanded (10% × 1.2) equals 12%. A 12% decrease in quantity demanded represents 100,000 × 0.12, or 12,000 sandwiches.

MODULE 12

12-1 Check Your Understanding

1. **a.** Elastic demand. Consumers are highly responsive to changes in price. For a rise in price, the quantity effect (which tends to reduce total revenue) outweighs the price effect (which tends to increase total revenue). Overall, this leads to a fall in total revenue.

   b. Unit-elastic demand. Here the revenue lost to the fall in price is exactly equal to the revenue gained from higher sales. The quantity effect exactly offsets the price effect.

   c. Inelastic demand. Consumers are relatively unresponsive to changes in price. For consumers to purchase a given percent increase in output, the price must fall by an even greater percent. The price effect of a fall in price (which tends to reduce total revenue) outweighs the quantity effect (which tends to increase total revenue). As a result, total revenue decreases.

   d. Inelastic demand. Consumers are relatively unresponsive to price, so the percent fall in output is smaller than the percent rise in price. The price effect of a rise in price (which tends to increase total revenue) outweighs the quantity effect (which tends to reduce total revenue). As a result, total revenue increases.

2. **a.** The demand of an accident victim for a blood transfusion is very likely to be perfectly inelastic because there is no substitute and it is necessary for survival. The demand curve will be vertical, at a quantity equal to the needed transfusion quantity.

   b. Students' demand for green erasers is likely to be perfectly elastic because there are easily available substitutes: nongreen erasers. The demand curve will be horizontal, at a price equal to that of nongreen erasers.

MODULE 13

13-1 Check Your Understanding

1. The cross-price elasticity of demand is 5%/20% = 0.25. Since the cross-price elasticity of demand is positive, the two goods are substitutes.

13-2 Check Your Understanding

1. By the midpoint method, the percent increase in Chelsea's income is

$$\frac{\$18{,}000 - \$12{,}000}{(\$12{,}000 + \$18{,}000)/2} \times 100 = \frac{\$6{,}000}{\$15{,}000} \times 100 = 40\%$$

Similarly, the percent increase in her consumption of albums is

$$\frac{40 - 10}{(10 + 40)/2} \times 100 = \frac{30}{25} \times 100 = 120\%$$

So Chelsea's income elasticity of demand for albums is 120%/40% = 3.

2. Sanjay's consumption of expensive restaurant meals will fall more than 10% because a given percent change in income (a fall of 10% here) induces a larger percent change in consumption of an income-elastic good.

13-3 Check Your Understanding

1. By the midpoint method, the percent change in the number of hours of web-design services contracted is

$$\frac{500{,}000 - 300{,}000}{(300{,}000 + 500{,}000)/2} \times 100 = \frac{200{,}000}{400{,}000} \times 100 = 50\%$$

Similarly, the percent change in the price of web-design services is

$$\frac{\$150 - \$100}{(\$100 + \$150)/2} \times 100 = \frac{\$50}{\$125} \times 100 = 40\%$$

The price elasticity of supply is 50%/40% = 1.25. So supply is elastic.

2. **a.** True. An increase in demand raises price. If the price elasticity of supply of milk is low, then relatively little additional quantity supplied will be forthcoming as the price rises. As a result, the price of milk will rise substantially to satisfy the increased demand for milk. If the price elasticity of supply is high, then there will be a relatively large increase in quantity supplied when the price rises. As a result, the price of milk will rise only by a little to satisfy the higher demand for milk.

   b. False. It is true that long-run price elasticities of supply are generally larger than short-run elasticities of supply. But this means that the short-run supply curves are generally steeper, not flatter, than the long-run supply curves.

   c. True. When supply is perfectly elastic, the supply curve is a horizontal line. So a change in demand has no effect on price; it affects only the quantity bought and sold.

MODULE 14

14-1 Check Your Understanding

1. The following figure shows that, after the introduction of excise tax, the price paid by consumers rises to $1.20; the price received by producers falls to $0.90. Consumers bear $0.20 of the $0.30 tax per pound of butter; producers bear $0.10 of the $0.30 tax per pound of butter. The tax drives a wedge of $0.30 between the price paid by consumers and the price received by producers. As a result, the quantity of butter bought and sold is now 9 million pounds.

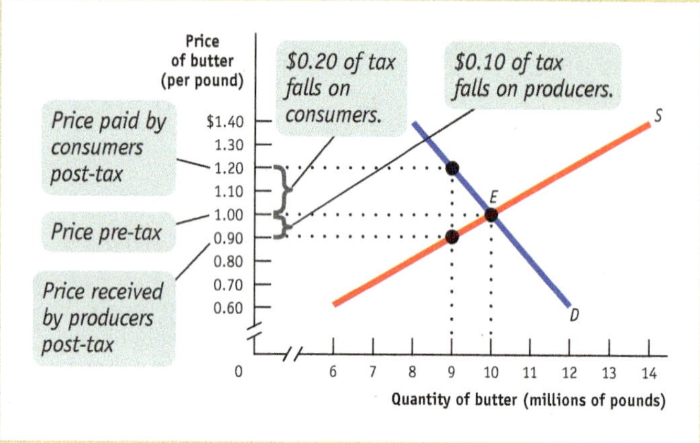

2. The fact that demand is very inelastic means that consumers will reduce their demand for textbooks very little in response to an increase in the price caused by the tax. The fact that supply is somewhat elastic means that suppliers will respond to the fall in the price by reducing supply. As a result, the incidence of the tax will fall heavily on consumers of economics textbooks and very little on publishers, as shown in the accompanying figure.

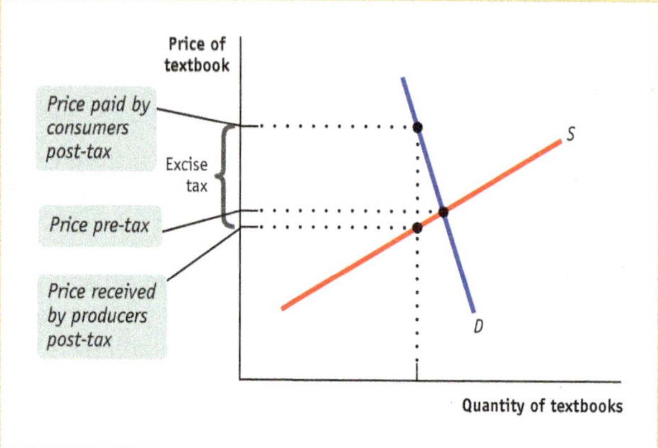

3. True. When a substitute is readily available, demand is elastic. This implies that producers cannot easily pass on the cost of the tax to consumers because consumers will respond to an increased price by switching to the substitute. Furthermore, when producers have difficulty adjusting the amount of the good produced, supply is inelastic. That is, producers cannot easily reduce output in response to a lower price net of tax. So the tax burden will fall more heavily on producers than consumers.

4. The fact that supply is very inelastic means that producers will reduce their supply of bottled water very little in response to the fall in price caused by the tax. Demand, on the other hand, will fall in response to an increase in price because demand is somewhat elastic. As a result, the incidence of the tax will fall heavily on producers of bottled spring water and very little on consumers, as shown in the accompanying figure.

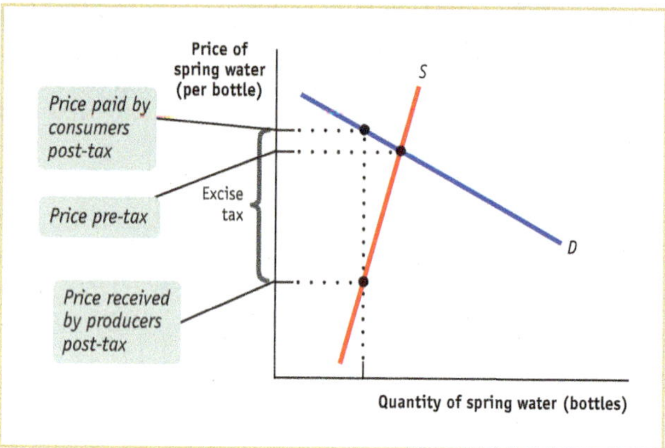

5. True. The lower the elasticity of supply, the more the burden of a tax will fall on producers rather than consumers, other things equal.

14-2 Check Your Understanding

1. **a.** Without the excise tax, Zhang, Yves, Xavier, and Walter sell, and Ana, Bernice, Chizuko, and Dagmar buy one can of soda each, at $0.40 per can. So the quantity bought and sold is 4.

   b. At a price to consumers of $0.60, only Ana and Bernice are willing to buy a can of soda. At a price paid to producers of only $0.20, only Zhang and Yves are willing to sell. So the quantity bought and sold is 2.

   c. Without the excise tax, Ana's individual consumer surplus is $0.70 – $0.40 = $0.30, Bernice's is $0.60 – $0.40 = $0.20, Chizuko's is $0.50 – $0.40 = $0.10, and Dagmar's is $0.40 – $0.40 = $0.00. Total consumer surplus is $0.30 + $0.20 + $0.10 + $0.00 = $0.60. With the tax, Ana's individual consumer surplus is $0.70 – $0.60 = $0.10 and Bernice's is $0.60 – $0.60 = $0.00. Total consumer surplus post-tax is $0.10 + $0.00 = $0.10. So the total consumer surplus lost because of the tax is $0.60 – $0.10 = $0.50.

   d. Without the excise tax, Zhang's individual producer surplus is $0.40 – $0.10 = $0.30, Yves's is $0.40 – $0.20 = $0.20, Xavier's is $0.40 – $0.30 = $0.10, and Walter's is $0.40 – $0.40 = $0.00. Total producer surplus is $0.30 + $0.20 + $0.10 + $0.00 = $0.60. With the tax, Zhang's individual producer surplus is $0.20 – $0.10 = $0.10 and Yves's is $0.20 – $0.20 = $0.00. Total producer surplus post-tax is $0.10 + $0.00 = $0.10. So the total producer surplus lost because of the tax is $0.60 – $0.10 = $0.50.

   e. With the tax, two cans of soda are sold, so the government tax revenue from this excise tax is 2 × $0.40 = $0.80.

   f. Total surplus without the tax is $0.60 + $0.60 = $1.20. With the tax, total surplus is $0.10 + $0.10 = $0.20, and government tax revenue is $0.80. So deadweight loss from this excise tax is $1.20 – ($0.20 + $0.80) = $0.20.

2. a. The demand for gasoline is inelastic because there is no close substitute for gasoline itself and it is difficult for drivers to arrange substitutes for driving, such as taking public transportation. As a result, the deadweight loss from a tax on gasoline would be relatively small, as shown in the accompanying diagram.

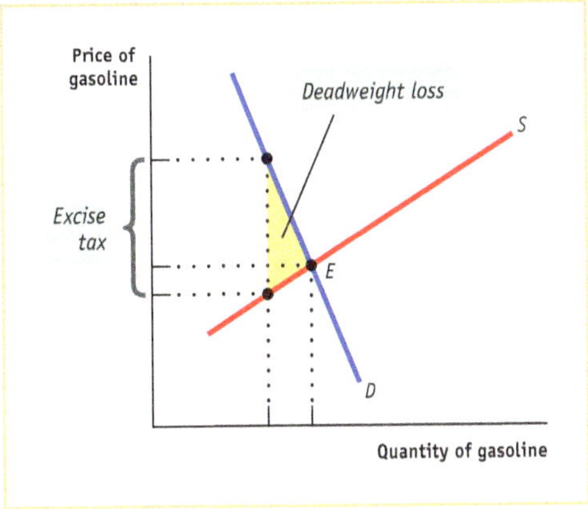

b. The demand for milk chocolate bars is elastic because there are close substitutes: dark chocolate bars, milk chocolate kisses, and so on. As a result, the deadweight loss from a tax on milk chocolate bars would be relatively large, as shown in the accompanying diagram.

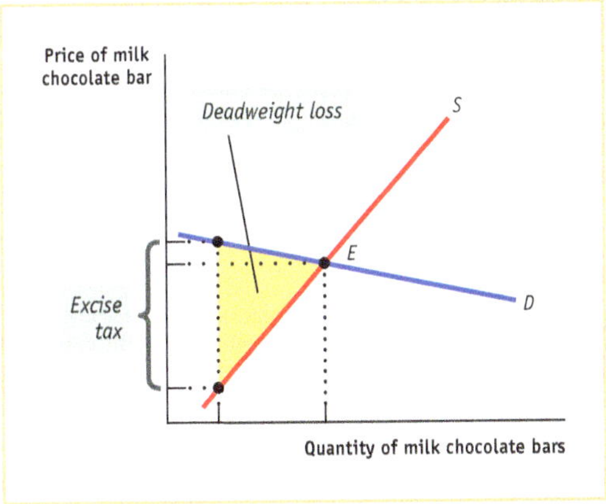

MODULE 15

15-1 Check Your Understanding

1. a. To determine comparative advantage, we must compare the two countries' opportunity costs for a given good. Take the opportunity cost of 1 ton of corn in terms of bicycles. In China, the opportunity cost of 1 bicycle is 0.01 ton of corn; so the opportunity cost of 1 ton of corn is 1/0.01 bicycles = 100 bicycles. The United States has the comparative advantage in corn since its opportunity cost in terms of bicycles is 50, a smaller number. Similarly, the opportunity cost in the United States of 1 bicycle in terms of corn is 1/50 ton of corn = 0.02 ton of corn. This is greater than 0.01, the Chinese opportunity cost of 1 bicycle in terms of corn, implying that China has a comparative advantage in bicycles.

b. Given that the United States can produce 200,000 bicycles if no corn is produced, it can produce 200,000 bicycles × 0.02 ton of corn/bicycle = 4,000 tons of corn when no bicycles are produced. Likewise, if China can produce 3,000 tons of corn if no bicycles are produced, it can produce 3,000 tons of corn × 100 bicycles/ton of corn = 300,000 bicycles if no corn is produced. These points determine the vertical and horizontal intercepts of the U.S. and Chinese production possibility frontiers, as shown in the accompanying diagram.

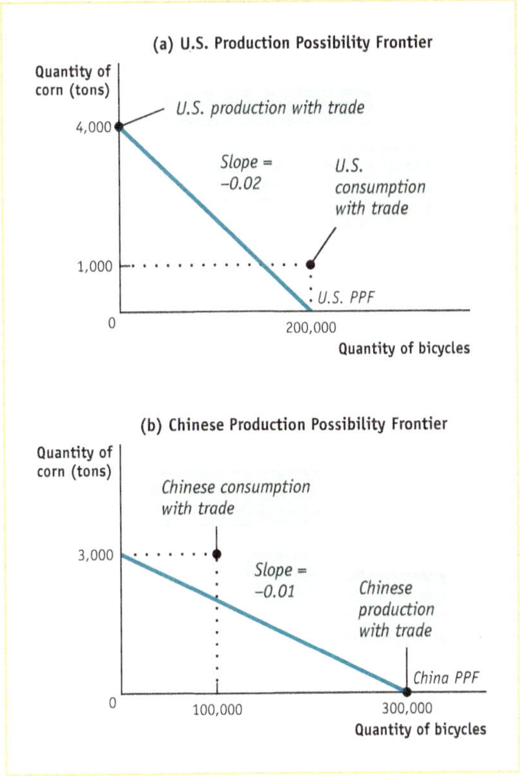

c. The diagram shows the production and consumption points of the two countries. Each country is clearly better off with international trade because each now consumes a bundle of the two goods that lies outside its own production possibility frontier, indicating that these bundles were unattainable in autarky.

2. a. According to the Heckscher–Ohlin model, this pattern of trade occurs because the United States has a relatively larger endowment of factors of production, such as human capital and physical capital, that are suited to the production of movies, but France has a relatively larger endowment of factors of production suited to wine-making, such as vineyards and the human capital of vintners.

b. According to the Heckscher–Ohlin model, this pattern of trade occurs because the United States has a relatively larger endowment of factors of production, such as human and physical capital, that are suited to making machinery, but Brazil has a relatively larger endowment of factors of production suited to shoe-making, such as unskilled labor and leather.

MODULE 16

16-1 Check Your Understanding

1. In the accompanying diagram, P_A is the U.S. price of grapes in autarky and P_W is the world price of grapes under international trade. With trade, U.S. consumers pay a price of P_W for grapes and consume quantity Q_D,

U.S. grape producers produce quantity Q_S, and the difference, $Q_D - Q_S$, represents imports of Mexican grapes. As a consequence of the strike by truckers, imports are halted, the price paid by American consumers rises to the autarky price, P_A, and U.S. consumption falls to the autarky quantity, Q_A.

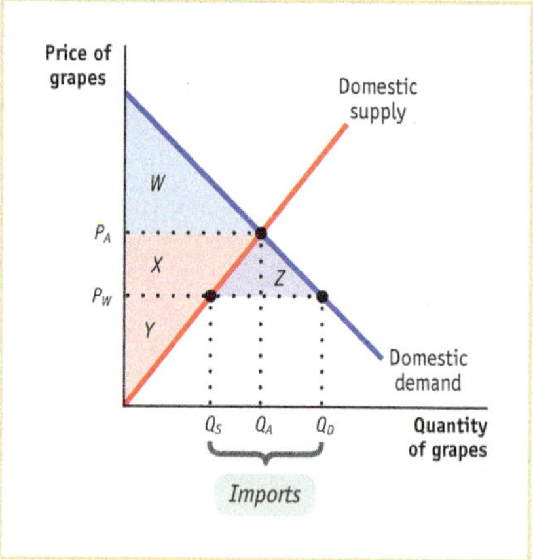

a. Before the strike, U.S. consumers enjoyed consumer surplus equal to areas $W + X + Z$. After the strike, their consumer surplus shrinks to W. So consumers are worse off, losing consumer surplus represented by $X + Z$.

b. Before the strike, U.S. producers had producer surplus equal to the area Y. After the strike, their producer surplus increases to $Y + X$. So U.S. producers are better off, gaining producer surplus represented by X.

c. U.S. total surplus falls as a result of the strike by an amount represented by area Z, the loss in consumer surplus that does not accrue to producers.

2. Mexican grape producers are worse off because they lose sales of exported grapes to the United States, and Mexican grape pickers are worse off because they lose the wages that were associated with the lost sales. The lower demand for Mexican grapes caused by the strike implies that the price Mexican consumers pay for grapes falls, making them better off. U.S. grape pickers are better off because their wages increase as a result of the increase of $Q_A - Q_S$ in U.S. sales.

16-2 Check Your Understanding

1. a. If the tariff is \$0.50, the price paid by domestic consumers for a pound of imported butter is \$0.50 + \$0.50 = \$1.00, the same price as a pound of domestic butter. Imported butter will no longer have a price advantage over domestic butter, imports will cease, and domestic producers will capture all the feasible sales to domestic consumers, selling amount Q_A in the accompanying figure. If the tariff is \$0.25, the price paid by domestic consumers for a pound of imported butter is \$0.50 + \$0.25 = \$0.75, \$0.25 cheaper than a pound of domestic butter. American butter producers will gain sales in the amount of $Q_2 - Q_1$ as a result of the \$0.25 tariff. But this is smaller than the amount they would have gained under the \$0.50 tariff, the amount $Q_A - Q_1$.

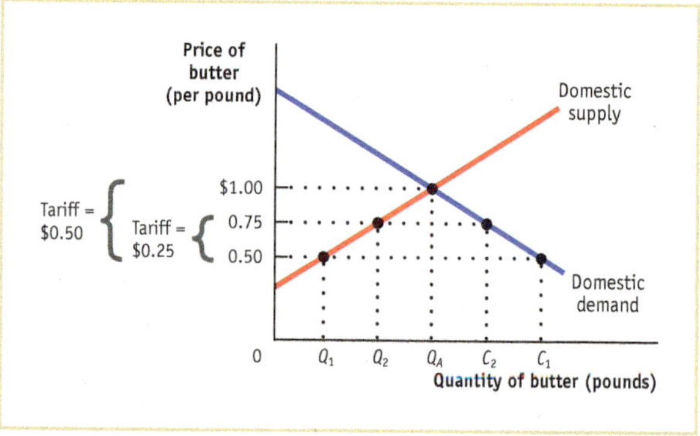

b. As long as the tariff is at least \$0.50, increasing it more has no effect. At a tariff of \$0.50, all imports are effectively blocked. A tariff of \$0.25 will increase the price to \$0.75 and reduce Q_D from C_1 to C_2. It will increase Q_S from Q_1 to Q_2.

2. All imports are effectively blocked at a tariff of \$0.50. So such a tariff corresponds to an import quota of 0.

16-3 Check Your Understanding

1. There are many fewer businesses that use steel as an input than there are consumers who buy sugar or clothing. So it will be easier for such businesses to communicate and coordinate among themselves to lobby against tariffs than it will be for consumers. In addition, each business will perceive that the cost of a steel tariff is quite costly to its profits, but an individual consumer is either unaware of or perceives little loss from tariffs on sugar or clothing.

2. Countries are often tempted to protect domestic industries by claiming that an import poses a quality, health, or environmental danger to domestic consumers. A WTO official should examine whether domestic producers are subject to the same stringency in the application of quality, health, or environmental regulations as foreign producers. If they are, then it is more likely that the regulations are for legitimate, non–trade protection purposes; if they are not, then it is more likely that the regulations are intended as trade protection measures.

MODULE 17

17-1 Check Your Understanding

1. a. Supplies are an explicit cost because they require an outlay of money.

b. If the basement could be used in some other way that generates money, such as renting it to a student, then the implicit cost is that money forgone. Otherwise, the implicit cost is zero.

c. Wages are an explicit cost.

d. By using the van for their business, Karma and Don forgo the money they could have gained by selling it. So use of the van is an implicit cost.

e. Karma's forgone wages from her job are an implicit cost.

2. We need to only compare the choice of becoming a machinist to the choice of taking a job in another state to make the right choice. We can discard the choice of acquiring a pharmacology degree because we already know that taking a job in another state is always superior to it. Now let's compare the remaining two alternatives: becoming a skilled machinist versus immediately taking a job in another state. As an apprentice machinist, Adam will earn only $30,000 over the first two years, versus $57,000 in the out-of-state job. So he has an implicit cost of $30,000 – $57,000 = –$27,000 by becoming a machinist instead of immediately moving out of state to work. However, two years from now the value of his lifetime earnings as a machinist is $725,000 versus $600,000 in advertising, giving him an accounting profit of $125,000 by choosing to be a machinist. Summing, his economic profit from choosing a career as a machinist over his other career is $125,000 – $27,000 = $98,000. In contrast, his economic profit from choosing the alternative, a career out of state over a career as a machinist, is –$125,000 + $27,000 = –$98,000. By the principle of "either–or" decision making, Adam should choose to be a machinist because that career has a positive economic profit.

3. You can discard alternative A because both B and C are superior to it. But you must now compare B versus C. You should then choose the alternative—B or C—that carries a positive economic profit.

17-2 Check Your Understanding

1. a. The marginal cost of doing your laundry is any monetary outlays plus the opportunity cost of your time spent doing laundry today—that is, the value you would place on spending time today on your next-best alternative activity, like seeing a movie. The marginal benefit is having more clean clothes today to choose from.

b. The marginal cost of changing your oil is the opportunity cost of time spent changing your oil now as well as the explicit cost of the oil change. The marginal benefit is the improvement in your car's performance.

c. The marginal cost is the unpleasant feeling of a burning mouth that you receive from it plus any explicit cost of the jalapeño. The marginal benefit of another jalapeño on your nachos is the pleasant taste that you receive from it.

d. The marginal benefit of hiring another worker in your company is the value of the output that worker produces. The marginal cost is the wage you must pay that worker.

e. The marginal cost is the value lost due to the increased side effects from this additional dose. The marginal benefit of another dose of the drug is the value of the reduction in the patient's disease.

f. The marginal cost is the opportunity cost of your time—what you would have gotten from the next best use of your time. The marginal benefit is the probable increase in your grade.

2. The accompanying table shows Alexa's new marginal cost and her new profit. It also reproduces Alexa's marginal benefit from Table 17-5.

Years of schooling	Total cost	Marginal cost	Marginal benefit	Profit
0	$0			
		$90,000	$300,000	$210,000
1	90,000			
		30,000	150,000	120,000
2	120,000			
		50,000	90,000	40,000
3	170,000			
		80,000	60,000	–20,000
4	250,000			
		120,000	50,000	–80,000
5	370,000			

Alexa's marginal cost is decreasing until she has completed two years of schooling, after which marginal cost increases because of the value of her forgone income. The optimal amount of schooling is still three years. For less than three years of schooling, marginal benefit exceeds marginal cost; for more than three years, marginal cost exceeds marginal benefit.

17-3 Check Your Understanding

1. a. Your sunk cost is $8,000 because none of the $8,000 spent on the truck is recoverable.

b. Your sunk cost is $4,000 because 50% of the $8,000 spent on the truck is recoverable.

2. a. This is an invalid argument because the time and money already spent are a sunk cost at this point.

b. This is also an invalid argument because what you should have done two years ago is irrelevant to what you should do now.

c. This is a valid argument because it recognizes that sunk costs are irrelevant to what you should do now.

d. This is a valid argument given that you are concerned about disappointing your parents. But your parents' views are irrational because they do not recognize that the time already spent is a sunk cost.

MODULE 18

18-1 Check Your Understanding

1. a. Jenny is exhibiting loss aversion. She has an oversensitivity to loss, leading to an unwillingness to recognize a loss and move on.

b. Dan is doing mental accounting. Dollars from his unexpected overtime earnings are worth less—spent on a weekend getaway—than the dollars earned from his regular hours that he uses to pay down his student loan.

c. Carol may have unrealistic expectations of future behavior. Even if she does not want to participate in the plan now, she should find a way to commit to participating at a later date.

d. Jeremy is showing signs of status quo bias. He is avoiding making a decision altogether; in other words, he is sticking with the status quo.

2. You would determine whether a decision was rational or irrational by first accurately accounting for all the costs and benefits of the decision. In particular, you must accurately measure all opportunity costs. Then calculate the economic payoff of the decision relative to the next best alternative. If you would still make the same choice after this comparison, then you have made a rational choice. If not, then the choice was irrational.

MODULE 19

19-1 Check Your Understanding

1. Consuming a unit that generates negative marginal utility leaves the consumer with lower total utility than not consuming that unit at all. A rational consumer, a consumer who maximizes utility, would not do that. For example, from Figure 19-1 you can see that Cassie receives 64 utils if she consumes 8 egg rolls; but if she consumes the nineth egg roll, she loses a util, netting her a total utility of only 63 utils. Thus, whenever consuming a unit generates negative marginal utility, the consumer is made better off by not consuming that unit, even when that unit is free.

2. Since Marta has diminishing marginal utility for coffee, her first cup of coffee of the day generates the greatest increase in total utility. Her third and last cup of the day generates the least.

3. **a.** Mabel does not have diminishing marginal utility of exercising since each additional unit consumed brings more additional enjoyment than the previous unit.

b. Mei does not have diminishing marginal utility of albums because each additional unit generates the same additional enjoyment as the previous unit.

c. Dexter has diminishing marginal utility of restaurant meals since the additional utility generated by a good restaurant meal is less when he consumes lots of them than when he consumes few of them.

19-2 Check Your Understanding

1. **a.** The accompanying table shows the consumer's consumption possibilities, *A* through *C*. These consumption possibilities are plotted in the accompanying diagram, along with the consumer's budget line, *BL*.

Consumption bundle	Quantity of popcorn (buckets)	Quantity of movie tickets
A	0	2
B	2	1
C	4	0

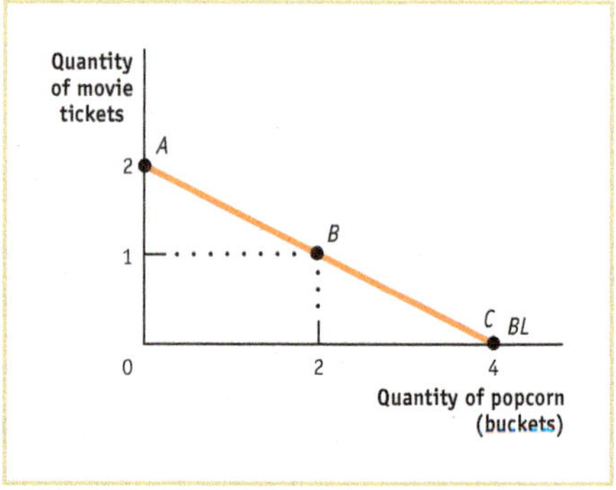

b. The accompanying table shows the consumer's consumption possibilities, *A* through *D*. These consumption possibilities are plotted in the accompanying diagram, along with the consumer's budget line, *BL*.

Consumption bundle	Quantity of underwear (pairs)	Quantity of socks (pairs)
A	0	6
B	1	4
C	2	2
D	3	0

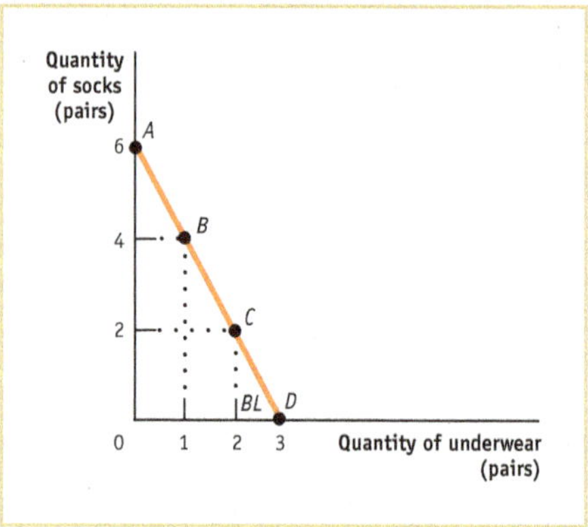

19-3 Check Your Understanding

1. From Table 19-3 you can see that Sammy's marginal utility per dollar from increasing his consumption of egg rolls from 3 rolls to 4, and his marginal utility per dollar from increasing his consumption of Coke from 9 bottles to 10 are the same, 0.75 utils. But a consumption bundle consisting of 4 egg rolls and 10 bottles of Coke is not Sammy's optimal consumption bundle because it is not affordable given his income of \$20; 4 egg rolls and 10 bottles of Coke cost \$4 × 4 + \$2 × 10 = \$36, \$16 more than Sammy's income. This can be illustrated with Sammy's budget line from panel (a) of Figure 19-3: a bundle of 4 egg rolls and 10 bottles of Coke is represented by point *X* in the accompanying diagram, a point that lies outside Sammy's budget line. If you look at the horizontal axis of panel (a) of Figure 19-3, it is quite clear that there is no such thing in Sammy's consumption possibilities as a bundle consisting of 4 egg rolls and 10 bottles of Coke.

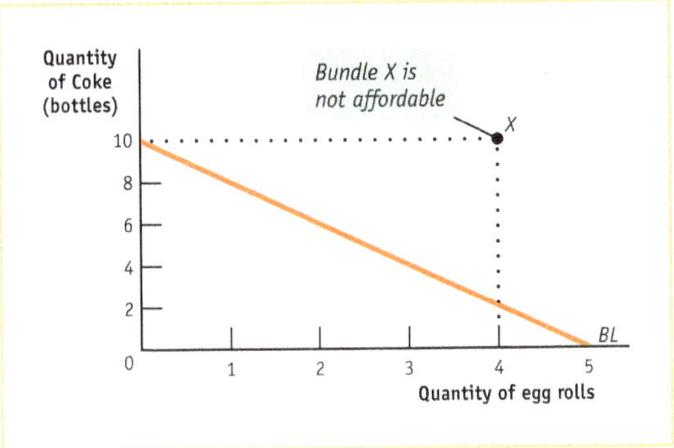

2. Sammy's maximum utility per dollar is generated when he goes from consuming 0 to 1 egg roll (3.75 utils) and as he goes from 0 to 1 bottle of Coke (5.75 utils). But this bundle consisting of 1 egg roll and 1 bottle of Coke generates only 26.5 utils for him. Instead, Sammy should choose the consumption bundle that satisfies his budget constraint and for which the marginal utility per dollar for both goods is equal.

19-4 Check Your Understanding

1. **a.** Since spending on orange juice is a small share of Clare's spending, the income effect from a rise in the price of orange juice is insignificant. Only the substitution effect, represented by the substitution of lemonade in place of orange juice, is significant.

   b. Since rent is a large share of Delia's expenditures, the increase in rent generates a significant income effect, making Delia feel poorer. Since housing is a normal good for Delia, the income and substitution effects move in the same direction, leading her to reduce her consumption of housing by moving to a smaller apartment.

   c. Since a meal ticket is a significant share of the students' living costs, an increase in its price will generate a significant income effect. Because cafeteria meals are an inferior good, the substitution effect (which would induce students to substitute restaurant meals in place of cafeteria meals) and the income effect (which would induce them to eat in the cafeteria more often because they are poorer) move in opposite directions.

2. To determine whether any good is a Giffen good, you must first establish whether it is an inferior good. In other words, if students' incomes decrease, other things equal, does the quantity of cafeteria meals demanded increase? Once you have established that the good is an inferior good, you must then establish that the income effect outweighs the substitution effect. That is, as the price of cafeteria meals rises, other things equal, does the quantity of cafeteria meals demanded increase? Be careful that, in fact, all other things remain equal. But if the quantity of cafeteria meals demanded truly increases in response to a price rise, you really have found a Giffen good.

MODULE 20

20-1 Check Your Understanding

1. **a.** The fixed input is the 10-ton machine, and the variable input is electricity.

   b. As you can see from the declining numbers in the third column of the accompanying table, electricity does indeed exhibit diminishing returns: the marginal product of each additional kilowatt of electricity is less than that of the previous kilowatt.

Quantity of electricity (kilowatts)	Quantity of ice (pounds)	Marginal product of electricity (pounds per kilowatt)
0	0	
		1,000
1	1,000	
		800
2	1,800	
		600
3	2,400	
		400
4	2,800	

   c. A 50% increase in the size of the fixed input means that Bernie now has a 15-ton machine. So the fixed input is now the 15-ton machine. Since it generates a 100% increase in output for any given amount of electricity, the quantity of output and marginal product are now as shown in the accompanying table.

Quantity of electricity (kilowatts)	Quantity of ice (pounds)	Marginal product of electricity (pounds per kilowatt)
0	0	
		2,000
1	2,000	
		1,600
2	3,600	
		1,200
3	4,800	
		800
4	5,600	

MODULE 21

21-1 Check Your Understanding

1. **a.** As shown in the accompanying table, the marginal cost for each pie is found by multiplying the marginal cost of the previous pie by 1.5. Variable cost for each output level is found by summing the marginal cost for all the pies produced to reach that output level. So, for example, the variable cost of three pies is \$1.00 + \$1.50 + \$2.25 = \$4.75. Average fixed cost for Q pies is

calculated as \$9.00/Q since fixed cost is \$9.00. Average variable cost for Q pies is equal to variable cost for the Q pies divided by Q; for example, the average variable cost of five pies is \$13.19/5, or approximately \$2.64. Finally, average total cost can be calculated in two equivalent ways: as TC/Q or as $AVC + AFC$.

Quantity of pies	Marginal cost of pie	Variable cost	Average fixed cost of pie	Average variable cost of pie	Average total cost of pie
0		\$0.00	—	—	—
	\$1.00				
1		1.00	\$9.00	\$1.00	\$10.00
	1.50				
2		2.50	4.50	1.25	5.75
	2.25				
3		4.75	3.00	1.58	4.58
	3.38				
4		8.13	2.25	2.03	4.28
	5.06				
5		13.19	1.80	2.64	4.44
	7.59				
6		20.78	1.50	3.46	4.96

b. The spreading effect dominates the diminishing returns effect when average total cost is falling: the fall in *AFC* dominates the rise in *AVC* for pies 1 to 4. The diminishing returns effect dominates when average total cost is rising: the rise in *AVC* dominates the fall in *AFC* for pies 5 and 6.

c. Alicia's minimum-cost output is 4 pies; this generates the lowest average total cost, \$4.28. When output is less than 4, the marginal cost of a pie is less than the average total cost of the pies already produced. So making an additional pie lowers average total cost. For example, the marginal cost of pie 3 is \$2.25, whereas the average total cost of pies 1 and 2 is \$5.75. So making pie 3 lowers average total cost to \$4.58, equal to (2 × \$5.75 + \$2.25)/3 When output is more than 4, the marginal cost of a pie is greater than the average total cost of the pies already produced. Consequently, making an additional pie raises average total cost. So, although the marginal cost of pie 6 is \$7.59, the average total cost of pies 1 through 5 is \$4.44. Making pie 6 raises average total cost to \$4.96, equal to (5 × \$4.44 + \$7.59)/6.

MODULE 22

22-1 Check Your Understanding

1. a. The accompanying table shows the average total cost of producing 12,000, 22,000, and 30,000 units for each of the three choices of fixed cost. For example, if the firm makes choice 1, the total cost of producing 12,000 units of output is \$8,000 + 12,000 × \$1.00 = \$20,000. The average total cost of producing 12,000 units of output is therefore \$20,000/12,000 = \$1.67. The other average total costs are calculated similarly. So if the firm wanted to produce 12,000 units, it would make choice 1 because this gives it the lowest average total cost. If it wanted to produce 22,000 units, it would make choice 2. If it wanted to produce 30,000 units, it would make choice 3.

	12,000 units	22,000 units	30,000 units
Average total cost from choice 1	\$1.67	\$1.36	\$1.27
Average total cost from choice 2	1.75	1.30	1.15
Average total cost from choice 3	2.25	1.34	1.05

b. Having historically produced 12,000 units, the firm would have adopted choice 1. When producing 12,000 units, the firm would have had an average total cost of \$1.67. When output jumps to 22,000 units, the firm cannot alter its choice of fixed cost in the short run, so its average total cost in the short run will be \$1.36. In the long run, however, it will adopt choice 2, making its average total cost fall to \$1.30.

c. If the firm believes that the increase in demand is temporary, it should not alter its fixed cost from choice 1 because choice 2 generates higher average total cost as soon as output falls back to its original quantity of 12,000 units: \$1.75 versus \$1.67.

2. a. This firm is likely to experience constant returns to scale. To increase output, the firm must hire more workers, purchase more computers, and pay additional telephone charges. Because these inputs are easily available, their long-run average total cost is unlikely to change as output increases.

b. This firm is likely to experience decreasing returns to scale. As the firm takes on more projects, the costs of communication and coordination required to implement the expertise of the firm's owner are likely to increase. As a result, the firm's long-run average total cost will increase as output increases.

c. This firm is likely to experience increasing returns to scale. Because diamond mining requires a large initial set-up cost for excavation equipment, long-run average total cost will fall as output increases.

3. The accompanying diagram shows the long-run average total cost curve (*LRATC*) and the short-run average total cost curve corresponding to a long-run output choice of 5 cases of salsa (ATC_5). The curve ATC_5 shows the short-run average total cost for which the level of fixed cost minimizes average total cost at an output of 5 cases of salsa. This is confirmed by the fact that at 5 cases per day, ATC_5 touches *LRATC*, the long-run average total cost curve.

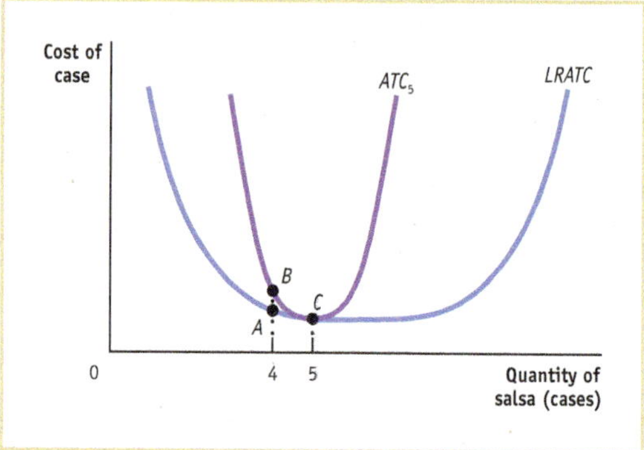

If Selena expects to produce only 4 cases of salsa for a long time, she should change her fixed cost. If she does not change her fixed cost and produces 4 cases of salsa, her average total cost in the short run is indicated by point *B* on ATC_5; it is no longer on the *LRATC*. If she changes her fixed cost, though, her average total cost could be lower, at point *A*.

MODULE 23

23-1 Check Your Understanding

1. **a.** With only three producers in the world, each producer will represent a sizable share of the market. Thus, the industry will not be perfectly competitive.
   b. Because each producer of natural gas from the North Sea has only a small market share of the total world supply of natural gas, and since natural gas is a standardized product, the natural gas industry will be perfectly competitive.
   c. Because each designer has a distinctive style, high-fashion clothes are not a standardized product. And thus the industry will not be perfectly competitive.
   d. The market described here is the market in each city for tickets to baseball games. Since there are only one or two teams in each major city, each team will represent a sizable share of the market. The industry will not be perfectly competitive.

23-2 Check Your Understanding

1. **a.** This does not support the conclusion. Texas Tea has a limited amount of oil, and the price has risen to equalize supply and demand.
   b. This supports the conclusion because the market for home heating oil has become monopolized, and a monopolist will reduce the quantity supplied and raise price to generate profit.
   c. This does not support the conclusion. Texas Tea has raised its price to consumers because the price of its input, home heating oil, has increased.
   d. This supports the conclusion. The fact that other firms have begun to supply heating oil at a lower price implies that Texas Tea must have earned sufficient profits to attract the others to Frigid.
   e. This supports the conclusion. It indicates that Texas Tea enjoys a barrier to entry because it controls access to the only Alaskan heating oil pipeline.
2. **a.** Extending the length of a patent increases the length of time during which the inventor can reduce the quantity supplied and increase the market price. Since this increases the period of time during which the inventor can earn economic profits from the invention, it increases the incentive to invent new products.
   b. Extending the length of a patent also increases the period of time during which consumers have to pay higher prices. So determining the appropriate length of a patent involves making a trade-off between the desirable incentive for invention and the undesirable high price to consumers.
3. **a.** When a large number of other people use Passport credit cards, any one merchant is more likely to accept the card. So the larger the customer base, the more likely a Passport card will be accepted for payment.
   b. When a large number of people own a car with a new type of engine, it will be easier to find a knowledgeable mechanic who can repair it.
   c. When a large number of people use such a website, the more likely it is that you will be able to find a buyer for something you want to sell or a seller for something you want to buy.

23-3 Check Your Understanding

1. **a.** The world oil industry is an oligopoly because a few countries control a necessary resource for production, oil reserves.
   b. The microprocessor industry is an oligopoly because two firms possess superior technology and so dominate industry production.
   c. The wide-body passenger jet industry is an oligopoly because there are increasing returns to scale in production.

23-4 Check Your Understanding

1. **a.** Ladders are not differentiated as a result of monopolistic competition. A ladder producer makes different ladders (tall ladders versus short ladders) to satisfy different consumer needs, not to avoid competition with rivals. So two tall ladders made by two different producers will be indistinguishable by consumers.
   b. Soft drinks are an example of product differentiation as a result of monopolistic competition. For example, several producers make colas; each is differentiated in terms of taste, which fast-food chains sell it, and so on.
   c. Department stores are an example of product differentiation as a result of monopolistic competition. They serve different clienteles that have different price sensitivities and different tastes. They also offer different levels of customer service and are situated in different locations.
   d. Steel is not differentiated as a result of monopolistic competition. Different types of steel (beams versus sheets) are made for different purposes, not to distinguish one steel manufacturer's products from another's.
2. **a.** Perfectly competitive industries and monopolistically competitive industries both have many sellers. So it may be hard to distinguish between them solely in terms of number of firms. And in both market structures, there is free entry into and exit from the industry in the long run. But in a perfectly competitive industry, one standardized product is sold; in a monopolistically competitive industry, products are differentiated. So you should ask whether products are differentiated in the industry.
   b. In a monopoly there is only one firm, but a monopolistically competitive industry contains many firms. So you should ask whether or not there is a single firm in the industry.

MODULE 24

24-1 Check Your Understanding

1. **a.** The firm maximizes profit at a quantity of 4, because it is at that quantity that $MC = MR$.

   b. At a quantity of 4, the firm just breaks even. This is because at a quantity of 4, $P = ATC$, so the amount the firm takes in for each unit—the price—exactly equals the average total cost per unit.

2. The lowest price that would allow the firm to break even is \$10, because the minimum average total cost is \$500/50 = \$10, and the price must at least equal minimum average total cost for the firm to break even.

MODULE 25

25-1 Check Your Understanding

1. **a.** The firm should shut down immediately when price is less than minimum average variable cost, the shutdown price. In the accompanying diagram, this is optimal for prices in the range 0 to P_1.

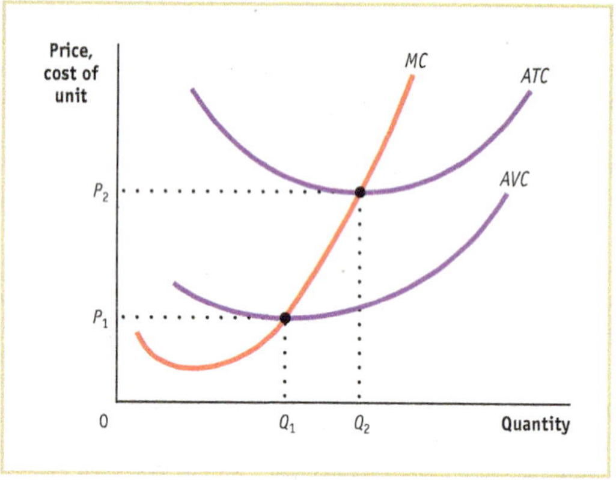

   b. When price is greater than minimum average variable cost (the shut-down price) but less than minimum average total cost (the break-even price), the firm should continue to operate in the short run even though it is making a loss. This is optimal for prices in the range P_1 to P_2 and for quantities Q_1 to Q_2.

   c. When price exceeds minimum average total cost (the break-even price), the firm makes a profit. This happens for prices in excess of P_2 and results in quantities greater than Q_1.

2. This is an example of a temporary shut-down by a firm when the market price lies below the shut-down price, the minimum average variable cost. In this case, the market price is the price of a lobster meal and variable cost is the variable cost of serving such a meal, such as the cost of the lobster, employee wages, and so on. In this example, however, it is the average variable cost curve rather than the market price that shifts over time, due to seasonal changes in the cost of lobsters. Maine lobster shacks have relatively low average variable cost during the summer, when cheap Maine lobsters are available. During the rest of the year, their average variable cost is relatively high due to the high cost of imported lobsters. As a result, the lobster shacks are open for business during the summer, when their minimum average variable cost lies below price. But they close during the rest of the year, when price lies below their minimum average variable cost.

MODULE 26

26-1 Check Your Understanding

1. **a.** A fall in the fixed cost of production generates a fall in the average total cost of production and, in the short run, an increase in each firm's profit at the current output level. So, in the long run, new firms will enter the industry. The increase in supply drives down price and profits. Once profits are driven back to zero, entry will cease.

   b. An increase in wages generates an increase in the average variable and the average total cost of production at every output level. In the short run, firms incur losses at the current output level, and so in the long run some firms will exit the industry. (If the average variable cost rises sufficiently, some firms may even shut down in the short run.) As firms exit, supply decreases, price rises, and losses are reduced. Exit will cease once losses return to zero.

   c. Price will rise as a result of the increased demand for the good, leading to a short-run increase in profits at the current output level. In the long run, firms will enter the industry, generating an increase in supply, a fall in price, and a fall in profits. Once profits are driven back to zero, entry will cease.

   d. The shortage of a key input causes that input's price to increase, resulting in an increase in average variable cost and average total cost for producers. Firms incur losses in the short run, and some firms will exit the industry in the long run. The fall in supply generates an increase in price and decreased losses. Exit will cease when losses have returned to zero.

2. In the accompanying diagram, point X_{MKT} in panel (b), the intersection of S_1 and D_1, represents the long-run industry equilibrium before the change in consumer tastes. When tastes change, demand falls and the industry moves in the short run to point Y_{MKT} in panel (b), at the intersection of the new demand curve D_2 and S_1, the short-run supply curve representing the same number of egg producers as in the original equilibrium at point X_{MKT}. As the market price falls, an individual firm reacts by producing less—as shown in panel (a)—as long as the market price remains above the minimum average variable cost. If market price falls below minimum average variable cost, the firm would shut down immediately. At point Y_{MKT}, the price of eggs is below minimum average total cost, creating losses for producers. This leads some firms to exit, which shifts the short-run industry supply curve leftward to S_2. A new long-run equilibrium is established at point Z_{MKT}. As this occurs, the market price rises again, and, as shown in panel (c), each remaining producer reacts by increasing output (here, from point Y to point Z). All remaining producers again make zero profits. The decrease in the quantity of eggs supplied in the industry comes entirely from the exit of some producers from the industry. The long-run industry supply curve is the curve labeled LRS in panel (b).

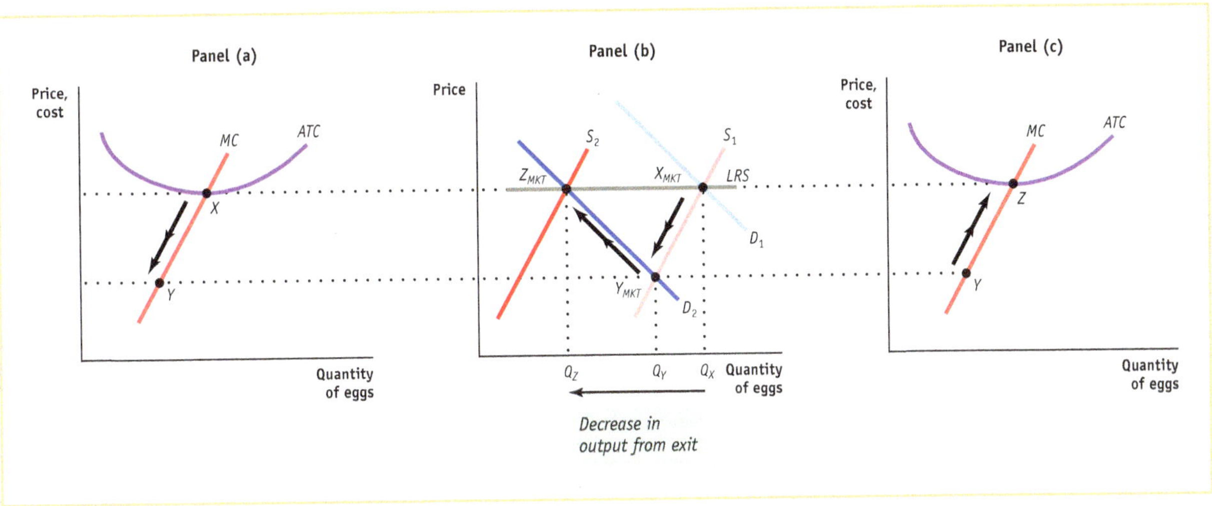

MODULE 27

27-1 Check Your Understanding

1. a. The price at each output level is found by dividing the total revenue by the number of emeralds produced; for example, the price when 3 emeralds are produced is $252/3 = $84. The price at the various output levels is then used to construct the demand schedule in the accompanying table.

   b. The marginal revenue schedule is found by calculating the change in total revenue as output increases by one unit. For example, the marginal revenue generated by increasing output from 2 to 3 emeralds is ($252 − $186) = $66.

   c. The quantity effect component of marginal revenue is the additional revenue generated by selling one more unit of the good at the market price. For example, as shown in the accompanying table, at 3 emeralds, the market price is $84; so when going from 2 to 3 emeralds, the quantity effect is equal to $84.

   d. The price effect component of marginal revenue is the decline in total revenue caused by the fall in price when one more unit is sold. For example, as shown in the table, when only 2 emeralds are sold, each emerald sells at a price of $93. However, when Emerald, Inc. sells an additional emerald, the price must fall by $9 to $84. So the price effect component in going from 2 to 3 emeralds is (−$9) × 2 = −$18. That's because 2 emeralds can only be sold at a price of $84 when 3 emeralds in total are sold, although they could have been sold at a price of $93 when only 2 in total were sold.

Quantity of emeralds demanded	Price of emerald	Marginal revenue	Quantity effect component	Price effect component
1	$100			
		$86	$93	−$7
2	93			
		66	84	−18
3	84			
		28	70	−42
4	70			
		−30	50	−80
5	50			

   e. To determine Emerald, Inc.'s profit-maximizing output level, you must know its marginal cost at each output level. Its profit-maximizing output level is the one at which marginal revenue is equal to marginal cost.

2. As the accompanying diagram shows, the marginal cost curve shifts upward to $400. The profit-maximizing price rises and quantity falls. Profit falls from $3,200 to $300 × 6 = $1,800 Competitive industry profits, though, are unchanged at zero.

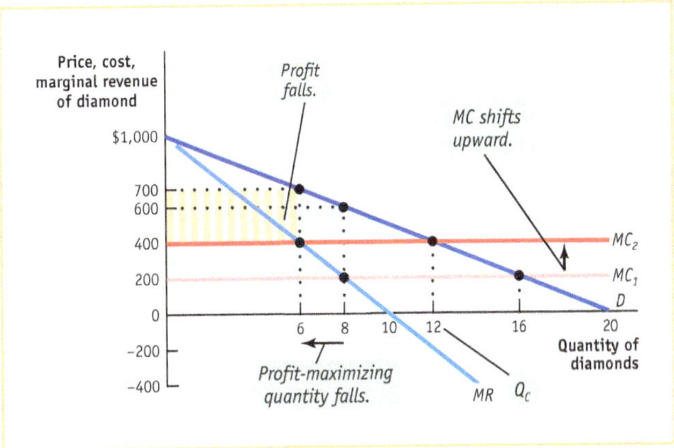

MODULE 28

28-1 Check Your Understanding

1. a. Because cable internet service is a natural monopoly, the government should intervene only if it believes that price exceeds average total cost, where average total cost is based on the cost of laying the cable. In this case, it should impose a price ceiling equal to average total cost. Otherwise, it should do nothing.

   b. The government should approve the merger only if it fosters competition by transferring some of the company's landing slots to another, competing airline.

2. a. False. As can be seen from Figure 28-1, panel (b), the inefficiency arises from the fact that some of the consumer surplus is transformed into deadweight loss (the yellow area), not that it is transformed into profit (the green area).

b. True. If a monopolist sold to all customers who have a valuation greater than or equal to marginal cost, all mutually beneficial transactions would occur and there would be no deadweight loss.

3. As shown in the accompanying diagram, a profit-maximizing monopolist produces Q_M, the output level at which $MR = MC$. A monopolist who mistakenly believes that $P = MR$ produces the output level at which $P = MC$ (when, in fact, $P > MR$, and at the true profit-maximizing level of output, $P > MR = MC$). This misguided monopolist will produce the output level Q_C, where the demand curve crosses the marginal cost curve—the same output level produced if the industry were perfectly competitive. It will charge the price P_C, which is equal to marginal cost, and make zero profit. The entire shaded area is equal to the consumer surplus, which is also equal to total surplus in this case (since the monopolist receives zero producer surplus). There is no deadweight loss since every consumer who is willing to pay as much as or more than marginal cost gets the good. A smart monopolist, however, will produce the output level Q_M and charge the price P_M. Profit equals the green area, consumer surplus corresponds to the blue area, and total surplus is equal to the sum of the green and blue areas. The yellow area is the deadweight loss generated by the monopolist.

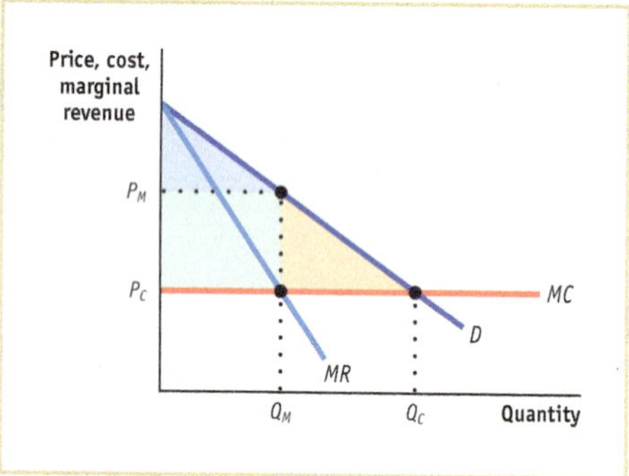

4. Facebook has nearly 2.5 billion users, which has created a network externality. At this point, Facebook is experiencing increasing returns to scale. But at the same time, there are many social media networks, including Twitter, Instagram, and Snapchat, which has reduced Facebook's market share.

MODULE 29

29-1 Check Your Understanding

1. a. False. A price-discriminating monopolist will sell to some customers that a single-price monopolist will refuse to sell to—namely, customers with a high price elasticity of demand who are willing to pay only a relatively low price for the good.

b. False. Although a price-discriminating monopolist does indeed capture more of the consumer surplus, inefficiency is lower: more mutually beneficial transactions occur because the monopolist makes more sales to customers with a low willingness to pay for the good.

c. True. Under price discrimination, consumers are charged prices that depend on their price elasticity of demand. A consumer with highly elastic demand will pay a lower price than a consumer with inelastic demand.

2. a. This is not a case of price discrimination because all consumers, regardless of their price elasticities of demand, value the damaged merchandise less than they would undamaged merchandise. So, the price must be lowered to sell the merchandise.

b. This is a case of price discrimination. Senior citizens have a higher price elasticity of demand for restaurant meals (their demand for restaurant meals is more responsive to price changes) than other patrons. Restaurants lower the price to high-elasticity consumers (senior citizens). Consumers with low price elasticity of demand will pay the full price.

c. This is a case of price discrimination. Consumers with a high price elasticity of demand will pay a lower price by collecting and using discount coupons. Consumers with a low price elasticity of demand will not use coupons.

d. This is not a case of price discrimination; it is simply a case of supply and demand.

MODULE 30

30-1 Check Your Understanding

1. a. The firm is likely to act noncooperatively and raise output, which will generate a negative price effect. But because the firm's current market share is small, the negative price effect will fall much more heavily on its rivals' revenues than on its own. At the same time, the firm will benefit from a positive quantity effect.

b. The firm is likely to act noncooperatively and raise output, which will generate a fall in price. Because its rivals have higher costs, they will lose money at the lower price while the firm continues to make profits. So the firm may be able to drive its rivals out of business by increasing its output.

c. The firm is likely to collude. Because it is costly for consumers to switch products, the firm would have to lower its price quite substantially (by increasing quantity a lot) to induce consumers to switch to its product. So increasing output is likely to be unprofitable given the large negative price effect.

d. The firm is likely to act uncooperatively because it knows its rivals cannot increase their output in retaliation.

30-2 Check Your Understanding

1. a. This is likely to be interpreted as evidence of tacit collusion. Firms in the industry are able to tacitly collude by setting their prices according to the published "suggested" price of the largest firm in the industry. This is a form of price leadership.

b. This is not likely to be interpreted as evidence of tacit collusion. Considerable variation in market shares indicates that firms have been competing to capture one another's business.

c. This is not likely to be interpreted as evidence of tacit collusion. These features make it more unlikely that consumers will switch products in response to lower prices. So this is a way for firms to avoid any temptation to gain market share by lowering price. This is a form of product differentiation that is used to avoid direct competition.

d. This is likely to be interpreted as evidence of tacit collusion. In the guise of discussing sales targets, firms can create a cartel by designating quantities to be produced by each firm.

e. This is likely to be interpreted as evidence of tacit collusion. By raising prices together, each firm in the industry is refusing to undercut its rivals by leaving its price unchanged or lowering it. Because it could gain market share by doing so, refusing to do it is evidence of tacit collusion.

MODULE 31

31-1 Check Your Understanding

1. When Margaret builds a missile, Nikita's payoff from building a missile as well is –10; it is –20 if he does not. The same set of payoffs holds for Margaret when Nikita builds a missile: her payoff is –10 if she builds one as well, –20 if she does not. So it is a Nash (or noncooperative) equilibrium for both Margaret and Nikita to build missiles, and their total payoff is (–10) + (–10) = –20. But their total payoff is greatest when neither builds a missile: their total payoff is 0 + 0 = 0. But this outcome—the cooperative outcome—is unlikely. If Margaret builds a missile but Nikita does not, Margaret gets a payoff of +8, rather than the 0 she gets if she doesn't build a missile. So Margaret is better off if she builds a missile but Nikita doesn't. Similarly, Nikita is better off if he builds a missile but Margaret doesn't: he gets a payoff of +8, rather than the 0 he gets if he doesn't build a missile. So both players have an incentive to build a missile. Both will build a missile, and each gets a payoff of –10. So unless Nikita and Margaret are able to communicate in some way to enforce cooperation, they will act in their own individual interests and each will build a missile.

2. **a.** Future entry by several new firms will increase competition and drive down industry profits. As a result, there is less future profit to protect by behaving cooperatively today. So each oligopolist is more likely to behave noncooperatively today.

   b. When it is very difficult for a firm to detect if another firm has raised output, then it is very difficult to enforce cooperation by playing tit for tat. So it is more likely that a firm will behave noncooperatively.

   c. When firms have coexisted while maintaining high prices for a long time, each expects cooperation to continue. So the value of behaving cooperatively today is high, and it is likely that firms will engage in tacit collusion.

MODULE 32

32-1 Check Your Understanding

1. **a.** An increase in fixed cost raises average total cost and shifts the average total cost curve upward. In the short run, firms incur losses. In the long run, some will exit the industry, resulting in a rightward shift of the demand curves for those firms that remain in the industry, since each one now serves a larger share of the market. Long-run equilibrium is reestablished when the demand curve for each remaining firm has shifted rightward to the point where it is tangent to the firm's new, higher average total cost curve. At this point each firm's price just equals its average total cost, and each firm makes zero profit.

   b. A decrease in marginal cost lowers average total cost and shifts the average total cost curve and the marginal cost curve downward. Because existing firms now make profits, in the long run new entrants are attracted into the industry. In the long run, this results in a leftward shift of each existing firm's demand curve since each firm now has a smaller share of the market. Long-run equilibrium is reestablished when each firm's demand curve has shifted leftward to the point where it is tangent to the new, lower average total cost curve. At this point each firm's price just equals average total cost, and each firm makes zero profit.

2. If all the existing firms in the industry joined together to create a monopoly, they would achieve monopoly profits. But this would induce new firms to create new, differentiated products and then enter the industry and capture some of the monopoly profits. So in the long run it would be impossible to maintain a monopoly. The problem arises from the fact that because new firms can create new products, there is no barrier to entry that can maintain a monopoly.

32-2 Check Your Understanding

1. **a.** False. As can be seen from panel (b) of Figure 32-4, a monopolistically competitive firm produces at a point at which price exceeds marginal cost—unlike a perfectly competitive firm, which produces where price equals marginal cost (at the point of minimum average total cost). A monopolistically competitive firm will refuse to sell at marginal cost. This would be below average total cost and the firm would incur a loss.

   b. True. Firms in a monopolistically competitive industry could achieve higher profits (monopoly profits) if they all joined together and produced a single product. In addition, since the industry possesses excess capacity, producing a larger quantity of output would lower the firm's average total cost. The effect on consumers, however, is ambiguous. They would experience less choice. But if consolidation substantially reduces industry-wide average total cost and therefore substantially increases industry-wide output, consumers may experience lower prices under monopoly.

   c. True. Fads and fashions are created and promulgated by advertising, which is found in oligopolies and monopolistically competitive industries but not in monopolies or perfectly competitive industries.

MODULE 33

33-1 Check Your Understanding

1. **a.** Ladders are not differentiated as a result of monopolistic competition. A ladder producer makes different ladders (tall ladders versus short ladders) to satisfy different consumer needs, not to avoid competition with rivals. So two tall ladders made by two different producers will be indistinguishable by consumers.

   b. Soft drinks are an example of product differentiation as a result of monopolistic competition. For example, several producers make colas; each is differentiated in terms of taste, which fast-food chains sell it, and so on.

c. Department stores are an example of product differentiation as a result of monopolistic competition. They serve different clienteles that have different price sensitivities and different tastes. They also offer different levels of customer service and are situated in different locations.

d. Steel is not differentiated as a result of monopolistic competition. Different types of steel (beams versus sheets) are made for different purposes, not to distinguish one steel manufacturer's products from another's.

2. a. Perfectly competitive industries and monopolistically competitive industries both have many sellers. So it may be hard to distinguish between them solely in terms of number of firms. And in both market structures, there is free entry into and exit from the industry in the long run. But in a perfectly competitive industry, one standardized product is sold; in a monopolistically competitive industry, products are differentiated. So you should ask whether products are differentiated in the industry.

b. In a monopoly there is only one firm, but a monopolistically competitive industry contains many firms. So you should ask whether or not there is a single firm in the industry.

33-2 Check Your Understanding

1. a. This is economically useful because such advertisements are likely to focus on the medical benefits of aspirin.

b. This is economically wasteful because such advertisements are likely to focus on promoting Bayer aspirin versus a rival's aspirin product. The two products are medically indistinguishable.

c. This is economically useful because such advertisements are likely to focus on the health and enjoyment benefits of orange juice.

d. This is economically wasteful because such advertisements are likely to focus on promoting Tropicana orange juice versus a rival's product. The two are likely to be indistinguishable by consumers.

e. This is economically useful because the longevity of a business gives a potential customer information about its quality.

2. A successful brand name indicates a desirable attribute, such as quality, to a potential buyer. So, other things equal—such as price—a firm with a successful brand name will achieve higher sales than a rival with a comparable product but without a successful brand name. This is likely to deter new firms from entering an industry in which an existing firm has a successful brand name.

MODULE 34

34-1 Check Your Understanding

1. a. The external cost is the pollution caused by the wastewater runoff, an uncompensated cost imposed by the poultry farms on their neighbors.

b. Since poultry farmers do not take the external cost of their actions into account when making decisions about how much wastewater to generate, they will create more runoff than is socially optimal in the absence of government intervention or a private deal. They will produce runoff up to the point at which the marginal social benefit of an additional unit of runoff is zero; however, their neighbors experience a high, positive level of marginal social cost of runoff from this output level. So, the quantity of wastewater runoff is inefficient: reducing runoff by one unit would reduce total social benefit by less than it would reduce total social cost.

c. At the socially optimal quantity of wastewater runoff, the marginal social benefit is equal to the marginal social cost. This quantity is lower than the quantity of wastewater runoff that would be created in the absence of government intervention or a private deal.

2. Yasmin's reasoning is not correct: allowing some late returns of books is likely to be socially optimal. Although you impose a marginal social cost on others every day that you are late in returning a book, there is some positive marginal social benefit to you of returning a book late—for example, you get a longer period to use it in working on a term paper.

The socially optimal number of days that a book is returned late is the number at which the marginal social benefit equals the marginal social cost. A fine so stiff that it prevents any late returns is likely to result in a situation in which people return books although the marginal social benefit of keeping them another day is greater than the marginal social cost—an inefficient outcome. In that case, allowing an overdue patron another day would increase total social benefit more than it would increase total social cost. So, charging a moderate fine that reduces the number of days that books are returned late to the socially optimal number of days is appropriate.

34-2 Check Your Understanding

1. A college education provides external benefits through the creation of knowledge. And student aid acts like a Pigouvian subsidy on higher education. If the marginal social benefit of higher education is indeed $29 billion, then student aid is an optimal policy.

2. a. Planting trees generates an external benefit since many people (not just those who plant the trees) benefit from the increased good air quality and lower summer temperatures. Without a subsidy, people will plant too few trees, setting the marginal social cost of planting a tree—what they forgo by planting a tree—too low. (Although too low, it may still be more than zero since a homeowner gains some personal benefit from planting a tree.) A Pigouvian subsidy will induce people to plant more trees, bringing the marginal social benefit of planting a tree in line with the marginal social cost.

b. Water-saving toilets generate an external benefit because they discourage wasting water, thereby reducing the need to pump more water from rivers and aquifers. Without a subsidy, homeowners will use water until the marginal social cost of water usage is equal to zero since water is costless to them. A Pigouvian subsidy on water-saving toilets will induce homeowners to reduce their water usage so that the marginal social benefit of water is in line with the marginal social cost.

c. Discarded plastic drink bottles impose an external cost by degrading the environment. Without a tax, people will discard plastic bottles freely—until the marginal social cost of discarding a bottle (what they must forgo in discarding a bottle) is zero. A Pigouvian tax or subsidy on drink bottles will bring the marginal social benefit of a drink bottle in line with its marginal social cost. This can be done two ways: via a tax or a subsidy. A tax will induce drink manufacturers to shift away from using polluting plastic bottles to less-polluting containers, like paper cartons. A subsidy for disposing of the containers in an environmentally sound way, such as recycling, will induce drink consumers to dispose of the bottles in a way that reduces the external costs.

MODULE 35

35-1 Check Your Understanding

1. This is a misguided argument. Allowing polluters to sell emissions permits makes polluters face the cost of polluting in the form of the opportunity cost of the permit. If a polluter chooses not to reduce its emissions, it cannot sell its emissions permits. As a result, it forgoes the opportunity of making money from the sale of the permits. So, despite the fact that the polluter receives a monetary benefit from selling the permits, the scheme has the desired effect: to make polluters internalize the externality of their actions.

2. **a.** If the emissions tax is smaller than the marginal social cost at Q_{OPT}, a polluter will face a marginal cost of polluting (equal to the amount of the tax) that is less than the marginal social cost at the socially optimal quantity of pollution. Since a polluter will produce emissions up to the point where the marginal social benefit is equal to its marginal cost, the resulting amount of pollution will be larger than the socially optimal quantity. As a result, there is inefficiency: if the amount of pollution is larger than the socially optimal quantity, the marginal social cost exceeds the marginal social benefit. A reduction in emissions levels will increase social surplus.

   If the emissions tax is greater than the marginal social cost at Q_{OPT}, a polluter will face a marginal cost of polluting (equal to the amount of the tax) that is greater than the marginal social cost at the socially optimal quantity of pollution. This will lead the polluter to reduce emissions below the socially optimal quantity. This also is inefficient: whenever the marginal social benefit is greater than the marginal social cost, an increase in emissions levels will raise social surplus.

   b. If the total amount of allowable pollution is set too high, the supply of emissions permits will be high and thus the equilibrium price at which permits trade will be low. That is, polluters will face a marginal cost of polluting (the price of a permit) that is "too low"—lower than the marginal social cost at the socially optimal quantity of pollution. As a result, pollution will be greater than the socially optimal quantity. This is inefficient and lowers total surplus.

   If the total level of allowable pollution is set too low, the supply of emissions permits will be low and so the equilibrium price at which permits are traded will be high. That is, polluters will face a marginal cost of polluting (the price of a permit) that is "too high"—higher than the marginal social cost at the socially optimal quantity of pollution. As a result, pollution will be lower than the socially optimal quantity. This also is inefficient and lowers total surplus.

   c. A carbon tax will increase the cost of using fossil fuels, including the prices of gasoline and coal. As the cost of fossil fuels increases, consumers will reduce their use of fossil fuels as energy sources. They will be increasingly likely to purchase more fuel-efficient cars and invest in solar technology for their homes.

35-2 Check Your Understanding

1. Types of fossil fuels are coal, oil, and gas. The main clean energy sources are wind and solar. The burning of fossil fuels creates greenhouse gas emissions, which cause climate change. Clean energy sources do not create greenhouse gas emissions, so do not contribute to climate change.

2. The market failure that led to climate change was the historical underpricing of fossil-fuel consumption. That is, the market price of fossil fuel was too low compared to the true cost of greenhouse gas emissions that they generated. The estimated loss to U.S. GDP from unmitigated climate change is 10%; the estimated loss to world GDP is 20%.

3. Government subsidies to innovations in clean energy are an important policy tool because it is unlikely that the clean energy sector would have become cost competitive with fossil fuels without them. Multilateral agreements between countries are an important policy tool because a country is likely to be unwilling to cut its emissions without a commitment by other countries to do the same. Individual incentives are important because they can lead to fast and effective ways to conserve energy and thus reduce greenhouse gas emissions.

4. Although the structural change required to address climate change will require some loss of GDP, it is small (1) compared to the costs of unmitigated climate change; and (2) compared to the projected growth rate of GDP over time. Also, the direct health costs of unmitigated climate change are significant, resulting in millions of excess deaths and as much as 5% of world GDP.

MODULE 36

36-1 Check Your Understanding

1. **a.** Use of a public park is nonexcludable, but it may or may not be rival in consumption, depending on the circumstances. For example, if both you and I use the park for jogging, then your use will not prevent my use—use of the park is nonrival in consumption. In this case the public park is a public good. But use of the park is rival in consumption if there are many people trying to use the jogging path at the same time or when my use of the public tennis court prevents your use of the same court. In this case the public park is a common resource.

   b. A cheese burrito is both excludable and rival in consumption. Hence it is a private good.

   c. Information from a password-protected website is excludable but nonrival in consumption. It is an artificially scarce good.

d. Publicly announced information on the path of an incoming hurricane is nonexcludable and nonrival in consumption. It is a public good.

2. A private producer will supply only a good that is excludable; otherwise, the producer won't be able to charge a price for it that covers the cost of production. So, a private producer would be willing to supply a cheese burrito and information from a password-protected website but they would be unwilling to supply a public park or publicly announced information about an incoming hurricane.

36-2 Check Your Understanding

1. a. With 10 Homebodies and 6 Revelers, the marginal social benefit schedule of money spent on the party is as shown in the accompanying table.

Money spent on party	Marginal social benefit
$0	
	(10 × $0.05) + (6 × $0.13) = $1.28
1	
	(10 × $0.04) + (6 × $0.11) = $1.06
2	
	(10 × $0.03) + (6 × $0.09) = $0.84
3	
	(10 × $0.02) + (6 × $0.07) = $0.62
4	

The efficient spending level is $2, the highest level for which the marginal social benefit is greater than the marginal cost ($1).

b. With 6 Homebodies and 10 Revelers, the marginal social benefit schedule of money spent on the party is as shown in the accompanying table.

Money spent on party	Marginal social benefit
$0	
	(6 × $0.05) + (10 × $0.13) = $1.60
1	
	(6 × $0.04) + (10 × $0.11) = $1.34
2	
	(6 × $0.03) + (10 × $0.09) = $1.08
3	
	(6 × $0.02) + (10 × $0.07) = $0.82
4	

The efficient spending level is now $3, the highest level for which the marginal social benefit is greater than the marginal cost ($1). The efficient level of spending has increased from that in part a because with relatively more Revelers than Homebodies, an additional dollar spent on the party generates a higher level of social benefit compared to when there are relatively more Homebodies than Revelers.

c. When the numbers of Homebodies and Revelers are unknown but residents are asked their preferences, Homebodies will pretend to be Revelers to induce a higher level of spending on the public party. That's because a Homebody still receives a positive individual marginal benefit from an additional $1 spent, despite the fact that their individual marginal benefit is lower than that of a Reveler for every additional $1. In this case the "reported" marginal social benefit schedule of money spent on the party will be as shown in the accompanying table.

Money spent on party	Marginal social benefit
$0	
	16 × $0.13 = $2.08
1	
	16 × $0.11 = $1.76
2	
	16 × $0.09 = $1.44
3	
	16 × $0.07 = $1.12
4	

As a result, $4 will be spent on the party, the highest level for which the "reported" marginal social benefit is greater than the marginal cost ($1). Regardless of whether there are 10 Homebodies and 6 Revelers (part a) or 6 Homebodies and 10 Revelers (part b), spending $4 in total on the party is clearly inefficient because marginal cost exceeds marginal social benefit at this spending level.

As a further exercise, consider how much Homebodies gain by this misrepresentation. In part a, the efficient level of spending is $2. So, by misrepresenting their preferences, the 10 Homebodies gain, in total, 10 × ($0.03 + $0.02) = $0.50—that is, they gain the marginal individual benefit in going from a spending level of $2 to $4. The 6 Revelers also gain from the misrepresentations of the Homebodies; they gain 6 × ($0.09 + $0.07) = $0.96 in total. This outcome is clearly inefficient—when $4 in total is spent, the marginal cost is $1 but the marginal social benefit is only $0.62, indicating that too much money is being spent on the party.

In part b, the efficient level of spending is actually $3. The misrepresentation by the 6 Homebodies gains them, in total, 6 × $0.02 = $0.12 but the 10 Revelers gain 10 × $0.07 = $0.70 in total. This outcome is also clearly inefficient—when $4 is spent, marginal social benefit is only $0.12 + $0.70 = $0.82 but marginal cost is $1.

36-3 Check Your Understanding

1. When individuals are allowed to harvest freely, the government-owned forest becomes a common resource, and individuals will overuse it—they will harvest more trees than is efficient. In economic terms, the marginal social cost of harvesting a tree is greater than a private logger's individual marginal cost.

2. The three methods consistent with economic theory are (i) Pigouvian taxes, (ii) a system of tradable licenses, and (iii) allocation of property rights.

i. *Pigouvian taxes.* You would enforce a tax on loggers that equals the difference between the marginal social cost and the individual marginal cost of logging a tree at the socially efficient harvest amount. To do this, you must know the marginal social cost schedule and the individual marginal cost schedule.

ii. *System of tradable licenses.* You would issue tradable licenses, setting the total number of trees harvested equal to the socially efficient harvest number. The market that arises in these licenses will allocate the right to log efficiently when loggers differ in their costs of logging: licenses will be purchased by those who have a relatively lower cost of logging. The market price of a license will be equal to the difference between the marginal social cost and the individual marginal cost of logging a tree at the socially efficient harvest amount. To implement this level, you need to know the socially efficient harvest amount.

iii. *Allocation of property rights.* Here you would sell or give the forest to a private party. This party will have the right to exclude others from harvesting trees. Harvesting is now a private good—it is excludable and rival in consumption. As a result, there is no longer any divergence between social and private costs, and the private party will harvest the efficient level of trees. You need no additional information to use this method.

MODULE 37

37-1 Check Your Understanding

1. Many college professors will depart for other lines of work if the government imposes a wage that is lower than the market wage. Fewer professors will result in fewer courses taught and therefore fewer college degrees produced. It will adversely affect sectors of the economy that depend directly on colleges, such as the local shopkeepers who sell goods and services to students and faculty, college textbook publishers, and so on. It will also adversely affect firms that use the "output" produced by colleges: new college graduates. Firms that need to hire new employees with college degrees will be hurt because a smaller supply results in a higher market wage for college graduates. Ultimately, the reduced supply of college-educated workers will result in a lower level of human capital in the entire economy relative to what it would have been without the policy. And this will hurt all sectors of the economy that depend on human capital. The sectors of the economy that might benefit are firms that compete with colleges in the hiring of would-be college professors. For example, accounting firms will find it easier to hire people who would otherwise have been professors of accounting, and publishers will find it easier to hire people who would otherwise have been professors of English (easier in the sense that the firms can recruit would-be professors with a lower wage than before). In addition, workers who already have college degrees will benefit; they will command higher wages as the supply of college-educated workers falls.

37-2 Check Your Understanding

1. a. As the demand for services increases, the price of services will rise. And as the price of the output produced by the industries increases, this shifts the *VMPL* curve upward—that is, the demand for labor rises. This results in an increase in both the equilibrium wage rate and the quantity of labor employed.

b. The fall in the catch per day means that the marginal product of labor in the industry declines. The *VMPL* curve shifts downward, generating a fall in the equilibrium wage rate and the equilibrium quantity of labor employed.

2. When firms from different industries compete for the same workers, then each worker in the various industries will be paid the same equilibrium wage rate, *W*. And since, by the marginal productivity theory of income distribution, $VMPL = P \times MPL = W$ for the last worker hired in equilibrium, the last worker hired in each of these different industries will have the same value of the marginal product of labor.

MODULE 38

38-1 Check Your Understanding

1. a. False. Income disparities associated with gender, race, or ethnicity can be explained by the marginal productivity theory of income distribution provided that differences in marginal productivity across people are correlated with gender, race, or ethnicity. One possible source for such correlation is past discrimination. Such discrimination can lower individuals' marginal productivity by, for example, preventing them from acquiring the human capital that would raise their productivity. Another possible source of the correlation is differences in work experience that are associated with gender, race, or ethnicity. For example, in jobs in which work experience or length of tenure is important, women may earn lower wages because on average more women than men take child-care-related absences from work.

b. True. Companies that discriminate when their competitors do not are likely to hire less able workers because they discriminate against more able workers who are considered to be of the wrong gender, race, ethnicity, or other characteristic. And with less able workers, such companies are likely to earn lower profits than their competitors that don't discriminate.

c. Ambiguous. In general, workers who are paid less because they have less experience may or may not be the victims of discrimination. The answer depends on the reason for the lack of experience. If workers have less experience because they are young or have chosen to do something else rather than gain experience, then they are not victims of discrimination if they are paid less. But if workers lack experience because previous job discrimination prevented them from gaining experience, then they are indeed victims of discrimination when they are paid less.

MODULE 39

39-1 Check Your Understanding

1. a. Clive is made worse off if, before the new law, he had preferred to work more than 35 hours per week. As a result of the law, he can no longer choose his preferred time allocation; he now consumes fewer goods and more leisure than he would like.

b. Clive's utility is unaffected by the law if, before the law, he had preferred to work 35 or fewer hours per week. The law has not changed his preferred time allocation.

c. Clive can never be made better off by a law that restricts the number of hours he can work. He can only be made worse off (case a) or equally as well off (case b).

2. The substitution effect would induce Clive to work fewer hours and consume more leisure after his wage rate falls—the fall in the wage rate means the price of an hour of leisure falls, leading Clive to consume more leisure. But a fall in his wage rate also generates a fall in Clive's income. The income effect of this is to induce Clive to consume less leisure and therefore work more hours, since he is now poorer and leisure is a normal good. If the income effect dominates the substitution effect, Clive will in the end work more hours than before.

MODULE 40

40-1 Check Your Understanding

1. a. A pension guarantee program is a social insurance program. The possibility of an employer declaring bankruptcy and defaulting on its obligation to pay employee pensions creates insecurity. By providing pension income to those employees, such a program alleviates this source of economic insecurity.

   b. The SCHIP program is a poverty program. By providing health care to children in low-income households, it targets its spending specifically to the poor.

   c. The Section 8 housing program is a poverty program. By targeting its support to low-income households, it specifically helps the poor.

   d. The federal flood program is a social insurance program. For many people, the majority of their wealth is tied up in the home they own. The potential for a loss of that wealth creates economic insecurity. By providing assistance to those hit by a major flood, the program alleviates this source of insecurity.

2. The poverty threshold is an absolute measure of poverty. It defines individuals as poor if their incomes fall below a level that is considered adequate to purchase the necessities of life, irrespective of how well other people are doing. And that measure is fixed: in 2014, for instance, it took $11,670 for an individual living alone to purchase the necessities of life, regardless of how well-off other Americans were. In particular, the poverty threshold is not adjusted for an increase in living standards: even if other Americans are becoming increasingly well-off over time, in real terms (that is, how many goods an individual at the poverty threshold can buy) the poverty threshold remains the same.

3. a. To determine mean (or average) income, we take the total income of all individuals in this economy and divide it by the number of individuals. Mean income is ($39,000 + $17,500 + $900,000 + $15,000 + $28,000)/5 = $999,500/5 = $199,900. To determine median income, look at the accompanying table, which ranks the five individuals in order of their income.

	Income
Vijay	$15,000
Kelly	17,500
Oskar	28,000
Sephora	39,000
Raul	900,000

   The median income is the income of the individual in the exact middle of the income distribution: Oskar, with an income of $28,000. So the median income is $28,000.

   Median income is more representative of the income of individuals in this economy: almost everyone earns income between $15,000 and $39,000, close to the median income of $28,000. Only Raul is the exception: it is his income that raises the mean income to $199,900, which is not representative of most incomes in this economy.

   b. The first quintile is made up of the 20% (or one-fifth) of individuals with the lowest incomes in the economy. Vijay makes up the 20% of individuals with the lowest incomes. His income is $15,000, so that is the average income of the first quintile. Oskar makes up the 20% of individuals with the third-lowest incomes. His income is $28,000, so that is the average income of the third quintile.

40-2 Check Your Understanding

1. The Earned Income Tax Credit (EITC), a negative income tax, applies only to those workers who earn income; over a certain range of incomes, the more a worker earns, the higher the amount of EITC received. A person who earns no income receives no income tax credit. By contrast, poverty programs that pay individuals based solely on low income still make those payments even if the individual does not work at all; once the individual earns a certain amount of income, these programs discontinue payments. As a result, such programs contain an incentive not to work and earn income, since earning more than a certain amount makes individuals ineligible for their benefits. The negative income tax, however, provides an incentive to work and earn income because its payments increase the more an individual works.

2. The second column of Table 40-3 gives the percentage reduction in the overall poverty rate by government programs. So the reduction in the overall poverty rate by the U.S. welfare state is given by adding up the numbers in that second column, which gives a 16.7% reduction in the overall poverty rate. For those aged 65 or over, the welfare state cuts the poverty rate by 43.6%, the amount given by adding up the numbers in the last column of Table 40-3.

40-3 Check Your Understanding

1. a. The program benefits you and your parents because the pool of all college students contains a representative mix of healthy and less healthy people, rather than a selected group of people who want insurance because they expect to pay high medical bills. In that respect, this insurance is like *employment-based health insurance*. Because no student can opt out, the school can offer health insurance based on the health care costs of its average student. If each student had to buy their own health insurance, some students would not be able to obtain any insurance and many would pay more than they do to the school's insurance program.

   b. Since all students are required to enroll in its health insurance program, even the healthiest students cannot leave the program in an effort to obtain cheaper insurance tailored specifically to healthy people. If this were to happen, the school's insurance program would be left with an adverse selection of less healthy students and so would have to raise premiums, beginning the adverse selection death spiral. But since no student can leave the insurance program, the school's program can continue to base its premiums on the average student's probability of requiring health care, avoiding the adverse selection death spiral.

2. According to critics, part of the reason the U.S. health care system is so much more expensive than those of other countries is its fragmented nature. Since each of the many insurance companies has significant administrative (overhead) costs—in part because each insurance company incurs marketing costs and exerts significant effort in weeding out high-risk insureds—the system tends to be more expensive than one in which there is only a single medical insurer. Another part of the explanation is that U.S. medical care includes many more expensive treatments than are found in other wealthy countries, pays higher physician salaries, and has higher drug prices.

Glossary

A

absolute advantage the advantage conferred on an individual or country in an activity if the individual or country can do it better than others. A country with an absolute advantage can produce more output per worker than other countries.

absolute value the value of a number without regard to a plus or minus sign.

accounting profit revenue minus explicit cost.

administrative costs (of a tax) are the resources used by the government to collect the tax, and by taxpayers to pay it as well as to evade it, over and above the amount of the tax.

antitrust policy legislative and regulatory efforts undertaken by the government to prevent oligopolistic industries from becoming or behaving like monopolies.

artificially scarce good a good that is excludable but nontrivial in consumption.

autarky a situation in which a country does not trade with other countries.

average cost total cost divided by quantity of output produced.

average fixed cost the fixed cost per unit of output.

average total cost total cost divided by quantity of output produced; also referred to as average cost.

average variable cost the variable cost per unit of output.

B

bar graph a graph that uses bars of varying heights or lengths to show the comparative sizes of different observations of a variable.

barrier to entry something that prevents other firms from entering the industry. Crucial in protecting the profits of a monopolist.

barter the direct exchange of goods or services without the use of money.

black market a market in which goods or services are bought and sold illegally, either because it is illegal to sell them at all or because the prices charged are legally prohibited by a price ceiling.

bounded rationality a basis for decision making that leads to a choice that is close to but not exactly the one that leads to the best possible economic outcome; the "good enough" method of decision making.

brand name a name owned by a particular firm that distinguishes that firm's products from those of other firms.

break-even price the market price at which a firm earns zero profits.

budget constraint the limitation that the cost of a consumer's consumption bundle cannot exceed the consumer's income.

budget line all the consumption bundles available to a consumer who spends all of their income.

C

capital the total value of assets owned by an individual or firm—physical assets plus financial assets.

cartel an agreement among several producers to obey output restrictions to increase their joint profits.

causal relationship the relationship between two variables in which the value taken by one variable directly influences or determines the value taken by the other variable.

circular-flow diagram a diagram that represents the transactions in an economy by two kinds of flows around a circle: flows of physical things such as goods or labor in one direction and flows of money to pay for these physical things in the opposite direction.

clean energy sources energy sources that do not emit greenhouse gases. Renewable energy sources are also clean energy sources.

climate change the man-made change in Earth's climate from the accumulation of greenhouse gases caused by the use of fossil fuels.

collusion cooperation among producers to limit production and raise profits in order to raise one another's profits.

commodity output of different producers regarded by consumers as the same good; also referred to as a standardized product.

common resource a resource that is nonexcludable and rival in consumption.

comparative advantage the advantage conferred on an individual or country in producing a good or service if the opportunity cost of producing the good or service is lower for that individual or country than for other producers.

compensating differentials wage differences across jobs that reflect the fact that some jobs are less pleasant than others.

competitive market a market in which there are many buyers and sellers of the same good or service, none of whom can influence the price at which the good or service is sold.

complements pairs of goods for which a rise in the price of one good leads to a decrease in the demand for the other good.

constant marginal cost each additional unit costs the same to produce as the previous one.

constant returns to scale long-run average total cost is constant as output increases.

consumer surplus a term often used to refer both to individual consumer surplus and to total consumer surplus.

consumption bundle (of an individual) the collection of all the goods and services consumed by a given individual.

consumption possibilities the set of all consumption bundles that can be consumed given a consumer's income and prevailing prices.

copyright the exclusive legal right of the creator of a literary or artistic work to profit from that work; like a patent, it is a temporary monopoly.

cost (of seller) the lowest price at which a seller is willing to sell a good.

cross-price elasticity of demand a measure of the effect of the change in the price of one good on the quantity demanded of the other; it is equal to the percent change in the quantity demanded of one good divided by the percent change in the other good's price.

curve a line on a graph, which may be curved or straight, that depicts a relationship between two variables.

D

deadweight loss the loss in total surplus that occurs whenever an action or a policy reduces the quantity transacted below the efficient market equilibrium quantity.

decreasing marginal benefit each additional unit of an activity yields less benefit than the previous unit.

decreasing marginal cost each additional unit costs less to produce than the previous one.

decreasing returns to scale long-run average total cost increases as output increases (also known as diseconomies of scale).

demand curve a graphical representation of the demand schedule, showing the relationship between quantity demanded and price.

demand schedule a list or table showing how much of a good or service consumers will want to buy at different prices.

dependent variable the determined variable in a causal relationship.

diminishing returns to an input the effect observed when an increase in the quantity of an input, holding the levels of all other inputs fixed, leads to a decline in the marginal product of that input.

domestic demand curve a demand curve that shows how the quantity of a good demanded by domestic consumers depends on the price of that good.

domestic supply curve a supply curve that shows how the quantity of a good supplied by domestic producers depends on the price of that good.

dominant strategy in game theory, an action that is a player's best action regardless of the action taken by the other player.

duopolist one of two firms in a duopoly.

duopoly an oligopoly consisting of only two firms.

E

economic growth the growing ability of the economy to produce goods and services.

economic profit equal to revenue minus the opportunity cost of resources used. It is usually less than the accounting profit.

economic signal any piece of information that helps people make better economic decisions.

economics the social science that studies the production, distribution, and consumption of goods and services.

economy a system for coordinating society's productive activities.

efficiency-wage model a model in which some employers pay an above-equilibrium wage as an incentive for better performance.

efficient description of a market or economy that takes all opportunities to make some people better off without making other people worse off.

elastic demand the case in which the price elasticity of demand is greater than 1.

emissions tax a tax that depends on the amount of pollution a firm produces.

environmental standards rules that protect the environment by specifying actions by producers and consumers.

equilibrium an economic situation in which no individual would be better off doing something different.

equilibrium price the price at which the market is in equilibrium, that is, the quantity of a good or service demanded equals the quantity of that good or service supplied; also referred to as the market-clearing price.

equilibrium quantity the quantity of the good or service bought and sold at the equilibrium (or market-clearing) price.

equilibrium value of the marginal-product the additional value produced by the last unit of a factor employed in the factor market as a whole.

equity fairness; everyone gets their fair share. Since people can disagree about what's "fair," equity isn't as well defined a concept as efficiency.

European Union (EU) a customs union among 28 European nations.

excess capacity the failure to produce enough to minimize average total cost; characteristic of monopolistically competitive firms.

excise tax a tax on sales of a good or service.

excludable referring to a good, describes the case in which the supplier can prevent people who do not pay from consuming the good.

explicit cost a cost that requires an outlay of money.

exporting industries industries that produce goods or services that are sold abroad.

exports goods and services sold to other countries.

external benefit a benefit that an individual or firm confers on others without receiving compensation.

external cost an uncompensated cost that an individual or firm imposes on others.

externalities external costs and external benefits.

F

factor distribution of income the division of total income among labor, land, and capital.

factor intensity the difference in the ratio of factors used to produce a good in various industries. For example, oil refining is capital-intensive compared to auto seat production because oil refiners use a higher ratio of capital to labor than do producers of auto seats.

factor markets markets in which firms buy the resources they need to produce goods and services.

factors of production the resources used to produce goods and services. Labor and capital are examples of factors.

firm an organization that produces goods and services for sale.

fixed cost a cost that does not depend on the quantity of output produced. It is the cost of the fixed input.

fixed input an input whose quantity is fixed for a period of time and cannot be varied.

forecast a simple prediction of the future.

fossil fuels fuels derived from fossil sources, such as coal and oil.

free entry and exit describes an industry that potential producers can easily enter into and existing producers can easily leave.

free trade trade that is unregulated by government tariffs or other artificial barriers; the levels of exports and imports occur naturally, as a result of supply and demand.

free-rider problem problem that results when individuals who have no intention to pay for their own consumption of a good take a "free ride" on anyone who does pay; a problem with goods that are nonexcludable.

G

gains from trade gains achieved by dividing tasks and trading; in this way, people can get more of what they want through trade than they could if they tried to be self-sufficient.

game theory the study of behavior in situations of interdependence.

globalization the phenomenon of growing economic linkages among countries.

government transfer a government payment to an individual or a family.

greenhouse gases gas emissions that trap heat in Earth's atmosphere.

H

Heckscher–Ohlin model a model of international trade in which a country has a comparative advantage in a good whose production is intensive in the factors that are abundantly available in that country.

Herfindahl–Hirschman Index, or HHI, the square of each firm's share of market sales summed over the industry. It gives a picture of the industry market structure.

horizontal axis the horizontal number line of a graph along which values of the x-variable are measured; also referred to as the x-axis.

horizontal intercept the point at which a curve hits the horizontal axis; it indicates the value of the x-variable when the value of the y-variable is zero.

household a person or a group of people who share their income.

human capital the improvement in labor created by the education and knowledge embodied in the workforce.

hyperglobalization the phenomenon of extremely high levels of international trade.

I

imperfect competition a market structure in which no firm has a monopoly, but producers nonetheless have market power that they can use to affect market prices.

implicit cost a cost that does not require an outlay of money; it is measured by the value, in dollar terms, of benefits that are forgone.

implicit cost of capital the opportunity cost of the use of one's own capital—the income earned if the capital had been employed in its next-best alternative use.

import quota a legal limit on the quantity of a good that can be imported.

import-competing industries industries that produce goods or services that are also imported.

imports goods and services purchased from other countries.

in-kind benefit a benefit given in the form of goods or services.

incentive anything that offers rewards to people to change their behavior.

incidence (of a tax) a measure of who really pays the tax.

income distribution the way in which total income is divided among the owners of the various factors of production.

income effect the change in quantity of a good consumed that results from the change in a consumer's overall purchasing power due to a change in the price of that good.

income elasticity of demand the percent change in the quantity of a good demanded when a consumer's income changes divided by the percent change in the consumer's income.

income-elastic demand the case in which the income elasticity of demand for a good is greater than 1.

income-inelastic demand the case in which the income elasticity of demand for a good is positive but less than 1.

increasing marginal cost each additional unit costs more to produce than the previous one.

increasing returns to scale long-run average total cost declines as output increases (also referred to as economies of scale).

independent variable the determining variable in a causal relationship.

individual choice the decision by an individual of what to do, which necessarily involves a decision of what not to do.

individual consumer surplus the net gain to an individual buyer from the purchase of a good; equal to the difference between the buyer's willingness to pay and the price paid.

individual demand curve a graphical representation of the relationship between quantity demanded and price for an individual consumer.

individual labor supply curve a graphical representation showing how the quantity of labor supplied by an individual depends on that individual's wage rate.

individual producer surplus the net gain to an individual seller from selling a good; equal to the difference between the price received and the seller's cost.

individual supply curve a graphical representation of the relationship between quantity supplied and price for an individual producer.

industry supply curve a graphical representation showing the relationship between the price of a good and the total output of the industry as a whole.

inefficient describes a market or economy in which there are missed opportunities: some people could be made better off without making other people worse off.

inefficient allocation of sales among sellers a form of inefficiency in which sellers who would be willing to sell a good at the lowest price are not always those who actually manage to sell it; often the result of a price floor.

inefficient allocation to consumers a form of inefficiency in which people who want a good badly and are willing to pay a high price don't get it, and those who care relatively little about the good and are only willing to pay a low price do get it; often a result of a price ceiling.

inefficiently high quality a form of inefficiency in which sellers offer high-quality goods at a high price even though buyers would prefer a lower quality at a lower price; often the result of a price floor.

inefficiently low quality a form of inefficiency in which sellers offer low-quality goods at a low price even though buyers would prefer a higher quality at a higher price; often a result of a price ceiling.

inelastic demand the case in which the price elasticity of demand is less than 1.

inferior good a good for which a rise income decreases the demand for the good.

input a good or service used to produce another good or service.

interaction (of choices) my choices affect your choices, and vice versa; a feature of most economic situations. The results of this interaction are often quite different from what the individuals intend.

interdependence a relationship among firms in which their decisions significantly affect one another's profits; a characteristic of oligopolies.

interim production decision rule the principles that when price lies between minimum average total cost (break-even price) and minimum average variable cost (shutdown price), the firm produces in the short run to minimize loss.

international trade agreements treaties in which a country promises to engage in less trade protection against the exports of other countries in return for a promise by other countries to do the same for its own exports.

invisible hand a phrase used by Adam Smith to refer to the way in which an individual's pursuit of self-interest can lead, without the individual's intending it, to good results for society as a whole.

irrational describes a decision maker who chooses an option that leaves them worse off than choosing another available option.

L

labor the economy's pool of workers.

land a resource supplied by nature.

law of demand the principle that a higher price for a good or service, other things equal, leads people to demand a smaller quantity of that good or service.

leisure time available for purposes other than just earning money to buy marketed goods.

linear relationship the relationship between two variables in which the slope is constant and therefore is depicted on a graph by a curve that is a straight line.

long run the time period in which all inputs can be varied.

long-run average total cost curve a graphical representation showing the relationship between output and average total cost when fixed cost has been chosen to minimize average total cost for each level of output.

long-run industry supply curve a graphical representation showing how the quantity supplied responds to the price once producers have had time to enter or exit the industry.

long-run market equilibrium an economic balance when the quantity supplied equals the quantity demanded, given that sufficient time has elapsed for entry into and exit from the industry to occur.

loss aversion an oversensitivity to loss, leading to unwillingness to recognize a loss and move on.

M

macroeconomics the branch of economics that is concerned with overall ups and downs in the economy.

marginal analysis the study of marginal decisions.

marginal benefit the additional benefit derived from producing one more unit of a good or service.

marginal benefit curve a graphical representation showing how the benefit from producing one more unit depends on the quantity that has already been produced.

marginal cost the additional cost incurred by producing one more unit of a good or service.

marginal cost curve a graphical representation showing how the cost of producing one more unit depends on the quantity that has already been produced.

marginal decision a decision made at the "margin" of an activity to do a bit more or a bit less of that activity.

marginal product the additional quantity of output that is produced by using one more unit of a given input.

marginal productivity theory of income distribution the proposition that every factor of production is paid its equilibrium value of the marginal product.

marginal revenue the change in total revenue generated by an additional unit of output.

marginal revenue curve a graphical representation showing how marginal revenue varies as output varies.

marginal social benefit of pollution the additional gain to society as a whole from an additional unit of pollution.

marginal social cost of pollution the additional cost imposed on society as a whole by an additional unit of pollution.

marginal utility the change in total utility generated by consuming one additional unit of a good or service.

marginal utility curve a graphical representation showing how marginal utility depends on the quantity of a good or service consumed.

marginal utility per dollar the additional utility gained from spending one more dollar on a good or service.

market economy an economy in which decisions about production and consumption are made by individual producers and consumers.

market failure occurs when a market fails to be efficient.

market power the ability of a firm to raise prices.

market share the fraction of the total industry output accounted for by a given producer's output.

market-clearing price the price at which the market is in equilibrium, that is, the quantity of a good or service demanded equals the quantity of that good or service supplied; also referred to as the equilibrium price.

markets for goods and services markets in which firms sell goods and services that they produce to households.

maximum the highest point on a nonlinear curve, where the slope changes from positive to negative.

mean household income the average income across all households.

means-tested program a program available only to individuals or families whose incomes fall below a certain level.

median household income the income of the household lying at the exact middle of the income distribution.

mental accounting the habit of mentally assigning dollars to different accounts so that some dollars are worth more than others.

microeconomics the branch of economics that studies how people make decisions and how these decisions interact.

midpoint method a technique for calculating the percent change. In this approach, we calculate changes in a variable compared with the average, or midpoint, of the starting and final values.

minimum the lowest point on a nonlinear curve, where the slope changes from negative to positive.

minimum wage a legal floor on the wage rate. The wage rate is the market price of labor.

minimum-cost output the quantity of output at which average total cost is lowest—the bottom of the U-shaped average total cost curve.

model a simplified representation of a real situation that is used to better understand real-life situations.

monopolist the only producer of a good that has no close substitutes.

monopolistic competition a market structure in which there are many competing firms in an industry, each firm sells a differentiated product, and there is free entry into and exit from the industry in the long run.

monopoly an industry controlled by a monopolist.

movement along the demand curve a change in the quantity demanded of a good that results from a change in the price of that good.

movement along the supply curve a change in the quantity supplied of a good that results from a change in the price of that good.

N

Nash equilibrium in game theory, the equilibrium that results when all players choose the action that maximizes their payoffs given the actions of other players, ignoring the effects of that action on the payoffs of other players; also known as noncooperative equilibrium.

natural monopoly a monopoly that exists when increasing returns to scale provide a large cost advantage to having all output produced by a single firm.

negative externalities external costs.

negative income tax a program that supplements the income of low-income working families.

negative relationship a relationship between two variables in which an increase in the value of one variable is associated with a decrease in the value of the other variable. It is illustrated by a curve that slopes downward from left to right.

network externality a network externality exists when the value of a good or service to an individual is greater when many other people use the same good or service.

noncooperative behavior actions by firms that ignore the effects of those actions on the profits of other firms.

noncooperative equilibrium in game theory, the equilibrium that results when all players choose the action that maximizes their payoffs given the actions of other players, ignoring the effects of that action on the payoffs of other players; also known as Nash equilibrium.

nonexcludable referring to a good, describes the case in which the supplier cannot prevent those who do not pay from consuming the good.

nonlinear curve a curve in which the slope is not the same between every pair of points.

nonlinear relationship the relationship between two variables in which the slope is not constant and therefore is depicted on a graph by a curve that is not a straight line.

nonrival in consumption referring to a good, describes the case in which more than one person can consume the same unit of the good at the same time.

normal good a good for which a rise in income increases the demand for that good—the "normal" case.

normative economics the branch of economic analysis that makes prescriptions about the way the economy should work.

North American Free Trade Agreement (NAFTA) a trade agreement among the United States, Canada, and Mexico.

O

offshore outsourcing the practice of businesses hiring people in another country to perform various tasks.

oligopolist a firm in an industry with only a small number of producers.

oligopoly an industry with only a small number of firms.

opportunity cost the real cost of an item: what you must give up in order to get it.

optimal consumption bundle the consumption bundle that maximizes the consumer's total utility given their budget constraint.

optimal output rule profit is maximized by producing the quantity of output at which the marginal revenue of the last unit produced is equal to its marginal cost.

optimal quantity the quantity that generates the highest possible total profit.

origin the point where the axes of a two-variable graph meet.

other things equal assumption in the development of a model, the assumption that all relevant factors except the one under study remain unchanged.

overuse the depletion of a common resource that occurs when individuals ignore the fact that their use depletes the amount of the resource remaining for others.

P

Paris Agreement a commitment by 196 countries, signed in 2015, to reduce their greenhouse gas emissions in an effort to limit the rise in the earth's temperature to no more than 2 degrees centigrade.

patent a temporary monopoly given by the government to an inventor for the use or sale of an invention.

payoff in game theory, the reward received by a player in a game, such as the profit earned by an oligopolist.

payoff matrix in game theory, a diagram that shows how the payoff to each of the participants in a two-player game depends on the actions of both; a tool in analyzing interdependence.

perfect price discrimination the price discrimination that results when a monopolist charges each consumer their willingness to pay—the maximum that the consumer is willing to pay.

perfectly competitive industry an industry in which producers are price-takers.

perfectly competitive market a market in which all market participants are price-takers.

perfectly elastic demand the case in which any price increase will cause the quantity demanded to drop to zero; the demand curve is a horizontal line.

perfectly elastic supply the case in which even a tiny increase or reduction in the price will lead to very large changes in the quantity supplied, so that the price elasticity of supply is infinite; a perfectly elastic supply curve is a horizontal line.

perfectly inelastic demand the case in which the quantity demanded does not respond at all to changes in the price; the demand curve is a vertical line.

perfectly inelastic supply the case in which the price elasticity of supply is zero, so that changes in the price of the good have no effect on the quantity supplied; a perfectly inelastic supply curve is a vertical line.

physical capital human-made resources such as buildings and machines.

pie chart a circular graph that shows how some total is divided among its components, usually expressed in percentages.

Pigouvian subsidy a payment designed to encourage activities that yield external benefits.

Pigouvian tax tax designed to reduce external costs.

positive economics the branch of economic analysis that describes the way the economy actually works.

positive externalities external benefits.

positive relationship a relationship between two variables in which an increase in the value of one variable is associated with an increase in the value of the other variable. It is illustrated by a curve that slopes upward from left to right.

poverty program a government program designed to aid the poor.

poverty rate the percentage of the population living below the poverty threshold.

poverty threshold the annual income below which a family is officially considered poor.

price ceiling the maximum price sellers are allowed to charge for a good or service; a form of price control.

price controls legal restrictions on how high or low a market price may go.

price discrimination charging different prices to different consumers for the same good.

price elasticity of demand the ratio of the percent change in the quantity demanded to the percent change in the price as we move along the demand curve.

price elasticity of supply a measure of the responsiveness of the quantity of a good supplied to the price of that good. It is the ratio of the percent change in the quantity supplied to the percent change in the price as we move along the supply curve.

price floor the minimum price buyers are required to pay for a good or service; a form of price control.

price regulation a limitation on the price a monopolist is allowed to charge.

price war a collapse of prices when tacit collusion breaks down.

price-taking consumer a consumer whose actions have no effect on the market price of the good or service he or she buys.

price-taking firm's optimal employment rule A price-taking firm's profit is maximized by employing each factor of production up to the level at which the value of the marginal product is equal to the factor's price.

price-taking firm's optimal output rule a price-taking firm's profit is maximized by producing the quantity of output at which the market price is equal to the marginal cost of the last unit produced.

price-taking producer a producer whose actions have no effect on the market price of the good or service it sells.

price-taking producer's optimal employment rule the principle that a price-taking producer's profit is maximized by employing each factor of production up to the level at which the value of the marginal product is equal to the factor's price.

principle of "either–or" decision-making the principle that when faced with an "either–or" choice between two activities, choose the one with the positive economic profit.

principle of diminishing marginal utility the proposition that each successive unit of a good or service consumed adds less to total utility than the previous unit.

prisoners' dilemma a game based on two premises: (1) Each player has an incentive to choose an action that benefits itself at the other player's expense; (2) when both players act in this way, both are worse off than if they had acted cooperatively.

private good a good that is both excludable and rival in consumption.

private health insurance a program in which each member of a large pool of individuals pays a fixed amount annually to a private company that agrees to pay most of the medical expenses of the pool's members.

producer surplus a term often used to refer to either individual producer surplus or total producer surplus.

product differentiation the attempt by a firm to convince buyers that its product is different from other products in the industry; it takes three main forms: by style or type, by location, or by quality.

production function the relationship between the quantity of inputs a firm uses and the quantity of output it produces.

production possibility frontier a model that illustrates the trade-offs facing an economy that produces only two goods. It shows the maximum quantity of one good that can be produced for any given quantity produced of the other.

profit determination rule whether a producer is profitable depends on a comparison of the market price of the good to the producer's break-even price—its minimum average total cost.

profit-maximizing principle of marginal analysis when faced with a profit-maximizing "how much" decision, the optimal quantity is the largest quantity at which the marginal benefit is greater than or equal to marginal cost.

property rights the rights of owners of valuable items, whether resources or goods, to dispose of those items as they choose.

public good a good that is both nonexcludable and nonrival in consumption.

public ownership the case in which goods are supplied by the government or by a firm owned by the government to protect the interests of the consumer in response to a natural monopoly.

Q

quantity demanded the actual amount of a good or service consumers are willing to buy at some specific price.

quantity supplied the actual amount of a good or service producers are willing to sell at some specific price.

quota rent the difference between the demand price and the supply price at the quota limit; this difference, the earnings that accrue to the license holder, is equal to the market price of the license when the license is traded.

R

rational describes a decision maker who chooses the available option that leads to the outcome they most prefer.

recession a downturn in the economy when output and employment are falling; also referred to as a contraction.

renewable energy sources inexhaustible sources of energy, such as solar or wind power (unlike fossil fuel sources, which are exhaustible).

reputation a long-term standing in the public regard that serves to reassure others that private information is not being concealed; a valuable asset in the face of adverse selection.

resource anything, such as land, labor, and capital, that can be used to produce something else; includes natural resources (from the physical environment) and human resources (labor, skill, intelligence).

Ricardian model of international trade a model that analyzes international trade under the assumption that opportunity costs are constant.

risk aversion the willingness to sacrifice some economic payoff to avoid a potential loss.

rival in consumption referring to a good, describes the case in which one unit cannot be consumed by more than one person at the same time.

S

scarce in short supply; a resource is scarce when there is not enough of the resource available to satisfy all the various ways a society wants to use it.

scatter diagram a graph that shows points that correspond to actual observations of the *x*- and *y*-variables; a curve is usually fitted to the scatter of points to indicate the trend in the data.

shift of the demand curve a change in the quantity demanded at any given price, represented graphically by the change of the original demand curve to a new position, denoted by a new demand curve.

shift of the supply curve a change in the quantity supplied of a good or service at any given price, represented graphically by the change of the original supply curve to a new position, denoted by a new supply curve.

short run the time period in which at least one input is fixed.

short-run individual supply curve a graphical representation that shows how an individual producer's profit-maximizing output quantity depends on the market price, taking fixed cost as given.

short-run industry supply curve a graphical representation that shows how the quantity supplied by an industry depends on the market price, given a fixed number of producers.

short-run market equilibrium an economic balance that results when the quantity supplied equals the quantity demanded, taking the number of producers as given.

shortage the insufficiency of a good or service that occurs when the quantity demanded exceeds the quantity supplied; shortages occur when the price is below its equilibrium level.

shut-down price the price at which a firm will cease production in the short run because market price has fallen below the minimum average variable cost.

shut-down rule the firm should cease production when price falls below the shut-down price, equal to the minimum average variable cost.

signaling taking some action to establish credibility despite possessing private information; a way to reduce adverse selection.

single-price monopolist a monopolist that offers its product to all consumers at the same price.

slope a measure of how steep a line or curve is. The slope of a line is measured by "rise over run"—the change in the *y*-variable between two points on the line divided by the change in the *x*-variable between those same points.

social insurance program a government program designed to provide protection against unpredictable financial distress.

socially optimal quantity of pollution the quantity of pollution that society would choose if all the costs and benefits of pollution were fully accounted for.

specialization the situation in which each person specializes in the task that he or she is good at performing.

standardized product output of different producers regarded by consumers as the same good; also known as a commodity.

status quo bias the tendency to avoid making a decision and sticking with the status quo.

strategic behavior when a firm attempts to influence the future behavior of other firms.

substitutes pairs of goods for which a rise in the price of one of the goods leads to an increase in the demand for the other good.

substitution effect the change in the quantity of a good consumed as the consumer substitutes other goods that are now relatively cheaper in place of the good that has become relatively more expensive.

sunk cost a cost that has already been incurred and is nonrecoverable. A sunk cost should be ignored in decisions about future actions.

supply and demand model a model of how a competitive market behaves.

supply curve a graphical representation of the supply schedule, showing the relationship between quantity supplied and price.

supply schedule a list or table showing how much of a good or service producers will supply at different prices.

surplus the excess of a good or service that occurs when the quantity supplied exceeds the quantity demanded; surpluses occur when the price is above the equilibrium price.

T

tacit collusion when firms limit production and raise prices in a way that raises one another's profits, even though they have not made any formal agreement.

tangent line a straight line that just touches a nonlinear curve at a particular point; the slope of the tangent line is equal to the slope of the nonlinear curve at that point.

tariff a tax levied on imports.

tax rate the amount of tax people are required to pay per unit of whatever is being taxed.

technology the technical means for producing goods and services.

technology spillover an external benefit that results when knowledge spreads among individuals and firms.

time allocation the decision about how many hours to spend on different activities, which leads to a decision about how much labor to supply.

time-series graph a two-variable graph with dates on the horizontal axis and values of a variable that occurred on those dates on the vertical axis.

tit for tat in game theory, a strategy that involves playing cooperatively at first, then doing whatever the other player did in the previous period.

total consumer surplus the sum of the individual consumer surpluses of all the buyers of a good in a market.

total cost the sum of the fixed cost and the variable cost of producing a given quantity of output.

total cost curve a graphical representation of the total cost, showing how total cost depends on the quantity of output.

total producer surplus the sum of the individual producer surpluses of all the sellers of a good in a market.

total product curve a graphical representation of the production function, showing how the quantity of output depends on the quantity of the variable input, for a given quantity of the fixed input.

total revenue the total value of sales of a good or service. It is equal to the price multiplied by the quantity sold.

total surplus the total net gain to consumers and producers from trading in a market; the sum of the consumer surplus and the producer surplus.

tradable emissions permits licenses to emit limited quantities of pollutants that can be bought and sold by polluters.

trade the practice, in a market economy, in which individuals provide goods and services to others and receive goods and services in return.

trade protection policies that limit imports; also known simply as protection.

trade war occurs when countries deliberately try to impose pain on their trading partners, as a way to extract policy concessions.

trade-off a comparison of costs and benefits of doing something.

U

U-shaped average total cost curve a distinctive graphical representation of the relationship between output and average total cost; the average total cost curve first falls when output is low, then rises as output increases.

unions organizations of workers that try to raise wages and improve working conditions for their members by bargaining collectively with employers.

unit-elastic demand the case in which the price elasticity of demand is exactly 1.

util a unit of utility.

utility a measure of the satisfaction the consumer derives from consumption of goods and services.

utility function (of an individual) the total utility generated by an individual's consumption bundle.

utility-maximizing principle of marginal analysis the marginal utility per dollar spent must be the same for all goods and services in the optimal consumption bundle.

V

value of the marginal product the value of the additional output generated by employing one more unit of a given factor, such as labor.

value of the marginal product curve a graphical representation showing how the value of the marginal product of that factor depends on the quantity of the factor employed.

variable a quantity that can take on more than one value.

variable cost a cost that depends on the quantity of output produced. It is the cost of the variable input.

variable input an input whose quantity the firm can vary at any time.

vertical axis the vertical number line of a graph along which values of the *y*-variable are measured; also referred to as the *y*-axis.

vertical intercept the point at which a curve hits the vertical axis; it shows the value of the *y*-variable when the value of the *x*-variable is zero.

W

wasted resources a form of inefficiency in which people expend money, effort, and time to cope with the shortages caused by a price ceiling.

welfare state the collection of government programs designed to alleviate economic hardship.

willingness to pay the maximum price a consumer is prepared to pay for a good.

world price the price at which a good can be bought or sold abroad.

World Trade Organization (WTO) an international organization of member countries that oversees international trade agreements and rules on disputes between countries over those agreements.

X

***x*-axis** the horizontal number line of a graph along which values of the *x*-variable are measured; also referred to as the horizontal axis.

Y

***y*-axis** the vertical number line of a graph along which values of the *y*-variable are measured; also referred to as the vertical axis.

Z

zero-profit equilibrium an economic balance in which each firm makes zero profit at its profit-maximizing quantity.

Index

Key terms and the pages on which they are defined appear in **boldface.**

N

O

P